18598

Beethoven's Concertos

ALSO BY LEON PLANTINGA

Schumann as Critic

Clementi: His Life and Music

Romantic Music: A History of Musical Style in Nineteenth-Century Europe

Anthology of Romantic Music

Beethoven's Concertos

HISTORY

STYLE

PERFORMANCE

LEON PLANTINGA

W · W · Norton & Company   New York   London

For information about permission to reproduce selections from this book,
write to Permissions, W. W. Norton & Company, Inc.,
500 Fifth Avenue, New York, NY 10110.

The text of this book is composed in 11/13 Fairfield LH Light
with the display set in Poetica Chancery I and Arabesque 2 ornament
Composition by Binghamton Valley Composition
Manufacturing by The Courier Companies, Inc.
Book design by Margaret M. Wagner

Library of Congress Cataloging-in-Publication Data

Plantinga, Leon.
Beethoven's concertos : history, style, performance / Leon
Plantinga.
p.   cm.
Includes bibliographical references and index.
ISBN 0-393-04691-5
1. Beethoven, Ludwig van, 1770–1827. Concertos.   2. Concerto.
I. Title
ML410.B42P6   1998

784.2'3'092—dc21   98-22552
CIP
MN

W. W. Norton & Company, Inc., 500 Fifth Avenue, New York, N.Y. 10110
http://www.wwnorton.com

W. W. Norton & Company Ltd., 10 Coptic Street, London WC1A 1PU

1 2 3 4 5 6 7 8 9 0

Contents

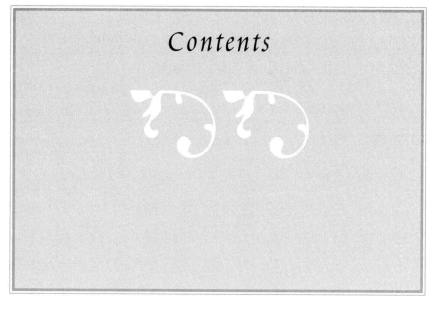

Preface · i x

Introduction · 3

1 Form in Beethoven's Concertos · 9

2 Bonn: The Court, the Composer, the Concerto · 2 2

3 The Virtuoso in Vienna · 4 2

4 Toward the LINGUA FRANCA: Piano Concerto No. 2 in B♭, Op. 19 · 6 7

5 Beyond the LINGUA FRANCA: Piano Concerto No. 1 in C, Op. 15 · 9 0

6 On the Origins of Piano Concerto No. 3 · 1 1 3

7 Toward the Middle-Period Style: Piano Concerto No. 3 in C Minor, Op. 37 · 1 3 6

8 An Interlude in the French Manner: Triple Concerto in C, Op. 56 · 1 5 9

9 To Sing of Arms and Men: Piano Concerto No. 4 in G, Op. 58 · 1 8 5

10 Of Purest Ray Serene: The Violin Concerto in D, Op. 61 · 2 1 7

11 The "Emperor": Piano Concerto No. 5 in E♭, Op. 73 · 2 5 1

12 On Performing Beethoven's Concertos · 2 7 9

Appendix I. The Bonn Concertos and Their Sources · 3 0 5

Appendix II. On Redating Piano Concerto No. 3: A Summary · 3 0 7

Abbreviations in the Notes and Bibliography · 3 1 0

Notes · 3 1 1

Bibliography · 3 7 3

Index · 3 8 5

Music Examples · i n p o c k e t

Plates appear on pages 167 to 178.

Preface

In some ways Beethoven's concertos are very well known. Five of them, four for piano and the one for violin, are fixtures in the repertories of all who play those instruments, and the inevitable companions of those of us who listen to concert music. They seem like trusted old friends from whom we expect few surprises, who for the most part simply continue to delight us with qualities we already know and admire. Much less familiar is the rich and varied historical background of these works: the particular social settings in which they emerged, the ways in which they were performed, the meanings they may have had for listeners in their own time, their role in the growth of what is distinctive in Beethoven's music. Inquiry into such matters will sometimes include rather exacting discussion of the time and place of composition and of early performances of this music. Technical talk about these matters, however, is as a rule relegated to the ends of chapters and to the notes. In the case of Chapter 6, the only one in clear violation of this rule, a short summary of the argument is given in Appendix 2.

This larger context involves a good bit of other music: the two less familiar concertos (the Triple and the "Second" Piano Concerto), of course, but also various concerto-like compositions of Beethoven's such as the Romances for Violin and Orchestra, Opp. 40 and 50, an extensive assortment of juvenilia, the beginnings of a sixth piano concerto (another candidate for inclusion, the Choral Fantasy, it was decided, lies just outside the pale), as well as many other compositions by Beethoven, his predecessors, and contemporaries. The hope is that a wide-ranging consideration of this historical context will serve to cast new light upon the music itself, which remains the central focus of this study.

Someone has said that writing about music is like dancing about architecture. Do we really add anything of value to the experience of, say, the slow movement of the Fourth Piano Concerto when we speculate about its entrenched literary associations or when we point to its kinship with certain dramatic techniques of opera? Yet underlying many a worthy scholarly or critical appraisal of things artistic there is probably an assumption that the search for comprehension itself yields enrichment. When we train our minds on the object and struggle for a closer appreciation of just what it is, how it achieves its effect, how it might have been understood in the past, the very effort represents a gain. For the discussion at hand the reader with a score will probably gain more than others. But for these others rather full examples are provided in the attached booklet—this format having been chosen so that one may follow a discussion of the music without leafing back and forth through the text. Since of the two forms in which this music is available—full scores or two-piano reductions—both are finally unsatisfactory (the one being impractical and the other insufficiently detailed) new reductions are offered for all examples.

To trace the scholarly efforts of one's more advanced years to childhood experience may be to stretch a point. But, in fact, my love of Beethoven's concertos began when my late father, Cornelius A. Plantinga, introduced me to the pleasures of concert attendance and insisted on quiet listening during Sunday afternoon broadcasts of the New York Philharmonic. My involvement with this music deepened when, as an ambitious young pianist during student days, I studied and performed the Third and Fifth Piano Concertos, encouraged by my early teachers, especially Robert T. Laudon and Ernst Victor Wolff. A mingling of such memories with work on this book has lent the enterprise a special sustenance and joy.

Others have made varied contributions of a more collegial and professional sort, which it is a pleasure to acknowledge here. Alan Tyson was always generous with his special expertise in Beethoven documentary studies; David Lewin, Lewis Lockwood, and Craig Wright graciously read the stretches of text I urged upon them and gave me good advice. To the principals, past and present, of the Beethoven-Archiv in Bonn I am indebted for hospitality and assistance; among them are Martin Staehelin, Sieghard Brandenburg, and especially Hans-Werner Küthen, who has repeatedly given me advance copies of his work and freely shared his thoughts during these years when we have been tilling the same field of inquiry. During my many periods of work in the Musikabteilung of the

Deutsche Staatsbibliothek (now the Staatsbibliothek zu Berlin, Preussischer Kulturbesitz) I could always count on help and kindness; for this I am grateful to Dr. Karl-Heinz Köhler, Fräulein Eveline Bartlitz, Dr. Helmut Hell, and particularly Dr. Clemens Brenneis, who even joined me one afternoon in poring over the autograph of the "Emperor" Concerto in a common effort to decipher the words written there in Beethoven's famous scrawl. The people at the Yale University Music Library are consistently helpful beyond the line of duty; especially deserving my thanks are the former head librarian Harold Samuel and the present one, Kendall Crilly, as well as Kathryn Mansi and Karl Schrom. The staff of the Music Division of the New York Public Library—whose riches never cease to amaze me—have made working there a pleasure, and upon my visits to the Gesellschaft der Musikfreunde in Vienna, Dr. Otto Biba and his staff have been similarly accommodating.

Several very able students—Elizabeth Bergman, Richard Boursy, John Gingerich, and Judah Adashi—have helped me greatly with this book, checking references, producing the examples, and making polite suggestions; other students, such as Alexander Solomon and Daniel Gien, have provided a certain stimulus to progress by forever asking when the thing would be finished. And my home institution, Yale University, has contributed to this work by attracting such a singular group of stimulating students and colleagues; I am also grateful for its generous leave policy and for two grants from the A. Whitney Griswold fund. The final stages in the long road to publication have benefited greatly from the attentions of W. W. Norton's knowledgeable and sympathetic music staff—editor Michael Ochs and assistants Martha Graedel and Anne White.

Woodbridge, Connecticut
April 1998

Beethoven's Concertos

Introduction

In his concertos Beethoven joined in a sort of human expression that seems almost universal: a discourse of the individual and the group, or of leader and followers who sometimes work together in harmony and sometimes appear pitted one against the other (early definitions of the concerto, indeed, were divided as to which was the main idea of the genre—cooperation or conflict). The concerto recalls familiar practices in Western religious ritual such as responsorial psalm-singing in which a soloist sings verses interspersed with choral responds, a practice the early church evidently inherited from its Hebrew progenitors. We recognize the idea again in the division of singing forces into *favoriti* and *complementa* that Schütz learned from early seventeenth-century Venetian models, in some of the finest moments in Gilbert and Sullivan, and, more remotely, in the interaction of soloists and corps de ballet of "classical" (i.e., nineteenth-century French) ballet.

But the paradigm is more widespread. It shows up in the popular European round-song (or dance), commemorated in such widely divergent works as the second act of Monteverdi's *Orfeo* and the first of Mozart's *Don Giovanni* (in the festivities that introduce Zerlina and Masetto), where a soloist emerges from the group, performs alone, and is reabsorbed. In many areas of sub-Saharan Africa, festive song and dance typically fall into analogous patterns of call-and-response and solo-and-circle or solo-and-line, the solo often presenting an embroidery on the utterance of the group; the parts overlap and combine, sometimes in agreement, sometimes at odds. The agreed-upon symbolism invokes the notion of "popular response to the actions of the ideal leader."[1] We see much the same pattern in the Brazilian and Salvadorian *capoeira*, a species of martial arts mixed with prominent elements of dance, drama, and music; here a soloist offers a musical statement, and a chorus responds in another enactment of the leader-follower paradigm.[2] And again in the music of the Balinese gamelan gong, the leading trompong part is an improvisatory, ornamented version of a nuclear melody played unadorned by the ensemble at large.[3]

In his concertos Beethoven typically cast himself as leader; the concerto was for him mainly a youthful preoccupation intimately bound up with his prowess and ambition as a public pianist. He began writing and playing concertos as a teenager in Bonn and continued to do so in Vienna until his middle thirties. His final complete work in the genre, the "Emperor," the first piano concerto at whose premiere someone else played the solo, broke that bond between concerto composing and concerto playing, and signaled the end of his involvement with the genre. In a curiously backward-looking gesture a half-dozen years later (1815), during a period of outward success but evident inward uncertainty, he set about writing one more piano concerto. The effort and the music seem oddly dated, and the project stalled before the first movement was finished. For Beethoven, as for J. C. Bach, Mozart, and Clementi before him, and Hummel, Moscheles, and Liszt after him, the concerto was mainly a personal vehicle for the composer-virtuoso's performances, a means for displaying new musical ideas of which a central feature was his own distinctive style of playing. When he effectively stopped playing in public in about 1809, the days of his attachment to the concerto also came to a close.

The concertos often have a compositional history—which, in turn, depends partly on their very ontological status—rather different from that of most of Beethoven's other music. Carl Dahlhaus, while pursuing the implications of Raphael Georg Kiesewetter's perception of an "era of Beethoven and Rossini" comprising two distinct musical cultures, wrote,

> Beethoven's symphonies represent inviolable musical "texts" whose meaning is to be deciphered with "exegetical" interpretations; a Rossini score, on the other hand, is a mere recipe for a performance and it is the performance which forms the crucial aesthetic arbiter as the realization of a draft rather than an exegesis of a text. Rossini's musical thought hinged on the performance as an event, not on the work as a text passed down and from time to time given acoustical "explications."[4]

This distinction—probably, in any case, much less clear in the nineteenth century before fidelty to a "text" became a first principle of performance—

is not one to be drawn simply between Beethoven and Rossini, and certainly not just between the Germans and the Italians. It has more immediately to do with genre. Operas were shows, and an opera score was a plan for a particular show. The three incarnations of Beethoven's *Fidelio*, for performances in 1805, 1806, and 1814, differ as widely as the various versions of a Rossini opera. What fixes a "text," truly makes it so, is publication. But even the prestige of the published score varies, hewing to lines of genre: we are much less upset by cuts in operas than in symphonies.

The primary destination of Beethoven's sonatas was clearly publication, and of his symphonies, performance to be followed as soon as possible by publication; these compositions, therefore, soon acquired texts (see p. 274). But for the concertos the performance itself was at the very heart of his intention. Particularly while focused upon making his name in Vienna as a public performer, Beethoven (like Mozart before him) was in no hurry to publish these pieces. He "held them back,"[5] as he once said, to allow for subsequent performance and successive revision; publication in the interim would dull the glimmer of novelty and, perhaps more important, fix the text in a way that Beethoven evidently wished to avoid. Thus so long as the concertos were in his active repertory, they—particularly their solo parts—operated in a kind of "aural" tradition whereby each new performance saw a new version. His practices of concerto composition and performance might remind us of certain modern theories about the Homeric epics: each new performance in an oral tradition produced a variant version, none of which could claim any special authority.[6]

The extreme case among the concertos is that of the "Second" Concerto in B♭, Op. 19. Beethoven first produced a version of it in Bonn and then played it time and again for well over a decade. Each time, the maturing composer felt driven to make changes, some as drastic as the replacement of movements. The corresponding period in which he saved the later C-major ("First") Concerto, Op. 15, for his own performances and for second compositional and improvisational thoughts, was about five years (1795–1800). So far as we know, Beethoven played his "Third" Concerto in C minor in public only once, in the spring of 1803. Most of his rethinking of the piece (and the autograph, now in Berlin, shows there was a lot) seems to have taken place in a very compressed period of time before that performance. In none of these three cases did he bother to get the piano part firmly written down before the performance; the orchestra needed an exacting script, but his own part of the dialogue was always to a large extent extemporaneous and hence ever variable.

What put a stop to both Beethoven's performances of his early concertos and his habitual improvisatory flights with them was their publication. So far as we know, he played a concerto of his after publication on only one occasion: the gargantuan concert of December 1808, in which the Fourth Concerto in G, published the previous August, was one of many compositions on the program. (In two cases he at least contemplated a bit of post-publication tinkering: some tentative changes in the autograph of Op. 19 and sketches for an elaboration of the solo part of the Fourth Concerto were evidently done after these works were published). Once in print, the text—insofar as a musical score is ever a "text"—was fixed, and for Beethoven the music seemed to assume a different status: now out in public for all to contemplate, it was no longer his own to mull over and redefine in performance. By its very nature, no musical composition can ever constitute a reified "work," the art object with a settled and precise identity so dear to later nineteenth- and twentieth-century thought. (As Isidore of Seville had already observed in the seventh century, music simply "flows by into the past and is left imprinted upon the memory.")[7] While in his active repertory, Beethoven's concertos remained far removed from this ideal of settledness. And even the degree of fixity and availability bestowed on them by publication seemed to end his interest in performing them.

Earlier in the eighteenth century, concertos typically figured in two of the three main venues of performance that provided a rough definition of musical genres: music for the church and music for the chamber (only the theater was missing). Corelli's Concerti grossi, Op. 6, are neatly split between the two types, *da chiesa* and *da camera*; Vivaldi's great profusion of concertos was composed largely for performance at the chapel services of the Ospedale della Pietá in Venice, where he was employed as *maestro di violino*; J. S. Bach wrote and performed his concertos as part of his regular duty to supply chamber music for the court at Anhalt-Cöthen. In the latter half of the century, the concerto altered its orientation, becoming a central fixture in that new urban institution created for the new middle-class audience, the public concert. In the 1760s J. C. Bach in London was probably the first to present his concertos on a regular basis to a paying public, and a generation later Mozart followed his example in Vienna, selling subscriptions to series of concerts that offered varied musical fare but almost always a new concerto.

While we cannot be entirely sure about the venues for Beethoven's concerto performances in Bonn, in Vienna he followed Mozart's example, playing them himself, in philanthropic benefit concerts, or between the acts of oratorios, or in (very substantial) programs of his own works. It was in the concerto that he offered the audience its fullest view of the composer's individuality and gift: here, together with the attractions of the music, was the exhilaration of virtuosity and, given the improvisational nature of the solo part, even a glimpse of the composer seemingly in the very act of creation.

In Beethoven's time, part of the effect of music still depended upon a certain repertory of widely understood conventional symbolism or "meaning." The associative idioms of the siciliano (signifying things pastoral), "Turkish" music (warlike, barbaric, but also a little comic), the French Revolutionary funeral march (solemn commemoration of the death of a hero), the waltz (carefree celebration, and maybe, more distantly, permissible physical contact between the sexes in public)—in the late eighteenth and early nineteenth centuries these and many other such associations were built up over long years of practice and broad acceptance within a musical culture.[8] Such conventional symbolism operates richly in Beethoven's concertos. The finales, without exception, are rondos, and to one degree or another their ritornello themes share the popular, implicitly rustic traits associated with the round dance: a certain singsong rhythmic uniformity and ironclad metrical regularity—sometimes projected on a very large canvas, as in the fifty-five-measure theme of the finale of the Third Piano Concerto—that urban Europeans associated with musical sounds of the countryside. The slow movement of the Violin Concerto is an adaptation of the chaconne, with far-reaching implications of gravity and antiquity. And in the Fourth Piano Concerto the astonishing slow movement, with its overtly delineated dialogue, its gestures of impassioned accompanied recitative (*récit obligé*, as Rousseau named this style) and somber arioso, seems to cry aloud for verbal clarification. Beethoven supplied none, leaving our imaginations free to make their own constructions of this stentorian declaration and poignant lyricism.[9]

But most pervasive, surely, of extramusical notions that Beethoven's concertos would reliably have evoked in the minds of contemporaneous listeners are images of things military. Here, as in the case of the rondo, the connection is made by invoking a musical idiom with established associations. With the exception, perhaps, of the Second Piano Concerto, adumbrations of the military march occur in all the concertos; even beneath the arching lyricism of the first movement of the Violin Concerto we hear its measured tread. In war-ravaged Europe of the younger Beethoven's lifetime, the military with its ritualized splendor, clamor, and menace was a constant; and its invocation was a useful means of summoning up, as well, those satellite notions of fate, struggle, and heroism that from early on loomed large in the composer's mind and music.

For Beethoven there was still a kind of innocence about it all that may be difficult for us to recapture. A half-century ago Jorge Luis Borges, contemplating some lines from the *Aeneid* ("My son, from me learn valor and true constancy; from others success"), from the Anglo-Saxon ballad of Maldon ("my people will pay the tribute with lances and with old swords"), and from the *Chanson de Roland*, Victor Hugo, Whitman, and Faulkner, reflected that "there is a flavor that our time (perhaps surfeited by the clumsy imitations of professional patriots) does not usually perceive without some suspicion: the fundamental flavor of the heroic."[10] At the dawn of the twenty-first century the heroic is if anything even more suspect because the coin seems further debased: the mode has been invoked in the service of too many unworthy causes, of imperialist and colonialist adventurism that we now more clearly see as such, and, more recently, of nationalisms run amok. The revisionist veil of censure rightly cast over European adventurers from the Crusaders to the settlers of the American West can also partly blur our vision of others—the Egmonts, William Tells, and Garibaldis of this world—who struggled for better causes.[11]

W. H. Auden said that the times were too late for the idealism of the nineteenth-century operatic world, that it was incompatible with the twentieth century's swirling mixture of alienations, when even the idea of free human agency seemed passé.[12] The same malaise threatens our perceptions of Beethoven's persistent vision of heroic struggle toward human perfection (in the composer's earlier days this idea was mingled with notions of a utopian socialism going back at least to Plutarch).[13] From the Joseph Cantata to *Fidelio* to the Ninth Symphony, we see played out the sentiments he wrote explicitly into his diary of 1812: convictions about ultimate triumph for the individual and for humankind achieved by selfless devotion and struggle.[14] The real struggle is an internal one, and the triumph exists largely in the moral sphere—a domain with which art, to Beethoven's mind, was always inextricably intertwined. Military imagery is only a handy metaphor plucked out of the *actualité* of the composer's world. If we apprehend what it stands for these days only with difficulty, the recovery effort is still worth our while. For us, too, this may require a certain struggle—the struggle for historical perspective.

C H A P T E R   1

Form in Beethoven's Concertos

A music student recently asked a puzzling question: "Does this piece have a form?" "Form," a name and notion that gained currency in music during Beethoven's lifetime and is now ubiquitous in our everyday talk about music, still has about it a certain penumbra of ambiguity.[1] Do we construe "form" so broadly as to allow that every composition has it (or one), or does musical form rather emerge only from the presence of certain kinds of properties in certain kinds of music? For most of us, the notion probably implies a degree of differentiation, the presence of some number of distinguishable events (distinguished by any number of stylistic elements: melody, rhythmic properties, key—or, as it will be argued here, instrumentation) that allows one to recount "what happens" in a piece. If a composition is without noticeable articulation from beginning to end— let us think, for the sake of argument, of a stretch of music from a movie soundtrack consisting of the continuous alternation of two chords played in a uniform rhythm—we might, with that student, question whether it "has a form." For if such an arrangement constitutes form, the term seemingly describes nothing more than "what a piece is like" and is so drained of specificity as to become virtually useless.

If, rather, some "series of events," is essential to the emergence of form, we can contemplate such a series in more than one way: as an abstraction, a model or pattern to be taken in at a glance, or as something more like a narrative whose nature and relationships are revealed moment by moment as we listen—during which we cultivate an illusion, at least, that we can be surprised. Both kinds of perception are essential, surely, to the apprehension of form (indeed to the larger enterprise of understanding music): the latter as we follow the formal progress of a composition, the former when the music is "recollected in tranquility."[2]

If the idea of musical form is beset with a certain ambiguity, it is also subject, in the present climate, to a certain suspicion. An interest in form easily attracts imputations of formalism, a belief that what is important about a composition are its internal relationships, what happens within its own skin, to the exclusion of things like value, social function, participation in a culture, and the like. The origins of the narrower view, it is often thought, are entangled with the roots of Beethoven scholarship in the work of that coryphaeus of formal theory in music and explicator of the music of Beethoven, Adolph Bernard Marx. His two- and three-part lied form, five varieties of rondo form, and sonata form in those familiar three parts, together with their schematic diagrams, are what remain in the minds of students of musical form these days,[3] to the near exclusion of the expansive idealistic theories that underlay Marx's thought. A musical composition for Marx was founded upon a "basic idea" (*Idee,* or *Grundgedanke*) that controlled all aspects of the music, most particularly its form.[4]

While such a notion, with its sonorous echoes of Schelling and Hegel, may fall largely on deaf ears at the turn of the twenty-first century, Marx may not in fact be irreparably removed from our ways of thinking. A characteristic rondo theme, for example (the opening of the finale of Beethoven's Violin Concerto will serve), creates some rather distinct expectations as to form. A spritely tune in the "familiar" style with perfectly regular periodization and transparently simple harmony gives a signal: it alerts the experienced listener that a salient "point" of the movement at hand will likely be a series of prominent returns of this ingenuous music. Anticipation of these returns (after intervals of distraction, and, often, teasing anticipation) becomes something of a "controlling idea" of the piece. And that much awaited theme always arrives with a cargo of associations: it calls to mind things such as a sanguine outlook, an uncomplicated (perhaps rustic) mode of life, and maybe a certain ironic distance from all this on the part of the present company.

If we can be convinced that Marx's basic notion—and by extension our own—that "form" grows out of "idea" is not hopelessly opaque and idle, we may also see here something of the intersection of musical form with that other slippery concept, "genre." Genre is of course a much broader notion that may include form—certainly it does so in the case of the rondo—while carrying other implications as well: the mere size of a composition may be involved, for example, and the forces needed to perform it, as are its customary venue of performance, and sometimes an implied social function and status.[5] Of the prominent generic properties of the instrumental concerto up to Beethoven's time (among them an association with virtuoso solo playing, for example, and an increasingly firm identification with the public concert), two, namely a particular deployment of performing forces and characteristic elements of musical form, are peculiarly intermingled.

A century before Beethoven, Corelli's Concerti grossi, Op. 6, differed from his trio sonatas only as to instrumentation. At certain points, especially as cadences approached, the four instruments of the trio-sonata setting were reinforced by others, creating a systematic alternation of texture, the familiar tutti-soli contrast of the concerto. A generation later, with the concertos of Vivaldi, and by extension those of J. S. Bach, this alternation coincided with a differentiation in musical style. The tuttis were now proper ritornellos; "presentational" in Schoenberg's sense, they tended toward harmonic stability and thematic consistency from one occurrence to the next. The solo sections, by contrast, were figurative and harmonically mobile. A coordination of thematic and harmonic design with alternation of performing forces became the defining trait of the genre; deployment of instruments had become an integral factor in the unfolding of "events," in the creation of form.

In the later eighteenth century, music theorists who wrote about larger structural issues (Riepel, Koch, Galeazzi, Kollmann) directed their attention almost exclusively to two variables, harmony and melody (or theme). In Beethoven's lifetime writers on musical form (Reicha, Momigny, Marx, Czerny) gradually shifted their focus, especially in discussion of first movements, from the one, harmonic events, to the other, the nature and disposition of themes. And in the mid-twentieth century, beginning in the United States, recognition of this shift instigated something of a reverse motion—roughly from the nineteenth- to the eighteenth-century view—in our way of thinking about form in Classical music.[6] But these elements, harmony and theme, even taken together, as we have seen, hardly suffice to permit a narrative of the major events, an explanation of "what happens" in a concerto. For here the main thing that happens—and this was attested before the mid-eighteenth century[7]—is still what is most obvious: the soloist and large group interact, alternating in their claims on our attention. What is special about the classical concerto is a particular kind of coordination of this first organizing principle, alternation of texture, with a second one that has to do with both theme and key. A collision of two quite opposed formal principles, the stark alternation of the old ritornello form and the "goal-oriented" forward momentum of the newer sonata form achieve a generally amicable, if at times uneasy, reconciliation.

This primary alternation of forces is played out in different ways in each of the piece's three movements (that there should be just three seemingly had been settled in the Italian repertory as far back as Torelli and Vivaldi and was overwhelmingly the rule for concertos everywhere by the later eighteenth century). The pattern occurs on both a local and long-term level. Sometimes, of course, the two groups answer each other in quick succession, creating an effect familiar in European music at least from the time of the Venetian polychoral compositions of the early seventeenth century. But the pattern is also played out on a larger, profoundly form-creating level, wherein long stretches of music are *primarily* the province of the solo or nearly exclusively the province of the orchestra. Solo sections usually have some orchestral accompaniment and permit occasional short interjections by the orchestra; roles are approximately reversed in the tuttis, where the solo part may simply merge into the larger ensemble, or, in a keyboard concerto, provide a continuo-like accompaniment. The single case in which the solo makes its presence forcefully felt during these sections is the intrusion of the cadenza in the final tutti section. In concertos of Mozart's and Beethoven's time, this larger organization is seen mainly in first movements,[8] where there is a fairly predictable and orderly alternation of this larger sort.

FIRST MOVEMENTS

So the first movements of Beethoven's concertos, for all their marvelous diversity of expression, are formally rather alike. They all follow, in a general way, a common late eighteenth-century paradigm: an alternation of four tuttis (labeled T in Table 1-1) with three solo sections (labeled S) as shown, in its bare bones, in Table 1-1.

Essential to the second organizational principle in such a movement is

TABLE 1-1

T_1		S_1			T_2	S_2		T_3	S_3		T_4	Cad	T_4
a	b . . . a	b . . . d						a	b . . . d				
I	I	I~~~V			V(~~)		~~	I~~	I		I		

the motion in S_1 to the secondary key, as in the exposition of a usual sonata form, and the restatement of much the same music in T_3 and S_3 together, now all in the tonic, as in a recapitulation. These central events, while creating the essential harmonic trajectory of the piece, typically account for just about all of its thematic matter as well. One more pre-dictable element occurs toward the ends of S_1 and S_3 ("d" in Table 1-1): the closing parts of these solos are regularly given over to ebulient virtuoso solo playing—Hans Engel named these sections "display episodes."[9] Here, thematic matter yields to brilliant passagework that drives inexorably to the end of the section; this takes place in the secondary key in S_1, of course, and in S_2, back in the original tonic. The second solo offers a diversion between those two central operations of the movement, that is, between the departure from and return to the tonic in S_1 and T_3 / S_3. S_2 is typically restless and often wide ranging as to harmony; yet (as in the splendid pastoral sojourn in F♯ minor in the first movement of the Fifth Brandenburg Concerto), it often quiets down and lingers for a time in a distant tonality as if to view the proceedings from afar.

The opening tutti offers a parade of the main ideas of the movement. Sometimes (as in the Third Piano Concerto) it has them all; but usually Beethoven, following Mozart's example, saves one distinctive tune for the soloist. T_1 begins and ends in the principal key; in between it may be more or less modulatory—more in Beethoven's early concertos, less in the later ones.[10] This section, as in most Mozart concertos, includes certain "sum-ming up" ideas, typically emphatic cadential gestures, earmarked in advance for those ritual incursions of the orchestra at the entrance of a tutti (T_2 or T_4, as T_1 and T_3 normally start with the first theme), or upon those occasional orchestral interjections that punctuate solo sections. In Beethoven's early concertos, as in most of Mozart's, the soloist breaks into the final tutti in a "surprise" last appearance to play the cadenza.[11] That ostensibly improvisatory solo excursion is obligingly set up by the orches-tra's pause on a grand cadential $^6_4$ sonority that fairly begs for resolution; the cadenza complies with fine discursive flair, after which the orchestra obediantly resumes where it had left off and finishes the movement. The closing sections are the only part of the eighteenth-century paradigm in which Beethoven unleashed his restless yen for formal innovation: starting with the Third Piano Concerto, the area of T_4 was to become the arena for far-reaching experiment and expansion.

A first movement of the sort we have just described, of course, shows essential features of the ubiquitous pattern (or procedure) in later eigh-teenth-century music that we call *sonata form*. And there are good histor-ical grounds for making the comparison. Several theorists of the time called attention to similarities between first movements of sonatas and concertos. Usually, the idea was that the big solos of the concerto movement were seen to correspond with the main formal sections of a sonata's first movement. The first to make the comparison explicit was probably the Abbé Georg Joseph Vogler, polymath composer, writer on musical subjects, and virtuoso keyboard player who reportedly once competed with Beethoven in a test of improvisatory playing.[12] Vogler wrote in 1779,

> Whoever wishes to compose a concerto does well if he first makes for himself an ordinary sonata. The first part of it becomes the first solo, the other part the second solo. Before the first, after the second, and between the first and second parts, the instruments play a Vor-, Nach-, and Zwischenspiel.[13]

Then, too, we know of a few examples from real musical practice in which composers more or less followed Vogler's recommendations. The child Mozart produced his earliest keyboard concertos by arranging sonata movements of J. C. Bach, Leonzi Honauer, J. G. Eckard, Johann Schobert, and H. F. Raupach;[14] what he did in first movements, essentially, was to add tuttis at the appropriate structural junctures of the original sonata movements. Some three decades later, Muzio Clementi did the same in reverse. His Sonata Op. 33, No. 1 (published in 1794), had had an earlier life as a piano concerto; to change it into a (more saleable) sonata he simply removed all the principal tuttis and transcribed the internal orchestral interjections for piano.[15]

The main thing the young Mozart had to add were the three tuttis of which Vogler spoke, one at the beginning, one after the sonata's exposition, and one at the end (other orchestral interjections are usually too fleeting to count as tuttis proper). But what Clementi removed were *four* tuttis, now including one after what was to be the "development," that section of the sonata form now steadily gaining in recognition as a third main division of such a movement. This corresponded with what Heinrich Christoph Koch, that magisterial explicator of compositional practice in the later eighteenth century, had to say about the matter in 1793. He compared first movements of concertos specifically with those of symphonies (always his principal exemplar for compositions of the sonata type). For him the second of two large divisions of the symphony movement is subdivided into two "principal periods" (what we have come to call development and recapitulation), necessitating, thus, the addition of four framing tuttis:

The first allegro of the concerto contains three principal periods, performed by the soloist, which alternate with four secondary periods
played by the orchestra as ritornellos. . . . As to the three principal periods of the solo part [of the first movement of a concerto], there remains
nothing more for us to say here; for they have the same outward organization, and the same course of modulation as the three principal
periods in the first allegro of the symphony.[16]

Immediately at issue, of course, is that additional tutti, the one coincident with the end of the development and the beginning of the recapitulation. This was an unstable point in the concerto movement, subject to
experiment throughout the second half of the eighteenth century;[17] and
here Beethoven and Mozart part company with their predecessors. What
Koch had in mind was a second solo (or development) that ends at a
certain tonal remove, most often in the relative minor. The ensuing tutti
is a short connective passage that steers the music back to tonic,
whereupon the third solo begins the recapitulation. This is precisely the
plan followed in many concertos of J. C. Bach and of the composers of
the Mannheim school; it appears in the first movement of Haydn's early
Klavier Concerto in F, Hob. XVIII:3, and in of several of Dittersdorf's
concertos. In his mature concertos of the 1780s, Mozart almost always
brought S_2 back around to the tonic, where the entrance of T_3 marks the
beginning of the recapitulation.[18] But it almost always does so unobtru-
sively, without fanfare, and only for a moment—the first theme then
passes quickly to the solo instrument, and S_3 is underway. But for Beethoven, however the details of his procedure at this juncture may vary,
this is always a moment of high drama, elaborately prepared and brought
off with great exclamatory force. Even if the first theme itself is on the
gentle side, as in the Violin Concerto and the Second and Fourth Piano
Concertos, here it comes back *fortissimo*.
    The shout of this homecoming creates one more point of rhetorical
emphasis within the first movement of the concerto. Mozart always had
just two such: the endings of S_1 and S_3 (i.e., of the exposition and recapitulation), each marked with the ritual trilled dominant-tonic close. Beethoven's addition of a third at the beginning of the recapitulation (which
in every case except that of the Fourth Piano Concerto coincides with the
entrance of the third tutti) invests the opening music with a heightened
insistence and urgency, driving home its function as an emblem, as the
identifying badge of the movement. Here we experience a happy marriage
of an older idea and a newer one: the ritornello, that venerable cornerstone

of the eighteenth-century concerto and aria, proves happily compatible with the much younger dramatic recapitulation.

While in the eighteenth century the concerto was often compared to the sonata, it did not seem to lose its identity in the process. Writers from Scheibe to Koch and Vogler saw the alternation of tutti and solo as the peculiarly defining property of the genre, as its first principle of organization. Toward the middle of the nineteenth century, especially in the descriptions of Czerny and Marx, the concerto became only a particular kind of sonata. What counted most was the presentation and development of themes; the special distribution of music among instruments in the concerto was only a matter of orchestration, of instrumental timbre. Czerny describes the piano concerto as "a combination of the Pianoforte with the full orchestra, in which however the latter, for the most part, merely accompanies, and is consequently subordinate." For Marx, the two forces simply combine in various ways to carry out the plan of a sonata ("Its form is that of the sonata in three movements"). The first movement adheres to "sonata form," the musical design to which he himself, in his previous volume, has given this name and devoted 100-odd pages of painstaking description that served to fix the dominant view of this sort of movement for a whole century. The second and third tuttis of the movement virtually disappeared in Marx's formulation; just who may be playing at any point in the execution of the formal plan seemed largely a matter of indifference.[19]

It is from these formulations that we inherit the rather facile transfer to the concerto of those names coined for sonata form: exposition, development, and recapitulation. This terminology, of course, ignores what had always been special about the concerto, the large-scale alternation between the soloist and orchestra. Nor can we point to consistently reliable correspondences between the concerto's succession of solos and tuttis and the parts of sonata form. The problems begin at the beginning: which is the "real" exposition, or are there two?[20] The first is harmonically wrong because it always stays in or returns to the tonic, and the second would seem redundant as an "exposition." The "recapitulation," in the later concertos of Mozart and those of Beethoven, is typically distributed over two of the concerto's textural divisions, T_3 and S_3. In three of Beethoven's five piano concertos (the odd-numbered ones), the second tutti belongs exclusively neither to exposition nor development, but rather straddles the two, closing out the music in the secondary key and modulating to the the area where the second solo begins. And the final tutti would seem, in a sonata-like scheme of things, a rather useless appendage, an afterthought to a drama that has already run its course (while in the concerto of the earlier eighteenth century it had been the essential concluding member of the system of framing ritornellos). To be sure, some operations of the parts of sonata form are clearly present in the first movements of Beethoven's concertos—conspicuously so is the function of recapitulation. Because of this, and because these words and their referents are so solidly rooted in our understanding of the music of this period, such terminology will occasionally make an appearance here. But in the main we will call the sections of the first movements of Beethoven's concertos by the less prejudicial names *first tutti, first solo,* and the like.

Writers on the concerto from the eighteenth century to the present have used the terms *ritornello* and *tutti* more or less interchangeably for the sections played by the orchestra. *Ritornello,* probably the word more often used in this context, was the usual name for recurring instrumental refrains within vocal music in the seventeenth and eighteenth centuries. The eighteenth-century concerto seemingly borrowed the designation from the operatic aria—that other genre in which a professional performer, supported by a group of instruments, displayed uncommon technical and musical skills in a (semi-) public venue. That concertos were thought akin to arias is clear from the time of Scheibe, who advised those interested in the construction of a concerto movement simply to read his section on the aria.[21] Both genres in the earlier eighteenth century, the concerto movement and the aria, typically began and ended with essentially the same instrumental music, all in tonic—in the aria the da capo feature decreed that this music would be heard four times, before and after the "A" section in each of its two appearances. Shortened versions of these ritornellos showed up internally, transposed to the tonalities at hand. But by the time Mozart and Beethoven wrote concertos, these framing orchestral statements had been much modified: the close resemblance of the first and last, in particular, had disappeared, and the musical content of the internal ones had grown vastly less predictable. When a solo section comes to a conclusion, we cannot be sure what will be played next; all we really know is who will be playing it. So while vestiges of the venerable ritornello lingered on, in discussions of first movement it has seemed best here to abandon that word, together with all its old associations, in favor of the more neutral *tutti*—a term that reliably describes what happens in the music.

FINALES

In last movements of the rondo type (the option Beethoven invariably chose for his concertos) exactly the reverse is true. What is predictable at the "returns" is not the performing forces but the music itself. What is bound to occur at the main formal junctures is the opening theme (though subsequent statements may be shortened, the theme's beginning, always immediately arresting, is always there). What we cannot be sure of is who will play this music—often it will be divided in entertaining exchanges between solo and orchestra, and either may go first. So the rondo theme in Beethoven's concerto finales, true to the genre's tradition, constitutes a genuine ritornello (or refrain, labeled R in Table 1-2; E is for episode), and here we can use the term in good conscience. But by the time Beethoven wrote his concertos, the rondo finale in the hands of Mozart, Haydn, and others had also taken on conspicuous features of sonata form.[22] A generic version of sonata-rondo, common among finales of the Classical concerto, including all of Beethoven's, is shown in Table 1-2.

As do his first movements, Beethoven's concerto finales represent something of a standardization of a rich formal diversity in the rondos of his predecessors. There had been a lingering fondness for the old Baroque habit of introducing ritornellos in contrasting keys, for example. In this arrangement the ritornello itself limns out the harmonic trajectory of the movement, thus pursuing an aesthetic premise quite at variance with the idea of the ritornello as return to an invariable starting point. This older practice persisted in the rondos of C. P. E Bach and was endorsed by music theorists until almost the end of the century.[23] Beethoven occasionally did something similar, but he was never sincere about it. His off-tonic ritornello openings, as in the finales of the First and Second Piano Concertos and in the *Rondo a capriccio*, Op. 129 (*Die Wuth über den*

TABLE 1-2

verlorenen Groschen), always come across as ironic: the key is wrong and plainly to be heard as such, much as in a false recapitulation—and it is soon resoundingly corrected. This play with the wrong key for the ritornello reappears, transformed, in the finale of the Fourth Piano Concerto. Here the theme comes, from the first, with an off-key beginning (subdominant) built in, but promptly rights itself, raising the perplexing question as to which key is to be prepared in advance, an issue going to the fundamental tonal bearings of the movement.

Among Mozart's various "deviations" from our hypothetical model shown in Table 1-2, a favorite of his was the omission of the third ritornello from the pattern, as in the finales of his Sonata in C, K. 309, and the Piano Concertos K. 456, 466 (here as one of a thicket of distinctive formal moves), K. 488, and K. 595. At this juncture of such movements he usually brings back the tonic key together with something other than the rondo theme, saving the third (and final) appearance of that theme to inaugurate a coda-like construction at the end. Here, once more, Beethoven parts company with his great predecessor over the matter of recapitulation. For Mozart a double return—the simultaneous revisiting of both main theme and key—is only one possibility among several. In the finales of all Beethoven's concertos it is the only solution: that third ritornello starts off a recapitulation, and dramatically so, with a decisive return to known narrative amid familiar surroundings.

The rondo theme at its initial appearance, too, plays something of a double role: it acts both as a ritornello—instantly offering the prospect of later return—and as the first in a series of events that constitutes a credible exposition. A purposeful modulation typically leads to a secondary key where new, vividly different music of one or more kinds is heard. This section and its equivalent after the third ritornello resemble the corresponding areas (exposition and recapitulation) in a sonata or a symphony enough to make the old terminology of the rondo, *episode* (or, worse, *couplet*) basically misleading: these parts of Beethoven's finales act essentially like sonata form. And because there is no standard large-scale deployment of tutti and solo to cloud the discernment of exposition and recapitulation, these functions of sonata form are paradoxically more visible here than in the first movements.

In Beethoven's earlier concertos the shape and spirit of the old rondo are still faithfully preserved in the single true episode that anchors the center of the movement (as shown in Table 1-2). The idea of the episode stresses juxtaposition as opposed to flow and continuity. The beginning of this section in Beethoven's finales separates itself vividly from its surroundings: the previous ritornello stops and the episode starts with quite different music in a different key. Its ending, however, typically drops the episodic guise and merges into a transition of sorts, usually laced with coy anticipations of the ritornello to come. This central section of the concerto finale in Mozart's hands had already edged closer to the procedures of sonata form, often growing harmonically unstable and quasi-developmental. Beethoven followed suit slowly: the first three Piano Concertos, the Triple Concerto, and the Violin Concerto have true episodes; in the Fourth and Fifth Piano Concertos, Beethoven writes a developmental section.

Still, all these movements remain easily identifiable as rondos, and what makes them so more than anything else is simply the character of the music. When Daniel Gottlieb Türk set out to characterize rondo-like music in 1789, he seemed to search for words, coming up with "gentle, sprightly, teasing, and the like." In 1802 Koch described the rondo as "informal and naive" in style, with a main theme typically cast in a simple binary antecedent-consequent pattern.[24] A half century after Türk, Czerny abandoned words, resorting to examples:

> We have already observed, that the commencement of the *first* movement of a Sonata may be either energetic, or melodious; excited, or soft and tranquil. The same may be said of the Rondo or Finale; but there must be a palpable difference between the two, in regard to the description of the leading idea: for rarely would a suitable commencement for a first movement, serve also for a theme of a finale.
>
> It is not easy to render this difference intelligible by words. . . . As this can be explained most clearly by examples, we here place the themes of the first movements and of the finales of several Sonatas opposite one another.[25]

There follow incipits of first movements and finales of a dozen piano sonatas by Mozart, Clementi, Haydn, Dussek, Beethoven and others. What seems to distinguish these and most other rondo themes, as Koch had observed, is an insistent simplicity and regularity of construction. Periodization on a small scale is overwhelmingly even and predictable, and on a larger scale rondo themes frequently fall into transparent binary forms whose "rounded" feature sets up the anticipation of return within the theme itself—playful delay of this internal return is a favorite sport of Beethoven's concerto-finales.[26] This harmonic and metrical regularity, typically felt as well in the remainder of the movement—particularly in central episodes—seemed to impress late eighteenth-century musicians as more essential to the identity of the rondo than adherence to any large-scale formal plan. (Thus Mozart's Rondo for Piano, K. 485, seemed to deserve the name by virtue of the nature of its themes, despite its structural similarity to sonata form.)[27] Beethoven's concerto finales are to a fair degree regular in both ways, in their "content" as well as their "form." (In some cases, as in the rondo theme in the finale of the First Piano Concerto, there is delightful play with an *expectation* of regularity.) Only toward the ends of these movements (once again) does Beethoven consistently break free from the inherited larger patterns: substantial codas are appended to the earlier concertos, and the later ones conclude with exuberant large summary structures, of which the final ritornello forms one constituent part.

MIDDLE MOVEMENTS

It is in the middle movements of the concertos that, from a purely formal standpoint, Beethoven shows the greatest range and originality. Only the first two piano concertos may be said to follow the most common pattern for slow movements, namely, an exposition and recapitulation with the requisite short transition from the one to the other—and they do so only approximately. In the Third Piano Concerto that transition is so expanded as to take on an expressive life of its own. Thereafter the slow movements follow divergent paths. The Triple Concerto and the Fifth Piano Concerto (a distinctly odd pairing!) offer solemn slow beginnings that turn by degrees into introductions to finales. In the Violin Concerto the intensely moving Larghetto is an intricately eccentric set of variations over an old bass pattern. The agonistic dialogue of the Andante con moto in the Fourth Piano Concerto is sui generis: aspiring to dramatic impersonation, the strings and piano conjure a scene where initial stark opposition gives way to rapprochement and finally something like reconciliation, none of which is easily subsumable in any usual formal account of a concerto movement.

If there is one consistent development in this succession of middle movements, it is their growing implication in the composer's efforts to bind together compositions as a whole. Beginning, once more, with the Third Piano Concerto (and perhaps excluding the singular Andante of the Fourth), those movements—following upon Beethoven's formal experiments with the Sonatas "quasi una fantasia," Op. 27, of 1800–1801—show increasingly explicit continuities with the finales, and, in some cases, with the first movements as well. "Form" in the concertos, as in the sonatas and symphonies, came to have robust new implications for works in their entirety.

C H A P T E R 2

Bonn: The Court, the Composer, the Concerto

Beethoven spent his early years in the town of Bonn and at its court, living a life not unusual for a musician growing up under the patronage system. Like his father and his grandfather before him, he was an employee at this court of medium size and importance, where duties were prescribed and rewards bestowed by a bureaucracy ultimately answerable to a single person. This person was the Elector, or *Kurfürst*,[1] one of the princes of the German realms; traditionally seven in number, Electors were entitled to cast a ballot for the election of successive Holy Roman Emperors and sat as members of the *Kurfürstenverein*, an assembly that often exercised palpable influence over the affairs of the empire. The office of Elector included a marked ecclesiastical component. Appointment was made by the concurrence of chapters of the church and the Pope (as well as the Emperor), and Electors commonly held other high ecclesiastical offices as well. All four Electors resident at Bonn in the eighteenth century were Archbishops of Cologne, the local see, and all held similar positions elsewhere at the same time. The last two, Maximilian Friedrich (1761–84), and Maximilian Franz (1784–94), the Electors under whom Beethoven served, were also Archbishops of Münster.[2] A thorough coalescence of the affairs of church and state at the Electoral court at Bonn was surely a factor in the routine distribution of its musicians' duties, including those of the Beethovens, among all three of those familiar genres: music for the church, for the theater, and for the concert room.

Bonn, situated on a plain on the left bank of the Rhine just downstream and across the water from the storied *Siebengebirge*, was chosen as the seat of the Electors and Archbishops of Cologne in the thirteenth century, and it remained so until the entire institution was swept away in 1794, shortly after Beethoven's departure, in the wars of the French Revolution. Never a large town, Bonn in the late eighteenth century had a population that hovered around ten thousand. Occupying a strategically sensitive position near the northeastern border of France and the southeastern border of the Netherlands, the town was in earlier times repeatedly overrun and occupied by foreign troops—three such attacks took place in 1673, 1689, and 1703. The eighteenth century, however, was a period of relative peace, leaving the last four Electors with the freedom to concentrate on courtly ceremony and entertainment, with ever-present music. Nor were they much encumbered by thoughts of governmental economies for the sake of their heirs, who in any case never had much hope of succession to their appointive office.

The Electors Joseph Clemens (1689–1723) and Clemens August (1723–61), using materials from the previous fortifications of the town, constructed the imposing palace that in its modern-day form is the central university building.[3] To the west and north of this splendid edifice were the handsome Rathaus, the adjoining market place, and the town streets with homes of the nobility and bourgeoisie, many of whose inhabitants were in the service of the court. Such was the case with the Beethovens, who lived successively in *Bürgerhäuser* in the Rheingasse (during more than one period), the Bonngasse (where Beethoven was born), and the Wenzelgasse, all within easy walking distance of the palace where they performed their duties. In one wing of the palace was the chapel, and in another (this one called the "Neue Quartier"), the *Akademiesaal*, or concert room, and the theater.[4] The Beethovens, grandfather, father, and son, rendered their services in all three places. During the same period the Electors built several other palatial retreats, or *Lustschlösser*, mainly for summertime festivities. One was the Poppelsdorfer Schoss, about a mile southwest from the main residence and connected with it by a handsome, tree-lined boulevard (still largely intact but now interrupted by the railroad). A yet grander one, with a lavish rococo music room, was built at Brühl, about a dozen miles to the northwest. At these places, too, members of the Electoral musical establishment were expected to entertain.

Clemens August, Archbishop and Elector of Cologne in the earlier eighteenth century, was also Bishop of Liège, to the west. At the cathedral there his attention seems to have been attracted by a young bass singer, Ludwig van Beethoven, whom he brought to Bonn in 1733.[5] Thus the grandfather of the composer began his forty-year service at the Electoral court, during the last twelve of which he was Kapellmeister, the supervisor of all its musical activities. Soon after his arrival he married a young woman from the area, Maria Josepha Poll. Apparently determining that their only surviving son, Johann (born in 1739 or 1740), should also serve in the court's musical establishment, he proceeded early on to train him in singing and clavier. Such an expectation and course of action repeated itself in the next generation. The eldest child of Johann and his wife Maria Magdalena, too, was destined by parental wish and enforcement to a career as a court musician—though in this case no very systematic instruction seems to have been provided. Thus the composer Beethoven, named for his grandfather, grew up in one of the several families of musicians employed at the Bonn court (others with well-known names were the Ries family—four members in three generations—the uncle and nephew Reicha, Johann Peter Salomon and his father, and the cousins Romberg). At this feudal court the succession of musicians hewed much more strongly to blood lines than did that of the appointed Electors.

It was usual for the younger musicians of a family to serve at court for a time without pay; thereafter, application might be made for salaries left vacant by attrition. Thus when the singer Mme. Lentner gave up her appointment at the end of 1763, her salary was divided, upon petition from both families, between Johann van Beethoven and the young singer Anna Maria Ries, daughter of the court trumpeter and violinist Johann Ries. The singer Beethoven, it was stated, had already served "a considerable time" and Anna Maria Ries "about a year."[6] Similarly, the thirteen-year-old Ludwig van Beethoven in early 1784 applied for the official position of assistant court organist (to substitute for his teacher Christian Gottlob Neefe), after having served de facto in that capacity for nearly two years. It is not quite clear what the response was to this petition; Thayer took it to be positive, and Schiedermair, negative.[7] But the point was moot. That spring the Rhine overflowed, and both the Elector Maximilian Friedrich and his prime minister, Count Anton von Belderbusch, died in a *Götterdämmerung*-like scene that left everyone's position in doubt.

The new Elector, Maximilian Franz, forced into stringent economic measures by the prodigality of his predecessors, reduced the salaries of many of his musicians. But resisting the recommendation that Beethoven ("of good capability, still young") should replace Neefe—thus effecting a considerable saving—he added the young musician to the payroll and simply subtracted his salary from that of his teacher. Thus by June 1784 Beethoven was an official member of the Electoral musical establishment,[8] eligible now to wear the court musician's livery, consisting, according to the reminiscences of the Beethovens' neighbor Gottfried Fischer, of "sea-green frock coat, green knee-breeches with buckles, stockings of white or black silk, shoes with a black bow-knots, embroidered vest with pocket-flaps, the vest bound with real gold cord, hair curled and with queue, crush hat under the left arm, sword on the left side with silver belt."[9] Beethoven's duties were for the most part what they had been the previous two years, that is, to substitute for Neefe when the latter's other obligations (usually having to do with the theater) prevented him from playing the services in the court chapel. These, according to the court calendar, involved Mass and Vespers on all Sundays and regular festivals ("gebotene Feyrtäg"), the Litanies on Saturdays, and special services with music in Lent.[10] One contemporaneous report, at least, seems to show that the organist's services were required even when the singing was plainsong. This is the Bonn physician Franz Wegeler's engaging recollection that Beethoven once improvised an accompaniment designed to "unhorse" the tenor Ferdinand Heller as he tried to sing the plainsong Lamentations on the weekdays preceding Easter. On this occasion, Wegeler remembered, Beethoven played piano, since the organ was not permitted to be heard during Holy Week—the clear implication being that plainsong was usually accompanied by the organ.[11]

Before and after his official appointment, the young organist's duties varied with the vicissitudes of Neefe's schedule. When the latter, as a member of the theatrical company, followed the Elector to Münster in the summer of 1782, for example, the eleven-and-a-half-year-old Beethoven was left fully in charge at the organ. But when the court's theatrical music was supplied by traveling troupes equipped with their own directors, as in in 1785–87, Neefe was mainly free to play the court organ himself, and his pupil's services were little required.[12] We also hear that when the need arose the boy Beethoven took over other duties from his teacher: when Neefe assumed the duties of the absent Kapellmeister Lucchesi for a time in 1783, Beethoven, now twelve, evidently took his teacher's place in the theater, accompanying rehearsals at the keyboard.[13] And somewhat later the theater provided an opportunity for the young Beethoven to exercise his musical talents in yet another way. In 1788 Maximilian Franz determined to renew the somewhat sporadic previous efforts of his predecessor toward the founding of a national theater similar to those at Vienna and Mannheim, a theater, that is, to produce either original German dramatic works or foreign works in translation. New dramatic and musical personnel were assembled, and resident musicians were pressed into service in the new undertaking. Among them was young

Beethoven, who now took up new duties as an orchestral violist, evidently in both theater and concert room. In the court calendar of 1790 he is listed in two separate capacities, as organist and violist.[14] For the last four years of his life in Bonn (1788–92), Beethoven's duties evidently remained much the same: playing services in the chapel (finally rebuilt in 1789 after the fire damage of 1777 and supplied with a new organ), playing viola for opera performances and concerts, and probably, at times, accompanying operatic rehearsals at the keyboard.

But such a portrait of the young court musician seems vastly too prosaic. In Beethoven's known musical activities for the court we see almost no sign of the budding piano virtuoso or of the young composer of growing powers—or of the musical genre that unites these two, the piano concerto. The first we hear of solo playing and the concerto in young Beethoven's life is in a setting far removed from the court. It occurs in a notice of a subscription concert organized by his father in 1778 in Cologne, featuring two of the elder Beethoven's pupils, the court contralto J. Helena Averdonck and young Ludwig, the latter performing "various keyboard concertos and trios."[15] There are vague reports that in early winter 1781, the boy undertook a voyage, this time with his mother—as in the case of Mozart's trip to Mannheim and Paris of 1777–78, the father could not be released from his duties—to the Netherlands (probably Rotterdam) where, according to one report, he "played a great deal in great houses."[16] There is firm documentary evidence, on the other hand, presented by Luc van Haselt in 1966, of a trip to that country in 1783. A payment record from the court of Prince Willem V at the Hague, dated 23 November 1783, includes a sum of 63 florins for "M. Beethoven, 12 [years]" for playing the forte piano with other instrumental players in a "funded concert." Whether there was one trip or two remains unclear; but the circumstances of the concert of 1783—eleven musicians were paid, and Beethoven's fee was the largest—suggest he may have been the soloist in a concerto.[17] There are also reports of early forays with his father (when the Elector was out of town) to Oberkassel, just up the river, and to other places, with the express purpose of performing for patrons of music.[18]

In 1791 the Elector gathered up some twenty-five of his musicians, including young Beethoven, for an expedition to Mergentheim,[19] an outing that yielded a good bit of testimony about the musical activities of the court and Beethoven's part in them. First, there was a stopover at Aschaffenburg-am-Main, where Beethoven and the noted composer-pianist Johann Franz Xaver Sterkel played for each other at Sterkel's home, Beethoven performing his *Righini* Variations and improvising some extra ones.[20] And in a long and chatty report in Bossler's *Musikalische Corres-*

pondenz of November 1791, the journalist and musical enthusiast Carl Ludwig Junker describes in some detail the musical activities of the court in Mergentheim. In addition to a performance of Paisiello's *Il Re Theodoro* (in German), Junker attended a concert at which the Romberg cousins played two (unidentified) concertos, one for cello, and a double concerto for violin and cello. He also heard Beethoven improvise at the piano, again in a private, informal gathering.[21]

Specific accounts of the personnel and activities of the Electoral musical establishment are notably silent about any solo performances by the young Beethoven. Neefe's lengthy and often-quoted report about musicians in the court and town, in C. F. Cramer's *Magazin der Musik* of March 1783, concludes a list of "dilettanti" in Bonn with the "very promising" Beethoven, who "plays the clavier very ably and with power." He does not even imply that the twelve-year-old demonstrated his prowess as a solo player at court.[22] And the much later list of musicians at the Bonn court in Bossler's *Musikalische Correspondenz* (July 1791) designates solo "virtuosi" with a single asterisk and those players who also compose with two. Beethoven's name, the year before his departure for Vienna, has none, though a laconic addition notes that "Herr Ludwig van Beethoven plays clavier concertos."[23]

It has often simply been assumed that Beethoven played those concertos and other piano compositions at court functions in the main residence or in the Lustschlösser at Poppelsdorf or Brühl. Deiters speculated that Beethoven's "official position necessitated his playing [concertos] before the Elector," and Willy Hess ventured that Beethoven "almost certainly" performed his very early Concerto in E♭ (WoO 4) at the Bonn court.[24] But we actually have no testimony whatever that he played a solo of any kind at court. Surviving evidence as to Beethoven's performances in the Bonn years is relatively sparse; if such appearances at court were for him at all usual, however, surely we would expect to read something about this in the Fischer reminiscences, from Wegeler-Ries,[25] or from the periodic reports of Neefe. Particularly Wegeler and Fischer, writing in later years, when Beethoven was famous, would likely have recalled such events. As it is, every reference from the Bonn years to solo performances by Beethoven testifies to an "extra-curricular" setting—to informal gatherings of various sorts, sometimes in the Beethovens' home, or, in the one event at Cologne, a public concert.

This, together with Beethoven's singular lack of official recognition as a solo player, suggests that he pursued his activities as a developing virtuoso and player of keyboard concertos quite apart from his role as a court musician. That this should be the case is not particularly surprising. The keyboard concerto in the 1780s was still a relatively new genre whose natural home was pretty clearly not the court entertainment, but rather the public concert. In London J. C. Bach's piano concerto became regular fare in his concerts of the later 1770s;[26] Mozart and Clementi played their piano concertos at subscription concerts in Vienna and London in the 1780s. At no court in Europe was there similar activity on this front, nor had there been, so far as we know, since C. P. E. Bach played his concertos at the court of Frederick the Great in the 1750s and 1760s; there is nothing unnatural about the Electoral court's failure to take advantage of its assistant organist's special gifts along these lines.

In another of his periodic communications to Cramer's *Magazin der Musik* about musical activities in Bonn, Neefe wrote in April 1787:

> The amateurs' zeal for music is increasing greatly among the inhabitants. The clavier is especially loved; there are here several *Hammerclaviere* by Stein of Augsburg, and other comparable instruments. Among the feminine amateurs who occupy their beautiful hands with these instruments, I shall name the Countesses Hatzfeld and Belderbusch, Felise Metternich, Frau von Waldenfels, Fräulein v. Weichs, Frau v. Cramer, Frau Belzer, wife of the Privy Councillor, Fräulein v. Gruben, Fräulein v. Mastiaux etc. The youthful Baron v. Gudenau plays the pianoforte right well, and besides young Beethoven, the children of the kapellmeister [i.e., Andrea Lucchesi] deserve to be mentioned because of their admirable and precociously developed talent. All of the sons of Herr v. Mastiaux play the clavier well, as you already know from earlier letters of mine.[27]

It is hard not to detect a certain patronizing tone in the well-intentioned Neefe's report. In Bonn as elsewhere in Europe, the piano—except for its role in the concerto—was evidently still thought of mainly in connection with amateur music, with music-making by women and the very young, and, by extension, with music in the home. (Evidently, such an association led Neefe to include the pianist Beethoven, both here and in his earlier report of 1783, among the amateurs.)[28] But music in the grander homes in Bonn often included performance before an audience. Such was the case in the home of the prime minister von Belderbusch and in those of other high officials such as the court counselor Altstädten.[29] The musical salon life of Bonn evidently reached its high point, however, in the home of Privy Councillor Johann Gottfried von Mastiaux, who, according to Neefe's report of 1783, "knew and wished no enjoyment but the enjoyment of music. . . . He is the only one who, now for some time, has through the entire winter held at his home a weekly concert in which every musical amateur, either foreign or local, may take part . . . among the great mass of his collected music he holds the following as the most important: 80 symphonies of Joseph Haydn, 30 quartets and 40 trios by him as well, and 50 clavier concertos, of the best authors."[30] Perhaps the young Beethoven played piano and piano concertos at musical gatherings such as these, where little in the way of a written record is to be expected.

If the Electoral court in its official capacity was not particularly nurturing of Beethoven's career as a performer, it also seems to have provided little encouragement to his growth as a composer. Musicians of the court who wished their children to receive musical instruction apparently arranged for it themselves without official supervision. In his earliest years Beethoven had a long series of teachers haphazardly engaged by his father. Some of this instruction apparently amounted to little more than child abuse, and at the same time the father actively discouraged his son's creative impulses.[31] It was surely a stroke of luck that a musician of the stature and sensibility of Neefe (from 1779 associated with the resident theater) was appointed court organist in 1781—just as Beethoven's prescribed years in elementary school came to an end, and he was able to devote himself exclusively to music. As Neefe himself reported in 1783, when he took Beethoven on as a pupil, he set him to studying the preludes and fugues of *The Well-Tempered Clavier* (circulating at this time only in manuscript copies), taught him thoroughbass "so far as his duties permitted," began instruction in composition, and arranged for the first publication of Beethoven's music, the Variations for Piano on a March by Dressler (WoO 63, 1782), at Mannheim. Other very early compositions evidently produced under the aegis of Neefe were the three "Kurfürsten" Sonatas (WoO 47), published in 1783 with a dedication to Maximilian Friedrich; the Piano Concerto in E♭ (WoO 4, 1784); and the three Piano Quartets (WoO 36, 1785).

Others who encouraged the young composer were Helene von Breuning and her family, with whom Beethoven had intimate associations from about 1784, and, a bit later, Count Ferdinand von Waldstein, who, after settling in Bonn in 1788, provided the young musician with both moral and financial support. Beethoven collaborated with him on the *Ritterballet*, produced at court in March 1791 (although the music for this production was Beethoven's, the court calendar attributes the work to Waldstein alone).[32] And the first major commission of the young composer's career, that for the Cantata on the Death of the Emperor Joseph II (1790), was granted, not by the court, but by the Bonn Lesegesellschaft, of which

Waldstein was a prominent member.[33] The Elector Maximilian Franz may have showed some interest in Beethoven's musical career when he permitted the ill-fated trip to Vienna of 1787 for lessons with Mozart.[34] But although by the time of his final departure from Bonn in late 1792 Beethoven had a list of some forty compositions to his name, we have no specific testimony, official or unofficial, that any of his music (with the single exception of that *Ritterballet*, for which he received no credit) was ever performed at court. Thayer's opinion that Maximilian Franz did not value Beethoven above his other court musicians, the Rombergs, the family Ries, the Reichas, seems amply justified.[35]

From the beginning, Beethoven's growth both as a composer and solo player seems to have been detached from the old-style courtly system in which he was raised. He surely benefitted from the attentions of those with high connections at court, particularly Belderbusch and Waldstein, and his salaried position enabled him to support himself and, toward the end, his younger brothers as well. But in what really counted, in his growth as a composer and player, he apparently made his way with precious little official support. It is a mistake to think of Beethoven's position as a liveried musician in Bonn as comparable, say, to Haydn's situation in Eisenstadt and Eszterháza in the early 1760s, where composition was Haydn's primary duty as Vice-Kapellmeister. Nor was Beethoven's relation to his court much like Mozart's experience in Salzburg (where for a time he held the very similar post of court organist) in the corresponding part of his career. However Mozart may have despised the "liederliche, lumpenhafte Kirchenmusik" he heard in the Archbishop's service, his own music, at least, was regularly performed at court, often under his own direction.[36] Beethoven seems not at all a usual product of the patronage system, for he apparently pursued his real career mainly in his spare time; this was surely the case in his cultivation—as composer and player—of the concerto.

We have only two meager reports that Beethoven played piano (or "clavier") concertos in his years in Bonn. They come from very early in that period (the concert at Cologne in 1778) and very late (the piece in Bossler's *Musikalische Correspondenz* of July 1791). We have no idea whose music the seven-year-old played in Cologne. This concert was evidently the opening salvo in Johann van Beethoven's campaign, which Neefe soon joined, to present the boy as a child prodigy. If Beethoven had also been the composer of the "various clavier concertos and trios" on the program, the promotional notice of this event probably would have said so.[37] By the time of the second notice, in 1791, Beethoven, we know, was both a player and composer of concertos. Nonetheless, we have no complete text of a

Beethoven concerto from the Bonn period; the most substantial surviving examples of music belonging roughly to this genre are as follows:[38]

1. The Keyboard Concerto in E♭ WoO 4, presumably from 1784.[39] The solo part is complete in three movements; the orchestral tuttis are in the piano score, with some instrumental cues. The surviving score is in hand of a copyist, with corrections by Beethoven.
2. A *Romance cantabile* in E minor for keyboard, flute, bassoon, and small orchestra, Hess 13, probably from 1786; the score breaks off after 57 mm.
3. Violin Concerto in C, WoO 5, ca. 1790–92. 259 mm. of a first movement in full score.
4. Fragments of the Piano Concerto in B♭, Op. 19.
   a. A leaf from an orchestral score, from ca. 1787–9 surviving in a collection of manuscripts in Berlin, the Fischhof Miscellany. Only the piano part is written in this passage, which is from the first movement.
   b. Another page of an orchestral score in a Paris manuscript from ca. 1790–92(?); from the development section of the first movement.
   c. A draft from ca. 1790–92 of the Andante that became the contrasting central episode of the Rondo in B♭, WoO 6, which itself was almost certainly an earlier finale of Op. 19.

THE CONCERTO IN E♭, WoO 4

The Concerto in E♭ (WoO 4) is an ebullient little piece, uneven in quality, hugely eclectic, suggestive of a thirteen-year-old who (as we may easily imagine) played rather better than he composed. The rough formal outlines of the three conventional concerto movements he seems to have had well enough in hand. The first movement follows the usual four-tutti plan, as described by Koch and practiced, with modifications, by Haydn in the 1770s, and by Kozeluch and the young Mozart in the early 1780s.[40] Beethoven's movement has a feigned modulation to the dominant in T_1; a second theme given there sits precariously on the dominant, then slides quickly back to tonic. The handling of this juncture in the first tutti was for some time to remain an issue for Beethoven—as it did much later for his critic Tovey.[41] There is a real modulation in S_1, where that second theme stays properly in the dominant. The second tutti duly rounds off the dominant section; the third coincides with the onset of a recapitulation; and the final one, interrupted by the expected signal for a cadenza, closes out the movement. The usual building blocks are all in place.

But the solos bear a peculiar relationship to these orchestral sections. The piano, for one thing, never plays the first theme at all; at both its principal opportunities to do so, at the start of S_1 and S_3, it states the barest head motive of the theme—just a rising fourth—using it as a springboard for protracted keyboard figuration. This might lead us to think the movement distinctly old fashioned, a recollection, perhaps, of Italian Baroque concertos, where motivic connections between solo and tutti were often minimal. But we might just as well consider this trait anticipatory of first movements of the virtuoso concertos of the first three decades of the nineteenth century, those of Hummel, Weber, and Moscheles—and even Chopin—where the solo part was also barely responsive to musical ideas proposed by the orchestra, but concentrated instead on its own protracted stretches of nonthematic figuration. The result here (insofar as we can judge, in the absence of the complete orchestral part) is a far cry from the intricate dialogue that graces the mature concertos of Beethoven or Mozart, from that musical conversation between an eloquent spokesperson and the massed group that seems sometimes acquiescent, sometimes contrary. Here the issue seems to be rather that the soloist simply has a number of remarkable feats to show us; the orchestra provides a backdrop, connective matter, and relief.

That first theme, so neglected by the piano (Example 2-1), sounds like a mildly childish conflation of two recognizable types: the third-fifth-sixth intervals of the rustic horn call, actually played by horns at the bottom of the texture, and the even tread and dotted rhythms of the quasi-military march that will be a recurring motif in Beethoven's concertos. The materials of the rest of the first tutti could easily have come from a Mannheim symphony of the previous generation: a typical rising crescendo leads to the second theme in trio texture with flutes in thirds above (that shift back to the tonic occurs between its two statements). This is really the sum total of thematic matter in the entire movement. The piece presents a stark contrast, of course, to the first movements of Mozart's concertos from any period, where we are typically offered a number of reasonably stable melodies together with bits of distinctive, easily recallable connective material, some of which will be useful later for internal tuttis. Here the young Beethoven greatly limits his choices. When the soloist comes to a cadence, the orchestra must play something recognizable. But as the repeated casual introduction of the first theme is a formal impossibility, we are again and again subjected at these junctures to that Mannheim-like second theme (in the middle of S_1 and S_3, at the beginning of T_2, and just after the cadenza), whose singsong regularity unfailingly checks any momentum the preceding section may have generated (see Example 2-2).

Central to this movement, and to the concerto as a whole, is an appealing display of keyboard agility and ingenuity, a celebration of the incipient virtuosity of Beethoven at thirteen. We have here something of an anthology of keyboard figurations. Standard patterns, like ordinary scales, broken chords, and arpeggios, abound. But there are also some unexpectedly modern figurations: fast scales in broken octaves (which the mature Mozart began to use sparingly in his concertos at just about this time[42]) and in double thirds, the figuration that Clementi had just made famous, but which failed to impress Mozart at the famous "contest" between the two musicians before Emperor Joseph II on Christmas Eve, 1781.[43]

The young Beethoven shows a special penchant for a pianistic figure comprised of a neighbor-note turn and octave leap, seen in the very opening of the solo part. This passage is distinctly awkward to play; its recurrence in S_2 (mm. 164–69, p. 8),[44] owing to the altered deployment of black keys, is a near impossibility (Example 2-3). As any pianist will instantly see, however, omitting the left-hand chords at the start of each measure makes the passage child's play. We might surmise that those chords represent the orchestra's music, included by the arranger of this reduced score simply to relieve the textural poverty of this solo material played alone.[45] A passage in S_1 (mm. 115–18, p. 6) gives the same impression, but more so. Here a supporting bass seems to have been added to a figuration borrowed from the Prelude in B♭ from the first volume of Bach's *Well-Tempered Clavier* (Neefe, we will remember, said he introduced Beethoven to this collection). Without the bass, as in Bach's version, this figuration is conveniently played with both hands; with it, the passage is gratuitously awkward, the sort of thing that would scarcely have repaid the young virtuoso's investment in practice time (see Examples 2-4, a and b).

The Larghetto of WoO 4 is the only movement of this work that strikes one as recognizably the work of Beethoven. Here the writing for keyboard in particular prefigures certain traits of the later slow movements of the first three numbered concertos. There is an extravagance of ornament that in more than one way steps well outside the usual stylistic boundaries of its time. First, there is the Beethovenian extended range of note-values, featuring a consistent use of sixty-fourth notes in $\frac{3}{4}$ meter, thus forcing an uncommonly slow tempo for the movement. And then there is a radical sweep and range to the ornamental figures themselves, such as the three-and-one-half-octave chromatic scale in sixty-fourth notes up to f‴ (the top note of Beethoven's piano) in m. 47 (p. 16).[46] The daredevil exuberance of the piano part in this slow movement was not to be exceeded until the Largo of the Third Piano Concerto (where Beethoven writes a good bit of figuration in 128th notes). But however prophetic in some ways, the slow movement of WoO 4 can scarcely be called a success. Its main theme—there really is only one—with its succession of even eighth-notes, is too bland and featureless to support the tempo dictated by the later figuration. Upon each of its three occurrences (two of them by the soloist, in contrast to the precedent of the first movement), this music simply dies a slow death (see Example 2-5). And the peculiar overall shape of the movement, a kind of compromise between a plain binary pattern and a ritornello form, has neither the compact economy of the one nor the repeated pleasure-in-recognition of the other—there can be little pleasure, in any event upon the return of that first theme.

The Rondo of WoO 4, also formally a bit eccentric, is the most satis-fying movement of the concerto. Its insouciant ritornello theme is played five times rather than the expected four of the usual rondo-with-episode (as shown in Table 1-2 above).[47] These appearances of the main theme are far and away the most distinctive moments in this movement, domi-nated otherwise by rather featureless keyboard figuration. After the first modulation to the dominant, a stable melody ("b") emerges briefly from the thicket, followed by the expected ritornello in the tonic. But then another discursive expedition to the dominant retraces the path just fol-lowed and presents a new bit of thematic matter ("c") that very closely resembles something from a Haydn sonata the young Beethoven may have played.[48] After this twice-told tale comes the episode, a self-enclosed, witty little sojourn in the tonic minor, its stiff-jointed alternation of tonic and dominant in the bass a recollection of the "Turkish" manner that never ceased to amuse European musicians. In gesture and tone this section anticipates the amiable irreverence of the corresponding places in the finales of the First and Second Concertos.

Toward the end, the movement seems to flounder; only a rough approx-imation of "b" is recapitulated—leaving us in doubt whether we should make the identification or not—and the piece is chopped off with childish abruptness as the last ritornello ends. But Beethoven has caught the joc-ular spirit of the genre. The ritornello is either ushered in with elaborate teasing lead-ups or abruptly plunked down before we expect it. And that ritornello itself, aggressively naive with its deadly regular peasant-dance rhythm, self-consciously undercuts its own declared ethos in its next-to-last appearance (R_4) by subtly turning into something with very different connotations, a horn call (see Example 2-6).[49]

After entertaining private audiences in Bonn with this concerto (as we may imagine), Beethoven seems to have kept the manuscript score of it all his life, for it was included in the auction of his papers the year after his death. And at some point he had moved to improve it. Among revisions he wrote in are cancellations that tend to curb the youthful exuberance of certain passages: four measures of the hackneyed I–VI–IV–V cadential pattern in the first movement,[50] six measures in the second, and five measures substituted for eighteen in the third.

But what was the original purpose of the manuscript itself? Now in Berlin, it is a complete copy in an unknown hand of the solo part, with the orchestral interjections in piano score. A title page proclaims "un Concert pour le Clavecin ou Fortepiano composé par Louis Van Beethoven agé douze ans," this seemingly written by the young composer himself. Such a score would not be very useful for a performance; parts could not be copied from the reduced tuttis, and the soloist would hardly need such a full version of them. But this score looks very much like the solo part in a concerto *publication*. The piano part in the first editions of Beethoven's Second and Third Piano Concertos (1804), for example, have just this arrangement: a full keyboard part and reduced tuttis. (In the other common format—more common in 1784—the keyboard part has a figured bass line during the tuttis.) So it seems reasonable to think that this manuscript was prepared for publication, as a sequel, perhaps, to the three *Kurfürstensonaten* put out the previous year by Bossler of Speier; even the wording of that printed title page, "von Ludwig van Beethoven /alt eilf Jahr," is approximated in the manuscript. But something evidently went wrong, and the concerto was not published. This is but one sign of a certain malaise that seems to have set in about this time in the young composer's progress and prospects.

THE *ROMANCE CANTABILE*

The *Romance cantabile* in E minor, Hess 13 (1786), is scored for the odd assemblage of solo piano, bassoon, and flute, together with an orchestra consisting of strings plus two oboes; it survives in autograph full score, apparently nearly complete, in a collection in London, the Kafka Miscellany. What is missing may well be only the continuation of a central *maggiore* episode that breaks off at the end of its first page (fol. 80v).[51] The instrumental romance, or *romanza*, was vaguely derivative of the vocal genre of the same name, much loved by amateur musicians in the later eighteenth century, especially in France. It frequently had a simple three-part episodic structure, ABA, and Beethoven's score has a clearly marked indication for a dal segno repetition of most of the first section. And there is good reason to think, following Nottebohm's suggestion,[52] that this piece was a movement of a larger work: its first page has "tacet" indications for four instruments (apparently brass) that are to be typically silent in the slow movement. Nor would there have been anything much out of the ordinary in writing a "romance" as an internal movement: in this matter symphonies of Gossec, Dittersdorf, and Haydn provided the young composer with good precedents.[53]

The *Romance cantabile* shares its peculiar instrumentation with an early chamber piece of Beethoven's, the Trio for Flute, Bassoon, and Piano, WoO 37.[54] Thayer presents evidence that the trio was written for the family of the head stable master (*Obrist-Stallmeister*) of the Bonn court, Freiherr von Westerholt-Giesenberg, an amateur bassoonist; his son played the flute, and his daughter, a pupil of Beethoven and for a time the object of his "Werther-like love," the piano. Deiters concludes with some justification that the *Romance* (and the larger work of which it was a part) was also intended for this singular family ensemble.[55] Nonetheless, there is reason to think that Beethoven meant the piano parts of these works not for his pupil, but for himself. All the instrumental parts in the autograph score of the *Romance cantabile* are written out in full except that for the piano, which is only partly notated. This document, like the autographs of the first three numbered piano concertos, has all the earmarks of a "performance autograph," a score from which parts could be copied; a sketchy piano part would have sufficed if Beethoven was to have been the pianist.

The piano part of the trio, too, must be suspect as a composition intended for somebody else. Especially in its finale, a theme and variations, it shows the distinctive and difficult keyboard figurations (particularly those involving drastic stretching of the hand) that also appear in the Concerto WoO 4 from 1784 and the Piano Quartets WoO 36 of 1785, and, more radically, in the Righini Variations WoO 65 of 1790. Specialized writing such as this is most easily explained, surely, as a product of Beethoven's own development as a virtuoso pianist. But this scarcely weakens the putative connection of these pieces with the peculiar flute and bassoon ensemble of the von Westerholts; in this case, once again, Beethoven's music and his playing of it were probably associated with private musical circles in Bonn.

As to musical style, there is nothing very ambitious or distinctive about the *Romance cantabile*. It has an appealing *affettuoso* main theme in E minor that reappears often enough in its episodic structure to dominate the piece strongly. One notices, especially, the consequent phrase of this theme, constructed so that its two parts fit together in a loose canon, providing thereby a contrapuntal interest almost totally absent from the fifteen-year-old's earlier music. The three solo instruments behave like equal partners, like a concertino to which the larger group of instruments acts alternately as a foil and as an accompaniment. In this they preserve the idea of the ensemble concerto or *concertant*, quite in contrast to the textures of the Trio WoO 37 and the Quartets WoO 36, where the prominence of the piano part betrays a kinship, instead, with the accompanied keyboard sonata. The *Romance cantabile* represents an essay for a combination of instruments to which Beethoven was to return more than once; from these efforts only one complete composition survives, the Triple Concerto Op. 56.

THE VIOLIN CONCERTO IN C, WoO 5

The torso of a first movement in full orchestral score is all we have of a violin concerto in C major (WoO 5) that Beethoven composed ca. 1790–92. The autograph score, now in Vienna, breaks off at the end of a verso side, suggesting that the movement may have been completed. If so, it must have been a big one: the T_1-S_1-T_2 and beginning of T_3 that survive—very likely less than half of it—comprise 259 measures in common meter. It starts with a unison triadic statement on the tonic in vigorous dotted rhythms, whose effect is largely vitiated by immediate literal repetition on the supertonic (Example 2-7).[56] What follows is at points radically experimental and often musically convincing. This opening tutti, an area in the concerto we are taught to think of as harmonically stable, courts tonal chaos. It halts portentously on the dominant (G) and resumes abruptly on the mediant (E), with a working of the original dotted motive (plus syncopated string chords à la Mannheim) that sets off a tortuous sequential passage, laced with accented dissonances. This leads stormily through Bb major and A minor and back to G (the dominant), where a tranquil "second theme" is heard—momentarily. A plunge in the flat direction now traverses Ab and C minor before the firm ground of the tonic major key—and once again the opening theme—is finally regained just as the soloist is about to enter.

Such disruption in the first tutti is an extreme example of what will come to be something of a habit for Beethoven; each of the first four numbered piano concertos indulges—in roughly descending order of temerity—in a degree of harmonic adventurism in this section. None of these opening tuttis is a docile introduction that presents the main matter of the piece in relatively neutral colors, as a prelude to subsequent adventures. Beethoven evidently had quite a different aesthetic principle in mind for this part of the movement: the mass of the orchestra comes on as active and even unruly, until the soloist takes matters in hand and for a time, at least, restores a measure of order.

We do not know for whom Beethoven intended the solo part; Deiters suggests he may have had in mind Franz Ries or Andreas Romberg, both violinists at the Bonn court and both friends of the composer.[57] At any rate, the soloist plays virtually all the melodic material of the piece in S_1 and is also given brilliant figuration that exploits the full range of the instrument. This is remarkably idiomatic and grateful violin music, written by one practiced in the art—or blessed with ready access to somebody who was. However violinistic this part may be, though, there is reason to think that Beethoven at a later point turned the piece into a movement of a piano concerto or at the very least contemplated doing so. In the Kafka Miscellany there is an extended cadenza draft, manifestly for piano, that is clearly a working out of the distinctive head motive of the first theme of this movement.[58] Since Beethoven typically worked on cadenzas when he was about to play a concerto in concert, there is a distinct possibility that he performed this piece on the piano in public. The sources do not permit a firm conclusion as to when this might have happened. But a gossamer thread of circumstantial evidence pursued by Douglas Johnson leads to 1793 as the date of the cadenza[59]—which would make the violin/piano concerto a likely concert piece for the young virtuoso during his first year in Vienna. Perhaps Beethoven wrote concertos for others when his opportunities for performing himself were very limited in Bonn—we know that during the Bonn period he also composed an oboe concerto, now lost[60]—but moved to refashion some of this music for his own instrument when his prospects improved in Vienna.

FRAGMENTS OF THE PIANO CONCERTO IN B♭, OP. 19

Another concerto Beethoven probably played during his first year or so in Vienna also has roots in Bonn: the Second Piano Concerto Op. 19. Some version of the first movement of this concerto, at least, was in existence before the move to Vienna. The earliest testimony to this is an (evidently rejected) autograph score fragment of a concerto in the Fischhof Miscellany (fol. 15), in which the piano part alone is notated; the music is a sequential treatment of the first theme of this movement. On the basis of paper type and handwriting, Johnson has suggested a date "sometime between 1786 and 1790" for this fragment. He also tentatively identifies the music as part of a cadenza.

But it would be most surprising to find a cadenza written out in an autograph score in this early period. Beyond their function as compositional documents, the scores of concertos generally served two purposes: they provided a model from which parts could be copied for a performance, or they became exemplars for publication. In neither case were the soloist's cadenzas included. Beethoven typically sketched these in his private papers in anticipation of performances at which he played the solo part. The first case we know of in which he wrote cadenzas into the score is in the autograph of Op. 73 (the "Emperor"), that is, the only one of the piano concertos that we know Beethoven did not himself premiere. Here he included them specifically to enjoin other soloists from supplying their own. The passage from Op. 19 in Fischhof, moreover, does not even look much like one of Beethoven's cadenzas. It lacks both the very fast harmonic rhythm and the ubiquitous trills that are hallmarks of his early ones.[61] It seems much more likely that it comes from an early form of the development section (or S_2) of this movement; that it moves out from a solid F major suggests that it may have begun this section.

The other bit of the first movement of Op. 19 deriving from the Bonn years is preserved on a bifolium of Bonn paper (now in Paris), dating, according to Johnson, from ca. 1790–92.[62] Following three sides of unrelated material, folio 2v is a single-page score fragment from the latter part of S_2 (as we know it) in the first movement. Because the concerto fragment does not begin on the first folio—nor would it if the bifolium were turned inside out—this manuscript can hardly be a rejected portion of a finished score or of one in progress. Very likely it was to have been a replacement page for an already existing score (that the music on its verso was not crossed out suggests that this intention was not realized). This music charts a harmonic course rather different from what we have at that point in the published concerto; the implications of this divergence will be explored in Chapter 4.

Another bit of music from Beethoven's last years in Bonn maintains an even more tenuous connection with Op. 19: the draft in Kafka of what was to be the contrasting Andante episode of the Rondo in B♭, WoO 6. This Rondo was almost surely the finale of the Concerto in 1793, soon after Beethoven's removal to Vienna.[63] But whether the Rondo as a whole existed in Bonn, or whether that episode was originally even intended for it, we simply do not know. The point to be made here is that while we cannot be sure what the other movements were like, the first movement of Op. 19 in some recognizable form was a concerto movement before Beethoven left Bonn. And this concerto, as we have seen, was only one of quite a number in his arsenal: as many as four for piano,[64] one for violin (soon evidently to be rewritten for piano), and one for oboe. For the developing virtuoso-composer in Bonn, the concerto loomed very large.

In 1972 Maynard Solomon called attention to a startling lack of consistency in the rate of Beethoven's output during the Bonn years.[65] Using the estimates (sometimes very subjective ones) of previous scholars as to the dates of the Bonn compositions, he concluded that Beethoven's career as a composer in Bonn fell into three subperiods. The first was 1782–86, which saw a good number of substantial compositions, including the three *Kurfürstensonaten* (WoO 47), the Concerto in E♭ (WoO 4), and the three Piano Quartets (WoO 36). The last was 1789–92, during which Beethoven again composed a good many works, such as the two cantatas on the death of Joseph II and the elevation of Leopold II (WoO 87, 88), the *Ritterballet* (WoO 1), several sets of variations including those on Righini's "Venni amore" (WoO 65, the original version), a rather large number of arias and songs, and perhaps the String Trio Op. 3 and the Piano Trio WoO 38.[66] But the intervening years, from sometime in 1785 until sometime in 1789, look barren; Solomon accordingly maintained "that Beethoven had abandoned a composer's career sometime in 1785 and resumed it sometime in late 1789 or early 1790."[67] More recent work, especially the paper and handwriting studies of Douglas Johnson, has to a considerable extent confirmed Solomon's hypothesis. Only one autograph of Beethoven's, according to Johnson, falls unequivocally within that slack period: the Trio for Piano, Flute, and Bassoon (WoO 37).[68] But the matching paper, staff lining, handwriting, and distinctive instrumentation of the autograph of the *Romance cantabile* (Hess 13) surely argue strongly for a similar dating. And Johnson's reasons for assigning a tentative date of 1787–89 to the earlier fragment of an orchestral score for the first movement of the Concerto in B♭, Op. 19, are persuasive.[69]

Beethoven's apparent inactivity as a composer in 1785–89 may be variously explained. Solomon calls attention to a bad review of his earliest published music in Forkel's *Musikalischer Almanach* for 1784; he probes, as well, for possible underlying psychological factors. But it may be most significant that the slack period began soon after the deaths of Beethoven's powerful supporters the Elector Maximillian Friedrich and the Minister von Belderbusch, and the accession of Maximillian Franz, who never showed any particular appreciation of the emerging genius under his roof. Perhaps it was a reflection of loss of official support that the Concerto WoO 4, and the Piano Quartets WoO 36, evidently prepared for publication, did not appear. The Elector, it is true, must have bestowed his blessing on Beethoven's ill-fated trip to Vienna in the spring of 1787, undertaken perhaps with a view to studying with Mozart (a composer Max Franz much favored),[70] a journey from which the young musician soon returned, as the Elector later complained, "with nothing but debts."[71] But Solomon has suggested that Beethoven went to Vienna not as a composer but as a pianist, and the rather shadowy reports we have of his contacts there with Mozart serve to confirm this impression.[72] Nor was there any apparent change in Beethoven's stock at court that might explain his emergence from these years of inactivity as a composer; the burst of new energy in 1790–92 may probably be associated instead with positive new influences in his life from Count Waldstein and the von Breuning family, both beginning in about 1788.

The course of Beethoven's stylistic development in the later 1780s seems discordant with the notion that he simply gave up composing for four or more years. The works of 1790–91 show clear gains in musical cogency and technical assurance over those of 1784–85—the nineteen-year-old, as one might expect, writes quite differently from the boy of fourteen. If we compare, for example, the Concerto WoO 4 and the Piano Quartets WoO 36 (1784 and 1785) with the surviving torso of the Violin Concerto in C, WoO 5, and the Minuet in A♭ for string quartet, Hess 33 (ca. 1790–92 and ca. 1790), robust stylistic growth, particularly in continuity of texture and phrasing, is unmistakable. And, as the new studies show, the slack years were actually not entirely barren. The little that we can be reasonably sure Beethoven composed in this period was without exception music that would have been useful to him for his own performances: the trio written for piano and the peculiar pair of accompanying instruments available at the Von Westerholts; the *Romance cantabile*, evidently the slow movement of an ensemble concerto for the same group plus small orchestra; and some version of the Concerto Op. 19, whose modest orchestration would be appropriate, once again, for private performance. It seems that in his darkest period in Bonn Beethoven continued to play the piano and to provide himself with at least some music for this purpose; thus even in these years he busied himself with the idea of the concerto.

C H A P T E R 3

The Virtuoso in Vienna

Early in November 1792, Beethoven left his native Bonn for good. The region was engulfed in political turmoil and threat of war, and the dire uncertainties of the time surely played a role in the Elector Maximilian Franz's ready assent to his departure. The previous Bastille Day, July 14, had been marked by two ceremonies that were emblematic of the opposed forces poised for violent international conflict: one representing tradition and the authority of received values, and the other, new ideas of social organization born of the Enlightenment and borne aloft in the French Revolution. But what was finally sought on both sides in this struggle was neither stability nor justice, but, rather, power. In Paris a vast throng from all over France gathered at the Champs de Mars (now the site of the Eiffel Tower) to rededicate itself to the principles of the Revolution, and to burn in solemn ceremony the icons of the ancien régime: "blue ribbons, gold chains, ermine mantels, parchment titles and all the baubles of the former nobility."[1] Louis XVI, still officially king, was on hand to reaffirm his allegiance to the constitution that everyone knew he had already repudiated. The next month the governing Assembly, responding to complex pressures of diverse interests, declared war on the Hapsburg Empire, with the purported aim of offering "aid and fraternity to all peoples wishing to recover their liberty," but with the more immediate objective of wresting Belgium from its Austrian rulers.

In Frankfurt, on that same Bastille Day, Beethoven's sovereign, Maximilian Franz, attended the coronation of his nephew Franz II as the new (and last) Holy Roman Emperor. The day was chosen quite deliberately, and all understood the event as an emphatic reaffirmation of the old order. Among those present were the highest ecclesiatical and secular personages of the realm (including Haydn's patron, Prince Paul Anton Esterházy, who gave a magnificent ball) as well as the flower of the French émigré nobility, many of whom were celebrating an expected imminent return to home and power.

In Paris, later that summer, a more radical phase of the Revolution (sometimes called the "Second Revolution") ensued; the Commune of Paris imprisoned the royal family, declared the sovereignty of the people, and pronounced feudalism to be ended. But "liberating" Prussian troops were already within French borders, and the clashes that followed marked the beginning of the continuous wars in Europe that were to form a sustained backdrop to most of Beethoven's life in Vienna, from his twenty-first to his forty-fourth year. Victorious French forces pushed into the Rhineland in the fall of 1792, forcing temporary evacuation of the Elector in Bonn in both the month before and the month after Beethoven's departure; the town was in French hands, and the court permanently dissolved late the following year. As Beethoven began his journey to Vienna, Revolutionary troops under General Dumouriez entered Brussels, and Beethoven's itinerary took him through Frankfurt, by now under French control for about a month.

Thayer notes that Beethoven's associates in Bonn did not see this journey as a permanent departure, but rather as a temporary move to further his education, something like the trip to Vienna of 1787 for study with Mozart; the expectation was that he would later return to Bonn and organize "artistic tours" from there.[2] If the idea was simply to seek out a major musical center to pursue his studies, though, why was it to be Vienna rather than, say, Paris? Paris was only half as far away; Bonn and its court had long participated in the French cultural orbit, and even during the current war the Elector, though a Hapsburg, cautiously maintained at least an appearance of neutrality. In those days, when "nationalism" was scarcely yet an issue, the sprawling and disparate empire of which Bonn and its court were a part probably inspired little more devotion in Beethoven than among its other far-flung subjects. Beethoven, moreover, was surrounded with people like the members of the local *Lesegesellschaft*, the group that in 1790 commissioned his cantata on the death of Joseph II; this group, at least in the days before high tide of the Terror in Paris, would probably have found current political developments in France rather to their liking. And the young musician himself, to judge from his later statements, shared something of their liberal sentiments.[3] The truth is that, however much quitting Bonn may look to us like a gesture of independence, Beethoven traveled at the behest of the court that had paid him such scant heed, and as its subject. The Elector paid some of his expenses—rather less than Beethoven had hoped—and considered calling him back as late as December 1793. The choice of Vienna (and of Haydn as his teacher) was surely for the most part out of Beethoven's hands.

Vienna, lying on the frontiers of Germanic, Slavic, and Hungarian populations, and on an ancient natural crossroads for trade by both river and land, presented the young Beethoven with a rich mixture of cultural contacts. He would have heard around him many languages and dialects; beyond those of the region, there was the usual French widely spoken among the aristocracy, and Italian among musicians (one remembers Mozart's fluent conversations with his Italian colleagues).[4] Vienna in late 1792, like all the empire, was of course in the throes of political upheaval. The forty-year reign of Maria Theresa had seen social, religious, and educational reforms that marked the transition in Austria from medieval feudalism to conditions resembling a modern state. Joseph II, upon his ascent in 1780, proceeded to extend his mother's progressive programs to unheard-of lengths. His "revolution from above," guided by a devotion to the more radical of the political views of Rousseau, prefigured oddly the principles of the revolutionary Constituent Assembly of 1789. He refused to be crowned and set about to reorganize the government of his realms (including that of the city of Vienna) along "reasonable" lines. The ancient internal boundaries of the empire were to be eradicated in favor of a division into thirteen departments governed under a uniform system. Humanitarian measures undertaken included the building of a public hospital in Vienna and the regular hosing of city streets with clean water during the summer.[5] Most controversial of Joseph's measures, and ultimately most damaging to the success of his program, were his actions in respect to the institutions of the church. The new regime completely subordinated the clergy to the state and closed monastic houses throughout the land, including twelve nunneries in the inner city of Vienna alone. Church graveyards were replaced by five communal burying grounds, one of which received the body of Mozart in 1791. The *Toleranzpatent* of 1781 permitted Protestant churches to function in this Catholic land—though without towers and bells—and a similar patent of the following year granted certain new rights to the Jewish population. But mounting opposition to Joseph's innovations forced the retraction of most of them by the time of his death in 1790.

Joseph was followed by his brother Leopold II, who came to the imperial crown with a record of enlightened rule as Grand Duke of Tuscany.

But the outbreak of revolution in Paris struck fear into the hearts of the privileged classes, and in the face of this alarm there was little possibility of carrying out or even stabilizing the remaining Josephine reforms. Leopold, in any case, lived only until the spring of 1792, whereupon his eldest and least able son assumed the throne, in the ceremonies at Frankfurt mentioned above, as Franz II. There had long been anxiety among the Hapsburgs as to the fitness of this heir apparent. His tutor had commented about the twelve-year-old boy: "Much egoism, likes to dissemble in all that he undertakes; mistrustful and jealous."[6] Even before he assumed the crown, Franz had laid the foundations of the police state that held sway in the Austrian dominions until the revolutions of 1848. Generally identified with the policies of Beethoven's fellow immigrant from the Rhineland, Prince Clemens Wenzel Metternich, the master plan for control and repression was in the first place the work of the Emperor-to-be, expressly drawn up in 1791.

What Franz feared most were conspiratorial societies of liberal or pro-French sentiment, and in 1794 his police ferreted out what seemed to have been a genuine nest of Jacobins. Though their offense had taken place before the law forbidding it was on the books, some were sentenced to death and some to life imprisonment. The regime instituted a pervasive system of censorship that extended even to musical productions of various kinds. In 1797 it was forbidden to perform or publish a certain *Friedenssymphonie* because of possible revolutionary implications of such a title.[7] Thus when the twenty-one-year-old Beethoven moved to Vienna, he exchanged an environment in which his liberal and humanitarian impulses were openly encouraged to one where they would be suspect and, perhaps, dangerous.[8]

Above the fears some harbored of the French and of revolution, and others of the police, there was in Beethoven's newly adopted city an overlay of the traditional Viennese love of public pleasures. Dwellers in the city's small apartments, including Beethoven, tended to spend time freely in inns and coffeehouses; of the latter there were, according to an estimate of 1793, over seventy in the city proper and about forty-five in the suburbs.[9] And there were public amusements of many sorts. In 1775 Joseph II (as regent) had opened the expansive Augarten for the delectation of the public at large, for strolling along the tree-lined avenues, for eating, and, a bit later, for musical performances. In 1784 a certain Herr Stüwer made a sensation with his daring hot-air balloon flights from the center of the city.[10] And from about mid-century there had been theaters devoted to the gruesome spectacle of animal baiting, a practice that continued until the mid-1790s, when Franz II, in one of his few constructive acts, forbade it.

Live theater was clearly the entertainment of choice for the nobility and the better situated bourgeoisie. The two court theaters, always administered as a pair, were the Burgtheater in the palace complex itself, and the nearby Kärnthnerthortheater; both presented plays and operas (in Beethoven's time the latter overwhelmingly Italian) during the regular season. At the time of his arrival, there were also two private suburban theaters, the Josephstadt and the Leopoldstadt (opened in 1776 and 1781, respectively); the latter, under the directorship of Carl Marinelli, provided a less exalted audience with somewhat lower-brow entertainment, at more reasonable prices, than the theaters in the city. A fifth theater, the one that was to figure most prominently in Beethoven's career, started out in 1787 as the Theater auf der Wieden (Mozart's *Die Zauberflöte* had its premiere there in 1791); in 1801 its director, Emanuel Schikaneder, moved it into a new building south of the city walls and gave it a new name, Theater an der Wien (though use of the old name persisted as well).

In the absence of a hall specifically intended for concerts—Vienna's first such, the great hall of the Gesellschaft der Musikfreunde, was opened in 1831—these theaters, with the apparent exception of the Josephstadt, had provided homes for public concerts, the natural habitat of the concerto, for most of the second half of the eighteenth century. After the model of the *Concert spirituel* in Paris, concerts in Vienna were concentrated in those seasons, primarily Advent and Lent, when dramatic entertainments were forbidden and audiences and theaters accordingly available. Other than the theaters, the two halls in the court complex used mainly for dancing, the *Grosser Redoutensaal* and *Kleiner Redoutensaal*, were also sometimes available for concerts, again most often in the "restricted" seasons, when the prohibition extended to balls as well.[11] Other concerts were held in restaurants and private dance halls. Two such, the Trattnerhof and the Mehlgrube, were the scenes of Mozart's subscription concert series of 1784 and 1785. In the latter hall the entrepreneur Philipp Jacques Martin organized a series of dilettante concerts in 1781; a public announcement called attention to the prevailing ambience of the place: "in the adjoining rooms gaming tables for all types of sociable games will be held in readiness, and each person will be served with all sorts of refreshments according to his wish."[12] Beethoven's Quintet for Piano and Winds, Op. 16, was first performed at Ignaz Jahn's restaurant in a concert organized by Schuppanzigh in 1797. In the summers of the late 1780s and the 1790s, concerts open to all without cost could be heard in the gardens of the Belvedere Palace and of Prince Liechtenstein's summer palace.[13] And by the mid-1780s concerts of various sorts were held in the Augarten, either out-of-doors or in the hall of the "Gartengebaüde," where from about 1784 music was one of many diversions offered by the enter-prising restaurateur Jahn.[14]

All of the musical events mentioned so far were open to the public. But conditions were still such that a composer-performer like Beethoven needed to direct his attention at least as much toward music that went on in private settings under some form of aristocratic patronage—an arrangement he had been quite accustomed to in Bonn. Although the number and rank of potential patrons in Vienna of course still far exceeded what Beethoven had known in Bonn, by the time of his arrival private music making in Vienna had evidently declined from its previous splendor. Standing orchestras in the great houses were virtually a thing of the past; by 1796 about the only one remaining was that of Prince Schwarzenberg. Nonetheless, ambitious performances, sometimes even with orchestra and chorus, were frequently heard in the homes of the nobility as well as of the wealthy bourgeoisie. In her helpful study of Viennese concerts Mary Sue Morrow divides these private events into six categories according to the centrality and formality of their music, as opposed to the other social activities involved.[15] The sixth, the most "concert-like," of these categories includes musical events that occured regularly, much like concert series.

As Beethoven settled in Vienna, such series took place in residences bearing the various noble names that we have come to associate with his own: Prince Golitzen, the two Princes Lobkowitz, and Prince Joseph von Schwarzenberg (concerts sponsored by the last-named, the only one of this group with a standing orchestra, are described as merely "occasional").[16] And however conflicted Beethoven's feelings may have been about the aristocracy and his place in their midst, soon after his arrival he could be seen outfitting himself with some of the necessities for entering their company: "Black silk stockings, winter silk stockings, boots . . ."[17] Other details of his behavior, too, such as his habit of fleeing the city for the pleasures of the countryside each summer, conformed with the patterns of a life spent among the upper classes.

PERFORMANCES OF THE PIANO CONCERTOS

Whatever the primary motivation may have been for Beethoven's previous expedition to study with Mozart, there can be little doubt that this one was undertaken largely to further his career as a composer. Within about a month of his arrival he was seeing Haydn for those famous lessons in counterpoint and in quick succession availed himself as well of instruction from Johann Schenk and J. G. Albrechtsberger in the same subject, from Salieri in Italian declamation, and perhaps from Schuppanzigh in violin playing.[18] Still, it was as a pianist that he made his strongest initial impression in his adopted city. In his autobiography Schenk describes his astonishment at the young virtuoso's improvisation, which he seems to have heard during Beethoven's first year in Vienna.[19] And as early as the summer of 1794, Beethoven wrote to Eleanore von Breuning (with a touch of his typical paranoia) of other pianists, "some of whom are my sworn enemies," who "palmed off with pride as their own" special features of his keyboard style.[20]

Thus Beethoven was clearly playing piano in Vienna with some frequency during his first two years in the city, mainly in private settings. A composition that surely figured in these performances was one or another version of the Concerto in B♭, Op. 19, which in 1793 underwent revision (including cadenza sketches for the first movement and a new, or possibly revised, finale, i.e., the Rondo WoO 6),[21] changes of the sort that Beethoven habitually made shortly before a performance. The presence of such revisions from this time provides evidence for performances not otherwise attested. Op. 19 was the only concerto from this period that underwent all the steps to publication and enshrinement in the canon, but we should not think it was the only one at his disposal. As was noted in the last chapter, there are signs of as many as four piano concertos from the Bonn period.[22] While it is hard to imagine the twenty-one-year-old dusting off the juvenile Concerto in E♭, WoO 4, for performance in his new surroundings, a piano version of the Violin Concerto in C is a distinct possibility. And a more distant one is the shadowy "Concert aus a," for which Beethoven sketched an Adagio in about 1790.[23] But by 1795, the time of Beethoven's earliest documented concerto performances, the Bonn pieces, with the exception of Op. 19, seemed to have disappeared. During the next eight years, so far as we can tell, he played just two concertos, roughly in alternation: the Concerto in C, Op. 15, and some version of Op. 19.

In 1796 Beethoven undertook two "artistic tours," the sort of thing he earlier contemplated upon his projected return to Bonn. The first, the most extensive of his life, took him northward to Prague, Dresden (perhaps Leipzig), and Berlin, and lasted from early February to about early July. The second, to Pressburg (Bratislava) and maybe Budapest, took place late in the year (the one secure date here being that of a letter written from Pressburg on November 19).[24] The purpose of these trips was to demonstrate his powers as a pianist and composer, and there is every reason to think that the playing of concertos—the genre precisely suited to the display of both—was regularly involved.[25] The surviving record of Beethoven's artistic tours, and indeed of his life as a performer at home in Vienna, is discouragingly sparse. But that there is no independent record of any of Beethoven's performances before 1795, for example, is surely an indication, more than anything else, that only the documentation is wanting. Bearing this in mind, we may construct the following list of reported events, extending to the turn of the century, at which Beethoven performed his concertos:

1 7 9 5

March 2. Prince Lobkowitz's residence. Beethoven played. (Morrow, p. 387)

March 29. Tonkünstler-Sozietät concert, Burgtheater. Beethoven piano concerto (Op. 19?). (TDR, vol. 1, pp. 398–400)

April 23. Count Razumovsky's residence. Beethoven played. (Morrow, p. 388)

December 18. Concert given by Haydn, Kleiner Redoutensaal. Beethoven piano concerto (Op. 15?). (TDR, vol. 1, p. 412)

1 7 9 6

January 8. Concert given by Maria Bolla, Kleiner Redoutensaal. Beethoven piano concerto. (E. Hanslick, *Geschichte des Konzertwesens in Wien*, vol. 1, p. 105; TDR, vol. 2, p. 7)

March 11. Concert given by Beethoven, Konviktsaal, Prague. (Bohumil Plevka, *Beethoven a Praha* [Prague, 1971] p. 96; includes facsimile of an admission ticket)

June. "Several appearances" at the Berlin court of King Friedrich Wilhelm. Performance of a Concerto (Op. 15?). (Wegeler-Ries, pp. 96–97); Hans-Werner Küthen, *Beethovens Werke*, Abt. III, Bd. 2, *Kritischer Bericht*, p. 6.)

November 23. Concert given by Beethoven at Pressburg. (*Letters*, vol. 1, p. 24)

End of December. Concert given by the cousins Romberg. Beethoven played. (Op. 15?) (Martin Staehelin in *Beethoven-Jahrbuch* 10 [1983], pp. 23ff; Küthen, *Kritischer Bericht*, pp. 6–7)

1 7 9 8

Two concerts given by Beethoven at Prague, Konviktsaal. Piano Concertos Opp. 15 and 19. (Tomášek, *Autobiography*; TDR, vol. 2, p. 73)

October 27. Concert directed by Schikaneder at the Theater an der Wieden. Beethoven piano concerto. (Morrow, p. 299)

1 8 0 0

April 2. Concert given by Beethoven at the Burgtheater. Beethoven piano concerto (Op. 15?). (TDR, vol. 2, pp. 171–73; Morrow, p. 304)

Most of Beethoven's recorded appearances during this period, thus, were at public concerts, though this may of course reflect practices in recording musical events more than Beethoven's actual participation in them.[26] The most frequent public concerts in Vienna of the 1780s and early 1790s were of the kind that in London would have been called "benefits," the beneficiary being the organizer and principal performer. And this musician needed to work very hard for whatever benefits accrued; tasks included renting the hall, seeking police permission, conscripting musicians, arranging for publicity, and copying parts. The orchestra was normally composed of a mixture of amateur and professional players, the latter mainly among the winds.[27] At such concerts a wide variety of compositions was usually heard, with vocal and instrumental pieces following in rough alternation. Concertos were standard fare whether the principal performer was a singer or instrumentalist; most often they occurred as the third offering, after an introductory symphony or overture and an aria. The concert given by Haydn on December 18, 1795, for example, was announced in the *Wiener Zeitung* thus:

> This coming Friday, the 18th of this month, Herr Kapellmeister Haydn will give a grand musical Academie in the small Redoutensaal, in which Mad. Tomeoni and Herr Monbelli will sing, Herr van Beethoven will play a concerto of his composition on the pianoforte; and three grand symphonies that the Herr Kapellmeister prepared during his last sojourn in London, not yet heard here, will be performed.[28]

The first public concert in which we know Beethoven participated, on the previous March 29, however, was of a different kind. This was one of two annual concerts given in Advent and Lent (each performed twice) by the Tonkünstler-Sozietät, the proceeds of which accrued to a pension fund for the widows and orphans of its deceased members. Founded by F. L. Gassmann in 1771, this institution was the city's closest approximation to a standing concert series. The Lenten concert for 1795 was given on March 29 and 30, and Beethoven played both evenings. The principal offering, as usual in this series, was an oratorio, on this occasion *Gioas, Re di Giuda* by Salieri's young student Antonio Cartellieri. So on March 29 we see Beethoven performing a concerto in its second-most common setting (after the "mixed" public concert), that is, between the two halves of an oratorio. The following evening, according to the records of the society, his contribution consisted of improvising at the piano.[29]

We know about these performances in a variety of ways. Hanslick first called attention to an announcement (in Italian) of the singer Maria Bolla's concert of January 8, 1796: "The music will consist of new compositions of Sgr. Haydn, performed under his direction. . . . Singers will be Sgra. Bolla, Sgra. Tomeoni, and Sgr. Mombelli. Sgr. Bethofen will play a Concerto on the Pianoforte."[30] The wording seems to imply that all the music on the program consisted of new compositions of Haydn. But this can hardly be true of the concerto Beethoven played, since in 1796 Haydn had no new concertos; this presents a possibility, at least, that Beethoven played one of his own. The concert at Prague of March 11 of the same year is attested to only by the chance survival of an admission ticket, and the one of November 23 in Pressburg by a letter Beethoven wrote from there to the piano maker Johann Andreas Streicher in Vienna.[31]

In some cases Beethoven's own musical documents supply or strengthen evidence for performances. In the Kafka Miscellany (fol. 57v) there is a cadenza draft that develops a motive similar to the opening of the first movement of the Concerto Op. 15. Directly below this Beethoven scrawled "Billet an duport Morgen Frühe," the last two words in very large and emphatic letters. The brothers Duport, Jean-Pierre and Jean-Louis, were both famous cellists at the Berlin court. The elder Jean-Pierre had been in Berlin from the time of his enlistment by Frederick the Great in 1772; Jean-Louis joined him there upon fleeing the French Revolution in 1789. Ries tells us that Beethoven, in Berlin in the summer of 1796, "played several times [*einigemal*] at court, where he also composed and played the two Sonatas with obbligato cello, Op. 5, for Duport (the King's first cellist) and himself."[32] Douglas Johnson, however, without explanation, associates the cadenza draft and the note with the concert of Haydn in Vienna the previous December—thinking, perhaps, that the "billet" was a note or letter Beethoven intended to send to Duport the following morning. Küthen takes it to be a ticket to a concert, one, he speculates, at which the concerto at hand was to be performed.[33] We, of course, know almost nothing about the nature of that "billet" itself; in the usage of the time it could be either a ticket or a letter. If it was an admission ticket, Beethoven would almost surely have been in Berlin at the time; a letter he could have sent from anywhere. But since there is no evidence that

Beethoven knew either of the Duports before he went to Berlin, a preference must be given to the supposition that the "billet" remark was written there. And the cadenza draft to which it is attached points to an imminent performance of a concerto, seemingly Op. 15. Thus the conjecture that he played that concerto in 1796 in Berlin is a reasonable one.[34]

A similar but even more tenuous trail of evidence suggests a visit to Pest after the sojourn in Pressburg in late 1796. Ries tells us, "Beethoven had hardly ever travelled. In his younger years, towards the end of the century, he had once been in Pressburg and Pest, and once in Berlin."[35] Küthen hypothesizes that a remark Beethoven wrote (upside down) on Kafka, fol. 138, refers to a performance of the Concerto Op. 15 in Pest shortly after his appearance in Pressburg in November 1796. This notation, "War's nicht Famös am 1ten december?" occurs here in conjunction with cadenza sketches for all three movements of the concerto; the handwriting and paper are consistent with a date of late 1796–97.[36] It is quite possible, of course, that the subject of Beethoven's happy reminiscence was a performance of the concerto in Pest. But one can daydream about many things (presumably even while composing), and any appearance of Beethoven in Hungary[37]—and, a fortiori, his performance of a concerto there—remains in the realm of speculation.

Beethoven's participation in the Rombergs' concert in December is similarly attested to by a combination of musical and nonmusical documents. The cadenza sketches for Op. 15 in Kafka (fol. 138), with the attached fond reminiscence about the "first of December," must have been written relatively shortly after *some* December 1. Johnson attempts resourcefully to connect these sketches, once more, with a performance of Op. 15 at Haydn's concert of December 1795, despite his earlier conclusion that Beethoven acquired the paper of Kafka 138 just after the Berlin trip of the following summer (1796) and used it for a period of about two years.[38] But a performance that neatly accommodates both criteria—placement shortly after some December 1 and not long after the return from Berlin— is that at the Romberg concert that took place at the end of December 1796. New information about this concert has shown up very recently. A letter from L[or]enz von Breuning to Wegeler of January 5, 1797 (previously only partly known in an extract printed by Wegeler), reports that "the Rombergs gave an *Akademie* here about a week ago, from which they received much applause and a quite considerable income. . . . Beethoven is here again. He played at the Romberg *Akademie*." And a fragment of a letter of Beethoven's to Lorenz von Breuning has turned up in which arrangements for an impending concert are apparently discussed; the recipient of the letter dated it December 28, 1796.[39] Thus it seems likely that Beethoven played Op. 15 at the Rombergs' concert on about December 30 or 31 (Friday or Saturday), 1796.

The only evidence we have for Beethoven's performances in Prague in 1798—indeed for his presence in that city in that year—is a commentary from the composer and pianist Václav Jan Tomášek. His colorful testimony merits quotation at length:

> In the year 1798, as I continued my law studies, Beethoven, the giant among pianists, came to Prague. He gave a concert, very well attended, in the Konviktsaal, in which he played his Concerto in C major, Op. 15, and then the Adagio and the graceful Rondo in A major [from the Piano Sonata], Op. 2, then closed with a free fantasy on the theme from Mozart's *La Clemenza di Tito* "Ah tu fosti il primo oggetto" (the Duet, no. 7), given him by the Countess Sch. . . . Beethoven's magnificent playing, and especially the bold development in the fantasy stirred my soul very strangely; indeed I felt myself in my most inner being so bowed down that for several days I did not touch my piano. . . .
>
> I heard Beethoven in his second concert, at which his playing and his composition no longer made such a powerful impression on me. This time he played the Concerto in B-flat, not composed until he reached Prague. Then I heard him a third time at the home of the Countess C . . . , where, in addition to playing the Rondo of the A-major Sonata, he improvised on the theme "Ah vous dirai je Maman." This time I followed Beethoven's artistic achievement in a more relaxed spirit; I certainly admired his powerful and brilliant playing, but did not fail to notice his often bold digressions from one motive to another, whereby organic connections, a gradual development of ideas, was precluded.[40]

One might well feel skeptical about the details of Tomášek's reminiscences, since his autobiography first appeared in the periodical *Libussa* in 1845, some forty-seven years after the events it recounts. As a trip of Beethoven's to Prague in 1798 is otherwise unattested, could Tomášek perhaps have been thinking instead of the amply documented visit of 1796, during which we know Beethoven had played in the very hall Tomášek mentions? One factor supporting the accuracy of his memory is the connection with a specific event in his own life: "As I continued my law studies . . ." We know that Tomášek embarked on those law studies in 1797;[41] hence it seems unlikely that he was thinking of events that really happened in 1796.

And once again we may compare such "external" evidence with that provided by Beethoven's own musical documents. There is ample sign of the sort of sketching that is consistent with an impending performance of both concertos in sources from 1798. Very early in Grasnick 1 (fol. 2v), the first of the "true" sketchbooks, which Beethoven used beginning in mid-1798, there are cadenza sketches for the first movement of Op. 15. And a little further on in the book (fols. 19ff.) he undertook a drastic revision of the first movement of the Concerto in Bb, Op. 19; adjoining are ideas for a cadenza for that movement as well as some revisions of the following Adagio. These sketches are complemented by those on Kafka, fols. 64–65, where there are extensive revisions of the Rondo of Op. 19.[42] Very shortly after making these revisions Beethoven wrote out a new score for the composition, almost certainly in anticipation of a performance.[43] Thus it seems clear enough that Beethoven prepared both concertos for performance toward the end of 1798; Op. 15 apparently needed only a new cadenza, while Op. 19, always something of a problem child, underwent renovation from beginning to end. We know of one other concert in this period at which Beethoven played a concerto, that directed by Schikaneder at the Theater auf der Wieden on October 27, 1798. But the exertions Beethoven put himself through to prepare *two* concertos surely adds credence to Tomášek's recollection of those other performances in Prague. And the concentration of the composer's efforts in the final months of 1798 also places those performances, for which Tomášek gave only the date 1798, late in that year.

The list of occasions for concerto performances on pp. 49–50 above, of course, does not include events at which other music of Beethoven was heard. One such was the concert Schikaneder gave just a few days after the one just mentioned. This program, on November 5, 1798, included an "Adagio by Beethoven," played on the violin by Ignaz Schuppanzigh. We cannot know for certain what this composition was, but it may well have been one of the two Romances for Violin and Orchestra, Op. 40 and Op. 50, that Beethoven composed roughly at this time; his brother Carl, in letters of 1802, described them as "2 Adagios für Violin, mit ganzer Instrumentalbegleitung."[44] The name and general character of these pieces recalls the *Romance cantabile* for solo instruments and small orchestra from the distant Bonn days.[45] But while that early composition was probably meant as a middle movement of a *concertant*, Beethoven seemed to regard Opp. 40 and 50 as independent compositions, as his brother's letters suggest. The Romance in F, Op. 50, seems to be the earlier of the two. Its autograph, now in the Library of Congress, probably dates from 1798, early enough for Schikaneder's second concert.

For the first public concert of his own in Vienna, on April 2, 1800,

Beethoven secured the most prestigious hall in the city, the Burgtheater. Tickets for the better seats could be bought at the box office or at Beethoven's fourth-floor apartment. The program for this event, singled out by the reviewer for the *Allgemeine musikalische Zeitung* (*AmZ*) as "probably the most interesting *Akademie* in a long time,"[46] opened with an unnamed symphony of Mozart and included two arias from Haydn's *Die Schöpfung*. Two new compositions of Beethoven's were heard for the first time in public, the Septet Op. 20 and, as the final number, the First Symphony. In addition, Beethoven improvised ("masterfully," the *AmZ* said) and performed a "grand concerto on the pianoforte" of his own composition.[47] The orchestra for the occasion was that of the Burgtheater itself; but according to the *AmZ*'s critic, it played in slovenly fashion. All of this orchestra's usual shortcomings—detailed in an earlier article in the *AmZ*— were exacerbated by the difficulty of Beethoven's music: "in accompanying they did not even take the trouble to pay attention to the solo player; thus there was no trace of delicacy in the accompaniment, of any compliance with the progression of the soloists feelings, and the like." The entire event had gotten off to a bad start, according to this report, when Beethoven attempted to replace the opera orchestra's usual director (i.e., concertmaster), Giacomo Conti, with his own choice, the composer-violinist Paul Wranitzsky, for whom the musicians had simply refused to play.

Neither the announcement in the *Wiener Zeitung*, the printed program, nor the review in the *AmZ* tell us which of his concertos Beethoven played under these stressful circumstances. A recent widespread opinion has it that in early 1800 Beethoven was composing a new concerto for this concert, namely, Op. 37 in C minor, but, failing to finish it in time, at the last minute substituted the C-major Concerto, Op. 15.[48] Johnson even entertains the possibility (for a moment, at least) that the C-minor Concerto was played at that concert after all.[49] This hypothesis about these two concertos and the performance of April 1800 will be taken up in Chapter 6. But for now let us be sure, simply, that a concerto other than Op. 37 was performed at that concert. Three usually reliable witnesses, all in a position to know, testify that the first performance of Op. 37 occurred three years later, at Beethoven's concert of April 5, 1803. And the autograph of the C-minor Concerto, which records much of the birth pangs of the composition, is clearly dated, in Beethoven's hand, "1803."[50] As to which Concerto he actually played in April 1800, the musical documents once more have something to say. A manuscript leaf formerly in possession of the Toscanini family in New York includes a cadenza draft for the third movement of Op. 15 as well as some brief readjustments of ornament in the piano part of the second movement; this leaf can be reliably dated in the spring-summer of 1800.[51] These notations, particularly the cadenza draft, give us very good reason to think that the concerto Beethoven performed at the concert of April 1800 was Op. 15.

THE RONDO WoO 6

The first substantial "concerto music" Beethoven composed after his arrival in Vienna, so far as we know, is the Rondo WoO 6 in B♭, dating from 1793. Persuasive arguments can be made that this Rondo was at that time the finale of the Concerto Op. 19. The key is right, of course, and its instrumentation (strings plus one flute, pairs of oboes, bassoons, and horns) also matches that of the concerto. The lack of a title or signature on the autograph suggests it was not an independent composition. The present finale to Op. 19 apparently did not yet exist in 1793, and there is no other visible alternative. The style of the rondo as a whole seems a bit "younger" than the first movement of the concerto as we know it (this is the only other movement we can be sure existed in 1793). But the first movement was probably rather different at that time from the one we know, and the Rondo may have been stylistically more compatible with that version.

It is easy to imagine the young virtuoso delighting his new audiences in Vienna with the Concerto in B♭ finishing with this Rondo.[52] True to the spirit of the Classical rondo, this exuberant piece has a bantering air that plays elaborately with the listener's expectations. The young pianist provided himself liberally with pauses before major new sections that he could turn into playful improvised anticipations and delays. The opening ritornello theme in the piano is notably short and at first hearing utterly ingenuous: four-plus-four measures of thin-textured dance music that moves predictably to the dominant and more predictably back to the tonic (Example 3-3a). But its detail will gain in significance. The strong beats sharpened with appoggiaturas become a typifying gesture of the movement. And further along, when the orchestra takes it over in mm. 131 and 202 (Example 3-1b), we discover that this first theme is fashioned around the familiar horn call—here inverted—that has further engaging echoes elsewhere in the piece. This figure is sometimes absorbed into the body of the "wind band" that often gains a kind of boisterous prominence (as at mm. 27ff.), invoking the sounds of the band-like *Harmoniemusik*.

One is immediately struck in this movement by the pervasive thinness of the writing. The piano starts off with a texture of two lines plus a dominant pedal. The first time we hear the orchestra, in mm. 8ff., it plays essentially one-voice music. Another favorite texture is the single line-plus-pedal heard in both piano and orchestra (mm. 86ff.). On the other hand, sometimes Beethoven writes a sonorous new oscillating left-hand accompaniment, spanning a tenth, that anticipates distinctive sounds of his later piano music (Example 3-1c). For now this texture seems reserved for concertos; it shows up again in the first movement of the Third Concerto (the continuation of the first theme, for example, mm. 122–28) but is absent from the early sonatas.[53] It seems to offer a small adjustment to the usual balance of piano and orchestra. While the solo instrument always counters the massed forces of the orchestra with brilliant speed and agility, here it claims some of that fullness of sound for itself.

This composition has an overall "sonata-rondo with episode" shape that (unlike the finale of the early Concerto in E♭, WoO 4) closely approximates that of many finales in Haydn's later works (see Table 3-1). Following in the train of the opening ritornello are a series of "attachments" in the course of which a modulation leads to the dominant and a two-member second group; this will all appear intact, with proper harmonic adjustments, in the recapitulation after the third Ritornello. This multiplicity of motives, following here in somewhat wooden succession, is not what became Beethoven's standard practice; the later rondos are thematically more compact and integral. Separating these two sonata-like sections in WoO 6 are two others that quite contradict its central premises. The second Ritornello, back in the tonic, plays its usual role in the sonata-rondo: it abruptly undoes that laborious trek to the new key, as if to insist that this is only a rondo, after all. And the Andante episode in E♭ that follows presents a strong contrast to the movement as a whole.

This Andante, dating back to the Bonn years,[54] is perhaps the most attractive feature of the piece. Its appealing *affetuoso* theme is laid out in a rounded binary pattern that becomes the subject of two variations, one strict, the other free. Two special moments stand out: another distinctively Beethovenian keybord figuration, in which the theme is submerged in full-throated moving chords (Example 3-2),[55] and its almost magical displacement in m. 190, via an augmented sixth progression, into the distant key of D major—exactly the transformation accompanying the entrance of Donna Anna and Don Ottavio in the sextet in *Don Giovanni*. In the opera it underlines a distinct reversal in the dramatic situation; in Beethoven's rondo it seems less motivated, an audacious step that in this context must be undone quickly in a return to the tonic.

The Rondo WoO 6 first came to light in the auction of Beethoven's *Nachlass* of November 1827, described as a "Rondo mit Orchester fürs Pianoforte, unbekannt"[56] This autograph (evidently written in 1793) was

TABLE 3-1 RONDO IN B♭, WoO6

8	21	31	40	69	86

R₁

S	T		S	T	S	T	S
a	a₁	a₂	a₃	b		b₁	

I ~~~~~~~~ V

122		138	154	178

R₂

E

S	S	T	T	S
a	(a)		C	var. 1 var. 2

I   IV

201	209	221	231	244	260	277

R₃

S	T		S	T	S	T	S		S
a	a₁	a₂	a₃	b		b₁			cad.

I ~~~~~~~~ I

295	311

R₄

T	S
a	coda (a)

I

bought by the dealer C. A. Spina, who arranged for publication of the rondo in 1829 by Diabelli. For this publication Carl Czerny elaborated the piano part that Beethoven had in some minor ways left incomplete; Czerny far exceeded the five-octave range of the instrument of 1793 and at many points added virtuoso passagework that sounds exactly like piano writing in 1829. The autograph, meanwhile, disappeared, and for the rest of the nineteenth century Czerny's arrangement was the only known version of the composition.[57] This arrangement gained a kind of official status when it appeared in the *Gesamtausgabe* of Breitkopf & Härtel. But in 1898 Carl Rouland discovered the autograph in the Peterskirche in Vienna, and it afterward became the property of the Gesellschaft der Musikfreunde. Eusebius Mandyczewski provided something of a comparison of the two texts in 1900 (praising Czerny's reconstructive efforts rather too handsomely).[58] Willy Hess printed the version of the autograph in his *Supplemente* to the *Gesamtausgabe* in 1960, giving us access, at last, to the work as Beethoven composed it.

THE ROMANCES OPP. 50 AND 40

It is not clear why Beethoven composed these two Romances for violin and orchestra, aside from Schuppanzigh's probable performance of one of them in October 1798. The music of both is agreeable enough, with engaging main themes that return periodically, as befits the genre, with some mild variation in the solo instrument. Formally, Op. 40 in G major has the sharper profile. Between the first two presentations of the theme, a recognizably separate motive is heard, set firmly in the dominant, and the next time around there is a genuine episode in the submediant minor. In Op. 50 in F the spaces between the three statements of the theme are filled mainly with improvisatory, florid lines in the violin that inevitably leave a certain impression of aimlessness. And the first theme of Op. 40 is itself arresting: the solo violin presents the tune alone, accompanying itself in unadorned double stops that remind us of the connotations of simplicity and "antiquity" that cling to the Romance (Example 3-5).

But neither of these compositions shows a trace of the gravity that Beethoven typically invested in the slow movements from 1795–1800— in the Piano Sonatas of Opp. 2, 7, 10, 13, and 22, for example, or in the slow introductions to the Piano and Cello Sonatas Op. 5, or even in the Andante of the Piano and Violin Sonata Op. 12, No. 2. Their manner is the easier one of the ingratiating Adagio cantabile from the Septet Op. 20, a composition that came to please Beethoven's audiences distinctly more than it did its composer.[59]

These Romances for Violin and Orchestra are determinedly elusive as to date of composition. Marginally less so is the one that seems the earlier, Op. 50 in F. In paper type and handwriting its autograph, now at the Library of Congress, corresponds closely to the principal autograph of Op. 19 (1798),[60] which accords well with the supposition that this was the "Adagio von Beethoven" that Schuppanzigh performed in November 1798.[61] But it is puzzling that no sketches have survived for this work; if it was indeed composed in the latter half of 1798, one would expect to find signs of this in Grasnick 1, along with the revisions of Op. 19. We should probably entertain the possibility that Op. 50 actually dates from a still earlier time when Beethoven worked on smaller gatherings and loose leaves, whose preservation is more tenuous. The sources for Op. 40 present a similar pattern. The autograph for this work (Bonn, SBH 553), according to Tyson, Johnson, and Winter, "could not have been written out before 1800,"[62] but once again there are no sketches to help, and it is not impossible that this work, too, was composed earlier. Beethoven's brother Carl offered both compositions to Breitkopf & Härtel in October 1802, as "2 Adagios für Violin, mit ganzer Instrumentalbegleitung";[63] they were finally published separately, Op. 40 by Hoffmeister of Leipzig in late 1803, and Op. 50 in Vienna by the Bureau des Arts et d'Industrie in 1805.

THE CONCERTOS IN B♭ AND C: ORIGINS AND HISTORIES

It is widely known that the Second Concerto, Op. 19, was composed earlier than the First—the reversed numbers simply reflecting the order of publication. This "Second" Concerto has by far the most complex history of any of Beethoven's works in the genre. As we have seen in the last chapter, its first movement existed in some recognizable form in Bonn, no later than 1790. Soon after the move to Vienna in 1793, a second version surfaced, including a finale, the Rondo WoO 6, probably a replacement for an earlier one now lost. Extensive cadenza sketches for the first movement (Kafka 89 and 46) from the same period point strongly toward performance at that time. A third version followed in 1794–95, including a new finale (a form of the present one) and a drastically revised or perhaps even newly-composed Adagio as well (this, too, is the one we know). Cadenza sketches indicate once more an intended performance, very likely that at the Tonkünstler-Sozietät concert in March 1795.[64] In

1798 a fourth version emerged, probably in connection with the performances in Prague and at Schikaneder's concert in October of that year. This
time there are thorough revisions of the last movement in some leaves
from Kafka, only recently identified by Johnson as belonging to 1798; the
first movement is reworked, together with some cadenza sketches in the
first pages of the sketchbook Grasnick 1, which Beethoven began to use
in about the middle of that year.[65]

Any of the four versions that actually led to a performance must have
involved writing out an autograph from which parts could be copied. Of
the pre-1798 versions only the autograph of the Rondo in B♭, WoO 6, of
1793 has survived; the sketches and drafts we have of the other movements leave us in considerable doubt as to how they looked in their earlier
incarnations. In 1798 Beethoven prepared a new autograph, this one preserved,[66] writing out all the parts in full except that for the piano, which,
of course, he was to play himself; this part he entered only in fits and
starts, leaving much to his celebrated powers of improvisation. Little more
is heard of the concerto until a pair of letters Beethoven wrote to the
publisher Anton Hoffmeister in Leipzig, early in 1801. In the first one
(dated by Anderson "January 15 or thereabouts") he offers Hoffmeister
the Septet, the First Symphony, the Sonata Op. 22, and the Concerto in
B♭, asking twenty ducats for each of the other works, but only ten for the
concerto: "I am valuing the concerto at only 10 ducats because, as I have
already told you, I do not consider it to be one of my best concertos."[67] A
deal apparently having been struck, Beethoven wrote again in April: "the
pianoforte part of the concerto was not written out in the score. I have
only written it out now, so that, as I am in a hurry, you will receive that
part in my own not very legible handwriting."[68]

That piano score, too, has survived,[69] and it is clear that Hoffmeister
used it and the main autograph, respectively, as the engraver's copies
(*Stichvorlagen*) for the piano part and the orchestral parts in his first edition of December 1801. But upon taking his old concerto in hand once
again, Beethoven apparently could not resist tinkering with it just a bit
more. In a distinctive gray ink he made a series of changes, almost all in
the first movement, and most of them in the opening tutti. Some are local
emendations, and some are deletions of passages with no substitutions
offered. These proposed changes address some details that (we may well
imagine) distressed Beethoven in 1801. But more "ideas for revisions" than
actual ones, they were soon abandoned, with only one (an emendation in
m. 77 of the opening tutti) finding its way into the Hoffmeister print.[70]
Dissatisfied though he may have been, Beethoven apparently could not
contemplate proceeding to a fifth version of the concerto.

THE CONCERTO IN C, OP. 15

The C-major Concerto has a far simpler story. Beethoven jotted down a few ideas for it, including the theme of the rondo, as early as 1793.[71] But composition of the piece did not really get underway until sometime in 1795, when he wrote large drafts for all three movements on Kafka 113 and Bonn, SBH 606. Beginning in that year Beethoven's concerto performances apparently fell into something of a routine: he played either Op. 19, which always seemed to need revision, or the new concerto, Op. 15. But just when did the new C-major Concerto appear on the scene? A central bit of evidence on this score has always been a famous anecdote of the composer's physician friend, Wegeler:

> Only on the afternoon two days before the performance of the first concerto (C major) did he write the Rondo. He was suffering at the time from the rather severe colic which plagued him frequently. I helped him with minor remedies as best I could. Four copyists sat in the hallway working from the manuscript sheets he handed over to them one at a time.
>
> Here I may be permitted another digression. During the first rehearsal which took place in Beethoven's room the next day, the piano was a semitone flatter than the wind instruments. Beethoven immediately ordered the winds as well as the other instruments to tune to B flat rather than A and he played his part in C sharp.[72]

This vivid bit of testimony has unleashed a torrent of argument and speculation. The mechanics of tuning Wegeler describes have been challenged: why should it have been necessary for Beethoven to perform the remarkable feat of transposing his part up to C♯ if the other instruments had already tuned up a semitone?[73] The answer, of course, is that the B♭ to which the orchestral instruments tuned was that given in the usual way by the piano—here the approximate equivalent of A. Thus they played their part more or less at standard pitch, while Beethoven needed to transpose up a semitone to compensate for his flat piano.

More far-ranging have been the debates as to just when and in anticipation of which performance Wegeler's little vignettes took place. He tells us himself that his stay in Vienna on this occasion lasted from October 1794 (after he was removed from his position as rector of Bonn University by the authorities of the French occupation) until "the middle of the year 1796," when he returned to Bonn; the date of his departure is exactly specified in his correspondence as May 31, 1796.[74] Three concerts at which Beethoven played concertos are known to have occurred during this period: the *Tonkünstler-Sozietät* concert of March 19, 1795, Haydn's concert of December 18, and Signora Bolla's concert of January 8, 1796. While it has been usual to assume that the concert in question was the one in March, on the basis of Wegeler's statement alone we have little reason to prefer any one of these over the others.

The question as to the time of the preconcert scenes Wegeler describes has also become mired in doubt about which concerto was involved. Though Wegeler unequivocally spoke of the Concerto in C, Nottebohm maintained that this was a mistake: that the B♭ Concerto must have been the one rehearsed that day in Beethoven's apartment.[75] He was prompted in this opinion by a belief—on very shaky grounds—that Op. 15 was first completed for the Prague performances of 1798. He also mentioned the difficulty of fitting a large orchestra, complete with the trumpets and drums of Op. 15, into "Beethoven's room"; the smaller orchestra for Op. 19 he found easier to visualize there. We might pursue Nottebohm's line of thought for a moment by noting that Wegeler made no claim that Beethoven wrote an entire concerto at the last moment before the concert, but only its rondo. It now seems reasonably clear that the finale of Op. 19 (evidently a replacement for the Rondo WoO 6) was in fact composed about that time, in 1794-early 1795.[76]

But Nottebohm was surely wrong about the date of Op. 15. Johnson has dated the large-scale drafts for all three movements in Kafka and on a leaf now in Bonn, as well as a series of cadenza sketches in other sources, rather securely in 1795.[77] And the very explicitness of Wegeler's reminiscence—his testimony is one of the few during this period that mentions the key of any Beethoven concerto—must surely count for something. In the absence of any convincing contradictory evidence, we should probably not dismiss his account lightly.

If we may assume, at least provisionally, that Wegeler knew which concerto he was talking about, it remains only to consider whether he referred to the concert in March or the ones in December or January: thus to determine whether the Concerto in C originated early in 1795 or at the end of that year. The sketches for the concerto are not very conclusive in this matter. Johnson has shown that the main drafts for the first two movements on Kafka 113 are associated with pieces dating from sometime in 1795, with a slight preference in one case (the *Rondo a capriccio*, Op. 129) for the later part of the year.[78] Although the Bonn leaf (SBH 606) with drafts of the finale—is this a leaf Beethoven had before him while preparing the sheets for the copyists in Wegeler's narrative?—

is of a paper type he used mainly for his counterpoint lessons with Albrechtsberger in 1794, Johnson believes it represents an unusually late use of that paper.[79]

A somewhat stronger case is made by some cadenza sketches on Kafka 72v, overleaf of drafts for the Deutsche Tänze WoO 8, composed for use at a ball on November 22, 1795, suggesting a performance of the concerto late in the year.[80] Sketches for Op. 15 from before 1795 seem distinctly tentative. The rondo theme appears in isolation on a leaf as early as 1793, and again on one in Washington that Johnson dates as late 1794–early 1795.[81] And a leaf now in Vienna,[82] whose paper type and handwriting match that of the Washington leaf, has a brief snatch of the orchestral continuation of the first theme from the second movement. But here it is clearly written for piano (with some spiky appoggiaturas that were later dropped), and it is in E♭ rather than the ultimate A♭ (Example 3-4). We may tentatively gather from all this that by the end of 1794 the composition of Op. 15 had not gotten very far.

But if the sources for Op. 15 only tilt in the direction of completion and performance of that composition late in 1795 (or early the next month), the much more decisive sketches for the other concerto in question, Op. 19, may shed light on the the dating of Op. 15. They chronicle revision of the first movement, fundamental revision or possibly even composition of the Adagio, and, almost surely, composition of the present finale, all occurring in late 1794–early 1795.[83] A draft of a cadenza for the first movement Johnson also dates (less securely) as early 1795.[84] Thus Beethoven carried out major renovations of the Concerto in B♭ at just the time it would have been needed for the March concert; this constitutes a strong argument, surely, that this was the concerto he played then, and that the Op. 15 Concerto, consequently, was not heard until December or January—a scenario perfectly in accord with Wegeler's report.[85]

We might, finally, note what sorts of events these were at which Beethoven played his concertos. The one in March was one of the semiannual Tonkünstler-Sozietät concerts in which, as was now usual, the principal offering was an oratorio. Salieri directed, and the musicians for this series were almost by definition professionals.[86] Beethoven provided the customary concerto between the acts; whatever his reputation in the city, at this event he could hardly have been the main attraction. For oratorio concerts there were normally two rehearsals, held on the two days preceding the performance. It seems doubtful that Beethoven, in his role as *entr'acte* performer, would be in a position to summon the professional musicians of the orchestra to his apartment on a day (Wegeler, we will recall, stated that the gathering in question took place the day before the concert) for which a general rehearsal was probably already scheduled. The Haydn concert in December, and Signora Bolla's in January, on the other hand, were the usual "benefits" in which most of the orchestral players were typically amateurs. For such concerts it was nonetheless the custom to have only one rehearsal, which took place on the morning of the concert itself.[87] It seems likely that Wegeler's "first rehearsal" was something of a preliminary run-through preparatory to such a full rehearsal the following morning; there is no suggestion that the entire orchestra was in attendance, and very likely the musicians participating were mainly willing amateurs. In a number of ways Wegeler's story rings true. And, attentively read, it joins the evidence of the musical sources to support a date of December 1795 or early January 1796 for the completion and first performance of the Concerto in C.

THE SOURCES FOR OP. 15

The sources from 1795 show the C-major Concerto in its general outlines largely in final form. For subsequent performances in 1796 and 1798 Beethoven seems to have contented himself for the most part with making new cadenzas; there is little sign of extensive revision of the composition as a whole. Then at his own concert of April 1800 he almost certainly played Op. 15 once again. And at about this time he wrote out the autograph that still survives, and entered a good many revisions that affected mainly figuration and ornamentation in the piano part.[88] By December 1800, he had made arrangements with the Viennese firm Mollo for publication of the concerto[89] as it stood in the final stage of the autograph, and publication followed the next March. That the piano part in the autograph was fully notated from the beginning, contrary to Beethoven's practice in the "performance autographs" for Opp. 19 and 37, suggests it was a part of the publication effort rather than one undertaken for a performance.[90]

We might construct a tentative scenario, then, like the following. Beethoven used an old autograph (from 1798?), now lost, for the concert of April 1800, one whose solo part probably allowed him considerable leeway for improvisation. Deciding afterwards that he had played this concerto often enough in public, he sought its publication—which evidently meant he was finished with the composition as his own performance vehicle—and proceeded to revise it to that end. He may have begun to work in the old autograph but decided at some point that the magnitude of changes he had in mind necessitated a new manuscript. He then wrote out the new autograph, concentrating on the piano part, which he now probably wrote down in full for the first time. In a second pass he revised both orchestral and solo parts, the latter much more heavily. He then turned it over to someone who marked up the score (in more than one stage) prior to engraving or—more likely—to the making of a fresh copy to serve as a *Stichvorlage*.[91] Thus, as with Op. 19, only publication finally stayed Beethoven's restless hand and fixed the concerto in the form in which we now know it.

In his first years in Vienna Beethoven presented himself to his new audiences with a variety of music, almost all of it newly composed. In all of this music, the trios, the early sonatas, and, most of all, the two concertos, we detect a kind of youthful exuberance, as if this young artist were not yet afflicted with doubts about his own powers. But a capacity for self-criticism appeared early in Beethoven's career and was manifestly built into the history of the Concerto in B♭. The various versions of the piece articulate various stages of youthfulness—all of them seemingly exuberant. The Concerto in C, by comparison, chronologically largely of a piece, reflects a certain consolidation, a settledness in style and expression wherein risks are calculated and enthusiasms under control.

Toward the LINGUA FRANCA: Piano Concerto No. 2. in B♭, Op. 19

The Concerto in B♭ as we know it represents only one of several forms—and not even quite the last one—that the piece assumed during its checkered history from the late 1780s to 1801. The version that has survived for posterity is essentially the one into which the concerto coalesced in 1798. And even at that, some of the music—most particularly in the Adagio—still reflected Beethoven's writing of 1794–95, the time of the Piano Trios Op. 1 and the Piano Sonatas Op. 2. It was not until December 1800, just after he had completed the String Quartets Op. 18, that the composer, with a gesture of embarrassment, offered the concerto to the publisher Hoffmeister: "A concerto for pianoforte, which, it is true, I do not make out to be one of my best. . . . At the same time it would not disgrace you to engrave this concerto."[1] Beethoven's modest assessment of his composition has not met with widespread disagreement. And the piece itself may be called modest. Its orchestra is small, with no clarinets or trumpets and drums, and the writing for instruments is little more than routine: the winds almost always play together as a choir, often simply doubling the appropriate strings, the latter also seen in conventional roles. The first two piano concertos, we should remember, are among Beethoven's first large-scale essays in writing for orchestra; the later triumphs in this music for this grandest of instruments remain, for now, in the future.

The solo part looks almost throughout like respectable late eighteenth-century piano music. It is mainly thin-textured, and it shows no great feats of virtuosity. It is a degree or two less flamboyant even than some of Beethoven's sonatas of the time (where virtuosity was, paradoxically, less de rigueur), as, for example, both outer movements of the Sonata in C, Op. 2, No. 3, of 1794–75, or the first movement of the Sonata Op. 7, in E♭ (1795–96). And in Op. 19—with the exception of one remarkably distended cadence pattern in the second movement (mm. 55–68)—the expressive extremes and the long-term mounting of tension associated with the earlier sonatas are not to be found.

The often-revised first movement (whose principal events are mapped in Table 4-1) is essentially an exercise in the *lingua franca* of the Classical style, a style in which the young Beethoven sometimes seemed not perfectly comfortable. The opening theme (Example 4-1),[2] with its two starkly contrasted elements (a_1 and a_2 in the table), a unison, triadic statement—its angularity heightened with sharp dotted rhythms—alternating with a legato, stepwise reply, recalls hundreds of similar themes in European music from the entire second half of the eighteenth century. Three well-known ones are the beginnings of Haydn's String Quartet Op. 1, No. 1 (ca. 1760), Mozart's Piano Concerto in E♭, K. 271 (1777), and his Piano Sonata in D, K. 576 (1789). The harmonic construction of such themes was variable (no two of the examples mentioned here are alike). Beethoven's first pair moves from tonic to dominant, and his second, in vaguely singsong fashion, back again. An impression of ironclad normality is reinforced by a periodization of 2+2, 2+2 measures. But each of the half phrases is of the type that resolves on the first beat of its second measure, threatening thus to leave the second halves of alternate measures silent. The problem is obviated in two ways: with the triple eighth-note anacruses of mm. 2 and 6, and the "filling" figure in the winds in mm. 4 and 8; but a feeling of discontinuity lingers nonetheless.

The continuation in mm. 9ff. (a_3) has a similar periodization, with the difference that unaccented (*feminine*) endings now occupy the interstices between half phrases; and any leftover time in the measure of the single accented ending (m. 16) is swallowed up by the early intrusion of a_1 in a good example of what Heinrich Christoph Koch called *Takterstickung* ("supression"—literally, "throttling"—of the measure).[3] As to melodic construction, the opening measures again may strike us as not perfectly assured: a source of unease here may be the fourfold endings (mm. 1–2, 2–3, etc.) where the melody sets out from a stressed pitch, makes its way to the fifth above, and immediately returns. This opening material comes to dominate the movement; all four tutti sections, for example, start off with those familiar deadpan dotted rhythms. It rules with particular force in the opening tutti, where there is no competition from other stable, distinctive thematic matter, and where a version of it (m. 63, borrowed from m. 16) is reintroduced, ritornello like, near the end of the section.

If in this beginning Beethoven seems to struggle with complexities of Classical periodization and phrasing, other thematic material in the movement sounds more at home in the style. A particularly happy bit of lyrical writing, one that the sources show as a part of this movement since at least 1794,[4] is the "soloist's second theme," b$_1$, starting in m. 127 (Example 4-2a). Again we have four-measure phrases (the pair of them shown in the example is immediately repeated, with a new ending). The first phrase of each pair falls into two halves, while the second is continuous. This, too, is one of the standard orderings of thematic matter in Classical style. (A familiar example is the beginning of Mozart's Sonata in A, K. 331; a much later one is the theme of Mendelssohn's *Variations serieuses*.)[5] While on the surface Beethoven's melody sweeps grandly through a wide range, it is fundamentally anchored to the third of the tonic triad, A, reached in m. 129, together with its auxiliary B♭ (and, at the very end, G). Melodic coherence persists despite those octave displacements. The harmonic syntax here is a rich one—with prominent submediant and supertonic sounds—and its continuity through each pair of phrases contributes a forward momentum quite lacking in the first theme.

The formal shape of this movement, broadly considered, is about what one expects in the first movement of a Classical concerto: the three sections in which the soloist participates correspond roughly to the exposition, development, and recapitulation of a sonata-allegro form; these alternate with four tuttis, the last of them interrupted by the soloist's cadenza. The final three tuttis are in the expected keys: T$_2$ rounds off the dominant area to which listeners were led by the the preceding solo, T$_3$ reintroduces the tonic (together with the first theme), and T$_4$, after a touch of last-minute disruption, effects a final confirmation of it. But the tonal plan of the first tutti, though it begins and ends in the tonic, is eccentric in the extreme. The music moves determinedly toward the dominant (minor) and pauses on three unison statements of *its* dominant, C; Beethoven then nudges the three unison strokes up a semitone and, having thus quite deprived listeners of their tonal bearings, launches unceremoniously into previously heard material (a$_2$) in the pitch at hand, D♭ (see Example 4-3). This abrupt detour—we cannot call it a modulation—is a particularly drastic version of the sort of harmonic jest for which Haydn's quartets and symphonies were already famous, and which in some form was to persist in Beethoven's music for many years (witness the stepwise slide from E♭ down to C at the beginning of the coda of the first movement of the *Eroica*, for example, and the similar device—using the same pitches—at the begin-

ning of the development of the Sonata Op. 110 of 1820–21, first movement). It is a gesture of defamiliarization; it severs the line of musical
thought, leaving the listener in doubt about the implications of the music
just heard, and quite in the dark as to what might come next. The opening
tutti of a concerto is up to this point perhaps the least likely venue for
such disruptive tactics. (That startling move from the dominant of F minor
to D♭ major is recreated in S_2, corresponding to a development section, at
m. 228; but now this wrenching motion forces the music from the dominant of G minor up a semitone to E♭, where, again, a_2 is heard.)

Beethoven had puzzled over this spot in T_1 more than once. A continuity draft in Grasnick 1 (fol. 19v, 1798) has the progression going not to
D♭ but (as in S_2) to E♭—sidling upward by semitone all the way from C.
Another draft on the following folio gives this passage from T_1 again, but
with its ending, the D♮ leading to the E♭, crossed out, and the written
notation "wie es war bis NB."[6] "NB" is marked above the measure further
along where the dominant of B♭ (m. 57) is regained, plainly suggesting
that in the source Beethoven was using (a score from 1794–95?), motion
from D♭ to the dominant of B♭ was achieved by a different route; this is,
of course, what happens in the *final* version of T_1, a version to which this
second draft in Grasnick 1 in other respects corresponds very closely.[7]
Thus it appears that in making this initial bizarre move from C to D♭ (and
rejecting the slide all the way up to E♭), Beethoven was reinstating an
earlier solution that for a moment in 1798 made him uneasy. There seems
to be some attempt to assimilate this tonal foreign body, D♭ in the first
solo section, where a motive in the second group, b_2, appears in that key
(in S_3 it is recapitulated, Schubert-like, in G♭, or ♭VI—that of course functions in the orbit around I as ♭III does in V). But, on the other hand,
removing the E♭ section in T_1 isolates the subdominant appearance of a_2
in the second solo section as the single occurrence of that tonality in the
movement.[8]

The initial tutti of the Classical concerto, like its close relative the
opening ritornello of a da capo aria, was by tradition a sturdy, straightforward thing. Something like a playbill, it alerted the listener as to the main
elements of what was coming: the leading thematic contents, with their
prevalent sorts of motion (specifying their affect, as it was earlier thought),
and the principal tonality that would govern the ensuing events. The action
itself, where these elements were elaborated, put on view in different
contexts, and imbued with the drama of dialogue and opposition, was
reserved in both aria and concerto for the solo sections. And this included
that purposeful modulation to a secondary key that in Beethoven's time
was a central structural and expressive component of virtually all big

pieces. It was perfectly usual, somewhere in the course of the first tutti, to deflect the tonality a bit in one direction or another. Of seven almost randomly chosen concertos by F. X. Sterkel, Leopold Kozeluch, and Muzio Clementi,[9] published in the 1780s and earlier 1790s, three have initial tuttis in which the tonic key is seriously undermined, usually by means of a somewhat extended secondary dominant to another key. But none actually modulates.

As we might expect, Mozart's concertos, especially his mature ones, are more than usually adventurous on this score. The first tuttis of a few (mainly the less well-known ones), K. 450 in B♭, K. 482 in E♭, K. 537 in D, and K. 595 in B♭, never waver in the least from their allegiance to the home key. In the Concerto K. 413 (387a) of 1782–83, the opening tutti moves to the dominant without firmly establishing it, plays a tune there, and moves quickly back. K. 453 in G (1784) dips to the flat submediant without quite modulating; K. 456, of the same year, moves strongly (amid one of Mozart's glorious thickets of suspensions) toward the minor sub-dominant but again turns back safely. K. 449 of the same year in fact modulates; it has a tilt toward the dominant built into its first theme, and its opening tutti spends time firmly in that tonality. The great Concerto in C of 1786, K. 503 (Tovey's strenuous protestations to the contrary not withstanding),[10] modulates unequivocally to the dominant in its first tutti, such that the pursuant abrupt return to the tonic (minor) is heard as a momentary discontinuity. And we might note that this point—G major reinterpreted as V of C minor—is marked by repeated unison strokes on that G in the full orchestra in a more artful version of the device Beethoven was to use in the first tutti of Op. 19 for the move to D♭.[11]

All these examples from Mozart are very models of tonal stability compared to Beethoven's first tutti. In addition to that abrupt shift to D♭, it has three strongly modulatory passages (they can be seen in Table 4-1 above): the motion to the minor dominant beginning in m. 22, the return from D♭ (m. 48ff.), and some quite exceptional tonal upheaval after the reappearance of a_1 in the tonic in m. 63. The effects of such radical disruption are not fully dispelled by the following two new bits of music, securely in the tonic, with which the tutti ends. The first of these (mm. 81–84), two statements of a cadential chordal "landing pattern," I–VI–II⁶–V–I, was a cliché borrowed from aria-endings in opera buffa. The second (derived from a_3) is a suddenly quiet, cantabile, eight-bar codetta, rather similar in effect to the first tutti endings in Mozart's K. 450 and (again) K. 503. Here it sounds vaguely disingenuous after the raucous cadences preceding, as if to claim that all disorder is now resolved and serenity quite restored—a claim promptly disputed by the two final fortissimo chords in the orchestra.

The soloist then enters with something new and unexpected: a single-line statement on the dominant and tonic accompanied with recitative-like interjected chords in the left hand (Example 4-4). Mozart had of course done something similar as early as the Concerto K. 271, where (after the soloist had already been heard in the surprise entry at the beginning of T_1) S_1 starts with ruminations in the piano not directly germane to anything yet proposed by the orchestra. This idea frequently returns in the Mozart concertos; and in some of the greatest of them, K. 466 in D minor, K. 491 in C minor, and K. 503 in C major, the piano's first utterances have highly distinct profiles that instantly set the soloist apart as a discrete persona. The effect is a little like the beginning of a dramatic scene that introduces a lead character who has not yet been firmly drawn into the central action. In Shakespeare's *Henry IV*, Part 2, for example, the king makes his first appearance in act 3 (Hotspur has already been killed, and the forces of insurrection are gathering) with a soliloquy about royal insomnia. He reveals something of himself, but little of his place in the events unfolding around him.

In both the play and the concertos the lead characters then quickly join the central action. In Op. 19 (as in all the concertos of Mozart just mentioned) the seemingly new material played by the soloist turns out to be a prelude to the reintroduction of the first theme and the full argument of the soloist's exposition. And, thinking back, we may even note a distant kinship of this first tune in the piano with certain thematic matter from T_1; the trajectories of its even motion in eighth notes somewhat resemble those of a_2 in mm. 2–3 (see Example 4-1) and, especially, their adaptation in mm. 34ff. It is surely such congruities that allow us to accept the opening of S_1 as an appropriate utterance, if not an immediately familiar one, in the musical context created by the first tutti (and by the time S_2 also begins with that figure, it sounds quite domesticated). Next comes the main theme stated in the piano, and the modulatory journey is promptly underway. A descending bass under virtually nonthematic keyboard figuration reaches the desired C (V of V) in m. 117; ten more measures of dominant preparation bring us to b_1, discussed above, and the momentary darkening to D♭ (reminiscent of the first tutti) for b_2, a miniature pastoral interlude played *pianissimo* entirely over the (local) tonic pedal. When F major, the ruling tonality of this area of the piece, is regained in m. 157, the music launches into the conventional drive to the conclusion that Hans Engel named the "display episode" (Dennis Forman calls it the "piano climax").[12] As usual, this section is dominated by brilliant figuration and nearly incessant motion in the solo part; and it permits no further harmonic dallying as it rushes to the end in F (the corresponding section of S_3, of course, will drive to Bb).[13] The second tutti, made up mainly of the opening and closing figures of T_1, then acts, conventionally enough, to confirm that tonality.

The following "development" section, or S_2, falls into four clear subdivisions:[14]

(1) Mm. 213–229: the first solo entrance from S_1 appears in F and moves to V of G minor.

(2) Mm. 230–46: the abrupt slide upward borrowed from T_1, mm. 39ff., leads to a relatively stable exposition of a_2 in Eb.

(3) Mm. 246–69: a more-or-less developmental treatment of x from m. 21, based nearly throughout upon the harmonically inert device of voice exchange (notably within diminished-seventh sonorities), and proceeding to the dominant of the home key.

(4) Mm. 269–84: 16 measures of dominant preparation, with added irritants, in turn, of the lowered sixth and second degrees (Db and Gb), as if—in a fairly conventional ruse—to usher in Bb minor.

In the first of these four passages, in mm. 213ff., Beethoven gives assurances that the seemingly indeterminate tune with which the soloist began S_1 (and now begins S_2) is in fact related to a_2, first heard as the contrasting strain of the first theme; now, at the beginning of the "development" section, we see the one changed by degrees into the other. But if that first solo section has left us with the impression of too much uproar and instability, this second one—where we might better expect such things—offers rather too little. Its first segment takes 16 measures to move, in the most orderly of progressions, from F major to the dominant of G; the ensuing derailment upward by a semitone, having already been heard in T_1, is no longer much of a shock. The tonality of the following stretch in Eb is rock solid; the third subsection, after an initial motion from Eb to C minor, is built mainly upon voice exchanges within a diminished sonority that guarantee tonal stasis of an indeterminate sort. And that leaves only the following dominant preparation, where the single remaining ambiguity is that most usual one between minor and major in the expected tonic.

Here, as in many Classical concertos, the onset of the third tutti coincides with the moment of recapitulation; but at its ninth measure the soloist breaks in, and we realize the tutti is already over. Mozart, too, often gave T_3 very short shrift, welding it, in effect, to the following solo section.[15] In this area of the movement, as in none other, the old concerto principle of schematized large-scale alternation gave way to a sonata-like idea, that of recapitulation, carried on jointly throughout T_3 and S_3. In the T_3 of Op. 19, the parade of events from T_1 starts out in a perfectly orderly fashion; then the soloist, without fanfare, simply takes one of them over, and from that point onward the forces combine in a spirit of polite competetion and dialogue. At the beginning of this section Beethoven follows the music of T_1; but from the point of its modulation toward V— here averted of course—the music recapitulates in tonic only the events from the dominant section of S_1, following them without incident to the end.

This avoids a good bit of trouble. It circumvents, in particular, that perilous slide to ♭III from m. 39, leaving only the gentle dip from the dominant to that key in m. 149 to be negotiated—which, as we have seen, Beethoven reproduced as I–♭VI, now in the context of the tonic key. And the plan of this section probably also conforms to Tovey's insistence that the S_3 should be a recapitulation of both T_1 and S_1[16]—Beethoven simply does them by turns. Then, after the piano's big cadence to end the section (mm. 378f.), T_4 duly enters with a combination of the first theme and some material adapted from x. This music sounds at first alarmingly unstable, moving at once to V of F and then to G minor; but some sequential figures from x bring it back under control, just in time for the $^6_4$ over the dominant and the cadenza. The section and the movement then finish off with the "reassuring" music from the close of T_1 and T_2, together with the two final sharp strokes on the tonic, sounding now, as they did twice before, vaguely incongruent.

There are some fine moments in this movement. Perhaps surprisingly, it is mainly the lyrical sections that seem most convincing: both the soloist's "second themes" (b_1 and b_2; see Example 4-2a for the former) and the continuation of the main theme in m. 9 (a_3; Example 4-1) are examples of this. The marcato "invertible" passages in the two versions of the display episode, despite some rough spots that we shall note in a moment, are stimulating stuff. But the movement as a whole leaves a disquieting impression of some failure of control; the tonal gyrations of T_1 and the extreme sectionalism and tonal inertia of S_2 do not seem like planned experiments (if they were, at least Beethoven never tried them again in a concerto). On a more local level there are instances of what look like youthfully inept writing. The chromatic parallel octaves in the bass and treble in mm. 56–57, and the resolution of suspensions in mm. 75–76 into pitches already present in the texture, comprise genuine syntactical errors in this style (in the autograph Beethoven moved to correct the suspensions, but, like many late revisions in that manuscript, this correction was not adopted in the published version).[17] A couple of uncertain places follow in the two versions of the display episode in S_1 and S_3. In mm. 165–66 the piano, playing alone, approaches F major using a common sequence-pattern of alternating sixths and thirds—or, more basically, descending thirds (Example 4-5). Accidentals in the ornamental pitches, particularly the alternating E♭-E♮ in the right hand, seem not to ring quite true, implying in very quick succession, as they do, conflicting tonal directions. One hesitates to suggest correcting Beethoven (he was never very receptive to suggestions about his music); but removal of the A♭ and the two E♭s would produce a surer effect. The same problem (and modestly offered emendation) applies to the inverted version of this passage in mm. 171–73 and the two analogous points in S_3, mm. 349–51 and 356–58.

THE ADAGIO

The Adagio of Op. 19, a movement that first shows up in the revisions of 1794–95, is a contemplative, serious piece. Like slow movements of many concertos, it might remind us of an aria sung by a character recently embroiled in high drama, but now pausing for introspection and reflection. The reflection here is not of Beethoven's most pessimistic sort. The triple meter alone sets it apart from the high pathos, for example, of the Adagio from the slightly later Sonata Op. 10, No. 3. Yet it has more expressive weight than either the Adagio cantabile or the Largo espressione of the almost exactly contemporaneous Piano Trios Op. 1, both of which in their basic materials exude a faintly perfumy effect, at the time very fashionable, of stock Classical phrase construction plus heavy (sometimes chromatic) ornament. Of all the other slow movements from about this time, the Adagio from Op. 19 is perhaps closest in spirit to the *Largo con gran espressione* of the Sonata Op. 7 (1796–97), with which it has in common triple meter and the contour and tessitura of the first theme. The two main thematic ideas of the Adagio of the concerto have a convincing directness to them. The first (best seen at the piano's entrance, m. 13, shown in Example 4-6) has a satisfying bass motion giving us two harmonizations each of the third and fourth scale degrees in the melody (I and VI; II⁶ and IV⁶), where leaps in the bass are effectively countered with conjunct motion in the other direction. A low melodic tessitura adds a degree of solemnity to this theme when it sounds on the piano; when played by low-lying violins, this effect is much less marked. The other leading motive (Example 4-7), fragmentary in the extreme, nevertheless again shows an active and shapely bass line and a separate harmonization of each melodic pitch—all this over a dominant pedal in the violas. Beethoven deals with these promising materials with a sureness and consistency not always evident in the first movement.

The overall form of this movement (see Table 4-2) is a member of the close-knit family of binary shapes that predominates overwhelmingly in slow movements in the later Classical style.[18] Sometimes called *sonatina form* and, more recently (and more cogently), *slow-movement form*[19] it con-

TABLE 4-2 OP. 19, II

T

a

I~~~~~~~~~~~~~V/I

12	18	23	31	
S			T	S

a   b   trans. (a+b)

I   ~~~   V   ~~~~~ V/I

37	49	55
S		

a   b   ext.

I   I   V/I

87		
T	Cad.	T

Coda (a)

I   ~~   I

sists of two essential tonal motions, I–V and I–I. It differs from the larger binary patterns and sonata-allegro form primarily in two ways. After the dominant is reached, there is no extended modulatory area, or development section, with its large-scale prolongation of harmonic tension, but, usually, only a brief transition of some sort back to the tonic. The other difference is that its two sections are not repeated. There is invariably thematic parallelism between the two parts, though the presence of distinctly new ideas in the dominant (later to be recapitulated in the tonic) is variable.

In concertos, as we might expect, a kinship with variants of this form found in arias of the period (as, for example, in the familiar "O Isis und Osiris" from the second act of *Die Zauberflöte*) is particularly clear. For one thing, both arias of this type and slow movements of concertos—until Mozart's last ones—were almost invariably prefaced by an orchestral introduction presenting one or more leading musical ideas of the piece.[20] Until disrupted by Mozart, this introduction seemed to be the single stable convention governing distribution of music between soloist and orchestra in slow movements, for here the schematic large-scale alternation of tutti and solo characteristic of first movements is entirely absent. But there is compensation in the typical arrangement of musical materials into repetitive patterns that allow for close dialogue between participants and for ornamented solo statements of music just heard in plain form in the orchestra— of which the second theme of the Op. 19 Adagio offers a good example.

The tutti introduction to this movement recalls something of the unruliness of T_1 in the opening Allegro—thus once more threatening to undermine one of the opening tutti's two main functions in establishing theme and key. It sets the first theme in motion and then promptly derails it. The normal half cadence of m. 2 is restlessly stated three times in an increasingly unstable harmonic context, as if it were simply impossible to get past the first half phrase. The task is simply abandoned, and a new melodic two-measure idea is heard—for the first and last time. Then some cadential material (that turns out to be related to the second theme, "b") leads to the solo entrance. Here the piano masterfully dissolves the accumulated uncertainties and presents the first theme whole, reserving any ornament for the end, when its character has become clear. A standard continuation, using the first idea as a point of departure, leads quickly to the dominant, the second theme (Example 4-7), and the cadence that closes the first segment of the binary form.

What happens next in this sort of movement is variable. Sometimes the tonic key is regained with a minimum of fuss, the first theme reappears, and the recapitulatory part of the binary scheme is underway. Mozart's Piano Concerto in C, K. 415 (= 387b), has only a V^7 to the tonic with a fermata signaling an improvised lead-in from the soloist. At the other extreme, in the Andantino of K. 449—where both first and second movements are elaborate studies in tonal eccentricity—an extensive middle section includes both main subjects, in the keys of ♭VII and IV. In Op. 19, after bringing the first section to a firm close in the dominant in the hands of the soloist, Beethoven articulates this juncture (as was relatively common) with a tutti statement. The music veers off in quick succession toward ♭VII and the minor tonic, using material fashioned from both main themes and recalling in its repeated half cadences (with sforzati on the dissonances) the turbulence of the tutti introduction. An augmented sixth chord on the lowered sixth degree then resolves properly to dominant, and the home key is secured for the reentrance of the main theme. All this is done with great efficiency in a mere six measures.

When the soloist now reintroduces the first theme, we expect to hear it in elaborated form, and Beethoven does not disappoint us. Most striking and original is the repetition of the first strain, where the decoration, itself remarkable, precedes the tune itself. The piano sets in motion a harp-like triadic figuration (Example 4-8), a variant of which Beethoven writes again as late as 1820 in the first movement of the Sonata Op. 109. In Op. 19 it anticipates by a full measure the sounding of the melody in the oboes. A different sort of elaboration just after the recapitulation of the second theme is yet more striking. Up to this point all the events of the movement have been relatively short lived: after fifty-four measures of $\frac{3}{4}$ meter, the introduction plus binary pattern is essentially complete. But the expected final cadence is averted. In its place there are two extravagantly extended cadential motions, the first of four measures, the second of ten; these produce the highest degree of tension of the entire composition (see Example 4-9 and the harmonic reduction in Example 4-9a). The first (mm. 55–58) proceeds from tonic I⁶ to a deceptive cadence on vi; the second goes back to the start and follows the same route but sticks fast on the B♭ $\frac{6}{4}$ (which the previous passage had reached just before the turn to vi).[21] There follows a vast "prolongation" of this sound—i.e., a postponement of its resolution—achieved through that favorite instrument of delay and obfuscation of Mozart's, parallel motion in $\frac{6}{3}$ chords.[22] This gives way in m. 66 to a $\frac{5}{4}$ over the dominant, which is next cleverly embodied in the piano's trill—the only harmonic movement accomplished so far, in this great stretch of music, has been the descent of the upper pitch of the $\frac{6}{4}$ down to the fifth degree. The suspension thus created is at last resolved to V⁷ in the second half of m. 68 (with the somewhat acrid additive of the lower semitone neighbor in the trill on e‴—the upper neighbor of the trill on f‴, which we would expect, was not available on most pianos of the time). When the final resolution to tonic comes in the next measure, the effect is nothing less than triumphant.

This passage is a vivid portent of the young Beethoven's future, an early look at his famous proclivity for creating high-voltage tension and climax through prolongation of dissonance. A familiar, rather literal example from about a decade later is the excruciating dissonance preceding the interlude in E minor in the development section of the first movement of the *Eroica*. Another admirable example from the time of Op. 19 may be seen in the Adagio from the Sonata Op. 2, No. 1. In the ternary plan of this movement the great bulk of the "B" section consists of three ornamented statements of a much extended cadential pattern (cleverly derived in the first place from the beginning of "A"). In the coda to the movement Beethoven returns to this idea, presenting it now four times in yet more attenuated form. As we have noted,[23] this movement is a drastic revision of the slow movement of the Piano Quartet in C, WoO 36, of 1785. In the original composition no trace of this sort of cadential extension is to be found; the technique seems to have taken hold in Beethoven's imagination from about the mid-nineties: from the time when his distinct musical persona began to emerge with clarity and—with a certain display of self-knowledge—he first dignified his publications with opus numbers.

The Adagio of Op. 19 closes with a final tutti, in which the hard-won tonic of the preceding section is for a moment threatened once more by the orchestra's characteristically turbulant treatment of the first theme. This quickly straightens itself out and pauses on an emphatic dominant $^6_4$, inviting a cadenza. But Beethoven refuses to leave anything entirely to the soloist. And instead of an ordinary cadenza, we get from the piano a single-line recitative-like solioquy, *con gran espressione*; presently, this alternates with fragments of the first theme from the orchestra in a somber dialogue that seems to prefigure, remotely, at least, that of the slow movement of the Fourth Piano Concerto. And the orchestra has the last word, repeating bits of the first theme in stable cadences—as if, after all the tonal violence it had visited on this musical idea, it has now been reined in by the eloquent pleas of the solo recitative. Herein is resolved a fundamental dichotomy of the movement, one in which the participants take on unaccustomed roles: the orchestra as maverick and eccentric, the piano as a force for order. The resolution convinces, and the movement emerges as a strong one. (It did not, however, escape its composer's censorious eye; only shortly after he had brought this movement nearly to its final form in 1794–95, Beethoven drafted an Adagio in D that he apparently intended as a substitute for it.)[24]

THE RONDO

The last movement of Op. 19, like the finales of all Beethoven's concertos, is of the prevailing rondo type (the great majority of Mozart's concertos, all but one of Kozeluch's and Sterkel's seen for this study, and the single surviving concerto of Clementi end with rondos; the only active alternative for Mozart seems to have been theme and variations). Writers on music from Beethoven's time, as we have seen, often leave the impression that the rondo was identified fully as much by the nature of its musical materials as by any patterns of thematic repetition or key relationships—a modern tendency to identify "genre" and "form" had not yet taken hold.

The rondo of Op. 19 (Example 4-10) begins with a theme that would fit well in Czerny's list of typical examples.[25] It is a member of a very numerous class of rondo themes in $\frac{6}{8}$ or $\frac{2}{4}$, surely influenced by the contredanse (which could be in either meter), that feature a profusion of even eighth notes or, in $\frac{6}{8}$, a trochaic alternation of quarters and eighths. Both kinds of motion, like the rondo itself, suggested associations with dancing and an ideal of rustic life. A familiar example of the type is the little round song and chorus "Giovinette che fate all' amore," in which Zerlino, Masetto and their rural companions are introduced, singing and dancing, in the first act of *Don Giovanni*. Themes of this sort often include a "hook," an intentional slip of the mask of naiveté as the predictable surface of the music is disrupted; Mozart's occurs at the chorus's "che sarà, la la la ra," where the prevailing even eighths suddenly give way to a sophisticated little rhythmic turn suggestive of a peasant's dance finishing off with, say, a stylish little pirouette. Haydn's instrumental finales from the 1780s and 1790s are full of themes of this sort. One might cite, for example, the three finale themes from the String Quartets Op. 33, Nos. 1, 2, and 4, those of Op. 74, Nos. 1 and 2, Op. 76, Nos. 2 and 5, and the Symphonies Nos. 88, 89, 92, 94, 96, 97, 99, 100, and 102. All of these have in common an implied metric regularity—which of course Haydn often delighted in upsetting[26]—and every one of them begins with a single or double eighth-note anacrusis. Themes of this kind were also ubiquitous in rondo finales of concertos. They often fell into schematic patterns of repetition—such as the popular rounded binary shape—that were perfect for quick alternation of tutti and solo; and the pleasure of recognition at each return could be heightened by a switch from one to the other.[27]

Beethoven starts his theme right off with the "hook": what we are conditioned to hear as an upbeat in the opening tune falls instead directly on the first beat, as if the pianist were playing the right hand part in this $^6_8$ meter an eighth note too late (Example 4-10). At every appearance of the theme—except the one at m. 261, which we shall note in a moment— the listener is buffeted by the opposition between the actual rhythm and the "right" one that is almost impossible to put out of mind. What is written seems askew for more than one reason. Within a context of perfect metrical regularity (2+2; 2+2 measures), the tonic scale degree and longer note value, reinforced with a *sforzato* (and in m. 3 with a fuller texture), all converge frustratingly on the second beat, creating an ungainly iambic (or "Lombard") rhythm that is a broad parody of the contredanse idea. And that iambic figure itself is promptly contradicted. As early as the second half of m. 2, the longer note and the new harmony fall properly on the (secondary) accent. And other thematic matter of the movement reinforces the correction: both b_1 and b_2 (Table 4-3 and Examples 4-11 and 4-12) are outspokenly trochaic. Two other passages in the movement, however, make reference to that opening rhythm. In m. 261, just before the final ritornello, the first theme is coyly introduced in a somewhat remote key (G major), now with the upbeat—to show us, as if we didn't know, what its rhythm really ought to be. But the main theme of the episode (c in Table 4-3) recalls and confirms that iambic rhythm: its open- ing figure inverts the initial falling third, and its systematic syncopation is jolted into motion by an iamb clearly reminiscent of the first theme.[28]

Beethoven's apparent interest in relating themes a and c—like his reuse in the episode of modulatory material from the transition to the second subject ("x" in Table 4-3)—apparently reflects a basic change of strategy subsequent to the composition of the Rondo WoO 6. There the episode, as in some of Mozart's earlier finales,[29] is radically "episodic"; it seems hermetically sealed off from the rest of the movement by a contrasting tempo, meter, and key. Beethoven never wrote another episode like that in a concerto; it may be that dissatisfaction with it contributed to his decision to replace that movement with the present one. What was per- haps at issue was a rather basic aesthetic question: to what degree should a rondo finale adhere to the principle of alternation and contrast of the rondo proper, or to what extent might the movement also embrace the directionality and developmental energy of sonata form?

By the time Beethoven wrote his earliest concertos, rondo finales almost invariably borrowed heavily from the procedures of sonata form, resulting in many variants of what we loosely term *sonata-rondo*. The rondo finale of Op. 19 is a fairly typical example (see Table 4-3). The rondo theme is heard in four ritornellos, each time in the tonic key. The first and third of these serve as springboards for the equivalents, respectively, of an expo-

TABLE 4-3 OP. 19, III

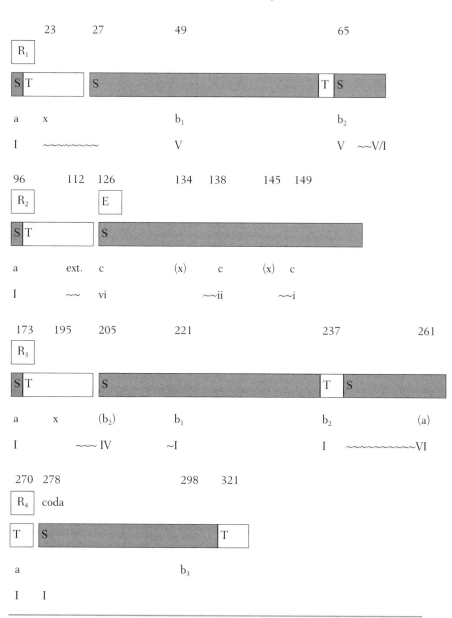

sition and recapitulation in sonata form. After the second ritornello comes the episode, ushered in by a swift modulation to its initial key of G minor (vi). A forty-bar coda, all in the tonic, follows the final ritornello. Such a shape has moved far toward the usual sonata-allegro plan, now differing from it formally only in a couple of ways. First is the undoing of the modulation to the secondary key: once accomplished, it is promptly negated by the second ritornello, that is, a return to the first theme in the main key. Then there is the more or less contrasting episode usurping the place of a "development" section (or, in a concerto first movement, an S_2). Of these two rondo-like features, only the first, the R_2 in the tonic after the modulation, is reliably present in concerto finales of the period.

For the section of the movement just after R_2, the location in Op. 19 of the episode, Mozart had presented a number of solutions. Sometimes there is a clear episode, either starkly contrasting (K. 271, K. 482) or, more commonly, bearing some continuity of motive or movement with what has preceded (K. 488, K. 503). In the Concerto for flute or oboe, K. 313 ($=285c$), the theme of the episode is merely a reworking of the main ritornello theme. Some of Mozart's concertos have no episode, but rather an out-and-out development section (K. 459, based on the audacious fugue that follows R_1; and K. 466), and one (K. 450) has both. When Beethoven decided on an episode painstakingly coordinated with the main thematic matter of the movement, he struck something of a middle course aimed at realizing the advantages of both rondo and sonata.

One potential trouble spot in a movement like this is the beginning of the final ritornello. The piece by this time has safely regained the tonic and there recapitulated most of the music that was previously heard in the dominant. This would hardly seem a favorable moment to bring on the first theme, also in the tonic, for the fourth time. Mozart, as usual, had offered some clever remedies. His problem, to be sure, was sometimes less acute than Beethoven's: he not infrequently omitted the R_3 altogether (K. 456, K. 459, K. 488, K. 537, and K. 595), and in these cases the ritornello, having last been heard before the episode (or development), arrived at the end of the piece sounding fresher.[30] But, even so, Mozart always took care to fan the fires of the listener's anticipation of this event. The most common way (as in K. 456, K. 459, K. 467, and others) was to insert a cadenza at this point—leaving it to the soloist, that is, to supply the desired tonal diversions and the lead-in to the theme. In other cases (K. 503 and K. 537), in order to create a demand for the ritornello Mozart himself provided florid transitional material full of portentous dominant sounds. This is the place in the finale of Op. 19 where Beethoven plays his genial little joke: he mysteriously shunts the music off into G major and presents the ritornello theme in that key with the "right" rhythm. This maneuver has the double effect of erasing the accumulated tonic sounds in our ears and placing the two versions of the main theme side by side for easy comparison. The ploy instructs while it entertains.

This movement has some very good things to offer. In addition to diverting flashes of wit, there are moments of engaging lyricism. As in the first movement, the first of the "second" themes, "b_1," (Example 4-11) is especially fine. This music, like the opening of the second movement, belongs to that class of themes, much beloved of Beethoven, in which a stationary melodic third degree sings over a descending bass. Its cantabile nature is enlivened by a pleasantly novel harmonic plan. Each of the paired phrases has a harmonic "sticking point" half way through, reinforced by a melodic leap and a *sforzato*. The first time it is on the subdominant, and the continuation is perfectly normal; but the second one lands on the submediant, and the phrase proceeds to finish unexpectedly on the dominant of that degree, as if with a question mark. This makes for an agreeable little jolt when the orchestra answers with the tonic chord upon launching into a restatement of the pair. The pattern of rapid repetitions here makes for the sort of close dialogue between tutti and solo—a dialogue in which the participants cooperate while revealing distinct musical identities—that is the glory of the genre.

But other features of the young Beethoven's rondo are bound to strike us as less successful. The episode is a systematic stop-and-go affair whose syncopated and very brief main theme is played in turn in G minor, C minor, and B♭ minor, with interspersed statements of the modulatory "x." Such unceremonious dislocations of this outlandish music surely suggest an intended buffo effect—we might think, say, of a "Turkish" character like Mozart's Osmin lumbering about the stage. But there is no very convincing parodic effect, and the passage comes off as more ungainly than witty. A good bit of the difficulty probably lies with the recurring "x" music, a bit of sparse two-voice counterpoint in rigidly even rhythm that merely outlines the dominant seventh to the new key—just barely getting the job of modulation done—and stops the proceedings dead both times it appears. Transitional material elsewhere, too, lacks the deftness that Beethoven is soon to acquire. The crucial return to the tonic for R_2 (mm. 82–94) is a case in point: the piano's single-line scales and questioning pauses, accompanied only by harmonically inconclusive chords in the orchestra, are simply too discontinuous (and too long) to heighten the listener's curiosity very much. In this movement Beethoven seems to do consistently better operating within a stable tonal area. The coda (beginning in m. 278), for example, all in the tonic, and mostly over a tonic pedal, unites a series of cadential gestures into a convincing whole. And some years later Beethoven himself paid one of these cadential gestures (b_3 in the table) a handsome compliment: he adapted it (in a slower tempo) for use at an analogous point in the second movement, in the same key and meter, of the *Pastoral* Symphony (see Example 4-13).

Beethoven's modest assessment of this piece in his letter to Hoffmeister, cited above, has been much quoted and little refuted. Apparent shortcomings in the work are always attributed to the composer's youth. But they have also typically been linked to the perception of a direct and strong dependence upon Mozart. A. B. Marx, showing only an approximate grasp of the chronology of the concertos, said that in all of the first three Beethoven "seized upon the tendencies and form of his great predecessor [Mozart]."[31] Guido Adler restricted a pervasive Mozartian influence to Op. 19, calling attention particularly to the ending of the first tutti of the opening movement as "stereotypically Mozartian" and, for Beethoven, "strikingly childlike" (thus invoking a real Mozartian stereotype).[32] Riemann (one assumes it is Riemann speaking at this point in the German edition of Thayer's biography), concurs: "in conception, invention, and piano technique the concerto yet remains in the Mozartian realm."[33] Basil Deane writes, "The influence of Mozart is strong, and not entirely digested."[34] Since Mozart so powerfully dominates our view of the concerto just before Beethoven, it is easy enough to assume that he similarly dominated Beethoven's view of it. But, as we have seen, the musical landscape probably looked rather different from the young Beethoven's standpoint. Other composers also loomed large in his musical upbringing; the question of Mozart's influence, insofar as such questions can ever be decided, will have to be decided on the evidence.

Quite aside from the particular circumstances of this case, surely it would have been a signal achievement for a composer in his twenties in the 1790s (and, indeed, for any composer at any time) to have provided even a plausibly convincing imitation of Mozart's masterpieces of the previous decade. Only radically "progressivist" presuppositions would lead one to think that what was magnificent in Mozart would in the next instant have been epigonous in Beethoven. But little that is specific, in any case, has been shown about the nature of the stylistic link to Mozart. Clear connections in the case of Op. 19 are not at all easy to see. The gentle little codetta to T_1 in the first movement (mm. 85ff.), which alternately leans on the dominant and resolves to the tonic, and which Adler called "stereotypically Mozartian," sounds plausibly like Mozart's music, all right. We have noted a similar passage with a similar function, in fact, in the first movement of the Piano Concerto in C, K. 503, mm. 82ff.[35]

But what we would need to show in order to make a strong case for Mozart's influence here is that other composers within Beethoven's ken never (or almost never) wrote such passages at analogous points in their compositions. But some did. Clementi often rounded off the expositions of the first movements of his sonatas with placid codettas roughly of this sort; more usually, they were built over a tonic pedal, but in some cases, such as the Sonata Op. 8, No. 2 (published in Paris in 1782), or the Sonata Op. 25, No. 2 (London, 1790), they alternate tonic and dominant. And Pleyel wrote similar closing gestures, as in the first movement of his Clarinet Concerto in C of ca. 1790.[36]

The basic stylistic language of Beethoven's concerto is one he shared with Western Europe as a whole. But what is *distinctive* about his writing in this work seems not at all an imitation of the special qualities of Mozart's music, either in Mozart's concertos or his other music. Mozart's contemporaries routinely saw his mature works as digressions from the norm in their intricacy, difficulty, and (over) abundance of detail. Fairly typical is the judgment of *Cramers Magazin der Musik* of 1787: the string quartets dedicated to Haydn, it said, were "too highly seasoned—and whose palate can endure this for long?" The composer and conductor Bernard Anselm Weber, according to a contemporary report, explained in more technical language that the music of *Die Entführung aus dem Sereil* was marred by the "frequent modulations and the many enharmonic passages," and progressions in which "the resolutions alternate too quickly with the discords, so that only a practised ear can follow the course of the harmony."[37] Mozart's music was widely seen as harmonically abstruse, "learned," and much given to counterpoint. These of course are what many of us now most admire in Mozart: the exquisite contrapuntal interplay, say, of the opening of the Andante of the Symphony in G minor, K. 550, in which a single melody is fashioned from the cooperative efforts of several voices, or the elusive modulatory course of the second subject of the String Quintet K. 516 (first movement) that within eight measures traverses B♭ major, C minor, and E♭ major before reaffirming B♭ major. Such flights of musical imagination seemed largely responsible for a general disaffection between the Viennese public and Mozart that set in after the performances of *Don Giovanni* there in 1788. But such elaboration and enrichment of the common Classical style was not the young Beethoven's way; any stylistic audacities to be found in Op. 19 seem very different.

In order to cast into relief the general contrast between the young Beethoven's innovations and those of the mature Mozart, it may be useful to compare two passages that are superficially similar in form and function. The first tutti in Op. 19, as we have seen, moves surprisingly to the flat mediant (D♭). The initial solo section of Mozart's Piano Concerto K. 503[38] does the same (the two passages would look very similar in the kind of structural tables we have been using). But their aesthetic effects are worlds removed. Mozart navigates to the new key (E♭) in the time-tested route through the parallel minor of the tonic (C minor), that is, the relative minor of his goal of E♭. But he does so with grace and elegance, moving an A♭ from the bass of an augmented sixth on that degree to the treble where, using the same rhythm, it turns into the melodic fourth degree of the new key. The usual resolution after the augmented sixth is (twice) denied, but an aural link between the old role of A♭ and the new one subtly creates a fresh continuation. Beethoven, we remember (Example 4-3), just moves the music up and insists upon the new key. The difference is similar to, say, that between being shown the way to an inviting courtyard below through a mysterious passageway or getting there upon being pushed unceremoniously out the window.

Contemporaneous responses to Mozart's music—from those not vexed with its intricacy—sometimes seemed to anticipate early Romantic views of the composer by evoking the eighteenth-century century affective category *wonder*. Schubart's *Vaterlandschronik* (1788) spoke of the "magic of his genius," and the *Dramatische Blätter* of Frankfurt (1799) said in reference to the graveyard scene in *Don Giovanni* that "Mozart seems to have learnt the language of ghosts from Shakespeare—a hollow, sepulchral tone seemed to rise from the earth."[39] The special effects of Beethoven's Op. 19 appear to incline much more strongly to that other contemporary psychological and aesthetic category, often paired with wonder as its antipode, *surprise*.[40] In some of the most distinctive passages in this concerto, such as the semitone slide in the first movement, the tonally disruptive opening tutti of the second, and the rhythmically displaced rondo theme of the finale, a principal effect is one of *unexpectedness*. Beethoven plays with the accepted procedures of the style, calling our attention to our own expectations as to tonal or rhythmic practice by partially frustrating them.[41] Thus the music in a sense enters into a dialogue with the system of norms that are its own point of departure, holding them up for inspection and questioning.

The composer known all over Europe in the 1790s for effects like this was, of course, Haydn, the most famous musician in the western world when Beethoven was composing Op. 19, and during a part of its incubation period (from late 1792 to late 1793), his teacher. Haydn's witty unorthodoxies seem most often to involve the manipulation of rhythmic patterns and phrase structure—as in the confounding of opening and closing gestures in the first movement of the String Quartet Op. 33, No.

5, and the last of Op. 33, No. 2 ("the Joke"). But his evocations of surprise also sometimes played on the listener's harmonic expectations. At the end of the exposition in the first movement of the Symphony No. 99 (to mention only one charming example), after the firm close in the Dominant, B♭, a questioning fragment of the first theme enters twice, separated by pauses, in the unrelated dominant of C minor; after another pause a different theme enters in C major. The most distinctive features of Op. 19— i.e., the points at which it digresses most markedly from the norms of composition of its time—clearly resemble such sallies of Haydn's wit more than anything in Mozart.

Influence, of course, is at best a slippery concept, and its operation can almost never be conclusively demonstrated. In the present case it may be, for example, that Beethoven depended upon intermediaries, upon others who imitated Haydn. One such intermediary, in a few compositions of the 1780s and 1790s, was the world's leading piano composer (in contemporary estimation), Clementi. His Sonata Op. 33, No. 1, dedicated to Haydn's London friend Theresa Jansen, seems a clear case in point. Its opening theme is an exercise in one of Haydn's favorite kinds of rhythmic ambiguity, one that confuses beginnings with endings; its last movement repeatedly makes a great show of preparing one key and then abruptly veering off in another.[42] This sonata was published in 1794—too late to have had any effect upon the earliest stages of Beethoven's work on Op. 19, but in time, perhaps, for the revisions of 1794–95. And some of the piano writing in Beethoven's concerto, particularly in its first movement, sounds for all the world like an imitation of Clementi. The thin scale-wise motion accompanied by a murky bass pedal at the start of the display episode (m. 157) was something of a speciality of the younger Clementi. And a few measures later (184ff.) Beethoven turns that thin keyboard texture into a figure strikingly like something from the first movement of Clementi's Sonata in F minor, No. 6 (see Examples 4-14a and b)—a composition of 1785, whose last movement, "Beethovenian" in the extreme, may well have supplied the contredanse theme in the finale of the *Eroica*.[43]

But much in the concerto is also quite recognizably Beethoven's own. What is inimitable in Beethoven illuminates the rest of the first movement's vigorous display episode, for example, and we feel it throughout the Adagio. This composition is probably the least of the Beethoven concertos. But that powerful musical persona of the decade to come is (if by fits and starts) already to be seen.

Beyond the LINGUA FRANCA: Piano Concerto No. 1 in C, Op. 15

The C-major Concerto was fixed in its present form when Beethoven wrote out the autograph in 1800. But this act apparently put to rest a far less tumultuous course of composition and revision than did the writing of the autograph of the Concerto in B♭ in 1798. While successive performances of Op. 19 always seemed to prompt Beethoven to work the piece over again—and he never seemed to do so entirely to his satisfaction—Op. 15 apparently remained reasonably close to what it was at its premiere in 1795.[1] And while Op. 19, whatever Beethoven did to it, never shook off a certain aspect of juvenility and patchiness, Op. 15 seems from the first more assured and more integral; in 1795 the C-major Concerto probably looked to be a more mature piece than the B♭ Concerto did in 1798.

The year of the C-major Concerto, 1795, was a good one for Beethoven. During this, his third year in Vienna, the Tonkünstler-Sozietät engaged him to perform at both their oratorio presentations in March. And he apparently presented his new concerto at a most auspicious occasion in December where Haydn, fresh from his triumphs in England, gave a first concert for the newly adoring home audience in Vienna. And Beethoven's concerto arrived on the heels of a succession of strong compositions, some of which he felt—for the first time—deserved the dignity of opus numbers. The outward circumstances of his life, too, were increasingly felicitous. Wegeler tells us that upon his arrival in Vienna in the fall of 1794

he found Beethoven living "as a guest" in the home of Prince Carl Lichnowsky, and that upon his own departure in mid-1796, the young composer was still there. Beethoven guarded his prized independence by
employing his own servant, hiring his own horse "though he had the
Prince's entire stable at his disposal," and choosing to eat out rather than
at the Prince's table.[2] On Friday mornings at Lichnowsky's, leading musicians of the city gathered for musicales where Beethoven's new compositions, notably the Piano Trios Op. 1 and the Piano Sonatas Op. 2, were
tried out and discussed.[3]

There is a good reason to think of this group of compositions from
1794–95, in particular the Piano Trios Op. 1, Nos. 2 and 3, the Piano
Sonatas Op. 2, and the C-major Concerto—this last something of a culmination of the series—as marking Beethoven's "first maturity." In expressive weight and technical sophistication these piano trios set a new
standard for their composer and for their genre. (The first of the set, in
Eb, seems to be an earlier piece.) These works firmly declare their independence from the most prominent models in the genre, Haydn's late
piano trios, which, for all their virtues, still cling to the old ways of the
accompanied keyboard sonata; the piano predominates strongly, the violin
is allotted only an occasional independence, and the cello remains for the
most part chained to the bass of the piano part.[4] Beethoven's trios, too,
are weighted in favor of the composer's own instrument. But they also
quite explicitly allow the cello to participate in imitative passages, to fulfill
textural functions in its mid and upper ranges, and to assume predominant
control of the bass line—thus releasing the left hand of the piano part for
other duties.[5]

And contrary to current expectations for their genre, these trios are big,
ambitious pieces, musically and technically demanding, each in four
movements with a sonata-form finale. Both first movements have tonally
equivocal principal themes whose ambiguities yield structural consequences later on. And the Trio No. 2 in G shows what may be Beethoven's
first experiment with explicit intermovement tonal architecture: its second
movement, in a rather distant E major, proceeds in a sudden passionate
outburst between the exposition and recapitulation to G major; and the
finale (back in G major), reaches E major in its development section.[6]
What Beethoven has done in these trios is to inject his most advanced
and adventurous kind of writing into a genre of "pleasant music" up to
now intended mainly for amateurs. This may help account for Haydn's
misgivings about at least one of them, the C-minor Trio, which he advised
Beethoven not to publish, and whose public success, he later told Ries,
had quite surprised him.[7]

To a degree, the same holds for the solo sonatas of Op. 2. Keyboard sonatas were normally directed toward one of two distinct destinations: for performance by the composer (or sometimes by another accomplished player),[8] or, more frequently, for publication and amateur performance. In the latter case they incurred the demand for accessibility that, at least in the opinion of the publishers, such an audience always presses. And one can often tell which sonatas were intended for which purpose. The distinction seems clear enough, for example, even within the group of sonatas Haydn published in 1780, Hob. XVI:35–39, and 20. The fluent regularity that reigns in this music, particularly in Hob. XVI:35–37, and 39, stands in stark contrast to the expressive urgency and radical disjunctions of texture—as well as technical demands—of the last sonata of the set, the famous one in C minor (Hob. XVI:20). The C-minor Sonata, composed much earlier, was evidently a last-minute substitution, probably added to the group in recognition of the pianistic abilities of its dedicatees, the sisters Auernhammer.[9]

But for Beethoven such a distinction hardly existed. With the exception of the two "easy Sonatas" Op. 49 (ca. 1795–97), his earlier piano sonatas were intensely personal vehicles that united the imaginative flights of his keyboard improvisation with a mounting distinctiveness of expression and structural cogency. The three sonatas of Op. 2 (the first of these, again, may be a bit earlier than the others) clearly mark a new stage in Beethoven's piano writing. The derring-do technical feats of the outer movements of the C-major sonata and the finale of the F-minor one, the insouciant abruptness of modulation and textural changes in the A-major sonata, the almost painful extension of the coda to the Adagio of the F-minor sonata (this movement marvelously adapted from the distinctly unripe Adagio of the Piano Quartet in C, WoO 36, of a decade earlier)—all this vividly evokes the image of the young composer at his own instrument, astonishing and delighting audiences with his newfound powers of expression and execution. It was from this atmosphere of a kind of *Spielfreudigkeit*, a pianistic euphoria, that the C-major Concerto emerged.

While the B♭ Concerto, even in its final embodiment, shows Beethoven struggling toward mastery of a high galant (or Classical) style long since achieved by Haydn and Mozart, in the best pieces of 1794–95 he seems already to have left that stage behind. No one can claim, of course, that these compositions surpass in any qualitative sense the best music of these older masters. Rather, at the moment he appeared equipped to join this august company, Beethoven had already struck out in directions of his own. The three movements of Op. 15 reflect a much wider range of affect (of "action and passion" in Descartes's language) than eighteenth-century decorum would usually have countenanced—from the tense urgency of the opening theme to the boisterous levity of the A-minor episode in the finale. And at every turn there is a certain virtuosity—both pianistic and compositional—that exudes the confidence of the young genius feeling for the first time something of the true extent of his powers.

This concerto stands in a particular tradition of C-major orchestral pieces with trumpets and drums (there are often horns as well). Works of this stripe, associated with festiveness and exaltation (trumpets and drums in Renaissance Europe had been the province of royalty), run like a "silver thread," as Robbins Landon says, through Haydn's long career, appearing in his symphonies of all periods.[10] Of Mozart's seven symphonies in C major only K. 128 of 1772 is without trumpets and drums, and those rousing instruments figure in three of his four piano concertos in that key.[11] One of these, K. 467 (1785), recalls a related but even older connotation of this instrumental partnership, that is, an association with things military. Its opening motive, with its rigid motion in even quarters with concluding flourishes at two-measure intervals, imitates the infantry march—as does the strikingly similar rhythmic pattern Mozart was to write later for Leporello's "Notte e giorno faticar" (Examples 5-1a and b).[12]

THE ALLEGRO CON BRIO

Beethoven's opening in Op. 15 is of the same military cast, but more earthy and explicit, with its miniscule melodic compass and its plain repetition of tonic chords followed by a rigid alternation of tonic and dominant. It moves with the same quarter-note gait and stiff even-measured periodization, and it even has the flourishes—though rhythmically repositioned—in the first violin (Example 5-2a; "a" in Table 5-1).[13] That opening motive is quickly heard in two versions, first quiet and anticipatory (much like its near contemporary in the same key, the beginning of Sonata Op. 10, No. 3) and next in all its trumpets-and-drums splendor. The effect of this last is heightened by a metrical elision at its beginning (Koch's *Takterstickung*) in which, given the ironclad metrical scheme by now in place, the peremptory new beginning rushes in one measure too soon. Rhythm has an overwhelming presence here. What the listener is left with, more than anything else, is that march-like tread of quarter notes set in motion by the initial half note; the second, in-between period (mm. 9–15) offers some relief in other aspects of the music, but that rhythm is still there. And Beethoven's explicit prescriptions for rhythm and meter

TABLE 5-1

FIRST PIANO CONCERTO, OP. 15, I

24	38	49		72	86	99
T_1						

a	a_1	a_2	b	ba	c	(a)
I		$\sim\sim\flat$III$\sim$iv$\sim$v$\sim$i		$\sim\sim$I		

106	154	182
S_1		

x (a)	b	c pass.
I	$\sim\sim\sim\sim$V	V

237	266	292	312
T_2	S_2		

ba	(b)	a
V	$\flat$III$\sim\sim\sim\sim$iv$\sim\sim\sim\sim\sim$V/I	

346	353	369	397
T_3	S_3		

a	a_1	b	c pass.
I		$\sim\sim$I	I

452	471	
T_4	cad	T_4 (cont.)

ba	c	a
$\sim\sim$I	I	

should be taken seriously. The piece is in common time, not *alla breve*, as one so often hears it; the quarter-note motion is essential.

What does such a beginning establish, and what implications would it have had for Beethoven's listeners about the movement as a whole? It is surprising how vigorously the old eighteenth-century notion of the "principal theme" as the embodiment of the central idea or feeling of a movement persisted in the late eighteenth century and across the divide into the nineteenth. In the article "Hauptsatz" in his *Musikalisches Lexikon*, published in 1802, one year after Beethoven's Op. 15, Heinrich Christoph Koch speaks of the matter thus: "The principal subject, or theme, is that melodic statement of a composition that defines its overall character, or that presents in a concrete shape or imprint the affect it is to express." As he so often does, Koch thereupon approvingly quotes Johann Georg Sulzer on this matter:

> Just as in an oration the principal idea or theme presents its essential content, and of necessity contains the material for the development of that principal idea as well as of the accessory ones, so too it is in music in respect to the modifications of an affect ("Empfindung") that the principal subject permits. And just as an orator passes over from his principal subject to secondary ideas, opposing ones, dissections, and the like, making use of rhetorical figures designed to reinforce the main subject, so too will the composer treat his principal theme . . . such that the episodes and secondary ideas, especially necessary in writing music, will not disturb the principal affect or mar the unity of the whole.[14]

And in a lengthy *Zusatz* to his translation of three of Reicha's treatises, published in 1832, Beethoven's former pupil Carl Czerny still said much the same: the opening theme or motive "will be developed throughout the movement as its basic idea [*Grundidee*]. The character it expresses, whether it be earnest, or imposing and brilliant, or mild and gentle, or passionate and gloomy, must be retained, insofar as the required variety of ideas permits, throughout the entire movement."[15] Thus from a historical point of view it seems to make sense for us to think about the *overall* character of a composition, and about the roles its various parts play in determining that character.

The first movement of Beethoven's Op. 15 has three fundamental musical ideas ("a," "b," and "c" in Table 5-1; Example 5-2) from which virtually all the music derives. The wind band motive "c," clearly enough, has much the same military character as "a": the marching quarter notes, and the distinctive rhythmic element that it adds, the dotted-note figure that was also a commonplace feature of military marches. Its little flurries of eighth notes act as accentuating anacruses, much like the flourishes in the first theme, and both its rhythmic and melodic profile recall march idioms of the French Revolution, of which the *Marseillaise* has become for us a prototype. Theme "b" of course is the contrasting lyrical statement, the proverbial second theme of A. B. Marx and the remainder of the nineteenth century, lyrical by virtue of its legato phrasing, stepwise motion, and low dynamic level. But it also has a certain swagger to it, with its expansive octave flourish in eighth notes. And in a subtle way it borrows elements from the first subject, which, as Sulzer told us, "of necessity contains the material for the development of that principal idea as well as of the accessory ones." That straight quarter-note motion reappears at the end of the first phrase of "b" (for a moment even with its familiar staccato articulation), and both phrases start with the initial half-note anchor from "a." Even the flowing eighths of "b" can be heard as a filling-in and smoothing-out of the basic motion of the first subject: there are no rhythmic events of a kind that would block or obscure the continuous quarter-note pulse. The relationship of "b" to "a" is an example of the "contrasting derivation" Arnold Schmitz saw as a fundamental constructive principal in Beethoven's works: music of widely differing character or affect is related by underlying motivic similarities. Here this process has two effects. It makes us feel (if only subliminally) that "b" is of a piece with a movement largely dominated by "a"; and insofar as we are aware of that motivic relationship, it compromises the purely lyrical nature of this "second theme."

The first subject predominates hugely here, and with just a bit of assistance from the other military motive, "c," its character of parade-like pomp prevails—just as the theorists prescribed. It serves to mark the beginnings and endings of things. In the first tutti it does both quite straightforwardly (mm. 1 and 99), a short way into S_1 (m. 118) it signals a renewed beginning, it starts off T_3 (m. 346, i.e., the recapitulation), and it ends the movement altogether (mm. 471ff). Its presence is felt elsewhere, too. Both the sixteenth-note flourish and the even quarters persist in the material immediately following that first theme ("a1," m. 24)[16]; then in the modulatory passage beginning in m. 72 ("ba"), both those elements of "a" are present once more, as they will be, of course, at subsequent recurrences of this music (mm. 237 and 452).

But however domineering the military music may threaten to become in this movement, its effect is also subtly but consistently undermined. This even happens in the initial eight measures of the first theme itself.

For all its declarative tonic-dominant resolve, it still has about it—in both its piano and fortissimo versions—a certain air of tentativeness brought on by the inconclusiveness of its two cadences, the first stopping on the dominant, and the second on a weak beat with the third on top. Such irresolution probably reflects in part a collision of formal considerations with expressive ones; in this period Beethoven increasingly favored open-ended first statements that allowed the "processive" features of the music to begin with the first bars (two examples close at hand are the first two sonatas of Op. 2). But such a procedure must inevitably detract from the decisiveness and declaratory force of the opening statement. And the answering phrase (mm. 8ff.), as so often happens with such peremptory beginnings,[17] is a mollifying agent; it presents the first subdominant sound of the piece together with a lyrical motion to a higher register. And though the initial rhythmic skeleton is still there, it is prefaced with legato eighth-note upbeats, and its detached repeated chords are softened to porta-mento. (Beethoven will forgo this lyrical continuation in the rush of events after the fortissimo repetition of the first motive; here in m. 24, that sub-dominant sonority launches instead the first of two kinds of vigorous tran-sitional material, "a_1" and "a_2," leading to the second subject.)

Thus the power and assertiveness inherent in the stuff of that first theme are brought into question even as we hear it for the first time. And however much this effect may have been a simple product of Beethoven's formal procedures, it is also congruent with the expressive posture of the movement as a whole. The solo sections to come make this clearer. In a transformation shortly before the end of S_2 (mm. 292ff.), the theme has turned almost meditative: it is modulatory (favoring minor keys), given to imitation, and subdued. And for a moment in S_1 we hear that theme subjected to something like parody; the piano decks it out in taunting appoggiaturas (mm. 126ff.) a bit like the idée fixe theme in the "Witches' Sabbath" of Berlioz's *Symphonie fantastique* (Example 5-3).

In these events in the solo part we sense certain differences in agenda between solo and orchestra that underscore an unusually outspoken oppo-sition between those two forces. The military motif dominates the first tutti, where both themes of that persuasion ("a" and "c") are fully aired, and the ending insists once more upon the hammer strokes of "a." Thereupon the solo at its first entrance responds (Example 5-4), as in the corresponding point in Op. 19, with a seeming irrelevancy—as if this lead-ing character had stepped onto the stage with thoughts left over from some other proceedings. (We might dimly perceive a connection between this statement and the lyrical "b" theme—a connection all the harder to make at this point, since we have not yet heard that melody in its entirety.)

When the piano has finished its enigmatic utterance, the orchestra tries to posit once more the straightforwardly militant "a." But the soloist silences its consequent half phrase with a flood of sound that quickly bends the music into modulatory directions, effectively annulling this new offering of the opening theme and forcing us in retrospect to hear the whole section (from m. 118) as the beginning of the transition.[18] And it is surely remarkable that in the movement as a whole the piano plays continuations, derivations, and paraphrases of "a," but never the theme itself. Something roughly similar happens with the other march tune, "c"; the winds of the orchestra play it twice, in the first and last tuttis, both times in the tonic. At the appropriate points in S_1 and S_3 (mm. 182 and 397), the piano participates in this music, all right, but festoons it with ornament—particularly Beethoven's favorite trill accompaniment from the cadenzas—such that its military character is quite compromised. It is as if the mass of the orchestra is easily roused to overt, forceful action, while its leader favors a more nuanced, artful approach.

The formal structure of the movement (mapped in Table 5-1) is for the most part unremarkable. The first tutti begins and ends in the tonic; S_1 takes us generally through the same music to the dominant; T_2 and S_2 are given over to modulation and paraphrase; and from T_3 to the end is a normal recapitulation and close that barely strays from the tonic. The major disturbance amid all this regularity, one any listener must be aware of, is the errant harmonic course, once more, of the opening tutti (Example 5-5).

In m. 46 the full orchestra comes to an exclamatory close on G major— still the dominant of C—whereupon the second violins balance delicately on that G and turn it into the third of E♭ for a first presentation of the second theme in that key. But we hear only the first segment of "b" before modulatory passages intrude to nudge the music up to F minor and then G minor for repetitions of this puzzling exercise. It finally takes a major effort of the sequential "ba" material (mm. 72–85) to restore order and usher in "c" in its proper key of C major. The disorientation brought on by these partial and harmonically errant statements of "b" is much abetted by the metrical scheme of the passage. Except for the one-measure elision at the fortissimo repetition of "a" (m. 16), the music up to this point has been a very model of Riemann's beloved *Vierhebigkeit*: everything falls into four-measure phrases. But in m. 49 "b" enters not only in the wrong key, but a measure too late; and because the intrusive modulating sequences here last only three measures each, the two subsequent statements seem to leap in a measure early.

In tonal music, turns toward the parallel minor are, of course, utterly commonplace: transitions, in particular, often aim toward minor so that ensuing music arriving in major sounds all the fresher. And that implied minor can, to be sure, easily summon up major keys based on *its* newly flatted pitches, the third and sixth (in Beethoven's sonata for Piano and Cello in F from 1796, the year after Op. 15, for example, the C-major music of the second group repeatedly veers toward C minor and A♭). But the first tutti of Op. 15, with the abruptness of nonmodulation to *three* unprepared keys coupled with metrical disorder, is quite another matter.

Tovey, in his amusing way, describes the modulation to the dominant at the corresponding point in the first movement of the C-minor Concerto, Op. 37, as an error or an accident—first tuttis of concertos, as Mozart has shown, need to stay at home in the tonic.[19] But the motion to the flat mediant in Opus 15, at least, was hardly undertaken casually; sketches in Kafka show that it was part of Beethoven's basic design for the movement. Two successive continuity drafts on fols. 113r and 113v record his efforts to settle on the continuation after the fortissimo version of the first theme in m. 16 ("a₁" and "a₂" of the final version). In his first attempt Beethoven works the head motive of the first theme, adding an eighth-note running motion, and later the new rhythm of "a₂"; the overall harmonic course of these twenty-eight measures is evidently a prolongation of IV–V–I, all in C major. The second time around he writes a shorter version, fifteen measures, first with a new conjunct melodic line growing out of the head motive and then, once more, the rhythm of "a₂" embedded in cadential runs. Both solutions end on the dominant of C major, and both thereupon proceed exactly as the final version does, with the quiet but abrupt shift to E♭ and the second theme. The harmonic goal of E♭ was evidently a fixed destination for Beethoven as he planned the movement. What came before and after was variable; in both drafts "b" appears only in E♭ and C minor, as opposed to the more radical E♭–F minor–G minor of the published version. But E♭, borrowed from the parallel minor, was settled.[20]

Thus the lyrical second theme, while retaining a certain rhythmic resonance with the assertive "a" (even the melody lines of their first cadences are curiously congruent) comes clothed in the surprising dark hues of minor—and in the final version, indeed, in two successive minor keys. As to effect and affect, this music remains richly ambiguous. Cantabile but vaguely reminiscent of the energy of the march, cheerful while inclining toward the somber flat side and the minor mode, it tends toward expansiveness, though (for now) its continuation is rudely cut off. It is only in the solo section to come that we will hear the melody in its entirety.

That that flat mediant was hardly desultory or incidental is confirmed later in the movement. The second tutti, playing one of its possible roles as solidifier of the dominant key established in the S_1 exposition, comes to a decisive close in G at m. 256, a close much resembling the one preceding the side step to the flat mediant and "b" in the first tutti. And here much the same thing happens again: an abrupt motion to E♭ prepares the start of S_2 (see Example 5-6).[21]

What the soloist plays now is at first hard to fathom; these arpeggiations on E♭ seem mere passagework until the turn around B♭ in m. 269, where we recognize the head-motive of "b" and in retrospect connect the succession of even eighths to the same source. Thereafter, holding fast to the key of E♭, Beethoven explicitly associates the even quarter-note motion in mm. 280ff. with "a": as the piano plays seemingly desultory scales in $^6_3$ chords, the link is firmly made by the head-motive of that theme played pizziccato in the strings. And if the flat mediant is by now established as the central tonality for this "development" section, the parallels with the opening tutti are not finished. The next harmonic motion in both places (mm. 56 and 288) is to F minor and then to G (the first tutti has G minor, while S_2 cuts the process short here, treating that pitch as the dominant of C in preparation for the reprise in T_3).

Those quirky harmonic gyrations of the second theme in T_1, from E♭ to F to G—all the more notable in that they occur within a large harmonic skeleton that is plainly conventional—now gain a measure of formal validation from the parallel harmonic motions in S_2: they are seen as part of a larger scheme. The conventional overall structure of a movement such as this leaves room, of course, for various local options in the harmonic plan: most of all, naturally, in S_2, but at other points as well. One such place—since transitions can be managed in various ways—is in the modulation toward the dominant in S_1; here the music aims toward G minor rather than major, touching E♭ major once more on the way (mm. 140–43). Further in the same solo section the approach to "c" also leans toward G minor, yet again lightly brushing against E♭ at m. 176 (its parallel passage in S_3 duly aims a fifth lower toward A♭). But most radical by far of such harmonic maneuvers (excepting the one in T_1) is the handling of the parallel display episodes that form the climaxes of S_1 and S_3. Here (mm. 216 and 431) Beethoven is willing to halt the forward rush of his brilliant piano music for a pianissimo meditative interlude; converging chromatic outer lines in m. 217 lead quickly to A♭, where we are presented in quick succession with two kinds of descending sequences (Example 5-7). The first falls to D♭, and the second, a type perfected by Mozart,[22] tumbles downward by fifths all the way through the enharmonic sharp keys back to C (which becomes the subdominant of G major). This is a radical encapsulation of a consistent trait of this movement. When Beethoven exercises his harmonic options, he does so, without exception, by moving in the direction of added flats.

Those corresponding motions to E♭ and F minor in T_1 and S_2 are more than an exercise in the simple aesthetic pleasures of symmetry. They are part of a consistent pattern in this movement by which the authority of the military topos, with its outspoken C and G-major brilliance, is systematically undercut by syntactical uncertainties, by eruptions of unscheduled lyricism, by injections of minor mode and consistent "regressions" in the flat direction. Analogous irregularities in Op. 19—and those of the still earlier concerto movements—are never thus bent to the service of larger aesthetic ends. The first movement of Op. 15 gathers up its rich variety of expression into a coherent design that marks a new level in Beethoven's composition of concertos.

But of course much of the joy of this movement lies also in its unabashed and exuberant pianism. The keyboard figurations often seem elemental—unartful, even, in comparison with those of the mature Mozart concertos.[23] The first great wave of sound that silences the orchestra's efforts to reinstate the main theme in m. 119 is nothing more than a run of one-handed descending broken chords of the sort every pianist remembers practicing. In the display episodes (mm. 191 and 406) two kinds of very straightforward figuration alternate (Example 5-8). The first, a simple ornamented descending scale, harmonically inert, depends for its bracing effect upon the figure in contrary motion that joins it in m. 195. (When writing the autograph in 1800, Beethoven made several attempts to elaborate the sixteenth-note figuration at this point by putting it in both hands at once in mirror imitation, but never worked it out to his satisfaction.) The other one, harmonically very active, acts as a foil: its stream of staccato triplets, easily invertible with their accompanying chords, comprise a series of moves to ever new local tonics. By their very simplicity and the transparency of their construction, passagework such as this lends the work an appealing freshness, an impression of vigor, and something like innocence.

Two other kinds of figuration here are specialties of Beethoven. One is the scintillating trill-plus-melody in the soloist's version of the "c" theme (mm. 186ff.), a figuration Beethoven much favored in his cadenzas. The other, already well practiced in Mozart's late concertos, is a quick alternation of tones in the same hand, one pitch remaining stationary while the others form a converging or diverging line with it (mm. 145ff. and 360ff.)—in the next concerto, Op. 37, the moving line will *cross* the fixed pitch, so that the pattern can be extended to two octaves. The close of the two outer solo sections introduces another mild innovation in piano writing. Instead of the fine old cliché of the Mozart concertos, the trilled dominant with some version of Alberti bass below, Beethoven leaves the lower parts to the orchestra, while the pianist does the trill in sixths. The famous ending of S_2 (m. 344)—a point in the movement Mozart tended to downplay—is much more drastic: a fortissimo sixteenth-note scale in octaves catapults down from the top of the piano to the bottom. The problem is that midway in its course Beethoven writes a low G for the left hand—already well occupied, presumably, playing the lower octave of the scale. A natural conclusion that Beethoven had in mind a glissando was confirmed by Czerny (together with a remarkable suggested alternative): "The return to the principal theme (after the second part) consists again of the octave slide, as in the Solo Sonata Op. 53, and small hands may therefore take the run in single notes, but with increased rapidity in order to extend it to eight notes lower."[24] While the run in octaves is clearly much too fast to be played one-handed with separate attacks, it is rather too *slow* for any hope of effective performance as a glissando—a tricky undertaking in any case on modern pianos. Pianists today usually either play the bass note first to free both hands for the scale or omit some portion of the scale in the left hand. But the only completely satisfactory solution—a solution, one suspects, that certain recent recordings may have quietly adopted—is to play the scales with both hands while enlisting an accomplice to add the low G.

THE LARGO

Beethoven's slow movements from 1794–95 show a new penchant for keys remote from the principal tonality.[25] The slow movements of the G-major Piano Trio of Op. 1 and the C-major Sonata of Op. 2 both move far in the sharp direction to E major. The C-major Concerto goes deter-minedly the other way (in accord with its already professed preference for the flat side) to A♭ major. The movement is Largo, evidently Beethoven's first with just this indication of tempo (or character). "Largo," with or without qualifiers, rare in Beethoven's music as a whole, appears more frequently in his early works than those of other periods. There had been the Largo con espressione of Op. 1, No. 2, and the Largo appassionato of Op. 2, No. 2, and there was about to be the Largo con gran espressione in the Sonata Op. 7 of 1796–97.[26] Except perhaps for this last, none of these movements suggests the extremes of slow tempo and gravity of expression that *largo* often implies nowadays; none is even in minor. Nor were eighteenth-century commentators by any means in agreement that largo was the slowest or gloomiest of the tempo indications. Some placed it between adagio and andante,[27] and Koch said simply that the term referred to the "most usual degree of slow motion," adding that it was appropriate for "such affects that reveal themselves in a ceremonious slowness."[28] Two of the Largos Beethoven composed within a year or so of Op. 15 may suggest such "ceremony": the slow movements of Op. 2, No. 2, and Op. 7 both have themes with procession-like staccato stepping basses (in Op. 7 it is the second subject, beginning at m. 25). The incidence of Largos in the concertos is high: the Third Piano Concerto Op. 37 and the Triple Concerto Op. 56 have them as well.

In the autograph Beethoven first added "cantabile" to the tempo indication, then crossed it out but wrote that word again in m. 15, where the clarinet takes the melody. If that "cantabile" indicates certain mental reservations about the idea of "largo"—a desire, perhaps, to avoid a connotation of the slow and lugubrious—the meter signature surely does so more decisively. For this Largo, quite exceptionally, is *alla breve*. Although the Breitkopf & Härtel collected edition and many subsequent printings have perpetuated the reading of common time for the movement, the autograph and the first edition (Mollo, pl. no. 153) leave no room for doubt. This *Largo alla breve* is virtually unique among Beethoven's works; the slow sections of the first movement of the Sonata in D minor, Op. 31, No. 2, provide the only other example that comes to mind, and there the *alla breve* indication may simply be a by-product of the rhythmic organization of the fast sections with which they are paired.[29]

Czerny insisted on a connection between the meter of Op. 15 and its affect: "This Largo is *alla breve*, and must consequently be played as a tranquil Andante. The noble melody must be performed softly, but with the most cantabile expression, and the simplicity of the passages must rise above the accompanying orchestra, by means of a refined tone and elegant delivery."[30] Thus we should probably think of the movement as more similar in tone to the Adagio cantabile of the Sonata Op. 13 (the *Pathétique*), rather than, say, the Adagio molto of the Sonata Op. 10, No. 1 (to recall two more-or-less contemporaneous movements in the same key). The opening dactylic rhythm, if felt in two rather than four, is only the first instance of "big upbeats" in this movement, of groups of quarters or eighths that unite to form extended anacruses. The orchestra's continuation in m. 8 ("a₁" in Table 5-2) is quite explicit about this, as is the transitional material in m. 19, and the motive "b" in m. 30, while the interlude that leads back to the reprise (m. 41) introduces the same idea in double-dotted rhythms (see Examples 5-9a–e). Although *alla breve* may suggest a somewhat faster absolute tempo,[31] the impression of cantabile

TABLE 5-2 OP. 15, II

	8		18		25		30	
S		T		S		T		S

a   a₁   trans   b

I   ~~~~~~~~~~~~~~~~V

41	44
T	S

(a)

V~~~~~~

	60	65	67		84		88	91		97
S		T	S			T			S	

53   ·   60   65   67   84   88   91   97

a   a₁   a   Coda

I   I   ~I   ~~I

tranquility Czerny wanted from this movement can be had more easily if we hear those upbeats whole.

Like the slow movements of several of Mozart's later piano concertos, this piece begins with the piano, but with a remarkable difference: the strings accompany alternate phrases with a subdued (*pianissimo* to the solo's *piano*), low-lying chordal reduction of the piano part. Such an "atmospheric" sound probably never before started off a movement of a keyboard concerto. The piano of course needs no help in accompanying its melody; it can and does supply its own harmonic support. The strings add pure sustained sonority, much like the string parts in what Rousseau called *récitatif accompagné*, a kind of recitative reserved for dramatic scenes of special gravity (or in German Passion settings for the words spoken by Christ). Beethoven seems to have relied upon such associations to give his theme an air of special solemnity.

And that theme itself has a familiar ring to it. It belongs to a rather numerous class of Beethoven's characteristic slow themes—they occur in all the stages of his career—in which the bass moves stepwise up from the tonic to create a tentative dominant sonority, V_3^4. Often, as here, this is part of a motion that continues to the third degree and a first inversion tonic. The soprano may move in parallel tenths (as at the beginning of the Sonata Op. 110)[32] or may have a simple $\hat{8}$–$\hat{7}$–$\hat{8}$ motion, as in the slow movement of the Sonata for Piano and Violin, Op. 12, No. 3, or the opening Andante of the Sonata Op. 26 (see Examples 5-10a–c). The theme from this concerto adopts elements of both those soprano motions, arpeggiating downward on the dominant sound to get from one to the other (another one that does just this is the Andante theme of the Sonata for Piano and Violin, Op. 12; No. 1).

There is nothing very distinctive about these contrapuntal shapes as such. Similar ones occasionally show up in slow themes of Mozart, for example in the slow movements of the Piano Concerto K. 414, the String Quartet K. 458, and the Piano Trio K. 502 (another example is the beginning of Brahms's Sonata in A for Piano and Violin, Op. 100). But in each of these cases the dissonant $_3^4$ occurs on a weak beat as a distinctly *passing* motion between one consonant sonority and another. When Mozart wishes instead to sustain and emphasize that dissonant (dominant) sound, he characteristically slides the bass down to the more conventional $_5^6$ position, as in the Poco Adagio of the Symphony K. 425 (Example 5-11).[33]

Beethoven makes the unstable dissonance a sticking point, a place of emphatic unsettledness. He routinely does this by placing the dissonance in the strong part of the measure; but what is more important, he frequently injects a disjunction of some sort between that dissonance and its resolution. In the case of this theme from Op. 15 (as well as in the movement from Op. 12, No. 1), the bass resolution is estranged from the dissonance by a rest and an octave registral shift (in Op. 26 it comes in late and offbeat). And, moreover, the strings just at that point withhold their support,[34] so there is nothing to soften that dissonance ringing in our ears. Through a small distortion of perfectly familiar materials, Beethoven places his distinctive mark on them.

This first theme has a rounded binary shape without modulation or repetitions of the two halves. But as it approaches the clarinet's restatement of the first strain (m. 11), the music is interrupted by an eruption of emphatic dominants: a simple cadential pattern (V/V–V), set in exclamatory new double-dotted rhythms and exchanged between the instrumental choirs, is repeated several times too often for the orderly progress of this little formal plan (see the end of Example 5-9b). Such blustery overstatement becomes a defining feature of this movement. Cadence patterns repeated *fortissimo* in the full orchestra with offbeat *sforzandi* usher in the theme in the dominant (m. 27); and because the recapitulation takes the repeat in the second half of the rounded binary form of the first theme, we hear the double-dotted dominants from m. 11 twice more (mm. 63 and 78). We may be reminded here of the unruly orchestra in the slow movement of the Concerto Op. 19, whose disruptive tactics also make use of intrusive chords in dotted rhythms.[35] But the procedures are very different. The orchestra in Op. 19 systematically upsets any orderly statement of the main theme itself, while in Op. 15 disruption becomes in a sense form-defining: music whose rhythmic and dynamic violence creates emphatic caesuras between its main events, forming a series of obtrusive signposts no one is likely to miss.

But these insistent place markers also contribute to the overall expressive posture of the movement. Their effect, anticipated in the milder dominant sticking point of the first theme itself, is to undermine the ruling lyricism of the movement. This lyricism, the "noble melody" and "*cantabile expression*" Czerny admired in the piece, comes in two particular colors; besides that of the solo piano there is the sound of the clarinet, which (in the absence of flutes and oboes in this movement) repeatedly assumes a soloist's role and impresses its darkish timbre on the overall song-like effect of this piece. But it is not only those punctuating dominant caesuras that come to disturb such an impression. At the piano's second presentation of the first theme in the recapitulation (this is m. 67, corresponding to the clarinet's solo in the exposition), Beethoven writes a peculiar spiky chordal accompaniment in eighth triplets with a detached marcato bass reinforced by pizzicato strings,[36] the effect is busy, maybe humorous, but certainly not lyrical. Then there is the second of two sorts of material in the second group (mm. 30 and 34) that has as its mission only the gaining of sufficient altitude to permit a downward melodic leap of a seventh (to a poignant II $^6_5$); this leap, expanded to a fourteenth the next time around, produces a moment of something like exuberant pathos—a strongly expressive moment, but hardly a lyrical one.

In his provocative article "Notes on Beethoven's Codas," Joseph Kerman laments a general oversight of the coda in virtually all accounts of Beethoven's sonata-form movements and sets out to supply something of a corrective.[37] But much more neglected, surely, are the slow-movement codas, though in Beethoven's music of the mid-1790s they came to bear ever more formal weight. Mention has been made of the coda of the Adagio of the Sonata Op. 2, No. 1, and its extraordinary long-spun extension—and final resolution—of tensions generated within the movement. And we have seen the conciliatory, reuniting function of the coda in the slow movement of Op. 19. The Trios Op. 1, Nos. 1 and 2, both have sizeable slow-movement codas, in each case accounting for about one fifth of the length of the movement. Their functions seem strikingly different. In the first trio the coda is a simple backward look at the thematic and formal events of the movement, a recalling, in partricular, of its plagal flavor, its inclination toward the subdominant. The coda in the slow movement of the second trio, however, is left with unfinished business to resolve. This movement, caught up in the ambitious and discursive tonal design of the composition as a whole, has strongly opposed both G and C major to its home tonic, E major. Its radical peregrinations just barely finished by the end of the movement proper, it leaves the restoration of tonic hegemony entirely to the coda. In the Larghetto con gran espressione of the Sonata Op. 7, Beethoven seems intent not upon assuring tonal order in the coda—he even risks a chromatic bass progression at the very end—but rather upon effecting something of a rapprochement between the materials of a central contrasting episode and the main theme of the movement.

The coda of the Largo in Op. 15, mm. 84–119, is more prominent and more experimental than any of these other examples. Accounting for about a quarter of the entire length of the movement, it more than compensates for the absence in the recapitulation of anything from the second group. This coda is much more than a retrospective glance or a closing conciliatory gesture. It threatens to mount an agenda of its own by introducing new ideas (always bound together by the eighth-triplet motion from the first theme in the recapitulation) and erupting in loud outbursts that threaten to desert the tonic key. The idea that a coda may advance further complications and intrigues—that themselves require reconciliation—is uniquely Beethoven's, and this is perhaps the first of his to do so. The experiment is of doubtful success. Primarily at fault is a series of intermittant plagal, "finishing" gestures (mm. 84, 91, and 101) that we might expect in a more usual (and shorter) coda. The piece simply says farewell too often without leaving. But its final warm exchange of first-theme material between piano and clarinet, once more with strong plagal coloring, proves to be the real end and compensates for any previous insincerities.

THE RONDO

A concert review of this concerto in the *Allgemeine musikalische Zeitung* of 1804 includes a curt remark about its last movement: "*All'Inglese*, distinguishes itself only by unusual rhythms."[38] With the expression *all'Inglese* the author probably intended to invoke that range of dance types of apparent English origin that included the older *Anglaise*, the hornpipe, and (particularly by 1804) the contredanse. All three principal themes of this rondo, like those of so many rondo finales from the period, are very much of the contredanse type: $\frac{2}{4}$ meter in this case (the finale of Op. 19, we recall, has the other contredanse meter, $\frac{6}{8}$),[39] with a great deal of motion in even eighth notes.

And the witty play with our expectations as to metrical structure—which itself we have come to expect—begins straightaway: a schematic repetition of one-measure rhythmic modules sets up an anticipation of metrical regularity, and, in the best Haydnesque fashion, whimsically defeats it (Example 5-12a). After two statements of the rhythmic cell (each starting with the upbeat) in mm. 1 and 2, m. 3 has a slight variation, a quickening that we expect to lead to closure in m. 4. But closure is not possible because the harmony in the second half of m. 3 turns out wrong; it leads to V of V instead of the dominant itself. Measure 4 consists entirely of this secondary dominant, and we then assume the close on the real dominant will follow at the beginning of m. 5. But no, that measure just alternates V of V and dominant, getting nowhere, until closure arrives at m. 6.

This phrase sets up a double-tiered expectation that could have been fulfilled as follows: (1) the second half of m. 3 could have been V of V and led directly to the present m. 6, making a regular four-measure group; that having failed, (2) m. 5 could have been skipped, resulting in an essentially four-measure phrase that, as often happens, spills over to the first beat of the fifth measure. In the music immediately following Beethoven gives examples of both the kinds of phrase structure he had just evaded. Beginning with the upbeat to m. 7 he writes a perfectly regular four-measure phrase that stays obediently within its boundaries (as in the first hypothetical option above); the next phrase, starting with the upbeat to m. 11, comes to a halt on the first beat of its fifth measure (the second option). That point of arrival then becomes the first beat of a new phrase, whose ironclad alternation of tonic and dominant measures and paired surface figurations should lead to a final cadence on the first beat of m. 19. But, repeating the ruse of m. 5, Beethoven delays things with a measure of superfluous tonic-dominant repetition. A mere three extra measures (mm. 4, 5, and 19) have transformed what could have been an unremarkable sixteen-measure musical period—a common exercise in contrived naiveté—into a contradictary, perplexing thing. The artist makes a show of adopting a popular manner, all the while artfully subverting it.

If that first theme is a particularly happy example of Haydn-like wit, the other two move a step or two beyond the pale of the Enlightenment decorum that even Haydn tended to observe. The first of these ("b") arrives after a modulation to the dominant, exactly like the second subject of any sonata form (Table 5-3 and Example 5-12b). Here again we hear the primitive harmony and unrelieved stream of eighth notes of the contredanse, roughened now by blunt accents on the final half beat of each measure. Symmetrical phrase structure is not just implied but actual: four times four measures, three times to dominant, and finally to tonic. The last pair is played by the soloist, who appends a little peroration, a repetition of the last phrase driving to the tonic. This gesture, however, had been constructed in the music just played to finish on the first beat of its fourth measure, leaving the remainder of the measure available for upbeats to a succeeding phrase. When the piano arrives there in m. 85, the orchestra enters with an insistent unison statement that forces a reinterpretation of that beat as the first of a new four-measure phrase (a good example of Koch's *Takterstickung*), and in comic-grotesque fashion leads the soloist off to the key of E♭ for a renewal of the theme in basso buffo garb. The effect, overall, is bluff, rude—surely a bit beyond what even Haydn would have permitted himself.

The episode (only the passage beginning in m. 191 qualifies as such) features the rambunctious theme (again contredanse-like) shown in Example 5-12c, part of whose charm is its very unexpectedness: on the heels of a decisive close of the second ritornello in C major, it leaps in unannounced in A minor (Beethoven wisely abandoned an intervening modulatory passage he contemplated in a sketch of 1794–95).[40] Like the first theme of the movement, it is made up of repetitive one-measure modules, this time with triple sixteenth-note upbeats, thumping bass, and off-measure accents whose irreverent swing might remind us of the samba. This tune, for all its insouience, is built into a rigidly schematic complex of repetitions. It alternates with a kind of a foil: a quasi-contrapuntal, modulatory passage (Example 5-12d) that determinedly pushes the music down the circle of fifths toward the mediant and submediant of the local tonic. But each time it relents, turning back at the last moment to the tonic A minor for another titillating round of the contredanse-samba. While the "b" theme surprises with its plodding directness, "c" sheds all stylization to revel in unadorned dance. Both probably overstep the bounds of what at the end of the eighteenth century might have been expected in a piece with the social standing of a concerto.

There is nothing very special about the larger form of this concerto rondo (see Table 5-3). Like most rondos of its time it has four statements of the ritornello in the tonic, the first followed by a transition and second

TABLE 5-3

FIRST PIANO CONCERTO, OP. 15, III

	40		66	85		108		128		138

R₁

| S | T | S | | | T | S | T | S | | | T | S | | |

| | a | a₁ | | pass. | b | x | b | | | x, a | | | (a) |

| | I | | | ~~~~~V | | | ~~♭III~~V | | | ~~ | | | iv |

171	191	273	283		299

R₂   E

| T | | S | T | T | | S | |

| | a | | c | xa | (a) |

| | I | | vi | ♭III~~v~~~~~V/I |

310	350			381	401		435		457	464	477

R₃

| S | T | S | | | T | S | T | | S | | T | | cad. | S | |

| | a | a₁ | | pass. | b | x | b | | b ext. | | | (a) |

| | I | | ~~~~~~~~~~I | | ~♭VI~~~~~I | | | | VII | V/I |

485		505		m.

R₄

| T | | S | | | T |

| | a | | coda (a, b, a) |

| | I |

theme ("b"), and the third by the corresponding elements of a recapitulation. After the second ritornello comes the episode (with its foil) in A
minor, and the final ritornello is topped off with a coda that casts both "a"
and "b" in a curious new light (more of this in a moment). While composing this rather standard-shape movement, Beethoven seems to have
directed his attention strongly toward the joining of sections. Should the
component members of the episodic structure simply exist side by side,
or should the junctures be softened by transitional passages? Beethoven
rejected a proposed modulatory transition between the second ritornello
and the A-minor episode, as we noted, in favor of a brusque juxtaposition.
At the end of the exposition following upon the first ritornello—that ending properly occurs at m. 120—he added a little eight-measure cadential
filler at some time late in the compositional process: it does not appear in
the Bonn sketch of 1794–95. This added passage, though, is in no way
transitional. It serves rather to stabilize the previous section; it restores a
solid four-plus-four metrical pattern after a previous deviation to six-
measure groups, thus tightening up the feeling of closure—and, hence,
abruptness of the ensuing juxtaposition. But in the end, impressions of
both "juxtaposition" and "transition" give way to the domineering presence
of return, to the inevitable reappearance of the ritornello.

In rondos, the ritornello, that sensation and expectation of "coming
round again," was always the central fact, and after Haydn there was often
an elaborate game about its return: a playful building of expectation by
intimation, evasion, and delay. In the rondo of Op. 15 Beethoven joins in
this sport with fine gusto. While Haydn tends to concentrate such tactical
maneuvers at just one return of the main theme,[41] Beethoven indulges in
them at all three return engagements, each time more elaborately hinted
at and longer delayed. The first time, after the exposition, coy anticipations
of the theme are heard on the lowered second, lowered third, and fourth
scale degrees (mm. 130ff.), reminding us of the first occurrences of the
"b" theme in the opening tutti of the first movement (mm. 49ff.). But in
this finale Beethoven separates these anticipatory bits of "a" with unceremonious unison upward slides in the orchestra (somewhat after the manner of the abrupt chromatic motion to ♭III in the first tutti of the Concerto
Op. 19, mm. 39ff.).

The second time around, just before the third ritornello (mm. 273ff.),
the same artless process brings anticipatory snatches of the theme on the
lowered third, fourth, and fifth degrees, this last extended as a long dominant preparation. Now Beethoven has only one more chance at this sort
of thing, and he makes the most of it. Before the final ritornello the orchestra plays its customary run up to the cadenza (supplied by the composer);

then comes a mysterious pianissimo slide into the final off-key anticipation of "a," this one in the remotest key of all, B major (m. 464). But Beethoven makes sure the listener will know something is wrong. The theme comes on *pianissimo*, with the opening sixteenth-note figure sharpened to a pert acciaccatura together with added off-beat leaping *Scotch snaps* (we are reminded of the off-key appearance of the ritornello theme with altered rhythm just before its last appearance in the finale of Op. 19). This trails off indecisively into a static passage of undifferentiated chordal sound, where we have B major, B minor, F♯ down to F♮, and, at last, the triumphant dominant-tonic to the final ritornello. All possible forces are marshaled for maximum anticipation of this moment. The obviousness of it all is part of the game; composer, performer, and listener participate in this agreeable little exercise in expectation, deception, and, finally, gratification.

A sizable coda is appended, one of the stabilizing, solidifying kind (beginning in m. 505). It never strays from the tonic while it reflects one final time on the nature of the first two themes. The head-motive of the ritornello theme is isolated as a vaguely nostalgic horn call even as the piano engages in the nonstop passages required of a brilliant closing section. But that is brought to an unexpected halt as the soloist pauses for a final word about the second theme. It too now seems retrospective, reconciled, its spiky off-beat accents gone, and its first segment given to easy harmonic resolution. One more brief flash of the first theme then dissolves into the coda's own cadenza, a tiny one-handed flourish again supplied by Beethoven, and a final cadence with the much prolonged dominant sound and abrupt resolution that will also end the *Eroica*. The coda's backward glance seems to take in not just the finale, but the entire composition.

CHAPTER 6

On the Origins of Piano Concerto No. 3[1]

When Beethoven played his C-major Concerto, Op. 15, at the concert of April 1800, the composition was not new to Viennese audiences: he had performed it in the city as many as three times before. But at least the concerto was not yet published—it did not have the sort of familiarity that comes with the presence of a score on the music racks of the city's amateur pianists. And for Beethoven this seemed important. He withheld his concertos from the press while they were still useful for his performances, and he only once, so far as we know, played a concerto of his that had already been published (this was the Fourth Concerto, which he performed in December 1808, a few months after publication). Toward the end of 1801 or early in 1802, he began to set plans in motion for a concert in April 1802. Since a concerto would be expected of him, and since both his piano concertos had been published by December 1801, it was clear that a new one would be needed. And, as we shall see, he labored earnestly to produce such a piece.

But things went wrong, and the concert of 1802 never took place. On April 22, 1802, Carl van Beethoven, acting during this period as his brother's amanuensis, wrote to Breitkopf & Härtel:

> My brother would have written to you himself, but he is at present not up to doing anything because the director of the theater, Baron von Braun, who is known to be a stupid and crude person, has refused him

the theater for his concert, and has reserved it for other, utterly mediocre artists.[2]

The Baron's action put an end, for the time being, to Beethoven's hopes of presenting his music, including any new concerto he might have contemplated, to the Viennese public.

A year later, on April 5, 1803, Beethoven finally succeeded in mounting a concert of his own works, this time at the Theater an der Wien, where he had taken lodgings in anticipation of the production of his projected opera *Vesta's Feuer*. The program was, typically, an ambitious one: there were two symphonies (his First and Second), the Third Piano Concerto in C minor, and the most ambitious offering of the evening, his new oratorio *Christus am Oelberge*. According to Ferdinand Ries, the concert was to have been even longer: "The concert began at six o'clock, but it was so long that a couple of the pieces were not performed."[3] Three of the four compositions on the program were new: the Second Symphony, the oratorio, and the piano concerto.[4] (The premiere of the first symphony had taken place at the concert of April 1800.)

Reviews of the concert were mixed. The *Freimütige* reported, "The symphonies and single passages in the oratorio were thought very beautiful, but the work in its entirety was too long, too artificial in structure and lacking expressiveness, especially in the vocal parts."[5] This oratorio—on Beethoven's own testimony composed at breakneck speed shortly before the concert[6]—marked his introduction to the Viennese audience as a composer of "dramatic" music, and for reviewers it was clearly the central attraction. Later Beethoven was to revise it drastically before publication by Breitkopf & Härtel in 1811.[7] As for the concerto, neither the composition nor Beethoven's playing of the solo part got much attention from the press. But the *Zeitung für die elegante Welt* of Leipzig, after speaking of the symphonies (much preferring the First to the Second), remarked curtly, "Less successful was the following concerto in C minor, that Hr. v. Beethoven, otherwise known as an excellent pianist, performed not completely to the public's satisfaction."[8]

So here, suddenly, is a new piano concerto. But when had Beethoven composed it? From what is known of his habits, we might well expect that he would have written this piece specifically for the concert at which it was first heard. During his early years as a public pianist, as we have seen in the cases of Opp. 19 and 15, he composed new concertos, or revised old ones, as concert deadlines loomed, typically not getting the solo part firmly written in the score—as he himself explained[9]—by the time of the performance. So it would not be unreasonable, barring evidence to the contrary, to suppose that the C-minor concerto would have been worked out in sketches in late 1802 or early 1803 and completed, except for the full writing out of the solo part, during the first months of 1803.

SOURCES FOR OP. 37

But for several reasons the history of this composition is difficult to trace. The most serious hindrance is an unusual paucity of surviving sketches. The following fragments are all we have:

1. Kafka Miscellany (London, British Library, Add. Ms. 29801), fol. 82r. Fragmentary sketches related to the first and third movements, with the verbal indications "Zum Concert aus C moll / Pauke bej der Cadent" and "Rondo dazu."[10] The seven-measure "Pauken" passage resembles the orchestral accompaniment just after the conclusion of the cadenza in the finished composition. The proposed theme for a rondo is a syncopated tune only vaguely similar to the rondo theme in the finale of Op. 37.
2. Fischhof Sammlung (Berlin, Staatsbibliothek, Mus. Ms. Aut. 28), fol. 13r. Another apparent reference to the first idea in (1) above, with the inscription "im Concert bej der Cadenz."[11]
3. Kafka Miscellany, fol. 155v. A two-part polyphonic working of the opening motive of the first movement.[12] This sixteen-measure passage bears some resemblance to the first part of the standard cadenza to the movement (starting with its m. 4), composed by Beethoven in ca. 1809.
4. "Kessler" Sketchbook (Vienna, Gesellschaft der Musikfreunde [GM], A 34), fol. 15r. A short-score draft of mm. 330–33 of the first movement.[13]
5. Bonn, Beethovenhaus, Bodmer Sammlung, SBH, 637, fol. 4r. Cadenza drafts for the first movement.

The first three of these entries are what Alan Tyson named "concept sketches,"[14] that is, fragmentary ideas jotted down before a piece has really got underway. Douglas Johnson has convincingly proposed that Beethoven acquired the paper for all three of these sketches during his travels to Prague and Berlin during the first half of 1796, and that all were written between that time and late 1797 or early 1798.[15] A feeling that only two concertos made a skimpy repertory for a traveling pianist may have led him to jot down these very preliminary ideas for a new one in C minor;

but no further progress was made on it, so far as we know, until much later. The final item in the list above, cadenza sketches for the first movement of Op. 37, occurs in a group of leaves that was once the final gathering (two bifolia) of the "Wielhorsky" Sketchbook.[16] The second half of this book (and this gathering) is dominated by sketches for *Christus am Oelberge* that were probably made shortly before the concert of April 1803. So drafts for a cadenza appear, just as we would expect them to, when the composer was about to perform the concerto in public.

The earliest extant full sources for Op. 37 are the autograph score (Berlin, Staatsbibliothek, Beethoven Autograph 14, hereafter "Aut. 14") and the first edition, in parts (Vienna, Bureau des Arts et d'Industrie, 1804). Aut. 14 was among the many musical documents removed from the Berlin Staatsbibliothek during World War II for safekeeping; in subsequent years its whereabouts were unknown until its eventual rediscovery and return (along with autographs of major works of Mozart and Bach) to the Berlin Staatsbibliothek in 1977.[17] But some information about this manuscript, including reports of an autograph date on its first folio, had been in circulation since before the war. In a survey of the Beethoven autographs in the Berlin library published in 1895, A. Ch. Kalischer gave a brief description of the document and quoted Beethoven's inscription on folio 1: "Concerto 1800 D. L. v. Beethoven."[18] In a reference to the manuscript Thayer also mentioned this date: "An important work bears, in the author's own hand, the date 1800. It is the great Third Concerto for piano and large orchestra in C minor."[19] And 1800 is the date for this autograph listed in the Kinsky-Halm *Verzeichnis* of 1955.[20]

For later Beethoven scholars, this reported date on the autograph, together with the near absence of sketches for Op. 37, seemed to coincide neatly with two other bits of information. First, there was the concert of April 2, 1800, at which Beethoven had played an *old* concerto—evidently Op. 15. Secondly, there seems to be a missing sketchbook from just before this time, one presumed to contain the sketches for two works performed on that program, the First Symphony and the Septet Op. 20 (and very likely for the String Quartet Op. 18, No. 4, as well).[21] Chronologically, this missing book would fall between "Grasnick 2" and the central section of the collection known as Autograph 19e ([Aut. 19e] both in Berlin, Staatsbibliothek). Grasnick 2, devoted mainly to work on Op. 18, Nos. 1, 2, and 5, was apparently filled by late summer 1799; the portion of Aut. 19e in question (i.e., fols. 12–31) has been dated late spring–summer 1800.[22] Thus Beethoven's work on those two books was apparently separated by a lacuna of about nine months.

Let us pause here to recall how Beethoven went about composing music. Throughout his career the initial stages of working on a piece seem almost invariably to have consisted of making sketches. At first he used single sheets and miscellaneous gatherings of paper, many of them now preserved in the Kafka and Fischhof collections; later he worked in the now-famous sketchbooks (beginning with Grasnick 1 in 1798). Some of these books were professionally made, and some he sewed together himself; some were intended for use at home, where he had pens and inkpot, and some (later in his career) he carried in his pocket and wrote in with pencil. In the years after 1798 he occasionally reverted to the use of loose leaves and smaller gatherings. But whatever he wrote with or on, Beethoven always sketched. For him this was the central act of composing. To say "this is a major piece for which no sketches ever existed" is tantamount to saying "this piece is not by Beethoven." So we can be perfectly sure that at one time there were sketches for Op. 37.

The four items of information mentioned above—the missing sketches for Op. 37, a missing sketchbook from 1799–1800, an autograph for Op. 37 with a reported date of 1800, and a concert on April 2, 1800, at which Beethoven played an old concerto—have led quite sensibly to the following hypothesis: in preparation for the concert of April 1800, Beethoven composed Op. 37 in 1799–1800 in the missing sketchbook and wrote it partly in score; but failing to finish his work in time for the concert, at the last minute he substituted the Concerto Op. 15.[23]

The reappearance of the autograph casts serious doubt on this explanation. In his report on the return of the previously missing manuscripts to the Berlin library, Karl-Heinz Köhler wrote, "One of the first results of research conducted after the return of the manuscript [Aut. 14] was the determination that this manuscript belongs to 1803 and not to 1800, as it is noted in Kinsky's *Das Werk Beethoven's* and elsewhere."[24] And the three people known to me to have studied the manuscript in detail after its return (Alan Tyson, Hans-Werner Küthen, and myself) agree that its date reads "1803."[25] Now two questions that immediately arise are these: can we really be sure of that "1803," and if so, how could practiced scholars like Kalischer, Thayer, and Kinsky all have made the same mistake? (Unlike the much publicized date on the autograph of Schubert's "Great" C-major Symphony, this one has all its digits intact.)

As this manuscript has apparently never been bound, some of the contents of its first folio, including the date itself, are very severely faded— so much so that photographic reproduction with the means available has been impossible. In good light, and with the aid of a magnifying glass, nonetheless, the date can still be made out; Figure 6-1 shows a reconstruction of it. The final digit comes close enough to forming a full circle

Figure 6-1. Reconstructed date, Aut. 14

that it is not hard to understand that these earlier investigators, especially if working under less-than-optimal conditions, could have mistaken it for an "0." But that the figure in question is "3" is certain; it resembles in shape Beethoven's usual 3s (with the hook placed high), and it is clearly formed, moreover, with a *clockwise* motion; Beethoven—like most of us—wrote both the number "0" and the script-letter "o" with a *counterclockwise* stroke.

So here we have an autograph dated 1803 by the composer; the composition, we know, was first performed in April 1803 and first published in summer 1804. Under any normal circumstances these unambiguous data—in the absence of compelling indications to the contrary—would simply settle the matter: the piece belongs to 1803. And its date does matter. The chronological position of a composition within any major composer's oeuvre must affect our perception of it, the way we listen to it and think about it. In the present case a difference between 1800 and 1803 determines whether we group the Third Concerto with the First Symphony, the Septet, the String Quartets Op. 18, and the Horn Sonata Op. 17, or, alternatively, with that very different and altogether remarkable series of pieces that stood on the threshold of the *Eroica*: the Second Symphony, the "Kreutzer" Sonata, the Piano Sonatas Op. 31, and the Piano Variations Opp. 34 and 35. The years in question were ones of rapid stylistic change for Beethoven as he moved into what is sometimes called his "heroic" period. Beethoven himself seemed aware of a major stylistic shift at about this time; according to Czerny he spoke of a "new way" in composition.[26] And two compositions of the period, the Variations Opp. 34 and 35, he claimed, were written "in an entirely new manner."[27] But whatever importance we wish to attach to such statements of the composer, the placement of Op. 37 among his works cannot be a matter of indifference.

THE "1800" HYPOTHESIS

As it turns out, there is reluctance in some quarters to give up the old date of 1800 for this concerto. In his finely detailed *Kritischer Bericht*, Küthen seizes upon various stages of writing in Aut. 14 in order to retain a connection with the older date. Thus he still maintains that the main work on the piece was done in 1799–1800 in preparation for the concert of April 1800, and that the date "1803" was added only in the process of revision in connection with the concert of April 1803. To test this theory we will need to to refer to the formidable tools for dating composers' manuscripts left us by modern Bach and Beethoven studies. Foremost among these are the exacting ways of studying paper that Alan Tyson, in particular, developed for the study of Beethoven's manuscripts. By establishing a detailed correlation between the differing types of paper Beethoven used and the times he is known to have used them—a process that is to a satisfying degree applicable to Mozart and Schubert as well—Tyson and others have brought an unprecedented precision to the dating of the composer's manuscripts. Let us see whether these methods will help us here.

We may begin by noting watermarks[28] in the paper Beethoven used for the autograph of Op. 37, reproduced in Figure 6-2. From this standpoint there are three types of paper in the manuscript. Types 2 and 3 appear only incidently: one double bifolium of Type 2 is used at the beginning of the second movement (fols. 59–62), and a double bifolium plus a single leaf of Type 3 appears near the end of the third movement (fols. 114–18). Type 2 is a paper Beethoven used in the autograph of his Sonata Op. 30, No. 3 (British Library, Add. Ms. 37767), composed in 1802; one leaf of this paper is also found in the sketchbook Landsberg 7 (Berlin, Staatsbibliothek) of 1800–1, and two more, originally part of the miscellany Aut. 19e of 1800, are now in private hands.[29] Type 3, found in both the Kafka and Fischhof collections, Beethoven had used mainly between 1795 and 1799, with a more concentrated use in the earlier part of the period.[30] In the autograph of Op. 37 both these papers appear to be replacement pages Beethoven used in the course of revision. These bits of Type 3 would appear to be old leftover leaves that came to hand for such a patch-up job (this is Beethoven's last known use of the paper), and Type 2 has a history of similarly fragmentary use. Neither paper seems to have much bearing on the date of this manuscript.

Paper Type 1 accounts for 111 of the manuscript's 120 folios, including, of course, fol. 1, where the date is written. Paper with the watermark elements of Type 1, AM with crossbow and a countermark of three crescent moons, occurs with great frequency in Beethoven's manuscripts from the years just after the turn of the century. Richard Kramer listed twenty sources from 1800–4 in which it is to be found, ranging from isolated leaves and bifolia to an entire sketchbook (Kessler, 1801–2) and a substantial portion of another (the "Wielhorsky," 1802–3).[31] Johnson added

Figure 6-2. The Watermarks of Aut. 14

a. Type 1

b. Type 2

c. Type 3

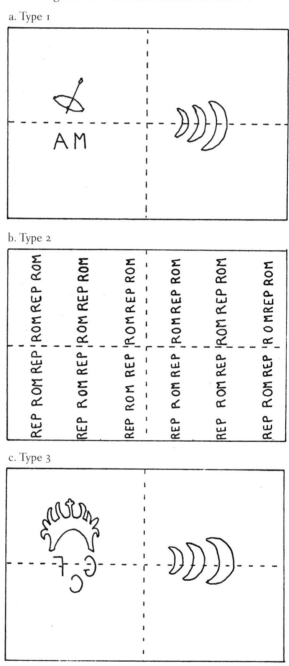

five more folios from 1798 that are included in the Fischhof Miscellany, and Tyson has pointed out several more in the "reconstructed" sketchbook of 1807–8.[32]

We have a grand total (now including Aut. 14) of some 485 leaves with these watermark elements in paper that Beethoven used over a ten-year period.[33] If watermark evidence is to be helpful for a precise dating of any of the manuscripts in question, it is clear that subclassifications of these papers will have to be made. Kramer reported some "eight variants of the archetype" and Johnson identified "six different molds" using these elements (in this last case including the variety with only a single moon).[34] In the classification of papers in Johnson, Tyson, and Winter's volume on the sketchbooks, there is a rough division of these papers into three subtypes, apparently made on the basis of placement and size of the component elements. But no information detailed enough to be helpful in any individual case is given, and the drawings provided are not to scale.[35] With the present state of research such information cannot be given because no one has yet done the basic work required: the lowly task of studying all the known examples of these papers in order to classify them according to the molds that produced them. This includes, first of all, taking careful measurements of the watermark elements. The next step is to match the resultant "subtypes" of paper with the compositional work for which they were used, and with what is known in other ways about the dates of such work. In this way, with a gratifying degree of predictability, patterns emerge that help establish probable dates for the manuscripts in question.[36] The AM papers still await such a study.

But a partial account can be given here of the AM paper used in the autograph of Op. 37. All of the Type 1 paper in this manuscript evidently originated from a single pair of molds; it is deployed, as usual, in pairs of nested bifolia (four folios, originally one sheet) from one mold in approximate alternation with similar gatherings from its twin mold. This sequence begins at fol. 1 with a double bifolium from Mold B, which is the mirror image of Mold A. These names for the molds reflect the true order of the letters AM (always read from the "mold side") in Mold A, and their reversed order in Mold B.[37] The elements in these two molds have very similar measurements (as shown in Table 6-1), the only significant difference being the length of the arrow.

While no one has yet sorted out the various subtypes of AM papers and the probable dates at which Beethoven used them, Küthen reports finding in two of the composer's manuscripts, dating from around 1800, "watermark proportions [dimensions?] identical" to those of type 1 in Aut. 14. The documents in question are Berlin, Staatsbibliothek, Aut. 19e, and

TABLE 6-1 WATERMARK ELEMENTS
IN TYPE 1

	Mold A	Mold B
AM (top to bottom)	33 mm.	32 mm.
AM (left to right)	55	56
Selenometry[38]	86	87
Length of bow	44	44
Length of arrow	70	66

Grasnick 24.[39] These two manuscripts, it turns out, were originally one: Grasnick 24 consists of a single bifolium whose stitch holes (and contents) show that it once belonged to the homemade sketchbook Aut. 19e.[40] But Küthen is mistaken: the subtype of AM paper in these manuscripts (Johnson, Tyson, and Winter call both examples "Type 7") is clearly not that of Aut. 14. The most striking difference is the much smaller size of the AM (and MA) in Grasnick 24 and Aut. 19e. In Aut. 19e, fol. 15 (from a Mold B according to our criteria outlined above), they measure 50 mm. across and 24–25 mm. vertically. In Grasnick 24 the horizontal dimension is also ca. 50 mm.; the vertical measurement cannot be made with precision because the tops of the letters in this single bifolium have been trimmed away. But, as the full-sized tracing in Figure 6-3 shows, the height of the letters is surely much less than the 32–33 mm. of Aut. 14. The AM paper of Grasnick 24 and Aut. 19e did not come from the same molds as that of Aut. 14, and can have no bearing on its date. As this single possibility for a chronological foothold vanishes into thin air, we are led to an inescapable conclusion: watermark evidence, by itself at least, offers no help at present in determining the period of Beethoven's main work on this manuscript.

STAFF-LINING

Another technique used together with the classification of watermarks in the dating of musical manuscripts from this period is a precise study of the characteristics of staff-lining, or "rastrology." A first rough application of this method will limit our consideration of AM papers to those that, like Aut. 14, have 16 staves. This reduces the total of known leaves of

Figure 6-3. Watermarks
a) Grasnick 24
b) Aut. 14

a.

b.

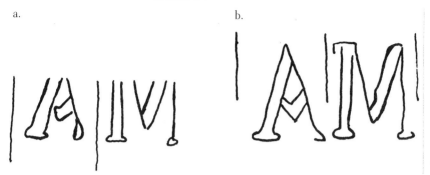

Type 1 paper in Beethoven's manuscripts from ca. 485 to ca. 406. And from the apparent overall range of dates (1798–1808), the papers from before 1800 (i.e., the leaves from the two early miscellanies) will be eliminated. The staff-lining in Aut. 14, with the exception of the five folios of Type 3 paper (odd sheets that Beethoven had evidently had in his possession for a long time), is entirely uniform, with an TS of 190 mm. and an SS of 6 mm.[41] The profiles of the edges of the staves, uniform from one folio to another, are highly distinctive; especially so are the irregular left edges of staves 3, 14, 15, and 16, visible in Plate 7.

While watermarks in the paper Beethoven used in the first years of the new century are relatively variable—even within the very numerous class of our Type 1 papers—the staff-lining in his sixteen-stave papers is startlingly uniform. Richard Kramer first called attention to the distinctive staff-lining described above, observing that it occurs throughout the Kessler, Wielhorsky, and *Leonore*[42] Sketchbooks, and in the autograph scores of the String Quintet Op. 29 (1801), the Sonatas for Piano and Violin Op. 30, Nos. 1–3 (1801–2), the partial score of the first movement of the "Kreutzer" Sonata, Op. 47 (1802–3), parts of *Christus am Oelberge*, Op. 85 (1803), the fragmentary opera *Vestas Feuer* (1803), and the Violin Concerto Op. 61 (1806). This distinctive staff-lining occurs in conjunction with a variety of watermarks; it appears on the Types 1 and 2 paper in Aut. 14 and on the subtype of Type 1 found in Aut. 19e and Grasnick 24. It is present in professionally made books like Kessler and Wielhorsky and conglomerations of paper that (like Aut. 14) have never been bound.

What are we to make of the ubiquity of this particular staff-lining? A simple solution would be to assume that Beethoven bought his paper blank and lined it himself (or, perhaps, had a copyist do it for him)—and did so with the paper of Kessler and Wielhorsky before turning it over to the binder who made up the books. This solution would permit us to hold to the assumption that underlies all use of paper studies in dating musical manuscripts, namely, that composers bought relatively small amounts of paper relatively often—the way we tend to buy stamps, as Tyson once said. This solution I think we may reject out of hand. The staff-lining in Kessler, Wielhorsky, Aut. 14, and the other examples seen for this study is precise, professional work that reflects high skill and good equipment— and, surely, a commercial origin.

In hope of maintaining the "frequent shopping" principle, we might then imagine that the firm where Beethoven bought his paper simply used the same staff-lining equipment for the sixteen-stave papers it sold from 1800 to 1805. But it seems unlikely that a rastral of whatever kind could have retained its idiosyncracies with such precision over such a long period of time while serving the needs not only of Beethoven, presumably, but of other Viennese musicians as well.

Reflections of this sort tend to support Kramer's conclusion that "at some point toward the end of 1800, Beethoven acquired the stock of sixteen-staff paper which was to supply most of the score paper of the following years."[43] If Beethoven in fact bought all this paper at once, then the traditionally held date for Aut. 14 (namely, that he began writing it in preparation for the concert of April 1800) would advance the date of first use of this paper by almost a year, from "toward the end of 1800" to near the beginning of that year. But Kramer's conclusion—requiring abandonment in this case of the "frequent shopping" principle—would also cast grave doubt on the reliability of all distinctions among physical features of these papers for purposes of dating Beethoven's use of them: he would have had access to all of them all the time. Nor can we count on someone of Beethoven's habits to use up such a large stock of paper in an orderly fashion (say, from the top of the stack to the bottom) during a period when he changed dwellings (including his characteristic summer removals) some twenty-one times. Physical characteristics of the paper Beethoven used for Aut. 14 is of next to no use—and, unhappily, may remain so—for determining whether the "1803" written on fol. 1 marks the beginning of his work on the manuscript or, as Küthen holds, the end of an extended process of writing, neglect, and revision.

STAGES OF NOTATION

Perhaps the notation itself can be of some help. In the writing of the first two movements in Aut. 14, three basic stages of work are distinguishable by function and by color of ink:[44]

Stage 1: Brown-grey ink. Here there is a fairly full writing out of the orchestral parts of the first two movements, and a piano part that is rather sketchy in the first movement and extremely so in the second.

Stage 2: Yellow-brown ink. At this stage there is revision of the orchestral parts (and some of the piano part) in the first and second movements, with the addition of articulation and dynamic markings and attempts to gèt the right number of beats in the measures. This looks like revision undertaken in preparation for the copying of parts for performance or publication. At this stage the third movement is first written down and revised.

Stage 3: Black ink. Fleeting, "private" revisions and elaborations of the piano part, written mainly in surrounding empty staves. In this notation it is often impossible to distinguish individual pitches and note-values; it is clear, nonetheless, that these revisions often correspond closely with readings in the first edition of 1804. Some revisions in the orchestral parts are also made in this ink.

In the absence of a scientific forensic finding, none of us can be certain beyond all doubt of the identification of one sample of ink with another (the pitfalls awaiting the amateur investigator were demonstrated a few years ago in the celebrated case of the forged "Hitler Diaries"). But even with this reservation firmly in mind, I am convinced that the words "Allegro,"[45] "Concerto 1803," and "Da L V Beethoven," all done in Roman script and centered across the top of fol. 1, are written in in the brown-grey ink of Stage 1: in the same ink as the names of the instruments, the bracing, the key and meter signatures, and the notation of the opening measures on that page. On this point I disagree with Küthen, who associates the writing of Stage 1 with Beethoven's purported plans to perform Op. 37 at the concert of April 1800, and the writing of Stage 2 with preparations for the actual performance in April 1803. It was at the end of this latter process, he suggests, that Beethoven wrote "Concerto 1803," in what, he says, "appears to be" the ink of Stage 2.[46] But whatever ink was used to write the date, there is no reason whatever to assume a long hiatus between any stage of writing in this manuscript and any other: the habit of doing so seems to revert to an earlier time when it was known that the concerto was first performed in 1803, but it was *thought* that the date on Aut. 14 read "1800."

A formidable barrier to assuming such a three-year hiatus between Stages 1 and 2 is the perfect continuity of paper between the end of the second movement (Stage 1) and the beginning of the third (Stage 2). This continuity includes an undisturbed sequence of Type 1 paper from a double bifolium of its "A" mold to one of its "B" mold. Nor can we think, apparently, that the "book" was assembled in advance and simply set aside for a long period: the sections of Aut. 14 with these two movements have never been bound or sewn together. If we wish to believe in that three-year gap between Stage 1 and Stage 2, we must also accept the astonishing coincidence that after the hiatus Beethoven should have (unwittingly) taken up a new double bifolium of the same run of paper at exactly the same point in its sequence of leaves where he had left it three years earlier.

One intriguing bit of evidence that might point to the existence of Op. 37 before the spring of 1803, however, is a very brief reference to its first movement on fol. 15 of the Kessler Sketchbook (this is the fourth item in our list of sketches for the concerto),[47] a book Beethoven used from late 1801 to ca. mid-1802. Here he jotted down on two staves a version of mm. 330–33 of the first movement, from the approach to the "second theme" in the recapitulatory third solo (see Example 6-1).[48] It is hard to know what to make of the presence of this fragment of Op. 37 in a source dating, apparently, from early 1802. Was this written down to settle a detail in a composition that was already largely complete? If the entry was made in Kessler by way of revision of a passage already notated in Stage 1 of Aut. 14 (as Küthen holds), one would expect to see some sign of the correction at that point in the autograph. But these measures in Aut. 14 (fol. 39) are virtually clean; Beethoven did make a minor slip in the first bassoon part (initially writing it a third too low, at the pitch of the second bassoons) and then corrected the mistake. The parallel passage on fol. 3v he had written without mishap, and the correction in m. 330 seems to have nothing to do, in any case, with the notation in Kessler. In the absence of any evidence to the contrary, it is probably best to regard the Kessler entry simply as another stray idea for the C-minor concerto, a composition Beethoven had contemplated as early as 1796 but never really got to work on until the 1803 concert was in view.

If the interpretation proposed here is accurate, that "1803" was one of the first things Beethoven wrote on the manuscript. Thus all the work on this document, from the writing of the date to a stage of readiness required for performance, must have taken place between the beginning of 1803 and April 5 of that year. The following sequence of events emerges: in early 1803 Beethoven put the first two movements up in score (doubtless working from earlier sketches and drafts, now lost) and wrote the heading, including the date, on the first folio (Stage 1). Very shortly thereafter, within a month or two, he set about correcting the orchestral parts—already much more fully written out than the piano part—in these two movements and wrote out and revised the third movement as well (Stage 2). After some clarifying marks were inserted by another hand,[49] all the orchestral music was now ready to to be copied into parts for the performance in April.

If we can be satisfied that the work of Stages 1 and 2 was in all probability done during the first months of 1803, let us then think about likely dates for Beethoven's elaboration of the piano part in the "private notation" of Stage 3. Küthen offers the attractive conjecture that this revision in black ink was associated with two events of more than a year later: Ferdinand Ries's performance of the composition at the Augarten Saal on July 19, 1804, and its publication by the Bureau des Arts et d'Industrie in November of that year. Regarding the former event Ries wrote:

Beethoven had given me his beautiful Concerto in C Minor (Opus 37), still in manuscript, so that I might make my first public appearance as his pupil with it. . . . We held two major rehearsals. I had asked Beethoven to compose a cadenza for me, which he refused, and instructing me to to write one myself, said he would correct it. . . . The piano part of the C minor Concerto was never completely written out in the score. Beethoven wrote it down on separate sheets of paper expressly for me.[50]

Beethoven sketched in these highly elaborate revisions for the soloist, Küthen feels, preparatory to writing out that separate part for Ries in the summer of 1804.[51]

But is there any compelling reason to posit (once again) a long hiatus between Stage 2 and Stage 3? The only reason Küthen gives, really, for connecting Stage 3 with Ries's separate piano score is that the writing in that stage is so strongly directed toward the piano part. This theory must assume, then, that Beethoven undertook a two-step procedure on his pupil's behalf: sketching out an elaboration of the keyboard part in the score and then making a readable copy on separate sheets. But perhaps we might think of an explanation involving rather less generosity on Beethoven's part. Could it be that the "private" notation of Stage 3 was actually intended for his own use—say, at his own concert of 1803?

To look into this possibility, let us consider one representative page of

Aut. 14: fol. 72v, shown in Plate 1. The second of the two measures of music on this page is m. 77 of the second movement. In Stage 1 (brown-gray ink) Beethoven wrote the succession of $^6_3$ chords seen on line 9 and transcribed in Example 2a. At Stage 2 (yellow-brown) he crossed out that measure and began to enter a new version in the blank staff directly above; but he crossed that out too, and wrote a different rhythmic solution to the measure—inadvertently doubling the note values—in line 14 below, also adding a bass accompaniment in the next measure (Example 6-2b). That version in turn he rejected for a single-line scalewise figure with accompaniment, written in lines 11 and 12, and cued in with Beethoven's characteristic "vi-de" (Example 6-2c). This is the final version of this bit of the piano part at Stage 2 (which also includes, especially in the preceding measure, some thoroughgoing revision of the orchestral parts). Later, using the black ink of Stage 3 in the bottom of the two staves, Beethoven sketched out for himself a much more flamboyant single-line solution, one that resembles the familiar reading of modern scores (Examples 6–2d and 2e).

While all versions proposed at Stage 1 and 2, we notice, have e''' as the highest pitch, the great sweeping scalewise curve written at Stage 3 rises to the b''' a fifth higher (in the first edition the main text goes only to e'''; the familiar version rising to b''' is given as an optional alternative). At Stages 1 and 2 in the autograph as a whole the highest pitch in the piano is g''', the "added G" that increased the standard five-octave piano keyboard by two semitones.[52] This pitch appears many times in the first two stages of writing, beginning with the first statement of the opening theme by the soloist—though in the course of tinkering with the register at this point Beethoven crossed out the top line. But the writing of Stage 3 has clearly been liberated from this upper limit; it exceeds g''' repeatedly, reaching c'''' at two points in the third movement (m. 86, Aut. 14, fol. 83v; and mm. 435ff., Aut. 14, fols. 116v–17). The first edition of 1804 also includes pitches up to c'''' (as optional versions) with some regularity, though its extensions of range do not always coincide exactly with those of Stage 3 in the autograph.[53]

In 1803 the Parisian piano maker Sebastian Érard gave Beethoven the handsome gift of a new piano. This instrument, now in the Kunsthistorisches Museum, Vienna, has a range up to c''''.[54] A connection has sometimes been made between the arrival of that instrument and Beethoven's revisions of Op. 37. H. C. Robbins Landon, for example, writes, "Beethoven radically changed his Third Piano concerto (autograph: 1800) after the French instrument's arrival."[55] Could Beethoven have made the revisions featuring this extended range in anticipation of his performance on that piano in April 1803? First we might entertain a prior question: is it likely that Beethoven would have played his own instrument that evening, or would one perhaps have been supplied by the theater? Here we should recall that the composer, following current custom, was at the time living right in that theater while (ostensibly) carrying out his commission to compose music for Schikaneder's libretto *Vestas Feuer*. So it seems plausible enough that he should simply have moved his piano to the stage for the concert.

But there is a chronological difficulty in assuming that the Érard was the instrument in question. The archives of the Érard firm show that their gift to Beethoven was given on the "18th of Thermidore, in the XIth year of the Republic";[56] that translates to August 8, 1803, some two months after the concert. It is of course possible that Beethoven expected the piano to arrive in time for the concert and made the revisions of Stage 3 in anticipation of performing on that instrument. Or the gift may conceivably have been given and received before the transaction was recorded. And other pianos with a range to c4 may have become available to Beethoven in 1803; Haydn brought one (with a Longman and Broderip label) from London to Vienna in 1795, and as early as 1801 he owned an Érard with the same range as Beethoven's.[57] But there is at present insufficient evidence to connect the extension of range in Stage 3 of the autograph with any particular piano.

One bit of work Beethoven did on this concerto was surely connected with his performance in April 1803: the cadenza sketches (shown in Example 6-3) that he wrote in the last pages of the Wielhorsky Sketchbook, the second half of which is almost entirely given over to sketches for *Christus am Oelberge* in anticipation of the April concert.[58] In these sketches Beethoven returned to the imitative treatment of the first theme broached long ago in Kafka, now juxtaposed with his current experiments in keyboard textures using extended trills as static "upper pedals." And he contemplated ending his cadenza with a drive to the climactic c''''—a dramatic gesture whose very point, it seems, is to emphasize the notes at the top of the expanded keyboard. Such a purposeful use of the extended range in this cadenza suggests a couple of things: that Beethoven expected to perform this concerto on an instrument that had those additional keys, and that incorporating this upper range into the piano part of the concerto was a preoccupation of his on the eve of the concert. And it certainly adds credibility to a supposition that the "private" notation (Stage 3) in Aut. 14, which also features such a preoccupation, was made in praparation for that concert as well.[59]

Here we might recall the testimony of Ignaz von Seyfried, at the time a director at the Theater an der Wien. He recounted his part in the concert of 1803 thus:

> For the performance of the concerto he invited me to turn pages. But—Heaven help me—that was easier said than done. I was looking at almost empty leaves; at most, on one or another page, a few unintelligible Egyptian hieroglyphics were scribbled down to serve as aids to his memory.[60]

Could Seyfried have been turning the pages of Aut. 14? Though there are many blank spaces in the piano part, his description of "almost empty leaves" is hardly applicable to the manuscript as a whole. But "Egyptian hieroglyphics . . . scribbled down to serve as aids to his memory" is distinctly plausible as a description of the very cursive and approximate notation of Stage 3. If this is indeed what he referred to, then of course Stage 3 was written by April 5, 1803. Perhaps the sudden availability of a piano with the "additional keys" prompted Beethoven to have another look at the solo part and jot down these elaborations, bringing that part—and what he played on April 5—closer to its final version as we know it. If this supposition is correct, we are led to the conclusion that the writing of Aut. 14 did not take place at various times between 1800 and 1804, but was compressed into no more than three months at the beginning of 1803.

WHEN WAS OP. 37 SKETCHED?

But for Beethoven the writing out of the autograph of course comprised only the final part of the act of composition. If he put this piece up in score and revised it early in 1803, when did the earlier stages of composition take place? Could he have done most of the sketches and drafts as early as 1799–1800 (as the claim goes), almost completely ignored them for three years, and finally completed work on the concerto in 1803? Let us see what reason we may yet have to associate the composition in any way with that earlier date.

Beethoven offered his Piano Concerto Op. 19, we will recall, to the publisher Hoffmeister of Leipzig in his somewhat jocular letter of December 15, 1800. After mentioning his other concerto, Op. 15, about to be published by Mollo of Vienna, he remarked, "I am still keeping back the better ones until I myself undertake a journey."[61] While "the better ones" might conceivably refer to Op. 37, this statement is in itself not good evidence for the existence of the piece at that early date. In his dealings with publishers Beethoven was not at all averse to exaggerating the state of readiness of his compositions. An example close at hand is the Triple Concerto Op. 56, which he proposed sending to Breitkopf & Härtel on August 26, 1804, even though most of the sketches for the work, scattered widely in Berlin, Staatsbibliothek, Mendelssohn 15 (the *Leonore* Sketchbook), were plainly done later.[62] In the case of his purported "better concertos," moreover, he was not even making a promise to which he could be held. And the accuracy of Beethoven's claim must aready be suspect in that it speaks of "concertos" in the plural—there is surely no sign, at this time, of a fourth piano concerto.

Let us return to the original reasons given for the supposition that the Third Piano Concerto is a product of 1799–1800. Among the four items of evidence offered in support of this position, the prize exhibit, an autograph dated "1800," has of course vanished; the autograph is dated "1803." And with the collapse of this structural member the rest of the argument falls of its own weight. That an *old* concerto (Op. 15) was played at the concert of April 1800 (purportedly a last-minute substitute for the not quite finished Op. 37) in no way argues for the existence of a new one—if anything, it suggests quite the opposite. All we are left with, really, is the coincidence of the missing sketches of Op. 37 and the presumptive missing sketchbook from 1799–1800—a convenient black hole, to be sure, into which we might drop this composition.

But perhaps we can locate other junctures in the record of Beethoven's compositional work into which Op. 37 might fit equally well. Using Table 6-2, a list of Beethoven's sketchbooks from the broader period in question,[63] let us begin, first, at the other extreme and consider the latest possible time in which Op. 37 could have been sketched, namely, the

TABLE 6-2 BEETHOVEN'S
SKETCHBOOKS, 1799–1803

Grasnick 1	mid-1798–February 1799
Grasnick 2	February/March 1799–late summer, 1799
Aut. 19e	Summer 1800
Landsberg 7	Summer 1800–March 1801
Sauer	April–November 1801 (?)
Kessler	Winter 1801–ca. July 1802
Wielhorsky	Fall 1802–May 1803

months just preceding the writing of the autograph and the performance at the concert of April 1803. If that was the time when Beethoven did the main work on this piece, we would expect to find evidence of it in the Wielhorsky Sketchbook from autumn 1802–May 1803, the book in which he sketched *Christus am Oelberge*, apparently the last-composed work for that concert. But there is no sign of it here except for the cadenza drafts, discussed above, that he wrote in the final leaves of Wielhorsky. By way of (perhaps idle) speculation we might take note of the way Beethoven went about using this book: much of its second half seems to have been "mapped out" in advance, with certain groups of pages allotted to the various sections of the oratorio.[64] It is conceivable that he was unwilling to disturb this plan and diverted work on Op. 37 to loose sheets that have subsequently been lost. But such an assumption (for which there is in any case no positive evidence) would require us to think that Beethoven produced another big piece in the same few weeks (as he described them) in which he composed the oratorio—not a very promising supposition. It is surely much easier to believe that by the period of the Wielhorsky Sketchbook, Op. 37 had already been sketched elsewhere.

Now let us think about possible times between these two extremes. Ignaz Sauer, owner of the sketchbook that bears his name, dismembered it shortly after Beethoven's death and sold many of its leaves individually. This book was apparently in use from ca. April–November 1801. Of its presumed original forty-eight or ninety-six leaves—the usual sketchbook sizes—only twenty-two have been located.[65] Since the sketches on these leaves concentrate almost exclusively on only three works (the Sonatas Opp. 27, No. 2 and Op. 28, and the Quintet Op. 29), it can be assumed that they did not originate from widely separated places in the book; Johnson, Tyson, and Winter even suggest that that they "represent a torso of one section of the sketchbook."[66] Thus there would seem to have been great stretches of contiguous leaves in the missing portions of the book—more than enough to accommodate the missing sketches for Op. 37. Those missing sections of the Sauer Sketchbook are surely at least as strong candidates for the location of the Op. 37 sketches as is the missing sketchbook of 1799–1800—especially since the candidacy of the latter book depended strongly on the mistaken reading of the date on the autograph as "1800." Thus the missing book no longer has any special claim for any connection with this concerto.

MUSIC FOR THE FAILED
CONCERT OF 1802

Turning to a different kind of evidence, let us recall that though Beethoven gave no concert (that we know of) between the two of April 1800 and April 1803, he clearly made plans for one: the ill-fated event contemplated in the spring of 1802 that we learned about from his brother Carl's letter to Breitkopf & Härtel. The composer's disappointed plans for this concert left clear traces in the Kessler Sketchbook of 1801–2.[67] Preparations there for "concert-type" music include sketches for the finale of the Second Symphony (fol. 15), as well as work on two movements for piano and orchestra, one a "marcia con variazoni" in A♭, and the other a movement[68] in A. In a later section of Kessler (beginning on fol. 38v), there is further serious work on music for piano and orchestra, again apparently undertaken in anticipation of the proposed concert of 1802. The drafting of a "rondo moderato" in F major and an apparent companion movement in C major, discussed by Richard Kramer,[69] did not advance very far.

But another composition, begun on the same page of Kessler, made much better progress. This is a "concertante" in D, evidently for violin, cello, piano, and orchestra, that Kramer describes in detail.[70] On nine folios of Kessler Beethoven sketched the two "expositions" of the first movement and entered ideas seemingly intended for the other two movements as well. He made sufficient progress with the first movement, in fact, to begin writing it out in score; a twelve-folio torso of this autograph survives in Berlin (Staatsbibliothek, Artaria 183). In this manuscript, which once clearly included additional leaves at its beginning and perhaps at its end as well, Beethoven worked out the music of (at least) the entire first solo section. We cannot be sure why he gave it up, but a possible reason lies close at hand: the concert for which this composition had been intended was cancelled.[71]

But why should Beethoven, working under time pressure from the impending concert, have put forth such effort to come up with a new concerto—effort sustained enough to bring the work to the first stages of an autograph—if all the while he had a powerful concerto in C minor at hand, mainly sketched and (according to Küthen) even largely written out in autograph?[72] Should we think, perhaps, that he was displeased with Op. 37, and felt it needed to be replaced? But, quite aside from the merits of the case, it would seem puzzling, then, that he should have changed his mind once more and put the C-minor concerto into shape for the following spring—with no further sign of work on the other concertos or the concertante.[73] Surely it is more reasonable to think that at the time Beethoven was working on these new compositions he had not yet made substantial progress on Op. 37: that the few fragmentary ideas for this piece that have survived (including the one in Kessler) represented, in early 1802, something like its true stage of development.[74]

If this last conclusion is to be trusted, then the likely period for serious sketching of of Op. 37 is narrowed to ca. May 1802–March 1803. At the beginning of this period Beethoven was working in the Kessler Sketchbook; sometime in the fall he began writing in Wielhorsky. Both these books (with the exception of one leaf in Wielhorsky) survive in their entirety, and each seems to give rather a full account of Beethoven's compositional activity during its period of use. But at the apparent time of transition between the two, a good many sketches are missing: those for the finale of the Piano Sonata Op. 31, No. 1, and for all of the Variations Op. 34.[75] It must be assumed that this work was done elsewhere, most likely on loose leaves that are now lost. This transition, falling in late summer–autumn 1802, seems to emerge as the most plausible time between the abandonment of the concerto projects of early 1802 and the concert of April 1803 for the main work on Op. 37. On November 23 Carl Beethoven, in response to solicitations from the publisher André of Offenbach, wrote,

> You have recently honored us with a letter and expressed the wish to have some of my brother's compositions, for which we thank you very much. At present we have nothing but a symphony and a grand concerto for pianoforte, the first at 300 florins, and the second at the same price.[76]

Here, for the first time since Beethoven wrote to Hoffmeister of Leipzig about his Concerto Op. 19, in April 1801, he actually offers a new concerto to a publisher (Breitkopf & Härtel gets the same offer, for the same price, the following January).[77] This offer seems to ring true. The new concerto is mentioned in the same breath with the Second Symphony, whose final movement had by this time been extensively sketched in Kessler. The modifier "grand" (*gross*) fits well the large proportions and full orchestration of Op. 37.[78] We have good reason to believe, of course, that there was as yet no autograph score for the work (since the date "1803" seems to apply to the earliest writing, Stage 1, in Aut. 14). But in the absence of any indication to the contrary, it seems sensible to take Beethoven's brother at his word and believe that by November 1802 a large new piano concerto—which can be no other than Op. 37—had taken shape. We cannot, with the present state of our information, prove conclusively that the principal work of sketching of this concerto was done in the summer–autumn of 1802. But the preponderance of evidence points strongly in this direction.[79]

Beethoven spent that period, the summer and early autumn of 1802, in the picturesque hillside village of Heiligenstadt, some four miles north of Vienna. Here, on October 10, he wrote (or at least copied) the celebrated Heiligenstadt Testament,[80] in which he records mounting despair over his deteriorating hearing, proclaiming that "only his art" held him back from suicide. The rhetorical pathos of this remarkable document has perhaps lent too dark a coloring to our view of this time in the composer's life. For whatever Beethoven's unhappiness, the period of Heiligenstadt and just after was one of prodigious productivity. During this time Beethoven did major work on a series of extraordinary compositions: the Second Symphony, the Sonatas for Piano and Violin Op. 30, the Piano Sonatas Op. 31, both sets of Piano Variations Opp. 34 and 35, and (to a lesser extent) the "Kreutzer" Sonata Op. 47. It now appears that we may, with a fair degree of confidence, add to this imposing list the Third Piano Concerto.

Toward the Middle-Period Style: Piano Concerto No. 3 in C Minor, Op. 37

The opening is unison, triadic, square, with terse dotted rhythms turning into the drum motive (*Pochmotiv*) of mm. 3–4. So, like the "First" Piano Concerto, Op. 15, the C-minor Concerto starts off with an unmistakable military topos,[1] a reminder of a continent in tumult that formed an ever-present backdrop to Beethoven's life. And, as in Op. 15, the warlike sound is at first quiet, tense rather than clamorous. But in Beethoven's musical universe C minor is worlds removed from C major, and in Op. 37 the winds, replying on the dominant to the unison strings, mount directly to an anguished (and unprepared) minor ninth. This sonority will not merely color the first theme in its various recurrences. Just before the piano enters (m. 99), it strikes once again its note of foreboding. Next, this Ab (disguised as G#) will return as the prominent third—the head-motive (*Kopfton*) in Schenkerian parlance—of the contemplative second-movement theme, and like an uncoiling spring it will launch the rondo theme in the finale.

However many separate motivic events we may wish to see in the music of the opening tutti—the breakdown in Table 7-1 risks looking like a vitamin list—they coalesce strongly around the two main themes (in Op. 15, as we recall, there were three), the one militant and the other songful, shown in Example 7-1. Even more distinctly than in the C-major Concerto, the military theme, "a," is a commanding force in the tutti and

TABLE 7-1 OP. 37, I

T_1

9	17	24	36	50		74	85	98	105
a	a_1	a_2	a_3	a_4	b	a_5	a_6	a_7	a_8
i			~~~~~~~~~~~III~I			i (→iv)			

S_1

111	122	131	138	146	164		186	199
a	a_1	a_2	a_3	a_4	b		a_6	pass. (a)
i			~~~~~~~~~~~III				(→iii)	III

T_2 | S_2

227	237	249	257	271	280	295
a_7	a_4	a	(a)	(a)	pass. (a)	8^{v} pass. (+a)
III~~~~v	V/v	v	~iv	~$^\flat$II		~~~~~~~~~~~~V/i

T_3 | S_3

309	318	326	334	340		361	375
a	a_1		a_4	b		a_6	pass. (a)
i				I		(→i)	I

T_4 | Cad. | S

403
a_5 Coda (a)
(→iv)   i

in the movement. The lyrical "b" is a complex of two dozen measures played once, sealed off from the rest of the section. The first theme, however, is initially much extended by developmental procedures. And when the lyrical "b" is over, "a" recurs in the guise of a multisectioned codetta (mm. 74ff.), a veritable parade of its derivatives that finishes out the tutti. The first solo section repeats these events in order—with fine elaborations from the solo instrument—almost to the end. But from the codetta Beethoven retains only the nostalgic sounding "a_6" from m. 85 (see Example 7-3); otherwise, he simply replaces it with the expected display episode. The motivic content of the latter, again, comes entirely from the first theme, with diminutions of its stepwise second segment in the piano and the *Pochmotiv* in the strings and horns.

And the same is true of the whole of T_2, T_3, the almost pastoral S_2, and so on to the end of the movement: with the exception of the three occurrences of "b" in the first tutti and the first and third solo sections, all the music of the movement is quite explicitly related to the first theme. This is cohesiveness carried to extreme. It is an experiment altogether new in Beethoven's concertos.[2] And it represents a distinct turning away from the Mozartean model, where melodic materials are dispensed with generosity, and the solo part typically has at least one contrasting theme of its own.

This is not at all to say that the movement is steadily bellicose in tone. Beethoven separates his ruling first theme into three component segments (marked in Example 7-1a). The descending stepwise motion in the second of these becomes the *espressivo* motive "a_6" in the codetta (m. 85). And in the S_2 section (mm. 257ff.), made up of all three segments, the stepwise one is again prominent, forming peaceful islands of G minor and F minor—a distant forebear to the development section of the first movement of the *Pastoral* Symphony—to the accompaniment of the now muted dotted rhythms of the third.[3] While in the movement as a whole the lyrical second subject provides an expressive foil to the latent aggressiveness of the first theme, this very theme—including the *Pochmotiv*—in time will contribute back on itself to much the same effect.

The opening tutti, to Tovey's chagrin, moves quickly to the relative major for the initial presentation of the lyrical theme. This, to be sure, is not a high point of the composition. But the problem is not simply that the opening orchestral section modulates (all Beethoven's concertos up to this point, do that, as we have seen, and they sometimes do it convincingly); rather, it is the particular nature of this modulation and return that leaves one uneasy. In m. 17 Beethoven innocently continues the kind of upward sequences he had just been writing to land on the relative major, E♭. The strings leap in (one measure early) with a furious confirmation of this key through a downward chromatic bass progression from its tonic to its dominant. In two dozen blustery measures (all of course constructed on the first theme) the composer assures us that E♭ is no passing fancy; we are really going there, and "b," as it now enters, sounds perfectly secure in these surroundings.

Then comes the problem: by an almost casual reference to C minor and the merest glimpse of an augmented sixth pegged to its dominant (shown in Example 7-2), we are jolted back into C major for the continuation of the second theme. In four measures, 58–61, the hard-won ground of the new key is given up without a struggle, and the tutti sails on in C major/minor, as though nothing had happened. In his earlier first movements, as in Opp. 15 and 19, and in the incomplete one of the C-major Violin Concerto, Beethoven had instituted tonal disruption—a deliberately created chaos calling for subsequent resolution—as a central premise of the first tutti. The C-minor Concerto is different; here a great show of purposeful modulation, common coin of sonatas and symphonies from the period, leads to a dead end. Beethoven seems to have called into question the very processive machinery by which large movements, including his own, usually operate: he has undone the drama of opposed tonalities, just established, with a single dismissive gesture. The point is hard to see, and Tovey has reason for puzzlement—though his censoriousness may be another matter.[4]

If the second theme sounds momentarily trivialized by this maneuver, it surely redeems itself in the first solo section (m. 164), where it sounds firmly in E♭ and benefits from fine decorative attentions from the solo piano. We may still feel a certain routine squareness about its first phrase, especially as the melody returns for the third time to the third degree.[5] But the deft voice exchange in mm. 54–55, with its melodic leaps to the fourth and sixth, are eloquent recompense (Example 7-1). And this motion establishes a subtle point of contact between the "b" theme and one of the incarnations of the stepwise segment of "a." The *espressivo* "$a_\flat$" in the codetta (the one bit of the codetta that Beethoven retained in the outer solo sections) is essentially an ornamented descent from the fifth degree to the first, deriving as it does directly from mm. 2–3. In its consequent segment (m. 89) this downward motion is interrupted by a rhetorical leap up to the eighth degree, a motion clearly akin to the second phrase of "b," one that becomes all the more impressive with the added major-minor chiaroscuro in the first solo section (Example 7-3). At this moment the militant-lyrical expressive polarity of the movement is bridged by an association of the most gentle aspect of "a" with the most assertive one of "b."[6]

Formally there is nothing much out of the ordinary about the first movement of Op. 37 (unless we wish to count a structural tightness much rarer in concertos than in symphonies). Even with its temporary deflection to the relative major, the opening tutti is more devoted to the tonic than that of any earlier Beethoven concerto. The first solo section does exactly what we would expect: it confirms the tonal polarity adumbrated in the opening tutti—there is no hint here of any key other than C minor and E♭—and reproduces with great faithfulness the melodic train of events of T_1, right up to the codetta, where, seemingly freed of formal constraints, it launches into a virtuoso excursion of its own, the ritual display episode. As often happens, the second tutti and second solo sections are of a piece: the orchestral portion simply serves to get us to the starting point of the becalmed, ruminating "development" section, with its stately motion from one tonal area to another. The third tutti and third solo again, quite unexceptionally, are formally a single entity corresponding to the recapitulation of a sonata-form movement. This section is much shortened from either T_1 or S_1; the only part Beethoven seems intent on preserving whole is the piano's display episode.

Then comes the final tutti, interrupted as always by the halt on a cadential $^6_4$ and the soloist's cadenza—in the first performance something no doubt resembling that profusion of counterpoint and decorative trills that Beethoven wrote down in the Wielhorsky sketchbook. Then comes the only formal surprise of the movement. The pianist does not resolve the dominant-plus-trill to the tonic—as had been much the point of the cadenza—but proceeds by means of what the reviewer for the *Allgemeine musikalische Zeitung* called a *Trugschluss*,[7] a deceptive close, to V^7/IV; here begins a coda that levitates between that sound and the subdominant in a long-spun plagal cadence played out above a pedal of solemn beats from "a" (third segment) in the timpani.[8] This hovering craft is finally grounded by repeated statements of an everyday opera-buffa ending, here vitalized by the minor key and an ever more urgent quickening of the motives at hand, drawn once again from the first theme (Example 7-4). The dark and driving passion of this ending encapsulates the familiar ethos of C minor inBeethoven's musical imagination.

It is tempting to think of this extraordinary ending as something of a response to the no less impressive coda of the first movement of Mozart's great concerto in the same key, K. 491. Mozart went about it just a bit differently; he allowed the tutti to close out in normal fashion in the orchestra before the piano rejoined it for the coda proper. But the two are yet startlingly similar: like Beethoven's coda, Mozart's (beginning with m. 501) is a series of plagal cadences over a tonic pedal accompanied by motivic fragments from the first theme and broken-chord figuration in the piano.

Is it responsible to think that Beethoven got this idea for a coda from Mozart's concerto? Here we might take note, first, of the charming anecdote about Beethoven's reaction to Mozart's concerto that Thayer has left us: walking in the Augarten with J. B. Cramer during a performance of the concerto, Beethoven "suddenly stood still and, directing his companion's attention to the exceedingly simple, but equally beautiful motive which is first introduced towards the end of the piece, exclaimed: 'Cramer, Cramer! we shall never be able to do anything like that!' "[9] This incident, reportedly told to Thayer by Cramer's widow, is generally supposed to have occurred during Cramer's visit to Vienna in 1799[10] (he spent almost all the rest of his life in England, and it is not known that he ever visited Vienna again). Unfortunately, this little narrative, like a disquieting number of those in the Beethoven repertory, does not hold up well under scrutiny. Since Cramer lived until 1858, the story must have been about sixty years old or more at its telling by his widow. In any event we have no record that any concerto of Mozart's was played in Vienna in 1799,[11] and his C-minor Concerto was not even published until 1800.[12] Yet another difficulty is this: there is no new motive "first introduced" toward the end of K. 491, only a new version of the familiar theme of this set of variations now put in compound meter[13]—a derivation that is not likely to have eluded either Beethoven or Cramer.

If the Cramer anecdote will not serve well to substantiate Beethoven's dependence upon Mozart's concerto, let us see what other reasons we might have to believe in it. Czerny mentioned (unspecified) "internal evidence" to this effect: "Individual traits of the C-minor Concerto of Mozart encourage the presumption that Beethoven allowed himself to be influenced by this work."[14] If we wish, with Czerny, to posit influence on grounds of internal evidence—always a risky venture—we must try, surely, to assess the distinctiveness of the musical traits to be advanced for this purpose. Should we manage to locate two compositions from this period that end with a diminished seventh chord (to use an extreme example), such an ending would be better evidence of influence between those two pieces than would a dominant-tonic final cadence. In the case at hand we may note that C minor was an exceedingly rare key for concertos in this period. K. 491 and Op. 37 are the only concertos of these two composers in C minor, and Haydn, Pleyel, and Dittersdorf, Vanhall, Kozeluch, and Viotti (for example) left us none in that key;[15] this much enhances the likelihood of a connection between the two concertos as a whole. In addition, Mozart's first movement is the only one of his that brings back the solo instrument after the cadenza interruption—the entire section being, after all, a tutti belonging to the orchestra—and the device is similarly unique, up to this time, in Beethoven's concertos.

As to further kinds of evidence, one might consider the legal categories of "motive and opportunity." Beethoven was surely motivated to match or exceed the artistic and popular triumphs of Mozart's concertos of the later 1780s. Nor is he likely to have been much inhibited from acting on that motive in a straightforward fashion; a degree of "model-composition" was an acceptable procedure at the time, and there are other cases in which he seems to have turned to Mozart's music as models for his own work.[16] As to "opportunity," we need only note whether or not Mozart's concerto was available to Beethoven when he composed Op. 37, and there is every reason—particularly if the conclusions as to the chronology of Beethoven's concerto offered in Chapter 6 are accurate—to think that it was.[17] Beethoven had contemplated writing a C-minor concerto since the mid-1790s, and from time to time he had jotted down a stray idea for such a composition. Perhaps an acquaintance with the Mozart concerto after it was published in 1800, the only concerto on the landscape in C minor and one whose dark urgency of expression was akin to Beethoven's idea of that key, provided an impetus for him to work seriously on his own.

One final point should be made about Beethoven's first movement: almost all modern editions of the piece get its meter wrong, and, naturally enough, almost all modern performances follow suit.[18] The autograph and first edition both show ordinary common time, **c**, while virtually all the editions in use these days make it *alla breve*. The first to do so (once again) was the old Breitkopf & Härtel *Gesamtausgabe* of the 1860s, and with the honorable exception of Franz Kullak's edition of 1881,[19] apparently all subsequent publications of the concerto—together with the magisterial Kinsky-Halm *Verzeichnis* of 1955—repeat the error.

With the benefit of hindsight we can easily see the rightness of the common time signature. Like the first movement of Op. 15, this movement features a vivid evocation of an infantry march in which the military cadence of even quarter notes is indispensable. And there are other suggestions that the measures need four beats. One is that Beethoven frequently writes *sforzati* on second beats (in the first tutti alone at mm. 10ff., 36ff., and 46ff.) such that one is almost compelled to hear the music in four. And then there is a particular kind of ornamentation at certain places, notably at the "b" theme in the solo sections where the nonharmonic tones in the piano always fall on the second and fourth beats (see Example 7-1); this poignant gloss on a second theme that otherwise verges on the pedestrian largely disappears in an *alla breve* performance.

In the two decades around 1800 Beethoven seems to have associated the *alla breve* meter with movements of particular characters. It shows up with some frequency in slow movements of a cantabile nature, as in the Concerto Op. 15, the opening Adagio sostenuto of Op. 27, No. 2 (the "Moonlight" Sonata), the Adagio cantabile of the Piano-Violin Sonata Op. 30, No. 2, and in both Romanzes, Opp. 40 and 50, where the attenuation of the beat adds loft and bouyancy to long-drawn phrases. Among fast movements *alla breve* is most often found in pieces with a touch of *scherzando*: in the finale of the Piano Sonata Op. 10, No. 1, and the first movement of Op. 10, No. 2, in the first movement of the First Symphony and the last movement of the Second.[20] In this connection it is instructive to compare the movement at hand with the first and last movements of the Piano-Violin Sonata Op. 30, No. 2, also in C minor. The opening movement has the tempo and meter of Op. 37, Allegro con brio in common time, and it has the special tension and urgency that Beethoven so often brought to that key. The finale is Allegro, *alla breve*; here all that taut energy has been exchanged for a kind of good-natured bluster in which, as in most of these other fast *alla breve* movements, the quickest motion is in eighth notes.

Beethoven has another kind of movement in cut time; this type is moderately fast, with a pronounced *cantabile* character distantly akin, at least, to the manner of the slow *alla breve* movements. Two early examples are the opening Allegro ma non troppo of the Sonata Op. 49, No. 2 (ca. 1796) and the Rondo (Allegro commodo) of the Sonata Op. 14, No. 1. Two others are the first movement of the String Quartet Op. 18, No. 3, in D major (Allegro) with its willowy opening theme, and the more sturdy but contemplative Allegro ma non tanto of the Sonata for Piano and Cello, Op. 69. All these movements have about them an amiable grace, a *Gemächlichkeit* that was as much a part of the younger Beethoven's musical persona as was the high-voltage tension of many of the minor-key first movements. He clearly associated the *alla breve* meter much more often with these two types—witty and bantering pieces or graceful and melodious ones—than with the urgent intensity of compositions like the first movement of Op. 37.[21]

THE LARGO

After the first movement closes with a furioso confirmation of C minor, the Largo enters, as if from another world, in E major (Example 7-5). The usually matter-of-fact Czerny said that this theme "must sound like a holy, distant, and celestial Harmony."[22] And the distance is easily measureable: C minor and E major stand at opposite points on the circle of fifths, poised at the maximum remove of seven accidentals. In the first edition Beethoven confirmed a "celestial" quality in those first sounds through his dynamic marking and pedal indications: *pianissimo* for the piano's entire statement—ignored by many performers—and *senza sordino* (i.e., with dampers raised).[23] Czerny reports that at the first performance in April 1803, Beethoven in fact held the pedal "during the entire theme"—a practice Czerny thought should be modified for later pianos.[24] However twentieth-century pianists approach the problem with their much more sonorous modern instrument, a certain blurring of harmonic junctures was the composer's clear intent.

Beethoven's atmospheric sound and Czerny's colorful diction ("holy, distant, and celestial") recall the contemporaneous vogue of the Aeolian harp, that mysterious instrument that Nature herself played upon, through whose nebulous sonorities she was thought to speak directly to humankind: the instrument that in an easy shift of sense became for early Romantic sensibilities a symbol for the poetic mind in touch with primal truths of the universe.[25] This elusiveness of sound and the poetic imagery attached to it were much of a piece with Beethoven's growing consciousness in this period of art as a transcendental force, and of the artist—in this case himself—as a Promethean figure, a fire-bringer from the gods to humankind. "Only my art held me back" from suicide, he wrote in the Heiligenstadt Testament of October 1802. And his calling as an artist entailed a responsibility to society: "Ah, it seemed impossible to leave the world until I had brought forth all that I felt was within me."[26] That prosaic instruction "senza sordino" in the Largo of Op. 37—as well as in the Sonatas Op, 27, No. 2 (the "Moonlight," first movement) and Op. 31, No. 2 (the Largo sections) from just before—may reflect a larger shift in Beethoven's thought, a new interest in musical sounds whose blurred surface forsakes clarity of immediate relationships to create a metaphor for a higher reality, "holy, distant, and celestial."[27]

The uncanny effect of this opening depends, of course, upon other factors as well. There is the close-packed spacing in the middle register that Beethoven had already used in a number of piano works (the Grave of Op. 13, the theme of the variations in the Sonata Op. 26) and that was to become a staple of Romantic piano sound in, say, Schubert's Impromptu D. 935, No. 2, and the opening theme of the late Sonata in B♭, D. 960. And the initial melody centers around the third degree an octave and a tenth above the bass, a sonority Beethoven much favored for starting off his slow movements for piano;[28] its special resonance derives from placing the third just where it occurs in the overtone series—and given the very slow tempo of this movement that sound has plenty of time to resonate.

But in the course of this theme Beethoven commits syntactical audacities that no softness or slowness of the music nor blurring by the pedal can obscure. The first of its three four-measure members pushes strangely toward the relative minor, ending with a long measure on its dominant. The second, after emphasizing that C♯ minor sonority in a higher register, recedes (with downward fifths in the bass) back to V/I. At this point one might expect an ordinary bar form continuation to assimilate this digression with a modified repetition of the first segment that closes on the tonic. But the third segment (mm. 8–12) is an utterly unforeseen intrusion. After an abrupt shift to the nonharmonic G major, the melody is borne aloft by a full measure of a celestial-wind-like tremolo in the bass on *its* fourth, C, before the music drops back (by reinterpreting that C as the lowered sixth of E) to the V/I where it had begun. Nothing has prepared us for this singular digression. Beethoven must have had some special purpose in mind (and presently we shall try to think what it might have been). Meanwhile, after these disruptions the orchestra now finishes as a proper bar form should, taking up the first strain again and releasing the accumulated tension in m. 17 with the first authentic cadence of the movement. What follows, until the reentrance of the piano in m. 25, is a codetta of cadential gestures, confirmatory and reassuring, but yet intensely expressive with its high melodic tessitura and insistent accents.

The familiar skeleton of "slow movement form" (Rosen's term) is easily visible here: the first large section of the movement goes to the dominant, and after a transitional passage there is a recapitulation (plus extensions) that stays in the tonic. What surprises is the scale and prominence of the transition. It starts out in G major, a key already pointedly alluded to in the the piano's first statement, and to get there Beethoven has to write a little transition to the transition (mm. 37–38). Thereupon, in its fourteen leisurely measures, the section moves through A minor to the dominant of E major. Always nebulous as to thematic derivation,[29] it has something of the static, hovering quality of the S_2 of the first movement, or of the beginning of the same section in the first movement of Op. 15. But here the music really seems to exist largely for the sake of the figuration in the piano. Arpeggios up and down the keyboard with long pedals—and some indistinct growling in the bass—renew the otherworldly Aeolian harp effect; the piano's ghostly undulation on a highly attenuated harmonic frame—in a sense the merest surface of the music—claims all our attention.

Ornamental figuration in the solo instrument comes strongly to the fore throughout this movement, and the autograph shows Beethoven's protracted struggles (in the inks of all three stages of work) to get it just the way he wanted. As early as the "celestial-wind" tremolo of m. 11 he already resorted to writing 128th notes. Sorting out the patterns of unaccustomedly small note values in the rest of the movement gave him trouble—the higher mathematics of writing down complex rhythmic patterns was in any case never Beethoven's strong suit—and some places he never got right.[30] The root of his problem was the huge variation here in rate of motion, from the initial melodic progression by quarter note to extravagant bursts of ornament in 128ths and faster.

The beginning of the recapitulation, with its exquisite exchanges between piano and orchestra, cost Beethoven great effort. These pages of the autograph became so cluttered with second and third thoughts that he resorted to the addition of a fresh bifolium (between the present fols. 67 and 70), sewing the new paper over the pages they replaced. The sewing has subsequently been undone (both old and new pages are now included in the foliation), so that we can see all the successive versions. Beethoven's main indecision was about the distribution of music between piano and orchestra; by slow stages he approached the happy solution of giving the orchestra the lion's share of thematic matter in the first eight bars (mm. 53–60), with ever more intricate piano commentary in its long interstices. The familiar music of the first theme is renewed by this difference, and the excurses of the piano, too, have a familiar ring due to similarities in figuration with the transition.

The precedent thus set he followed, with less indecision, in the codetta (mm. 69ff.). This music, entirely for orchestra in the exposition (mm. 17–24), is now enriched with solemn upward scales in the solo instrument. In m. 75 it veers off from its model in the exposition as the harmony points toward a stopping place on the cadential $^6_4$. The piano, ever voluble and agile, assumes the upper hand, finally even ushering in its own cadenza. This is a single-line affair, *sempre con gran espressione*, much like the beginning of the recapitulation of the first movement in the Sonata Op. 31, No. 2 (*con gran espressione e semplice*). Both have the effect of a displacement (an *ecstasy* in the root meaning of the word) from the main discourse of the music, a somber reflection, as if from without, on the events at hand. The orchestra, echoed by the piano, then closes this movement, called by the *Allgemeine musikalische Zeitung* reviewer "one of the most expressive and richly sensitive instrumental pieces ever written,"[31] with a reminiscence of its very first cadence, there a deceptive one, here resolved and becalmed in the home tonic.

THE RONDO

In the opening ritornello theme of the finale, shown in Example 7-7a, the rigidly square phrasing of the right-hand melody is much softened by the fluid running figure below, an accompaniment reminiscent of the *grazioso* rondo theme of the *Pathétique* Sonata Op. 13, in the same key. That left-hand accompaniment actually occurred to Beethoven rather late in the game, at Stage 3 (black ink) in the autograph. What he first wrote is the unabashedly primitive version shown in Example 7-7b, where the aggressive squareness of this music is enhanced in mm. 3 and 7 by huge offbeat accents (accomplished solely by reinforcement of texture). The theme in this form leaves a radically altered impression of what Beethoven had in mind for this ritornello: it is a rough-hewn thing, here, artless and boisterous throughout, but most of all in those blunt syncopations of the penultimate bars of its two halves. Just what importance we should attach to such a first conception—that is, to an artist's preliminary idea for a work, an idea later partly rejected—remains a vexed question, and one much debated in Beethoven's case. But knowing the origins of this theme must color our feeling about it by calling attention to its less refined aspects; at the very least we will wish to give the *sforzati* in mm. 3 and 7— all that remains of those great thick chords—their full due.

The most distinctive feature of this theme, as in many of Beethoven's rondo themes, is its head-motive. That opening A♭, the minor ninth over the dominant, reminiscent of countless Baroque fugue themes and already having played an expressive role in the first movement, propels the piece out of the starting blocks. It then serves as a melodic target toward which subsequent returns may aim (and sometimes amusingly overshoot). And all the while that pitch remains in the back of our minds as something of a sticking point, for it never resolves decently, either in the short or long run, to the expected G below.[32] Each renewed entrance of the ritornello thus brings with it a small abrasion, a slight affront.

This ritornello, an expansive, fifty-five-measure rounded binary statement with written-out repeats, takes on the mantle of naive predictability we come to expect of rondos. Its schematic structure is like a homely objet trouvé; what matters is what the artist can make of it. The form fosters engaging exchanges between piano and orchestra characteristic of concerto rondos. More specifically, it provides ample opportunity for internal "return," the heart of the rondo idea at large. The point Beethoven chooses to focus on, more than any other, is the moment of recapitulation in the binary form (at m. 26, shown in Example 7-8). The first part of the second segment, beginning at m. 17, directs its melodic and harmonic motion strongly toward the dominant G (the G to which the theme always refuses to resolve) with a broadly comic ritard as the goal is approached. The piano then takes that G, decorates it in an extravagent little cadenza while holding out (in a curious reversal of expectation) the implicit promise that the A♭ of the head motive will follow; instead, borrowing the chromatic scale from the first return in m. 4, the piano flies exhilaratingly all the way up to f‴ for the beginning of the theme.[33] The corresponding point in the orchestra's repetition of this segment (m. 42) surely requires *some* sort of response to all this carry-on in the piano; so Beethoven cleverly ushers in a quite unexpected major version of the theme, *piano*, followed by an instant *buffo fortissimo* correction in minor plus rounding-off cadences.

The other major structural member of this movement, the episode (the overall shape of the movement is shown in Table 7-2), is similarly a large rounded binary form with repeats, this one rigidly periodized in $8+(8+8)$ measures. Once again the built-in repetitions provide inviting opportunities for exchanges between solo and orchestra, and Beethoven makes the most of them. But much more striking than the exchanges themselves are his alterations of the initial materials. The opening in m. 181 (Example 7-9) is a presentable enough clarinet theme with that characteristic upward motion in tenths to a V_2^4 that we hear in so many of Beethoven's slow movements, followed by a rather run-of-the-mill cadential pattern—a measure each of dominant and tonic, both in root position. The final melodic gesture of the first phrase, $\hat{5}$–$\hat{8}$, mirroring the bass motion just heard, can only be described as weak. But the piano thereupon transforms this music into something that marvelously transcends its origins. The melody is an octave higher, there is an added dominant pedal, a smooth bass motion to I_3^6 replaces the plain dominant of m. 190, and—probably most important—the clarinet's feeble upward gesture of the following measure has disappeared.[34] The theme in the piano, now airborne, wheels and soars high above the orchestra. There are to be two more occurrences of the melody in the "recapitulation," and both times the improved version prevails.[35] Beethoven seems to have treated his initial formulation like a mere sketch, a first idea subject to renovation.

Since the episode happens only once, its rigid schematic form and elaborate internal repetition constitute no particular structural peril for the movement. The equally systematic and repetitive ritornello, however, we expect to hear four times, and four of those fifty-five-measure statements, however fine in themselves, would never do. Only one more time, at its second appearance in m. 127, does Beethoven let us hear the theme in its entirety (this time he writes an even fancier piano cadenza at the

TABLE 7-2 THIRD PIANO CONCERTO, OP. 37, III

	57	68	83	103	115

R_1

S	T	S			T	S

a   trans. b_1 b_2 b_3

i   ~~~~~~~~III   ~~V/i

	127	181	229	264

R_2 E

S	T	T	S	T	T	S

a   c   trans. (a)

i   VI   ~~~~~~   ~~~♯III~~~~v/i

	298	320	331	346	376	387

R_3

S	T	S					T

a   trans. b_1 b_2 a

i   I   ~~~~~~~~~♭II~~~~~~

	407	415	443

R_4

S	T	S		T	S

Coda (a)   (b_2)

I

"recapitulation"). The third ritornello (m. 298) seizes upon that other opportunity offered by such programmatic internal repetitions: it leaves most of them out. What purports to be the orchestra's repeat of the first segment, we are suddenly aware, has become the minor mode "correction" within the second one (within its *repetition*, at that)—fifty-five measures have become twenty. And instead of the final ritornello, what we get is a startling transformation of its theme, now in major, $\frac{6}{8}$, and presto, as the opening sally of a rousing coda (see Example 7-10).

In this coda the pivotal A♭/G♯, once agonized or foreboding, is now drained of all its intensity to become only a piquant decoration to the new sixth degree in the theme, A♮. The answering woodwinds, moreover, offer a frivolous mimicry of that opening gesture. For an eight-measure period a darker mood intrudes—a suggestion of nostalgia, perhaps, for what has passed—as the piano's somber downward steps (in sixths and tenths with voice exchanges) are enveloped in rippling chords played off against a tonic pedal in the winds. From here to the end, all is scintillating cadential passagework in the piano. For his final motivic offering, at m. 443, Beethoven recalls two elements from his second group, a syncopation from b_2 (m. 83) and a precipitous downward scale from b_1 (m. 68);[36] but this too is woven into the repeated cadential landing patterns that finish the movement. Here Beethoven has struck something of a middle course between the conclusions of Mozart's two minor-key concertos: between the nearly irrelevant good cheer of the end of the D-minor Concerto and the unrelentingly dark and entirely apposite close to the one in C minor. Beethoven's coda leaves behind all the C-minor gravity of this composition, but it does so with a persistent, even compulsive, care for motivic integrity.

THE MUSIC AND THE DATE

Speaking of the opening of the Largo, Tovey remarked, "the shock of the first chord, in its remoteness from the C minor of the rest of the work is in itself a feature of Beethoven's second period." And Wolfgang Osthoff opened his informative little monograph on Op. 37 with the assertion that this composition "belongs to the so-called second creative period" in which "the inimitable Beethovenian character breaks through."[37] So both seem to place the concerto in the second of those familiar three periods of Beethoven's creative life—a division clearly formulated as early as 1837 in Fétis's article on the composer in his *Biographie universelle des musiciens* and perpetuated in Wilhelm von Lenz's *Beethoven et ses trois styles* of 1852[38] and countless later writings.

The chronological boundaries proposed for these divisions, including that between the first and second periods, the one of immediate interest to us here, have been various. Fétis's opinion was firm: the second period began unambiguously with the *Eroica* (1803–4). Von Lenz (whose book in a later edition of the *Biographie universelle* Fétis blasted as a "tissue of extravagances and silliness, written in a ridiculous style") showed a more nuanced approach: dating of the first works of the "second style" varies by genre. The *Eroica* is the first of the symphonies, Op. 59 (1805–6) the first among the quartets, but Op. 30 (1801–2) the first among the piano-violin sonatas, and (he decides with difficulty) the slow movement of Op. 22 (1800) the first among the piano sonatas.[39] However erratic his writing (and it is very much so), Von Lenz came to the clear conclusion that Beethoven's sonatas for piano (alone or with other instruments) tended to be more original and "advanced" than his compositions in other genres. He surely had good reason for this opinion. Beethoven seemed most in control—and at the same time most audacious—when writing for his own instrument in a genre that had been less than central among his illustrious forebears, but that he made his specialty. He composed his String Quartets Op. 18 (1798–1800) in the face of towering achievements in that sector by Haydn and Mozart. They are at many points frankly imitative: this music could be mistaken for the work of his great predecessors much more readily than could any of his early piano sonatas, going back even as far as Op. 2 of 1794–95.

Beethoven himself cooperatively made some reference to a change in style shortly before the *Eroica*. According to Czerny, he said "around 1803" to Wenzel Krumpholz, "I am not satisfied with the works I have written so far. From now on I am taking a new path."[40] And his letter of October 1802 to Breitkopf & Härtel includes protestations about the "entirely new manner" of the Variations Opp. 34 and 35 (both 1802).[41] These statements, of course, have been taken to point directly to the onset of that proverbial "middle period" in the composer's career in which, with certain variations, almost everybody seems to believe.

But there is much less accord as to just what it is that Beethoven began to do differently in this period. For some the idea of the "heroic" looms very large in designating and delineating a middle period. Alan Tyson, in his "Beethoven's Heroic Phase," embarked from a position set down in Joseph Kerman's *The Beethoven Quartets*:

> It can be no coincidence that these these two works [the *Eroica* and *Fidelio*] are so strongly, so unusually shot through with extra-musical ideas, and that the ideas should be ideas of heroism. . . . Even the few

sonatas are now heroic—the "Waldstein" and the "Appassionata." With this set of works Beethoven made his revolution.[42]

Tyson sees the *Eroica* as the "most characteristic product" of that "heroic phase." He wishes to root the origins of this phase in the psychological turmoil attendant to the onset of Beethoven's deafness, in the nearly manic-depressive alternation of despair and resignation with a defiant will to overcome (and something like elation) that is so striking in certain of his letters from 1801–2 and in the Heiligenstadt Testament of October 1802.

However convincing we find such an explanation of the emotional origins of Beethoven's heroic manner, we must be aware that the popular and pat name "heroic" is a very poor designation for Beethoven's middle period as a whole. While most of us easily associate that term with *Fidelio*, the "Waldstein," the *Appassionata*, and the Third and Fifth Symphonies, there is no ignoring that this was also the period of the "Pastoral" Symphony, the Violin Concerto, the String Quartet Op. 59, No. 1, the first movement of the Fourth Piano Concerto, the Sonata Op. 54, and the sacred songs after Gellert, Op. 48. Any general characterization of Beethoven's music from, say, 1802 to 1812 must take account of an immense diversity as to genre, medium, and expressive intention and effect. And what we can easily observe about this repertory as a whole will probably consist largely of approximations and generalities. Leaving aside for a moment the vocal works, we might say (for example) that instrumental movements tend to be longer than before and explore unprecedented extremes of expressivity; they often show an intricate organization with forays into remote harmonic regions (such as the median relations in the basic structures of the "Waldstein"'s first movement and in the *Leonore* Overtures Nos. 2 and 3); they feature longer-term gestures (such as the prolonged building of climaxes in the *Eroica* or the extended islands of stasis in the "Pastoral" Symphony); they tend to shift their centers of gravity sharply toward the end with bigger development sections and structurally significant codas; and they gravitate toward architectural coherence that often clearly transcends the boundaries of movements.[43]

And in keeping with the tenor of some of this repertory's extramusical associations—with Prometheus the fire-bringer, with Napoleon the destroyer of the old older, with Florestan's and Egmont's noble resignation—musicians and listeners of every generation since Beethoven's have sensed in it intimations of the transcendental or otherworldly, of the ethical or hortatory. For E. T. A. Hoffmann this music "unveils before us the realm of the mighty and the immeasureable . . . , sets in motion the machinery of awe, of fear, of terror, of pain, and awakens that infinite yearning which is the essence of romanticism."[44] A century later Romain Rolland wrote,

> But when, underneath these first strata of commonness, the artist is vigorous enough to delve down to the great laws of the general life and the essential rhythms of the soul, the masterpiece of the individual genius becomes, without effort or intention on his part, the natural expression of all humanity. And I affirm that this oneness is the highest harmony that can be realised on earth. Beethoven has accomplished it in the *Eroica*.[45]

And Kerman and Tyson, in the unlikely venue of a modern encyclopedia article, say, "The combination of his musical dynamic, now extremely powerful, and extra-musical suggestion invests his pieces with an unmistakable ethical aura."[46]

Convincing formulations of a more specific and technical nature as to what makes the music of the middle period what it is are harder to come by. Carl Dahlhaus, perhaps surprisingly, has made an intriguing contribution along these lines in his article "The 'New Path.' "[47] Equating this "new path" mentioned by Czerny and the "entirely new manner" the composer attributed to his sets of variations, Dahlhaus seeks to show that in several diverse genres of composition Beethoven began, around 1802, to redefine the nature and function of "theme" within his instrumental movements. Using four compositions (the Variations Op. 35, the Sonata Op. 31, No. 2, the *Eroica*, and the String Quartet Op. 59, No. 3) as models, Dahlhaus contends that themes are no longer presented as premises from which consequences can be drawn in the course of the movement, or as "texts" upon which the movement comments (always returning, in circular fashion, as it refers again and again to the beginning). Rather, these movements present no single definitive statement of the theme, but only elements of themes ("thematic substance") or "thematic complexes" such that the processes of working out and development begin at the very outset. Ambiguity as to "subject" and "treatment of subject" are central to the formal idea of the movements.

One might cavil at several points. Dahlhaus never stopped believing in the mid-nineteenth-century formulation of sonata form—in which the nature of "themes" and their treatment stood at the center—as the norm from which Beethoven deviated. And his discussions concentrate almost exclusively on first movements, indeed usually on their first few measures; he declines to show in any detail how the "new manner" works in a movement as a whole. But the arguments are nevertheless in some cases convincing, and in all, provocative.

So where does the C-minor Concerto stand in all this—does it belong to the "new path" of 1802 and the years after, or does it fit with the First Symphony and the String Quartets Op. 18? Does the style of the music complement or contradict the "physical" evidence for a date of 1802–3 presented in the last chapter? While bearing in mind the perils attendant to matching a piece with a period on internal evidence, we might begin by noting that twice in the course of the Rondo of Opus 37, Beethoven strays well outside the ordinary formal boundaries of the genre. After the episode in A♭ he writes a fugato working-out that seems well on track toward the home tonic.[48] But its progress is suddenly deterred by a mystifying turn to a distant tonality and a static, placid rendition of the rondo theme (beginning at m. 264).[49] This pastoral interlude, we quickly realize, strongly recalls the expressive world of the Largo: the key is the same, E major, and the Aeolian-harp pedal effect of that movement is repeated. This key is arrived at through an explicit reinterpretation of G♯/A♭, and the return to C minor exploits the same ambiguity, employing the rondo head-motive (beginning in m. 279) as the very instrument by which the harmonic connection is made.

This is the same strategem, in fact, that had led from the Largo to the Rondo in the first place. Both the first and last sounds of the Largo are E-major chords with very prominent G♯-*Kopftöne*; the head-motive of the Rondo takes up that pitch (as A♭) together with the fifth (B) of the chord just sounded, "reining in" these two tones into the starkly opposed expressive and tonal context of the C-minor Rondo (see Example 7-11). (Beethoven's clever maneuver should have consequences for performance; no *attacca* is written, but the connection ought to be made plain.)

The Rondo's other unauthorized detour (a "frolic," our legal colleagues might call it) comes just before the presto coda, where once again we hear the main theme in placid guise and in a distant tonality, this time in D♭. Here, too, a connection with the Largo is not hard to detect: its first theme, we recall, moves immediately to the relative minor, C♯, enharmonic equivalent of D♭. And now that other harmonic peculiarity of the Largo theme begins to make sense. Its second phrase turns unexpectedly to G and then with great emphasis to *its* subdominant, C—the tonic, of course, of the third (and first) movement (see Example 7-5). It is important to note that these tonal acrobatics are exceptional, startling measures; they are contrived, it seems clear, to make that remarkable E-major movement assimilable in a composition in C minor.

Tovey was probably right that the very remoteness of E major for the second movement of a piece in C minor was a sign of Beethoven's "second period." But such deliberately worked-out relationships between movements as those between the Largo and the Rondo are a clearer sign, surely much more to be expected from Beethoven in 1802–3 than in 1799–1800. The two sonatas *quasi una fantasia* of Op. 27 (1800–1), particularly the first one in E♭, seem to have been proving grounds for the use of "cyclic" procedures.[50] The Sonata Op. 31, No. 2 (the "Tempest"), whose sketches fall rather clearly into that gap between Kessler and Wielhorsky—the same period that is suggested here as the time for the composition of this concerto—is an elaborate exercise in intermovement reference: its opening Adagio-Allegro, doing duty for both slow introduction and first theme, provides motivic material for all three movements.

Beethoven's decisive innovations usually showed up in his solo piano music first; we would expect that the references between movements in Op. 37 would follow the experimental Sonatas of 1800–2 rather than anticipate them. In so doing this concerto joins other middle-period works that owe a debt to those experiments; the Fifth Symphony is an obvious case, and Lewis Lockwood's study of the early sketches in Wielhorsky for the *Eroica* have shown a plan for the whole symphony that in outline and detail grew out of its last movement.[51] And the manner in which these connections in Op. 37 are made is important. Beethoven manipulated the very themes of the Largo and Rondo so that their shapes have significance overstepping the boundaries of the movements. The forceful bending of the Largo theme anticipates a wayward feature of the Rondo and then recalls the home tonality from which it itself so strongly digresses; this music is "text" in Dahlhaus's sense, and at the same time "commentary." And the Rondo theme, gathering bits of what has just been heard in the Largo to make of them something startlingly different, projects a similar duality of function. These are strategems, surely, of the "new path." In the concertos a building of continuities between second and third movements pointed toward Beethoven's future practice: all his subsequent concertos showed such connections, while all his earlier ones lacked them. And that intricate conceptual unity of the Largo and Rondo of Op. 37 would itself argue for approximate contemporaneity of their composition— this in opposition to Küthen's hypothesis that the Largo, written at Stage 1 of the autograph, dates from 1799–1800, and the Rondo (Stage 2) from 1802–3.

Much of the writing for piano in Op. 37 also seems distinctly later than, say, that of Op. 15, whose surviving autograph, with extensive revision of the piano part, Beethoven wrote out in 1800. But here we must be careful to exclude from consideration any revision in the piano part of Op. 37

that may have been done just before the concert of 1803 (or, as Küthen believes, even later) and confine our attention to the very rudimentary version of it that is present in Stage 1 of the autograph. The saturated chordal texture at the opening of the second movement, for example— and particularly the massive doublings in mm. 5–6—might lead one to comparisons with passages like the beginning of the Fourth Piano Concerto. But at Stage 1 of the autograph, the piano part at that point showed nothing but the melody line; those chords were added at Stage 3.

One feature of the piano part that Beethoven bothered to write down at that early stage are the highly distinctive dive-bomber-like cadences ending the three big solo sections of the first movement. The first of these, the grand descent to E♭ in mm. 225–27, initially occurred in a somewhat different form that observed the upper limit of the keyboard range at Stage 1, g‴ (Examples 7-12a and b show both that version and the final one that first appeared as an option in the first edition). This new sort of dramatic exit for the solo instrument, doing duty for the familiar trilled dominant-tonic endings of the Mozart concertos, also seem more plausible in 1802–3 than in 1799–1800. Those cadential points in the first movements of his previous concertos show, with one exception,[52] some version of the trilled dominant-tonic ending. In the later piano concertos this venerable cadence has disappeared.[53] At the corresponding points in the first movement of the "Emperor" Concerto (1809), Beethoven elaborates upon the idea of Op. 37, with exhilarating scales in both hands running in contrary motion, a singular pianistic effect that was anticipated at major cadential points in the first movement of the "Waldstein" Sonata" of 1803–4.

In deciding whether Op. 37 belongs stylistically to the period of the First Symphony or that of the Second, we should probably take notice of a separate mini-tradition in which the concerto participates, that of pieces in C minor. Beginning with the Piano Trio Op. 1, No. 3,[54] Beethoven seems to have felt a compulsion to include a C-minor piece in most of the principal collections: Opp. 3, 9, 10, 18, and 30—an even half dozen of them by the time of Op. 37. In these compositions first movements are the ones most invested with C-minor passion and fury; finales often have a touch of *scherzoso*, as in the Sonata Op. 10, No. 1, or the *alla Zingarese* of the Quartet Op. 18, No. 4; the characters of internal movements are various.

As it happens, two of these C-minor compositions coincide rather closely in time with the two proposed dates for the composition of Op. 37. First is the Quartet Op. 18, No. 4, whose lost sketches were likely done in that missing sketchbook of 1799–1800, the very book, according to the standard theory, that also included the sketches for the C-minor Concerto.

While probably undeserving of the opprobrium Kerman once heaped upon it,[55] this piece—especially in its first and last movements—has a certain jarring unevenness in tone and an apparent uncertainty in technique. This can be seen in the merest details. In its first phrase Beethoven trains all the expressive weapons in his arsenal on the dissonant crux of the second measure (a vii[7] over the tonic pedal). Indeed, he does nearly as much just *before* that point—a V$^4_2$ with an onbeat appoggiatura over the same pedal—in a clear excess of pathos as yet unjustified by the musical discourse (Example 7-13). This is in vivid contrast to the generically similar gesture at the beginning of Op. 37, where such a stressed dissonance (the memorable minor ninth) is cast into relief by a graduated approach—a more mature handling of a moment of similar expressive content. The construction of the first movement of the quartet has about it a distinct start-and-stop patchiness, as does the finale, a true episodic rondo without sonata-like procession to a second key. When comparing these two first movements, and perhaps especially the two Rondos, one is hard pressed to believe that the quartet and the concerto could have been companion pieces, two big compositions in C minor composed together.[56]

The other C-minor piece, the Sonata for Piano and Violin Op. 30, No. 2 (1801–2), the first member of its genre, von Lenz said, to participate in the "second style," shows some of the restless experimentation and expansion of the piano sonatas of that time. In the first movement a quiet, backward-looking codetta merges imperceptibly into the development section as it turns to a very distant B major; in the recapitulation this music fades away again, now into a substantial developmental coda. The finale is a radical exploration of the consequences of the Haydnesque sonata-rondo: the returns of the rondo are all there, but Beethoven has replaced the episode with a contrapuntal development of a subsidiary theme. This finale, like the first and second movements of this piece, ends with the expansive coda that Beethoven increasingly relies upon as a weight-bearing member of his musical structures. The sonata as a whole is fully believable as a near predecessor of the concerto. And there are some tantalizing specific similarities in detail. The first movement of the sonata and the finale of the concerto finish up with the same keyboard figuration. And in the sonata's Adagio cantabile the coda starts out in the usual "farewell" manner with *dolce* reminiscences over a dominant pedal. But this suddenly gives way to furious upward scales in the piano utterly unrelated to anything yet heard in the movement (Beethoven later moves to make them credible). These are almost precisely the scales forming the run-up to the piano's first theme in Op. 37. Perhaps a stray thought about that other big C-minor piece, long in the back of Beethoven's mind, intruded upon this sonata—a companion thought to that other tiny idea for the first movement of the concerto that shows up, just after this time, in Kessler.[57]

While on the subject of codas in C-minor compositions, let us recall here the striking similarities of idea between the codas to the first movements of Op. 37 and Mozart's Concerto in C minor, K. 491.[58] Should we believe that in composing his concerto Beethoven consulted Mozart's? Mozart's concerto, we recall, was composed in 1786 but first published by André in Offenbach at some undetermined day in 1800. The period during which Beethoven did the bulk of the work on his C-minor concerto, according to the old theory, was before April 2, 1800, the date of that spring's concert. But surely it is much more likely that Mozart's concerto— published at some point in 1800 in another city—would have been available to him in 1802–3 than at any time before April 2, 1800. The strength of any apparent connection between the two pieces constitutes an argument for the later date of Beethoven's. There is a danger of circularity here. Earlier, under the rubric "motive and opportunity," Beethoven's probable access to Mozart's concerto was included in the argument for its probable influence on Beethoven's concerto. One cannot have it both ways: (1) using the later date for Beethoven's concerto to support the contention that Mozart's music influenced it; and (2) using a claim of Mozart's influence to support the later date. One part of the argument or the other probably needs to be relinquished; the reader may decide which has to go. Yet the beauty of such a circular argument is that if the conclusion of either of its parts wins agreement, the remaining part gains credibility. There may yet be hope for the argument from/for the Mozart connection.

CHAPTER 8

An Interlude in the French Manner: Triple Concerto in C, Op. 56

The two years following the concert of April 1803—the onset, that is, of Beethoven's proverbial middle period—were for him a time of breathtaking productivity. Six weeks after that concert he managed to finish the "Kreutzer" Sonata just in time to perform it with the violinist George A. Polgreen Bridgetower at the Augartensaal. Shortly after this concert he began to work in Landsberg 6, the *Eroica* Sketchbook; into this book he crowded work on all four movements of the Third Symphony, sketches for the "Waldstein" and its original slow movement (the Andante "favori," WoO 57), first drafts for the abortive opera *Vestas Feuer* as well as for the opening numbers of *Leonore*, preliminary ideas for the Fourth Piano Concerto and the Fifth and Sixth Symphonies, and sketches for various other works.[1] And an accelerated rate of publication of his music from a bit earlier testifies to Beethoven's burgeoning fame during this period. In a blizzard of correspondence with publishers in Vienna, Leipzig, and Edinburgh, Beethoven and his brother Carl negotiated energetically for high honoraria, speedy publication, and accurate texts—roughly in that order of importance.[2] Such was the forward thrust along the trajectory of his career that the works for which Beethoven was reading proofs, despite reasonably efficient publication schedules, belonged to a distinctly earlier phase than those he was composing.[3]

The central focus of all this activity, after the completion of the *Eroica* in early 1804, rapidly narrowed to the composition of *Leonore*, the work that ultimately cost Beethoven more effort than any other: one, he claimed, that would win him a martyr's crown.[4] That he was even in a position to pursue that crown depended upon external factors. The ownership and management of the Theater an der Wien shifted rapidly (and repeatedly) at the end of 1803 and the beginning of 1804, with final ownership falling into the hands of Beethoven's imagined nemesis who also controlled the court theaters, Baron von Braun. With Schikaneder's departure from the theater, Beethoven gave up working on his libretto, *Vestas Feuer*—with which he had in any case become disaffected—and moved out of his rooms there. But soon he took up *Leonore*, "an old French libretto," as he called it, in a translation by the new temporary director, friendly to Beethoven, Joseph Sonnleithner,[5] and in time moved back into the theater. However demanding and absorbing the composition of *Leonore* proved in the following months, Beethoven found time for certain other projects as well. Mendelssohn 15 (the *Leonore* Sketchbook), in which he began to work in early summer 1804, has the great bulk of the sketches for the first version of the opera, but also the principal ones for the Sonata Op. 54, for "An die Hoffnung," Op. 32, and for the first movement of the Appassionata Sonata Op. 57.

Another composition largely worked out in Mendelssohn 15, the first big orchestral piece after the *Eroica*, and exactly contemporaneous with the 1805 version of *Leonore*, is the Triple Concerto for Piano, Violin, Cello, and Orchestra, Op. 56.[6] One of the least performed of all Beethoven's large-scale instrumental works, and probably no one's favorite piece, this concerto figures in Joseph Kerman's list of "certain Cinderellas and ugly ducklings." From Kerman's idol Tovey it calls forth a somewhat limp explanation: "Once or twice in the middle of Beethoven's career we meet with what is usually described as a reversion to an earlier style. . . . certain works make a less powerful and less definite impression on us than others."[7] But Tovey assigns the piece a heuristic function: it is "in some sense a study" (in what sense he does not say) for the greater concertos to come. Certain features of this composition, such as its less than dazzling piano part, according to an explanation current since Schindler's biography made it so result from its having been composed expressly for the sixteen-year-old Archduke Rudolph—who just about this time became Beethoven's piano pupil—and the string players Seidler and Kraft. At what he (apparently wrongly) took to be its first public performance at an Augarten concert in the spring of 1808, the unnamed players, Schindler suggests further, did not think much of the piece: it was badly received because they took it "too casually."[8] And in his laconic section on the Triple Concerto, the always partisan Czerny manages to come up with only a few indifferent words of praise: "grand," "tranquil," "harmonious," "lively."[9]

The composition does seem vulnerable to criticism. There is at least some justice in thinking the first movement prolix and the last awkward—and the Largo perhaps overly high minded for both its length and the company it keeps. But it is too simple to attribute any prolixity in the opening movement, as some do, to the longueurs mechanically brought about by the three solo instruments, each demanding a fair share of attention. The movement is long, all right (531 measures of allegro, common time), and Beethoven seems to have been at some pains to give each solo part its due. But the first movements of both the "Emperor" Concerto and the Violin Concerto, with their single soloists, are longer, and few would think them prolix. Any flagging of the listener's interest in this movement likely has more to do with a certain indistinctness of expression, and a kind of sponginess of construction that tends to neutralize rather than heighten expectation.

The disposition of thematic matter in this movement is superficially much more like Mozart's concertos than Beethoven's earlier ones. Three themes ("a," "b," and "c") appear in the first tutti, and two more new ones ("d" and "e") in the first solo (see Example 8-1 and Table 8-1). The "d" idea (m. 114), moreover, has two detachable endings, the second of which (m. 130) accomplishes the initial modulation to the second principal key, and later proves valuable, as we shall see, in other contexts as well. Deiters with some justification complained that these themes—unlike those Mozart usually gives us in a similar context—"are too much alike, and all suffer from a certain lameness and shortness of breath."[10] None of them has a very sharply etched character of its own; none seizes our attention as forceful or assertive, and none is notably lyrical. Of these five (one might arguably also recognize the endings of "d" as independent thematic events), all have very prominent dotted rhythms that foster an impression of interchangability. As a result, significant events in the movement, or those which the context makes out to be significant, come off with a certain air of randomness. Hard pressed to tell whether or where we have heard just *this* music before, we are deprived of those feelings of either grateful recognition or welcome surprise that often attend such points of arrival.

Such indeterminacy of thematic matter might remind us of the radical experiment Beethoven had just finished in the exposition of the first movement of the *Eroica*, where the themes (if we may even call them that) also lack firm identities. But the cases are very different. In the *Eroica* exposition Beethoven presents an initially bewildering succession of the-

TABLE 8-1 OP. 56, I

	29				33	44	52
T₁							
a					b	~~	c
I	~				(V) I		I

	77		114	121	130	157	170	182
S₁								
a			d	ending1	ending2	b	~~	e
I				~~~~~VI				vi

	225	243
T₂		**S₂**
d	x	a
IV~vi	VI	♭VII

	325	342	359	368	395	407	419
T₃	**S₃**						
a		d,end.1	end.2	b	~~	e
I		~~~IV	~V/I	I		i

	462	470		492	506	512
T₄	**S**					
d	c	c ext.				(a)
♭VI	~~I			~~IV	~~IV	I

matic fragments (as many as ten or eleven, depending on how one counts); while their beginnings may be decisive, their endings are not; the boundaries between them are accordingly indistinct, and they vary widely in character.[11] In the Triple Concerto the themes are fully formed and intelligible in themselves, one of them (b) even having a symmetrical eight-measure antecedent-consequent construction. What they lack is expressive distinctiveness, vividness, and, above all, contrast. Nor do the melodic similarities here resemble the compact thematic construction of a piece like the first movement of the C-minor Concerto, where the whole fabric of the movement is woven from the two featured themes.

This seems a different sort of experiment, one defined by a set of concerns and constraints peculiar to the piece and quite different from those attending the first movement of either the *Eroica* or Op. 37. At the heart of Beethoven's plan, it seems, was the simple fact of his three-member solo group. His most general scheme for managing this piano-trio ensemble was apparently something like this: the instruments shall enter singly, in turn, in roughly imitative fashion, and (for some reason) the cello goes first. And the sort of imitation Beethoven prescribed for himself with some consistency follows the old fugal alternation of entries on first and fifth (or sometimes fourth) degrees.

These constraints leave recognizable traces in the very shapes of the themes. The first one, "a," in accord with the rule that the cello—or cellos in the tuttis—go first, is plainly a bass theme; in fact, it turns into a standard bass line when the melodic function passes, as it had in the opening measures of the *Eroica*, to an upper voice.[12] Simultaneously, the music trails off to the dominant for easy imitation at the fifth when the occasion demands, as it presently will, in the first solo section. Similarly, "b" moves to the subdominant because the imitation in S_1 will be at the fourth. But in "a" and "b" and elsewhere there is a textural sleight of hand at work: the imitation in the violin behaves very much like a simple continuation of the melody, a consequent phrase that just happens to be played by a different instrument. And the nearly invariable sequel, played by the piano back in the tonic, sounds like a normal repetition in ordinary Classical phrase structure. This is only seeming polyphony, fashioned explicitly for the task at hand, namely, for the systematic presentation of melodies by three soloistic instruments. And Beethoven has it both ways: such constructs conjure up the Baroque fugue while at the same time holding to familiar "Classical" phraseology.

Such an easy exchange of tonic and dominant becomes a kind of working idea in this movement, one we find replicated on a somewhat larger scale. In the opening tutti Beethoven faced his—and most particularly

Tovey's—old problem of tonal organization: should this section be a solid pillar of unassailable tonic, or may it be drawn into the tonal argument of the movement? Here there are clear echoes of that tonic-dominant ambiguity that was broached right at the start in the first theme. We first hear "b" (Example 8-1b) precariously poised on the dominant; not enough has been done to establish the dominant key as such, but enough so that we at least provisionally accept the placement of this theme there. But when for its repetition "b" slides back down to the tonic (m. 41), that sounds all right, too. Beethoven has struck a delicate balance that epitomizes the idea of the "bifocal close": the music hovers between dominant and tonic, and the ear accepts it as either.

This idea is again much in evidence at the close of the first tutti. The motive "c," introduced in m. 52, though set in its entirety over a dominant pedal, is solidly in the tonic C major. But in what follows (Example 8-2) we hear nothing but G major and *its* dominant; these two sonorities, relentlessly repeated, are enough to weaken greatly the C-major tonic, but are in themselves powerless to establish G as a new tonic. Beethoven then encourages this feeling of ambivalence as the texture dissolves to a unison line, inviting the listener to provide a mental harmonization; its first half points straight at G, but the second carries on resolutely down to C, where the first solo can now begin. This exercise in ambiguity is a far cry from the tonal audacities in first tuttis of the earlier concertos, especially Opp. 15 and 19. It is subtle, suggestive rather than disturbing; here Beethoven seems safely back in the Mozartean fold.

This delicate balancing act between tonic and dominant is a relatively local occupation, in the long run not very consequential for the shape of the movement. Like the first movement of the "Waldstein" Sonata and the *Leonore* Overture No. 2—its companions in the *Leonore* Sketchbook— this movement is constructed on a large-scale thirds relation, in this case between C major and A major/minor. The second ending of "d" in the first solo moves resolutely to that A, where we get both old ("b") and new ("e") material, the first in major and the second in minor. This new tonal terrain will be much belabored in the second solo section, where, in a curiously old-fashioned gesture, Beethoven simply transposes "a" from the first solo—a kind of "Mannheim crescendo" figure—to the new key, much as some of Haydn's early symphonies bring back the first theme in the dominant at the beginning of the development section (see Table 8-1, above).

But Beethoven quite undermines the solidity of A as the secondary tonality, and indeed any overall polarity between it and the principal key, with what can only be understood as a musical joke (which he tells us twice, so that there will be no misunderstanding). At the ending of S_1

(from m. 211) we get the familiar build up to the big cadence of the section in the new key. At the corresponding point in the first movements of Mozart's concertos (and in Beethoven's Op. 19), such a dominant preparation in the secondary key culminates in the formulaic trilled dominant-tonic ending; this is utterly expected, a frank cliché, but for that very reason an unmistakable position marker and a maker of form. But here, after the uncommonly protracted "solo exposition," the preparation for the close is suspiciously overdone, proceeding from a coy *pianissimo* dwelling upon V/V to a protracted series of upward rushing scales crowned by a huge crescendo with trills in all the solo instruments (a triple trill, finally, in the piano). All this feverish anticipatory activity is then deflated in a stroke by a deceptive cadence (V–♭VI in A) that launches the second tutti in the unlikely key of F major (Example 8-3).

Beethoven repeats this maneuver at the end of S₃, another spot where one expects to hear the comfortably hackneyed old close. This cadence (corresponding to the end of the recapitulation) was to have left us four-square in the tonic; instead we land in A♭ major (♭VI in C major). In both cases the music quickly gets back on track, so that neither of these wayward gestures has lasting consequences. They give listeners a momentary jolt (even those without absolute pitch or a score) and raise confusion as to just where we are situated in the movement. Beethoven had already discarded the old place-marking trilled cadence in Op. 37; this revisit, overdone as it is and capsized by a deceptive resolution, has about it more than a hint of burlesque. It holds up for critical scrutiny not only the formulaic cadence itself, but the very idea of tonal polarities in this movement. The two strongest form-making moments, the culmination of music in the contrasting key and then of the tonic recapitulation, seem, if not trivialized, at least compromised. It is as if for Beethoven the time had passed when he could simply reuse the old cadential formula; he serves it up, instead, with a vigorous twist of irony—one with certain questionable formal consequences—instead of offering anything substantive in its place. If, as Schindler reports, early public performers of the concerto failed to take it seriously, amusement or perplexity at these unserious endings probably played a role.

So here, at m. 462, we have the fourth tutti. In the ordinary parlance of concerto first movements, a swift ending should follow: an orchestral statement of familiar motives, a declamatory pause in mid-cadence for the soloist's cadenza—really only an elaborated conclusion of that cadence—and some final exclamations from the orchestra. In his C-minor Piano Concerto, as we have seen, Beethoven followed Mozart's innovation in *his* C-minor concerto by bringing the soloist back after the cadenza to join in for a coda. But this point in the Triple Concerto offers special problems. All the soloists, presumably, would need to take part in a cadenza, thus seriously undermining any illusion of improvisation (for his Symphonie Concertante K. 364, Mozart had frankly supplied a cadenza à 2). And Beethoven has just steered his movement, via the huge deceptive cadence, to the unlikely key of A♭, thereby precluding a summary close of any kind. He instead writes a fairly extended final section in which all the solo instruments participate. It regains the tonic key, offers great plagal gestures of departure (together with a concluding *stretta*), and makes no reference whatever to the matter of the cadenza.

As we would expect in any extended work from Beethoven's most productive years, this movement has beautiful and memorable passages. One such is the "purple patch" (as Tovey calls such things) in theme "b" that suddenly turns for an introspective moment far to the flat side (mm. 44ff. and 407ff.)—and then, as if caught uncomfortably in a reverie, just as quickly rights itself. A concluding gesture in m. 506, neatly imitative, leaning on F in a protracted plagal motion while delicately rubbing the leading tone B♮ against the B♭ of the F scale, is another. And the opening of S_1, on the surface only a kind of solo version of the "Mannheim crescendo" from the orchestral opening, cleverly starts its three participating instruments on a single pitch from which two diverge by suspensions while the third holds on as an acrid "upper pedal" until that pitch again fits the harmony (see Example 8-4). But there are, in all, four occurrences of the "Mannheim" opening or its imitation, the last such (m. 337) coming within the third tutti just after a grand statement of that very theme by full orchestra; a good enough idea at first, the device in the end palls. This movement is middle-period Beethoven, all right, and easily recognizable as such. But it has about it a curious out-of-focus quality, as if its ideas never quite manage to come clear. If Jove nodded, the explanation may be not mere somnolence, but that his attention lay elsewhere—that is, in his current struggles with *Leonore*.

THE LARGO-RONDO

As in his other C-major concerto, Op. 15, Beethoven drops far in the subdominant direction to A♭ for the slow movement. The opening sounds, darkly luminous in the low range of the orchestral strings, fall into one of the composer's habitual patterns for slow themes: contrary contrapuntal motion between treble and bass passes from tonic to a solemn questioning stop on an inverted dominant, this time enfolding another inverted dom-

Plate 1. Beethoven in 1802. Miniature
on ivory by Christian Horneman.
*(By permission of Beethoven-Haus,
Bonn. Collection H. C. Bodmer)*

Plate 2. Bonn, the Electoral Palace (now the principal building of the university), where the Beethovens—grandfather, father, and the composer—performed their duties.
(*By permission of Beethoven-Haus, Bonn*)

OPPOSITE. *Plate 3.* Vienna, der Kohlmarkt, a street just to the north of the palace complex. On the right is the shop of Artaria & Company, publishers of Beethoven's early works from 1793–97.
(*From Wien in alten Ansichten: Das Werden der Wiener Vedute, by Alfred May. Salzburg, Residenz-Verlag, 1965. Courtesy Arts of the Book Collection, Yale University*)

Plate 4. The village of Heiligenstadt, north of Vienna, where Beethoven underwent the psychological crisis that produced the "Heiligenstadt Testament." (*Historisches Museum der Stadt Wien*)

Plate 5. The Theater an der Wien, Vienna, where the opera *Leonore* was first performed in 1805. The Third Piano Concerto was premiered here in 1803, the Violin Concerto in 1806, and the Fifth and Sixth Symphonies in 1808. (*Historisches Museum der Stadt Wien*)

Plate 6. The Érard piano, now in the Kunsthistorisches Museum, Vienna, presented to Beethoven by the Parisian piano builder Sebastian Érard in 1803. Its upper range extends to c′′′′. (*Oberösterreichisches Landesmuseum, Linz, Austria*)

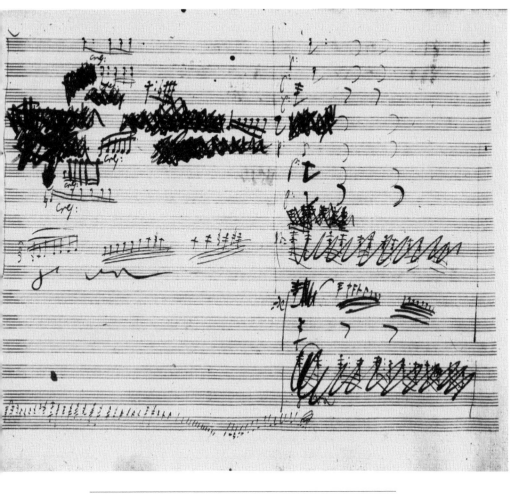

Plate 7. From the autograph of the Third Piano Concerto,
second movement, mm. 76–77, showing the three
main stages of composition.
(*Staatsbibliothek zu Berlin, Beethoven Aut. 14, fol. 72v*)

Plate 8. The concert hall in the Augarten, Vienna, where
various of Beethoven's compositions were performed;
one was the "Kreutzer" Sonata, first heard here in 1805,
played by the English violinist George Polgreen
Bridgetower with the composer at the piano.
(*Historisches Museum der Stadt Wien*)

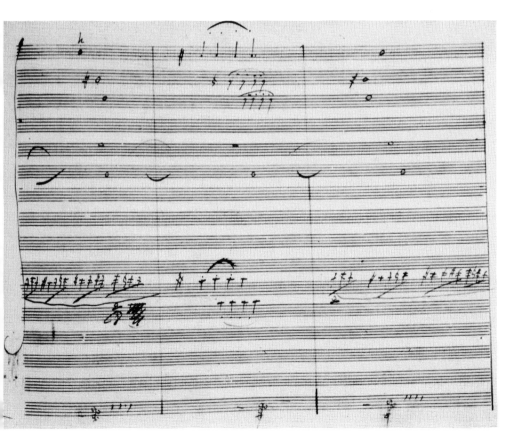

Plate 10. Napoleon's bombardment of Vienna in
May 1809, from a contemporaneous engraving.
(*Historisches Museum der Stadt Wien*)

Plate 11. A leaf from Beethoven's autograph score of the first
movement of the Fifth Piano Concerto, Op. 73. This page shows
mm. 231–36, from the second tutti, where Beethoven has entered
a reduction of the orchestral part into the piano staves
(fifth and sixth staves from the bottom),
together with basso continuo figures.
(*Staatsbibliothek zu Berlin, Beethoven Aut. 15, fol. 33v*)

Plate 12. The music room at the home of Prince Lobkowitz, where many of Beethoven's compositions were performed; the "Eroica" Symphony was first heard here in 1804, and possibly the Fourth Piano Concerto in March 1807. *(Photo by Niebuhr)*

inant—all leading, by reversing over ground already covered, to the real dominant that ends the phrase in m. 4 (see Example 8-5). This melody, a grave and meditative interrogative, is next heard in the solo cello (here always first among equals) an octave higher, sounding newly urgent and tense high up on the A string.[13] These two short utterances turn out to be the initial pair of *Stollen* of a barform that after some cadential extension ends in m. 20. Next comes an exacting ornamented repetition, the melody in close-position thirds in the winds followed by an open-spaced duet in solo violin and cello, all accompanied by the harp-like figuration in the piano (an idiom Beethoven had disapproved in 1796[14] but nonetheless practiced regularly) that becomes something of a trademark of this piece.

This is compelling music, altogether a worthy opening for a middle-period slow movement, and one from which we would surely welcome a full continuation (a modulation to a new key, say, and an eventual recapitulation). But the two statements of the bar form, forty measures, are really all Beethoven gives us. What follows is only a transition to the finale: the Ab tonic in the bass drops easily to G, which becomes a long-held dominant to the movement to come. This transition takes up the slow movement's gravity of tone and raises the stakes. A portentous tremolo in the low strings warns of dire things to come (see Example 8-6). This music borrows its dramatic idiom directly from the *récit obligé* that introduces the desperate Florestan in the dungeon at the beginning of Act 3 of *Leonore*—music Beethoven was just now working out in neighboring pages of Mendelssohn 15.

The consequence of all this turns out to be not dire in the least, but only a jolly *Rondo alla polacca*. The jollity, to be sure, is muted at first as the solo cello and violin play the rondo theme, in turn, sotto voce.[15] It is as if Beethoven is directing attention to the peculiar harmonic shape in which he has cast that theme, whose effect might be marred by any instrumental clamor. First, the music is all bland tonic over a tonic pedal; next, after the barest hint of modulation through the augmented sixth, the violin, in a delicately wistful gesture, plays it on the third degree, again with the appropriate pedal (see Example 8-7). As easy as it was to get to that third degree, it is just as easy to get back; the music then continues with no further harmonic disturbance, forming a broad rounded binary form with a specially elaborate lead-in to the return (mm. 23–33). The whole—with an appended codetta—occupies sixty-one measures. Any *alla polacca* elements in this music seem at first rather distant (just what the term implied at the time is in any case not perfectly clear). The second measure vaguely emphasizes the second beat, a stressed point in the old polonaise, by duration and by approach with a melodic leap.[16] But it is only in the final *fortissimo* statement with full orchestra (mm. 37ff.) that Beethoven actually writes this accent into the score and allows us to hear his rondo theme in all its raw vigor and presumed folkloric color.

After m. 61 the movement carries on, from a formal point of view, much as we would expect. The soloists, starting as usual with the cellist, embark on running imitative passages that lead to the dominant and a second subject. Then more running passages in the solo instruments round out this section brilliantly and bend it back to the tonic for a full statement of the ritornello. Next comes the episode, in A minor, a shortened ritornello, the second theme back in the tonic key, and a combined fourth ritornello and coda (Table 8-2 shows the movement's formal plan). In the sonata-like aspects of this movement, Beethoven has exactly reversed the procedure of the first movement—and each of these ventures is in its own way effective. In the first movement local play with surface ambiguities of tonic and dominant was embedded in a large-scale construct founded on a thirds relation; here a thirds relation colors the opening music, while the movement as a whole—exclusive of the episode—is founded on the familiar tonic-dominant polarity. But the endings of the two movements seem governed by a single idea: the final tutti (or ritornello) does double duty as a coda. In the finale Beethoven opens this last ritornello in duple meter and a presumably faster tempo, allegro (the movement is originally marked only *Rondo alla polacca* with no mention of tempo). Here the rondo theme is transformed into a rushing variation of itself in even sixteenths, complete with the deflection to E major. Presently, the original meter and tempo are restored, and an emphatic (and distinctly *alla polacca*) treatment of the rondo theme merges into the sort of leave-taking cadences on tonic and dominant that grace the exit of many a Mozart aria.

In 1812 Beethoven wrote to the Archduke Rudolph (intent on implicating him, seemingly, in the composer's preferences), "in our finales we like to have great roaring passages (*rauschendere Passagen*).[17] The finale of the Triple Concerto has such passages in abundance, and it was probably with this movement still ringing in his ears that the correspondent for the *Allgemeine Musikalische Zeitung*, reviewing the first Viennese performance, arrived at this hyperbole: "It consists almost entirely of passages, about equally divided among the [solo] instruments, that in time grow tiring for listener and player alike."[18] Such passages accord with an exuberant—not to say raucous—tone to this movement, in keeping, more or less, with the ideas both of *rondo* and *alla polacca*. If the rondo theme itself, always the main setter of mood and character in such a finale, inclines toward the boisterous, the second subject in G major (mm. 76ff.)

does so more pointedly. The episode with its sharp polonaise rhythms and short-breathed schematic alternations of A minor, C major, and E minor—recalling the thirds relation of the rondo theme—has about it aspects of a cavalry charge; this, however, is quickly mitigated by a second strain to which Tovey aptly attributes a "note of reproachful pathos"[19] (see Examples 8-8a and b). In this latter passage special qualities of Beethoven's genius have a local redeeming effect in a movement and a concerto that we may well think not up to his usual standard.

This composition of 1804 can hardly be seen as a natural extension of Beethoven's cultivation of the concerto. It was, for one thing, the first mature concerto-like work of his that was quite detached from his own career as a virtuoso pianist: there is no record that he ever played the piece. Whatever credence we wish to grant Schindler's explanation that it was written for the Archduke and his collaborators, any proper understanding of this work must also take into account its generic affiliations. Though use of a piano trio for a solo group was apparently unique at the time,[20] a concerto-like piece with multiple soloists would hardly have seemed an anomaly to Beethoven's European contemporaries. For there was a great proliferation of such works published and played during the decades before and after 1800. Barry Brook showed that such pieces were seen as a distinct genre; although known by various names, their central designation was *symphonie concertante*, and their origins in (and continuing ties with) Parisian musical practice were widely understood.[21] One of the things understood about the *symphonie concertante* was that it was a "happy" genre with a distinctly popular tilt; virtually none were in minor keys, and more often than not they were in only two movements. Op. 56 seems to accord well with the genre: its extroverted expression, rushing motion, that jolly *alla polacca* finale, and its singular lack of a genuine middle movement all point in this direction.

An abbreviated name for the *symphonie concertante*, one seemingly confined to non-French composers, was the adjectival *concertante*.[22] In this connection we will recall that Beethoven's brother Carl prematurely offered Op. 56 to Breitkopf & Härtel in October 1803, calling it a "Konzertant für alle Instrumente für Klavier, Violonzello [*sic*] und Violin," and that when the composer himself (more realistically) offered it again in August 1804, it was similarly a "Konzertant für Violin, Violoncelle und Pianoforte mit dem ganzen Orchester."[23] Thoughts of a composition embodying the idea of *Konzertant* had been at least at the back of Beethoven's mind for some time. There was of course his unfinished *concertante*—so called by the composer himself in the Kessler Sketchbook—

seemingly for the same ensemble, and probably intended for the abortive concert of spring 1802.²⁴

There may be a simple explanation for Beethoven's forays into this kind of composition. Beginning shortly after 1800 we see in the composer's life a growing preoccupation with things French. There is no need here to go back to Beethoven's purported association with Count Bernadotte, the French ambassador to the Austrian court—for only about two-and-a-half months—in 1798; only Schindler attests to such an association (together with its alleged role in the genesis of the *Eroica*). The very early date and fleeting nature of Bernadotte's visit, as well as the lack of corroboration of Schindler's report, give us even more reason than usual to be skeptical.²⁵ But in a curious passage in Beethoven's letter of January 1801 to Franz Anton Hoffmeister, he mused about a *Magazin der Kunst* to which "the artist would only bring his artworks in order to take what he needed."²⁶ This remark probably reflects, as Maynard Solomon's elegant analysis suggests, the composer's familiarity with recent French utopian-socialist views, in particular, very likely, with those of François Noël Babeuf.²⁷ And despite the composer's deliberate blurring of the *Eroica's* association with Napoleon—and despite Beethoven's vacillating opinion of him—the original programmatic connection of the symphony with the First Consul seems clear enough. When Cherubini's post-Revolutionary operas took Vienna by storm in 1802 and 1803, Beethoven shared the popular enthusiasm of the city (later, in an unguarded moment, even pronouncing Cherubini "the greatest living composer").²⁸ That in 1804 Beethoven abandoned Schikaneder's classical subject *Vestas Feuer* for "an old French libretto" of the "rescue" type was surely not unrelated.

That same letter of 1801 to Hoffmeister includes the first of a series of veiled references—veiled, surely, because of their political implications—to a plan that Beethoven long entertained for a trip (even a move) to Paris. This letter, while offering Hoffmeister the Concerto Op. 19, claims he is holding back his "better" concertos until "I myself have made a trip"—the odd locution alluding, perhaps, to Hoffmeister's own recent removal from Vienna to Leipzig. As to the concertos in question, Beethoven probably had in mind only projected pieces such as the *concertante* he would begin to sketch in the Kessler book the following year and the C-minor concerto, ultimately Op. 37, for which he had made desultory notations since about 1796. The next references to such a trip are in two letters of August and October 1803 from Beethoven's student Ries to Nikolaus Simrock in Bonn: "Beethoven will remain here at the most 1½ years. Then he will go to Paris, which makes me extremely sorry," and

"Beethoven is to receive the libretto [Subjet] for his opera soon. After that he plans to leave; with each passing day my hope justifiably rises that I shall accompany him."[29] Early the following year Beethoven's own letter to Sonnleithner, busy at this time translating and editing *Leonore*, returns to the subject:

> I received yesterday another letter about my journey, and this one has made my decision to travel irrevocable—Hence I most earnestly request that by *the middle of next April* the book, which forms *the poetical part*, will be quite finished, so that I can press on with my work and so that the opera can be produced in June at the latest, when I myself can help to produce it.[30]

And Beethoven's favorable words about Rodolphe Kreutzer, as well as the dedication that same year of his Sonata for Piano and Violin, Op. 47[31] to the Parisian violinist (whose only meeting with Beethoven had occurred years before upon the French musician's visit to Vienna in the entourage of Count Bernadotte) hints at the cultivation of useful contacts in the French capital. Ries's letter of October 1803 mentions another plan of Beethoven's to dedicate the sonata jointly to Kreutzer and Louis Adam, as the "first violinist and pianist of Paris." The composer is in Adam's debt, Ries explains, "because of the Parisian piano"—a reference, no doubt, to the Érard piano Beethoven had received just the previous summer.[32] In a later letter to Simrock (December 11, 1803) Ries even reports that Beethoven wishes to postpone publication of the *Eroica* (whose firm connection with Napoleon Ries maintains in the earlier letter) so as to "reserve it for his trip."[33] Beethoven's "unshakable plans" for a trip were never realized, perhaps partly, at least, because of delays in the production of *Fidelio*—whose first performance then coincided with the French attack on Vienna. But the *concertantes*, one finished and one not, fall neatly into place as a factor in the composer's hopes for a sojourn in Paris; they may well be seen as a commentary on—and perhaps an intended concession to—French taste.

CHAPTER 9

To Sing of Arms and Men: Piano Concerto No. 4 in G, Op. 58

There is in souls a sympathy with sounds;
And, as the mind is pitch'ed the ear is pleas'd
With melting airs, or martial, brisk, or grave:
Some chord in unison with what we hear,
Is touch'd within us, and the heart replies.

SAMUEL COWPER, *The Task*, Bk. 5

What is most arresting about the Fourth Piano Concerto, Beethoven's most captivating work in the genre, is surely that middle movement (given in its entirety in Example 9-1). Its less than five minutes of playing time—significantly less if the players are serious about the *con moto* Beethoven appends to his Andante—describe no expectable formal design but offer us instead a vividly etched dialogue between piano and strings, one that seems to begin in dead earnest discord and distance but in the end achieves at least an uneasy resolution. The strings start off in stentorian tones, in severe octaves, jagged and detached, delivering a proclamation that would seem to brook no opposition. The piano answers with what sounds less like opposition than near irrelevance; lost in its own musings it steps up to its apex, then traces a subdued songful octave-long downward melodic path, heavy with resignation, tonic to tonic, supported by plain chordal harmonies. A note in the first edition instructs the pianist to use the *una corda* pedal continuously for most of the movement, until the trills of m. 55, where it is by degrees disengaged. Understatement enhances the poignancy of this music.

As at other crucial points in the solo part of this concerto (the opening of the first movement is an example), there is a hint here of improvisation, as if the pianist, in nonresponse to the orchestra, is trying out an idea that we imagine could have taken many forms. And like many improvisations, it has something formulaic about it, with its even eight measures neatly bisected by a cadence on the relative major, together with a prominent bass motion downward by fifth before each cadence—this last contributing to that sense of grave inevitability that pervades these two sentences. But the melodic coherence of the piano's nonanswer—and Beethoven's performance direction, *molto cantabile*—also suggests voice and song, arioso in contrast to the disjunct and brittle instrumental gestures in the strings. Yet this instrumental idiom, too, has a familiar ring to it, one distantly linked in musical practice to the idea of arioso; its staccato dotted figures recall the agitated orchestral interjections—always in the strings— in the most dramatic style of eighteenth-century accompanied recitative, what Rousseau called *récit obligé*.[1] Invoked in opera at moments of high gravity or alarm, especially in confrontation with things supernatural, this style, at least for Beethoven's more knowledgeable listeners, would have come with just such ready-made associations.[2]

So this movement joins many others among Beethoven's instrumental works that conjure up the idea of voices and song and dramatic situation, works such as the "Tempest" Sonata (Op. 31, No. 2), the Sonata Op. 110, the middle movement of the "Waldstein" (more tenuously), the introduction to the finale of the String Quartet Op. 132, and (of course most explicitly) the finale of the Ninth Symphony. In the movement before us the "vocal" part of the recitative is at first missing; we have only its agitated string accompaniment, followed by contemplative arioso so unlike in character that it would scarcely have been joined to *that* recitative. We are given the merest sketch, with only the most essential elements intact, of a scene in which implacable demand—or prohibition, or censure—is met with something like grave reflection on a subject of only tenuous pertinence. The strings, so far, have stayed well in the home key of E minor, while stressing the minor sixth degree (C), with a fleeting hint at its use as the seventh of a dominant to the relative major (mm. 3–4) that the following solo will give us explicitly at its midpoint—this being about the only plainly perceptible connection, so far, between the two. When they resume in m. 14, the strings stay in character, confirming their recitative affiliations with the all but clichéd ending of mm. 17–18 (here with a fleeting invocation of the *vocal* component of dramatic recitative), but now offering distinct harmonic motion toward the D major suggested earlier only as a dominant function. The piano too insists on its own character (now *molto espressivo* and explicitly *pianissimo*) but shows signs of accommodation; it accepts that D major and adopts as well something of the harmonic mobility of the orchestral statement, while leading in its insistent way, as it always will, back to the original E minor.

So far, there has been an almost ritual symmetry to these exchanges, each participant allowing the other sufficient time to speak: the orchestra gets five measures each time, the piano, four-plus-four. But now, beginning at m. 28, the piano crowds in on its imperious adversary, cutting it short with an ever more insistent (but still generally *pianissimo*) ascending sequence of plaints, but at the same time bringing itself around to something of the manner of singing recitative for which the orchestra had all along been implying a fierce accompaniment. As the two forces contend, they come to inhabit the same musical universe.[3] Reaching the highest tessitura so far and the dominant of E minor in m. 34, the piano breaks into a more florid version of its familiar falling arioso; the strings, suddenly soft, increasingly acquiesce, and the newly dominant piano rises up once more to new heights for a third lyrical disquisition (m. 47), this one most eloquent and rhetorical of all—an intimation of the aria forecast by all that implied recitative and arioso. Edward Cone has rightly called attention to the interdependence of the second and third of these lyrical statements (or arioso sections) in the piano.[4] But both of these, surely, refer back to the piano's very first utterance in m. 6. All three are essentially falling stepwise melodic lines (each having a prefatory "run-up," or *Anstieg*) with escalating ornamentation and ever higher starting points, all showing certain plain similarities of harmonic scaffolding. These correspondences lend a certain expressive consistency to the piano part at large, as it engages in a gradual rapprochement with the strings (it also suggests a modification of Edward Cone's rather rigid division of the movement into two parts plus coda, in which the piano's first arioso is part of "A," and the second and third ones fall within "B").[5]

Each of these piano segments aims toward a cadential $\frac{6}{4}$ (mm. 12, 38, and 51ff.) that forms an expectant stopping point, an intimation of closure but also a kind of psychological crossroads that invites retrospection and elaboration. In the first two cases resolution comes with little fuss, the first time all the way to tonic, the next time to a half cadence on the dominant. But the third time around (at m. 51) Beethoven turns that sonority into a real way station, a pause for reflection. The strings have been reduced to pizzicato punctuation. The piano, having just finished off a dramatic two-octaves-and-a-third descent, skips back upward for some cadenza-like complication featuring a chromatic descent of diminished sevenths. All this is heard as a prolongation (as the Schenkerians say) of that cadential $^6_4$—the standard signal, after all, for an elaborative cadence (or cadenza)—that finally reaches its expected resolution on the dominant, with the requisite trill, only at m. 55.

Joseph Kerman registers puzzlement over this passage: "It [the piano] swoops down too fast, perhaps, hitting some obstacle that drives it up again as though on a rebound, its harmonies turned anxious and chromatic."[6] The "obstacle," of course, is that stopping place $^6_4$, a harmonic and psychological barrier approached twice before, now expatiated upon as the piano gains ever greater mastery and expansiveness (still, strangely, at that eerie *pianissimo* with the *una corda* pedal engaged). But the expressive momentum gathered in this elaboration seems to foreclose, even now, any summary resolution of that hard-won dominant goal. With the orchestra now silent, the piano abandons the *una corda* by stages—as Beethoven's piano allowed—rises within a single measure of trilled chord members to *fortissimo* on a ninth above the dominant, and is already launched into a newly impassioned cadenza continuation on the dominant itself.[7] The space between chord members is filled with *furioso* chromatic scale anacruses to the lower D♯ answered by jolting semitone appoggituras to the upper A, together with the continuing trill on the C inside—a device that in Beethoven's piano writing had by now broken out of cadenzas into movements proper, famously so in the finale of the "Waldstein." The effect is one of nearly manic surface assaults on a harmonic object that remains immovable, an act of desperation whose futility recalls and validates the *una corda* resignation of the movement as a whole. We may think of *Fidelio* and Georg Friedrich Treitschke's characterization of the second part of Florestan's aria "In des Lebens Frühlingstagen" as "the last blazing up of life before its extinguishment."[8]

The concerto movement's fortissimo is extinguished as it had arisen, by degrees, and the piano wanders into forlorn single-line recitative (reminiscent of the lead-in to the recapitulation of the first movement of the "Tempest" Sonata, Op. 31, No. 2) that at last permits closure of the cadenza with recovery of the low B dominant under a renewed cadential $^6_4$ and resolution with no further protest to $^5_3$ and tonic. The orchestral strings now end their silence in a brief coda to declare near-total acquiescence with the thought and mood of the solo instrument. Taking on the piano's *pianissimo*, they propose in the bass only despondent fragments of their old imperious dotted rhythms (reminding us vaguely of the close of the *Marcia funebre* in the *Eroica*); they push only tentatively toward the subdominant they had twice before proposed (mm. 26–8 and 38–40) and submit easily to the piano's correction (back to dominant-tonic) while giving up their own unison assertiveness and even adopting the piano's peculiar chord spacing (m. 69) and doubled version of that dotted rhythm. The solo instrument then has the final word. And word-like it is, once more implying voice and speech, as the final descending third, in imitation of recitative, is filled in with the intervening lingering passing note.

What are we to make of all this? The sort of musical rhetoric Beethoven gives us seems intimately bound up with situation, character, speech. And there can be no doubt about elements of implied human drama here: a protagonist and antagonist, a relationship between the two that changes over time from implacable opposition—even their very worlds of discourse seem at first opposed—to some agreement, reconciliation, maybe sympathy. In his intriguing essay of 1985 Owen Jander argues intricately for this movement as "Beethoven's most elaborate venture into the realm of program music. . . . It may well be the most totally programmatic piece of music—great art music—ever composed."[9] The program he detects here—despite a total absence of commentary on the matter by Beethoven or his contemporaries—is the story of Orpheus's confrontation with the shades in Hades. The force of the mythic singer's music gradually persuades his adversaries to grant him entrance and to permit an attempt to retrieve his beloved Euridice from that infernal place. (Though, as we know, like Lot's wife in the Genesis narrative, Orpheus violates the stipulation that he shall not look back, bringing on ultimate catastrophe.) Sources of the story upon which Beethoven seems to have drawn, Jander points out, range from Gluck's *Orfeo ed Euridice* and operas on that theme by Johann Gottlieb Naumann and Friedrich August Kanne back to Virgil's *Georgics* and Ovid's *Metamorphoses*.

Jander mentions several previous sightings of a link between the concerto movement and the exploits of Orpheus, the earliest appearing in the 1859 monograph on Beethoven of Adolph Bernhard Marx, whom Jander credits with the "discovery" of this connection.[10] A bit earlier, as he also mentions, Czerny had encouraged a more nebulous programmatic association: "In this movement . . . one cannot help thinking of an antique tragic scene, and the player must feel with what intense, pathetic expression this solo is performed, in order to contrast with the powerful and austere orchestral passages, which are, as it were, gradually withdrawn."[11] Later Tovey atypically muddied the waters by attributing to Liszt a comparison of this movement to *another* episode in Orpheus's adventures, his taming of the wild beasts with the music of his lyre. (Although Liszt composed the symphonic poem *Orpheus* with an appended prose introduction, and an essay on Gluck's *Orfeo ed Euridice* appeared under his name, he is not known to have associated either Orphic story with Beethoven's concerto.) Tovey declared himself sympathetic to "Liszt's" idea about the wild beasts and endorsed as well an association of the opening of the Andante con moto with the initial confrontation of Orpheus and the furies in Gluck's opera.[12] And it is just this latter connection that E. M. Forster said "slipped into my mind to the detriment of the actual musical sounds"—this was in 1936, the year Tovey's essay was published and some sixty years after Marx made the notion public.[13] So we can see among writers on Beethoven, beginning in the mid-nineteenth century, a rather persistent (if shadowy and at times confused) tradition of Orphic associations with this middle movement of the Fourth Concerto.

But what, exactly, is being asserted when various people see "connections," "associations," and "links" between the Orpheus stories and the concerto movement? Sometimes the claim, it seems, comes only to this: that thinking about Orpheus and the Furies may further an appreciation of the expressive import of Beethoven's music (though Forster said it impeded another kind of understanding), whether or not any such specific connection ever existed in the minds of the composer or of his early nineteenth-century listeners. Perhaps this is only a friendly suggestion to listeners in search of images or associations that they might find useful in comprehending or defining the experience of this music. Recognition of an underlying kinship among seemingly diverse ideas and acts of the imagination might find ready acceptance in the wake of certain strains of structuralist anthropology and literary theory. There is the Levi-Straussian notion of a kind of collective unconscious that routinely produces ever-recurring patterns of thought quite apart from the conscious control of individuals, and structuralist critics in the tradition of Vladimir Propp find in myth and narrative an unending repetition of a relatively small repertory of elements. Ovid and Beethoven, according to such theories, might both be unwitting transmitters of such common archetypes or patterns of thought.

But recognition of some such commonality of theme, situation, and character in diverse contexts was an article of faith in musical thought long before Durkheim, Levi-Strauss, or Propp. Musicians from at least the seventeenth century trusted in a recognizable kinship among situations or affects that recur in poetry, drama, and music. Baroque theorists described a fairly standard repertory of affects or passions common to dramatic situations and rhetorical and musical utterances. In a later variant of this general idea, Schumann espoused a Romantic belief that scenes, poems, and music could be intricately and mysteriously united by a commonality of "states of the soul" (*Seelenzustände* or *Stimmungen*); programs for musical compositions or invocation of poetic "counterparts" for them are fitting and effective, insofar as they bring to light correspondences of such "states of the soul," thereby clarifying and enriching the expressive message of the music.[14]

Marx's discussion of the Andante con moto of Beethoven's concerto is very much in this latter vein.[15] Here we are, he says, in the midst of a dramatic scene: the "brazen," "pitiless" chorus of strings united in resistance to the "shy, weak, gently imploring" voice of the piano. Presently, "the song of the piano, in the face of the orchestra's harsh refusal, grows more imploring and ardent; words in flight from the two sides press upon one another, and the rigid determination of the orchestra, at first seemingly so unbending, softens before this show of gentle courage." (So far, the dramatis personae are exactly what we hear and see: the piano and the orchestral strings.) Next, clearly signaled with the inconspicuous but crucial word *wie*, comes an analogy, a simile: "just as once in Gluck's Orpheus the No! of the Eumenides melted before the entreaties of song and love." Marx congratulates himself a bit on the aptness of his analogy:

Hardly could two poems in their basic nature show a closer kinship than this chorus of Gluck's and the Beethoven andante. The contrast between a single person, unarmed, without power except for the depth of his feeling . . . against the assembled force of an obstructing . . . chorus: this is the content of the one as well as of the other musical poem.

But then he hastens to qualify his analogy by pointing out ways in which the expressive import of the two compositions diverge:

But if one penetrates more deeply, the unlikeness of the two emerges. In Gluck the chorus of the Eumenides is more melancholy, filled with sorrow, as it were, about itself and its bitter duty; in Beethoven the chorus appears more energetic, with a more pronounced, Nordic strength—and yet more human, exactly because it has none of the marble-like chill and statuesque repose of the Hellenic form such as it also assumes in Gluck, but partakes rather of flesh and blood. Orpheus, the singer and lover, could hardly avoid a certain softness and sweetness, while the piano by its very nature has about it a kind of idealism, and in Beethoven's hands dedicates itself in ideal purity to the expression of the noblest, most ardent entreaty.

In making these distinctions, Marx revives certain familiar notions of intellectual history by now rather long in the tooth. The cool Hellenic, statuesque quality of Gluck's chorus and the sensuousness of his hero are opposed to the strength and idealism in Beethoven's piano part and a "Nordic" energy in his orchestra. This is another invocation of the old Classical-Romantic, southern-northern distinctions formulated around the beginning of the century (and reformulated in the *Aesthetic Lectures* of Hegel, Marx's colleague at the Berlin University). But the point here is the opposition itself: for Marx Beethoven's concerto movement and Gluck's operatic scene, whatever their surface similarities, also have marked differences in character and expressive import. Nor does he for a moment suggest either that Beethoven had Gluck's chorus in mind while composing his Andante, or that recourse to the opera is necessary for understanding the concerto.

During his long career as a music critic, Marx developed the notion of an underlying *Idee* inherent in all great compositions (which for him meant increasingly the large-scale works of Beethoven). While this *Idee* could involve individual personalities and events (the hero Napoleon in the *Eroica*, the life and death of Beethoven himself in the Piano Sonata Op. 111), it was typically something rather more abstract than a particular scenic depiction or specific narrative.[16] And Marx certainly does not present Gluck's Orpheus scene as the *Idee* of Beethoven's Andante but offers it rather in the spirit in which Schumann compared the Allegretto of the Seventh Symphony to a rustic wedding ceremony or, on another occasion, suddenly discovered a poetic correspondence between the story of Hero and Leander and his own piano piece *In der Nacht* from the *Fantasie-stücke*.[17] Each of the two writers subscribes to a version of the transcendental vision of musical expression descended from E. T. A. Hoffmann: the best of musical expression inhabits a realm removed from that of our everyday thoughts and feelings; it eludes the ordinary operations of rational discussion, prompting recourse to imaginative modes of discourse, to flights of poetic fancy, to analogies with the expressive effects of other great works of art and literature.

But this apparently is not at all what Jander has in mind. Taking a much more radical stance than his nineteenth-century predecessors, he proposes that what Marx made was not an analogy but a discovery: he discovered the "truth" that Beethoven, in composing this movement, consciously set about to create a detailed and specific musical counterpart to the story of Orpheus and the Furies, and that "to analyze this work without the program misses the point of the form."[18] He "reassembles" Beethoven's putative poetic model from a number of sources: Gluck's opera, operas on the same subject by Naumann and (most prominently) Beethoven's acquaintance Kanne, and the versions of the myth in Ovid and Virgil. Jander does this with skill and ingenuity. Most provocative are the data he musters to show that the composer would likely have been acquainted with the sources named (Ovid's *Metamorphoses* had recently been printed several times in Vienna after decades of Jesuit prohibition; Kanne's opera was being prepared for performance at the Burgtheater shortly after the premiere of Beethoven's concerto; both composers at the time had as their patron Prince Lobkowitz, who was a subscriber to the initial Viennese printing of Ovid, and the like).

But questions leap to mind. If knowing about this Orphic connection is essential to understanding the piece, was Beethoven unaware of this requirement (despite having consciously constructed the movement in accord with that story)? For he left no hint that we know of about any such program. Nor was it that he was particularly reticent at the time about specifying extramusical associations for his compositions. In the case of the *Eroica* shortly before this, he had composed the symphony "on Bonaparte" but then upon reflection (and perhaps out of political prudence) expanded this extramusical reference into the general idea of "the heroic" (its *marcia funebre* would in any case have been easily understood as a ceremony for a hero's death). And just prior to that, he was a bit more specific about another funeral march, the one in the Piano Sonata Op. 26, designated *sulla morte d'un eroe*. The first public performance of the Fourth Concerto at Beethoven's concert of 1808 also saw the premiere of the Pastoral Symphony with its programmatic titles, and, perhaps more significantly, of the Choral Fantasy, which urges an explicit comparison of music in its "absolute" state with the same music equipped with words and ideas; it doubles back to present with voices and text what was previously played by instruments alone—in anticipation, as Beethoven himself noted in 1824, of the finale of the Ninth Symphony.[19] If Beethoven had wanted us to think of Orpheus and any of his exploits while listening to the Andante of this concerto, he probably would not have hesitated to let us know about it.

And many may be troubled by individual incongruities that arise along the course of the two "narratives" as Jander presents them. In all of the operas, and in Ovid, for instance, Orpheus speaks first (in the *Metamorphoses* to the point of downright garrulity, after which the spirits instantly relent), [20] and the Furies initially have very little to say (only a repeated interjection of "No!" in Gluck); the utterances of Beethoven's "shades" begin the movement and, especially at first, wax rather expansive about it. And Jander's strong implication that the initial question of the Furies in Kanne's tetrameters is a metrical fit with Beethoven's opening[21] must be discounted—it requires matching the single-syllable contraction *na'hn* with four staccato notes. A claim that the intense music of mm. 56–59, with its two short segments followed by a longer one, illustrates a line Beethoven took directly from Virgil ("And three times a crash was heard in the swamps of Avernis") should probably take into account that such a deployment of phrases is commonplace in the style. Kerman is certain that the sudden crisis-like flaring up of the piano in this section "can have nothing to do with Orpheus regaining and then losing Eurydice, as Owen Jander believes," but arises in response to the conflict (the "agon," as he calls it) already in progress.[22] That the "program," even those parts of it that Jander sees as "incontrovertible," needs to be drawn from so many different sources, moreover, saps one's confidence in the enterprise.[23]

Nonetheless, a comparison with the Orphic scene (I mean here a comparison in Schumann's sense as a guide to thought and feeling) is in its general outlines provocative, and one would be hard pressed to think of another literary counterpart as appropriate. We might wish to reflect on the initial conflict and ultimate reconciliation of King Lear and his youngest daughter, Cordelia, together with the stormy events—battle and death, Lear raging on the heath—that intervene. Or, turning to themes with which Beethoven had a direct association, one might think of Egmont, resigned but impassioned before his judges, or of Christ facing his. (The oratorio *Christus am Oelberg* had been premiered in 1803, and the incidental music to Egmont was to follow in 1809–10.) Then there is a brief review in the *Allgemeine musikalische Zeitung* of March 1820 of something called "To Psyche: a Melodramatic Essay after the Andante of Beethoven's Concerto, Op. 58" by one J. H. Clasing.[24] The reviewer tells us that the text is "spoken rhythmically to the music" instead of alternating with it (as is normal in the melodrama). We are also offered the enigmatic hint that the supplied poem is "a kind of imitation, with an altered orientation, of Goethe's *Kennst du das Land.*" But which installment of the Psyche story is presented here one can only guess. Is it perhaps the part in which she wanders the earth in search of Cupid, who remains in a distant land? The truth is that we cannot have any clear idea about scenes or events Beethoven may have had in mind when he composed this movement; he did not tell us, and the music cannot. But we do know that in this riveting dialogue he decided to leave any dramatis personae unnamed, and what they said and did unspecified. He thus kept our imaginations unfettered, free to make our own constructs, or to ponder, perhaps, a more general idea of human conflict and concord within a genre of musical expression for which such matters stand at the very center.

THE ALLEGRO MODERATO:
ASCENDANCY BY PERSUASION

The concerto begins with the solo instrument; this simple fact has been much noted—together with the ritual naming of its nearest known precedent in Mozart's Concerto in E♭, K. 271. And such a reversal of roles is to be sure startling; it calls attention at the outset to issues about the individual and the group that will be raised to a higher power in the second movement, and it suggests from the first a particular musical persona for the soloist. The simple fact that the first musical statement is given out by the piano is less remarkable, surely, than the nature of that statement (Example 9-2).[25] The soloist starts with a distinctive eight-fingered tonic chord in radically "close" position (skipping no notes), an instant announcement of that new piano sound of the nineteenth century, a saturated, intensely colored sonority in a middle register.[26] The initial sound, now thinned, resonates by even repetitions throughout the first measure; nothing is added but this throbbing effect that only preserves and focuses it. Then on the second eighth of m. 2 comes the first harmonic event of the piece, a gesture that forms the very kernel of this theme and a kind of emblem of the movement, a melodic motion, 3–2, supported by I–V. An everyday figure it is, a simple, quiet, questioning move from tonic to dominant. But here it is transformed by the soprano-tenor doubling—recalling the saturation doubling of the first chord—a motion that explicitly sacrifices voice leading orthodoxy to that resonant sonority. The kernel reappears at the end of the piano's five-measure opening, as if to say that, despite any intervening events, this single interrogative motion, devoid of closure, is the central force of that first utterance. What intervenes is an upward melodic struggle, marked by a slowing and destabilizing of rhythmic motion, first to the strongly accented fourth degree of m. 3, and then in the next measure, surprisingly, up one more step, to the fifth, D. But even amid this short burst of energy the priority of the dominant ending—the uncertain query—is supported by the close of the first of the statement's two (unequal) segments on a root-position dominant in m. 4. The soloist persona comes across as a calm inquirer, this calm born not of perfect serenity, the music hints, but of strong affect that is for now under control.

The strings then enter with much the same music, matching the soloist's *piano, dolce* with an orchestral pianissimo. But the initial thirds-shift from G major to a B-major sonority is crucial, sowing doubt as to the syntactical function of this music. Are we hearing the second of a matching pair of phrases (the metrical irregularity of the piano's five-measure opening discourages such a reading), or is this in the nature of a continuation, the sort of thing that carries on *after* the theme? The latter seems confirmed when, in m. 8, the strings fall into a common sequence (descending fifths with alternating first inversions), borrowing the amphibrachic rhythm of m. 3. But this harmonic mobility, it quickly becomes clear, serves only to lead from the local B major in the flat direction back toward home, overshooting G by one degree, and landing on its subdominant, C. Marking this point with a dramatic upward melodic leap of a sixth, Beethoven breaks out of the sequence with a clear reference to—actually an expansion of—the ending the piano statement. The strings overreach the piano's high points of C and D by one step, with E, and proceed with a descent back to A. Once there, however, they avert the tonic-dominant "query" with a willful reinterpretation: the dominant is replaced by a first-inversion II chord (an echo, surely, of m. 3) that leads to conventional closure on the tonic. Two things in particular have happened here. Recovery of the piano statement's tonality with a parallel of its ending now allows the ear to accept the two opening utterances as a pair of phrases, the string response simply having been expanded by the sequence in the middle and the cadence at the end. But at the same time the orchestra pushes the discourse beyond where it had yet gone: it poses a quick resolution (too easy an answer, we might think) to the piano's question.

In what follows, the inquiring tonic-dominant motion continues to hang heavy in the air. The orchestra, with gradually growing participation of the winds, launches into what sounds like a true "continuation" (a signal of this is a steady new busyness in the second violins). First Beethoven boldly puts a version of his opening theme into imitative counterpoint (soprano and bass) that by any ordinary standards simply does not work: it produces a series of acrid dissonances of which none conforms to the prevailing rules of part writing (Example 9-3).[27] What counts is not the infraction of the formal standards of counterpoint, but a distinctly unsettling effect, like a storing up of irritants that comes to require broad resolution. And recompense is immediately at hand in the magnificent ascending crescendo that follows (beginning in m. 19). A faultlessly consonant version of those same first-theme materials, this passage mounts to a climax of straight exclamatory repetitions with full orchestra of the piano's original tonic-dominant question, the last of these rhythmically drawn out for maximum emphasis (Example 9-4). But once more we must be in doubt as to formal function. This continuation shows little of the expansion and "progress" one might expect: the music is all clearly first theme, and strays not a hair's breadth from G major.[28] The waywardness of the orchestra's initial off-key entrance had been reined in to the regularity of a thematic statement. Something similar happens in this passage. And particularly when Beethoven follows it with utterly unlike material in a sudden, new key—effecting closure with the wave of a wand as it were—we may wonder in retrospect if everything up to this point (m. 28) has been the mere presentation of a theme.

At any rate, the listener has every reason to expect that this opening tutti at last has done with the first theme. But after the contrasting music, "b" (in its own right altogether remarkable), there it is again, in fact in two versions. The first (Example 9–5; "a_1" in Table 9-1), entering on the crest of another grand rising crescendo, gives an emphatic full orchestra rendition of the piano's "question" in its original context, the descent from D–A; the first of two following cadential expansions twice adds the *sforzato* subdominant that we remember from the orchestra's first answer (mm. 55 and 58), and the second (m. 60) returns to the eternal 3–2 question but offers no resolution. Then the winds end the tutti (this is the second added version of the first theme) by recapturing the very opening of the movement in a retrospective codetta suffused with sixths doubled in three registers, all over a tonic pedal (m. 68). But once more there is no closure, only an exasperated clash of tonic and dominant. As we can see, the first theme dominates the opening tutti enormously. Heard in whole or in part, or in whatever adaptation, that theme is always plainly recognizable, and despite a resolute resistance to closure, it serves almost invariably to shore up the home key. Although a questioning gesture is at the heart of this theme, a sameness and solidity in its treatment confers upon this section a large-scale stability to be found in no first tutti in Beethoven's earlier concertos. And that this music was first given out by the piano has ongoing consequences; there is almost a reversal of usual roles, as the orchestra redirects the soloist's opening inquiry, expatiates upon it, offers one (premature) resolution, and finally, so to speak, leaves the question open.

The contrasting matter, "b" in Table 9-1, contrasts in every way (Example 9-6), this effect heightened as it enters, not with a modulation, but with a harmonic shift. Its brusque dotted rhythms and initial upward thrust signal "military," a topos familiar enough from the earlier concertos; here it seems at first a surprising bit of foreign matter. But is this a "theme" in any usual sense, or is it only transitional material? Its very distinct rhythmic and metrical profile (three identical march-like four-measure modules) argue for the former, while a radical harmonic volatility suggests the latter. Its three statements come in two harmonic types: the first segment, starting in minor, modulates up a fifth, while the other two, beginning in major, finish a semitone down.[29] Beethoven compounds the harmonic instability of the passage by abrupt third shifts downward between statements (there is also a fleeting reference to the third above, filling out the triad of the tonality to come), such that in twelve measures we have a bewildering series of implied keys: A minor, E minor, C major, B minor, G major, and, finally, F# minor. The effect is at least vaguely reminiscent of the harmonic disruption that occurred at the corresponding point in the first movements of Op. 19 and Op. 15. In both these earlier cases disorienting harmonic moves came just before (or upon) the introduction of contrasting thematic material, as if to cast it in a strange and vivid new light; here the new material itself is the destabilizing factor.

Still, can we decide on its function: is it thematic or connective matter? On balance the music urges the former: its sharply delineated phrases, rhythmic distinctiveness, and contrast with its surroundings tip the scales fairly decisively in that direction. Modulating themes, in any event, are no stranger to this concerto; two others are the "soloist's theme" of this movement (m. 119; "c" in Table 9-1) and the remarkable rondo theme of the finale. The mobile, yet neatly measured out passage at hand plays its part in a brilliant solution to the problem of the opening tutti. The unity of an "introductory statement"—one of which even Tovey approved—is assured by the ubiquity of the first theme and its derivatives, always supportive of the home key; yet in "b," harmonic motion, color, and thematic variety are had without adding stretches of goal-oriented symphonic-style transitional music. And this contrasting theme cuts enough of a figure to shift appreciably the ethos of this section and of the movement as a whole. Another voice seems to be speaking, proposing, perhaps urging, soldierly action and adventure as an antipode (or answer?) to the questioning posture of the main theme. In the solo section to come, its fraternal twin, "c" (m. 119), similarly a military tune and a modulating one, relays much the same message.

If the opening theme with its eloquent indecision is to be heard almost everywhere in the first tutti, it is missing where we expect it at the reentry of the piano at the start of S_1, where Beethoven writes a little cadenza-like passage instead (though the articulation of its even eighths are a clear derivative of that theme).[30] The next time we expect an intact statement is at the onset of the recapitulation (m. 253), and this time we do hear it, but astonishingly transformed: starting as a fortissimo proclamation by the soloist, it quickly draws back at its midpoint, once more, to *dolce, piano*, and finishes in a flourish of ornament (Example 9-7). Kerman finds this inexplicable (and as he says on another occasion, a "mistake"):

My difficulty is that almost alone among such moments in Beethoven, this one leaves me bewildered. What is being represented here? Of course it is clear that the opening theme is completely transformed in mood. . . . But as the dynamic fades, continuous piano figuration or filigree [m. 258] appears high above the string's consequent phrase, so that the all-important sense of solo-orchestra exchange is lost. It is also clear that the buoyant new mood of this recapitulation has been carefully prepared . . . but that is not to say that it has been rationalized. I don't come up up with any association to "explain" it.[31]

It is a surprise, all right, that the piano's opening inquiry, grave and controlled as it was, should now return as this huge exclamation. But surely we must construe this outburst, at least partly, as an element in a formal plan. A formidable weight falls on the onset of the recapitulation in any such movement: recovery at once of the tonic key, tonal stability, and the first theme make this a point of arrival second in significance only to the final chord of the movement. In concertos this point is reinforced, by custom, by the return of the orchestra after the soloist's domination of the S_2 (or development) section. A decisive reentry of the orchestra marks the moment of recapitulation in all of Beethoven's concertos so far, and in almost all of Mozart's.[32] But Beethoven had begun this movement with the soloist and seems bent upon a symmetrical repetition of that anomaly here; thus the piano becomes the weight-bearing member of the ensemble. And we must remember, too, that we have already heard the heart of this quiet theme, the "question" itself, played with great emphasis at high volume as early as m. 24 and again in "a_1" (m. 50 and elsewhere). Beethoven has a penchant for shifting the expressive stance of his thematic materials, particularly those that start out on the lyrical side. The Violin Concerto brings back its idyllic opening music in a stentorian pronouncement at exactly this point in the first movement, and the Quartet in F, Op. 59, No. 1, does the same, only more exaggeratedly, in its first-movement coda.

The effect in the Fourth Piano Concerto is a double one. The point of formal articulation is marked off in no uncertain terms, but there is also a sudden loosening of bonds, almost a loss of control, as what was tentative becomes insistent, even exasperated. The part of this that is hardest to fathom—and here Kerman has something of a point—is the immediate pulling back to a prevailing gentleness of tone and dynamic for the orchestra's off-key reply (with added filigree from the soloist), as if the piano's outburst was an embarrassment to be quickly smoothed over. But this moment of recapitulation is an exception; in the third solo Beethoven seems as intent on developing the lyrical qualities of this opening music as he had been in the corresponding part of S_1. Both times he steers resolutely around the fine crescendo in the first tutti (mm. 20ff) enroute to a distant island of tranquility (mm. 105 and 275; "sx" in Table 9-1). The pressing demands of the crucial point of recapitulation deter him from that preoccupation only in passing. Beethoven wanted it both ways; formal and expressive ends collided, it appears, leaving the onset of the recapitulation something of an enigma.[33]

In all the big sections of this movement endings are at least as inventive as beginnings. The first tutti sets the stage by introducing at its close a series of fast-moving events: a rhetorical high-volume distillation of the opening theme ("a_1") with two cadential attachments (mm. 55 and 60; "ext. 1 and 2" in the diagram) followed by the sixth-laden codetta with its tonic pedal—the first theme as if recalled in reverie. In the first solo section "a_1" arrives in its proper position in the winds (m. 157), festooned with pianistic decoration but curiously retreating from its former declamatory *fortissimo* to *piano* for the descent to the tonic-dominant "question." After the first of the two cadential extensions, this also newly muted, the soloist glides into a trill on the dominant (a difficult triple trill, actually, for which the first edition offers an easier alternative) that would seem to signal the end of the section (Example 9-8). But something is wrong; the piano's lowest sounding tone is the fifth of the dominant chord, effectively undercutting a true dominant function. This trill then dissolves instead into a repetition of "a_1," now entirely *dolce e con espressione*—an altogether new expressive stance for this music. But without letting the piano finish its thought, the orchestra suddenly breaks in with great impatience to play (once more) the first extension, after which it presents in orderly fashion the second extension and codetta, all solidly in the local tonic. The piano's first big solo section did not really end; it was cut off. The orchestra has by main force taken for itself all the closing gestures, and only in retrospect do we see that this act of appropriation actually constitutes the second tutti, a section that normally acts rather as an addendum after the close of the soloist's exposition, or as a transition to new ground for the development-like S_2. If the piano had seized the beginning of the concerto from its rightful owner, in this section the orchestra has now taken over the piano's rightful ending.

The end of the movement is an artful extension of this elaborate play with agency and role. Again we have the piano's compromised cadential trill (now of course aimed toward the tonic), the protean "a_1" in its new, tender guise, and the orchestra's blustery intrusion with the first extension, this being (as we can now guess) the beginning of the final tutti. Were this movement to proceed conventionally, the soloist would now be finished (except for a cameo reappearance in the cadenza), dismissed in mid-sentence, as it were, with a reprimand. This peremptory first extension has a built-in pause on the subdominant (a clear reference to the subdominant surge of the orchestral response in the first theme; compare m. 10 in Example 9-2 with m. 178 in Example 9-8). Here in the last tutti Beethoven seizes upon this handy topographical feature for a sudden detour to a cadential $^6_4$, where everything stops for the cadenza, which is now inserted into a known sequence of events—that is, at the close of the first cadential extension—rather than occurring as it usually does in a tutti that has been built explicitly for its inclusion. Nor is this the last we hear from the piano. Having gained the upper hand in the cadenza, the solo part presses its advantage; but instead of proceeding with the second extension, it doubles back for one more try at its own calmly eloquent version of "a_1."[34] This time the orchestra relents, accompanying the theme respectfully to the end; it then even cooperates in a quiet rendition of that first extension (m. 352), the very music it had twice used to quash the piano's reveries. The codetta follows, played for the first time by the soloist and invested with a heightened ethereal nostalgia as it sounds in octaves, with dampers lifted, from the highest register of the keyboard. Ten measures of scurrying piano figuration, from *pianissimo* to *fortissimo*, end the movement on a note of tonal security and untroubled affirmation—of which we will hear more in a moment.

It is not only the beginnings and endings of the main solo sections that make this movement a radical exercise in redefinition of the solo-tutti relation. The solo persona Beethoven creates (for himself, in the first place) has repositioned itself with respect to the orchestra almost throughout. This often has much to do with the piano sound of the new century, and in particular with the freedoms afforded by the newly expanded keyboard. In his earlier sonatas and concertos we hear Beethoven forever struggling against the restraint at the top of his instrument. Now he positively luxuriates in the added upper reaches of piano tessitura (up to c''''),[35] writing long stretches of luminous commentary on the orchestra's more straightforwardly thematic fare, as if from on high. We have noted one or two such places: the joint reply to the recapitulatory outburst of the soloist (Example 9-7) and the new version of the first extension of "a_1" after the cadenza (m. 352). Another notable example is the treatment of "b" in both S_1 and S_3 (mm. 141 and 308); joining the fray for only the last of this theme's three segments, the piano soars skyward with ghostly *pianissimo* figuration, rewritten the second time around to accommodate the change of key, but both times staying pinned to the top of the keyboard. But the new freedom apparently comes with new restrictions. Beethoven seems chary of writing straight thematic material in the piano's high range (the codetta just before the end is a rare exception; here he takes the precaution of putting it in octaves), and probably with good reason: the pianos of the time were always weak-sounding in this tessitura, particularly so in the additional keys above f'''. (And by 1808, when the work was finished and performed, any weakness in the upper range of his piano would likely have seemed all the more severe to the increasingly deaf composer.) So necessity was probably the mother of invention; the marvelous textural innovation that so strongly marks this movement—at the same time reducing the amount of thematic matter in the solo part—may be partly due to the current state of piano technology and Beethoven's own auditory equipment.

If in the first movement of the C-major Concerto, Op. 15, one may detect certain differences between piano and orchestra as to expressive emphasis, such an effect is vastly more striking in this movement. In a useful oversimplification we might separate this music into two expressive camps: the mainly gentle, questioning, but potentially intense—A. B. Marx would probably have added "idealistic"—music of the first theme and its derivatives, over against the military themes, "b" and "c." These latter, in their brusqueness and urgency, remain overwhelmingly the province of the orchestra; this is particularly notable in the case of "c," a new "solo" theme in S_1 that in the mature Mozart concertos would characteristically have been sounded first by the solo instrument. But here they belong to the orchestra, and when the piano joins them, in both S_1 and S_3, it does so only to add commentary: tart, almost trivializing semitone collisions in "c," and a kind of subversion of expressive intent as it bends the sternness of "b" into something ethereal and reflective (mm. 123 and 286, 142 and 308).

What the piano adds entirely on its own are two fleeting passages—too fleeting to be called themes—in distant tonal lands, "sx" and "sy." The first of these, in m. 105, is a tiny island of relaxation far on the flat side ($B\flat$ in S_1 and $E\flat$ in S_3) at which the piano pauses for rest and reflection on its journey toward the secondary materials in the first solo (Example 9-9a). Again, the right-hand part is pinned to the top of the keyboard (rewritten in S_3 to keep it there), and the legitimacy of this stop-off is furthered by a subtle reference in rhythm and articulation—note especially m. 106 in the piano and the augmentation of the opening rhythm in the strings—to the first theme. While the piano simply steps down to the $B\flat$ island in S_1, the other new passage, "sy," arrives as the end point of a long and determined harmonic process in the developmental S_2. Solo arpeggiated figuration starting early in the section (m. 204) leads ineluctibly to C♯, first broached in m. 212 and ushered in with a huge flourish in m. 230. What the piano thus introduces, indeed insists upon, is another pastoral island, in C♯ minor, four measures of *dolce* and *pianissimo* music again high up on the instrument and related once more by rhythm to the first theme (Example 9-9b). The solo part seems to be making a point. Taking charge as never before in this movement, it finally forces its own agenda; but what it urges, as it turns out, is an anomalous message of gentleness, almost passivity.

Upon hearing Beethoven's performance of this concerto in public at his concert of December 1808, the Berlin composer and author Johann Friedrich Reichardt called it "a new piano concerto of monstrous difficulty, which Beethoven played astonishingly well in the fastest possible tempos."[36] Since thereupon Reichardt proceeds immediately to a characterization of the second movement ("a masterpiece of beautifully developed song"), it seems fair to assume that the "difficulty" and "fastest possible tempos" refer mainly to the first movement. Tovey, making this very assumption, has an explanation: the solo part in this movement routinely has figuration in sixteenth triplets (the "demisemiquavers" he refers to are only incidental), thus more than compensating for any potential lack of pianistic brilliance in this Allegro moderato.[37] And this points to a ruling conundrum of the movement: the piano as leader, showing occasional fine bursts of virtuosity, but remaining all the while devoted to the cause of tranquil and nuanced reflection, a curb on the orchestra's propensity for energetic motion, for direct action. There is a developmental aspect along these lines in the movement as a whole. Gaining ascendency in S_2, the solo part maintains its upper hand only precariously in what follows; finally, after the cadenza, it successfully imposes its version of a_1, takes control of the codetta—all, typically, at levels of *piano* and *pianissimo*—and allows itself only a few measures' celebration in a surging crescendo of passagework at the very close. As in the second movement, the voice of the piano achieves mastery of a very particular kind, and it does so only as the end result of a process of working-out, a dialectic, we might say, whose conclusion is a greatly enriched encapsulation of its parts.

THE RONDO

Charles Rosen hears the Andante con moto as a kind of introduction to the concerto's finale; he cites its "theatricality" by way of comparison to Haydn's slow introductions to symphonic first movements, as well as its kinship—of which a signal element is its virtual lack of modulation—with the introduction to the finale of Mozart's G-minor Quintet, K. 516.[38] One might object that what is often most "theatrical" about Haydn's introductions is their harmonic errancy[39]—just the reverse of the tonal stability Rosen sees in the Mozart and Beethoven. And theatricality in Beethoven's movement-in-dialogue is so much more palpable than in any of those earlier introductions that the comparison seems fruitless. Still, for all its intensity, there does seem to be something introductory about Beethoven's movement: it is far shorter than his usual slow movements, by its very nature lacking extension or elaboration of musical ideas; its limited harmonic scope, to be sure, is also a factor, and it is quite explicitly joined to the finale both by Beethoven's direction "Segue il Rondo" and by a clear melodic-harmonic connection. To start the Rondo, the same strings—this is the only Beethoven concerto that begins the finale with the orchestra[40]—proceed in the same tessitura, at the same *pianissimo*, and with the same uppermost pitch. The bass shifts down a third, from the key of E minor to a C-major sound, but it is the rousing new rhythmic figure that catapults us into a different world (Example 9-10 and the ending of 9-2). Binding this ending to this beginning radicalizes the contrast between the two, escalating, in particular, the vividness of the rondo theme—an effect Beethoven had already realized, but in very different fashion, in the Third Concerto.

This new beginning projects a double persona. Its drum-like double anacruses and upward-thrusting arpeggio sound (once again) vaguely military, foreboding but controlled. At the same time the theme plays an elaborate intellectual game (seemingly an unmilitary thing to do) with its own musical design. It begins on (not necessarily *in*) C major, but over ten measures makes its way to the "right" key, G major (or is it the dominant of C?). Neither key is really settled here: there is no syntax in C—it is merely stated—and both "tonics" have the indecisive third on top. Next, as in a miniature binary form in C major, this segment is repeated (in an elaboration by the piano). The C-major binary phantom proceeds: G is extended after the imaginary double bar by a kind of counterstatement in the piano, leading back to a rowdy repetition, with trumpets and drums, of the initial music (so it is to be a *rounded* binary form in C?). We await the ending, the moment of truth when Beethoven will have to commit himself one way or the other. But he eludes us; after moving for the third time in the direction of G, the music temporizes, grows modulatory, and puts us on the road leading to the true dominant, D major, for the second theme. The rondo theme thus leads the ear with about equal force in two directions: toward acceptance of C as home with its expectable dominant in attendance, and toward a surmise that the piece starts with a big plagal cadence, a subdominant-tonic. (This last would not be entirely without precedent in Beethoven's music: both Allegro movements of the Sonata for Piano and Cello in G minor, Op. 5, for example, have such openings.)

This sally of wit has consequences. How one hears the ritornello depends strongly on the interpretation of its harmonic plan: is it a binary shape in C that fades into obscurity toward its end, or is it a theme that simply keeps returning obstinately to that subdominant beginning? And there are consequences for the movement as a whole. For this is the opening ritornello of a rondo, bound to come back repeatedly, each time, if ordinary rondo etiquette is observed, with elaborate preparation. What, then, is to be prepared, C or G? To what lengths is Beethoven prepared to go to press the (in the end illusory) tonic, C? To considerable lengths, it turns out: there are two formal reappearances of the ritornello, at mm. 160 and 416, plus an abbreviated one in the coda (at m. 568), and each time all forces are marshalled for a return of C major (see Table 9-2). And each time all this preparation of course makes C major sound more secure than it did at the beginning, where it had none; all these prolonged deflections tilt the whole movement strongly toward C major—to this end Beethoven even finds it convenient to have his trumpets and drums permanently in that key.

But before the main statement of the ritornello theme in the coda, he offers a covert "solution" to the riddle: at m. 519 the winds quietly play the theme (against another of those radiant tapestries in the high register of the piano) beginning this time in the "right" key.[41] He has simply appended an initial G-major statement of the first rising figure (with a tonic pedal under all); this version of the theme is almost a cliché of harmonic regularity (I–IV–V–I) and seems to imply that all the other occurrences had been incomplete. To make sure we get the point, Beethoven follows this explanation directly with the theme in its original form, complete with that ceremonious build up for the wrong key. As a military topos this music distantly relives something of the C-major bravado of the first movement of the First Concerto. But here any bluster or combativeness is largely neutralized by a certain passive composure that comes with all that emphasis on what turns out to be the subdominant, and no less so by the substantial distractions of this central ambiguity.

The movement really has only one prominent formal preparation for the true tonic: when after a central development-like section we begin to expect the third statement of the ritornello together with its recapitulation-like continuation, the piano puts down an anchor on a dominant D (m. 272) and with help from the orchestra prolongs this function for twenty-seven measures. But all this anticipation is rewarded not by the ritornello (which, of course, always takes a preparation for the false tonic), but for the second theme (m. 299). As in a number of Mozart's later rondos, thus, this movement simply dispenses with a ritornello at this point. Return to the tonic comes with the reintroduction of the second theme, thereby casting this theme into high relief as the main instrument of recapitulation. It might seem a slender reed for such an assignment. Its texture is attenuated in the extreme, stretched out from the isolated single-line melody high up in the piano to the solo cello's tonic pedal three and one-half octaves below (Example 9-11). One is reminded of Beethoven's Sonata Op. 109, written some fourteen years in the future, whose first movement forces the essentially meditative main theme into a declamatory (or perhaps despairing) shout at the recapitulation, its single-line melody again soaring four octaves above the bass. In both cases this great void in the texture isolates the melody, presenting it exposed and vulnerable, a tender plant seemingly in alien soil.

The orchestra has quite a different notion about that second theme. Taking it up directly after the piano's presentation in both appearances, it makes of this melody a gnarled contrapuntal web, studded with dissonance, given to dense doublings, and driven by a compulsion to turn back on itself (see the latter part of Example 9-11). Acerbic clashes result, as Beethoven insists on writing lines that do not quite fit together (the two lines in the same range make "impermissible" dissonaces from the outset). The procedure and effect are strongly reminiscent of what he had done with the orchestral continuation in the first theme of the first movement (Example 9-2). In both cases an atmosphere of subdued meditation is disturbed by a new pungency, an unsettling harbinger of struggle ahead. And if the rondo's second theme reminds us of that earlier one, there may be another reason as well: they share a topology dominated by a $\hat{3}$–$\hat{2}$ motion over the dominant, that partly resigned, partly questioning half cadence that puts its stamp so strongly on the first movement. But in the rondo the orchestra goes further. The half cadence becomes an instrument of self-renewal as the theme evades closure, circling back upon itself, growing ever richer and warmer through massive doublings, inviting us to think ahead once more to Beethoven's late style, in particular to the transcendant second theme (also in D major) in the slow movement of the Ninth Symphony. This remarkable treatment invests the theme with a specific gravity enabling it to function credibly as the main vehicle for recapitulation. But, as we shall see in a moment, Beethoven is not yet done with this music.

The Rondo of the G-major Concerto is the first of Beethoven's to feature a central developmental section rather than an episode. At the point where the first ritornello veers off in the sharp direction (disappointing our hope for clarification of that tonal ambiguity about C or G), the second one turns decisively toward the flat side (m. 204). The music quickly settles into a curiously static stretch (despite the piano's insistent *fortissimo*) consisting of literally nothing but arpeggios on the local tonic alternating with its first-inversion dominant, four measures each, successively on Eb, Bb minor, and F minor. The modulations between these keys are effected each time by scherzando interpolations based on the ritornello theme, these too in rigid four-measure modules. But the interpolations serve a more subtle function: they nudge us into accepting all those arpeggios as thematic, as bland abstractions of the arpeggiated trajectory of the ritornello theme itself.[42] The piano then assumes control (m. 248), working the overtly thematic material of the interpolations through another half dozen four-measure modules, while traversing G minor and C minor on the way to the dominant pedal, D, and the second-theme recapitulation. It is perhaps something of a paradox that this "development" should be the most rigorously schematic section of the movement—as if some vestige of the episodic idea remained in the face of the decision to write a development instead. The experiment seems not perfectly successful, and this section comes off as something of a holding action for more striking things to come.

Tovey rightly marvels at the movement's "enormous coda." But just how enormous is open to question. He has it beginning "after the recapitulation of the second subject," and thus accounting for "exactly five twelfths of the whole movement"—that is, at m. 350.[43] Such an interpretation would be fair enough, were this a sonata-form movement. But this is a rondo, where we expect and get (at m. 416) a final ritornello after the recapitulation has run its course; here this is presented with a full-dress preparation for the wrong key (C major) exactly parallel to the trappings of the second ritornello in m. 160. To subsume this standard formal member of the rondo within a gigantic coda is to court confusion. There is, however, an anomalous (and marvelous) stretch of music after m. 350 that needs explanation. Following the recapitulation of the second theme, a new and unexpected turn toward the flat direction leads to a sustained sonority of Eb where *divisi* violas give out a *dolce* version of the ritornello theme in warm thirds and sixths—moving, as that theme does, to its dominant— while the piano plays quiet arpeggios above. Concerted winds then sound an alarm in diminished sevenths, and the preparation for the final ritornello is underway. Such a confluence of piano arpeggios, play with the ritornello theme, and a tonal center of Eb/Bb must be taken as a reference, surely, back to the development. That section, short, schematized, almost routine, had left unfinished business that is now concluded by this much more fanciful addendum. It is as if the missing third ritornello, expected just after the development, has been transplanted to the position of the fourth—taking with it on its travels a piece of the developmental material it required by way of preparation.

The most sensible place to put the beginning of the coda, surely, is at about m. 443 (making it just over a fourth the length of the movement), where the crossroads following upon the ritornello presents itself for the third time. After the first ritornello things had moved in the sharp direction and on to the second theme; after the second one the music had turned in the opposite direction and moved into the development; this time it cleaves to the tonic with *fortissimo* plain broken chords in the piano and attenuated hints of the ritornello theme in the winds—as if we were now to have a straightforward peroration, a stable summing-up of a movement essentially finished. But Beethoven's plan is rather more elaborate. The piano, wavering tonally, and thinning and calming as it always does in approaching the second theme, now offers that melody in a kaleidoscopic series of juxtaposed keys: F♯, C, and, with a fine sense of homecoming, the tonic G. The orchestra has always seen potential for depth and elaboration in this theme and now positively luxuriates in it, alternating entries in bass and treble that pit the first half of the tune against the second in wonderful dissonance, but dissonance easily contained by the overall affirmative stability of this music. This could well be the end of the concerto. That calm, poignant, questioning theme, a palpable revisitation of the central expressive stance of the first movement, emerges in a kind of serene triumph. But Beethoven has more on his mind for this coda— three things, actually, that tumble out in short order: a cadenza that shifts attention for a moment entirely to the soloist (who is warned to be quick about it);[44] the "solution" to the ritornello theme, sounding entirely in the tonic G; and that theme in its original form, but now ratcheted up to presto, bringing closure quickly.

OP. 58: HISTORY AND TEXT

At his concert of December 22, 1808, Beethoven presented his Fourth Piano Concerto to the Viennese public. It was one of a remarkable number of major new compositions on this long program: besides the concerto there were the Fifth and Sixth Symphonies, the Choral Fantasy (composed at top speed shortly before the concert), and sections of the

Mass in C major in German translation. Hectic last-minute preparations for this event, misunderstandings between Beethoven and the performers, and exhaustion all around produced confusion and disruption.[45] Various accounts agree that during the performance of the Choral Fantasy—for which, according to Seyfried, there was a single rehearsal, "with wet voice parts as usual"—the orchestra broke down, prompting Beethoven to shout from the piano for a new beginning. Reichardt, who sat with Prince Lobkowitz in his box directly above the stage, reported their patience sorely tested by "many failures in performance" in this four-hour concert in a cold hall. But the concerto seems to have gone well: Reichardt described (as we recall) "a new forte-piano concerto of monstrous difficulty, which Beethoven played astonishingly well at the fastest possible tempos."[46] This was the last time, so far as we know, that Beethoven played a concerto in public; burgeoning fame as a symphony composer (and local fame as a conductor of his own works), as well as international success in publishing his music, finally made concerto playing—that preferred means of putting his musical persona before audiences in the Bonn and early Vienna years—ever more dispensable.

Of all the music on the program of the concert of December 1808, the concerto had probably been finished the longest, and it may possibly have been heard earlier in one or more private gatherings. Its first performance is always confidently assigned (as in the editorial report of the new *Beethoven Werke* and the list of works in the *New Grove*)[47] to one of two concerts of Beethoven's music at the home of Prince Lobkowitz in March 1807. Here, according to reports in journals from Weimar and Leipzig, Beethoven's first four symphonies were performed, as well as the *Coriolan* Overture, some airs from *Fidelio*, and (as one report has it) an unidentified piano concerto.[48] In a series of letters from the spring of 1806 to the spring of 1807, Beethoven had offered his new concerto to several German publishers and included it in a contract for a group of five major compositions (Opp. 58–62) that were to have been published by Muzio Clementi's firm in London.[49]

The meager surviving manuscript evidence suggests that Beethoven did extensive work on the concerto, especially its first movement, in 1805–6.[50] Since the work was likely finished by the spring of 1807, it is tempting to think this was the composition performed at Lobkowitz's concerts in March of that year. But the evidence is weak. There seemed to be no hesitation at these concerts about presenting earlier works (the first three symphonies date from 1800 to 1804). As the reports make no mention of Beethoven as soloist, the piano part for the concerto may well have been taken by another pianist, and there were several such in Vienna who had earlier concertos of his in their fingers.[51] Then too, one might well wonder why Reichardt, listening to the December 1808 concert from Lobkowitz's box, should speak of the concerto he heard as "new" if it had been performed some twenty-one months earlier at the home of the man sitting next to him. In the absence of further information we should probably regard the performance of December 1808 as the true premiere of this concerto.

But Beethoven seems to have planned matters otherwise and in so doing betrayed a major shift in perspective on his own career. Ries, generally a reliable witness, tells this engaging story:

> One day Beethoven visited me, carrying his Fourth Concerto in G major tucked under his arm, and said: "Next Saturday you have to play this in the Kärnthner-Thor Theater." Only five days remained to practice it. Unluckily I remarked to him that the time was too short to learn to play it well; would he not permit me to perform the C minor Concerto. Beethoven was annoyed about this, turned on his heels and went to young Stein, whom he did not really like much. Stein was also a pianist, and in fact had played longer than I. He was clever enough to accept the suggestion immediately. Since he could not finish learning the Concerto either, he went to Beethoven the day before the performance and asked, as I had, if he could play the other one, in C minor. Beethoven more or less had to give in and agreed to this.
>
> However, whether the fault lay with the theater, with the orchestra, or with the pianist himself, the performance was not successful. Beethoven was most annoyed, especially since he was asked by several people: "Why didn't you let Ries play it, since he had such a success with it?" These remarks gave me a great deal of pleasure. Later Beethoven said to me: "I thought you just did not particularly care to play the G major Concerto."[52]

Thayer implicitly associates these events with the Tonkünstler-Sozietät concert on the evening following Beethoven's own performance of the Fourth Concerto.[53] But Ries makes no such connection, and although an unidentified Beethoven concerto was on the program for that evening, no pianist is named.[54] But during the period when two necessary conditions were met, that is, that Ries was in Vienna and the Fourth Concerto was likely complete, there was in fact a single concert whose program included the performance of a Beethoven concerto by Stein, namely, the Public Charities (*Wohltätigkeitsanstalten*) concert of November 15, 1808.[55] (Both concerts in question, it turns out, took place, not at the Kärnthnerthortheater, but at the other court-controlled theater a few hundred yards away, the Burgtheater. The discrepancy probably results from Ries's faulty recollection, some thirty years after the event, of this detail.) For the concert of November 15 two other works of Beethoven, one of his symphonies and the *Coriolan* Overture, were on the program, and Beethoven himself was engaged as conductor; this probably explains why it was he who made arrangements for the performance of his concerto.

But if it was for the November 1808 concert (as seems most likely) that Beethoven set about to engage a soloist, we see him actively conscripting another pianist to play his *new* concerto in public a month before he had a chance to do so himself. Participation in such a scoop—which of course was aborted when Stein switched concertos—would have been unthinkable in Beethoven's earlier years as an ambitious keyboard virtuoso. And in this connection we might ask just what physical object Beethoven carried "tucked under his arm" when he offered Ries the concerto. The most reasonable answer is that it was a copy of the piano part of the first edition, published the previous August in Vienna by the Kunst und Industrie Comptoire. For in this case he did not, as had been his habit, withhold his concerto from publication until he had got sufficient mileage out of it in performance; he had it printed—indeed, he had made several earlier efforts toward this end—before it had ever been heard in public. This shows, surely, a newly cavalier attitude toward his own career as a pianist, and perhaps it shows as well a shifting view of the concerto as a genre. Less a personal vehicle designed for his own—or anyone's—pianistic exploits, it seems now to have moved toward status as an oeuvre in that distinctly nineteenth-century sense: a monument to its creator, a work of art whose identity stands firm through the vicissitudes of various performances by various executants. The Fourth Concerto, in its intricacy and profundity, seems an altogether worthy representative of such a work.

Still, just what this work consists of, what we should regard as its "text," remains in some details uncertain. Since the autograph disappeared many years ago, all modern editions are ultimately based on the first printing, in parts, from 1808. But there is another surviving primary document, now at the Gesellschaft der Musikfreunde in Vienna, that records something of Beethoven's intentions for this work, namely, a copyist's score of the concerto with a large number of markings in the composer's hand.[56] The first and third movements of this manuscript appear to have served as the engraver's copy (*Stichvorlage*) for the first edition; it bears engraver's markings and the plate number of the edition, as well as a number of corrections in Beethoven's "Röthel," the red crayon he characteristically used in proofreading. There is a very close correspondance—most significantly in the reduction of the orchestral tuttis entered into the piano part—to the text of that edition. The second movement in this manuscript is a much later copy, with no relevance for the establishment of the text.[57]

The great bulk of Beethoven's autograph entries in the manuscript, written in ink, are confined to the piano part (mainly entered into two blank staves immediately above the piano) and are limited largely to the first movement. In an often fleeting, "private" notation they record a startling elaboration of the solo part as we know it, an elaboration that clearly represents a stage of Beethoven's ideas subsequent to that of the first edition, from which all later ones were derived. Of the various kinds of changes Beethoven indicated, Nottebohm emphasized those that extend the upper range of the keyboard part. In the first edition the piano part had not risen above c'''', and at certain places Beethoven had made some rather visible adjustments to conform to this limit; this is particularly noticeable in the recapitulatory S_3 of the first movement, where it was necessary to reorient toward the tonic music that in S_1 had centered around the dominant.[58]

But the revisions in the Vienna manuscript take no particular note of these passages. Rather, they consistently explore the uppermost reaches of the expanded keyboard, all the way up to f'''', in the interests of new brilliance in the solo part, particularly in cadential passages leading to important structural junctures. At the end of S_1, for example (and at the corresponding point in S_3), the sustained double trill in the piano is replaced by a paroxysm of leaping double-third trills whose acrobatics cover two-and-a-half octaves (Examples 9-12a and b).[59] A series of similar leaping trills replaces the scalewise passage ushering in the "b" theme in S_3 (Examples 9-13a and b). At a number of points in the Vienna sketches, Beethoven enlivens keyboard figuration that in the original versions he may have thought somewhat routine; one such figuration, from near the beginning of the second solo (or development section), is shown in Examples 9-14a and 9-14b. At the repetition of "a_1" just after the cadenza, use of the higher range seems to be the main idea. Already lying very high, the melody is put up another octave (reaching e'''') and decorated with Beethoven's characteristic accompanying trills (Examples 9-15a and b).[60]

Another kind of revision is the unsettling addition of a bass reply to the already surprising off-key entry of the piano at the beginning of S_2 (Example 9-16); these new notes clarify that Beethoven thought of the initial F♮ in the context of D minor as the music prepares to set off on its modulatory course. And sometimes the sketches make adjustments evidently designed to correct textural or voice leading problems in the original version; at the first occurrence of "a₁," for example, he writes a new left-hand figuration that does away with the parallel octaves between the two hands (Example 9-17).[61] In the same passage, the repetition of the two-measure melody (*dolce e con espressione*) is supplied with an emphatic "ri-tar-dan-do"; another *dolce* passage, "sy" beginning at m. 230, has a "ritardando" in its second measure, with an "a tempo" three measures later. These indications suggest a distinct willingness to bend tempo in the service of expression in cantabile passages.[62]

But perhaps the most arresting addition of all is the single measure of arpeggios that Beethoven prescribed for the piano at a point in S_3 (m. 286), for this occurs in a passage in which the piano ostensibly rests while the strings play theme "c" alone (Example 9-18). The context here is close dialogue: the soloist is about to answer the orchestra's straight presentation of that theme with its own ornamented version. This passage, of course, becomes something very different if the strings do not in fact play alone but present their statement in competition with those rolling arpeggios from the piano. And the implications here transcend this passage and this concerto: this is one case, at least, in which Beethoven specified solo playing during an orchestral tutti—an issue we shall consider more closely in Chapter 12.

Nottebohm suggests two possible occasions for Beethoven's elaborations of this piano part: for a performance of his own, or as an aid to another pianist who planned to play the work, such as Stein.[63] In considering the matter we should take note of the "private" nature of the entries in the Vienna manuscript. Sketchy in the extreme, they often serve only to get a passage started, leaving the continuation to surmise; and sometimes they consist only of a stream of noteheads—these on occasion even disintegrate into a continuous broad line—without rhythmic values. If such suggestions were to be of use to another pianist, Beethoven would have needed to make them much more explicit. As they stand, these notations look very much as if they were for his own use. Much like the sketches he typically made for cadenzas shortly before his performances of the earlier concertos, they appear to be an aide-mémoire for a performance that retained a strong element of improvisation. We know of only one performance of this concerto by Beethoven, that at his concert of December 1808. (In fact, this is the only known performance of this concerto in Vienna during the composer's lifetime.) And of this performance Czerny told Nottebohm (the careers of these two in Vienna overlapped by about eleven years) that Beethoven had played the concerto very "roguishly" (*mutwillig*), adding many more notes in the passages than were written.[64]

If we may reasonably suppose that Beethoven made these revisions for his own use at the concert of 1808, we might further surmise that the impetus for doing so arose from the upward expansion of the keyboard of Viennese pianos from c'''' to f'''' at just about this time.[65] The circumstances of Beethoven's notations in the Vienna manuscript, it seems, thus closely resemble those of Stage 3 of the autograph of the C-minor Concerto:[66] a newly expanded keyboard and an imminent performance prompted Beethoven to think about just what it was he intended to play.

So what the audience at the Theater an der Wien heard that long December evening in 1808 was probably not quite the Fourth Concerto as we know it, but a richly elaborated version of it, the piano's expansive music partly planned, partly improvised. To whatever degree Beethoven had begun to dissociate the idea of the concerto from his own performances, in its creator's hands the Fourth Concerto continued to be less the presentation of a "work" than a live activity, a unique event subject to whim, its nature flowing partly from the mood of the moment. The piece seemed to exist for Beethoven on two levels. One was for publication, probably in most cases for performance with reduced forces or even with piano alone in private; the intricacies of balance between solo and tutti, and a certain intimate and subdued quality in the piano remind us of chamber music. But Beethoven also had his public conception of this music, in which the solo part (at least at points) commands, dazzling and astonishing a rapt audience in a large hall.[67] What we have, of course, is the former version of the work, one belonging to a particular moment, a moment before performance. The special magic of Beethoven's public version must remain mostly in our imagination.

Of Purest Ray Serene:
The Violin Concerto in D,
Op. 61

Of all that is most beauteous—imaged there
In happier beauty; more pellucid streams,
An ampler ether, a diviner air,
And fields invested with purpureal gleams.

WORDSWORTH, *Laodamia*

There seems to be something of a consensus about Beethoven's Violin Concerto. Writers as diverse as Tovey and Tyson speak of it with the same words: "The whole gigantic scheme is serene"; and ". . . coming to terms with this serene masterpiece."[1] Hans Engel speaks similarly of a *stiller Friede* in the first two movements (the other writers, like most who comment on symphonies and concertos, seem to to be thinking mainly of the first movement).[2] But whence all this serenity? For one thing, the opening theme quietly announces its expressive world in concerted wood-winds with conjunct melody, plain and slow harmonic motion, and a saturated doubling in thirds. Together with tonic and dominant pedals, partly implied, and an avoidance of firm resolution—the melody always aims away from the tonic—this is old and widely understood musical symbolism for "pastoral," for that complex of impressions and feelings of which the musical *locus classicus* was the pastorale or siciliano.[3] It summons up the imagined simplicity and contentment of bucolic life in the countryside that Beethoven had recently evoked in his Piano Sonata in D, Op. 28, and would soon do so again, with similar means but greater explicitness, in the first movement of the Sixth Symphony. The point is even clearer in the "second theme," mm. 43ff. ("b" in the diagram in Table 10-1), where oboes, clarinets, and bassoons sing in thirds, doubled in three registers, above nothing but tonic and dominant pitches alternating at two-bar intervals. In the intervening music at mm. 18ff. ("t" in the diagram), we hear much the same: massive doubling of thirds in the woodwinds, tonic and dominant exchanges every two measures. But here the music ascends with a crescendo to forte—for Beethoven pastoral sentiments could be exuberant as well as placid. (The three passages are shown in Example 10-1.)

But what, then, can we make of the famous but still perplexing initial four tonic strokes of the timpani? Like the first chords of the *Eroica*, they fall outside the highly structured metrical scheme—and they will do so twice more at the beginnings of the first solo and the third tutti. At first they strike us as something exterior, something left behind when the true business of the movement is underway. But, not easily to be got rid of, they become a persistent presence that colors even the repose of the second theme. Measured drumbeats, with their distant implication of military ceremony, suggest a background of sternness and struggle (the sharp and peremptory sound of the timpani in Beethoven's day would have underscored this implication). And in one way or another this other expressive sphere intrudes upon the lyrical tone at almost every step of the way. Each of the three pastoral statements shown in Example 10-1 is undermined by a contradictory gesture. Following hard on the heels of the first theme is the rasping nonharmonic unison D♯ of m. 10, a discordant echo of the opening timpani strokes that proceeds—one can hardly say resolves—to a seeming non sequitur, a dominant seventh of the tonic with the C♯ on top ("ax"). A similar maneuver ("bx," shown in Example 10-1d) follows upon and similarly threatens to subvert the second theme in m. 65, where, as Tovey says, "the mysterious D♯ is now explained away."[4] But although the D♯, now harmonized as a diminished seventh, moves in a more satisfying way to E, this progression (vii^7/ii–V$^4_2$/I) still disquiets because an element is still missing. What that element is Beethoven hastens to clarify in the next measures, where in one of this movement's sudden bursts of enthusiasm that diminished chord mounts upward to resolve with a certain triumph (and perfect syntactic propriety) to ii^6, V$^4_2$, and arrival at the tonic. The "explaining away" of which Tovey speaks is there, all right, but it comes in two distinct steps. And the final effect is that Beethoven has it both ways: things are thrown into disorder, but swift redress makes this seem in retrospect quite justifiable.

TABLE 10-1 OP. 61, I

	18			43	65	77		
T_1								
a	ax	t	t_1	b	bx	b_1		
I		($\flat$VI/I)		I, i				

89	103	126		141	166	178	206	
S_1								
cad.	a	ax	t	b	bx	b_1	ext.	(ax)
V/I	I	~~~~		V, v		V		

	221		239	261	272	
	T_2					
	t_1		b	bx	b_1	
	$\flat$VI/V ~~~V	V, v			~~~$\flat$VII	

284	301	331		357
S_2				
cad.		a	(atb)	
V/$\flat$VII~~vi~~~~iv			$\flat$II ~ ~ ~ ~ V/I	

	365	386		418	440	452	480	
	T_3	S_3						
	a	ax	t	b	bx	b_1	ext	(ax)
	I		~~~	I, i		I		

497		511
T_4	cad	
t_1		Coda (b, b_1)
($\flat$VI/I) ~ i		I

Nor does Beethoven allow the prevailing sunny equilibrium of the intervening music ("t"; Example 10-1c) to stand unchallenged. Its quiet ending is broken off by an abrupt deceptive cadence, *pianissimo* to *fortissimo* (with the first deployment of the trumpets) at m. 28 ("t_1"). This outburst on the lowered sixth also proceeds quickly to harmonic self-justification, as it takes its place in an orderly procession back to the tonic minor, followed by the switch to major and the second theme. But that instrument of disruption has bigger implications. For in both the first and third solo sections, corresponding to exposition and recapitulation, Beethoven curiously omits this element (and this one alone). He is saving it, we soon learn, for the pivotal entrances of the second and fourth tuttis. Here, where we might expect a rousing confirmation of the achieved dominant and tonic keys, we get instead those great exclamatory deceptive cadences, throwing these two essential structural points of the movement into temporary confusion.[5] In each case Beethoven patiently sets about picking up the pieces: the following music explains the explosive flat sixth as a temporary diversion into the tonic minor—a sidestep for which the second theme had already shown a marked predilection. It is as if a placid tone in this movement is maintained only with difficulty, as if a prevailing idyllic serenity is but an interlude in the midst of a harder and more tumultuous world that threatens at every turn to intrude. Though the warrior's arms, as we might imagine, have been left behind for now, thoughts of that other life can never be wholly suppressed.

Even the leading themes themselves have a tinge of expressive ambiguity. The second one ("b"), as we have seen, shows a marked tonal mobility: it darkens easily into its own tonic minor, thus providing ready access, as well, to *its* relative major, F.[6] In the second tutti, m. 246, this swerve into minor erupts into a *fortissimo* declaration that surprisingly persists for the rest of that section; the minor-colored version of the theme, it turns out, has the latent energy to ignite high pathos of remarkable staying power. And "a" itself, with its graceful smoothly descending thirds, returns as a stentorian pronouncement at the onset of the recapitulation (T_3; m. 365). The orchestra announces the new section with the four timpani strokes now played at full volume by everybody, top to bottom, and the first theme carries right on, *fortissimo* and insistent in the extreme. The two expressive modes have not collided, it seems, but somehow joined forces, as if in some sudden-dawning vision of a commonality between two divergent worlds of expression.

It is the quiet music, not the military topos, that makes the adjustment. Beethoven's lyrical first themes of the middle period often have this protean aspect: at some crucial point later in the movement, they turn assertive and powerful, sometimes verging on the boisterous. We have seen this at the moment of recapitulation in the first movement of the Fourth Concerto, where the opening theme bursts forth with great declamatory force, as if suddenly freed of a prior restraint. In the F-major String Quartet, Op. 59, No. 1, first movement, this moment is saved until the beginning of the coda, where what was originally a composed, placid bass theme appears quite unexpectedly with startling power (and a necessary adjustment in harmony) at the top of the violin range. Much the same happens in the first movement of the Sonata for Piano and Cello Op. 69, where the central event of the coda, once more, is the quiet first theme, now no longer quiet, but peremptory and insistent.[7] One issue governing these maneuvers may be a simple compulsion to do something startling and memorable at important structural junctures. In the Violin Concerto, as we have seen, Beethoven was willing to put tonal equilibrium seriously at risk in the attention-grabbing off-key entries of the second and fourth tuttis; that a decisive marking of just these two junctures was the point of the exercise seems clear from his subsequent haste to restore order in this generally orderly piece.

The conduct of the recapitulation seemed to command Beethoven's attention in particular ways. In outspokenly "heroic" first movements like those of the Third and Fifth Symphonies, such a moment, though signalled in each case with portentous anticipation, quickly gives way to gestures of relaxation, to a kind of retrenchment.[8] Though the start of the recapitulation demands and receives full notice, the drama and drive of the preceding development section seems to discourage at this point a protracted dose of more of the same. Beethoven's solution is to bring on the return itself with full panoply—and then draw back. In the Fifth Symphony the famous oboe solo, with its plangent world-weary meditation, stops the forward drive; the corresponding music in the *Eroica* treads water quietly on the flat side of the harmonic stream. Variants of this latter solution show up as well in the Sonata for Piano and Violin in C minor, Op. 30, No. 2, and in the "Waldstein" Sonata.

But the moment of recapitulation in the Violin Concerto is a very different case, because the recapitulation of a *lyrical* theme was always quite another problem for Beethoven. How is the drama of return and arrival to be reconciled with words softly spoken? The first movement of the "Pastoral" Symphony remains perfectly steadfast and content in its expressive world: the placid opening music reenters just as it is, but ingeniously borne aloft by an expansive plagal cadence that is in any case something of a hallmark of that marvelous piece.[9] The music just before this does the work of preparation with a purposeful bass descent by fifth, in four stages from A to F (overshooting by one step to effect the plagal cadence). In the Fourth Concerto and the Violin Concerto, Beethoven marks this moment with the somewhat blunt expedient of simply playing the gentle music with great force; the themes turn insistent, as if fed up with their own gentleness when they have an important structural task to perform. Such changeability of expressive stance in the presentation of thematic material (as opposed to any transformations it may undergo in the process of working out) is in any case a notable and novel development of Beethoven's middle years. It takes its place beside that related penchant of his for a certain planned obscurity in identity and function of musical ideas: the ambiguity of introduction and theme at the beginning of the "Tempest" Sonata and of the Sonata for Piano and Cello Op. 69, the lack of a settled thematic statement to start the *Eroica*.[10] Musical "process" in these examples is less a discursus on something already plainly stated than it is the very stuff of the musical discourse. As in the Fourth Concerto and Violin Concerto, idea and structure bend in mutual accommodation.

But in the first movement of the Violin Concerto, such expressive variability occurs within a larger frame of uniformity that is another essential ingredient of the serenity everybody hears in this piece. The opening tutti, for one thing, despite the disruption of the big deceptive cadence in t_1 (m. 28), never strays from the home tonic. This represents an extreme endpoint to a long progression in Beethoven's concertos whereby this section grows ever more stable. The Third Concerto, we recall, had offered a modulation as a kind of temporary glitch quickly corrected; the Fourth had ingeniously substituted a modulating second theme for any transitional motion to another key. The Violin Concerto allows nothing more by way of tonal variation in this section than the two momentary descents into the parallel minor (i.e., after the deceptive cadence and in the continuation of the "b" theme). In an older article on the formal shapes in the Violin Concerto, Hans Joachim Moser became confused on this point and boldly questioned his own father's (Andreas Moser's) view of the matter:

> When A. Moser in his analysis takes the idea with the rising D-major scales [our "b"] for the "second theme," then one would have to add a question mark to this identification; for a review of the full deployment of themes in the opening tutti shows that *all* its ideas, including this one, are in the main key. And in what sonata movement since Philip Emanuel Bach can one simply designate as second theme an idea that appears for the first time in the tonic?[11]

The point, of course, is that this is not a sonata, but a concerto. And in putting his opening tutti all in one key—making it more like an introduction or ritornello and less like a sonata exposition—Beethoven is in effect returning to the tradition of concerto writing of J. C. Bach, Haydn, and Mozart, a tradition whose treatment of the opening tutti is rooted in practices of the Baroque ritornello. But in so doing Beethoven is surely responding less to any antiquarian impulse than to the particular expressive ideals of this concerto.

Another force for uniformity in this movement is its extraordinarily regular scheme of periodization, or hypermeter. Once the "external" timpani strokes have been heard, the phrases unfold with near-perfect predictability in modules of four bars (this even includes the violins' imitation of the timpani strokes on D♯ in m. 10). There are two kinds of exceptions to this calculated regularity. First, before important points of arrival there is often a two-measure extension or addition, creating a sensation of "stretching out" as the music approaches something new. This happens just before the off-key "t_1" at m. 28,[12] at the violin's cadenza-like first entrance (which itself promptly turns perfectly regular); it signals the coming of "b" in the first solo (m. 144), the G-minor music in the second solo (m. 331), and so on.

The other kind of exception to this comfortable uniformity of periodization is an occasional disruption plain and simple, done for special expressive effect. The opening measure in the timpani is thus (in retrospect) designated as an interloper in this bucolic landscape, a reminder of another world from which this movement seems to offer temporary respite. Such an effect is confirmed when those four strokes again intrude as an extra measure in S_1 (m. 101) and again in a great exclamation at the beginning of T_3 (m. 365). Then there is something of a jolt within the already disruptive "t_1," where an elision at m. 35—the fourth measure equals the first—adds a further edge of urgency to the proceedings (it happens again in the parallel passages at mm. 231 and 504). But these are exceptions made for particular purposes. The ruling disposition of the movement remains one of calm, one in which the listener's defenses relax in response to a uniform, vaguely singsong playing out of benevolent musical discourse.

Such an effect in this movement is also much abetted by a settled uniformity in its overall shape (see Table 10-1). Its events—except for that calculatedly disruptive one, "t_1"—follow upon one another with an air of unruffled orderliness. But for the omission of "t_1" and a modest extension at its end, the first solo follows exactly the course of the opening tutti, and the third tutti and third solo together repeat precisely the events of that first solo. Even the second tutti (m. 224), from which we expect only a summarizing gesture or two (and possibly a transitional motion to the developmental second solo), after leaping in with the off-key "t_1," pursues as if by inadvertence the train of events that had followed "t" in the first tutti, repeating in order the ideas "b," "bx," and "b_1." This quite relieves Beethoven of the task of making up any new music for this section. And the second solo, from which we expect contrast and development, enters with an imitation of the improvisatory opening of the first solo, as if we were about to start over again from that point. Thereafter we do get some of the tonal motion of a development section: a dominant seventh on G is reinterpreted as an augmented sixth (m. 300) for a magical, shimmering reenactment, very high in the violin range, of the first theme in B minor. But a return from these distant lands to the tonal goal of the section, G minor, is achieved in a process of almost regimented regularity, namely, by five steps around the circle of fifths in the flat direction, from B to C (overshooting, as often happens, by one degree).

Having arrived at G minor, Beethoven presents a hushed melancholic idea (Example 10-2; "atb" in Table 10-1) that seems at once both new and familiar. Rather than deriving clearly from any single earlier event, it convokes properties of several: its overall trajectory (a forthright rise to an afterbeat resolution—what we used to call a feminine cadence) resembles that of "b"; the distinctive staccato eighths just before the resolution recall "t"; the resolution itself reminds us of cadences in both "a" and "b"; and all the while horns and bassoons in the background explicitly invoke the never-to-be-forgotten timpani strokes of "a." This is a specially artful example of the highly abstract ways in which Beethoven leads us to hear connections between disparate events. In the same section of the first movement of the Third Concerto, we are lulled into accepting plain even-note downward scalewise motion as integral, even thematic, because it had featured so prominently in the opening idea; here a generalized shape combines with a collection of musical details, none on its face especially distinctive, to establish the "rightness" of this passage, to domesticate it within its surroundings. The process is a near relative of the "contrasting derivation" Arnold Schmitz found in relations among many of Beethoven's themes: strong contrast in aesthetic character between two themes is mediated by motivic similarities.[13] Here the similarities do not mitigate direct oppositions of expressive character—the G-minor passage only adds certain darker shades to the bucolic landscape—but the principle is the same: correspondences of the seemingly inessential underlie the unity we perceive in the face of clear diversity.

Now, when all that purposeful harmonic motion has led to an obvious destination, we might expect the music to stay put for a time, perhaps to form something like the similarly placed island of gentle pathos in F♯ minor in the first movement of the Fifth Brandenberg Concerto. The G-minor theme itself persists, but the music resumes its harmonic travels. A temporary resting place at E♭ soon proves to be the Neapolitan of the home D (initially minor), which we now approach with large, unhurried motions for the onset of the recapitulation. This quasi-developmental second solo generates little in the way of momentum; in the end it makes its own contribution to a pervasive sense of a pre-ordained succession of events played out in slow orderly fashion (this procession is little disturbed even by the repetition of the "t_1" gambit at the start of the final tutti—which the second time around is no longer much of a surprise).

A reviewer for the *Wiener Theater-Zeitung*, commenting on the first performance of the Violin Concerto (December 1806), reported a complaint of connoisseurs that "endless repetitions of certain common passages (*Stellen*) could easily be tiring."[14] And that inevitable seeming train of events in the first movement, to be sure, does include a lot of leisurely and unashamed repetition. Even without counting, listeners can hardly be insensible to hearing the lyrical "b" five times, the extra occurrences coming from the "borrowed" music in the second tutti and the playing of this theme yet again in the coda. (We hear it more like six or seven times if the violinist uses either the Joachim or Kreisler cadenza.) Repetition of a sort is a familiar staple of music in the pastoral mode. The mantra-like reiteration of unvaried motives in the Sixth Symphony, particularly in the development of the first movement, creates a prevailing impression of stasis, a perfect counterpart—and inducement—to the spiritual calm at which Beethoven aimed. There is some such local repetition in the Violin Concerto movement, as within "b_1" (mm. 77ff.; see the end of Example 10-1d)—which is also played five times in its entirety.

But the pastoral element in the concerto—less pronounced, in any case than in the symphony—is more a matter of musical line, harmony, and instrumentation than of repetitive syntax. Repetition here occurs more typically on a larger scale and to somewhat different expressive ends; we hear things stated again (and again) at a considerable distance in the slow unfolding of a highly uniform structure. The effect is almost like a ritual that thrives on such repetition, on the comforts of the familiar; and in such a context few would wish to complain about knowing what comes next. Beethoven's music engages us not in heroic drives toward musical climax, nor in any ongoing mental exercise in measuring implication against realization, or (at the other extreme) in a passive presence in a motionless landscape, but rather in a quiet act of contemplation and assent to what we had expected all along.

THE LARGHETTO

The coda of the first movement ends with a little flash of brilliance that seems no more than de rigueur: a brief cadential tail to the "b$_1$" melody mounts in four measures from a prevailing *pianissimo* to *fortissimo*, as the solo violin scurries upward through four octaves to d''''. This does not begin to dispel the overall mood of calm or to alleviate the prospect, should the second movement be at all of the traditional sort, that we will hear two lyrical movements in succession. In symphonies, sonatas, and quartets the composer could easily settle the matter with a simple exchange of the two middle movements: the dance-like piece could follow a first movement of gentle persuasion, as in four of the six Quartets in Haydn's Op. 33, Mozart's String Quartets K. 387 and 464, Beethoven's Sonatas Op. 26 and Op. 27, No. 1, his String Quartet Op. 59, No. 1, and many other examples. But in the concerto Beethoven's unwavering devotion to the traditional three-movement form foreclosed any such easy solution. (The problem did not come up in the Fourth Concerto, of course, because of the highly idiosyncratic and essentially nonlyrical second movement.) The Violin Concerto confronts this matter head-on: the second movement is *larghetto*, begins *pianissimo*, and uses muted orchestral strings throughout. In some respects it even returns to that comfortable repetitiveness to which we became accustomed in the opening movement. It is essentially a theme-and-variations structure, and an exceedingly literal one at that, with all the quotidian repetition such an arrangement entails.

But this movement is nonetheless so strikingly distinctive in character as to preclude any impressions of redundancy. The theme (Example 10-3) and its variations are built on a descending ground bass reminiscent of a species of chaconne: four pairs of measures with a caesura (on the seventh degree) in the middle and a two-measure epilogue at the end. An invocation of antiquity in the use of such a formula is furthered by a slow dance-like rhythm that pauses emphatically on the second beat, thus— despite its duple meter—distantly recalling, as well, the sarabande.[15] This bass line is built on a major version of the descending diatonic tetrachord, G–D, with the semitone on top. Each of the principal tones is harmonized as a root of its triad—most strikingly the F♯—and each (except the F♯) is preceded by its dominant. Such movement by fifths was common in various of the old ground basses: the passamezzo antico, the romanesca, and in some versions of the chaconne.[16] Here the pattern, as it happens, also approaches a bass behavior rather more common in Beethoven's day, simple downward motion by fifth (the G–F♯ being the single exception), and Beethoven seizes upon the standard but splendid opportunity for attendant chromatic downward motion in an upper voice that such a bass progression offers. In Example 10-3 (mm. 2–6) this chromatic line, B down to F♯, is divided between the viola and second violin, and it is unerringly present within the orchestral strings in each variation.[17] Still, the aroma of antiquity persists, at least until m. 7, where the mask slips with a plain (and premature-sounding) dominant-tonic cadence with parallel sixths above, a sound belonging distinctly to the nineteenth century. What follows is only a short cadential summing up, but one that again recalls a usual ending formula of the chaconne.

What would move Beethoven to take up a technique so long outmoded as this basso ostinato? Any answer to this question should take into account that this is not at all an isolated occurrence; during Beethoven's middle years schematic bass patterns, some of them distinctly associated with earlier times, show up with conspicuous frequency. Closely contemporaneous with the Violin Concerto is the set of Thirty-two Variations in C minor (WoO 80), its theme built upon a descending chromatic tetrachord—again with adjustments at the end. An even better known example is the opening theme of the "Waldstein" Sonata Op. 53.[18] The second theme of the first movement of the "Emperor" Piano Concerto, as we shall see in the next chapter, follows exactly, both in bass and melody, a late-seventeenth-century version of the *folia*. The first theme of the second movement of the Fifth Symphony is built strictly upon a bass descending by fifth, downright Vivaldian in its reach, from A♭ back to A♭ (with the typical substitution of a tritone, D♭–G, in m. 3, so as to shorten the trip around the circle of fifths by half). How it is that Beethoven came to use such techniques is far from clear. The descending chromatic tetrachord, the "lament" bass, was common enough in Beethoven's Vienna, especially in church music.[19] But one can only guess as to whether he actually knew examples of the *folia* or simply hit upon the pattern independently (the distinctive sound of the third degree in the bass, 1–5–1–7–3–7–1–5, also shows up in the minor version of the second theme of the first movement of the Violin Concerto). The use of these bass patterns, wherever he got them, is a distinct eccentricity in the first decade of the nineteenth century. Some preterite impulse lends an aura of retrospection to a number of Beethoven's middle-period compositions,[20] an arresting blend of exoticism and severity. However much the sheer sound of these old patterns appealed to Beethoven, he may also have valued such techniques for the very reason of their technical severity, for their limiting function—just as in a few years he would turn to those most restricting of procedures, fugue and variations, as cornerstones for his late style.

In this movement the bass pattern is not perfectly consistent from variation to variation: the initial tonic note is sacrificed in variations 1, 3, and 4, as the opening is turned into an ascending horn call with the typical $^6_3$ configuration. What is perfectly invariable are the pitches of the melody above, ritually repeated note for note in all four variations. The variability of these variations, anything but conventional for either their own century or for that of the chaconne, comes about in two ways: by changing instrumental color from one variation to the next, and by increasingly fervent— and growingly thematic—commentary in the solo violin. The theme, shown in Example 10-3, is in the orchestral strings alone; the first two variations (mm. 10 and 20) put the melody (except for the prefatory horn call) in the first clarinet and first bassoon, respectively. The third one (m. 30) curiously reverts to the orchestral strings, but now filling the empty rests with solemn full-voiced echoes in the winds;[21] the soloist stands silent. In the final variation (m. 55), the melody becomes something of a ghost, played pizzicato and *perdendosi* (dying away) in the strings—something like the conclusion of the Scherzo in the Fifth Symphony. But now the soloist, having heretofore provided ornament and eloquent commentary to the theme, plays the tune itself in an only lightly elaborated fashion, often staggering the notes in echo of the pizzicato first violins as in the eighteenth-century version of *tempo rubato* (Example 10-4, mm. 58, 63–65). We come to expect successive variations to grow increasingly abstract—hence the stark and unforeseen drama when the theme returns naked at the end of the *Goldberg Variations* and of Beethoven's Sonata Op. 109. But here there is something of a long-term drive toward explicitness, first in the orchestral strings (third variation) and finally in the solo violin itself. The archaic theme follows its inevitable course with dignity, standing conspicuously on its own merits.

That ghostly fourth variation has what turns out to be a new theme wrapped around it; this unexpected melody, entirely the province of the solo violin, arrives unheralded in the home key at m. 45 (see the beginning of Example 10-4). While its bass rises by fifths, roughly mirroring the motion of the main theme, its character is starkly different: a soaring melody floats over a long tonic pedal, then rises in tenths with the bass toward a cadential dominant. It sounds settled, almost inert, utterly modern in its time. But then that cadence sticks fast, as if this other melody were only a passing distraction, and imperceptibly the music merges back into the fourth variation on the main theme. When the variation has run its course, we hear four measures of mysterious solo rumination over a tonic pedal (Example 10-4, mm. 65–69). Our suspicion that this is really the missing ending to that *other* theme is confirmed in what follows: the soloist (mm. 71–86) plays a somewhat ornamented version of the music that preceded and followed the fourth variation; those four ruminating final tonic measures prove to be the missing resolution and a convincing counterweight to the initial tonic pedal of the *other* theme. Use of this second theme leaves nothing of the impression of double variations, or alternating variations, of the type canonized by Haydn; it adds, rather, a reflective gesture, a placid present-tense meditation on the archaic structure unfolding around it, and which, on a smaller scale, it enfolds. The main theme is the central essence here, a settled, serene presence; the movement—which Tovey calls a "case of sublime inaction"—stands or falls on it. The other theme registers real time in the face of archaism; it records the distance from which Beethoven contemplates this revisitation of the past.

THE FINALE

As the second movement with its stylized solemnity comes to a close, there is a final pondering of the placid second theme, perfect, with its tonic pedal, for this last backward glance. Then an alarm sounds: the orchestral strings (like the disrobing nuns in the graveyard scene of *Robert le Diable*) cast off their mutes, and a rousing double-dotted, jagged-edged imitation of the first theme's rhythm drives to a portentous augmented sixth, perched where it belongs on the lowered sixth degree; in the dominant resolution that follows the solo violin assents to these proceedings with a prolonging cadenza. The alarm is by design a false one; what it good-humoredly signals, of course, is only a traditional finale, a rondo and a particularly lighthearted specimen at that. This famous movement starts with the dominating ritornello theme in the solo violin, played very low, by explicit instruction on the G string. The sound is gruff and gritty—like a cabaret soprano belting out a strain at the bottom of her range for semi-comic effect. And upon its repetition the soloist with a certain perversity plays two octaves *up (delicatamente)*, skipping the normal soprano range of the violin altogether—or, as we soon learn, leaving it entirely to the orchestral instruments when they play the music over again (Example 10-5, m. 20) upon repetition of the second strain.[22] We get two more chances to hear this amiable manipulation of tessitura, at the second and third ritornellos (mm. 93 and 175), where the whole theme is repeated verbatim (in the autograph Beethoven simply wrote a da capo). Surely there is something of a comic intent here, quite in keeping with the expectations built into the genre of the rondo; Beethoven probably intended this agile leaping among registers—while studiously ignoring the obvious one—as a gentle parody of violinistic vanity, an effect that for most of us may have worn off with repeated hearings.

That theme itself, ingenuous, unabashedly square, bumpkinish, is pared away to the bare bones. At the outset its only accompaniment is some dull tonic drumming in the cellos faintly reminiscent of the timpani strokes of the first movement; this presently turns into a fragmentary bass counterpoint, always appealingly offbeat. When the tune vaults up two octaves, so does the drumming, landing in the orchestral violins; these tonic strokes find their true home in the timpani only when the full orchestra—joined even by the horns, insofar as they are able—restates the theme *fortissimo* in the second run-through of the "recapitulation" at m. 20. Elaboration here is minimal; there is nothing after the implied double bar of the binary shape except for the two-measure teasing lead-in and the restatement of the theme. So in the twenty-eight measures of this complex, all but four are theme pure and simple.

This theme achieves its overwhelming prominence in the movement largely because everything else is at least equally minimalist, and nothing else has the advantage of three-fold repetition (see Table 10-2). An extension of the theme at m. 28 introduces a fetching new rhythmic dotted-note motive that promptly disappears; a phantom of a second theme in the dominant (m. 58) with a life span of ten measures dissolves, almost before we are aware of it, into the soloistic pyrotechnics of the rondo's equivalent of a display episode. The only other integral stretch of music laying claim to our attention for any duration is the charming central episode in G minor (m. 126), built very much along the lines of the ritornello theme, with two eight-measure halves, each repeated with ritualistic exchanges between solo violin and first bassoon.[23] It floats weightlessly above a long tonic pedal, turns firmly toward the relative major, and returns to its beginning: a darkly peaceful island of thirty-two brief measures that we will not hear again (Example 10-6). We are reminded that the central section (S_2) of the first movement had also retreated for a quiet interlude in the minor subdominant (Example 10-2). The effect here, if only because of its context, seems more memorable. While in the listener's mind the G-minor passage of the first movement tends to fade into its more similar surroundings, this episode projects a stark contrast with its ambient music as if a pensive yet vivid new character has walked onstage, for only a moment. But upon its exit—which comes all too soon—it leaves behind faint traces in a listener's memory of that similar quiet passage, heard some twenty-five minutes earlier. Of all the central episodes we have seen in Beethoven's concerto rondos, this is the most sober and appealing; it is also the most fleeting.

The third ritornello, as usual, kicks off the formal recapitulation, where everything falls into place pretty much as expected. The brief second theme (b) comes in the tonic instead of the dominant; the ensuing brilliant passages for the solo instrument (the equivalent, we remember, of a display episode in a first movement) that in the exposition had inclined strongly toward the Neapolitan, E♭, now leans toward the corresponding flat fifth degree, down a fifth (mm. 68ff. and 242ff.). Running out of music to transpose in m. 263, Beethoven fashions an extension featuring some horn-call music, borrowed from the transition, that now leads to the cadenza. Somewhere in here we expect the fourth ritornello. We do now get the ritornello theme, in fact two versions of it; but neither turns out to be the real thing. First, a deceptive resolution of the cadenza leads back to the lowered fifth for a playing of that theme in this remote key (all Beethoven's concerto rondos at some point bring the ritornello theme back in a distant tonality, usually as a teasing precursor of the genuine article). After an ornamented version of the tune rights itself with the help of a fine chromatic falling bass line (mm. 296ff.), we have the theme back where it belongs. But it is too late for a final ritornello proper; this is a coda-like backward-looking statement, *pianissimo*, all over a static tonic pedal, with the answering phrase in the solo violin altered to accommodate this new harmonic context. All that remains after this moment of retrospection is a regrouping of forces for some brilliant cadential passagework to make the requisite vigorous close.

The finale of the Violin Concerto is a robust, jolly piece. It is also short, over with in barely more than a third the playing time of the first movement. Compared with most Beethoven finales of the middle period, there are fewer gestures here to temper a pervading air of joviality, fewer pauses for doubt or reflection or second thoughts. There is little here to compare with the soaring expanse of the central episode in the Third Concerto's finale or that movement's elaborate musical references back to the previous one, or with the expressive and formal intricacy of the finale of the Fourth Concerto. Except for the short-breathed central episode in G minor, any structural ambiguity or expressive dissent is saved for this movement's final minute-and-a-half. Following upon the tranquil expanses of the first movement and the ritual archaism of the second, this finale might be said to create a certain imbalance in specific gravity among the concerto's parts—a consequence, we might suppose, of the enormous

TABLE 10-2 OP. 61, III

	45	58	68
R₁			

S|T S

a	trans.	b	pass.
I		~~~ V, v	V (♭ II) V

	92	126
R₂	E	

S|T S

a	c	ext.
I	iv	~

	174	218	233	242	279
R₃					

S|T S .... cad.

a	trans.	b	pass.	ext.
I		~~~ I, i	I (♭ V) I	

	293	314
(R₄)		

S

a	Coda (a)
♭ V ~~~	I (IV, ♭ VI) I

time pressure under which it was composed. But the sympathy and joy with which generations of listeners have received this finale suggest other thoughts: forthright good humor and uncomplicated rejoicing may rank high as human values, quite fit to stand together in the artistic enterprise with expressions of the most profound sort.

WRITING FOR SOLO VIOLIN

Upon composing this concerto Beethoven was not wholly inexperienced in writing soloistic music for violin. In Bonn he had composed most of a movement (or more) of that early Violin Concerto in C, in which the solo writing is at least plausible; then there are his two Romances for violin from about 1802, and the "Kreutzer" Sonata of 1802–3, the latter "scritto in un stilo molto concertante, quasi come d'un concerto," as he said—a qualification evidently meant to separate this piece from the genre of the accompanied keyboard sonata with which all sonatas with piano and one or two other instruments were naturally associated. The advanced intricacy of the violin part fully justifies Beethoven's distinction. On evenhanded scrutiny the solo part of the Violin Concerto, especially in comparison with the *concertante* writing of the sonata, might seem a bit primitive. There are none of the dramatic double stops so characteristic of the first movement of the "Kreutzer,"[24] nor any other of the special effects—with the tame exceptions of the *sul G* in the ritornello of the finale and the orchestral mutes in the concerto's second movement—that were common currency in the violin literature of the time. Even the concertos of Viotti, composed about a decade earlier, are much more adventurous than Beethoven's in this respect (Example 10-7a shows the second theme of the first movement of Viotti's Concerto in A minor from the mid-1790s). Beethoven's solo violin has long stretches of harmonic figuration in uniform sixteenths that in a lesser composition might easily be thought a bit boring (Examples 10-7b and c). But these passages have simply become part of the familiar and well-loved sound of this composition; indeed, their very ordinariness, particularly in the first movement, contributes to that sense of majestic slow inevitability at the heart of this work.

But another device in Beethoven's violin writing, equally determinative of the sound of this composition, is far from ordinary. This is a technique for which we might borrow the old term *heterophony*, one in which the solo instrument rings changes on the melody as it is played in the orchestra. A particularly fine moment of this sort is heard in the stately downward motion by fifths (five steps, from B to C) in the second solo of the first movement: while the bassoons traverse this great span with a sequence in thirds derivative of the first theme, the violinist spins out an eloquent commentary that incorporates all its pitches (Example 10-7d). This kind of writing is still more characteristic of the variations of the second movement (Example 10-7e), contributing essentially to the measured dignity of this piece, and to its vaguely "antique" physiognomy.

Sometimes the violin writing in this composition becomes what it is because Beethoven is working against the restraints imposed by transposition from a parallel passage; this is clearly the case in Example 10-7c (from the third solo of the finale), where, taking mm. 81ff. as a model, he transposes everything down a fifth until forced by the range of the instrument to rewrite. The rewriting is minimal, and for this fleeting instant the result (if one dare say it) oversteps the commonplace to verge on the banal. But the original solo part at mm. 81ff. may already have had its own problems. As Example 10-7f shows, the violin figuration in mm. 81–82 and 85–86 is laid out in pairs of measures in which the second is an octave below the first. But in mm. 83–84 the parallel figuration for no visible reason breaks the pattern and puts both measures in the lower octave.[25] This is only one example of an unusual number of textual anomalies that have always afflicted this composition we think we know so well.

TEXTUAL ORIGINS AND UNCERTAINTIES

The first performance of the Violin Concerto took place on December 23, 1806, at the benefit concert of Franz Clement, first violinist and director at the Theater an der Wien. Other works heard that evening were overtures of Méhul and Cherubini, an aria of Mozart, a vocal quartet by Cherubini, and a Fantasy and Sonata "on a single string with a reversed violin" played (and evidently composed) by Clement.[26] Despite such diversions, the correspondent for the Leipzig *Allgemeine musikalische Zeitung*, writing some two weeks later, confined his remarks to the performance of the concerto: "To the admirers of Beethoven's muse it may be of interest that this composer has written a violin concerto—the first, so far as I know—which the beloved local violinist Klement, in the concert given for his benefit, played with his usual elegance and luster."[27]

Such elegance and luster seem to have been all the more to the agile violinist's credit, since by all accounts Beethoven, barely getting the concerto written down in time for the performance, had left him no time to practice. Czerny reported in later years that Beethoven had composed at breakneck speed, finishing the work a scant two days before the concert, and other witnesses mentioned that Clement was obliged to play the solo part at sight, without a rehearsal.[28] Czerny's recollection is to a degree confirmed by other evidence. There is little to be known about the earlier stages of composition, since all we have in the way of sketches for the concerto are some fragmentary notations for the beginnings of the first and third movements on a single page of the miscellany Landsberg 10 (p. 64); these jottings are what Tyson calls "concept sketches," which probably preceded serious work on the composition, and that in any case cannot be very securely dated.[29] But in the letter to Breitkopf & Härtel of September 3, in which he offered for publication five major works including the "Rasumovsky" Quartets and the Fourth Concerto, there is no mention of a new violin concerto. And another letter to the Leipzig publisher of November 18 likewise mentions the piano concerto and the quartets but is again silent on the subject of a violin concerto.[30] In view of Beethoven's obvious eagerness to get his works published during this period, and the well-known optimism of his predictions as to when they were likely to be finished, this curious absence would lead one to think he had made little progress with the concerto by the latter part of November.[31] If this is the case (as appears likely), the time of its composition was evidently compressed into a period of little more than a month.

The solo part Clement read at sight that December evening seems to have differed appreciably from the version we know. In the autograph of the work, dated 1806,[32] now in the Nationalbibliothek, Vienna, the solo part, especially in the outer movements, is a battleground of competing versions. But an early layer of writing, the version written into the staff originally reserved for the solo violin plus its corrections, is made with a certain purposefulness and consistency—with the supplanted reading carefully expunged—that bespeaks the necessities of either performance or publication. As preparations for publication are clearly associated with later stages of revision, we have good reason to believe that this earlier layer presents the text used in preparation of parts for the performance in December 1806.[33]

Substantial variance from the solo part as we know it comes to light almost immediately in the first movement, in the transitional material "t" (mm. 126ff.) leading to the second theme (as well as in the parallel passage in the third solo, mm. 386ff.). In the earlier version the entering run in broken octaves—reminiscent, surely, of the very opening of the violin part—reasonably carries on upward to the high a''' rather than giving up the octaves for a more conventional alternating-note figuration, as in the final version (Example 10–8a).[34] In the third movement Beethoven wrote another very long passage in broken octaves that did not survive alteration; this occurs in the continuation of the far-away *pianissimo* reappearance of the ritornello theme in A♭ shortly before the close of the movement (mm. 292ff.; see Example 10–8b). The issue, in both cases, may have to do simply with the difficulty of playing all those octaves in tune—a problem violinists still fret about in respect to the celebrated but much more moderate opening of the first solo. The successive alternations Beethoven made in the violin part often improved its playability on the instrument, as various commentators have observed. Whether he made these changes of his own accord or on the explicit advice of the violinist Clement, as some have assumed, we are not in a position to know.[35]

The audience on that December 1806 evening apparently also heard a distinctly different version of the fine contemplative episode in G minor in the second solo of the first movement, at mm. 330ff. The trajectory of the solo melody, as we know it, reaches g‴ in its exhilarating ascent to the dominant; a matching phrase aimed at the tonic then reproduces this line essentially a fifth lower, after which a concluding segment (moving now toward the key of E♭) with obscure motivation leaps back up, reaching over the previous high point to a♭‴. This odd shifting of register, it turns out, is a remnant of the earlier version in which the entire second phrase was set in the upper octave, soaring all the way up to c⁗—and providing for a smooth and seamless descent back down toward the new key (see Example 10–8c). The sound of the theme here, as Beethoven first thought of it, was distinctly different from what we know and really quite wonderful: there was a silveriness, a kind of ghostly sheen that was later replaced by the warmth—and one might almost say conservatism—of the lower octave. Was Beethoven's decision to reconfigure the theme with its middle segment down an octave an aesthetic or practical one? Did he favor the richness and heft of the lower tones, or was he moved by the danger of loss of melodic continuity—and accurate intonation—in that risky highest register?[36]

The most startling variance the autograph shows from the ultimate published versions of the concerto did not survive the first round of Beethoven's corrections and was apparently stricken before the first performance. The passage in question is the beginning of T₃ in the first movement, the famous moment of recapitulation where the orchestra enters with the first theme now turned huge and insistent. This point in all Beethoven's concertos but the Fourth, Op. 58 (and almost all of Mozart's), belongs to the orchestra: the full forces of the tutti proclaim the crucial return of the original musical idea in the original tonic. The soloist, of course, rests. But in Beethoven's first conception the violinist was anything but silent: beginning with the *fortissimo* "drumbeats" at m. 365, the soloist flails away for seventeen measures with virtuoso wide-ranging scales and arpeggios—relentless, exhausting, at points nearly unplayable (Example 10–8d)—leaving, finally, only four measures of rest before the next solo entrance at m. 335. (In a similar but less flamboyant early idea at this stage of the autograph, the matching internal tuttis in theme "b$_1$" at mm. 178 and 452 are also decked out with broken-chord figuration by the soloist).

So once again, as in the case of the Fourth Concerto,[37] we know that Beethoven contemplated solo playing during the principal orchestral tuttis. In neither case was this to be anything like a doubling of orchestra parts, as in, say, the concertos of Corelli from a century earlier. Nor did it resemble either a continuo realization (as might conceivably be appropriate in the piano concerto) or a reduction of the orchestral music for keyboard (which in fact occurs in the autograph of the "Emperor" Concerto, together with continuo figures). In these notations in the Violin Concerto, the soloist participates enthusiastically in the business at hand, adding a texture that is once again "heterophonic," with the theme plainly embedded within the coils of the violinist's figuration.

In both concertos this music is assertive, apodictic, a prominent feature of what is being said at the moment. Both passages were evidently recorded in preparation for a first performance. But Beethoven preserved neither for posterity: the one he jotted down only in fleeting, private notation meant for himself alone; the other he obliterated before the first performance. In neither concerto were prescriptions for solo playing during the tuttis ultimately preserved in writing that had a "public intent," in notation, that is, from which performance parts were to be copied (though with the Violin Concerto there may have been moments of indecision on this point), or parts engraved for publication. Like cadenzas in the earlier piano concertos, some such music was evidently meant to be heard but was ultimately excluded from the written record. Its precise nature Beethoven probably saw as the prerogative of the soloist—even if, as in the case of the Violin Concerto, that soloist was another musician playing another instrument. Here Beethoven seemingly still paid lip-service, at least, to a distinction between a concerto as a "work" and as something more like an "event" subject to the whim of the moment. But as he gradually turned his concertos over to other players (and presently stopped writing them altogether), he plainly trusted their whim less than his own. His directions grew more specific: the cadenza for the last movement of the Fourth Concerto was to be short ("la cadenza sia corte" says Beethoven's note); all the cadenzas for the Fifth are written out; and in 1809, the year of that concerto, he supplied cadenzas for all the previous piano concertos as well.

But if this notation for soloistic playing during orchestral tuttis has the approximate "authenticity" status of Beethoven's indications for cadenzas (i.e., if they instruct only that something improvisatory is expected at this point from the soloist), should modern performers pay any attention to such a thing? We have grown accustomed to hearing a bit of continuo-like playing during the tuttis of Mozart's piano concertos (as in Malcolm Bilson's fine recordings), while such a practice is still very rare among modern performers of Beethoven's works—a fortiori in the Violin Concerto. Two notated examples that the composer (for whatever good reason) chose not to preserve of course provide slim grounds for changing modern habits of performance. But the sources as a whole suggest a much greater degree of variability and leeway for the performer than we are accustomed to: the solo part usually remained in the rough until some version of it was fixed by publication; new performances were the occasion not only for fresh cadenzas, but also more often than not for far-reaching changes in the solo part proper. The score for a concerto was a rough script for a particular event, subject to change for the next one. While Beethoven tended to be cautious about other players' liberties, the modern performance in which certain freedoms are taken—original cadenzas, even solo playing in the tuttis—is probably in the end less anachronistic than the one that faithfully renders every note, not one more nor fewer, of the authorized score.

The music for solo violin Beethoven first wrote into the tutti sections all but robs the orchestra of its most dramatic "solo" function and radically readjusts, from our latter-day perspective, the balance between the two forces. The first movement was to have been cast more in the mold of the concerto of the 1830s and 1840s, with the virtuoso soloist very much in command and almost continuously in evidence. This abetted an impression of pervasive uniformity in that first version, a uniformity owning not only to the almost continuous presence of the soloist, but also to the sometimes dogged consistency of the figuration in that part. While in the concerto as we know it there are many passages in languorously constant sixteenth notes, strategic changes in motion—partly because of that prevailing uniformity—can have a telling effect. This happens particularly at the approach to important points of arrival. In the display episode following "b_1" in the first movement (mm. 181ff.), for example, the soloist launches into two pages of determined sixteenth-note passagework, broken at m. 195, finally, as a big cadence approaches. This change of surface motion is allied with a metrical "stretching" effect, as the prevailing four-bar hypermeter gives way to a group of six, effectively braking the forward momentum on a larger and smaller scale at once. This refinement was entirely missing in the concerto as Clement evidently played it: the sixteenth-note motion barreled along right into those cadential measures with an invariance that would probably have sounded, to those of us who know the final version, at least, somewhat unreflective.[38] In this case, the changes made between performance and publication seem a net gain.

An integral first stage of composition ("Stage 1") that apparently produced the version of the violin part heard at its premiere is relatively easy to discern in the autograph (A). It is written in the staff allotted to the solo part; its corrections, written in lower blank staves (usually the bottom one) and cued in with Beethoven's customary signs such as "vi-de," are in what appears to be the same ink. A second layer of writing ("Stage 2"), also entered in blank staves below, but in a much darker ink, presents a much less satisfying prospect: at many points it offers alternative readings, often where that of the first stage apparently remains in force (first movement, mm. 115–116, 151–55, 162–65, etc.), and very occasionally it suggests two such alternatives at once (first movement, mm. 173–74, 334). This stage does not therefore present an integral version, and the autograph could not at this later point have been used to create parts for performance or publication.[39] Another document was needed to clarify the composer's intentions. The next source that survives is the copyist's score (B), since 1952 in the British Library.[40] (See Table 10-3 below for a schematic account of the sources for this work.) As Alan Tyson has convincingly shown, the orchestral parts in this manuscript are taken directly from the autograph. The solo violin part, appearing virtually in the form in which it has come down to us, obviously came from some intermediate source, now lost. This has become the "definitive" version by virtue of its publication (in parts only), early in 1809, by the Bureau des Arts et d'Industrie in Vienna (C).[41]

This, the current form of the violin part, bears an odd, fragmented relationship to the text of the autograph: sometimes it follows Stage 1 of Beethoven's writing, sometimes Stage 2, and occasionally it offers entirely new readings. Switching among versions can occur at very short intervals, and any rationale for the choices made is far from obvious—even parallel passages do not always agree. Such considerations led one commentator, Fritz Kaiser, to the remarkable conclusion that the violin part as we know it (in the outer two movements, that is, since the slow movement shows few of these problems) was probably assembled by someone other than the composer; he called it "a kind of corruption of the original text that appears to exclude its having been made by Beethoven. Its stylistic disunity shows an illogic that cannot be found in any Beethoven concerto, and that has no parallel, particularly in any solo part."[42] But (in one more illustration of the dangers of forming conclusions solely on stylistic evidence) Kaiser's conclusion has since been seriously questioned: Shin Augustinus Kojima has pointed out a whole series of autograph corrections in the violin part of B that were destined for the first edition.[43]

Whatever we may think of the violin part of Beethoven's concerto, or its manner of construction, we can hardly doubt that he sent it into the world with his blessing. The elusive history of this solo part may, finally, have something to do with the matter of genre. At two points in that history textual precision was needed because parts were to be made for performance or publication; these two junctures correspond to the first stage of the autograph and the final redaction as we have it in B and in the first edition. Between these two points Beethoven allowed competing versions of soloistic playing to coexist in suspension—recalling the customary sketchiness of the solo part in his earlier piano concertos—as if to replicate in writing something of the fluidity of an improvisatory style proper to the concerto.

While the history of the solo violin part is complex and in important ways obscure, the orchestral parts arrive on the scene with a relatively unclouded pedigree. Beethoven wrote and corrected them in the autograph, which then served as the model for copy B; he made further corrections in this copy, which was thereupon used to make the first edition. Nonetheless, the orchestra's music also retains a great many textual anomalies and some clear mistakes. It is not only a question of an unusual number of the usual problems with text—disagreements in the sources about ties and slurs, say, or dots and dynamic marks. There are basic questions here about the notes. In his article of 1967 Tyson called attention to a number of these problems and offered suggestions as to their solution. What are we to make of the suspicious isolated g″ in the flute in m. 88 of the third movement, as all the traditional scores and parts show it—is this note perhaps a fortuitous remnant of Beethoven's onetime plan for the flute to double the first violin in mm. 85–89? In mm. 278ff. of the first movement, why does the second bassoon abruptly stop doubling the cellos and basses as they answer the melody in the violins? In the second solo of the first movement, mm. 304–17, as the music begins its stately descent by fifths from B minor, the strings play sustained tones and reminiscences of the opening timpani strokes, all approximately in unison. But in all the older editions the violas and cellos keep dropping in and out, while the first violin joins in only after an inexplicable two-measure rest.

None of this can possibly be what Beethoven intended.[44] Many such difficulties must surely be ascribed to simple inadvertence, to Beethoven's evident haste in writing out the autograph—particularly from lapses in continuity at page turns—or from pointlessly literal interpretation in B of the composer's timesaving abbreviations (such as indications for doubling), and from careless proofreading by Beethoven himself. Often there is no solution to these problems that is clearly right, only reasonable responses to difficulties once they have been understood. In 1968 Eulenburg put out a new printing of its miniature score (made from the old plates newly altered) with corrections made by Tyson, changes that sometimes follow the suggestions he made in the article of 1967 and sometimes do not. The edition in the new *Beethoven Werke*, edited by Kojima, comes up with a very similar set of solutions.[45] These editions go a very long way toward solving the textual conundrums that have always plagued this concerto; their use among violinists and orchestras would add an increment of clarity to our understanding and appreciation of the work.

The Violin Concerto played a part in a new plan for "simultaneous publication" that Beethoven had tried to carry out, beginning in 1804, in order to block the alliances publishers made to the disadvantage of composers—as well as to counter the common practice of international piracy—and get full payment for his music. On April 26, 1807, he wrote identical letters to Simrock in Bonn and Pleyel in Paris, offering for a fixed price six works that were to be published on specified dates (September 1 and October 1), thus depriving publishers of the chance of trading, or simply appropriating, music from one another. Shortly thereafter Beethoven entered into similar negotiations with the Viennese publisher the Bureau des Arts et d'Industrie.[46] And, as we have noted above in Chapter 9, just a few days before this he offered the same group of compositions (the others being the Fourth Piano Concerto Op. 58; the "Rasumovsky" Quartets Op. 59; the Fourth Symphony Op. 60; and the *Coriolan* Overture Op. 62) to the London firm of Muzio Clementi, who was at the time in Vienna. By April 22, 1807, negotiations were complete and Clementi wrote exuberantly to his business partner, William Collard, that after several previous efforts[47] he had finally secured publishing rights for Beethoven's much-coveted music:

> By a little management, and without committing myself, I have at last made a compleat conquest of that *haughty beauty*, Beethoven: who first began at public places to grin and coquet with me which I took care not to discourage: then slid into familiar chat, till meeting him by chance one day in the street—Where do you lodge, says he; I have

not seen you this long while! . . . In short, I agreed with him to take in MSS from *three quartettes*, a *symphony*, an *overture*, a *concerto for the violin*, which is beautiful and which, at my request, he will adapt for the pianoforte with and without additional keys; and a *concerto for the Pianoforte*: for *all* which we are to pay him two hundred pounds sterling. The property however is only for the British Dominions. Today sets off a courier for London thro' Russia, and he will bring over to you 2 or 3 of the mentioned articles. Remember that the violin concerto Beethoven will adapt himself and send it as soon as he can.[48]

Beethoven and Clementi had signed a contract for publication of these five works two days earlier, on April 20.[49] This contract stated that the violin concerto, symphony, and overture had just been dispatched to England. Clementi's letter to his partner Collard of two days later had it slightly differently: the courier was to leave "today" and would travel (through Russia) with two or three of the compositions. These negotiations took place during the height of the Napoleonic wars, and the long detour through Russia was necessitated by Napoleon's "Continental System," which aimed to prevent any movement of goods between England and the European mainland. In fact, having capitulated to the French pursuant to the invasion of 1805, Austria was at the moment Napoleon's ally, and in planning this shipment of musical goods to London, Beethoven and Clementi were evidently breaking Austrian law as well. Probably owing at least partly to such vicissitudes, things went very wrong with these plans for publication: Clementi's firm first published the quartets in 1809–10, not from any manuscript sent by the composer, but, apparently, as a reprint (*Nachdruck*) of the Vienna print of 1808, and the Violin Concerto in the autumn of 1810. The other three compositions never appeared at all in the lists of Clementi's company, and it seems clear that much of the music to be sent according to the terms of the contract never arrived in London.[50]

Only one of the publications stemming from these negotiations shows signs of direct communications between composer and publisher, and was thus likely part of the manuscript materials sent from Vienna at about the time the contract was signed: the orchestral parts of the Violin Concerto in Clementi's edition represent a stage in their textual history prior to the Viennese first edition of early 1809, and even of the copy B from which that edition was made. They were evidently based on a set of parts copied directly from the autograph as it existed before Beethoven made corrections preparatory to the writing out of B.[51] The solo parts of Clementi's edition are quite another matter: they seem to be of distinctly later provenance, derived from neither the autograph nor the copy B, but (like the Quartets Op. 59) from the first edition of 1808–9. Table 10-3 summarizes the somewhat complex interrelations among the sources for the concerto.

THE PIANO TRANSCRIPTION

The contract and Clementi's letter both specify that Beethoven is to supply the London publisher a piano version of the Violin Concerto. A few desultory sketches of a left-hand part for this transcription already show up in the bottom staves of the autograph. Like the solo violin part, it appears complete in copy B and in the first edition[52] (and, derived from the latter, in Clementi's edition). This version of the concerto has led a shadowy existence: while there were very few performances of the original version for violin until Joachim championed its cause at mid-century, the piano transcription seems to have been virtually unknown until modern times (though it was included in the old Breitkopf & Härtel *Gesamtausgabe* of 1863). It has always been regarded as Beethoven's own and is listed in the Kinsky-Halm catalogue without apparent reservation. But even now the transcription is seen more as a curiosity than as a true member of the Beethoven oeuvre. It enjoys nothing of the status, say, of the two-piano versions of works of Brahms, such as the Variations on a Theme of Haydn, and perhaps justifiably so.

The part for right hand of the piano transcription is, to put it simply, yet another version of the violin line; it differs from all the printed editions, and while it does not correspond in detail to any version of the violin line in the autograph, its most extensive affinities lie with the earliest layers (Stage 1) of that manuscript. Listeners will be struck by the higher octave in the G-minor interlude in S_2 of the first movement (less grateful in this range for the piano, surely, than for violin), by the much higher incidence of broken octaves (better for the piano), by a greater uniformity of motion in the figuration—all remnants of the earlier writing in the autograph. Some have assumed that Beethoven, having made the changes leading to the first edition mainly for the sake of performability on the violin, gratefully restored to the piano version those earlier readings that he had probably preferred all along.[53]

But Kojima, pointing out that Beethoven's sparing indications for the piano transcription in the autograph apparently predate the revisions he made at Stage 2—the dark ink of that stage on occasion crosses out the pencil sketches for the piano version—concludes that the right hand of the piano part reflects an earlier stage of the solo voice simply because

Table 10–3 Sources for the Violin Concerto Op. 61

A (Autograph)

Lost solo parts

orch. parts

Orch. parts from
early stage of A

Copy with
B   both solo parts
(British Library)

D   Clementi ed.
1810

B used by Beethoven
for reading proof

solo parts

First ed.
C   Vienna, 1808–9

GA (1863) from A and C
Peters Min. Score, ed. Altman, from C alone
Eulenburg Min. Score, 1967, ed. Tyson,
    from Peters plates, with corrections

that earlier stage was all the autograph showed at the time it was made.[54]
This explanation is too simple. At about a dozen points in the transcription,
the right-hand part corresponds not to Stage 1, but to the revisions of
Stage 2. One such place occurs shortly after the solo instrument enters,
at m. 128, where in Stage 1 the solo part continues up in the broken
octaves from the previous measures; the piano part (this time eschewing
the broken octaves) follows the altered figuration of Stage 2 and the
printed versions (as in Example 10-8a). The same sort of thing happens
in m. 357 of the first movement, where Stage 1 carries on with sixteenth-
note figuration, while Stage 2, the piano part, and the final violin

version all break into eighth-note triplets. In the finale, mm. 140–41, the piano follows the revisions of Stage 2, while yet a third version appears in the final violin part.[55] This should suffice to show that the right hand of the piano part is not just another rendition of the violin line that Clement played at the premiere; it takes part to a degree in the later welter of second and third thoughts that ultimately led to publication. And at some points, especially in the finale, it simply goes off on its own: the double stops in mm. 68ff. (and 243ff.) of that movement have been adjusted for playability on the piano, and—in another modest example of solo playing during a tutti—mm. 345–46 have some rather ungainly broken octaves for the piano where in all other versions the orchestra plays alone.

But making a few adjustments in a single musical line written for violin is barely a start toward a satisfactory transcription for piano. What we value in the two instruments is much too different: we delight in the richness and flexibility of tone color in a single line played in almost any register of the violin, while the same line played alone on the piano will seem by comparison poverty stricken.[56] What counts in transcribing music from the one instrument to the other is the invention of textures that sound convincing on the piano, an art in which Beethoven's solo piano works from all periods of course excel. This virtue is conspicuously missing in the transcription of the Violin Concerto. In a great many passages the violin line is simply doubled down an octave: the merest expedient, it seems, adopted only to give the left hand something to do. But these passages seldom do any real harm, either, and one may appreciate them when contemplating the places where something really new has been added to the texture. An accompanying figuration that promises to move in tenths with the treble in the first movement (m. 357) is subverted by raw-sounding chromatic parallel octaves, two to the measure (Example 10-9a).[57] At isolated points the added left hand commits what are in this style fairly elementary harmonic errors; in Example 10-9b, from the second movement (m. 27), the ornamental note b''' in the melody is mistaken for a harmonic tone and, to somewhat queasy effect, reproduced in the accompaniment below.

When in Beethoven's or Mozart's piano concertos (or in Clementi's single surviving one) the solo instrument has a texture of melody with accompaniment, what the piano plays invariably makes sense by itself—whatever the orchestra may add to the sound. This accords well with what we know about contemporaneous uses of published piano concertos. A piano part with the tuttis suitably reduced to two staves, as publishers usually provided after about 1790, could be played to plausible effect by the amateur pianist at home. Such a destination for the piano version of the Violin Concerto—as opposed to public performance, of which none is known for the entire nineteenth century—is surely the sort of thing Clementi had in mind for this transcription. But this requires that the piano part be largely self-sufficient, most especially when the memorable "tunes" are heard. That often does not happen in this transcription, which in many such passages simply abdicates all responsibility for the bass line. The second half of the "b" melody in the second movement (mm. 65–69 and 79–83), for example, is set over a resigned, immovable tonic pedal, G, in the cellos and basses; the transcription has no such thing, but implies a distinctly unsatisfactory dominant pedal (Example 10-9c).[58]

But the most spectacular casualty of this neglectful part writing is surely the second theme ("b") of the first movement in its continuation by the solo instrument (Example 10-9d shows this as it occurs in the coda, mm. 515–23). Here there are octaves between melody and accompaniment (m. 515) and an absence of bass function almost everywhere, but especially in those outlandishly inept mm. 521–22.

There are a few places where the transcription sounds well. One such is in the finale (in general, this movement comes off best), upon the return from the last playing of the rondo theme, in A♭: here the transcription features the broken octaves of Stage 1 of the autograph and adds to good effect a left-hand arpeggiation with a real bass (Example 10-9f).

We are left with the impression that the piano transcription of Beethoven's Violin Concerto ranges in quality from satisfactory to incompetent—and that it is more heavily weighted toward the latter end of this scale. The inevitable question is, "Could Beethoven possibly have written all this music?" Whatever the perils of judging matters of authenticity on stylistic evidence, Examples 10-9a–e (and these are only selected instances of questionable writing) make a strong prima facie case, surely, for believing that someone else must be largely responsible for this work. Let us review quickly what is known about Beethoven's own connection with the transcription. The contract with Clementi speaks (in its original French) of the concerto "arrangé pour le piano avec des notes additionnelles," with no specification as to who is to do the arranging; Beethoven's letters of April 1807 to the publishers Simrock and Pleyel speak of the transcription in the same way.[59]

Clementi's letter of April 22, 1807, to Collard, however, mentions that Beethoven is to make the arrangement himself, and two of the composer's associates remembered him as having done so. Czerny, writing many years later, said as much, and Ferdinand Ries included the Violin Concerto among the four compositions he claimed Beethoven himself had transcribed for other instruments.[60] The pencil notations in the lowest staves of the autograph show that Beethoven at least got started with that task. When next we hear of the piano part, however, it is written out in final form by someone else in copy B, the *Stichvorlage* for the first edition; there is nothing in between. Thus the gap in our knowledge about the lineage of the piano transcription is enormous, far greater than in the case of the solo violin part. Of the latter we have one complete early version and manifold alternate readings in Beethoven's own hand, with only a few places in the final version that do not exist in autograph. If someone else assembled that part, as Kaiser believed,[61] what that person did was largely restricted to choosing, passage by passage, among readings that Beethoven himself supplied. In the case of the piano transcription, for which music in Beethoven's hand barely exists, we might attempt to narrow that huge gap by examining its near and far sides, that is, by comparing those few autograph pencil sketches with the final product.

What the sketches do in most cases is to get a measure or two of a new left-hand figure started at the beginning (or sometimes *near* the beginning) of a new section of music. And usually these figures correspond at least roughly to what appears in the final transcription. There are, luckily enough, fragmentary sketches bearing on several of our dubious examples above. The left-hand notes of the first measure of Example 10-9a, with the first of those unfortunate parallel octaves, are plainly there in Beethoven's hand; there are no sketches for the following measures, and the transcription simply replicates the pattern of the first one, with a resultant proliferation of parallel octaves. But in this passage Beethoven has changed the violin figuration at Stage 2. And if, as generally seems to be the case, the pencil sketches were made before the revisions of that stage of writing, then this bass was probably planned to go with the violin figuration of Stage 1—with which it fits far better. The composer also left some indications for Example 10-9c. His sketch for the piano (as we see in the bottom staff of that example) has the sustained tonic pedal so conspicuously lacking in the final transcription; the transcription here ignores to bad effect the intentions for this passage that Beethoven suggested in the bass part of the orchestra and clearly prescribed in the sketch.

Example 10-9d is from the coda of the first movement. At this point the bottom staves of the autograph are blank. This second theme had already appeared in the same key, however, in the third solo, at m. 418, where it is begun by the clarinets and bassoons, and continued by the soloist at what corresponds to the beginning of Example 10-9d. In that measure in the autograph the bottom staves have several fragmentary sketches evidently intended as possible alternatives for the violin line itself. One of these (though written an octave higher) exactly matches the first two measures of the left-hand part in the piano transcription. Those bald parallel octaves between melody and accompaniment are clearly a mistaking of the composer's intentions—*that* "accompaniment" was originally intended, surely, as an elaboration of the *melody*.

One more case in which departure from the composer's sketch did not turn out well occurs in the first movement toward the end of the S$_1$ ("bx," mm. 166–72; Example 10-9e). Here the diminished- and dominant-seventh harmonies are supplied in the orchestra with repeated string chords in the even quarter notes of the opening timpani strokes. Beethoven's sketch supplied an equivalent harmonization, off-beat, for the left hand of the piano part (shown in the lowest stave of the example); the final version of the transcription, however, ignores those chords, substituting a threadbare repeated pitch, e″, which—though it is the single common tone of the chords involved—is nonsensical as a harmonization. Again, there is a faint trace in the autograph of something that might bear on this misguided accompaniment. At that point the oboes have a long-sustained e″ that partly survives in the transcription. And in the bottom staff, in mm. 167 and 169 of the autograph, Beethoven wrote a minuscule four quarter notes on that pitch, the idea evidently being that the oboes might alternate with the solo violin and orchestral strings in tapping out that quarter-note rhythm (see Plate 9). That the pitch e″, with those quarter notes repositioned in the even-numbered measures, should have become the piano accompaniment, seems like an egregious misunderstanding. Thus for some of the least acceptable writing in the transcription, there is an explanation: a misinterpretation—surely by someone else—of the instructions the composer left in the autograph.

If those sketches in the autograph largely absolve Beethoven of responsibility for the most glaring inadequacies in the piano transcription, later stages in the textual history of the Violin Concerto might seem once more to implicate him. In reading the proofs for the first edition, the composer used copy B, which contained both solos, the piano version written directly above the part for solo violin. He made many detailed corrections, often corroborating in ink changes already made in pencil, in the solo violin and orchestral parts—and a few, as well, in the piano part. These markings have exclusively to do with "secondary properties": with missing verbal directions and accidentals, imprecise dots and slurs, and the like. The substance of the music is untouched. For the crucially unsatisfactory Example 10-9e, for instance, Beethoven offered no improvement but simply reaffirmed in ink the pencil addition of a treble clef for the left hand.

Surely the level of inadequacy of passages like Example 10-9d is such that extremely good evidence would be needed to attribute such music to Beethoven. This evidence is lacking, and there are rather far-reaching explanations as to how such passages came into being. But on the face of it, Beethoven seems to have approved them when reading the proofs. We might easily imagine a scenario such as this: Beethoven made some notations for the left hand in the belief that he would do the transcription himself, but under time pressure during the steps to publication turned the work over to someone else.[62] This person partly followed those notations, but—perhaps with only limited access to the autograph—increasingly struck off on his own; Beethoven did not care enough about the matter to have the work done over. He behaved as though the transcription were not really his concern, as if it were a commercial project of Clementi's (one of whose usefulness the Viennese publisher was also persuaded) and not really a part of the artistic undertaking at hand.

THE PIANO CADENZAS

A subsequent encounter of a sort between the composer and the transcription—one which again might be taken as some recognition of its legitimacy—probably took place later in 1809: when writing out a series of cadenzas for all his published concertos, he included a set for the piano version. There are two brief internal cadenzas for the finale, to precede the second ritornello and the final one in A♭, as well as a short one to bridge the gap between the second and third movements. The modesty of these ornamental additions contrasts vividly with the cadenza for the first movement, a gigantic, powerful thing. More than four minutes in duration, featuring all the virtuoso piano playing so conspicuously absent from the body of the movement, it might remind us of a showpiece aria added in the third act to mollify a singer in an otherwise colorless role. It is launched with the disruptive off-key tutti figure (t_1) on the lowered sixth degree—a jolt all the more unexpected in that we have just had it at the onset of T_4 only fourteen measures before. It continues with careening chromatic scales above, measured off with fragments of thematic matter in the left hand that soon assume the rhythm of those ubiquitous timpani strokes. This brings on a second formal section of the cadenza, in which the timpani (both of them, in D and A) actually join in to play their own even-note strokes in a protracted duet with the piano (one is reminded of the piano-timpani duet just *after* the corresponding cadenza in the Third Concerto). This second section is designated *Marcia*; the third and final one (*Meno Allegro*), in which the timpani figure persists, reverts to the brilliant pianism of the opening, exclaims aloud the first theme of the movement, and closes with the usual cadential trills.

The Marcia is surely revelatory of Beethoven's thoughts about this movement. The measured tread of the timpani is placed in the explicit context of a military march, one more than a little reminiscent of the March of the Guards ("Offiziere mit einem Detachement") that opens the second act of *Fidelio* (see Example 10–10).

The timpani strokes that introduce the movement while standing just outside it, and hover about it, ubiquitous but unspecific, are indeed once more a military metaphor, an emblem of struggle that illumines the joys of tranquility—as in the "Dona nobis pacem" of the *Missa solemnis*, where peace is defined by the invocation of its opposite. The movement—and by extension the concerto—are indeed serene, but that is only part of the story. Like the Fourth Piano Concerto, the Violin Concerto in both its lyricism and forcefulness bears eloquent witness to the range and richness of expression in Beethoven's middle period, to the many faces of the heroic.

CHAPTER 11

The "Emperor": Piano Concerto No. 5 in E♭, Op. 73

Ein ruheloser Marsch war unser Leben
Und wie des Windes Sausen, heimatlos,
Durchstürmten wir die kriegbewegte Erde.

SCHILLER, *Wallensteins Tod* (1799)

. . . and all of past reflection, all of
future dread, made the whole
grandeur of the martial scene, and all
the delusive seduction of martial
music, fill my eyes frequently with
tears. . . .

The Diary of Fanny Burney, 1802

Beethoven grew up in Bonn as a subject of the Holy Roman Empire; as a resident of Vienna he witnessed the final decline and demise of this feudal dinosaur, with its lumbering bureaucracy and ceremony. The wars stemming from the French Revolution first chipped away at its western edges, detaching the Electoral court at Bonn shortly after Beethoven's departure. The armies of Napoleon severed dependent states in northern Italy and southern Germany from traditional Hapsburg control, and occupied imperial Vienna twice during the first decade of the new century. In the summer of 1806 Napoleon established the Confederation of the Rhine under French control. This was a very large agglomeration of German states including many former members of the Holy Roman Empire; he now felt fully justified in viewing France as the new seat of empire and himself as the true heir to Charlemagne. Franz II, the titular emperor in Vienna, accepted the inevitable and abdicated his meaningless throne to rule henceforth with the hastily created title Franz I, Emperor of Austria. This put a formal end to that increasingly tattered system of governmental administration and ritual that had played a major role in European affairs for a thousand years.

Beethoven's life and fortune intersected at many points with the meteoric career of Napoleon, the central agent of these events. Like many Europeans of a generally liberal persuasion, he apparently vacillated in his view of the man whose enterprises were throwing the continent into such confusion. Should he be seen as a liberator bearing gifts of equality and freedom born of the Enlightenment and the French Revolution? Or was he an imperialist pure and simple intent upon brute conquest and power? In the spring of 1804, according to the famous story reported by Ries and Schindler, Beethoven eradicated Napoleon's name from the title of the Third Symphony in a fury at Napoleon's assumption of the title of Emperor of France. (He may not have known that two years earlier Napoleon had been named First Proconsul for life with the privilege of naming his successor.) But when offering the composition to Breitkopf & Härtel only three months later, he confided, "The title of the symphony is really *Bonaparte.*"[1] Later, upon what appeared to be Napoleon's final defeat at the Battles of Vittoria and Leipzig in 1813, Beethoven joined the general celebration with his "battle symphony," *Wellingtons Sieg*—a potboiler surely meant at least partly as a spoof, but taken by the Viennese at face value.

For persons of monumental productivity, intensity of focus often comes out as something like compulsive self-interest; their ideas and opinions— social, political, even religious—tend to be immediately bound up with the central work of their lives. That Wagner, the fiery revolutionary atop the ramparts at Dresden in 1849 should have turned into a compliant monarchist when in 1864 he became the favorite of King Ludwig II had little or nothing to do with any abstract convictions he held about how society might best be ordered; it had everything to do with the fortunes of the Wagnerian music drama. Beethoven, too, viewed Napoleon and his reorderings of the European map mainly through the prism of his own work's progress: the implications for uninterrupted composition in peaceful summertime surroundings, opportunities for performance, prospects for publication at home and abroad. Napoleon's activities impinged strongly upon these central concerns of Beethoven's life in 1805. After laying elaborate plans for a cross-channel invasion of England (and before their scuttling by Nelson's great naval victory at Trafalgar in October 1805), Napoleon abruptly turned his attentions toward land conquest in central Europe. France sided with princes of Bavaria, Würtemberg, and Baden in their quarrels with the Hapsburg Emperor. Austria attacked Bavaria in the mistaken impression that troops of their Russian allies would soon come to their aid. But the vastly superior French army drove the Austrians back to Salzburg and Ulm and thence marched on Vienna. By November 15 Napoleon had taken up residence in Schönbrunn Palace, and just five days later Beethoven's *Fidelio*, after vexatious delays, took the stage at the Theater an der Wien. But the Austrian upper classes, the theater's natural audience, had fled the city before Napoleon's advance, and the opera closed after playing for three nights to almost empty houses. Beethoven, in the prudently oblique manner of the letters, fretted about a "distressing crisis."[2]

In 1807 Napoleon's Continental System, a European-wide blockade designed for the economic strangulation of England, clearly disrupted arrangements with Clementi for the London publication of a group of Beethoven's major compositions. By this time, Austria was an ostensible ally of the French, and in seeking to evade the blockade Beethoven was, as noted above, actually an infraction of Austrian law. But the following year, Napoleon's bent for establishing dynastic ties (and, perhaps, for simple feathering of the familial nest) worked at least temporarily to the composer's advantage. His power approaching its apogee, Napoleon systematically put his relatives on the thrones of vassal states: his brother Joseph was given the Kingdom of Spain, his brother-in-law Joachim Murat went to the Kingdom of Naples, and Josephine's son, Eugène de Beauharnais, became viceroy of the newly established Kingdom of Italy. A Kingdom of Westphalia centered at Kassel was pieced together from bits of various German principalities and entrusted to the youngest Bonaparte brother, Jérôme.

Napoleon advanced this Kingdom of Westphalia as a model of the enlightened governance that was to prevail in the new empire ("Men of no rank, but of marked ability, shall have an equal claim upon your favour and your employment. . . . and every trace of serfdom, or of a feudal hierarchy between the sovereign and the lowest class of his subjects, shall be done away with.")[3] and personally took a hand in drawing up its constitution. One item in Jérôme's agenda, apparently, was a measure designed for cultural improvement at court: in the autumn of 1808 he invited Beethoven to become Kapellmeister there at an annual salary, the composer reported, of 600 gold ducats.[4] In January 1809, complaining in a long letter to Breitkopf & Härtel of the vexations of his career in Vienna—the indignities of the concert of December 1808 still fresh in his mind—Beethoven firmly declared his intention to make the move.[5] The issues emerging from this and other letters of his have nothing to do with any virtues of the new regime in Kassel, or even its stability, but only with Beethoven's prospective freedom to do his work, and perhaps even more importantly, the honor to be accorded him as an artist. Both these matters were promptly addressed, it turns out, in a singular action taken by his most prominent supporters in Vienna: on March 1, 1809, the Archduke Rudolph and the Princes Lobkowitz and Kinsky drew up an agreement whereby they would collectively pay Beethoven an annuity of 4,000 florins "until he receives an appointment that pays him the equivalent of the above-mentioned sum," or, that failing, for life.[6] In return, Beethoven was required only to remain and work in Vienna or in "another city in the hereditary lands of his Austrian-Imperial Majesty."[7] This agreement sealed the matter, and Beethoven remained in Vienna for the rest of his life.

This tactfully obscure talk of an "appointment that pays him the equivalent"—at least in Beethoven's understanding—had to do with a hoped-for position at the local Austrian imperial court of Franz I. In a letter of February 1809 to his friend Baron Ignaz von Gleichenstein, Beethoven clarified this point as he plotted the wording of the annuity agreement:

> As to the *Imperial services*, well, I think that this point must be dealt with tactfully—and certainly not so as to suggest that I am asking for the title of Imperial Kapellmeister—but purely with a view to being able, by means of an income paid by the court, to relinquish the sum which these Lords are now going to pay me. I think that this point might best be expressed by saying that I hope, and that it is my most ardent desire, to enter the service of the Emperor, and that in this event I would immediately draw a smaller sum, namely, smaller by the amount of the income which I should receive from His Imperial Majesty.[8]

The Imperial Majesty in question is manifestly the one in Vienna, Franz I of Austria, whose employment of Beethoven would involve assuming some or all of the payment to the composer stipulated in the annuity agreement—and would of course assume compliance with its requirement that he remain in the city. So at the beginning of 1809 Beethoven first contemplated attaching himself to the emerging new world order of Napoleon by joining the court of his brother; shortly thereafter he proposed to declare in writing his "ardent desire" to enter the service of that other emperor, Franz I.

In May of that year Napoleon once again marched on Vienna with his very large and efficient army. This time, unlike 1805, a decision was taken to defend the city, and an armed force was hastily assembled. The nobility, seemingly not very sanguine about the outcome, packed their bags once more for a retreat to more peaceful places. An intense bombardment followed during which, according to Ries's recollection, Beethoven retreated to the cellar of his brother Carl's home in the Rauensteingasse, covering his head with pillows to shield his sensitive ears from the explosions.[9] The Austrian army cut the bridges to the city and concentrated their forces north of the Danube, where in July, after a terrible battle at Wagram, they were defeated and sued for peace. Beethoven, in a letter of July 26 to Breitkopf & Härtel, complained bitterly:

> Let me tell you that since May 4th I have produced very little coherent work, at most a fragment here and there. The whole course of events has in my case affected both body and soul. I cannot yet give myself up to the enjoyment of country life which is so indispensable to me— The existence I had built up only a short time ago rests on shaky foundations—and even during this last short period I have not yet seen the promises made to me completely fulfilled—So far I have not received a farthing from Prince Kinsky. . . . What a destructive, disorderly life I see and hear around me, nothing but drums, cannons, and human misery in every form.[10]

Beethoven had good reason for anxiety about the singular financial arrangements he had made with his benefactors, for his annuity was to become a casualty of the Austrian defeat. A severe devaluation of the currency according to the *Finanz-Patent* of 1811 vastly reduced the worth of the sum to which he was legally entitled; in November 1811, moreover, Prince Kinsky died after a fall from his horse, and Prince Lobkowitz's bankruptcy soon ended payments from that quarter.

During the tense period of the French advance and invasion in early 1809, Beethoven was composing the concerto the English-speaking world calls "the Emperor." The name (used here simply for its recognition value) is a later invention and historically suspect, to say the least—as early as 1879 Sir George Grove deplored it.[11] Should Beethoven have had in mind any such association, one would be hard pressed even to say which emperor he might have been thinking of: Napoleon, whose activities were just now making life so miserable for him,[12] or the hapless Franz, defeated once more and about to yield up substantial territory to the French in the treaty of Schönbrunn? The truth, of course, is that this concerto has no identifiable connection with any emperor. And though it fairly bristles with musical topoi of a military cast and with modes of expression we easily identify as "heroic," one can hardly imagine that Beethoven, fed up with all the "drums, cannons, and human misery" on all sides, could have intended this piece as a celebration of any military hero or anyone's victory in war. Symbolism here, as usual in music of substance, is a far subtler thing, at once richer and more diffuse than the mere property of being "about" an emperor, an army, a battle, or even battles or military action in general. Any invocation of such things in this music we should think of as metaphorical: thoughts of the military, that constant presence in Beethoven's world, may have reminded him (and now us) of a generalized human struggle, and its heroic gestures pointed to a nobility of character required to prevail.

THE FIRST MOVEMENT

The concerto begins with those well-known great cadenza-like flourishes (Czerny called them "three very powerful and brilliant cadences")[13] set in motion by *fortissimo* tonic, subdominant, and dominant chords (Example 11-1). Mozart's concerto in the same key, K. 271, and Beethoven's Fourth Piano Concerto, had also featured the solo instrument at the very start, but in both cases it presented the opening theme, thus involving the soloist immediately in the business at hand. The present concerto intimates instead something like character: the protagonist as brilliant, masterful, in control of a purposeful march toward tonal arrival—and yet operating with a certain reserve and forethought, turning *espressivo* as each of the stations along the way is approached. Until the tutti proper begins we have no idea of the movement's musical substance or the piano's part in it, only a portrait of a decisive lead character with imaginative flair tempered by a habit of reflection. In the Concerto in B♭, Op. 19, and the Violin Concerto (and in several of the later Mozart concertos), the first solo arrives, at its appointed place after the first tutti, with unanticipated new improvisatory music; it is like an aside about the main character's state of mind just before his plunge into the action at hand. But here we know something about the nature of the protagonist from the very beginning, such that our hearing of all the following music, including the first orchestral tutti, will be colored by it.

That first tutti, like the one in the C-minor Concerto, is a model of economy, constructed on just two themes ("a" and "b" in Table 11-1; shown in Example 11-2). The other motives one might identify in the movement—they all make an appearance in this first tutti—consist of derivatives or appendages, never really distinct or sustained enough to achieve independent status. These two fundamental themes illustrate a special case of Arnold Schmitz's "contrasting derivation." Instead of presenting differing characters with a common motivic bond, they show similarity of character in the face of constructive and even expressive diversity. The first theme is (on the surface) an assertive, swashbuckling march in which the force of the first beats is magnified by two kinds of emphatic anacruses: the distinctive snapping turn plus detached eighths, or jagged dotted-note upbeats. The "b" theme is *pianissimo*, tense with pent-up energy perhaps, but understated. The common element is an underlying motion of straight quarter-note strides, in both themes reinforced at strong beats with those attention-getting anacruses. In somewhat differing ways both get across the idea of a military march, the one extroverted with brass blaring, the other evoking martial motions only at a distance, as in imagination or memory.

The first theme has a blunt force, owing partly to an overt inelegance in its harmonic-metric design. There are three modules of two measures each, xxy. The melody of the two "x's," like the similarly constructed opening theme shared by the *Leonore* Overtures Nos. 2 and 3 (both themes consisting solely of the tones of the tonic triad plus the sixth), shows a certain penchant toward expansion that is instantly suppressed by those imperious anacruses and the unrelenting tonic harmony. The snippet "y" wanders off into subdominant and dominant sounds, but it too is brought back into the fold with crisp military precision for a replay of the entire theme. Each of these three members, though on the surface regular in length, is cut off as its ending coincides with what comes next, sounding incomplete, as if forced into a predetermined regimen; the assured progress of the march seems bought at a price. This music predominates enormously in the movement. It returns insistently later in the first tutti; all the subsidiary motives (a_1–a_4 in Example 11-2) spin off from it. And the developmental second solo will be built exclusively from its parts.

But as the first tutti ends, the solo-protagonist, whose acquaintance we have already made, returns as something of a liberator. The first bassoon in m. 105 heightens our expectation by adding an abrasive minor ninth to the dotted-note march of dominant chords. The piano, less like a foot soldier than a ballet dancer gliding to the center of the stage for a new beginning, enters on a chromatic run (during which the ninth is safely resolved)[14] to offer a transformed version of the theme. Now it is *dolce*,

TABLE 11-1 OP. 73, I

11	23	29	41	62	78	97
T	Cad.	T₁				

	a	a₁	a₂	b	a	a₃	a₄
I	I		~V/♭VI	i, I	~I		

107	111	126	136	151	166	184	205	217	221
S₁									

Eing.	a	a₁	a₂	b	pass. (a)	a₃	(a₃) pass.
I		~V/♭VI	♭vi	♭VI { ~V	V	I, vi { ~V ♭VI { V	V/V

227	242	264	310	333	343
T₂		S₂			

a	a₄	Eing. (a) pass.	b	a₄	a₃
V	~III	V/III vi iii ii	♭vi ♭VI { ~V vi~III	♭VII	I (VI)

362	372	380	393	408	423	441	462	474	478
T	Cad.	T₃	S₃						

a	a₃	a	a₂	a	b	a, a₂	pass. (a)	a₃	(a₃) pass
I	V	~III	V/♭VII	♭vii ♭VII { I	I	♭VII	I	IV, ii { i ♭II { I	V/I

484	496	515	529	542	549
T₄	cad.				

a	b	Coda	a	a₂	a₁	a₄
I	i	I				

meditative, the rigid tonic replaced by a varied harmonization in eight-fingered chords (mainly in sturdy root position) that gradually dissolve back into the glissading cadenza-like flourishes familiar to us from the soloist's opening a hundred bars earlier. The regimented march bends to the will of the lead character; it emerges nuanced, with variable expressive potential. Such variability will be fully exploited in the *dolce* opening section of the second solo (mm. 276ff). Here, revisiting the plan of the corresponding place in the C-minor Concerto, Beethoven presents the theme successively at stations along a solemn procession from one minor tonality to another, C, G, and finally F; and shorn of its jagged dotted-note upbeats, the music seems diffident, even vaguely repressed.

That other main theme, "b," appears early on, in m. 41, also ushered in by non-harmonic irritants, with both the minor ninth and minor sixth applied, this time, to the dominant. It comes in two versions, minor and major, but both solidly tonic. Here Beethoven has gone the full distance: by stages the opening tuttis of his concertos have approached tonal unity, and in this one there is no hint of modulation (Tovey, who had decried the earlier variability, now speaks ungratefully of "a severe monotony of key").[15] But the second theme itself, in its minor and major variants, has a harmonic fascination that is more than ample recompense for the sameness of key. As was noted in the previous chapter, its minor version follows the harmonic pattern of the old *folia*, in 1809 a piece of forgotten exotica (while this dance type was in triple time, Beethoven has transformed its distinctive sounds into a duple four-square march). Perhaps the best known *folia* these days is the first movement of Corelli's Sonata for Violin and Continuo, Op. 5, No. 12 (*La Follia*). Example 11-3 shows the fifth variation of Corelli's piece,[16] together with Beethoven's theme, transposed to the same key for easy comparison.

What sounds archaic to modern ears here (and must have seemed more so in Beethoven's time, in the absence of present-day folk and pop music) are that distinctive downward bass motion, tonic-flat seventh, and a tonal goal on the mediant. The *folia*-march, sounding *pianissimo*, seems distant in both place and time. But its attendant aroma of antiquity is instantly dispelled when the theme turns major: the $\hat{3}$–$\hat{2}$–$\hat{1}$ melodic motion is transformed into a perfectly up-to-date horn call, easily playable in two parts from beginning to end by the E♭ horns now operating in their familiar world of tonics and dominants.

When next we hear this music, in the first solo, the horns are necessarily left with nothing to do, for the soloist plays this theme in the distant key of the flat submediant (the section in minor is written in B minor for convenience; the proper C♭ major follows)[17] in a very early example of an unambiguous "three-keyed exposition" in a major tonality. This is a practice usually associated with a younger generation of composers, most particularly with Schubert, beginning in the third decade of the nineteenth century.[18] In about 1802 Beethoven had begun to experiment with true substitute dominants (as opposed to temporary diversions to other keys) in the Sonata Op. 31, No. 1, followed by the "Waldstein" Sonata (1804) and the *Leonore* Overtures Nos. 2 and 3 (1805 and 1806), in all cases establishing the mediant, and in no case reverting to the dominant. In the first movement of the Fourth Concerto, we recall, there was a pause on the flat mediant (the serene *pianissimo* island in B♭ in mm. 105ff.) enroute to the dominant, this in addition to local tonal disturbances brought on by the use of a modulating second theme. But the present concerto movement creates an unambiguous tonal area on the lowered sixth for the presentation of the *folia*-march and then, in an imperious, almost theatrical gesture, resolves it downward to the proper dominant. The agent of that harmonic motion is the second theme itself, now entering intrusively in yet a third incarnation: shorn of all exoticism or reserve, it has become a march pure and simple, and a highly extroverted one at that (Example 11-4). The wrenching semitone motion down to the dominant B♭, coincident with the final transformation of the second theme, emerges as a denouement of the entire section, a moment that registers something like triumph.

That grand shift down to the dominant is part of a pattern of semitone relations that leaves a distinct mark on the overall sound of this concerto. The ♭6–5 motion is rather elaborately prepared in advance of the "b" theme. It all really begins in m. 136, when the motive a_2, which in the opening tutti (m. 29) had been perched on the dominant, now appears on G♭, dominant to the new key, C♭. Then, in mm. 144ff., the piano's surging upward figure is constructed on that tone together with its upper semitone appoggiatura, G-F♯, thus replicating in miniature—and one dominant higher—the larger motion to come. (Such advance warning may remind us of a similar strategem in the late Schubert Sonata in B♭, D. 960, where the first theme is diverted for a time to the flat submediant, and, even earlier, some mysterious rumbling trills in the bass, ♭6–5, interrupt it to signal at a distance this central harmonic motion of the movement.) Beethoven revisits the issue late in the first solo, at m. 205, where the piano plays the transient but glorious motive a_3, almost Wagnerian in its aspiration, in C♭, subject to immediate retrieval back to the dominant by the orchestra.[19] That semitone upper appoggiatura to the dominant, B, never to be got rid of, reappears once more as the key of the second movement. At its end, the correction is made again without mediation, get through. It may then surprise us that in the recapitulatory third solo of the first movement Beethoven seems to depart from his big plan. We will recall that Schubert, with his penchant for literalism and symmetry in recapitulations, tends in their later sections simply to repeat the corresponding events of the exposition, however remarkable, a fifth lower. Thus in both the Sonata in B♭ and the Trio in E♭, the motion ♭vi-V in the exposition is matched in the recapitulation with ♭ii-I. Beethoven's recapitulation, while revisiting in a general way that forceful motion toward stability in the playing out of "b" (m. 408), now gives up, or at least alters, its constructive component. Instead of starting the second theme in the Neapolitan so as to produce the symmetrical ♭II–I, he puts it in the seemingly irrelevant key of the flat seventh, C♯/D♭. The "correction" deposits the music firmly back where it belongs, in the tonic, and the shift, this time up a tone, startles us again (though in a different way). A relation to anything else in the movement is obscure; the effect remains, but the cause is elusive. The unfinished business here is finally dispatched in two ways: "a₃" (m. 462) has the expected ♭II–I shape, and in the following cadenza—Beethoven insisted on his own—the *folia*-march is heard one last time, now wholly naturalized in the tonic, with no adjustments needed.

One of the great joys of this concerto is, of course, its wealth of splendid keyboard sound. Beethoven makes palpable further advances in the surge of pianistic inventiveness that was so conspicuous in the Fourth Concerto (and so sorely wanting in the piano transcription of the Violin Concerto). Especially intriguing is the intricate interplay of thematic matter and figuration; the one may dissolve into the other while both somehow remain clearly present. When in the first movement the soloist takes up the minor version of the "b" theme (m. 151), the melody is irregularly projected into a triplet figuration while the familiar strong-beat march accents are preserved with conflicting duple upbeats, all played in a very high range, *pianissimo*, as if from another world.[20] When presently the theme turns major, the *folia*-march is further disembodied, the melody now the merest phantom, essentially absent as the piano serenely plays out the pattern of its harmony and meter to attenuated quiet chords in the orchestra (Examples 11-5a and b).

Some of the gorgeous new textures Beethoven creates are more distinctly ornamental. In the first solo, for example, "a₂" arrives perched on G♭ (dominant of C♭ and the second theme to come) played in dialogue among the woodwinds and festooned with a piano figuration that ranges over five octaves (m. 136). The harmonic interest of these figures is just about nil[21]; what counts is texture and tessitura—and joy of playing (*Spiel-*

freudigkeit), a joy that the listener is bound to share (Example 11-6). In the retransition of the last movement, Beethoven needs some piano sound as he traverses the great harmonic distance, proceeding by descending fifth, from the flat supertonic, F♭ (or E) to the tonic for the third ritornello. He really gives us nothing but the harmonies along the way (plus some drumming in the strings on the rhythm of the ritornello to come). What he counts upon to fill this void is a fine roaring wide-spaced unmelodic arpeggiation in the piano (reminiscent of the tempestuous C-major episode just before the coda in the finale of the "Waldstein"), a figuration that spans the instrument's entire middle register (Example 11-7). This figuration, too, is patently ornamental, but what it ornaments is not melody or motive, but a humble harmonic progression; and the central attraction, again, is sheer piano sound. Yet more memorable for its piano writing is a passage just before the end of the first movement, starting at m. 558 (Example 11-8). Here even the harmonic motion has been suspended; the winds simply play rhythmic tonic chords that are then distilled to a single sustained pedal tone in the second horn. The piano has the only motion: a shimmering downward scalewise progression starting at the top of the keyboard, really a novel adaption of the old cadential sequence of falling $^6_3$ chords, now sounding transfigured and of another time and place.

The area of the first movement where we might expect maximum deployment of virtuoso keyboard figuration is the close of the first solo (and the corresponding point in the third), the standard display episode of the Classical concerto. In Mozart's concertos this section typically saw a shift of emphasis. Presentation and elaboration of musical ideas gave way to "performance" by the soloist: thematic matter was largely suspended, and harmonic rhythm slowed and evened out as the pianist drove toward the finish of the section with scalewise and arpeggiated figures in the fastest note values of the work. A full generation later this practice became both more extreme and more routine. In the concertos of Mozart's student Hummel,[22] composed in the second and third decades of the nineteenth century, this section typically added new pianistic devices: various leaping figures, for example, and parallel thirds in both hands. But the old pattern is still easily discernible in a dissolution of musical discourse into straight passagework—brilliant surface motion in regular rhythms with no perceptible motivic connection to the rest of the movement. It was by now a standard feature of the concerto, a ritual but riveting sprint to the wire.

Beethoven, in his own way, had adhered to this practice in all his earlier concertos with the exception except the Fourth. But his treatment of the section ran counter to historical currents eddying around him: his display episodes tended to become successively more motivic and less continuous. In the Fourth Concerto that section has all but disappeared (the only possible reminder of it here is a cadenza-like interruption of a closing theme, "a₁," at m. 164). In the Fifth it is back, but with a difference. This section (beginning at m. 184 and the corresponding m. 441) pays lip service to the old—and new—practice with its downward chromatic scales crackling in the bass.[23] But the real business of the passage is fiercely thematic: a determined working of the head-motive of "a" with its distinctive turn at the beginning, together with the finely idealistic "a₃" at its end. There is a feeling of regularity about the beginning of this section that might remind us of the even harmonic periods Hummel would write later at this juncture: four measures of Bb, four of Eb, four each of C minor and G minor, and back to Bb. But it seems that at one point Beethoven had something else in mind. Among the sketches for this movement is a sheet in Bonn,[24] some of whose (maddeningly fragmentary) contents seem to bear on the first display episode.[25] The music starts in a single line with the beginning of "a," just like the right hand of m. 184, but presently adds another voice in counterpoint at the lower fifth. There are several attempts to create an imitative polyphonic texture here; but they finally come to nothing, and the large section of the sheet containing these attempts is crossed out. One tiny remnant of such an abortive plan for an imitative polyphonic texture at this point may still be visible in the single-line start of m. 184, followed by its doubling in thirds. Another may be that schematic disposition of harmonies, as if designed to accommodate the successive entries of constituent voices that in the end remained unsung. In any case, the very thought of writing that sort of passage at this juncture of a concerto, whether viewed from the past or the future, was distinctly radical.

In closing the first movement Beethoven pursued a new variation of the corresponding sections in the G-major and C-minor concertos. There are really four constructive elements here to be ordered and juxtaposed: the ending of the recapitulatory third solo, a final tutti, a cadenza, and a coda. In the Third Concerto they came in just that order except that the cadenza, as was normal, interrupted the final tutti—the real novelty being the coda with piano at the end. The Fourth Concerto, in its gentler way, eliminated the drive to the finish of the third solo (which usually also marks the end of the recapitulation), closing out the section instead with a chain of events in which the final tutti simply enters at some point to lend a hand. As befits its temperament, the Fifth Concerto restores the drive to the close of S₃ and its dramatic conclusion: but now the place-marking dominant trills of the Mozart concertos—and the plunging diatonic runs of the Third Concerto—have been replaced with vertiginous chromatic scales, careening in opposite directions to their tonal goal.

The last tutti, again clearly outside the recapitulatory process, brings back the martial first theme and some of its satellites, now smoothed out, tonic and triumphant. The piano's cadenza seems less an interruption than an eager assent: it brings into conformity, at last, even the errant *folia*-march, now heard solidly in the tonic (this may provide a structural reason for Beethoven's insistence upon the use of his own cadenza). But the piano does not drop out. We only gradually become aware that the cadenza is over and that something like a coda has begun as the horns takes up the strain in major, realizing the perfect affinity of that version of the theme with the idiom of these instruments, as the piano adds unclouded triadic figuration above. This grounding in the tonic with music that has rid itself of all previous complication recalls the horns' play with the main theme in E♭ at a corresponding point in the first movement of the *Eroica*; both are the elemental sounds of a celebratory homecoming. The first theme joins in, followed by a glimpse of the motives a_1 and a_4. All is benign and bouyant until, in a closing flashback, the bassoons add their monitory minor ninth to the music poised on the dominant (m. 554); the piano's rising chromatic scale recalls the anticipation of past solo entrances, only to dissolve into the luminous closing descent followed by an easy resurgence to the heights amid the ringing of the old martial rhythms, and the last chords.

THE ADAGIO AND RONDO

Of the slow movement Czerny claimed, "When Beethoven wrote this *Adagio*, the religious songs of devout pilgrims were present to his mind, and the performance of this movement must therefore perfectly express the holy calm and devotion which such an image naturally excites."[26] "Hymn-like" and "meditative" are surely words that come to mind upon contemplating this movement. The opening melody is played by low-lying violins, con sordino, to almost mystical effect (Example 11-9). There is a certain modest hesitancy to its motions as it unfolds in two-bar modules that are sometimes further divided by questioning rests (the effect is abetted by the indecision of that pivotal deceptive cadence in m. 10). But Czerny used "adagio" simply as a generic designation for a slow movement. Beethoven had added the qualification *un poco mosso*, and Czerny cautioned that "The *Adagio* (*alla breve*) must not be dragging."[27] This *alla breve* meter signature has figured hardly at all in the modern textual history of the movement, although it is incontrovertibly present in both the autograph in the Berlin Staatsbibliothek and in Breitkopf & Härtel's first edition (early 1811) for which the composer read the proofs; it was silently changed to common meter in the later Breitkopf & Härtel collected edition and appears thus in virtually all modern sources.[28] So this movement (like the Largo of Op. 15 and the first movement of Op. 37) has taken its place in the canon and in the repertories of pianists around the world with the wrong meter signature.

This makes a big difference. It is not mainly a matter of tempo; Czerny gives a metronome marking of ♩ = 60, not a great deal faster than the tempo at which one usually hears the movement these days (Alfred Brendel's recording for Phillips, 1983, takes it at about ♩ = 50, which seems close to average). Rather, a basic pulse of two to the bar creates a certain fluency of motion toward those sharply delineated syntactical stops—endings of what Koch called "incises" (*Einschnitte*)—in mm. 2, 4, 7, 8, 10, and 13, investing them with a greater prominence and poignancy than is possible if we hear the music in four. This smooth-flowing character contrasts strangely with a feeling of sturdiness about the very opening, with its strict contrary motion between soprano and bass and exclusive use of root-position chords (with resultant disjunctions in the pizzicato bass line)—and this is surely part of the intended effect. As it continues, the music expands from these rather constricted beginnings, making use of that contrary motion to push the melody up and the bass down, but ending, in the tonic extension of mm. 13–15, with the melody poised on the questioning third.

This melody returns in its entirety twice (mm. 45 and 60), first in a fleshed-out and mildly ornamented version for the solo instrument, then as a trio for woodwinds with unhurried ethereal figures in the piano on high. These three statements of the theme, all in the tonic, are the main substance of the movement, giving it, overall, something of the static feel of a leisurely theme and variations. When Beethoven writes in this genre, he usually offers some significant diversion from its confinements, and he does so here. The piano in m. 16 responds to the first statement in the strings with a passage of limpid descending figures over long-held tones in the bass, its fine atmospheric sound enhanced by Beethoven's liberal prescription of pedal. Tovey calls it a second theme. But this is to miss the subtle but perfectly audible derivation of this passage from the opening music. It follows the bass of that first theme, note for note and chord for chord, in an artful augmentation that makes six measures out of two. With that structure in place the piano's figures may indulge in great melodic abstraction without destroying the relationship, and this they do; still, where the voice leading takes on a more distinctive shape with the ascending tenths of mm. 20–22, the music adheres faithfully to its model (Example 11-10).

Having established its roots, this passage then moves further afield for a brief sojourn in the rather distant D major. Here a show of repeating that derivative passage in its new surroundings quickly gives way to a cadenza-like excursion that leads the music elegantly back to the tonic for those two almost formal variations on the main theme. The second of these finishes at m. 71, where we hear nine leisurely measures of simmering down: over a tonic pedal the piano plays its musing figuration, now adding the expressive flat-sixth ornament, G–F♯, passing on through a *diminuendo* that reaches beyond *pianissimo* to a final *morendo*. So the larger topography of this movement is mainly flat, virtually devoid of development or drama of its own. We hear the same ruminative theme three times in the same key, relieved only by a fleeting diversion modeled directly on that theme. Vastly shorter in its reach than the theme and variations of the Violin Concerto, and more static in effect than any other of the slow movements in Beethoven's concertos, it leaves the impression, finally, of a great unhurried introduction to the finale (an effect paradoxically furthered by an *alla breve* performance), a protracted moment of quiet before the storm to come. It is a moment of nostalgic reflection, of pathos that gives pause to the scenes of unbounded energy and struggle developing around it.

And while all the concertos since the Third had created some link between the second and third movements, this one does so with a new insistence. In a blunt Beethovenian gesture the tonic B slips unceremoniously down to B♭ (that ♭6–5 motion again), which draws the discourse back to the orbit of the prevailing E♭, at a stroke undermining the tonal independence of the entire movement and pointing to its place in the larger scheme of things. Then with an obstinately crabbed and elusive rhythm (units of dotted eighths? or eighths?), the piano limns out in slow motion, like momentous tidings gasped out in a stage whisper, the shape of the rondo theme to come. Beethoven was very particular about this connection. The horns (having changed crooks from D for the second movement back to E♭) hold a long B♭ that bridges the gap, and the piano's upbeat B♭ to the rondo theme has a fermata (m. 82) to which the composer appended a cautionary footnote, *semplice poco tenuto*, to keep the pianist from holding it too long.

As that theme then comes on with a rush, the perplexing rhythm of its foreteller is simplified, but not immediately clarified (Example 11-11). This is one of those rambunctious creations of Beethoven's whose main point seems to be simple ungainliness. It may recall for some listeners the main theme of the *Leonore* Overture No. 1 (which, we now know, was composed just the preceding year); that theme, too, is prepared with great panoply, and upon its arrival galumphs upward with similar good-humored bounds. The concerto theme, of course, serves as the ritornello of a rondo, where we expect certain violations of metrical decorum (the odd accentuation in Op. 19, a toying with periodization in Op. 15, the bluff off-beat accents in Op. 37). Here the piano starts the theme right off, *fortissimo*, with what remains a rhythmic anomaly. The upward leaps in the right hand imply $\frac{3}{4}$ meter, while the left hand keeps time incontrovertibly in $\frac{6}{8}$ (creating a hemiola many pianists seem intent upon concealing); the *sforzato* on the second beat of the following measure is ill fitted to both.

But clarification comes quickly in the downward reply: this is a hunt-like theme in $\frac{6}{8}$, it turns out (recalling, for example, the galloping motions in the first movement of Mozart's "Hunt" Quartet K. 458, and the finale of Haydn's Symphony No. 73, "La chasse," originally composed for a hunting scene in his opera *La Fedeltà premiata*). The beginning of Beethoven's theme seems distorted from an excess of energy—behaving more like a large puppy than a reliable steed. The hunting motif is reinforced at every turn in this movement (tonality permitting) by a great prominence of that instrument of the chase, the French horn: it sounds its dominant note throughout the first playing of the main theme (and its growling tonic pedal tone during "b"), and upon repetition of the opening motive (mm. 99ff.) it shows that this music also fits nicely with the classic horn call. And at many points in the movement (mm. 36–41, 160–61),[29] the horn marks time, announces new beginnings, and ushers in new tonalities by tapping out its equestrian rhythms.

This repeated opening phrase comprises the first segment of the sort of schematic pattern into which rondo themes so often fall. Beethoven's often have a rounded binary shape, with repeats that can be variously omitted upon later occurrences. The rondo theme of Op. 73 can best be viewed as a compact rounded binary form with two modifications: the initial repeated four-bar segment is also repeated in the "rounded" feature of the second segment—at the point where the orchestra first enters—and the music exits from the pattern during the repetition of this second segment, avoiding thereby the final statements of the principal motive. Upon subsequent occurrences (shown in Table 11-3) the ritornello is twice modified. R_2, at m. 93, is typically shortened, exiting during the initial statement of the second segment. (R_3 is an exact replica of R_1, and Beethoven did not even bother to write it out again in the autograph). In keeping with a disinclination in his later concertos to present the ritornello

TABLE 11-3 OP. 73, III

37	42		49	72

R₁

| S | T | S | | |

| a | a₁ | | b | c |

| I | | | I | ~~~~~V |

93	109	138	155	161	182	188	209	212	220

R₂

| S | S | | T | S | T | S | T | S |

| a | (a) | a | a₁ | a | a₁ | a | a₁ | (a) |

| I | I | ~~~~~~~VI | | ~~ IV | | ~~ ♭II | | ♭ii~~~~V/I |

246			294	319

R₃

| S | T | S | | |

| a | a₁ | | b | c |

| I | | | I | I ~~~ |

341	370		399	402	425

R₄

| S | T | S | | T |

| a | | | a₁ | Coda (a) | (a) |

| IV, I |

four times in the home key, the last time around (m. 341) Beethoven brings the theme back in A♭, the subdominant, then bends it sharply back to the tonic during the "exit music" of its second segment—a tame modification, surely, in comparison with the thematic complexities of the finale of the Fourth Concerto.

Despite its initial unruliness, this theme conveys a feeling of almost singsong regularity because all its parts are measured out strictly in two- and four-bar modules, each leading like clockwork to either the tonic or dominant. Music for the hunt comes across here as a distant relative of the military sounds of the first movement;[30] but it also bears a clear family resemblance to the contredanse, whose rhythms had been at home in rondo themes since the later symphonies of Haydn.

There are two other distinct thematic ideas in the movement (Example 11-12; "b" and "c" in Table 11-3), both of them *dolce*. Both are perfunctory and passing; the first (m. 49), still in tonic, is a very short-lived lyrical gesture that fades away after eight measures, and the second (m. 72), now in dominant and pinned to *its* dominant, behaves like a cadential formula that after six measures dissolves into pure figuration over the new tonic. Both bits of themes make their requisite cameo appearances in the recapitulatory section after R₃, "c" now safely relocated in the tonic. Neither plays any further role in the movement, and both in any case compromise their identity by accepting rhythmic patterns dictated by the rondo theme. These propulsive rhythms dominate enormously, driving the movement from beginning to end (or almost the end) at a full gallop, breathless and exhilarating.

As in the finale of the Fourth Concerto, Beethoven decided upon a development-like central section rather than an episode. But in both movements there is a marked schematic regularity to this section, like the ghost of an episode that might have been. (We recall the comic rigidity of the episode in the finale of the Concerto in B♭.) In Op. 73 it comes in four distinct subsections. The first (mm. 109–120) seems partly introductory, serving to get the music to the first somewhat distant tonal goal of the section (and, indeed, of the movement), C major. This is done the hard way. The piano adds a tracery of quiet scales to accompany the strings as they embark on the only sustained contrapuntal music of the concerto: a working of the ritornello theme in which imitative entries crowd in, once every measure, while the music ascends the circle of fifths, finally stopping on the dominant of C. After a celebratory cascade of broken-chord figuration from the pianist, we have the main business of this development: three set pieces at three successive tonal levels, C, A♭, and E (this last shown in Example 11-12). In each the pianist makes a (successively shorter) allusion to the ritornello theme, then wheels off into glittering figuration built upon the simplest harmonic framework within the key at hand, and doled out in even eight-bar segments,[31] the end of which is signalled by the the orchestra's interruption (suggesting a mini-ritornello) with the rounding-off motive "a₁." The effect is a series of rousing excursions that, in accord with the larger idea of the rondo, keep circling back to their starting point. This is an adventure played out within carefully measured bounds.

There is, however, progress; the enclosure itself seems to expand with each subsequent tour as the music traverses the augmented triad of keys downward from C. The last installment of this exercise, situated on the Neapolitan E, is again closed out by the little rounding-off motive "a₁," (shown in Example 11-12), whereupon the piano sets about negotiating a way out of this arena by means of the final big semitone motion of the concerto. The exit is leisurely and lawful: arpeggio figures in both hands, roaring in place, slowly pick their way down to the dominant of E♭, the descent quietly secured by sinking fifths in the pizzicato bass line, as the strings keep the old equestrian rhythm going in the background. Once this dominant is secured, the piano figuration narrows to trills on B♭ that now take on the function of the horns from the very beginning of the movement: they serve as a long-drawn dominant pedal, while the strings anticipate in wide-spaced snippets—the meter now clearly identifiable as ⁶⁄₈, deception along these lines no longer being possible—the grand reentry of the third ritornello.

This third ritornello and the recapitulatory matter that follows are a faithful copy of their models from the outset of the movement, with the necessary exception of the appearance of "c" in the tonic instead of the dominant, the adjustment being made with a minimum of fuss during the sequential figures that follow "b" (mm. 53ff. and 298ff.). So faithful is the copy, in fact, that the music formerly in the dominant, but now in the tonic, leads ineluctably to a start of the fourth ritornello in the sub-dominant (m. 341). Listeners without absolute pitch are tipped off that something is amiss by the noticeably higher tessitura in the piano and the absence of accompanying horns (which in this key Beethoven could easily have supplied); the necessary adjustment is again made effortlessly, without even disturbing the metrical pattern. This time it comes in the connective tissue just before the orchestra's restatement of the theme—which then follows full blast in the tonic. Beethoven pursues the continuing music from just after the ritornello, and even expands it with splendid new exchanges between solo and orchestra. The little melody "a₁" makes a final appearance, once again (as in the development section) the signal of an ending.

All that remains is the coda, and for this Beethoven has saved a final dramatic gesture (Example 11-13). The two timpani, tonic, then dominant, tap out the hunting rhythm, *pianissimo*, in a sixteen-bar duet with the piano, a simmering-down gesture at once valedictory and premonitory of the final mad rush to the end. The choice of timpani for this final playing of the primal rhythm of the movement, and their sudden emergence into a solo role for such a purpose, seems rife with symbolism. Until now these instruments have only added their supporting sounds to the big climaxes of the movement, while the hunting rhythm has typically been heard either from the more "neutral" strings and high winds, or from the hunting instrument itself, the horn (as we heard in the preparation of the section of the recapitulation in A♭). But now the timpani instantly transform that amiable, galloping rhythm into something quite different: it has become tense, portentous, martial. It recalls the military music of the first movement. Perhaps Beethoven was even stirred by a memory of the timpani strokes that had haunted the Violin Concerto, whose martial intent he had made clear in the cadenza to its piano transcription, composed at about the same time as the Fifth Concerto. His last concerto ends with a closing reference to that archetypal emblem of the genre, a vision of leader and followers engaged in common struggle and cooperation. The imagery is military, the meaning ultimately human and humane.

The symbolism seemed now to leave Beethoven the pianist largely out of the picture. Gradually giving up his career as a public performer during this period—for reasons of both growing deafness and growing fame as a composer—he never played this concerto in public and probably never intended to.[32] The first performance we know of took place at the Gewandhaus in Leipzig late in November 1811, with Friedrich Schneider as soloist. In a composite review of a series of Gewandhaus concerts, Friedrich Rochlitz fairly brimmed with enthusiasm for this performance of "Beethoven's newest concerto": "It is doubtless one of the most original, most inventive, most effective, but also most difficult of all existing concertos . . . so it could not be otherwise but that the numerous audience was in transports of delight."[33] Czerny played the concerto in Vienna the following February at a charitable event featuring the exhibition of paintings described in Goethe's *Wahlverwandschaften*; here its reception was reportedly indifferent at best.[34] That others were giving the first performances of the composition shows how the function of the piano concerto in Beethoven's life had changed from the time of the early concertos. We could note the beginnings of such a shift with the Fourth Concerto, when he allowed the work to be published before its public premiere: the concerto was no longer a vehicle for demonstrating his fabled prowess as a pianist.

Even the autograph of the concerto, now in the Berlin Staatsbibliothek, reflects the change. In this manuscript, in stark contrast to his scores for all the earlier piano concertos, Beethoven wrote out the solo part meticulously, including articulation marks, pedaling, verbal performance directions, and even alternative passages (marked "o sia") for shorter keyboards.[35] And he wrote a good bit of music into the piano part in the orchestral tuttis, with the intriguing addition of systematic figured bass notation. All these features of the autograph are familiar from printed piano concertos of the period and strongly suggest that its immediate destination was not performance (certainly not by Beethoven) but publication. A bit earlier the piano part, during the tuttis, in published keyboard concertos often showed only the bass line plus the old fashioned continuo figures. The first edition of Beethoven's First Piano Concerto (1801) follows this practice. The idea, evidently, was to allow the pianist to accompany the orchestra in continuo-fashion or at least to follow its progress between sections of solo music. The first editions of the Second, Third, and Fourth Concertos (1801, 1804, and 1808) followed another (generally newer) practice, in which the keyboard part has a skeletal reduction of the tuttis. This arrangement would, of course, allow the soloist to follow the orchestral part in performance and to participate in it at will. But it had another outstanding virtue: in the absence of an orchestra, the entire work could now be played on piano alone, an inestimable advantage for publishers intent upon attracting the amateur pianist.

The first edition of the Fifth Concerto (Breitkopf & Härtel, February 1811) avails itself of both alternatives: during tuttis the piano part has a somewhat skimpy reduction of the orchestral music, usually consisting only of bass and melody, plus a profusion of continuo figures. Beethoven had provided both the reduction and the figures in the autograph (both were silently dropped from all later published scores).[36] Example 11-14 offers a sample of the composer's handiwork from the first movement, mm. 64ff. (fol. 9v). Here the presence of the reduction tends to make the figures redundant. The "3s" in mm. 66 and 68, for example (which in standard figured-bass practice would in any case be understood), are superfluous in the presence of the melody note supplied above; the same is true of the 2–3 sequences in m. 70.

But there is a likely reason for this redundancy. The intent is apparently to fulfill the expectations of two different sorts of users. The amateur player can perform the tuttis, after a fashion, from the reduction, perhaps using the figures at points to fill out harmonies. That the reduction is actually meant to be played (and not merely followed) is strongly suggested by certain adjustments made to ease performance on the keyboard, one being the pianistic tremolo (shown in Example 11-14) at m. 64 (though such concessions, as the following measures show, are far from consistent). And the soloist at a concert with orchestra who wishes to play during tuttis will find the familiar enabling figures on the page. At certain places in the orchestral music where the bass line is particularly active (for example the first movement, mm. 76, 84, 241, 244), Beethoven even wrote in the old continuo direction "tasto solo" that instructs the soloist to play only the bass line, without chords. This is an explicit signal, surely, of his expectation that the harmonies will usually be realized—that is, that the pianist will play during tuttis.[37]

The first edition, and by extension the autograph, were not directed first of all toward a particular performance, or even a particular type of performance. They were an exercise in a much broader sort of dissemination that sought to make the work accessible not only to public players and orchestras, but also to the large and growing ranks of amateur musicians who wished to replicate something of the splendors of the concert stage at their own instruments. But such an arrangement, permitting an approximation of all the music at a single piano, presents special problems in Beethoven's later concertos, owing to the heightened intricacy in these compositions of the relationship between solo and orchestra; the second solo of the first movement of the Fifth Concerto, for example, can never make much sense without the orchestral part.

And to offer such a work in such a form to a diverse public involved another implied contradiction. In his review of the first performance Rochlitz[38] reluctantly put his finger on the nettlesome reality: this, "one of the most difficult of all existing concertos," is technically beyond the reach of all but the most accomplished amateur players. In the autograph Beethoven showed himself in a mood to make certain concessions to some players, namely, those with shorter keyboards, by prescribing alternative versions for passages at the top of the piano's range, alternatives that were taken up in the first edition.[39] At one point the publication offers a more substantial concession to the amateur pianist. The shimmering descent in double notes at the end of the first movement (mm. 562ff.) has a right-hand replacement (marked "o sia più facile") in single notes.[40] But the basic difficulty of course remains; the splendid display episodes (mm. 184ff. and 442ff.) in the first movement, for example, remain untouched and will spell sure defeat for most amateur pianists. With this concerto Beethoven and Breitkopf & Härtel confronted a central conundrum of the nineteenth-century virtuoso's address to the public. Glittering virtuosity in concert performance was counted on by publishers to spur sales of printed music to an admiring public; but the technical wizardry that had most excited audiences in the first place was the element least reproducible at the living-room piano. Publishers and pianists collaborated in various forms of simplification, but the central problem remained.

In the years of the Fourth and Fifth Concertos (1808–9), as Beethoven effectively gave up his career as a public pianist, he seemed in a more general way to shift his focus from getting his works performed to getting them published. There was a distinct falling off in the composition of new works, especially noticeable in 1810, as he invested prodigious effort in seeing older ones through the press. The year 1809, during which his schedule was thrown off by the French invasion, saw the publication of the Fifth and Sixth Symphonies, the Sonata for Piano and Cello Op. 69, the Trios Op. 70, and various lesser compositions. Among the publications of 1810 were the second version (1806) of *Leonore* (with piano), the *Leonore* Overture No. 3, the Overture to *Egmont*, the Fantasy for Piano Op. 77, the Sonata Op. 78, and the Sextet Op. 81b. Shortly after completing the Fifth Concerto, Beethoven offered it to Breitkopf & Härtel, along with a fine list of other large-scale pieces, including the Choral Fantasy, the Piano Sonatas Op. 78, 79, and 81a, and the String Quartet Op. 74.[41] There was no plan, so far as we know, for early performance of the concerto, and certainly no talk of holding it back until it had been heard; this concerto simply joined that majestic flow of major works to be recorded in print and preserved for posterity.

Beethoven seemed intent, beginning in these years that coincided with the waning of his own career as a performer, upon producing and preserving "works," creations with a fixed identity that in a modern sense are represented by (or sometimes are even said to consist of) "texts."[42] For a composer this of course involved ultimate reliance on musical notation, that notoriously blunt instrument for the symbolization and preservation of musical events that always requires an attendant battery of interpretive information and skills.[43] Beethoven's letters of the period show an almost compulsive attention to getting the text just right as he harangued Breitkopf & Härtel about their carelessness ("and now I have very lively reproaches to make to you, such as, why is this very fine edition not without inaccuracies???? Why did you not send me first a copy to check, as I have so often asked you to do?").[44] But the notion of a work with a fixed and inviolable text seems fundamentally at odds with both Beethoven's older—but nonetheless rather recent—idea of the concerto score as a rough script in the service of a particular performance. For this distinction between settledness and contingency of the musical text was to a degree genre specific, and for Beethoven the concerto was the last holdout of the older view of the matter.

The emergence of the musical text as a fixed entity, independent of the exigences of any single performance, was a natural result of publication. In the first half of the eighteenth century, the instrumental compositions of Corelli, Vivaldi, Handel, and many other composers were engraved, assigned opus ("work") numbers, and sold to an anonymous market for preservation and performance under varying conditions at some future time. As early as 1709 such musical publications had copyright protection in Britain by registry at Stationers Hall, and similar arrangements—always applicable only within individual countries—soon followed elsewhere in Europe. But when music was thus treated as a commodity addressed to a market, that very fixity of its texts afforded by publication came to be a hindrance, an impediment to wide adaptability for various kinds of users. As Beethoven's later concertos became "texts of works," they faced just this difficulty. And whatever his belief in a settled score as the record of a work, in his later concertos Beethoven was ready to make concessions (whether from commercial motives or from more lofty ones) to widely differing tastes and conditions for performance. He was complicit— though that was probably the extent of it—in the reworking of the Violin Concerto for piano, and it seems he could contemplate the performance of the "Emperor" by the amateur pianist at home.

A BACKWARD GLANCE

The story of Beethoven's concertos has a postscript. At the end of 1814, Napoleon, having tendered his abdication as Emperor and surrendered to the British, was living under house arrest on the island of Elba, off the west coast of Italy. Representatives from the major countries of Europe deliberated at the Congress of Vienna about how to put the continent back together. Beethoven, now well past the monumental deeds of his "heroic" period and going through a fallow phase in his career, a time of regrouping and refocussing, played a tiny role around the edges of these worldshaking events. In 1813, in celebration of Napoleon's downfall, he offered the Viennese public, delirious now with patriotism, his battle symphony, *Wellingtons Sieg*, a musical absurdity originally composed for J. N. Maelzel's mechanical instrument, the *panharmonicon*, with which the composer and inventor vainly hoped to mount a lucrative tour of England. Rewritten for orchestra, the work was presented, together with the first performances of the Seventh Symphony, at two concerts of December 1813, for the benefit of soldiers wounded in battle against Napoleon. Then at his academy a year later, as a forthright celebration of the Congress itself, Beethoven presented a new cantata, *Der glorreiche Augenblick* (The Glorious Moment). Audiences applauded him as never before, and this great burst of public acclaim led in the same year to the revival of *Leonore*, now titled *Fidelio*. At this time of outward success but artistic uncertainty his thoughts seemed largely occupied with ephemera of the present—no doubt influenced by financial worries—or a reliving of the past.

In early 1815, just as Napoleon escaped from Elba and launched a campaign to revive past glories, Beethoven was also at work on a retrospective project—one equally abortive, as it turned out—a new piano concerto in D major. This attempt can be tracked through rather a full set of surviving sketches for a first movement to a partial score for that movement that survives in Berlin.[45] Nottebohm left a brief description of the score and some of the sketches (including a transcription of an extended single-line draft from what came later to be called the Scheide sketchbook), but there was no full account of this project before Lewis Lockwood's detailed article on the subject in 1970.[46] Here we were given our first clear view of what was to have been the opening movement of Beethoven's Sixth Piano Concerto. A rising triadic theme in unison octaves leads to an insistent fanfare-like alternation of tonic and dominant cadential chords punctuated by dotted-note rhythms in the timpani (Example 11-15). The physiognomy of this theme is instantly recognizable: it is the old "hymnic" manner, born in the fervor of French Revolutionary celebration, and familiar to us from Beethoven's most "heroic" music, the first themes of the *Eroica*, the "Emperor" (more remotely), and, most strikingly, the C-minor Concerto and the finale of the Fifth Symphony.

This theme is introduced in the woodwinds with the interesting addition of double bass; like the opening of the C-minor Concerto, it is apparently soft (a faint pencil marking in Beethoven's hand specifies *pianissimo*). After the music veers off toward the dominant, the piano enters, rather after the manner of the "Emperor" Concerto, with a cadenza-like flourish: cascades of scales and broken chords—together with leaping trilled notes reminiscent of the ornamented version of the Fourth Concerto—establish a mastery and brilliance of the solo persona at the outset. In other ways, the complexion and plan of the movement seem to reach even further back into Beethoven's past. It has just two sharply defined themes, for one thing, with much less in the way of memorable subsidiary thematic matter than either the Fourth or Fifth Concertos. Its first solo follows the events of the opening tutti with almost no deviation save the expected modulation to the dominant. Both of these characteristics recall not the previous two piano concertos, but the Third Concerto from a dozen years before. All we really have of this abortive movement is the first tutti and the first solo—the two expositions.[47] But the music we have does not make one long for the rest of this composition. There is a certain lassitude to the phrase construction that we are not used to in Beethoven's music in this manner (at the juncture of two ideas in m. 5 of Example 11-15, for example). It is as if he no longer really believes in his old heroic gestures. Their time, and that of the concertos, has passed.

CHAPTER 12
On Performing Beethoven's Concertos

The etymological affiliations of "perform" lie with the old French *perfournir*, "to furnish or supply." And performers, indeed, furnish music, bring it to consciousness, in a profound sense bring it into being. In the Western imagination the role of the musical performer has undergone notable change during the past two centuries. London concert programs of the late eighteenth century often simply announced the presentation of a sonata or an aria by a certain performer. Whether that person was also the composer of the sonata was not revealed because this was a matter of relative indifference—just as no one cares much these days about the unnamed hired writers who supply material for our television comedians. At the other extreme, a half-century ago it was fashionable to think of performers (ideally) as neutral executants, faithful transmitters of a composer's work who take care to insinuate into the process as little of their own personalities and preferences as possible. In Europe of the late 1700s, the solo concerto was situated close to the first-named pole of this dichotomy; it was by its very nature essentially a "performance." Composers of concertos were often virtuoso players who fashioned such pieces for their own public appearances, tailoring them to fit their own special technical and expressive strengths. And even when it was others doing the playing, reactions of critics often suggested that the main point of the concerto was still the occasion it created for fine displays of the soloist's prowess.[1] This is the main explanation for a lingering suspicion toward the genre among the cognoscenti—for the aversion that E. T. A. Hoffmann, for example, felt toward piano concertos (though he was willing to make exceptions for Mozart and Beethoven).[2]

During his first dozen or so years in Vienna, Beethoven clearly saw his piano concertos first of all as vehicles for his own performances. In keeping with this special status he made a visible textual distinction in the autographs of the first three piano concertos[3] between the solo and orchestral music. The latter, of course, needed to be written out exactly so that parts could be copied for performance. Beethoven (like Mozart) was able to leave the solo parts in sketchy form, trusting to his well-known powers of improvisation for their realization in performance. Getting all the details of a score fixed, that is, making a final text, was associated not with performance but with publication. So when the concerto was a vital instrument of the composer's own music-making, there was not yet a full score, and the solo part could (and clearly did) undergo radical alteration from one performance to the next.

So what were these performances like? How did Beethoven's concertos sound when he played them? We may seek answers to these questions for a variety of reasons. Performers may want to know how Beethoven's concertos were done in his own day out of an honest desire to respect the composer's wishes. And they may do so without any intention of allowing historical verisimilitude to displace all other values, of single-mindedly pursuing that elusive and by now rather tarnished Holy Grail of "authentic" historical performance. The difficulties attendant to such a pursuit, of course, are legion. Should the test of historical accuracy extend to the external circumstances of the performance? If so, some of Beethoven's concertos would apparently require renting a cold hall and seeking out amateur string players who would be permitted only a single rehearsal. And if the goal is limited to replicating as closely as we can the *sound* of Beethoven's performances, those underrehearsed string players are surely still a factor, as are the weak-sounding pianos of which Beethoven perpetually complained, and, above all, far-reaching uncertainty about the very notes the composer played in the free-flight of improvisation.

The most satisfactory approaches to historical performance practice, surely, are those that seek information from a variety of sources (a score that distinguishes between a composer's writing and editorial surmise, verbal testimony of the composer, observations of contemporaries, and the like) in order to get at the composer's *intentions* about a composition, the range of its ideal sound and expression free of the limiting exigencies of particular performance.[4] And we might even wish to lower our sights a bit and ask what sort of performance the composer would have contemplated or found acceptable.

Judging what the composer was thinking is naturally a hazardous undertaking (quite aside from the ritual warning of the hoary "intentional fallacy," that misnamed bit of opinion still sometimes invoked, even by those who might be expected to deplore its ideological underpinnings). For such a judgment involves not just evidence, but myriad acts, large and small, of interpretation. And those who make the final decisions must be the ones who bear responsibility for the success of their implementation, the performers themselves. Scholars working with primary sources may offer suggestions and advice about what the composer intended, but in the end it must be the convictions of performers that count. Judging what musical effect and affect the composer had in mind is in their hands. And these are of course people with perfectly legitimate aims that go well beyond the accurate recreation of something done or thought in the past. All of them, even faithful early-music advocates, must operate in a present-day social context, addressing themselves to an audience variously attuned to Verdi, Debussy, jazz, and rock—not to mention Freud, Chomsky, and Derrida. If Beethoven's music attracts anything beyond esoteric interest, as it manifestly does, this is because it makes its way successfully in these contemporary surroundings: because performers of various stripes have been persuasive in offering the composer's musical ideas, with varying degrees of literalness, to this modern audience.[5]

The questions "What were performances of Beethoven's music like in his own time?" and "How should that music be performed these days?" then, are best seen as two separate ones that may be related in complex ways and for which none should presume to prescribe a rule. But surely we may also interest ourselves in that first question, quite apart from its connection with the second. We may wish to look into early nineteenth-century performances of Beethoven out of simple historical curiosity. (Historians, after all, often study events—the Crusades, the Irish potato famine—without advocating their modern reenactment.) So, hoping to sharpen our image of Beethoven and his contemporaries bringing his music to life in their own surroundings—and to offer a friendly suggestion or two to present-day performers—we will take up a few basic questions about the concertos as performed during the composer's lifetime.

THE ROLES OF THE SOLOIST

The keyboard concerto, an offspring of the concerto for strings, had been around for only about a half-century when Beethoven began to cultivate the genre in the late 1780s. We have seen lively controversy about the manner of performance of these pieces, from the first examples, the transcriptions J. S. Bach made of his and others' string concertos in Leipzig in the late 1830s, until those of Beethoven's time. Particularly at issue has been the question of just what the soloist was expected to do. For the earliest part of the repertory, the matter seems to be relatively settled. Following upon the researches of Hugo Daffner and others early in the twentieth century, there seems to be general agreement that a single keyboard player in J. S. Bach's concertos fulfilled two (or three) roles: as virtuoso performer in the solo sections and as director-continuo accompanist during the tuttis.[6] The central evidence for this was the appearance of the keybord part in contemporaneous prints, which at the onset of tuttis changed from soloistic writing to a simple bass line for the left hand, often supplied with figures for realization. In principle, this style of notation remained a standard practice for printed keyboard concertos in German-speaking lands right through the century, including those of Mozart, and extending in part to the concertos of Beethoven published after 1800. But when the editors of the *Neue Mozart-Ausgabe*, beginning in 1959, decided to print the figured bass part in the piano staves during the tuttis, a storm of protest ensued.[7] And much more recently, when Hans-Werner Küthen, editor of the concerto volumes for the new *Beethoven Werke*, decided instead to leave those staves blank, there was objection from the other side.[8]

The basic question is whether a relative consistency in notation during these fifty years reflected a similarly consistent tradition in performance practice, or whether the figured bass in Mozart's and Beethoven's concertos had become a mere "place-keeper" for the soloist—or indeed a meaningless notational relic left over from an earlier time. The final three decades or so of the eighteenth century were a time of notable change all over Europe in the way large musical ensembles were directed. Speaking very broadly, we may say that the accompanying director at the keyboard was gradually replaced by the first violinist-leader, and then with a time-beating conductor. But, as we might expect, these changes occurred at varying rates in different geographical areas, and, more notably for our purposes, among the different musical genres.[9] For orchestral performances, direction from the keyboard continued longer in England than on the Continent. That Haydn should conduct his symphonies from the harpsichord and pianoforte in London concerts of 1791–92 and 1794–95 (and play his famous little piano solo in the Symphony No. 99) was purely a concession to local practice.[10] As late as 1816 Muzio Clementi, following English custom, conducted his compositions, a symphony and an overture, from the piano at a Paris *Concert spirituel*—to the evident puzzlement of both the orchestra members and French and German reviewers.[11] By the 1790s performances of purely orchestral music on the Continent were more typically under the control of the leader of the violins.

Other genres saw the cultivations of other habits in directing performances. Composers of Italian opera by custom conducted the first few performances of a new production from the cembalo—Rossini still did so for the disastrous premiere of *The Barber of Seville* in Rome in 1816—and simple recitative, accompanied in the old way with bass and keyboard—persisted far into the new century. In late eighteenth-century and early nineteenth-century sacred music, too, continuo playing remained a familiar feature. And the sources by and large reflect this. While the rich trove of autographs and authentic copies of Haydn's symphonies from the Esterháza years show no indications of a continuo accompaniment, such indications abound in the sources of operas, sacred music, and concertos.[12] Both the autograph and first edition of Beethoven's *Missa solemnis* still have elaborate indications of the practice, and as late as 1849 Bruckner provided a figured bass for his Requiem. In opera and church music, musical scores and parts testify abundantly to performance with basso continuo, and few seem seriously to doubt that this testimony is to be trusted. Why, then, should there be such doubt about similar indications in keyboard concertos, and so much resistence to their performance with realized continuo?

There are probably two main reasons for this. The first is obvious: most of us have learned to know and love the concertos of Mozart and Beethoven in styles of performance that grew up in the later nineteenth century, and we remain wedded to the joys of the familiar. In modern public performances, moreover, the orchestra is almost always larger than those typically available to Mozart or Beethoven, and it is routinely led by a baton-wielding conductor; thus two primary functions of a continuo player, reinforcing the sonority and holding the ensemble together, seem to be otherwise provided for. But even if one wishes to reject modern habits and aim for the actual or ideal practice of late eighteenth-century music-making, the information at hand to guide us is hardly straightforward. This results mainly from two interrelated historical factors: concessions made to amateur performers, and the expectation that solo concertos would be played with a variety of instrumental accompaniments, or sometimes with none at all. From early on in the century these factors together produced alternate ways of notating the solo part during tutti passages, all of them involving the provision of notes for the right-hand part in addition to, or instead of, the (figured) bass.

Notation of the tuttis in a keyboard concerto with a figured bass alone is of virtually no use except to a trained cembalist playing with a full complement of instruments. But beginning with the earliest keyboard concertos, many musicians, particularly amateurs, evidently wished to perform them under less than such optimal conditions. An early and radical solution was simply to do without the accompanying instruments altogether: J. S. Bach's Concerto in the Italian Style (1726) is the best known of a considerable number of early eighteenth-century concertos for keyboard alone.[13] Whether original compositions or transcriptions, pieces of this sort typically simulated "tutti" and "solo" by alternating harmonically stable "thematic" sections with florid, modulatory music—all, of course, written out for keyboard alone. Another solution was the keyboard concerto with ad libitum accompaniment (a close relative of the accompanied keyboard sonata) that made an appearance in Germany beginning about 1730. Concertos of this sort were essentially solo pieces with "tutti" sections written out (often in simple two-or three-part textures), at which points doubling violins or flutes might be added as wished.[14] The keyboard concerto thus joined a fledgling repertory of music designed primarily for a bourgeois amateur consumership, circulated by publishers naturally interested in accommodating a maximum variability of performance conditions.

So before mid-century there were two well-established ways of notating the tuttis in keyboard concertos: a simple bass line, with or without figures, by tradition tied to the double basses, intended for a trained player-director performing with a full group of instruments; or a bass line, still often with figures, together with at least the melody of the tutti supplied for the right hand—this latter method maximally adaptable for playing with a full accompaniment, with reduced accompaniment, or with keyboard alone. The second option appeared as early as 1738 and 1740, with the publication of two sets of Handel's organ concertos by Walsh of London. Both arrangements had remarkable staying power, each appearing, with some variation, in published concertos until past the turn of the nineteenth century. After about 1770, however, we hear complaints that the ability of musicians, even professional ones, to realize a continuo part is declining; about this time inclusion of bass figures similarly declines (though more slowly in Vienna, it seems, than elsewhere).[15] In a set of six concertos published in his *Betrachtungen der Mannheimer Tonschule* of 1777–79, Georg Joseph Abbé Vogler, a future rival of Beethoven's, supplied bass and melody but omitted the figures; an appended explanation clarified that "one can play the six concertos without accompaniment, like sonatas, since the ritornellos are written out in notes . . . ," and that (presumably for a fully accompanied performance) "in the place of the old *Generalbass*, a solid knowledge of harmony can thoroughly and more effortlessly guide the accompanist."[16]

For us it is Mozart's concertos, of course, that form the *locus classicus* of the late eighteenth-century keyboard concerto. While exacting information about Mozart's own performances of his concertos is hard to come by, it is clear that some version of the old basso continuo practice was very much alive in the Mozart family. In at least one case (the *cembalo terzo* of the Triple Piano Concerto K. 242), Mozart himself wrote in bass figures for the tuttis, and he provided—or promised to provide—figures for the tuttis of the Concerto in D minor, K. 466, for his sister Nannerl's use.[17] He routinely sent the scores of his concertos from Mannheim and Vienna to his father, Leopold, in Salzburg, who had them copied and himself provided the basses with figures for Nannerl's and his students' performances. Mozart's autograph scores regularly have the direction *col basso* in the left hand of the keyboard staves, an instruction for the copyist or engraver to enter the bass line of the strings into the left hand of the keyboard part, to which the published version most often added figures.[18] But even more conclusive are certain *negative* instructions: rests where the bass line is not wanted, and (in additions, possibly by Leopold, to the autographs of K. 238, K. 246, and K. 271) the indication *tasto solo* where the soloist is to play the bass line but refrain from adding chords. Apart from an expectation that the soloist normally plays a realization in such passages, these indications serve no purpose.[19]

The intent of a bass part with figures had always been perfectly clear: the chords indicated were meant to be realized in performance; if for some reason another meaning was intended, such a thing surely would have required a special explanation. So it seems that Mozart expected some performers, at least, to realize the bass during tuttis. We cannot reasonably think that this expectation would have applied mainly to amateur musicians, for such a supposition flies in the face of widespread contemporaneous testimony that these were the players least able to deal with the figures—whose neglect of the rigors of basso continuo, indeed, the musical profession often looked upon with a certain indulgence.[20] Nor can we assume that a figured bass realization was used largely to make up for the absence of winds. In no case would a realization have served to replace missing wind melodies; the figured bass was always expressly tied to the bass of the string choir, and in wind passages where the strings rest, it rests as well.[21] Rather, in the keyboard concerto of Mozart's time a realized figured bass was associated with performance by a soloist who played with a full complement of instruments. We may easily imagine the incisive attack of the quick-speaking struck string adding definition to the ensemble, in many cases, indeed, proving indispensable for holding it together.

If the sources for keyboard concertos of Mozart and his contemporaries testify unmistakably to performance with a realized continuo in the presence of a full accompaniment, published versions and circulating copies often provide as well for the less formal practices that had been associated with the genre for half a century. The format Walsh once adopted for the publication of Handel's organ concertos had continued to thrive in England: J. C. Bach's Concertos Op. 1, for example, came out in 1763 with figured bass for the left hand and the violin melody (or *soprano seguente*) in the right hand of the keyboard part. Vogler, as we have seen, followed that example in 1779, but without the bass figures, appending an explanation that the added melody line permitted the soloist to replace missing instruments. And beginning in the 1780s German and Austrian publishers developed a typographical practice to help performers distinguish one performing situation from another: notes printed large represented what always had to be played, while small ones, often labeled with the names of their proper instruments, showed the soloist how to proceed in the absence of these instruments—or acted simply as place-keeping cues if they were present.[22] In tuttis the bass line of keyboard parts, whether figured or not, was almost without exception printed in large notes. But even the exceptions are instructive. Publishers tried to show that the keyboardist could be exempt from playing the orchestral bass in very short tuttis, particularly those that alternated quickly with solo statements. Such segments, previously shown with rests in the keyboard part, might now appear with small notes in both hands, as in André's print of Wanhal's Concertos Op. 14.[23] The soloist would omit these notes in the presence of an orchestra and play them in its absence.

For Mozart the keyboard concerto was a personal vehicle for his appearances as soloist, and he was usually in no hurry to see them in print. Only about a half-dozen of his keyboard concertos, mainly the earlier ones, were published during his lifetime. Most of the great later ones first saw print in the series André published beginning shortly after the composer's death and extending into the first years of the new century. These publications, together with the earlier ones, extend from about 1784 to 1802 and partake of the full range of common practices in printing keyboard concertos. In the piano parts the tuttis all have have large-note bass lines, in nearly all cases with figures. Many have melody lines in the right hand, sometimes cued to specific instruments, and some distinguish among various possibilities for the right hand by the use of large and small notes. The idea was to make the concerto as usable as possible in a variety of venues: the concert hall, the small gathering of chamber players, the pianist playing alone at home. There is no reason to think Mozart objected to any of these possibilities. But Mozart's primary intention for his concertos, surely, was that they should be played as he played them, with a full accompaniment and, we have every reason to believe, with a realized bass line in the tuttis.

The role of the concerto in Viennese musical life scarcely had time to change in the half decade between Mozart's playing of his own works and Beethoven's arrival on the scene in 1792. Like Mozart, Beethoven came to Vienna as an ambitious piano virtuoso for whom playing concertos was the principal way of presenting himself to the public. And, like Mozart, he tended to withhold these pieces from publication until he had gotten full use of them at his concerts. The publications, when they materialized, for the most part looked not unlike Mozart's. The keyboard part of the first of them, Mollo's print (1801) of the "Grand Concert" in C, Op. 15, has the traditional figured bass in the left hand and rests in the right during the tuttis. That this figured bass was not intended (by whoever made it for the publisher) as a mere formality, a "relic" from an earlier time, as Lebermann contended,[24] can be seen by a glance at the opening tutti, where full and meticulous figures are supplemented by various other explicit instructions for performance: the marking "unis." on the first beat of m. 7 prevents the pianist from adding other pitches (the strings are in unison for that one beat); similarly, the "all' ottava" markings at mm. 70 and 100 call for adding just the octave above; m. 21 has rests because only the winds play there. Such instructions have no meaning aside from an assumed realization of the continuo. Here, just after the turn of the century, Beethoven's concerto is put on the market in a form useful only for playing with orchestra, one that specifically directs that the soloist shall play continuo.

None of the first editions of the subsequent concertos shows such an old-fashioned reliance on the availability of a full accompaniment and of a soloist who understands basso continuo. Hoffmeister's print (later in 1801) of the Second Concerto in Bb, Op. 19, has a variant of the other common format: a large-note bass line without figures in the tuttis of the piano part, together with a small-note *soprano seguente* for the right hand. This arrangement (as Vogler had explained) allows the pianist playing alone to produce at least some likeness of the tuttis, and (as he implied) such a two-part reduction also permits continuo accompaniment in performances with full orchestra. And in this case, at least, we know that Beethoven himself approved the format, for we have that solo part in his own hand; his two separate autographs for the piece, one for the solo, the other for the orchestra, in fact served as *Stichvorlagen* for the edition.[25]

At a few places in the solo autograph (and the published piano part) of Op. 19, Beethoven supplemented the right-hand melody in the tutti with one or two other voices to fill out the harmony, thus facilitating either a credible solo rendition of the music or a performance with continuo accompaniment. This procedure is expanded (in sporadic fashion) in the first edition of the Third Piano Concerto (Vienna, Bureau des Arts et d'Industrie, 1804), whose format otherwise closely resembles that of Hoffmeister's edition of Op. 19. Here, during the tutti, especially in wind passages (first movement, mm. 5ff., 85ff.), the soloist is occasionally offered something resembling a full reduction of the orchestral music. And tremolos in the strings are sometimes reduced to a form conveniently playable on the piano. But such provisions for playing without accompaniment are not permitted to compromise the solo part where quick exchanges with the orchestra make things difficult; at such places (as in the second solo section of the first movement) the accompanying instruments are represented by mere fragments of melody or by rests, leaving gaping holes in the texture. This is perfectly in keeping with established practices in the notation of keyboard concertos for performance with orchestra: in brief internal tutti little or nothing is expected of the soloist. This first edition of the Third Piano Concerto thus represents an uneasy compromise: it is meant to be useful in both contexts, but when priorities must be chosen, it is the performance with accompanying instruments that prevails.

For Beethoven's first three piano concertos the relationship between autograph and first edition, and what we know about the composer's endorsement of the edition, is different in each case. As we have seen, in the two autographs of the Concerto in B♭, Beethoven literally provided the text for the first edition. The autograph score of the C-minor Concerto, missing from before the Second World War but returned to Berlin in 1977, has full orchestral parts, but even in the solos the writing in the piano staves sometimes degenerates into unresolved sketchy alternative readings; it shows nothing for the keyboard player to do in the tutti. This leaves us rather in the dark as to the composer's role in making the piano reduction for the edition, though we may perhaps draw some comfort from its general resemblance to that of the print of the B-flat Concerto. As to clarity and completeness, the autograph of the First Piano Concerto falls somewhere between the other two. The orchestral parts, as usual, are nearly complete, and Beethoven seemingly made a determined effort to write out a definitive version of the piano music. But at points[26] an impenetrable maze of revisions defeats his resolution to produce a readable result. There is no sign in the blank piano staves of the orderly bass-with-figures of the first edition. But for two points of some harmonic complexity in the second movement (mm. 84 and 105), Beethoven worked out appropriate figured bass symbols in the margins, symbols that then appeared unchanged in the first edition.[27]

When Lebermann chose the autograph of the C-major Concerto[28] as the authoritative guide as to what Beethoven expected the soloist to do during tuttis, he failed to distinguish among two quite separate functions the autograph scores fulfilled. In the cases of the first three concertos, at least, Beethoven initially wrote out the music with the aim of performing it himself with an orchestra. What was needed at this stage was a full version of the instrumental parts, written clearly enough so that a copyist could produce the parts. The keyboard part (whether in the score or, perhaps, written out separately) was for Beethoven's private use and as such could remain in a state of considerable chaos. The autograph of the Concerto in C minor is just such a document, prepared (as has been argued above) for Beethoven's concert of April 1803; the orchestral parts are essentially complete, but the keyboard staves leave much to the composer's powers of improvisation. That Beethoven left those staves blank during the tuttis says nothing about what he did or expected any other performer to do in these passages.

The pair of autographs for the Concerto in B♭ is very different: together they were meant expressly for *publication*. And here Beethoven follows a well-established practice that allows for alternative modes of performance: playing alone, playing with instrumental accompaniment (either partial or full), the latter with the option, at least, of realizing an accompaniment from the bass and treble notations during the tutti. The autograph of the C-major Concerto was possibly once used to copy parts for a performance (perhaps in December 1800);[29] but at some point Beethoven went to work at it again, bringing it closer to a condition—but without achieving that condition—where it could be used for publication. That the piano staves in the tuttis remained blank at this juncture means nothing.

If the bass-cum-treble notation in the piano autograph and first edition of the B♭ Concerto leaves some ambiguity as to whether Beethoven contemplated a chordal accompaniment of some sort in the tuttis when an orchestra was present, corresponding documents for the Fifth Concerto (the "Emperor") would seem to settle the matter. The autograph of this concerto, written in 1809–10 when Beethoven had ceased to play his concertos in public, was clearly aimed from the beginning toward publication, which followed in quick succession in two somewhat differing versions by Clementi in London and Breitkopf & Härtel in Leipzig.[30] While the figured bass of the first edition of the C-major Concerto had favored performance with full accompaniment, and the bass-with-melody of the B♭ Concerto facilitated playing with lesser forces, the primary documents for the "Emperor" did both. The autograph and German edition are a publisher's ideal, designed for usefulness in a maximal variety of settings. In the tuttis of the autograph Beethoven wrote out a melodic reduction of the instrumental parts, a fuller and vastly more skillful one than those in the first editions of the First and Third Concertos, one in which idiomatic writing for orchestral instruments, such as violin tremolos, are revised to facilitate playing at the piano. And here we have as well, in Beethoven's hand, a full set of meticulous figured bass symbols, including explicit directions for basso continuo realization—that is, *performance*—such as selective octave doublings of the bass, the instruction *tasto solo* ("play only this key"), and careful arrangement of figures for specific ordering of chord tones. These symbols, absent from Clementi's edition, are reproduced in almost all particulars in the Breitkopf & Härtel edition of early 1811.[31]

One could scarcely wish for more conclusive evidence that Beethoven contemplated continuo playing in the tuttis of this concerto; one writer, Tibor Szász, has argued at length that this is the case.[32] But Hans-Werner Küthen, editor of the piano concertos for the new *Beethoven Werke*, has uniformly followed the modern practice of dropping the figures and substituting rests for whatever may have appeared in the tuttis of the right-hand piano staves in the original sources. And in the special case of the "Emperor," where we have the composer's own continuo notations, he has a special explanation. He offers the intriguing theory that the composer's bass figures have nothing whatever to do with performance of the concerto but came about as part of a course of instruction in figured bass for his patron and pupil, the Archduke Rudolph—that Beethoven wrote out these figures in his own music, destined for publication, for this wholly extraneous purpose.[33] In the absence of overwhelming evidence that this is the case, it is much easier to believe that Beethoven's figures mean what they say, that in his final completed concerto he clung persistently to entrenched traditions of the genre, whereby the pianist performing with orchestra could be expected to play multiple roles: as virtuoso soloist, as accompanist during the tutti, and sometimes as director.

There are also provisions for performance under other conditions. Cues for wind instruments in the first violin part, partly specified by Beethoven in the autograph, allow for direction by the first violinist when that is needed; and Beethoven's reduction of the orchestral music, while an aid, surely, to a pianist/director, also makes it possible to play the piece in the absence of some of the melody instruments or, if need be, alone. When he wrote out the score of the "Emperor," Beethoven acted as a willing participant in a publishing venture, an undertaking intended to put his music at the disposal of the widest possible range of customers: musicians professional or amateur, who could be expected to play it, well or badly, under whatever circumstances might pertain. The scope of Beethoven's tolerance in this matter recalls his apparent acquiesence in the reduction of the Fourth Concerto for performance with a string quintet and the arrangement of the Violin Concerto in a version (at points a shockingly maladroit one) for piano.[34] But despite all this willingness to participate in the popular musical culture of his time, performance of his piano concertos with full orchestra surely remained Beethoven's ideal, as it had been Mozart's; and for such performances the soloist, whether directing or not, was rather explicitly invited to play continuo during the tuttis.[35]

As in the case of Mozart, we have little precise information about just how Beethoven performed his own concertos, and we know almost nothing about what he played during the tuttis.[36] The sources create an impression of great variability in the piano part from one performance to the next, and between performing versions and the published one. The Concerto in B♭, played and revised many times, seemed to arrive at a final form when Beethoven sent the autograph score to the publisher Hoffmeister in 1801. But in that score (as Beethoven said was his custom)[37] the piano part is absent except for a few sketchy notations; and the written-out part Beethoven sent Hoffmeister separately does not even correspond very well with those sketches. The piano part of the Third Concerto was not yet written down in anything like final form when the composer first performed it in 1803; what he had on the music rack at the time (according to Ignaz von Seyfried, who turned pages)[38] was some private sketches that looked like hieroglyphics. When Beethoven played his own concertos, the soloist's music was a changeable thing, subject to the composer's whim until the moment it was fixed in print.

The single concert of Beethoven's about which we have the most information is the memorable *Akademie* at the Theater an der Wien of December 1808, that saw the first public performances of the Fifth and Sixth Symphonies, the Choral Fantasy, parts of the Mass in C, and the Fourth Piano Concerto. One member of the audience, the visiting composer and musical commentator J. G. Reichardt, described the event as one in which Beethoven seemed to be in complete control. We will recall that he reported having sat with Prince Lobkowitz in the latter's box, which "was in the first balcony near the stage, so that the orchestra with Beethoven in the middle conducting it was below us and near at hand."[39] However he may have conducted the symphonies—by this time it is clear that he sometimes did so standing before the orchestra in the modern manner—it is safe to assume that for the concerto he directed the other musicians from the keyboard. Another listener, Carl Czerny, as we also recall, reported that in the concerto Beethoven had played "roguishly" (*muthwillig*), adding many more notes than were written.[40] The Vienna manuscript copy that served as the *Stichvorlage* for the first edition (as we have argued) evidently documents something of this *Muthwilligkeit*: elaborate, startlingly agile ornament that appreciably escalates the degree of virtuosity in the solo part and sometimes palpably alters its effect.[41] And where the soloist's second theme of the first movement reappears in the recapitulatory third solo (m. 286), Beethoven sketches in the beginning of an arpeggiated accompaniment for the pianist (see Example 9-18): a continuo realization, that is, and a startlingly elaborate one at that. Here is one place where Beethoven, almost by happenstance, offers us a glimpse of what he might have done as a soloist in his own concertos. His was a freely improvisatory style of playing that (true to Rochlitz's general observation about soloists in keyboard concertos)[42] evidently did not stop when the tuttis began.

But when Beethoven as a performer was through with a concerto—typically when it was published—he seems to have countenanced various other freedoms. Someone other than the soloist, for example, might direct the performance. When his student Ferdinand Ries played the Third Piano Concerto at an Augarten concert in 1804, according to Ries's later report, "Beethoven himself conducted, though he only turned the pages, and it may well be that no concerto was ever accompanied more beautifully."[43] The cues for the first violinist in the autograph of the "Emperor" apparently authorize a performance in which the concertmaster conducts, and the composer's own reductions for piano of the orchestral melodies both here and in the Second Concerto provide for performance with reduced forces—as, of course, does the arrangement he evidently approved of the Fourth Concerto for piano and string quintet. As Beethoven moved into the magnificent years of his middle period (as we have seen), he seems to have thought of his compositions, including his concertos, less as grist for the mills of performance than as "works," as monuments to his artistry with a certain fixedness and durability. But this fixedness could be had only through publication: which meant his music entered the public domain, in some sense now belonging to the public and participating in a diversified public musical culture—which, paradoxically, entailed great variability in conditions and kinds of performance.

Beethoven seems to have understood and accepted the situation. There is no reason to believe that he would have been less understanding about still other conditions under which his concertos are heard in our day.

INSTRUMENTS, TEMPERAMENTS, AND TEMPOS

One kind of variability Beethoven provided for in the autograph of the Fifth Concerto was differing compasses of keyboards. While the composition includes pitches up to f'''', nicely accommodated by the new six-octave keyboard, FF–f'''', of German and Austrian pianos, Beethoven wrote in alternate (*ossia*) passages for pianists whose instruments stopped at c'''' (in some few cases he seemed to assume the availability of the d''''). Similarly, the final version in the autograph of the Third Concerto from a half-dozen years earlier, almost surely prepared for Beethoven's premiere performance of April 1803, included pitches up to c''''; but the first edition of 1804 still has *ossia* alternatives for the older upper limit of f'''. This is just one symptom of the rapid change the instrument underwent during the period in which Beethoven composed and played his piano concertos.[44] Mozart (and, in all but his latest keyboard works, Haydn) had lived comfortably with the Classical five-octave double-strung Viennese piano, FF–f''', with its poignant, rather reedy-sounding treble and clear-speaking bass. But in the first years of the new century, as the Viennese piano grew appreciably in string tension, compass, and volume of sound, Beethoven, in something of a revolution of rising expectations, remained dissatisfied. In 1817 the increasingly deaf composer asked the piano makers Nannette and Johann Andreas Streicher to adjust one of their instruments for him, to make it "as loud [stark] as possible."[45] But in 1826, after having had in his possession some fourteen pianos, he still declared, as his friend Karl Holz reported, that the piano "is and remains an inadequate instrument."[46]

In Beethoven's writing for piano, range had always been an issue. From his very early sonatas (such as in the finale of Op. 2, No. 1) he was frustrated by the upper limits of available keyboards, rewriting the transpositions of parallel passages so as to keep within the prescribed limits. And he was quick to respond when liberated from those limits. As keyboards expanded, particularly in the treble, his piano music began to luxuriate in that wash of very high sounds so familiar to us in the music of composers of the younger generation like Schubert and Weber. Beethoven's concertos availed themselves of this expansion in 1803–6; while the Concertos in B♭ and C had (reluctantly) remained within the old five-octave confines, the Third and Fourth Concertos and the Triple Concerto moved upward to c'''', and by 1809 the "Emperor," as we have seen, included pitches up to f''''. This upward expansion of range is no mere technical detail; the resultant piano sound became a distinctive stylistic trait, an instantly recognizable emblem of early nineteenth-century music.

One area in which an intersection of style and keyboard range impinge directly on modern-day performance is in the selection (or creation) of cadenzas. It was evidently in 1809 that Beethoven composed a series of cadenzas for the first four piano concertos (there are also extra ones for the first movements of the First and the Fourth).[47] This music shows no interest in the niceties of historical verisimilitude: it is written in the more expansive and complex manner of 1809 and for the pianos of that time. This presents little difficulty for the Third and Fourth Concertos (for the Fifth he wrote cadenzas directly into the score); the discrepancy as to style and piano sound in the first two, however, is potentially troublesome, and performers have dealt with this problem in various ways. The traditional approach has been to ignore it: simply to shift gears in the cadenza to Beethoven's style and instrument of 1809. The gnarled chromatic counterpoint of the cadenza to the first movement of the B♭ Concerto, reaching almost an octave higher than the movement proper, has come to be simply an obligatory, if somewhat indigestible, appurtenance to the piece.[48] Other pianists have used newly-composed cadenzas, often, it seems, out of motives other than a zeal for stylistic uniformity.[49] But for his recording of the complete set in 1987, Steven Lubin[50] diligently used four different instruments and composed his own cadenzas for the first movements of the first two concertos. These seem stylistically apt and (perforce) stay within the five-octave range of the pianos at hand, while sacrificing nothing in the way of virtuoso flair. If one wishes to correct Beethoven's evident disregard for historical scruples, this would seem a convincing way to do it.

Richard Taruskin begins his expansive review article of Roger Norrington's recording of Beethoven's Ninth Symphony[51] by reporting his impulse to congratulate the timpanist, Robert Howes. But the drum sound that so impresses Taruskin surely has more to do with the instrument—a "period instrument," the sort of thing Taruskin routinely disparages—than he credits. The timpani of Beethoven's time, typically smaller than its modern counterpart and normally played with hard-headed sticks, gave off a sharp crack of a sound vividly recalling its not-so-distant origins in cavalry regiments. Such a sound throws a revelatory new light on the coda of the first movement of the Third Piano Concerto, the concluding measures of the

Fifth (where on modern drums the rhythms are never heard distinctly), and the beginning of the Violin Concerto.

Early nineteenth-century timpani differed from modern ones, in fact, much as pianos from the time differ from concert grands of today. In each case an increase in size and the introduction of felt as a striking agent has yielded a certain velvety effect, that stronger and longer-lasting but less focused sound we are used to hearing in large performing spaces. A parallel later nineteenth-century development in string instruments (such as the use of steel strings) and ways of playing them (with increased bow pressure and vibrato as an assumed component of the sound) has aimed single-mindedly at greater volume and brilliance. This, too, is all for the good for performance in large concert halls. But the variety of conditions under which we hear this music today (such as listening to the easily controlled sound systems in our living rooms) clearly allows for other solutions, including a return to the use of period instruments and the ways they were once played.

"Which is the right instrument for this piece?" is a quintessentially twentieth-century question. In the eighteenth century such matters were characteristically viewed with an air of sensible pragmatism. J. S. Bach evidently tried out the new pianoforte at the court of Frederick the Great with an open mind, simply to see how it might work for his music. In Haydn's second London season he performed his symphonies in an unaccustomedly large hall with an orchestra of unprecedented size, even playing continuo himself (on the piano) because that was the local practice. Beethoven collaborated with his publishers in issuing his concertos for widely variable forces. A similar streak of pragmatism is needed to maintain the vitality of this music today. The relatively weak upper range of the Viennese piano of the turn of the nineteenth century is clearly better matched with strings of its own time than with a modern violin section, and the nine-foot grand with a steel frame (despite a certain inevitable muddiness of its bass register that requires particular care in many passages of Beethoven's concertos) will obviously stand a better chance of surviving with a modern orchestra in a big hall. But Beethoven's music has flourished under a wide variety of conditions. What finally counts is not choice of instruments, but what musicians do with them in a particular setting: the critical judgments and adjustments they must make at every moment as to articulation, sonority, and balance—all needed, in any case, in the service of those ever-present larger concerns of style and expression.

In an open letter of 1799 to a (presumably imaginary) young composer, Friedrich Rochlitz lamented the gradual elimination of the accompanying keyboard instrument from orchestras of his time. He gave a surprising reason for his regret:

> So you are yet in doubt as to the appropriateness and wisdom of the current practice of banishing the harpsichord from the orchestra? Allow me to share my thoughts on the matter with you. . . . If one wishes to do away with the harpsichord as a *keyboard instrument*, then one also excludes its substitute, the pianoforte, turning over the direction [of the ensemble], as becomes ever more usual, to the violin. . . . One thus forgoes the surest and most convenient means of preserving in performance the so-called irregular temperament [*schwebende Temperatur*], upon which, however, our entire present tonal system is based. And one runs the danger of reintroducing all the well-known abuses that result from the playing of mathematically perfect fifths by the violins—abuses of which we have only recently managed to rid our orchestras. (That our violinists now use a tempered tuning you will not deny.) . . . But if a tempered keyboard instrument of some kind is present, the other instruments will tune in accordance with its fifths, and all will be in order.[52]

The ancient problem in tuning instruments of fixed pitch was to achieve reasonably pure thirds and fifths (i.e., close to the "just," or nonbeating forms of these intervals that corresponded to the low-numbered ratios of the overtone series, 3:2, 4:3, 5:4, etc.) in a reasonable range of keys. "Temperament," or patterns of deviation from just tunings of intervals, had always represented something of a compromise: the more impurity in individual intervals one was willing to tolerate, the more keys there would be available. "Just intonation" yielded perfectly pure intervals in about half the range of keys, leaving the others unusable; meantone tunings permitted the use of more keys but paid the price with intervals (especially fifths) that were less pure; equal temperament distributes the basic "error" (the ditonic comma, or the difference between twelve fifths and seven octaves) equally throughout the system, so that all keys are equally usable—and equally out of tune.

Equal temperament has become such a fixture of our musical life that we easily forget what a recent institution it is. Despite a persistent modern tendency to associate Rameau, J. S. Bach, and other eighteenth-century musicians with the practice, it is rather clear that equal temperament was not in regular use for keyboard instruments until the twentieth century.[53] During Beethoven's time keyboard instruments were tuned in a variety of irregular temperaments (or well-temperaments) in which all keys were acceptable, but some were smoother, and some more pungent—the general rule being that purity declined as one ventured toward the remoter reaches of the circle of fifths.[54] This is surely what Rochlitz had in mind when he spoke of temperament not as a compromise, but as a positive virtue, a basis, as he said, for "our entire present tonal system." And he was far from alone in this opinion: Johann Philip Kirnberger of Leipzig, pupil of J. S. Bach and a central figure in the theory of later eighteenth-century music, maintained that a good temperament "must not injure the variegation of the keys." And according to his disciple Tempelhof, without variations in the purity of intonation from one key to another, music would become "nothing more than a harmonious noise that tickles the ear but leaves the heart slumbering away in a disgusting indifference."[55] An unabated interest in discerning the affective qualities of the keys, as in the famous characterizations of C. D. F. Schubart (published in 1806) and Robert Schumann (1834),[56] would be hard to explain but for a general practice of these irregular tunings.

According to Anton Schindler, Beethoven's amanuensis during his later years and his not very reliable biographer, Beethoven read Schubart and particularly admired his characterization of the keys. In a somewhat obscure passage Schindler seems to give an account of a fine distinction the composer made between transposing from one key to another and simply moving a given key to a higher or lower pitch: "Beethoven based his counter-claim [in reply to the composer and critic F. A. Kanne] on his unfailing ability to recognize each key even if it were pitched a whole tone higher or lower than the ear was accustomed to hearing it. . . . The orchestral pitch had been raised, but the difference was imperceptible, because our feeling for the psyche of each key had risen along with it, for this psyche is implicit in the scale of each key."[57] If we can believe that Schindler got it right, and if (as seems likely) the "psyche of each key" was related to differences in tuning, then we have a strong suggestion that Beethoven thought about key coloration in the tunings available to him as a factor in musical expression.

There is reason to think that the surprise and wonder, and sometimes shock value of increasingly exotic keys and remote modulations in early nineteenth-century music, such as became nearly routine for Schubert, was materially abetted by these irregular tunings. Beethoven's music too, almost from the first, easily lends itself to such an interpretation. As early as the first movement of the Sonata Op. 2, No. 2, in A (1795), the E-major ending of the development moves abruptly to C major (a favorite pairing of keys for Beethoven), then quickly to A♭—a traversal, that is, of eight steps in the flat direction within a few measures.[58] In the recapitulation of the first movement of the Sonata in C minor, Op. 10, No. 1 (1796/98), the transition slips far down to Gb and its relative Eb minor en route to the placid F major of the second theme. The Funeral March of the Sonata Op. 26 juxtaposes Ab minor and B minor (the former a key of "difficult struggle," said Schubart, the latter one of "patience"); the opening of the "Moonlight" Sonata is *delicatissimamente e senza sordini* but cast in C♯ minor, a "despairing" key in the contemporary estimation. Tonal audacities in these passages and countless others are safely tamed by the homogenized temperament in which we always hear them.

The concertos abound in harmonic relations, especially in connection with secondary themes, that seem predicated on contrasting key colors. In the coda of the last movement of the Fourth Concerto (mm. 459–83), for example, statements of the magical second theme in F♯, C, and G are placed side by side, as if to invite comparison; the remarkable modulating theme of the opening movement (first heard in mm. 29–40) moves with ceremonial gait along a distinctly radical path from a to e, C, b, g, and f♯ (in the first and third solos the fixed-pitch piano joins the sequence, in two transpositions, only in its more colorful later portions). In the second theme of the first movement of the "Emperor," a pivotal lowered-sixth relation—later so beloved by Schubert—pits (enharmonic) Cb major/minor against its large-scale resolution to Bb; that Cb then returns as the key of the second movement, renewing not only a tonal center but also the special piquancy of its basic third, B–D♯.

Something similar can be heard in the Third Concerto when the second movement of this C-minor work enters with a quiet jolt in E major, a tonality that will return, with its "penetrating" sound, for a poignant retrospective moment before the third ritornello in the finale (mm. 264–74). The two earlier concertos have less to show in the way of juxtaposition of distant keys and their colors. But Beethoven moved to remedy this a bit when he took these pieces up again, evidently in 1809, to provide them with cadenzas: the third cadenza he supplied for the first movement of the C-major Concerto, for example, brings us the more lyrical of the two secondary themes at the far remove of Db. These compositions open a fertile field for exploring the enhanced effects of the tunings with which they were associated. Musicians who take equal temperament as a given (as almost all do, together with their piano tuners), miss an opportunity not just for another badge of authenticity, but for rediscovery of expressive resources that were once a part of this music.

If present-day players of Beethoven's concertos give little or no thought to the tuning of their pianos, they must reveal, from the first notes played, what they think about tempo. The composer himself showed a lively interest in getting the tempos of his music right. Schindler, reporting on this matter of general interest in which he had no particular stake (and is thus more likely to be trustworthy) recalled, "When a work by Beethoven had been performed, his first question was always, 'How were the tempi?' Every other consideration seemed to be of secondary importance to him."[59] In 1817–19 this interest, in addition to a sudden burst of enthusiasm for the new mechanical device given him by its putative inventor, Johann Nepomuk Maelzel, led to those famously troublesome metronome markings Beethoven supplied for a number of his compositions: for all his symphonies but the Ninth (which he added later), the first eleven string quartets, the Septet Op. 20, the "Hammerklavier" Sonata Op. 106, and a half-dozen other works.[60]

The main problem with Beethoven's metronome markings has always been that musicians thought them too fast (or, in a very few cases, too slow). This has led to speculation that the composer's metronome was faulty, or that he made consistent mistakes in recording tempos, or that we have simply misunderstood his system in noting these values.[61] But for some years now, beginning with an article by Rudolf Kolisch in 1943, a conviction has been growing that those metronome markings for the most part reflect Beethoven's intentions, and that in this case, at least, we have some tangible, objective evidence as to how he wished his music to be performed.[62]

There can be little doubt that at the time he engaged in his metronomizing (*Metronomisierung*), Beethoven felt he was departing sharply from tradition in the matter of tempo. A good summary statement of later eighteenth-century notions of tempo can be had from J. J. Quantz, who divided the whole range of tempo indications (in common time) into four general categories, Allegro assai, Allegretto, Adagio cantabile, and Adagio assai. Each of these classes of tempo could be coordinated, following ancient practice, with the human pulse, which Quantz estimated in a "jovial and high-spirited" person (in the afternoon) at eighty beats per minute. In Allegro assai the half note matched the pulse, and each of the successively slower tempos halved the note-value corresponding to it (thus Adagio assai would be $\flat$ = 40). In *alla breve*, or *tempo maggiore*, all the notes "are taken twice as fast as in common time." And one more tempo in common time, falling between Allegro assai and Allegretto, was "a kind of moderate allegro" with a pulse for every three eighths ($\flat$ = 120) that "occurs frequently in vocal pieces, and is also used in compositions for instruments unsuited for great speed in passage work."[63]

In the first flush of his infatuation with the metronome, Beethoven wrote to Ignaz Franz Mosel (an official at court and musical author who was about to publish an adulatory article on Maelzel and his device), abjuring the "four standard tempos": "as for those four chief movements, which, however, are far from embodying the truth or the accuracy of the four chief winds, we would gladly do without them. . . . As for me, I have long been thinking of abandoning those absurd descriptive terms, Allegro, Andante, Adagio, Presto; and Mälzel's metronome affords us the best opportunity to do so."[64]

He did not, of course, abandon the words, but the metronome markings he provided for the symphonies and quartets, distributed across a broad spectrum of tempos, showed few signs of the older standard groupings. Two students of the subject, Rudolf Kolisch in the 1940s and Hermann Beck in the mid-1950s, have attempted to demonstrate that these tempo indications nevertheless show a certain consistency and system—though one much more complex than that outlined by Quantz.[65] Both Kolisch and Beck consider factors other than Quantz's verbal indications, meter signatures, and fastest note-values, taking into account as well the character of movements and types of rhythmic motion. Using these criteria, both writers—Kolisch freely and often subjectively, Beck more systematically and cautiously—proceed to extrapolate from the movements for which Beethoven supplied tempos to those for which he did not.

Beethoven himself left no metronome markings for any of the concertos. But in the fourth volume of his *Complete Theoretical and Practical Piano Forte School*,[66] his student Czerny provided them for all the movements (but one) of all the concertos that involve piano (including the piano transcription of the Violin Concerto). Although this work was not published until about 1840, Czerny tells us (speaking in the third person) that he wrote in a retrospective frame of mind, drawing on his experience as Beethoven's pupil and trusted musical colleague in Vienna during the first decade of the century: "he [Czerny] was extremely partial to Beethoven's piano music, studying all such works immediately as they appeared, some of them under the master's own supervision."[67] Among the works he studied under Beethoven's tutelage, he later reported to Gustav Nottebohm, were all the published piano concertos but the Second.[68] Czerny's reputation for reliability is good; his suggestions for tempo in these compositions, given in Table 12-1, are surely worth taking into account.

The opening movements of the first three piano concertos are all in common time, Allegro con brio, a very frequent combination in Beethoven's compositions up to the time of the Third Concerto. Czerny's tempos for these movements, compared to most modern performances, are somewhat on the fast side. But the recording of Steven Lubin with Christopher Hogwood (L'Oiseau-Lyre, 1987) closely approximates these tempos; they fall behind only in the First Concerto, playing at about ♩ = 80 rather than Czerny's 88. But others have shown that Czerny's marking for this movement is practicable enough: on period instruments both Anthony Newman and Melvyn Tan hold to that tempo, and Rudolf Serkin and Glenn Gould (at ♩ = 82 and 84, respectively) almost did so on modern pianos.[69] In the first movement of the Second Concerto, Gould, Lubin, and Tan are almost squarely on Czerny's mark; an informal survey of some performances of the first movement of the Third Concerto shows a preference for a tempo just a little slower than Czerny's ♩ = 144.[70] The only account of the tempos of these movements that seems quite unrealistic is that of Kolisch (who appears better attuned to pieces for violin than for piano). Extrapolating from Beethoven's markings for the first Allegros of the first two symphonies and the Septet, he lumps all three of the concerto movements together with a suggested tempo range of ♩ = 184–224—an impossibly fast pace for any of them.[71]

For the first movement of the "Emperor" (Allegro, **c**) Czerny suggests a tempo of ♩ = 132, and at least three recent recordings, by Lubin, Newman, and Levin[72]—all surely knowing about Czerny's recommendation—are almost exactly on the mark. The music, energetic and exuberant at this speed, shows scarcely a hint of breathlessness or loss of control. In this case, too, Kolisch's generalizations seem to lead him very far afield; this movement lands in a group for which he recommends an inconceivable tempo of ♩ = 168–76.[73] There is nothing remarkable about the tempo (♩ = 126) Czerny recommends for the opening movement of the Triple Concerto (also Allegro, ⁴⁄₄); it is usually performed at just about this rate.[74] Beethoven pointed to the more lyrical character of the first movements of the Fourth Concerto and the Violin Concerto with his modifiers: (Allegro) moderato and ma non troppo. Czerny's recommendations are again only a trifle faster than the tempos at which we are used to hearing these pieces.[75]

For the finales of the first two piano concertos, Czerny's tempos are easily attained (and a couple of times exceeded) by Gould, Lubin, Newman, and Tan. Czerny makes no suggestion for the body of the Rondo of the Concerto in C minor, but his ♩. = 112 for the Presto coda of this movement is a notch below the tempo taken by Gould and Tan (both at about 116), while Schnabel in 1947 and Perahia in 1986 played it even faster, at 120. The marking Czerny gives for the finale of the Fourth Concerto (♩ = 138) is distinctly brisk, but Lubin approaches it at about ♩ = 132, and Schnabel had already equalled it in 1946. Most performances of the finale of the Violin Concerto (e.g., Heifetz, Perlman and Grumiaux) seem to hover just below Czerny's ♩. = 100, while his ♩ = 104 for the Rondo of the Triple Concerto accords well with the inclinations of modern players. There are no real anomalies, thus, among Czerny's metronome markings for the outer movements of the concertos: none that is impossibly fast or in any way wildly out of kilter with what we are used to hearing. He simply urges us to play some of them—mainly first movements—a little faster than we are accustomed.

It is possible to compare Czerny's tempos for these movements with modern ones in general because there has been a remarkable consensus on this matter among performers of the past fifty years or so.[76] Such a consensus is much less to be found among performances of the slow movements. Quite apart from audacious eccentricities such as Gould's rendition of the second movement of the Fourth Concerto at a highly unsteady ♪ = ca. 44 (Czerny says ♪ = 84), there is a considerable variety of opinions as to just how slow these movements really are. Performances of three (among the seven in question) find little agreement on this matter either with Czerny or among themselves. A contributory factor in one of these, the Largo of the First Piano Concerto, may be confusion as to meter signatures. Beethoven clearly designated the movement ¢, which the editors of the old Breitkopf & Härtel *Gesamtausgabe*—the source for all subsequent performing parts—arbitrarily changed to **c**.[77] At any rate, a sampling of modern performances showed a range of ♩ = 38 to 66 (with most in the lower 40s), as compared to Czerny's 58. All performances of the Larghetto of the Violin Concerto noted here, ranging from ♩ = 42 to 50, fall well short of Czerny's ♩ = 60. The same holds for the Largo of the Triple Concerto, where the range is about ♪ = 60 to 80, to Czerny's remarkably spritely 104.

Czerny's prescriptions for tempos are as close as we are likely to get to Beethoven's ideas about how fast his concertos ought to be played. If there is a general lesson here that performers might wish to consider, it is this: fast movements, according to Czerny, go somewhat faster than we usually hear them, and slow movements, on the whole, considerably faster. Some present-day pianists (Lubin, Tan, Newman, Levin) seem to have taken Czerny's prescriptions to heart, and one from an earlier time, Schnabel, arrived at a number of very similar conclusions, probably out of simple musical conviction; in both cases the results are enlightening.

Beethoven's concertos belong to history, but also to a live modern-day culture of performance and listening. Like all living things, this tradition

APPENDIX I

The Bonn Concertos and Their Sources

WoO 4. Keyboard Concerto in E♭, presumably from 1784, surviving in a copy (Berlin, SPK, Artaria 125) with an apparently autograph inscription on fol. 1: "un Concert / pour le Clavecin ou Forte-piano / Composé par / Louis Van Beethoven / agé de douze ans." There are some later autograph corrections. The solo part is complete; in the tutti sections the orchestral part is in piano score with some instrumental cues. Published in *GA*, Ser. 25, no. 310.

Hess 13. *Romance Cantabile* in E minor for keyboard, flute, bassoon, and orchestra. This orchestral fragment, written on fols. 74–80 of the Kafka Miscellany, probably dates from 1786. Transcription in Kerman, *Kafka*, vol. 2, pp. 50, 55–58. Published in Hess, *Supplemente*, vol. 3, p. 33.

WoO 5. Violin Concerto in C. Part of a first movement only, surviving in autograph, Vienna, Gesellschaft der Musikfreunde, A 5, dating from ca. 1790–92. Published in Schiedermair, 427, and Hess, *Supplemente*, vol. 3, p. 44.

Adagio in D to a concerto in A, in Kafka 154v, ca. 60 mm. on two staves, inscribed: "adagio zum Concert aus A." Dated by Johnson 1790–92. *Fischhof*, vol. 1, pp. 253–55. Transcr. J. Kerman, *Kafka*, vol. 2, pp. 127–28.

Fragments associated with Piano Concerto No. 2 in B♭, Op. 19:
   (1) A page from an orchestral score, Berlin, Staatsbibliothek, Aut. 28 (the Fischhof Miscellany), fol. 15, from ca. 1787–89. In this extract from

the first movement, only the piano part is notated. Transcr. D. Johnson, *Fischhof*, vol. 2, p. 71.

(2) An autograph score fragment from the development section of the first movement, in Paris, Bibliothèque nationale, MS. 61, fol. 2v, from ca. 1790–92. Transcr. D. Johnson, *Fischhof*, vol. 2, p. 75.

(3) A sketch of the Andante that appears as the contrasting central episode in the Rondo in B♭, WoO 6, at one time the finale of the Concerto in B♭. Kafka 75v. 1790–92?

(4) A draft of an Adagio in D in Kafka 127, 65 mm. in one and two staves with an inscription on its verso: "Concerto in B dur adagio in D dur." Dated by Johnson as "Spring 1795," Fischhof, 371–72. Transcr. J. Kerman, *Kafka*, vol. 2, pp. 48–49.

Oboe Concerto in F, Hess 12, slow movement sketches. Dated by Johnson, 1793, and sent to the Elector in Bonn in that year. *Fischhof*, vol. 1, pp. 94, 99. Transcr. J. Kerman, *Kafka*, vol. 2, pp. 126–27.

On Redating Piano Concerto No. 3: A Summary

The generally accepted account of the origins of the C-minor Concerto was this: Beethoven composed it mainly in 1799–1800 and planned to present it at his concert of April 1800. But failing to finish it on time, he substituted an older concerto (almost surely Op. 15) at that concert and finally played the C-minor one for the first time at the concert of April 1803. The foremost reason for believing in this sequence of events was that the autograph score of the work, missing since the Second World War, was reportedly dated "1800." There are, moreover, almost no surviving sketches for the concerto; a missing sketchbook from just this time (1799–1800) seemed a good explanation for their absence.

But the autograph reappeared in 1977, and the date on its first page, in Beethoven's hand, is indisputably "1803." Hans-Werner Küthen, in his *Kritischer Bericht* for the *Beethoven Werke*, attempted to retain the older dating for the work, relying partly on watermark evidence but mainly on the presence of several stages of writing—with the use of at least three different inks—in the autograph, the first of which he associated with Beethoven's purported work on the piece in 1799–1800.

But an identification of the principal watermark in the autograph with that of two sources form ca. 1800 turns out to have been a mistake; these papers clearly came from different molds. And the study of watermarks to date the manuscript is in any case largely futile, since Beethoven used the type of paper found in this manuscript (with minor variations in its watermarks) over a very long period of time. A similar situation holds in respect to the other potentially useful physical property of the paper in question, the distinctive traits of its staff-lining: this, too, is ubiquitous in Beethoven's manuscripts from 1800–ca. 1804. And with these means of dating—the date on the autograph and the physical characteristics of the paper—rendered useless for maintaining a connection with 1799–1800, there are no longer any presumptive periods of time with which to connect the various stages of notation in the autograph. No one claims to distinguish Beethoven's hand of 1800 from that of 1803; the two principal stages of writing in the autograph, as far as we know, could have taken place equally well shortly before the concert of 1803.

But much of the act of composition for Beethoven consisted of sketching before writing out an autograph. Could we perhaps still hold to the theory that the missing sketches of Op. 37 were made in the missing book of 1799–1800? With the collapse of a connection with 1800 that the misreading of the date on the autograph had provided, that missing book no longer has any special claim on our attention as we try to place the missing sketches. And there are other lacunae in the surviving record of Beethoven's compositional work into which the missing sketches of Op. 37 could fit at least equally well. One such is the dismembered "Sauer" Sketchbook of mid-1801, only a fraction of whose leaves have survived.

In the spring of 1802 Beethoven made preparations for a concert of his own works at one of the court theaters—a concert that never took place, as it turned out, because use of the theater was finally denied him. The "Kessler" Sketchbook of late 1801–mid-1802 testifies to his strenuous efforts to provide compositions for that concert. Included are signs of serious work on music for piano and orchestra such as a Rondo moderato in F major and an apparent companion movement in C major. While these compositions did not progress very far, Beethoven sketched another one, a *concertante* in D major, evidently for piano, violin, cello, and orchestra, and partly wrote it out in autograph before finally abandoning the project (because the concert was canceled?). It is hard to believe that he would have labored so assiduously at these other concerto-like pieces—working under time pressure of the approaching concert—if the C-minor Concerto had at the time been anywhere near completion. (A fortiori, it is hard to think, with Küthen, that even the autograph of Op. 37 would by this time have been largely written.) In light of these considerations, the most likely time for the sketching of the concerto must fall after the collapse of the concert plans of 1802. As it happens, there is a lacuna in the record of Beethoven's sketches that falls just at the most appropriate time: the period between the Kessler and Wielhorsky Sketchbooks, that is, from mid- to late-1802.

The surmise, then, is that the C-minor Concerto was very likely prepared explicitly for the concert of 1803: that it was sketched sometime toward the end of 1802 and written up in score and revised during the first three months of 1803. No conclusive proof can be offered, but this explanation is more congruent with the evidence than any other.

Abbreviations in the Notes and Bibliography

BN	Bibliothèque nationale
AmZ	*Allgemeine musikalische Zeitung*
JAMS	*Journal of the American Musicological Society*
Kafka	Beethoven, Ludwig van, *Autograph Miscellany from Circa 1786 to 1799: British Museum Additional Manuscript 29801, ff. 39–162 (The Kafka Sketchbook),* ed. Joseph Kerman, 2 vols., (London: Trustees of the British Museum, 1970)
Kinsky-Halm	Georg Kinsky, *Das Werk Beethovens: Thematisch-bibliographisches Verzeichnis,* compl. and ed. Hans Halm (Munich: Henle, 1955)
Mf	*Die Musikforschung*
ML	*Music & Letters*
MQ	*The Musical Quarterly*
MR	*The Music Review*
MT	*The Musical Times*
NZfM	*Neue Zeitschrift für Musik*
ÖMz	*Österreichische Musikzeitschrift*
SBH	Sammlungen Beethoven-Haus
SIMG	*Sammelbände der Internationalen Musikgesellschaft*
SPK	Staatsbibliothek zu Berlin, Preussischer Kulturbesitz
SzMw	*Studien zur Musikwissenschaft*
TDR	Thayer, Alexander Wheelock, *Ludwig van Beethovens Leben von Alexander Wheelock Thayer nach dem Original-Manuskript,* ed. Hermann Deiters and Hugo Riemann, 3d ed. (Leipzig: Breitkopf & Härtel, 1907–17)
Thayer-Forbes	Thayer, Alexander Wheelock, *Thayers Life of Beethoven,* rev. and ed. Elliot Forbes (Princeton: Princeton University Press, 1964)
VfMw	*Vierteljahrschrift für Musikwissenschaft*
ZfMw	*Zeitschrift für Musikwissenschaft*

Notes

NOTES TO THE INTRODUCTION

1. See Robert Farris Thompson, *African Art in Motion* (Los Angeles: University of California Press, 1974), p. 27.
2. See J. Lowell Lewis, *Ring of Liberation; Deceptive Discourse in Brazilian Capoeira* (Chicago: University of Chicago Press, 1992), especially pp. 152–55.
3. See Colin McPhee, *Music in Bali: A Study in Form and Instrumental Organization in Balinese Orchestral Music* (New Haven: Yale University Press, 1966), p. 67. I am grateful to Michael Tenzer for calling my attention to this practice.
4. *Die Musik des 19. Jahrhunderts* (Laaber: Laaber-Verlag, 1980), trans. J. Bradford Robinson as *Nineteenth-Century Music*. (Berkeley and Los Angeles: University of California Press, 1989), p. 9.
5. This in a letter of December 1800 to the Leipzig publisher Franz Anton Hoffmeister. Ludwig van Beethoven, *Briefwechsel Gesamtausgabe*, ed. Sieghard Brandenburg (Munich: Henle, 1996), vol. 1, p. 54; Emily Anderson, ed., *The Letters of Beethoven* (London: Macmillan, 1961), vol. 1, p. 43.
6. This is a central argument in Gregory Nagy, *Poetry as Performance: Homer and Beyond* (Cambridge: Cambridge University Press, 1997).
7. *Etymologiarum*, Bk. III. This quotation is from Oliver Strunk, ed., *Source Readings in Music History* rev. ed., Leo Treitler, ed., (New York: Norton, 1998), p. 149.
8. These associations were rife with distinctions as to social milieu (the contredanse and Ländler over against the minuet and sarabande; the canzonetta as opposed to the ornamented da capo aria). And distinctions as to gender were surely involved. Gretchen Wheelock has shown with convincing evidence that certain manners of expression and, most strikingly, the use of the minor mode in Mozart's operatic arias were strongly associated with female characters. See her "*Schwarze Gredel* and the Engendered

Minor Mode in Mozart's Operas," in Ruth Solie, ed., *Musicology and Difference: Gender and Sexuality in Music Scholarship* (Berkeley: University of California Press, 1993), pp. 201–21. Other attempts to read a master narrative of the preservation and celebration of male social hegemony into the whole repertory of seventeenth- and eighteenth-century music—not just certain of its idioms or types—reflect more imagination and political enthusiasm than historical study. See Susan McClary, *Feminine Endings: Music, Gender, and Sexuality* (Minneapolis: University of Minnesota Press, 1991), Chapter 1, passim, and "Narrative Agendas in Absolute Music," in Solie, ed., *Musicology and Difference*, pp. 330–32.

9. See Chapter 9 for a discussion of Owen Jander's artful attribution of specific literary associations to the movement.

10. Jorge Luis Borges, *Other Inquisitions*, trans. Ruth L. C. Simms (Austin: University of Texas Press, 1952), p. 169. For this reference I am grateful to Nicolas Shumway.

11. A later association of Beethoven's "heroic" music with incipient German nationalism (an association Richard Taruskin, for example, seems determined to cement, as in his combative piece "Another Beethoven Season?" in the *New York Times* of Sept. 10, 1995) is probably not something we should hold against the composer; he worked in cosmopolitan Vienna (under intermittent French domination) long before there was a Germany.

12. W. H. Auden, "Notes on Music and Opera," in *The Dyer's Hand and Other Essays* (New York: Random House, 1962), p. 474.

13. See Maynard Solomon, "Beethoven's Magazin der Kunst," *19th Century Music* 7 (1984), pp. 199–208; repr. in Solomon, *Beethoven Essays* (Cambridge, Mass.: Harvard University Press, 1988), pp. 195–200.

14. "Submission, deepest submission to your fate, only this can give you the sacrifices— for this matter of service. O hard struggle! Do everything that still has to be done to arrange what is necessary for the long journey. . . . You must not be a *human being, not for yourself, but only for others*: for you there is no longer any happiness except within yourself, in your art." See "Beethoven's Tagebuch," in Solomon, *Beethoven Essays*, p. 246.

NOTES TO CHAPTER 1

1. Anton Reicha, music theorist, composer, and a companion of Beethoven's in Bonn and during the early years in Vienna, was perhaps the first to describe instrumental movements as conforming to preexisting patterns or sequences of events that resemble the modern notion of "form." His ideas are developed mainly in three treatises written in Paris, where Reicha was professor at the Conservatoire: *Traité de mélodie* (1814), *Cours de composition musicale* (1816–18), and *Traité de haute composition musicale* (1824–26). All three of these reappeared in a bilingual French and German edition with commentary by Carl Czerny, *Vollständiges Lehrbuch der musikalischen Composition* (Vienna, 1832). At the beginning of his book *Wordless Rhetoric* (Cambridge, Mass.: Harvard University Press, 1991), p. 1, Mark Evan Bonds locates the persistent ambiguity of "form" in an opposition between two of its common uses: "Form is commonly used to denote those features a given work shares with a large number of others, yet it is also often understood as the unique structure of a particular work." But this does not seem to be the main problem. In ordinary language this kind of multiple

reference is often negotiated with ease. The closely related word "shape," for example, can refer to something often replicated (say, a pear), or to one of an infinite variety of unique configurations (as in the formations of clouds) without much confusion. A more central problem with musical form, surely, is the question as to what constitutes it: which properties of a musical composition count as defining form?

2. The Schenkerian view of tonal compositions as elaborations on a small number of structural archetypes—and particularly the graphic presentation adopted to show this—seems explicitly designed to allow an instantaneous overview of the basic shape of a piece. Poles apart is the moment-by-moment measure of possible relationships and continuations in Gottfried Weber's famous analysis of the opening of Mozart's String Quartet K. 465 (the "Dissonance"), in *Versuch einer geordneten Theorie der Tonsetzkunst*, 3d ed. (Mainz, 1830–32), pp. 196–226; trans. Ian Bent, in *Musical Analysis in the Nineteenth Century* (Cambridge: Cambridge University Press, 1994), vol. 1, pp. 157–83. Methodologically similar to Weber's approach is that of the "implication-consequence" school of Leonard Meyer and his followers. Carl Dahlhaus in effect aligned himself with this latter camp with his repeated insistence on the "processual" (*prozessual*) nature of musical form. But he characteristically—and, surely, correctly—allowed for seeing the matter both ways. See, for example, *Ludwig van Beethoven und seiner Zeit* (Laaber: Laaber Verlag, 1987), trans. Mary Whittall as *Ludwig van Beethoven: Approaches to His Music*. (Oxford: Clarendon Press, 1991), pp. 113–14 and 166.

3. One other detail of Marx's thought has recently achieved great prominence in some segments of American musicology: his metaphorical use of the terms *masculine* and *feminine* respectively, to characterize the principal theme and secondary theme of sonata form has been used to buttress the characterization of that form as an allegory of male sexual domination. See McClary, *Feminine Endings*: pp. 12–16; and Marcia Citron, *Gender and the Musical Canon* (Cambridge: Cambridge University Press, 1993), pp. 132–42. An informed and fair-minded assessment of this matter is Scott Burnham, "A. B. Marx and the Gendering of Sonata Form," in Ian Bent, ed., *Music Theory in the Age of Romanticism* (Cambridge: Cambridge University Press, 1996), pp. 163–86.

4. See, for example, A. B. Marx, *Die Lehre von der musikalischen Composition*, 2d ed. (Leipzig: Breitkopf & Härtel, 1841–51), vol. 3, p. 259. See also Scott Burnham, *Aesthetics, Theory, and History in the Works of Adolph Bernhard Marx* (Ann Arbor: UMI, 1988), pp. 50–51, 85–86, 90–91, and passim; Carl Dahlhaus, "Formenlehre und Gattungstheorie bei A. B. Marx," in Günter Katzenberger, ed., *Heinrich Sievers zum 70. Geburtstag* (Tutzing: Hans Schneider, 1978), pp. 29–35; and "Aesthetische Prämissen der 'Sonatenform' bei Adolf Bernhard Marx," *AfMw* 41 (1984), pp. 73–85.

5. A thoughtful consideration of the matter is Dahlhaus, "Was ist eine musikalische Gattung?" *NZfM* 135 (1974), pp. 620–25. Here Dahlhaus stresses the historically variable standards for formation of genres; while social function and venue of performance predominated until the later eighteenth century, with the advent of "autonomous" concert music of the late eighteenth and nineteenth centuries, standards derived from instrumental music such as performance forces (*Besetzung*) and form came more prominently into play. Adopting something of a "strict constructionist" approach (similar to that taken here with respect to form), he maintains that not all compositions are representive of a genre—one doubtful candidate is the fugue, which he describes as determined solely by compositional procedure and lacking the other specifications included in the idea of genre.

6. This first occurred mainly in the context of investigations of eighteenth-century views of sonata form. See Leonard Ratner, "Harmonic Aspects of Classic Form," *JAMS* 2 (1949), pp. 159–68; and William Newman, "The Recognition of Sonata Form by Theorists of the 18th and 19th Centuries," *Papers of the American Musicological Society* (1946), pp. 21–29. German scholarship was slow to take these developments into account until Fred Ritzel offered a broad synthetic overview in his admirable dissertation, *Die Entwicklung der "Sonatenform" im musiktheoretischen Schrifttum des 18. und 19. Jahrhunderts* (Wiesbaden: Bretkopf & Härtel, 1968; 2d ed., 1969).

7. In 1739 Johann Adolph Scheibe began his description of the first movement of a concerto thus: "The instruments that are added to the solo part as an accompaniment . . . generally start with the principal theme . . . When this comes to an end, the solo part itself finally enters." J. A. Scheibe, *Critischer Musicus* (Leipzig, 1745) vol. 2, pp. 631–62 (originally from the Dec. 1739 issue).

8. A generation earlier, as in the concertos of Dittersdorf and the young Haydn, finales often followed a similar pattern.

9. His original term is "Spielepisoden." Hans Engel, *Das Instrumentalkonzert* (Wiesbaden: Breitkopf & Härtel, 1974), vol. 2, p. 2. In the 1840s Beethoven's student Czerny described this section thus: "To this ['the melodious middle subject'] succeed brilliant passages, which are indispensable in a Concerto, and which again are ordinarily built upon that continuation, which has previously followed the middle subject in the first tutti." Carl Czerny, *School of Practical Composition, or, Complete Treatise on the Composition of All Kinds of Music*, trans. John Bishop (London, [1848]) p. 160.

10. In 1793 Heinrich Christoph Koch gave three alternate plans for the opening tutti. In the first there is no modulation; in the second a modulation leads to contrasting material in the new key (before a return to the tonic); a third alternative, "the most usual one in newer concertos," has a modulation to the new key for a contrasting idea but no "proper close" in that key, followed by a quick retreat to the original tonic. See *Versuch einer Anleitung zur Composition* (Leipzig: Adam Friedrich Böhme, 1793), vol. 3, pp. 334–35. Beethoven's concertos offer examples of all these designs.

11. A generation before Mozart, as in the concertos of J. C. Bach and Dittersdorf, the cadenza was commonly attached to the ending of S_3 or separated from it by a very short orchestral transition. This latter is the arrangement Koch still described in 1793. See *Versuch einer Anleitung zur Composition* vol. 3, p. 339. See also Jay Lane, "The Concertos of Carl Ditters" (Diss., Yale, 1997), pp. 125–26. But Mozart's later concertos and Beethoven's earlier ones clearly present the cadenza as an interruption of the final tutti. This point, still often misunderstood, was accurately pointed out by D. F. Tovey as early as 1903. See "The Classical Concerto," repr. in *Essays in Musical Analysis* (London: Oxford University Press, 1936), vol. 3, p. 16.

12. This likely occurred in 1803 when both were temporarily engaged as composers at the Theater an der Wien.

13. Georg Joseph Vogler, *Betrachtungen der Mannheimer Tonschule* (Mannheim, 1779, repr. Hildesheim: Georg Ohms Verlag, 1974), vol. 2, p. 36. This translation is adopted, with some changes, from Jane Stevens, "Theme, Harmony, and Texture in Classic-Romantic Descriptions of Concerto First-Movement Form" *JAMS* 27 (1974), p. 33.

14. These are the Concertos K. 37 and 39–41, all composed in Salzburg in 1767; the Mozarts had come into contact with all these composers in Paris and London during their grand tour of 1763–1766. Edwin Simon gives a detailed account of Mozart's

arrangements in "Sonata into Concerto: A Study of Mozart's First Seven Concertos," *Acta musicologica* 31 (1959), pp. 170–85.

15. See Leon Plantinga, *Muzio Clementi: His Life and Music* (London: Oxford University Press, 1977), p. 162.

16. H. Ch. Koch, *Versuch*, vol. 3, pp. 333 and 336. See the able discussion of Koch's description of the concerto in Jane Stevens, "An 18th-Century Description of Concerto First-Movement Form," *JAMS* 24 (1971), pp. 85–95.

17. In the article on the concerto in his *Musikalisches Lexikon* (Frankfurt-am-Main, 1802), col. 305, Koch curiously reverted to a description of the form as previously outlined by Vogler, with three tuttis and two solos. Two good discussions of the vicissitudes of this point in the first movement of the classical concerto are Shelley Davis, "H. C. Koch, the Classic Concerto, and the Sonata-Form Retransition," *Journal of Musicology* 2 (1983), pp. 45–61; and Jane Stevens, "Patterns of Recapitulation in the First Movements of Mozart's Piano Concertos," in Nancy Kovaleff Baker and Barbara Russano Hanning, eds., *Musical Humanism and Its Legacy. Essays in Honor of Claude V. Palisca* (Stuyvesant, N.Y.: Pendragon Press, 1992), pp. 397–418.

18. On this point Jane Stevens somewhat misleadingly says that "J. C. Bach and Mozart customarily omit this ritornello." See "An 18th-Century Description," p. 91, fn. 22. All of Mozart's mature piano concertos, beginning with K. 413, have at least a short section for orchestra at this point, and all of these tuttis but one—the exception being in K. 413—begin with the first theme. But the soloist typically reenters after some 6–10 measures. Only two of his later concertos, K. 467 in C, and K. 595 in B♭, have an extended tutti here.

19. Czerny, *School of Practical Composition*, vol. 1, p. 159; Marx, *Die Lehre von der musikalischen Composition.* (1847), vol. 4, p. 439. For Marx, the concerto makes an appearance seemingly as an afterthought, at the end of his final volume, in the course of an exposition of the ways in which his compositional principles may be applied to various instrumental combinations.

20. Marx evades this problem by describing the orchestral opening and first solo as together comprising "the first part" of the form. A few years later Otto Jahn called attention to a similarity of the "double exposition" to the usual repetition of the first part in sonata form—a comparison that must ignore the difference in harmonic plan. See Stevens, "Theme, Harmony, and Texture," pp. 52–53.

21. Scheibe, *Critischer Musicus* 2, pp. 632. "Aria" in Scheibe's time ordinarily meant the da capo aria, that seemingly rigid musical construct that was adaptable to almost any dramatic situation. Its opening section (the one that returns da capo, at the end) shows distinct formal similarities to the first movement of a concerto, particularly in its structures resembling exposition and recapitulation framed by related orchestral statements. Charles Rosen provides an enlightening discussion of the formal properties of eighteenth-century da capo arias (and their kinship with both the contemporary concerto and the later sonata) in *Sonata Forms* (New York: Norton, 1988), pp. 28–70.

22. Elements of ritornello structures, conversely, had appeared regularly in first movements of pieces of the sonata type from shortly after the mid-eighteenth century. See Fritz Tutenberg, "Die Durchführungsfrage in der Vorneuklassischen Sinfonie," *ZfMw* 9 (1926–27), pp. 90–94; and Joel Galand, "Heinrich Schenker's Theory of Form and Its Application to Historical Criticism, with Special Reference to Rondo-Form Problems in Eighteenth- and Nineteenth-Century Instrumental Music" (Diss., Yale,

1990), pp. 114–28. On the sonata-rondo see Malcolm Cole, "Sonata-Rondo, the Formulation of a Theoretical Concept in the 18th and 19th Centuries,"*MQ* 55 (1969), pp. 180–92.

23. As, for example, D. G. Türk, in his *Klavierschule, oder Anweisung zum Klavierspielen* (Leipzig and Halle, 1789); repr. E. R. Jacobi, ed. (Basel: Bärenreiter, 1962), p. 398.

24. Türk, *Klavierschule*, p. 398 (". . . von einem zärtlichen, muntern, tändelnden etc. Charakter"); Koch, *Lexikon*, p. 1272.

25. Czerny, *School of Practical Composition*, p. 67

26. In some of his earlier rondos, uncertainty of continuation is exalted to a principle. Examples can be seen in the finales of the Sonatas in C minor and D of Op. 10. In the systematically eccentric Sonata in D, the rondo theme is so fragmented as to generate maximum insecurity on a small scale; but then, as if by magic, it turns out to form a perfectly regular period of four-plus-four measures.

27. Galand provides an extended and enlightened discussion of this piece, departing from Schenker's view of it, in "Heinrich Schenker's Theory of Form," pp. 93–100. A rondo in which Mozart seemed to compose deliberately against the generic norm is that profoundly expressive one in A minor, K. 511.

NOTES TO CHAPTER 2

1. From Old High German, *kiosan*, "choose," and *Fürst*, "prince."

2. Maximilian Franz was in addition Grand Master of the Teutonic Order (*Der deutsche Orden*), that quaint remnant of the medieval institution, at once secular and religious, that was originally founded in Jerusalem to further the goals of the Crusades. Its later efforts focused upon the *Drang nach Osten* of Germanic power and influence in the Baltic regions, where at one time it governed vast stretches of land. In the eighteenth century, much weakened and of uncertain intent, the order had its headquarters in Mergentheim on the Taube river; in the autumn of 1791 Beethoven joined a band of musicians who accompanied the Elector on one of his periodic excursions there.

3. See Gebhard Aders, *Bonn als Festung* (Bonn: Rohrscheid, 1973), pp. 120–27; and Plate 2.

4. Ludwig Schiedermair gives a protracted and enthusiastic description of the eighteenth-century palace and its rooms in *Der junge Beethoven* (Leipzig: Quelle & Meyer, 1925), pp. 16–20.

5. A brother of this Beethoven, Cornelius, a chandler, had preceded him to Bonn about two years previously. Elliot Forbes gives an able summary of the genealogical studies of the Beethoven family in *Thayer's Life of Beethoven*, rev. and ed. Elliot Forbes (Princeton: Princeton University Press, 1964 [hereafter Thayer-Forbes]), pp. 41–5.

6. Thayer-Forbes, 18–19.

7. The question seems to be somewhat garbled in both Thayer-Forbes, pp. 70–71, and Schiedermair, p. 166. A reproduction of the relevant documents in Alexander Wheelock Thayer, *Ludwig van Beethovens Leben von Alexander Wheelock Thayer nach dem Original-Manuskript*, ed. Hermann Deiters and Hugo Riemann, 3d ed. (Leipzig: Breitkopf & Härtel, 1907–17 [hereafter TDR], vol. 1, pp. 164–66, shows that the Obristhofmeister (an official charged with the administration of various court functions,

including music), in a rather discursive statement, recommended the appointment. Appended to this document is a shorter summary of his opinion (which both Schiedermair and Forbes took as the final disposition of the matter but disagreed as to what it said). Riemann offers the convincing suggestion (TDR, vol. 1, p. 166) that the notation "beruhet" on the document means that no action was taken. Perhaps it was an issue that the appointment of young Beethoven, as proposed, was an incremental one.

8. Consisting, according to the court calander of 1783, of just over forty singers and players. See Schiedermair, *Der junge Beethoven*, p. 47.

9. See Joseph Schmidt-Görg, ed., *Des Bonner Bäckermeisters Gottfried Fischer: Aufzeichnungen über Beethovens Jugend* (Bonn: Beethovenhaus, 1971), pp. 51–52. This translation is from O. G. Sonneck, ed., *Beethoven: Impressions by His Contemporaries* (New York: G. Schirmer, 1954), p. 8.

10. Thayer-Forbes, p. 68; Schiedermair, p. 49.

11. Wegeler, Franz Gerhard, and Ferdinand Ries, *Biographische Notizen* (Koblenz: K. Bädeker, 1838), trans. Frederick Noonan as *Beethoven Remembered* (Arlington, Va.: Great Ocean Publishers, 1987 [hereafter Wegeler-Ries, trans. Noonan]), pp. 20–21. The organ in the chapel at this time was a temporary "chamber" instrument, as the principal organ had been destroyed in a fire at court in 1777.

12. See Thayer-Forbes, 65 and 81.

13. See TDR, vol. 1, p. 158. Thayer implies that the young Beethoven on these occasions actually conducted the orchestra from the keyboard instrument; and Solomon, in *Ludwig van Beethoven* (London: Granada, 1980), p. 53, repeats this claim. But orchestras in the eighteenth century were directed either from the keyboard or by the leader of the violins. Schiedermair, citing Carl Ludwig Junker's exacting description of a performance of the court orchestra with the violinist Franz Ries in charge, argued persuasively that the twelve-year-old Beethoven probably only played continuo; Schiedermair, p. 164.

14. See Schiedermair, pp. 60–61. About Beethoven's training as a violist we know very little; the Fischer document says that he studied violin and viola with Franz Georg Rovantini, a court musician who was related to Beethoven's mother and who for a time, like the Beethovens, lived in the Fischer house in the Rheingasse. The lessons could not have continued very long, as Rovantini died in 1781, before Beethoven reached the age of eleven. There is testimony that in about the mid-1780s Beethoven also studied violin with the music director Franz Ries. See Thayer-Forbes, p. 82.

15. This according to a playbill surviving in the Beethovenhaus in Bonn and reproduced in Schiedermair, p. 130. The playbill further states that both musicians had already been heard "by the entire court," without specifying in which capacities.

16. Thayer-Forbes, p. 63.

17. See Luc van Hasselt, "Beethoven in Holland," *Mf* 18 (1965), pp. 181–84; and Theodore Albrecht, ed. and trans., *Letters to Beethoven and Other Correspondence* (Lincoln, Neb.: University of Nebraska Press, 1996), pp. 3–4. One of the musicians who participated was Carl Stamitz, the composer and string player from Mannheim, resident at this time in the Hague.

18. Thayer-Forbes, ibid. p. 63.

19. See above, note 2.

20. This report of Wegeler (Wegeler-Ries, trans. Noonan, p. 23) is confirmed by Nikolaus Simrock, who was present at this event. See TDR, vol. 1, p. 266.

21. Beethoven played in private, not in the "public hall," Junker speculated, "because perhaps the instrument did not meet his requirements." The entire text of Junker's report is given in TDR, vol. 1, pp. 268–73.

22. Schiedermair, pp. 73–82, reprints Neefe's entire article. This report repeats the common error of understating Beethoven's age by one year.

23. See TDR, vol. 1, p. 262.

24. Ibid., p. 350; and Willy Hess, *Beethoven-Studien* (Bonn: Beethovenhaus, 1972), p. 80. In TDR it is suggested that Beethoven wrote the Concerto WoO 4 for the purpose of introducing himself to the new Elector, Maximilian Franz, in 1784.

25. Wegeler recalls an event in which Beethoven—evidently playing piano—took part in a piano trio of Pleyel performed for the Elector. Wegeler-Ries, trans. Noonan, p. 21. In TDR, vol. 1, p. 262, it is conjectured that this performance took place in 1791, since trios by Pleyel published in 1789–92 were his "first works in this form," and in March of 1791 the music shop of Beethoven's Bonn colleague Nikolaus Simrock advertised a trio of Pleyel. But the case for this dating has subsequently been weakened; we now know that Deiters (who seems to be writing at this point) was mistaken about Pleyel's first published trios: a good many were published between 1785 and 1790, several sets appearing in Paris and London in 1788 alone. But the earliest publication of Pleyel's trios (Ben. 428 and 429, printed by Forster) appeared in London under Haydn's name in 1785. See Rita Benton, *Ignace Pleyel: A Thematic Catalogue of His Compositions* (New York: Pendragon Press, 1977), pp. 188–91, and Alan Tyson, "Haydn and Two Stolen Trios," *MR* 22 (1961), pp. 21–27. In any case, the Elector in question would have been Maximilian Franz.

26. Bach's first solo performance on the piano was announced in London's *Public Advertiser* of June 2, 1768. As to his concerto performances, see my *Muzio Clementi: His Life and Music* (London: Oxford University Press, 1977), p. 277.

27. This translation (with corrections) from Thayer-Forbes, p. 86.

28. See p. 27.

29. Schiedermair, pp. 53–54.

30. Schiedermair records the program of Mastiaux's concert of November 1779, "from his own testimony," as including two symphonies of Haydn, two unidentified arias, and two clavier concertos performed by his son and daughter. Schiedermair, p. 54.

31. The stories of the "tiny boy, standing on a little stool in front of the clavier and weeping" and of middle-of-the-night lessons from his father's drinking companion Tobias Pfeiffer are too well attested to be discounted. See Friedrich Kerst, ed., *Die Erinnerungen an Beethoven* (Stuttgart: J. Hoffmann, ca. 1925), vol. 1, p. 10; and Fischer, p. 32. And Beethoven's father seemingly did his best to suppress his son's later celebrated talent for improvisation. See Fischer, pp. 32–33. Through Czerny and Otto Jahn we hear of Beethoven's own testimony to "harsh treatment from his father" and his "unsatisfactory instruction"—to which, however, he added, "but I had a talent for music." See TDR, vol. 1, p. 203.

32. See Thayer-Forbes, p. 98.

33. The cantata was planned for a memorial ceremony for the enlightened Emperor (who had died in February 1790) by this liberal society that heartily approved his reform measures. The cantata was not performed, perhaps because it was not finished in time. Beethoven later adapted the music of one aria, "Da stiegen die Menschen ans Licht," for use in the finale of *Leonore* and *Fidelio* ("O Gott! welch' ein Augenblick").

34. Beethoven evidently was in Vienna only about two weeks before being called home

because of his mother's illness. According to the Fischer document, precedent for sending young court musicians away to study was established by the previous Elector, Maximilian Friedrich, who allowed Beethoven's temporary teacher Franz Rovantini and the violinist and tenor Christoph Brand a similar opportunity to study in Berlin and Dresden. See Fischer, p. 29.

35. See Thayer-Forbes, pp. 106–7. Yet it should be noted that, according to Wegeler, a cantata of Beethoven's, presumably either the Joseph Cantata or the Leopold Cantata, was rehearsed at Mergentheim, with a view to performance in 1791. But the performance never took place because the wind players found their parts too difficult. Wegeler-Ries, trans. Noonan, p. 22. See Thayer-Forbes, p. 106. Perhaps the nearest approximation we have to evidence that his music was played at court is in the Elector's letter to Haydn of November 1793. Haydn had sent the Elector what he took to be five very recent compositions of Beethoven as proof of progress made since the latter's move to Vienna about one year earlier. The Elector replied testily that all but one of the pieces were "composed and performed here in Bonn before he departed on his second journey to Vienna." Thayer reports that the letter is "in an official hand, corrected by the Elector himself"; Thayer-Forbes, pp. 144–45. This information about "performances in Bonn" could, of course, have come from someone who knew about Beethoven's activities outside the court. There is a faint suggestion, finally, of possible performances of Beethoven's music at court in the instrumentation of the Octet Op. 103 (probably one of the compositions Haydn sent the Elector) and the Rondino WoO 25, both from ca. 1792–93. In both pieces the pairs of clarinets, oboes, horns, and bassoons correspond to the ensemble, described by Junker, that supplied the Elector's *Tafelmusik* at Mergentheim. See TDR, vol. 1, p. 268.

36. There are many accounts of Mozart's performances and performances of his music for the Salzburg court. The child prodigy played there as early as February 1763; "Cammer-Musique" of his was performed at the court when he was off on his journey to London in 1765; the court staged *La finta semplice* in 1769; Mozart composed his sacred music mainly for performance at the cathedral to which the Archiepiscopal court was attached. See Otto Erich Deutsch, *Mozart: A Documentary Biography* (Stanford: Stanford University Press, 1965), pp. 20, 38, 88–89. And shortly before his release from court service with that celebrated "kick on his ars," Mozart composed two rondos and a sonata for the Archbishop's concert. See Emily Anderson, ed., *The Letters of Mozart and His Family*, vol. 2, pp. 723 and 741.

37. See p. 26.

38. Details about original sources and modern publications of this music, together with a list of further fragments of concertos from the Bonn period, are given in Appendix I. The first movement of a piano concerto in D major was also regarded for a time as a work of Beethoven's from the Bonn period and has been printed as such in the old *Gesamtausgabe*, Serie XXV (*Supplemente*). This movement was first described and put forth as genuine by Guido Adler in *Vierteljahrschrift für Musikwissenschaft* 4 (1888), pp. 451–70. See also Schiedermair, pp. 380–83; and TDR, vol. 1, p. 315. But in 1925 Hans Engel convincingly identified this piece as the work of Johann Josef Rösler (it was published as his Op. 15 by André in ca. 1809). See *Neues Beethoven-Jahrbuch* 2 (1925), pp. 167ff. More recently, the authenticity of Beethoven's autographs of 1784–86, and by implication their music (including WoO 4, with its autograph corrections), has been challenged by Andreas Holschneider. See "Unbekannte Skizzen Beethovens zur Cello-Sonate Op. 5 II, WoO 36, WoO 37, und Hess Nr. 13 sind nicht im Auto-

graph überliefert," *Bericht über den Internationalen Musikwissenschaftlichen Kongress Bonn 1970* (Kassel, 1972), pp. 444–47. These radical suggestions have been convincingly countered by Douglas Porter Johnson's arguments in *Beethoven's Early Sketches in the "Fischhof Miscellany," Autograph 28* (Ann Arbor: UMI Press, 1980, 1977; [hereafter *Fischhof*]), vol. 1, p. 223.

39. Dating of this and certain other compositions of this period depends upon the sources' fairly consistent representation of the composer as one year younger than his actual age. In this case an apparently autograph inscription on the title page says "composé par Louis Van Beethoven agé douze ans." Since he was born in December 1770, it is assumed that the work was composed sometime between his thirteenth birthday, December 1783, and his fourteenth, December 1784.

40. See p. 15.

41. See p. 138–39.

42. In K. 449 in E♭, third movement; and K. 450 in B♭, first and third movements (both 1784).

43. In the solo sonatas of Clementi's Op. 2 (1779) and his Toccata Op. 11, published in 1784 but evidently played at the contest with Mozart in 1781. See my *Clementi: His Life and Music*, pp. 43–45 and 61–68.

44. Page references are to the old Breitkopf & Härtel *Gesamtausgabe* [GA], series 25, which includes no measure numbers.

45. The Musical Heritage Society's recording of the concerto, in a "reconstruction" by Willy Hess, in fact assigns these left-hand chords to the orchestra. It should be noted, however, that in the first movement of the Piano Quartet in D, WoO 36, of the following year there are two spots where a troublesome version of this figuration must be played with no hope of outside help.

46. One two-measure ornamental flourish was inadvertently omitted from the GA edition (after p. 17, m. 11); Deiters supplies these measures in TDR, vol. 1, p. 170.

47. The two rondo finales in the Piano Quartets WoO 36 of 1785 move in the opposite direction with a three-ritornello plan.

48. Hob. XVI:35 in C major, closing material of both halves of the first movement. This sonata was published in 1780.

49. This occurrence of the ritornello (m. 200, p. 26) is another of those places where the arranger of this score has evidently written some of the orchestra's music into the keyboard part. The usual left-hand part of the keyboard is replaced with horn-like music—third, open fifth, sixth—marked "corni."

50. Similar obvious "landing patterns" in the second of the *Kurfürstensonaten* (WoO 47, No. 2, first movement) of the previous year, indelibly recorded in print, were beyond reclamation. The Piano Quartets (WoO 36) of 1785, like the concerto, remained unpublished in Beethoven's possession and underwent similar later revision.

51. Willy Hess "completed" the composition and provided critical commentary in the Breitkopf & Härtel edition, PB 3704, 1952.

52. Nottebohm, *Zweite Beethoveniana: Nachgelassene Aufsätze*, ed. Eusebius Mandyczewski (Leipzig: Peters, 1887), p. 70.

53. See Roger Hickman, "Romance," *The New Grove*, vol. 16, p. 125. The Romanze of Haydn's Symphony No. 85 ("La Reine"), probably composed in 1785, the year before Beethoven's piece, is cast as theme and variations, another form common to the genre. But we must resist a temptation to associate Beethoven's piece with another composition that has a *romanze* as a slow movement, Mozart's Concerto in D minor, K. 466,

composed two years earlier, in 1784. This concerto (the only one of Mozart's with a movement by this name) would one day be a favorite of Beethoven's; in about 1809 he wrote out cadenzas for its first and last movements. And the opening melody of Beethoven's *Romance cantabile* is strikingly like one in Mozart's first movement (see Example 2-8). Nonetheless, it is most unlikely that Beethoven would have known Mozart's concerto in 1786, since it was first published by André of Offenbach in 1792.

54. GA, series 25, no. 31. Douglas Johnson has shown that the autograph of the *Romance cantabile* has the same staff-lining as the autograph of WoO 37 (i.e., Berlin, Staats-bibliothek, Grasnick 31) and shows the same stage of Beethoven's handwriting. He assigned them both—the *Romance cantabile* somewhat cautiously—to the year 1786. This date was arrived at a bit circuitously on the strength of a notation on Grasnick 31, "age 41," by assuming a transposition of the digits and the usual miscalculation of Beethoven's age. See *Fischhof*, vol. 1, p. 245.

55. See Thayer-Forbes, p. 124, and TDR, p. 320–21. The reports of Beethoven's emotional attachment to "the beautiful and cultured Fräulein von Westerholt" come from Wege-ler. See Wegeler-Ries, trans. Noonan, p. 43.

56. This theme bears more than a slight structural resemblance to the opening of the first Allegro in Beethoven's First Symphony in the same key. Why the repetition on the supertonic works better there probably has to do with more than one factor: the symphony has a clear connection between the two degrees (via an applied dominant), and this connection is emphasized by two extra measures allotted to it.

57. TDR, vol. 1, p. 318.

58. It is a later addition to the pages containing the *Romance*, Hess 13. See Joseph Kerman, ed., *Autograph Miscellany from circa 1786 to 1799* (London: Trustees of the British Museum, 1970 [hereafter *Kafka*]), vol. 1, fols. 76v–79v; vol. 2, pp. 100–101. Richard Kramer, who first pointed out the connection between the cadenza and the violin concerto in his review of *Kafka* (*Notes* 28 [1971–72], p. 32), suggested that it was intended for the pregnant pause toward the end of S_1 (mm. 205–6). The music here is in G major, as is the cadenza. But the cadenza really does not fit there; it begins with a traditional D $^6_4$ (mistranscribed, in my opinion, in *Kafka*, vol. 2, p. 100), while the fermatas in S_1 occur over a C♯; diminished seventh followed by C $^4_2$. It would in any case be very odd to have so large and grand a cadenza in the course of a solo section. It seems much more likely that the piano version of the concerto was—or was to have been—in G major.

59. Johnson, *Fischhof*, vol. 1, pp. 405–6. That this concerto movement was on Beethoven's mind in 1793 is attested to by a lengthy sketch from that year in the Fischhof Mis-cellany for a movement in E♭ based upon its first theme—modified so as to counteract the debilitating effect of literal repetition one step up (cf. Example 2-7). See Johnson, *Fischhof*, vol. 1, pp. 86–88, and vol. 2, p. 195.

60. This from the exchange of letters between Haydn and the Elector Maximilian Franz of November-December 1793. See p. 319, n. 35. Incipits of the three movements of an oboe concerto are given in a manuscript at the Beethoven-Archiv in Bonn. See TDR, p. 126. These allow the identification of sketches on Kafka 150 as belonging to this piece.

61. See Johnson, *Fischhof*, vol. 1, pp. 365–66, and vol. 2, pp. 71–73.

62. Ibid., vol. 1, p. 366.

63. Ibid., p. 368.

64. In addition to the Concerto in E♭, the one that included the *Romance cantabile*, and

an early version of Op. 19, rather extensive sketches from ca. 1790 survive in Kafka for an Adagio in D marked "zum Concert aus a." See Appendix I.

65. Maynard Solomon, "Beethoven's Productivity in Bonn," *ML* 53 (1972), pp. 165–72.

66. This early dating of Op. 3 relies upon reports from the mid-nineteenth century of the usually reliable William Gardiner (1770–1853), to the effect that he had played a Beethoven string trio in E♭, brought from Bonn, in Leicester in 1793. See TDR, vol. 1, pp. 312–13. The autograph of this work (part in Paris, part in Washington, D.C.) is associated with Artaria's first edition of 1796. No sketches or autograph survive for the posthumously published Piano Trio WoO 38; a Bonn provenance is asserted by a notation in Anton Gräffer's handwritten catalogue (1844) of the Artaria collection of Beethoven manuscripts: "Komponiert 1791 und ursprünglich zu den 3 Trios Op. 1 bestimmt, aber von Beethoven als zu schwach weggelassen." See Georg Kinsky, *Das Werk Beethovens*, completed and ed. Hans Halm (Munich: Henle, 1955 [hereafter Kinsky-Halm]), p. 480. Solomon includes both these pieces in his list for the period in question.

67. Solomon, ibid., p. 169.

68. That is, Berlin, Staatsbibliothek, Grasnick 31. See the "strict constructionalist" list in Johnson, *Fischhof*, vol. 1, p. 220.

69. Ibid., vol. 1, pp. 365–6.

70. Maximilian Franz, son of Maria Theresa and brother of Joseph II, had known Mozart since about 1775. See Thayer-Forbes, p. 77.

71. Thayer-Forbes, p. 145.

72. Solomon, ibid., p. 170, and Thayer-Forbes, pp. 87–88.

NOTES TO CHAPTER 3

1. R. R. Palmer, *The Age of Democratic Revolution* (Princeton: Princeton University Press, 1964), vol. 2, p. 9.

2. Thayer-Forbes, p. 114.

3. Beethoven adopts an unmistakable antibourgeois tone in his well-known remark to Simrock of 1794: "it is said that a revolution was about to break out—But I believe that so long as an Austrian can get his brown ale and his little sausages, he is not likely to revolt." Anderson, *Letters*, vol. 1, p. 18; *Briefwechsel*, vol. 1, p. 224. In 1811 Beethoven wrote to Joseph von Varena in Graz: "From my earliest childhood my zeal to serve our poor suffering humanity in any way whatsoever by means of my art has made no compromise with any lower motive." Anderson, *Letters*, vol. 1, p. 345; *Briefwechsel*, vol. 2, p. 224.

4. As in Emily Anderson, ed., *The Letters of Mozart and His Family*, 2d ed. (New York: St. Martin's Press, 1966), vol. 2, p. 717.

5. Peter Csendes, *Geschichte Wiens* (Vienna: Verlag für Geschichte und Politik, 1981), p. 93. A centralized water system was installed in Vienna at the beginning of the nineteenth century, largely putting an end to the epidemics of cholera that had plagued the city for centuries.

6. Stella Musulin, *Vienna in the Age of Metternich: From Napoleon to Revolution, 1805–1848.* (London: Faber and Faber, 1975), p. 19.

7. See Alice M. Hanson, *Musical Life in Biedermeier Vienna* (Cambridge: Cambridge University Press, 1985), pp. 44–5.

8. Stephan von Breuning reported that on a trip from Nuremberg to Vienna in 1796 he, his brother Christoph, and Beethoven, "three natives of Bonn together aroused the attention of the police, who were sure they had discovered something. I do not think that one could find a less dangerous man than Beethoven." From a letter of January 1796, quoted in Wegeler-Ries, trans. Noonan, p. 156, Wegeler adds, "Beethoven also never came into contact with the police, even though he is supposed to have drawn the attention of those authorities to himself with sharp criticism of administrative regulations and with his democratic ideas."

9. See Jost Perfahl, ed., *Wien Chronik* (Salzburg: Das Bergland-Buch, 1969), p. 186.

10. Ibid., p. 167.

11. The so-called Norma Edict, enacted in 1752 in the reign of Maria Theresa, stipulated many other days on which drama and dancing were not permitted—and concerts were accordingly possible—such as Corpus Christi, the birth and death dates of members of the royal household, and all Fridays. When in 1786 Joseph II began to ease these restrictions, drama gained and concerts lost. The court theaters and the Redoutensäle were leased in 1794 to Baron Peter von Braun, who greatly restricted the use of these halls for concerts, which apparently brought in little in the way of revenues. Beethoven was much put out by his policies in 1802. See TDR, vol. 2, p. 612, and the recent study by Mary Sue Morrow, *Concert Life in Haydn's Vienna: Aspects of a Developing Musical and Social Institution* (Stuyvesant, N.Y., 1989), pp. 39, 68–70.

12. *Realzeitung*, July 10, 1781. Cited in Morrow, p. 486.

13. See Otto Biba, "Concert Life in Beethoven's Vienna," in *Beethoven, Performers, and Critics*, ed. Robert Winter and Bruce Carr (Detroit: Wayne State University Press, 1980), p. 80.

14. Morrow, p. 93.

15. See above, note 11.

16. Morrow, pp. 16–17. It should be borne in mind that evidence for private musical events survives very much by happenstance. For example, someone in attendance may have mentioned such an affair in a diary or a letter—and this too happened to survive. The actual numbers of these events are surely much larger than the evidence shows.

17. Thayer-Forbes, p. 135.

18. These seem to have been his first systematic lessons in (Fuxian) counterpoint. See Richard Kramer, "Notes to Beethoven's Education," *JAMS* 28 (1974), pp. 73–74. As to the violin lessons, see Elliot Forbes, "Schuppanzigh," *The New Grove*, vol. 16, p. 871.

19. Thayer-Forbes, 140–41.

20. Anderson, *Letters*, vol. 1, pp. 14–15; *Briefwechsel*, vol. 1, p. 18. Beethoven specifically mentions the coda of the Variations for Piano and Violin on "Se vuol ballare," WoO 40, as an example of the style he had in mind, instructing von Breuning that she "need only play the trill and can leave out the other notes, since these appear in the violin part as well." The music in question shows a texture of trill-plus-melody in one hand that is also a trademark of the early cadenzas Beethoven sketched for his concertos.

21. See Kerman, *Kafka* vol. 1, p. 89, and vol. 2, pp. 45–46; and Johnson, *Fischhof*, vol. 1, pp. 367–68. Johnson's arguments (*Fischhof*, vol. 1, pp. 368 and 384–85) for regarding WoO 6 as an earlier finale of Op. 19 are persuasive.

22. See p. 40.

23. See Appendix I.

24. *Briefwechsel*, vol. 1, p. 33; Anderson, *Letters*, vol. 1, p. 24. Regarding the trip to Prague, Dresden, and Berlin see Douglas Johnson, "Music for Prague and Berlin: Beethoven's Concert Tour of 1796," in *Beethoven, Performers, and Critics*, ed. Winter and Carr, pp. 24–40.

25. In a letter of 1801 to Wegeler, Beethoven speaks of his frustrated desire to undertake tours as a composer and player: "Had it not been for my deafness, I should have long ago travelled half the world over; and that I must do—for to me there is no greater pleasure than to practice and display my art." Anderson, *Letters*, vol. 1, p. 67 (with corrections); *Briefwechsel*, vol. 1, p. 33.

26. Otto Biba points out that the police registration records, otherwise an important source of information about concerts of the time, were destroyed in a fire at the Wiener Justizpalast in 1927. See "Beethoven und die 'Liebhaberconcerte,'" *Beethoven-Kolloquium 1977*, ed. Rudolf Klein (Kassel: Bärenreiter, 1978), p. 83.

27. For Mozart's subscription concerts at the Mehlgrube in 1785, he undertook the extraordinary step of hiring a theater orchestra, evidently that of the Burgtheater. See Otto Biba, "Concert Life in Beethoven's Vienna," in *Beethoven, Performers, and Critics*, p. 79. The abilities of the amateur players ("Dilettanten") of Vienna have been variously estimated. Periodic reports in the *AmZ* of Leipzig were very critical of both professional and amateur orchestral playing in the city around the turn of the century. See Clive Brown, "The Orchestra in Beethoven's Vienna," *Early Music* 16 (1988), pp. 4–6. A commentator in the *AmZ* of 1800–1 (3, pp. 622–63), however, attributes such criticisms largely to simple reciprocal contempt between North and South Germans; some of the amateurs, this report claims, are, to be sure, mediocre, while many others could even be called virtuosi. Ibid., col. 638. Otto Biba maintains that amateur musicians played their instruments "perfectly" but for pleasure rather than for a living. See "Concert Life in Beethoven's Vienna," *Beethoven, Performers, and Critics* ed. Winter and Carr pp. 78–79. Clive Brown is more persuaded of their mediocrity, Brown, ibid.

28. TDR, vol. 1, p. 412.

29. See TDR, vol. 1, p. 400. And on the next evening of this busy week, March 31, Beethoven reportedly played a Mozart concerto between the acts of a performance of *La Clemenza di Tito* at the Burgtheater, organized by Constanze Mozart. Thayer speculates that the concerto was K. 466 in D minor, a suggestion that in later accounts has with little justification been elevated to the status of a certainty. See Thayer-Forbes, vol. 1, p. 175.

30. Eduard Hanslick, *Geschichte des Concertwesens in Wien* (Vienna: W. Braumüller, 1869–70), vol. 1, p. 105.

31. *Briefwechsel*, vol. 1, p. 33; Anderson, *Letters*, vol. 1, pp. 24–25. This letter shows that Streicher had sent a piano to Pressburg, probably for Beethoven's concert, and that Beethoven agreed to sell it for him afterwards.

32. See Kerman, *Kafka*, vol. 1, fol. 57v, and vol. 2, p. 215; and Wegeler-Ries, trans. Noonan, p. 109. It had always been assumed that the Duport in question was the older one, Jean-Pierre. But Lewis Lockwood has made a case for the younger brother; he notes that in 1795 Jean-Louis alone was listed as cellist in the court *Kapelle* (in 1786 Jean-Pierre had been elevated to *Oberintendant* of the court's chamber music), and that Ries's designation, "the King's first cellist," thus would apply more properly to him. See "Beethoven's Early Works for Violoncello and Contemporary Violoncello

Technique," *Beethoven-Kolloquium 1977*, ed. Klein, pp. 176 and 181. It is hard to know how literally we should take Ries's statement.

33. See Johnson, *Fischhof*, vol. 1, pp. 354–55; and Küthen, *Kritischer Bericht*, p. 6.

34. There is a faint bit of evidence that Beethoven also played the Concerto Op. 19, either in Berlin or at an appearance shortly thereafter, perhaps in Pest. Johnson identifies the paper of a sketch for the revision of a passage in the second movement (Fischhof 16v) as one Beethoven acquired during this trip and used mainly in Berlin. See Johnson, *Fischhof*, vol. 1, pp. 164–65 and 372–73.

35. *Wegeler-Ries* trans. Noonan, p. 96.

36. Küthen, *Kritischer Bericht*, pp. 6–7. See also Johnson, *Fischhof*, vol. 1, pp. 182 and 185–86.

37. In a supplement to the *Biographische Notizen* published in 1845, Wegeler quotes from a letter that casts serious doubt upon a visit by Beethoven to Hungary after the concert in Pressburg on November 11: it testifies that Beethoven was back in Vienna before November 23. The letter is from Stephan von Breuning, written, Wegeler reports, from Mergentheim on November 23, 1796: "I do not know whether Lenz [the youngest of the brothers von Breuning] has written anything about Beethoven; if he has not, here is the news. I saw him while still in Vienna, and in my opinion, which Lenz also confirms, the journey (or perhaps the outpouring of friendship upon his return!) has made him more stable, or actually a better judge of men, and has convinced him of the rarity and value of good friends." See Wegeler-Ries, trans. Noonan, p. 156.

38. Johnson, *Fischhof* vol. 1, pp. 185 and 355. Papers that are used mainly during a particular period and then in isolated later occurrences form a familiar pattern among Beethoven's autograph sources—odd bits of paper being left over after completion of a task or tasks. But the isolated *earlier* occurrence of a paper whose main period of use is yet to come (suggesting that the composer acquired it, used just a leaf or two, and left it lying about) is virtually unknown.

39. See Küthen, *Kritischer Bericht* p. 6, and Martin Staehelin, "Brieffragment an Lenz von Breuning," *Beethoven Jahrbuch* 10, 1978–81 (Bonn, 1983), pp. 23–33. Küthen was the first to make an explicit connection between Kafka 138 and the Romberg concert. Thayer reports, without offering any evidence, that Beethoven played the piano-cello sonatas with Bernhard Romberg at that concert. See Thayer-Forbes, p. 196.

40. From TDR, vol. 2, p. 73.

41. See Adrienne Simpson, "Tomášek," *The New Grove*, vol. 19, p. 33.

42. Johnson has transcribed the cadenza sketches for Op. 15 in Grasnick 1 in *Fischhof*, vol. 2, p. 64. He was the first to date the sketches for the Allegro of Op. 19 in Kafka, f. 64–65, securely in 1798. *Fischhof* vol. 1, pp. 373–74. The fullest and most detailed catalogue of the sources for Op. 19 is Geoffrey Block, "Some Gray Areas in the Evolution of Beethoven's Piano Concerto in B♭ Major, Op. 19," in Lewis Lockwood and Phyllis Benjamin, eds., *Beethoven Essays: Studies in Honor of Elliot Forbes* (Cambridge, Mass.: Harvard Music Department, 1984), pp. 123–26.

43. Berlin, SPK, Beethoven Aut. 13. Much of the revision of Op. 19 and the writing out of the autograph may have been done in Prague; all this activity may have misled Tomášek to think the concerto was newly composed there.

44. TDR, vol. 2, pp. 358 and 614. See the discussion in Johnson, *Fischhof*, vol. 1, pp. 217–18.

45. See pp. 31 and 35–36. One commentator, Basil Deane, has suggested that "one or both" of the Romances may have been intended as slow movements for that other

Bonn work, the Violin Concerto in C, WoO 5. "The Concertos," in *The Beethoven Reader,* ed. Denis Arnold and Nigel Fortune (New York: Norton, 1971), p. 379. There is no support for this in the sources.

46. *AmZ* 2 (1800), col. 49.

47. A surviving program is reproduced in TDR, vol. 2, pp. 171–72.

48. See Alan Tyson and Douglas Johnson, "Reconstructing Beethoven's Sketchbooks," *JAMS* 25 (1972), p. 150; and Küthen, *Kritischer Bericht,* pp. 43–44.

49. Johnson, *Fischhof,* vol. 1, p. 358.

50. The witnesses are Ries, Ignaz von Seyfried, and Czerny. See Chapter 6, note 4. The autograph is Berlin, Staatsbibliothek, Beethoven Autograph 14.

51. See Richard Kramer, *"The Sketches for Beethoven's Violin Sonatas, Opus 30: History, Transcription, Analysis"* (Princeton diss., 1970), pp. 138–40; and Johnson, *Fischhof,* vol. 1, p. 358, and vol. 2, pp. 65 and 68–69 (transcription). Küthen, *Kritischer Bericht* p. 9, reports that this leaf is now in private hands in the Netherlands.

52. Printed in Willy Hess, *Beethoven Werke: Supplemente zur Gesamtausgabe* (1960), vol. 1, p. 7.

53. The finale of the Piano Sonata Op. 2, no. 1, composed about two years later than WoO 6, is a veritable anthology of experimental keyboard textures; but it does not include this one.

54. See pp. 31 and 39.

55. This texture can be seen again in the Andante "favori", WoO 57, that Beethoven first planned as the slow movement of the "Waldstein" Sonata, Op. 53.

56. See Kinsky-Halm, p. 435. The auction and its catalogues are ably discussed in *The Beethoven Sketchbooks,* Douglas Johnson, Alan Tyson, and Robert Winter, eds. (Berkeley: University of California Press, 1985), pp. 15–17, and ibid., pp. 567–72.

57. This arrangement has been recorded more than once. In the Monitor recording (1966) of Lili Kraus and the Vienna State Opera Orchestra, for example, the Czerny version is given without explanation. Alfred Brendel's fine recording with the Orchestra of the Vienna Volksoper (Turnabout, 1967) presents the original version with some tasteful added embellishments.

58. Eusebius Mandyczewski, "Beethoven's Rondo in B für Pianoforte und Orchester," *SIMG* 1 (1899–1900), pp. 295–306.

59. In 1802 he urged Hoffmeister to hurry with the publication of the composition because the "rabble" (*der Pöbel*) was waiting for it. See *Briefwechsel,* vol. 1, p. 105; Anderson, *Letters,* vol. 1, p. 73.

60. Berlin, SPK Aut. 13.

61. See Johnson, *Fischhof,* vol. 1, pp. 34, 214, and 217–18, and above, p. 54. The autograph shows two clear stages of writing, the second consisting mainly of corrections and clarifications that Beethoven may have made just prior to publication in 1805. But this stage includes one substantial modification, a four-measure extension of the concluding coda.

62. Page 117.

63. TDR, vol. 2, p. 614. A month later he also offered them to Andre of Offenbach. Ibid., vol. 2, p. 358.

64. See above, pp. 50–51, and Johnson, *Fischhof,* vol. 1, pp. 368–73.

65. See Johnson, *Fischhof,* vol. 1, pp. 373–74, and Johnson, Tyson, Winter, p. 77ff.

66. Berlin, Staatsbibliothek, Beethoven Aut. 13. Johnson concludes on the basis of the handwriting and paper that the autograph was written not long after the revisions in

Grasnick 1 that it incorporates. And this document was almost certainly prepared in anticipation of a performance; the ones of late 1798 occur at exactly the right time.

67. Anderson, *Letters*, vol. 1, p. 48; *Briefwechsel*, vol. 1, p. 64.

68. Anderson, *Letters*, vol. 1, p. 50; *Briefwechsel*, vol. 1, p. 72.

69. Bonn, SBH 524.

70. See Block, "Some Gray Areas" in *Beethoven Essays*, ed. Lockwood and Benjamin, p. 115. Since Hoffmeister otherwise ignored the additions in gray, he must have had some instruction on the matter from Beethoven.

71. Bonn, Universitäts-Bibliothek, Velten-Sammlung, fol. 64. See Johnson, *Fischhof*, vol. 1, p. 356.

72. *Wegeler-Ries*, trans. Noonan, p. 38.

73. Theodor Müller-Reuter pointed out Wegeler's "mistake" in *Die Musik* 50 (1913–14), offering the bizarre alternative explanation that the concerto in question was the one in B♭, that Beethoven transposed his part up a whole tone to C major, and the other instruments tuned a semitone higher than their normal pitch (probably an impossibility for the winds). His misimpressions were corrected by Fritz F. Steffin and Arthur Rydin in *Die Musik* 50 (1913– 14), pp. 281–84.

74. See *Wegeler-Ries*, trans. Noonan, p. 5; and Küthen, *Kritischer Bericht,* p. 5.

75. *Zweite Beethoveniana*, (Leipzig: Peters, 1887) pp. 65–68.

76. See Johnson, *Fischhof*, vol. 1, pp. 370–71.

77. Ibid., pp. 353–36.

78. Ibid., pp. 354, 410–11, and 152. Erich Hertzmann in 1946 suggested that the *Rondo a capriccio* was written in response to the finale of Haydn's Piano Trio, Hob. XV:25, a piece he brought back with him from London in August 1795. See "The Newly Discovered Autograph of Beethoven's 'Rondo a capriccio,' Op. 129," *MQ* 37 (1946), pp. 171–95.

79. *Fischhof*, vol. 1, p. 152.

80. See *Kafka*, vol. 1, 72v and vol. 2, 36–37; and Kinsky-Halm, p. 440. Johnson's attempts to connect Kafka 57 and 138 to the December performance (*Fischhof*, vol. 1, p. 355) are not convincing. See above, p. 51.

81. Bonn, Universitäts-Bibliothek, Velten Sammlung, f. 64; and Washington, D.C., Library of Congress, acc. 318077, SV387. See Johnson, *Fischhof* vol. 1, p. 356.

82. Gesellschaft der Musikfreunde, A 62.

83. The sources are Kafka 134 and 97. See Johnson, *Fischhof* vol. 1, pp. 370–71 and Block, "Some Gray Areas," in *Beethoven Essays*, p. 124. Beethoven evidently also began to compose a new slow movement in D major for the B♭ Concerto; a notation on Kafka 127v "Concerto in B dur adagio in d dur," seems to refer to a draft in D major on the overleaf whose "tutti" and "solo" markings point to a concerto.

84. Kafka 45; see *Fischhof*, vol. 1, p. 372.

85. Küthen, *Kritischer Bericht*, p. 5, though he does not explicitly dispute Johnson's dating of the sources, believes it more likely that Beethoven played the C-major Concerto in March (and, likely, the B♭ one in December). His reason is that the concerto for the March concert was advertised as "new," while that for the December concert was not. A poster for the Tonkünstler-Sozietät oratorio concert on March 29 announced the entr'acte entertainment for the evening as "a new concerto of his own invention played by the master Herr Ludwig van Beethoven," and the subsequent report in the *Wiener Zeitung* of April 1 concurred that the concerto was "entirely new," adding that it won "undivided applause." TDR, vol. 1, p. 400. While this argument certainly has some

attractions, the factor of "newness" should not, perhaps, weigh too heavily. Tomášek thought the B♭ Concerto was new in 1798 ("not composed until he reached reached Prague"), and the review in the *AmZ* had it that the concerto Beethoven performed at his own concert in April 1800 (almost certainly Op. 15, composed in 1795) was "new." *AmZ* 2 (1800), col. 49. Both of these reports may have mistaken revised concertos for new ones. And of course in March 1795, Beethoven had just subjected Op. 19 to thorough revision in the course of which certainly one, and perhaps two of its three movements were in fact newly composed. And it is not impossible that Beethoven himself, having most probably played his B♭ concerto at least twice before in Vienna, may have permitted descriptions that exaggerated what was now new about it.

86. See Otto Biba, "Concert Life in Beethoven's Vienna," in *Beethoven, Performers, and Critics*, p. 80.

87. See Morrow, p. 187. Ries describes the single rehearsal for Beethoven's concert of April 5, 1803: "The rehearsal began at eight o'clock in the morning. . . . It was a dreadful rehearsal, and by half past two everyone was exhausted and more or less unsatisfied." See Wegeler-Ries, trans. Noonan, p. 66.

88. Berlin, Staatsbibliothek, Beethoven Aut. 12. For the dating of the manuscript see Johnson, *Fischhof*, vol. 1, p. 358–59. The changes in this manuscript are mainly of a "local" nature; they affect figuration, registration, instrumentation, and the like, rather than structural features.

89. As he told Hoffmeister in his letter of December 15. See *Briefwechsel*, vol. 1, p. 54; Anderson, *Letters*, vol. 1, p. 43.

90. Johnson points out that the score is ruled so as to accommodate long measures in the piano part; *Fischhof*, vol. 1, p. 358. And in a number of places it is clear that the piano part was in fact written first. For example, two measures Beethoven initially wrote in the solo part after m. 542 of the third movement (striking out in a harmonic direction quite different from that of the final version), he was able to delete and then carry on without disturbing any other parts. Küthen, on the other hand, proposes that the autograph served as a model for copying twice: for the orchestral parts preparatory to the April concert, and for the solo part preparatory to publication. He finds corroboration for this idea in the multiple sets of markings (numberings of measures and of multiple rests) obviously intended to facilitate copying. He feels, moreover, that Beethoven's first stage of writing in the solo staves grows sketchy and hurried toward the end of the third movement, and he hypothesizes that such haste was occasioned by the deadline of the concert on April 2 (the piano part was the single one that could be sacrificed at that stage, since Beethoven was to play it himself). The corrections, then, written in a different ink, would have been made later in anticipation of publication. But there is very little evidence anywhere in the manuscript of an incomplete piano part in the first stage of writing (there are plenty of places where Beethoven's vigorous crossings-out have rendered that stage illegible, showing nonetheless that there was a good bit there to cross out). The prominence of the solo part at the first stage and the strong indication that even very late in the finale it was written down first, distinguish this document clearly from the autographs for Opp. 19 and 37, made specifically for performance. It seems much more likely that Beethoven wrote it out with publication in mind.

91. That a copy intervened between the autograph and the print is suggested by the great difficulty an engraver would likely have had with Beethoven's much-altered manu-

script, and by minor discrepancies between its final readings and the Mollo publication.

NOTES TO CHAPTER 4

1. *Briefe*, vol. 1, p. 54; Anderson, *Letters*, vol. 1, p. 43.
2. The first segment of this theme shows up in the very earliest surviving traces of the concerto. Douglas Johnson has suggested a date of 1787–89 for a score fragment in the Fischhof Miscellany in which the opening motive is treated sequentially. See *Fischhof*, vol. 1, pp. 365–66, and vol. 2, pp. 71–73. But it is not clear to me why Johnson should identify this music as a cadenza. See above, pp. 38–39.
3. *Versuch einer Anleitung zur Composition* (Leipzig, 1782–93), vol. 2, p. 453ff.
4. A sketch of a cadenza for this movement in Paris, BN, Ms 70, evidently dating from that year, includes this theme. See Johnson, *Fischhof*, vol. 1 p. 371.
5. In revising the theme of the Adagio of the Piano Quartet in C, WoO 36 (1785), for use as the second movement of the Sonata Op. 2, No. 1 (1795) Beethoven rewrote the second of two pairs of highly regular and predictable phrases, making of this music a seamless unity—and transforming an ordinary theme into a distinguished one.
6. See Johnson, *Fischhof*, vol. 2, pp. 83 and 85.
7. That final shape of the passage is in all essentials present in the autograph (Berlin, SPK, Beethoven Aut. 13, fol. 3v). But there the composer could not resist tampering with it some more; in those mysterious emendations in gray ink (see above, p. 61), he has crossed through the chromatic motion to D♭ and inserted in the first violin and cello parts the merest skeleton of a *modulation* to that key, with A♭ below and G♭–C above. It was not the tonal destination that troubled him at that point, apparently, but rather the method of getting there. Like many of the emendations (or "sketches" for them) in this ink, this one was not realized in the published concerto. See Geoffrey Block, "Some Gray Areas," *Beethoven Essays*, ed. Lockwood and Benjamin, p. 114. Block makes mistakes in his description of the tonalities involved.
8. Two earlier sources, Paris, BN, Ms 61 (1790–92) and Bonn, SBH 609 (1794–5), suggest that the latter section in E♭ did not then yet exist. Thus it seems likely that Beethoven first introduced *both* of these passages in E♭ in 1798—the second draft in Grasnick 1, fol. 20v (1798), shows the one in S_2—giving this tonality a real presence in the movement. By subsequently removing one of them, that in T_1, he may have weakened the rationale for having the other. See Johnson, *Fischhof*, vol. 1, pp. 379–80.
9. Sterkel, Concerto for Piano in C, Op. 20, published by Schott of Mainz in 1784–85; Kozeluch, Concerto for Clarinet in E♭ (Budapest, 1975, from a set of parts perhaps copied in Berlin in 1792), Concerto for Piano, Four Hands, in B♭ (Padua, 1980; listed in the Breitkopf Catalogue, 1785–87), Concerto in D, in *Storace's Collection of Original Harpsichord Music* No. 2 (London, n.d. [No. 1 dated 1787–88]), Concerto pour clavecin . . . No. 2 [in F] (Paris: Sieber, ca. 1790), Troisieme concerto pour clavecin . . . Oeuvre 13 [in B♭] (Paris: Boyer, ?1785), Concert pour le clavecin . . . Oeuvre IX [in G] (Vienna: Artaria, ca. 1785); Clementi, Concerto for Piano in C (Milan, 1966; first published in a later arrangement as a piano sonata in 1794).
10. *Essays in Musical Analysis*, vol. 3, p. 18. In this famous essay of 1903, "The Classical

Concerto," Tovey is bent upon establishing "true concerto form," as opposed to "symphonic form," which he detects (with strong displeasure) in the T_1 of the first movement of Beethoven's Third Piano Concerto. The principal issue for him seems to be the mere presence or absence of the "dramatic" element of modulation. But perhaps, as has been suggested above, we should rather think whether or not aberrant harmonic motion and the intrusion of secondary tonalities loom large enough to subvert this section's introductory character. At any rate, Tovey's insistence that Mozart's passage in question (presumably mm. 44ff.) is *on* the dominant rather than *in* it is belied by the very long V/V preparation in mm. 36ff. The key to the ultimate unity of the section, perhaps, is how little music is actually presented in the dominant—and this could be said for Beethoven's C-minor Concerto as well. It is perhaps just as well that Tovey omitted Op. 19 from his discussions of Beethoven's concertos.

11. It is possible that Beethoven knew Mozart's concerto at the time he made the revisions in the first movement of Op. 19 late in 1798; K. 503 had been published earlier that year. But if this passage was a restoration of an earlier reading, as suggested above, it is unlikely that Mozart's composition could have been at hand to serve as its model.

12. Hans Engel, *Das Instrumentalkonzert*, vol. 2, p. 2; Dennis Forman, *Mozart's Concerto Form: The First Movements of the Piano Concertos* (London: Hart-Davis, [1971]), p. 56.

13. This section surely shows signs of the composer's youth. It starts off with four measures of "murky bass" in the piano virtually unmitigated by anything of interest above—this is quite unlike Beethoven's later urgent and dramatic use of the murky bass, as in the first Allegro of the *Pathétique* Sonata.

14. These have been noted by Johnson in *Fischhof*, vol. 1, pp. 379–80.

15. Of his last fourteen piano concertos (beginning with K. 413 = 387a) only four (k. 453, 456, 467, and 595) have a T_3 of more than 8 measures.

16. "The Classical Concerto," p. 23. The footnote with this insight was evidently added in 1936, when the essay, originally published in 1903, was anthologized.

17. See Block, "Some Gray Areas," *Beethoven Essays*, ed. Lockwood and Benjamin, p. 115.

18. In Owen Jander's description of this movement as "strophic," the orchestral introduction, with its partial statement of the opening material (in the tonic), the full exposition (I–V), and the recapitulation (I–I) all seem to count as "strophes." See Jander, "Romantic Form and Content in the Slow Movement of Beethoven's Violin Concerto," *MQ* 69 (1983), p. 175.

19. Charles Rosen, *Sonata Forms*, pp. 29ff. Rosen's distinction of three sorts of binary forms (pp. 18ff. and 29), however, seems to me forced and not entirely clear. The suggestion that "minuet form" begins after the double bar with contrasting material is surely misleading as a description of the usual Classical minuet. And the distinction between *simple binary* form and *slow movement form*, according to which the former has a contrasting theme in the dominant that is missing in the latter, would work better if the descriptions were simply reversed.

20. All of the slow movements of Mozart's concertos begin with the orchestra until the Romance of K. 466 (1785), where the plaintive tones of the first theme are first given out from the piano. Mozart seemed to like the effect; four of his seven following piano concertos and the Clarinet Concerto use this arrangement.

21. The Schenkerians are quite right that this functions as a dominant sonority with a $^6_4$ that must resolve to $^5_3$.

22. Mozart frequently prolonged important dominant functions through descending parallel $^6_3$ motion over V; examples are the preparation for the "second theme" (it is really

the first theme again) in the first movement of the *Haffner* Symphony, and the exquisite passage just before the recapitulation in the first movement of the Symphony in G minor, K. 550. Beethoven used this device many times, as in the dominant preparation for the second theme in the first movement of the Third Piano Concerto Op. 37. This construction appears distinct from another in which Mozart used $^6_4$ passages for temporarily obscuring the key. The enigmatic opening of the "Dissonance" Quartet, K. 465 is an example (though Schenker and others would dispute this). In a virtuoso tour de force in the String Quartet in E♭, K. 428, second movement, Mozart actually wrote parallel descending root-position chords, successfully avoiding the literal parallels through evasive maneuvers in the bass. This second, more extended prolongation in Op. 19 may have been mainly a product of 1798; it is sketched in Grasnick 1 (transcription in *Fischhof*, vol. 2, pp. 91–92). Thus, this most forward-looking passage in the movement is likely to have been a late addition.

23. See above, note 4.

24. See *Kafka*, vol. 2, p. 48, and *Fischhof*, vol. 1, pp. 371–72. This piece bears some striking resemblances to the Adagio Beethoven retained. It, too, appears to belong to the ornamented aria type, and its melody also begins with repetitions of the third scale degree over a moving bass (written at the first tutti indication)—here moving surprisingly from tonic down a diminished fourth to the lower semitone neighbor of the sixth degree.

25. See p. 20.

26. An intriguingly complex example of this is the finale theme of the Symphony No. 66.

27. Mozart's later concertos abound with splendid examples of these themes; see the finales of K. 449, 450, 456, 459, 467, 482, 503, and 537, and the Concert Rondo K. 382. Beethoven's friend Reicha commented upon the usual closed binary shape for the rondo theme in his *Traité de haute composition musicale*, trans. Czerny (Vienna, 1832), p. 1167.

28. In the course of writing and revising this movement, Beethoven vacillated fitfully between versions of the first theme with and without an upbeat. Sketches in the Kafka Miscellany (fol. 147v) from 1794–95 show the iambic idea in the main theme. And in what seems to be a lead-in to it, there is a most persistent hammering away at that rhythm in alternating dominant seventh and ninth block chords that Beethoven marked "8 mal." See *Kafka* vol. 2, p. 53. Yet in 1798 (Kafka, fol. 64v; dating according to *Fischhof*, vol. 1, pp. 373–74), the piece starts out with the "normal" trochaic rhythm (i.e., with the accented note on the first beat). The related theme of the episode, with its characteristic syncopation, makes its first appearance—initially in B♭ minor—at a slightly later point (fol. 97r), but at a time when the first theme was still iambic. Thereafter Beethoven seemed to think of these two passages as complementary, and he dealt with them in tandem. When he "normalized" the rhythm of the first theme in 1798 (fol. 64v), he changed the pattern of syncopation in the episode to match (fol. 65r). Then in Autograph 13 (probably late 1798) they both revert to the iambic rhythm of 1794–95. A problem with the trochaic version is that it needs some remedy for the motionlessness of the entire second half of the first measure. In both the sketches of 1798 and in m. 261 of the final version, Beethoven adds a third D upbeat on the final eighth of the bar—surely a somewhat lame solution.

29. Those of the Violin Concertos K. 216, 218, and 219, and of the Piano Concerto K. 271. The practice appears once more in the Piano Concerto K. 482 in E♭.

30. In some earlier movements (the Bassoon Concerto K. 191 [=186e]; the Flute Con-

certo K. 313 [=285c]; and the Rondo for Violin and Orchestra, K. 373) Mozart did away with the problem altogether by eliminating the fourth ritornello. Kozeluch came up with a novel solution in his Concerto for Piano, Four Hands (first published, Padua, 1980): the recapitulation after R_3 modulates to the dominant exactly as the exposition had, thus providing the necessary tonal contrast with R_4.

31. A. B. Marx, *Ludwig van Beethoven: Leben und Schaffen*, 2d ed. (Berlin, 1863), vol. 1 p. 183.

32. "Ein Satz eines unbekannten Klavierkonzerts von Beethoven," *VFMw* 4 (1860) p. 469.

33. TDR vol. 2, p. 87.

34. "The Concertos," *The Beethoven Reader*, p. 320.

35. See p. 72. That Beethoven could have had this particular passage in mind when composing his codetta is unlikely. Mozart's concerto was not published until 1798; Beethoven's codetta theme appears in the course of a cadenza surviving in a manuscript apparently dating from the first half of 1794, Paris, BN, Ms. 70. See *Fischhof*, vol. 1 p. 371, and vol. 2, p. 89.

36. Ed. G. Balalla (Budapest: Editio Musica, n.d.) originally published by Sieber of Paris, ca. 1790.

37. O. E. Deutsch, ed., *Mozart, a Documentary Biography*, pp. 290 and 328.

38. Measures 143–38. The first movement of the Clarinet Concerto, K. 622, has a similar tonal pattern and would have worked equally well for this comparison.

39. O. E. Deutsch, *Mozart, a Documentary Biography*, pp. 312 and 341.

40. As in Dugald Stewart, *Elements of the Philosophy of the Human Mind* (London, 1792). For this reference I am indebted to Gretchen Ann Wheelock, "*Wit, Humor, and the Instrumental Music of Joseph Haydn*" (Diss., Yale, 1979). Henry Home, Lord Kames, attempted to explain the difference between "wonder" and "surprise" as follows: "An Indian in Britain would be much surprised to stumble upon an elephant feeding at large in the open fields; but the creature itself, to which he was accustomed, would not raise his wonder." See *Elements of Criticism* (Edinburgh, 1762) vol. 1, p. 321.

41. The "implication-realization model" of musical analysis of Leonard Meyer and his disciples, in its various embodiments, takes some such process to lie at the heart of the effect music (in a known style) exerts upon its listeners. For a theoretical defense of this position, see Eugene Narmour, *Beyond Schenkerism: The Need for Alternatives in Music Analysis* (Chicago: University of Chicago Press, 1977), pp. 122ff. Eighteenth-century aesthetic theory advanced a great many other models—ranging from the association of affect with rhythmic motion to explanations of music as primitive language. And even in the analysis of the "unforeseen outcome" a distinction was made between cases in which the focus is on the special character of an ensuing event (giving rise to "wonder") and those in which the principal effect was the unexpectedness itself (exciting "surprise"). See the discussion of this point in Wheelock, op. cit., pp. 55ff.

42. See Leon Plantinga, *Muzio Clementi* pp. 167–69.

43. See Alexander Ringer, "Clementi and the 'Eroica,'" *MQ* 56 (1961), pp. 742–58, and Plantinga, *Muzio Clementi*, pp. 103–5.

NOTES TO CHAPTER 5

1. We can tell this partly from the sketches of 1794–95. The draft of the opening tutti of the first movement on Kafka 113 shows the main ideas of that movement in place

(though the connective materials were later to be altered). Sketches for the second movement on the same leaf are much less conclusive; though the main theme and a later idea or two are intact, the shape of the movement does not emerge, and the whole is presented in the remarkable key of D♭. But the Rondo is in all essentials present in its final form in the draft on Bonn, SBH 606. See Kerman, *Kafka*, vol. 1, fol. 113r, and vol. 2, pp. 34–35, and Johnson, *Fischhof*, vol. 1, p. 118, and vol. 2, pp. 67–68. Revisions in the autograph itself consist in large part of changes in piano figuration and (to a much lesser degree) details of orchestration.

2. Wegeler-Ries, trans. Noonan, p. 36. But a note of uncertainty as to Beethoven's place of residence at this time is introduced by an advertisement for the Piano Trios Op. 1 in May 1795, that gives his address as the "Ogylyisches Haus in the Kreuzgasse behind the Minorite Church." TDR, vol. 2, p. 177. Possibly he was reluctant to conduct his public business out of the Prince's house.

3. According to Wegeler and Ries, both sets were played at these gatherings in the presence of Haydn, who expressed his reservations about the third trio (C minor) and advised Beethoven not to publish it. Wegeler-Ries, trans. Noonan, pp. 32 and 74.

4. Hence the difficulty one has conscripting cellists to play these pieces. But the pianist Charles Rosen is high in their praise. See *The Classical Style* (New York: Norton, 1972), p. 351–65.

5. Taking the cello part at Lichnowsky's musicales was probably Anton Kraft or his son Nicholas, both of them respected professional players. See Wegeler-Ries, trans. Noonan, p. 32, and Alfred C. Kalischer's editorial comment, ibid., p. 174.

6. See the provocative article of Douglas Johnson, "1794–1795: Decisive Years in Bee-thoven's Early Development," in *Beethoven Studies* 3, ed., Alan Tyson (Cambridge: Cambridge University Press, 1982), pp. 1–28. Johnson sees the innovations of Bee-thoven's style in this period as a response to Haydn's recent symphonies; the C-minor trio of Beethoven's Op. 1—the one Haydn advised him not to publish—Johnson says, is specifically modeled after Haydn's Symphony No. 95 in the same key. But one is moved to urge more leniency with the young Beethoven when Johnson (p. 23) pro-nounces all his most ambitious pieces from the period (the Trios Op. 1, Nos. 2 and 3, the Sonatas Op. 2, Nos. 2 and 3, and the Concerto Op. 15) "pretentious." "Brash," perhaps, or "impetuous" might be more acceptable.

7. Wegeler-Ries, trans. Noonan, p. 74.

8. Haydn's most ambitious keyboard sonatas were usually intended, not for the press, but for specific pianists of note such as Maria Anna von Genzinger (Sonata in E♭, Hob. XVI:49).

9. See A. Peter Brown, *Joseph Haydn's Keyboard Music: Sources and Style* (Bloomington: Indiana University Press, 1986), p. 316. A similar distinction is often visible among Clementi's sonatas; it is particularly obvious in the stylistic differences between the accompanied keyboard sonatas (intended mainly for amateur players) and the solo sonatas (often composed for himself). See Plantinga, *Muzio Clementi*, pp. 126–29 and 159–60.

10. His Symphonies Nos. 32, 33, 38, and 48 from the 1760s, Nos. 41, 50, 56, 60, and 69 from the 1770s, Nos. 82 and 90 from the 1780s (written for Paris), and the London Symphony, no. 97, of 1792. See H. C. Robbins Landon, *Haydn: Chronicle and Works* (Bloomington and London: Indiana University Press, 1976–1980), vol. 2, p. 289.

11. K. 415, K. 467, and K. 503. The exception is K. 246 of 1776.

12. See Wye Jamison Allanbrook's admirable *Rhythmic Gesture in Mozart: Le Nozze di*

Figaro & Don Giovanni (Chicago and London: University of Chicago Press, 1983), pp. 201–2. In the concerto Mozart's distribution of rhythmic patterns over the measures is more straightforward than in the opera; it corresponds, in fact, to what Allanbrook (speaking of the opera) says "a lesser composer, attending to the conventional expectations of meter and period structure, would have fashioned . . ." Ibid., p. 202.

13. A large collection of military march rhythms from this period is given in Georges Kastner, *Manuel général de musique militaire* (Paris: Didot Frères, 1848), supplement, "Battéries et sonneries de l'armée française," pp. 12–18. A common denominator of these rhythms is the even tread of repeated quarter notes, in some cases sharpened with dotted figures or ornamented with occasional subdivisions and accentuating flourishes.

14. Koch, *Musikalisches Lexikon*, col. 745. The quotation is from the article "Hauptsatz" in Johann Georg Sulzer's *Allgemeine Theorie der schönen Künste* (Leipzig, 1792–99).

15. Anton Reicha, *Vollständiges Lehrbuch der musikalischen Composition*, trans. Carl Czerny, vol. 1, p. 1, 316. Very much later Brahms still seemed to say something similar: ". . . one has not written a sonata if one holds together a few ideas merely with the outward form of a sonata; on the contrary, the sonata form must of necessity result from the idea." See Walter Frisch, *Brahms and the Principle of Developing Variation* (Berkeley: University of California Press, 1984), p. 34.

16. This is a continuation that Beethoven evidently settled on somewhat late in the process; it does not appear in the Kafka draft.

17. Examples of this are legion; two are the opening of Haydn's String Quartet Op. 1, No. 1, and Beethoven's Sonata Op. 10, No. 1.

18. This procedure resembles the beginning of the *Eroica* Symphony, where the second appearance of the initial idea (m. 15), to which the listener had looked for an integral statement of the theme, begins at once to modulate. Dahlhaus describes the initial statement of the motif in m. 3 as "not yet" the theme, and its recurrence in m. 15 as "no longer" the theme. See Carl Dahlhaus, *Ludwig van Beethoven und Seiner Zeit* (Laaber: Laaber-Verlag, 1987), *Ludwig van Beethoven: Approaches to His Music*, trans. Mary Whittall (Oxford: Clarendon Press, 1991), p. 173.

19. Tovey, *Essays in Musical Analysis*, vol. 3, p. 64.

20. A comparison has sometimes been made with the corresponding passage in Mozart's Concerto in C, K. 503, where a new theme (one rather resembling "c" of Beethoven's movement, actually) appears in C minor and lightly touches for a moment on E♭, foreshadowing the reuse of that key in S_1. But Mozart's procedure is more conventional; the harmony (even in the deliberate fits and starts of S_2) always moves with at least a modicum of modulation rather than by abrupt about-face. It is most unlikely in any case that Beethoven could have known Mozart's concerto, first published in 1798, when he was working on Op. 15 in 1795.

21. The procedure here even more closely resembles the sliding nonmodulation to the flat mediant in the first tutti of Op. 19 (see pp. 70–71).

22. In one of the most satisfying properties of the tonal system, chromatic downward motion in the top voice fits with a bass that descends by fifth to produce 7–3, 7–3, allowing thus for a pattern of alternating V⁷ chords and their tonic resolutions. A most splendid example of this technique occurs in the second theme of the first movement of Mozart's Symphony in G minor, K. 550. Upon its repetition Mozart intensifies the effect by making *each* step of the sequence a V⁷ chord, and then overshoots the goal

of B♭ to dip bemusedly down into A♭ major. Beethoven's first type of sequence (mm. 220ff.) has a bass with which downward soprano motion by whole tone produces that 7–3 alternation.

23. Czerny wrote of Op. 15 that "the first movement of the present Concerto must be played in a rapid and fiery manner, and the passages, which in themselves are not difficult, must acquire an appearance of bravura through a brilliant style of playing." See Carl Czerny, *On the Proper Performance of All Beethoven's Works for the Piano*, ed. Paul Badura-Skoda (Vienna: Universal 1970), p. 103.

24. Ibid. The quotation comes ultimately from *Die Kunst des Vortrags der älteren und neueren Klavierkompositionen*, Op. 500, originally published in 1842. The C-major concerto is one of the compositions that Czerny, according to his own testimony, had studied with Beethoven. See Nottebohm, *Beethoveniana*, p. 136. Küthen's argument that the octaves were meant to be played by one hand with separate attacks—and legato at that—is not convincing. See Küthen, *Kritischer Bericht*, p. 17.

25. See the table in Johnson, "1794–1795: Decisive Years," *Beethoven Studies 3*, ed. Tyson, p. 15.

26. The first of the "Kurfürsten" Sonatas (WoO 47) and the early Piano Concerto in E♭ (WoO 4) have Larghetto slow movements.

27. See the article by David Fallows in *The New Grove* vol. 10, p. 469.

28. Koch, *Musikalisches Lexikon*, col. 890.

29. There are a few movements with some form of Adagio together with *alla breve*: the first movement of the Sonata Op. 27, No. 2 (the "Moonlight"), the Romance Op. 50, and the opening Adagio of the Fourth Symphony.

30. Czerny, *On the Proper Performance, of All Beethoven's Works for the Piano*, ed. Badura-Skoda, p. 104.

31. Czerny suggests ♩ =58, a tempo at which the half note pulse can be effectively maintained.

32. Ignored here for the moment are the attractive voice exchanges between outer parts in this example and certain ornamental features in the other ones.

33. More commonly Mozart proceeds directly to the $^6_5$ sonority by dropping the bass a semitone from the tonic, as in K. 458, third movement; K. 481 Adagio; K. 488, Andante (with ravishing inner-voice movement); and the motet *Ave verum corpus*, K. 618. This motion appears in many of Beethoven's slow movements as well, particularly from about 1795–1807 (Op. 7; Op. 10 No. 1; Op. 18, No. 3; Op. 28; Op. 30, No. 1; Op. 31, No. 1; Op. 36; Op. 37; Op. 69; and others). There are several other contrapuntal patterns in which Beethoven moves directly from an initial tonic to an inverted dominant. The $^4_3$ inversion over 2 in the bass can occur in bass motions of 1–2–7–1, 1–2–7–5, or 1–2–1, and the $^4_2$ inversion is seen in a bass pattern that leaps to the subdominant degree, 1–4–3. These motions from tonic to inverted dominants together account for the beginnings of a very large proportion of Beethoven's slow themes.

34. In the clarinet's version of the melody in m. 15ff., the resolution to the tonic is evaded through a motion to II$^6_3$.

35. See p. 78.

36. This figuration was evidently not present in 1795. In the autograph of 1800, Beethoven first wrote a version of the passage that included the eighth-triplet motion but without the staccato articulation or marcato bass, and subsequently substituted the reading of the final version.

37. In *Beethoven Studies 3*, ed. A. Tyson, pp. 141–59.

38. *AmZ* 6 (1804), col. 198.

39. See p. 81.

40. Bonn SBH 606r. This eleven-measure transition is transcribed in *Fischhof*, vol. 2, p. 67.

41. As in Symphonies No. 85 and 88 before the third ritornello, and in Nos. 99 and 102 before the second. Sometimes the device appears before the reprise in the opening rounded binary theme (Symphony No. 96) or very late, before a final consolidation of the tonic (Symphonies No. 89 and 94). Among the earlier rondos Beethoven may have known, those of C. P. E. Bach bring back the ritornello theme very often and in various keys, with an effect that is altogether different.

NOTES TO CHAPTER 6

1. An earlier version of this chapter appeared as "When Did Beethoven Compose His Third Piano Concerto?," *Journal of Musicology* 7 (1989), pp. 275–307. Appendix 2 offers an abstract of its argument.

2. TDR, vol. 2, p. 612. The auditorium in question was either the Burgtheater or the Kärnthnerthortheater; the Baron von Braun had been in charge of these two court establishments since 1794. The Kärntnerthortheater under his control was seldom let out to givers of concert, and the Burgtheater almost never. In the latter case an exception was made for the pianist Josepha Auernhammer, who may well have been one such "mediocre" artist to whom Carl van Beethoven referred. See Morrow, *Concert Life* p. 50.

3. Wegeler and Ries, trans. Noonan, p. 66.

4. Three witnesses confirm that this was the first performance of the concerto: Ries, who assisted Beethoven in preparations for the concert (Wegeler-Ries trans. Noonan, p. 66); Ignaz von Seyfried, who reports that he turned pages while the composer played (*Caecilia* 9 [1828], pp. 291–92); and Czerny, who attended the concert (*On the Proper Performance of All Beethoven's Works for the Piano*, ed. Badura-Skoda, p. 9).

5. Quoted in Thayer-Forbes, p. 330.

6. A year later Beethoven reported that he had composed the oratorio in "a few weeks" (*in nur einigen Wochen*). In 1811 he described this duration as "fourteen days amidst all possible tumult." *Briefwechsel*, vol. 1, p. 219 and vol. 2, p. 216; Anderson, *Letters*, vol. 1, pp. 116 and 338–39.

7. See Alan Tyson, "The 1803 Version of Beethoven's Christus am Oelberge," *MQ* 56 (1970), pp. 551–84.

8. *Zeitung für die Elegante Welt*, April 16, 1803.

9. Letter to Hoffmeister, April 22, 1801. In *Briefwechsel*, vol. 1, p. 169; Anderson, *Letters*, vol. 1, p. 50.

10. Kerman, *Kafka*, vol. 1, fols. 82r and 155v; vol. 2, p. 58.

11. Johnson, *Fischhof*, vol. 1, p. 390, and vol. 2, p. 98.

12. Ibid., vol. 1, fol. 155v; vol. 2, p. 58.

13. See Sieghard Brandenburg, ed., *Kesslerisches Skizzenbuch* (Bonn: Beethovenhaus, 1976–78), vol. 1, fol. 15, and vol. 2, p. 54. Bathia Churgin first identified this little passage in her review of the *Kesslerisches Skizzenbuch*, in *Israel Studies in Musicology* 3 (1983), p. 177. See also Küthen's discussion in the *Kritischer Bericht, Beethoven Werke*, Abt. III, Bd. 2, p. 38.

14. Tyson, "The 1803 Version of Beethoven's *Christus am Oelberge*," p. 571.
15. *Fischhof*, vol. 1, pp. 161, 164–65, and 169–70.
16. See Johnson et al. *The Beethoven Sketchbooks*, pp. 132 and 136.
17. See Karl-Heinz Köhler, "Return of Treasures to the Deutsche Staatsbibliothek," *Fontes artes musicae* 26 (1979), pp. 86–87.
18. A. Ch. Kalischer, "Die Beethoven-Autographe der königlichen Bibliothek zu Berlin," *Monatshefte für Musikforschung* 27 (1895), p. 161.
19. TDR, vol. 2, p. 179.
20. Kinsky and Halm, p. 92. It is highly unlikely that Hans Halm, working on the *Verzeichnis* in Munich after the war, would have seen Aut. 14. But Kinsky certainly did. His name, together with the date 13 October 1937, is the first entry in the register attached to the manuscript in the Berlin Staatsbibliothek. It may be that he did not study the the sources for this composition very carefully: the incipit he provides for the first movement shows a meter signature of ¢, a signature for the movement that was unknown until the Breitkopf & Härtel collected edition of the 1860s. The autograph and first edition both show ¢.
21. See Sieghard Brandenburg, "The First Version of Beethoven's G Major Quartet, Op. 18, No. 2," *ML* 58 (1977), p. 127.
22. See Johnson et al., *The Beethoven Sketchbooks*, pp. 87 and 96.
23. This course of events was first described by Alan Tyson and Douglas Johnson in "Reconstructing Beethoven's Sketchbooks," *JAMS* 25 (1972), p. 150.
24. Köhler, "Return of Treasures," p. 86.
25. Küthen, *Kritischer Bericht*, p. 39; Tyson, personal letter, December 1987.
26. See below, Chapter 7, note 40.
27. See below, Chapter 7, note 41.
28. A pioneering study of watermarks is A. H. Stevenson, "Watermarks are Twins," *Studies in Bibliography* 4 (1951), pp. 57–91. In the musical literature Tyson has described the role of watermarks in paper making a number of times, most recently in the chapter "New Dating Methods: Watermarks and Paper Studies" in his collected essays, *Mozart: Studies of the Autograph Scores* (Cambridge, Mass.: Harvard University Press 1987), pp. 1–9.
29. See Richard Kramer, *The Sketches for Beethoven's Violin Sonatas, Opus 30: History, Transcription, Analysis* (Diss., Princeton, 1973; Ann Arbor, Mich., 1979), p. 100; Alan Tyson, introduction to *Facsimile of the Autograph Manuscript in the British Library, Add. MS 37767*, p. viii; and Küthen, *Kritischer Bericht* p. 38.
30. See Johnson, *Fischhof*, vol. 1, pp. 134–41.
31. Kramer, *The Sketches for Beethoven's Violin Sonatas*, pp. 96–99. The Kessler Sketchbook has appeared in facsimile and transcription, edited by Sieghard Brandenburg (see above, note 13); the Wielhorsky Sketchbook has been published, also in facsimile and transcription, by N. L. Fishman (Moscow, 1962).
32. *Fischhof*, vol. 1, p. 95; Tyson, "Beethoven's Home-Made Sketchbook of 1807–8," *Beethoven-Jahrbuch* 10 (1983), pp. 185–200; and Johnson et al., *The Beethoven Sketchbooks* pp. 162 and 546. There is one more leaf in the Kafka Miscellany; see Kerman, *Kafka*, vol. 1, pp. xxvi–xxvii.
33. This total does not include occurrences of a similar watermark from this period with only one crescent moon.
34. Kramer, "The Sketches for Beethoven's Violin Sonatas," p. 104; and *Fischhof*, vol. 1, p. 197.

35. Johnson, et al. *The Beethoven Sketchbooks* p. 546.

36. The predictability of this process relies upon the precise nature of the patterns left in paper at the artisan's shop through the use of given molds at a given time (distinctions can even be made between paper produced early or late in the life of a given mold). Specific runs of paper, thus identifiable, are thought to remain together, for the most part, in the retail establishment where they are sold, and ultimately in the composer's workshop.

37. Küthen provides a schematic account of these gatherings and accurate full-sized drawings of the watermarks from fols. 5–8 (Mold A) and fols. 9–12 (Mold B), in *Kritischer Bericht*, pp. 86–91.

38. The measurement of an axis passing through the centers of of all three crescent moons, from the inside curve of the smallest to the ouside curve of the largest. (Tyson whimsically coined this name—perhaps in the hope of avoiding any Latinate alternative that might resemble "lunacy.") During the making of this run of paper (at fol. 56 of Aut. 14), the outer edge of the largest moon in Mold 1 was bent, reducing the measurement to 83 mm.

39. *Kritischer Bericht*, p. 38.

40. See Johnson et al., *Beethoven Sketchbooks* pp. 92–93, and 98.

41. I.e., "total spann" (from the top line of the highest staff to the bottom one of the lowest) and "single spann" (the width of a single staff).

42. Berlin, Staatsbibliothek, Mendelssohn 15, 1804–5. The sketchbook between Wielhorsky and *Leonore*, however, the *Eroica* Sketchbook of 1803–4 (Krakow, Biblioteka Jagiellońska), shows a different staff-lining.

43. *The Sketches for Beethoven's Violin Sonatas*, pp. 83–84.

44. It is easy to determine the order in which the inks were used from the placement of notation on the staff, and from what is used to cross out what.

45. The "con brio" was added later in what looks like the ink of Stage 2.

46. *Kritischer Bericht*, pp. 7 and 44. Küthen may have been misled by a certain fading of the ink on this folio, particularly near the edges of the pages, that imparts a somewhat yellowish tinge to the writing.

47. See p. 115.

48. This music occurs twice earlier, in the opening tutti and in the first solo section, both times in E♭ minor. In S₃, as in the Kessler Sketchbook, it is in C minor.

49. Küthen identifies this hand as that of Beethoven's copyist Schlemmer. See *Kritischer Bericht* p. 38.

50. Wegeler and Ries, trans. Noonan, pp. 101–3.

51. He also speculates boldly that Ries's piano part, now lost, was written in that same black ink of Stage 3, and that it served as the *Stichvorlage* for the first edition. And certain "cue-crosses" (*Hinweiskreuze*) written in black ink into the margins of orchestral staves in the autograph he connects with revisions of those parts for publication. See *Kritischer Bericht*, p. 40.

52. Czerny reports that in 1799–1800 he played a piano in Beethoven's possession built by Anton Walter, a builder whose keyboards often extended to g‴. See Czerny, *On the Proper Performance of All Beethoven's Works for The Piano*, ed. Badura-Skoda, p. 4; and Edwin M. Good, *Giraffes, Black Dragons, and Other Pianos* (Stanford: Stanford University Press, 1982), p. 70. Pianos of other Viennese builders of the 1790s also included the "added G." One such is the instrument of Johann Jokob Könnicke, dated ca. 1790, in the Yale Collection of Musical Instruments. On only a very few occasions

before writing Aut. 14 did Beethoven exceed the five-octave FF–f‴ range. The Piano Trio WoO 38 (ca. 1791) has a g‴ (for which information I am indebted to Penelope Crawford); the Piano Trio Op. 1, No. 2 (1794–95), the Piano Sonata Op. 14, No. 1 (1798), and the published version of the Piano Concerto Op. 15 (1801) all include an f♯‴. On this subject see also William Newman, "Beethoven's Pianos versus His Piano Ideals," *JAMS* 23 (1970), 491–93. "Additional keys" made a somewhat earlier appearance in Britain. Shortly after 1790 Broadwood began to produce both grands and squares with a range to C⁗, and William Southwell of Dublin entered a patent for fitting older square pianos with additional keys in 1794. See Rosamond E. M. Harding, *The Piano-Forte: Its History Traced to the Great Exhibition of 1851* (Cambridge, 1933), p. 333; and Horst Walter, "Haydn's Klaviere," *Haydn-Studien* 2 (1969–70), p. 269. Clementi's Sonata Op. 33, No. 1, published in London in 1794, includes optional readings for "additional keys" up to b‴.

53. The triumphant run up to C⁗ at the end of the first movement, which fairly demands a conclusion in that high register, appears for the first time as an option in the first edition. In the autograph (Stage 1) the final eight notes drop down an octave, and there is no revision in Stage 3.

54. See Good, *Giraffes, Black Dragons, and Other Pianos* pp. 71–76.

55. Robbins Landon, *Haydn: Chronicle and Works* vol. 3, p. 414.

56. Thayer-Forbes, p. 335. Richard Kramer has more recently confirmed Thayer's reading of the Érard archives in "On the Dating of Two Aspects in Beethoven's Notation for Piano," in *Beiträge 76–78*, ed. Klein p. 170.

57. See Walter, "Haydn's Klaviere," pp. 279 and 283–84.

58. The pages with the cadenza sketches were at some point detached from the book and survive separately in the manuscript Bonn, SBH 637. See above, p. 116. The "inverted suspensions," with their sharp dissonances in mm. 4–6 of Example 6-3, are seemingly intentional.

59. William Kinderman has recently favored the traditional dating of Op. 37. He attributes the "1803" reading of the date on Aut. 14 to me alone (whereas, as we have seen, it was first ascertained by Karl-Heinz Köhler and subsequently confirmed by Alan Tyson and Hans-Werner Küthen). And Kinderman claims that "the thoroughgoing compositional changes in the score [i.e., Aut. 14] lend more support to the older view that the concerto was revised after an interval." *Beethoven* (Berkeley and Los Angeles: University of California Press, 1995), p. 65. But "thoroughgoing compositional changes" may be misleading. Revisions at Stages 2 and 3 of the autograph neither add nor delete a single measure nor alter a single harmony. The changes have to do almost exclusively with figuration, especially in the solo part, or with details of instrumentation. Revisions of the same sort—if anything, more drastic than these—occur in Beethoven's reworking of the piano part of the Fourth Piano Concerto very shortly after its publication; the autograph of the Violin Concerto, moreover, has several layers of widely differing figurations in the solo part, all apparently written in a very brief period of time. See above, pp. 213–16 and 235–40. Kinderman does not address the main structure of my argument for the later date. Among its parts are these: a total lack of any documentary evidence to connect the Third Concerto with 1799–1800, the absence of this composition from Beethoven's plans for the abortive concert of 1802, and the lacuna between the Kessler and Wielhorsky Sketchbooks as a plausible juncture for the sketching of this work.

60. *Caecilia* 9 (1828), p. 220.

61. *Briefwechsel*, vol. 1, p. 54; Anderson, *Letters* vol. 1, p. 43.

62. See Johnson et al., *The Beethoven Sketchbooks*, pp. 149–51.

63. Compiled mainly from Johnson et al., ibid.

64. See Tyson, "The 1803 Version" pp. 569–71. Tyson speculates (p. 577) that there may possibly have been another sketchbook between Wielhorsky and the following *Eroica* book, one perhaps containing missing sketches for the ending of the oratorio and for the variation movement of the "Kreutzer" Sonata. A conjecture that such a book would also have contained the sketches for Op. 37, however, would require us to believe that Beethoven sketched the cadenza to the first movement before composing the concerto.

65. See Kramer, *The Sketches for Beethoven's Violin Sonatas*, pp. 34–41, and Johnson et al., *The Beethoven Sketchbooks* pp. 113–18.

66. Ibid., p. 116.

67. See p. 113.

68. Brandenburg identifies this movement as a rondo. See *Kesslerisches Skizzenbuch: Uebertragung*, p. 19. Folio 15, we will recall, also has the notation of a fragment of the first movement of Op. 37.

69. Richard Kramer, "An Unfinished Concertante by Beethoven," *Beethoven Studies 2*, ed. Alan Tyson (London: Oxford University Press, 1977), p. 34.

70. Ibid., pp. 34–50.

71. Brandenburg suggests that the concertante may have been given up before the collapse of plans for the concert. See *Kesslerisches Skizzenbuch: Uebertragung*, p. 14.

72. According to Küthen's theory, the first two movements of the concerto were written up in score (Stage 1 of Aut. 14) by this time. If we are to assume further, in the context of this theory, that the finale (written in the autograph at Stage 2, it is agreed, early in 1803) had already been sketched by the spring of 1802, it is all the more astonishing that Beethoven should not simply have planned to use this concerto at the proposed concert rather than to work on others. But if the sketches to the finale were *not* made by this time, the theory would have to admit the remarkable coincidence that they, like the sketches to the other movements, were lost, but under quite independent circumstances.

73. Kramer, "An Unfinished Concertante," *Beethoven Studies 2*, ed. Tyson, pp. 42–43, suggests some interesting ways in which the concertante may have served as a kind of preparatory exercise for the Triple Concerto Op. 56.

74. On March 28, 1802, Carl Beethoven wrote to Breitkopf & Härtel that "in three or four weeks we will have a grand symphony, and a concerto for piano." And in the letter of April 22 he informed Härtel that he would have to wait a while longer for the two works. See TDR, vol. 2, pp. 610–12. These letters must refer to music Beethoven was working on for the planned concert; their imminent completion was apparently no longer contemplated when the concert was canceled. The symphony in question was clearly the Second, and the concerto very likely one of the projected ones, or the concertante; sketches for a concerto in F, the concertante, and the Second Symphony all appear on the same page (fol. 38v) in Kessler.

75. See Brandenburg, *Kesslerisches Skizzenbuch: Uebertragung*, pp. 15–16; Johnson et al., *The Beethoven Sketchbooks*, p. 133; and Christopher Reynolds, "Beethoven's Sketches for the Variations in E♭ Op. 35," *Beethoven Studies 3*, ed. Alan Tyson (Cambridge, 1982), p. 69. Reynolds concludes (pp. 65–67) that for a time Beethoven worked in both sketchbooks. The pattern of work on the Sonatas Op. 31, however, clearly points to a chronological gap of at least one or two months between them.

76. Thayer-Forbes, p. 314.
77. TDR, vol. 2, p. 616.
78. Czerny wrote, "The style and character of this concerto are much more grand and fervant than in the two former." Czerny, *On the Proper Performance*, ed. Badura-Skoda, p. 107.
79. It is unlikely that Beethoven would have composed a concerto without the prospect of its performance at a concert. It is not known when the negotiations with Schikaneder, involving the composition of *Vestas Feuer*, Beethoven's move into the theater, and (in all likelihood) the use of the theater for a concert, were concluded. But when the move was made, Beethoven took his brother Carl in to live with him, and in the letter of January 22 to Breitkopf & Härtel Carl reports that the two or them now resided together. See TDR, vol. 2, p. 617. The conclusions reached here would suggest that that the negotiations with Schikaneder had been made some months earlier than this.
80. Printed in Thayer-Forbes, pp. 304–6.

NOTES TO CHAPTER 7

1. See Chapter 5, note 13.
2. The extensive review of the first edition of this concerto in the *AmZ* of 1805 (7, cols. 445–57), takes note of this peculiarity: "In the course of the whole [movement] this idea and this rhythm, sometimes as a whole and sometimes in part, underlie the figurations and are subject to development" (col. 446).
3. The stepwise segment has a certain protean adaptability. In "a₁" (mm. 9ff.) punctuating upward octave leaps and offbeat *sforzati* keep it within the expressive orbit of the first theme as a whole.
4. See p. 99.
5. Arnold Schmitz found a rather convincing model for this theme in an accompanied sonata of J. F. X. Sterkel, whom, we recall, Beethoven had met in Aschaffenburg-am-Main in 1791. A Schmitz, *Beethovens zwei Principe: ihre Bedeutung fur Themen-und Satzbau* (Berlin: F. Dümmler, 1923), p. 16.
6. Another fleeting association of the two themes can be heard, perhaps, when the $\hat{3}$–$\hat{2}$–$\hat{1}$ melodic motion in each is incorporated into the traditional horn call ("a," mm. 139, 220, and 395; "b," mm. 50, 172, and 348).
7. *AmZ* 8 (1805), col. 450. In the now standard cadenza to this movement (probably written in 1809), Beethoven elaborates on the piano's trilled cadence by moving the top line chromatically up to E for a firmer connection with the V⁷ of IV.
8. Beethoven settles for the presence of the timpani's dissonant G against the subdominant rather than to prescribe a retuning (or a third instrument) for this section.
9. Thayer-Forbes, p. 209; TDR vol. 2, p. 78.
10. Most recently by Joseph Kerman in "Notes on Beethoven's Codas," *Beethoven Studies* 3, ed. Tyson, p. 143.
11. See Morrow, *Concert Life in Haydn's Vienna*, pp. 300–3.
12. André of Offenbach first printed K. 491 together with five other Mozart concertos in 1800; the plate number of K. 491 in this publication is 1417. See O. E. Deutsch, *Musikverlags Nummern* (Berlin: Mersburger, 1961), p. 6.

13. This in the finale; nor is there a new motive introduced toward the end of the first movement, should that have been the one in question.

14. *Vollständiges Lehrbuch*, ed. Czerny, vol. 2, pt. 3, pp. 334–35.

15. Among earlier composers, C. P. E. Bach apparently left us three in that key. Among earlier concertos from the Vienna orbit we might note a C-minor concerto by Wagenseil and two C-major concertos with C-minor introductions by Josef Antonín Stepán. See Helga Scholz-Michelitsch, *Das Orchester-und Kammermusik von Georg Christoph Wagenseil: Thematischer Katalog* (Vienna, 1972), p. 45; and Howard J. Picton, *The Life and Works of Joseph Anton Steffan (1726–1797)* (Diss., University of Hull, 1976; New York and London: Garland, 1989), vol. 1, p. 520. For this information I am indebted to Jay Lane.

16. Czerny urged aspiring composers to choose a masterwork—the example he gives is the first movement of Beethoven's "Waldstein" Sonata, Op. 53—and reproduce all its formal features, such as modulations, metrical structure, and the like, measure for measure in a new composition. See *Vollständiges Lehrbuch*, ed. Czerny, vol. 2, pt. 3, pp. 324–30. Beethoven's three early Piano Quartets WoO 36 are generally conceded to be modeled on specific violin sonatas of Mozart. See Douglas Johnson, "1794–95: Decisive Years in Beethoven's Early Development," *Beethoven Studies* 3, ed. Tyson, p. 14. A work from Beethoven's "first maturity," the String Quartet in A, Op. 18, No. 5, is thought to be to be (at least in part) an imitation of Mozart's Quartet in A, K. 464. In his interesting article on this relationship, Jeremy Yudkin points to some rather convincing parallels, especially between the two finales. See "Beethoven's 'Mozart Quartet,'" *JAMS* 45 (1992), pp. 30–74. But he is insufficiently attentive, in my opinion, to a difficulty to which he himself alludes, that of distinguishing between what is common musical property of the period and what is peculiar to a certain piece of a certain composer—that is, distinctive enough to allow us to identify specific imitation with some confidence. This is the case, I believe, in the parallel Yudkin draws between the beginning of Mozart's Piano Concerto K. 595 in B♭ and that of Beethoven's Op. 19 in the same key (ibid., p. 34, n. 12). The contrast between forceful and lyrical statements and between winds and strings that he points to are common currency of the period. And in this case a dependence of Op. 19 on K. 595 can be rather conclusively ruled out. Beethoven's movement existed in recognizable form (including the first theme upon which the comparison is based) in Bonn, certainly by 1790, and probably earlier; Mozart's appears in his *Verzeichnis* in January 1791 and was first published in 1800 (by André, in the same series as the C-minor Concerto).

17. Before subscribing fully to this argument, however, we ought to recall that something very like those timpani strokes of Beethoven's coda shows up among the fragmentary early sketches in the Kafka Miscellany (*Kafka*, vol. 1, fol. 83r; and vol. 2, p. 58): the passage in question, marked "zum Concert aus C moll/Pauke bei der Cadent," apparently dates at the latest from the beginning of 1798—a good two years before the publication of Mozart's concerto. But it is perfectly clear that here Beethoven intended to use this passage just *before* the cadenza: it concludes with a descending bass to a cadential $^6_4$, marked with bass figures in the source. The transferral of this timpani idea (also present at various other points in the movement) into the context of a coda with long-drawn plagal cadences could well have happened in 1803 in response to Mozart's example.

18. An exception is the recording by Alfred Brendel and the Chicago Symphony Orchestra,

with James Levine conducting (Philips, 1983). In his program notes Brendel makes it clear that he knows about the movement's correct signature.

19. This volume of the *Gesamtausgabe* (series 9, no. 16) was edited by Carl Reinicke. Kullak's edition was published (in a two-piano arrangement) by Steingräber. In a footnote Kullak calls attention to the common time signature of the autograph.

20. There are many other examples; some are Op. 9, No. 1, IV; Op. 9, No. 3, IV; Op. 10, No. 2, III; Op. 18, No. 5, IV; Op. 18, No. 6, I; and Op 20, I.

21. Two exceptions are the first movements of the Sonatas Op. 13 (the *Pathétique*) and Op. 31, No. 2, in D minor; both have urgent, driving Allegro sections that alternate with slow statements. That all this music is *alla breve* must have some relationship (obscure to me) with the coordination of the two very divergent tempos. Two borderline cases of the use of *alla breve* are Op. 1/3/III and Op. 2/1/I, both minor-keyed movements that one might characterize as, say, "impetuous" rather than highly charged and dead serious.

22. Czerny, *On the Proper Performance of All Beethoven's Works for the Piano*, ed. Badura-Skoda, p. 108.

23. These indications, missing in the autograph, were probably supplied in the *Stichvorlage* for the first edition.

24. Ibid., pp. 107–8. The first edition of 1804 shows pedal changes (*con sordino-senza sordino*) at mm. 4, 7, and 11.

25. See M. H. Abrams, *The Mirror and the Lamp: Romantic Theory and the Critical Tradition* (New York: Oxford University Press, 1953), p. 51. Two well-known poems that play on this imagery are Coleridge's "The Eolian Harp" and Eduard Mörike's "An eine Aeolsharfe." Goethe's *Faust, Part Two*, opens with the protagonist "lying on a flowery greensward," surrounded by celestial spirits, while Ariel sings to the accompaniment of Aeolian harps.

26. Thayer-Forbes, p. 305.

27. The orchestra, unable to continue the celestial sound in the same way, approximates the effect, with some irony, by playing its version of *con sordino*.

28. Op. 2/2/II, Op. 2/3/II, Op. 7/II, Op. 15/2, Op. 27/1/III, Op. 30/2/II, and, much later, Op. 90/I, Op. 109/III, and Op. 110/I. The initial contrapuntal motion of this movement is the $\hat{1}$–$\hat{7}$ bass progression, I-V$^6_5$, common in both Mozart's and Beethoven's slow movements; but here, exceptionally for Beethoven, the V$^6_5$ is a transient sound leading to the root position dominant of m. 2. See above, Chapter 5, note 33.

29. We might possibly associate the falling subsidiary figures in the flutes and bassoons with the shape of the piano's ornamental gestures in m. 7.

30. See Plate 7 and Example 6-2 for a passage with many consecutive revisions. His mistakes in the figuration of m. 33 (all values are doubled) persisted in the first edition. At m. 63 (Example 7-6), the "celestial-wind" tremolo in the recapitulation, in the first edition the third note in the right hand is an eighth—necessitating 256th notes in the following downward run, but showing 128ths. (The autograph shows only earlier versions; the last of these, in Stage 3 black ink, first proposes the leap to the high g''' but omits all note values.) Later editions have corrected that eighth to a sixteenth and repositioned the run in respect to the bass. Kullak and Küthen, correctly, I believe, have instead made the necessary changes in the run, and this is the version shown in Example 7-6.

31. *AmZ* 7 (1805), cols. 452–53.

32. A familiar example of this melodic type is the opening of the subject of Bach's *A Musical Offering*, which resolves the ninth in somewhat delayed fashion. Mozart's Concerto in C minor, K. 491, starts out with a version that resolves the ninth immediately, while the subject of the Kyrie from his Requiem, like Beethoven's theme, never does. In the very preliminary sketch for the theme of this movement in Kafka, the G–A♭ is already there, but with an immediate resolution back to G.

33. The cadenza is more lavish in the second ritornello (m. 158). In both versions of this return, one wonders whether Beethoven would have continued his chromatic run to a♭‴ had his revision at Stage 3 in the autograph (which extended the range of the piano part from g‴ to c″″ been more systematic.

34. In the first stages of the autograph, the high A♭ of this gesture was not available to the piano; whether by luck or design Beethoven did not add it in his Stage 3 revision. A texture very similar to the one heard here will be heard again in the *dolce* melody at the beginning of the Rondo from the Sonata for Piano and Cello, Op. 69 (m. 9).

35. The last time around, in m. 231, the clarinet's upward gesture to A♭ recurs, but a stepwise continuation (borrowed from a middle voice) provides it with an ex post facto rationale.

36. Tovey recognized only the latter derivation. See *Essays in Musical Analysis*, vol. 3, p. 75.

37. Tovey, *Essays in Musical Analysis*, vol. 3, p. 73; and Wolfgang Osthoff, *Ludwig van Beethoven: Klavierkonzert Nr. 3, C-moll, Op. 37, Meisterwerke der Musik*, Heft 2 (Munich: Wilhelm Fink, 1965), p. 3.

38. François Joseph Fétis, "Beethoven," in *Biographie universelle des musiciens* (Paris: Libraire de H. Fournier, 1837) vol. 2, p. 59; Wilhelm von Lenz, *Beethoven et ses trois styles* St. Petersburg, 1852; 2d ed. Paris, 1909, repr., with a foreword by Joseph Kerman, New York: Da Capo, 1980). See also Maynard Solomon's "The Creative Periods of Beethoven," in his *Beethoven Essays*, pp. 116–25, for an able summary of the history of the idea of "three styles."

39. Von Lenz, *Beethoven*, pp. 56, 156, 159–60.

40. In notes made by Czerny for Otto Jahn in 1852. Translated in Carl Czerny, *On the Proper Performance of All Beethoven's Works for the Piano*, ed. Badura-Skoda, p. 13. There is some confusion about details of Czerny's text. Badura-Skoda and Walter Kolneder, in Carl Czerny, *Erinnerungen aus meinem Leben* [Strassburg, 1963], p. 43, correctly give Czerny's reported date for Beethoven's statement as "1803"; this corresponds with Czerny's original notes now in Berlin, Staatsbibliothek, Czerny, Karl, Mus. Ms. Aut. theor. 2 (second pagination, p. 5). The parallel passage in Sonneck, *Beethoven: Impressions by His Contemporaries*, p. 31, has "1800." The compositions Czerny mentions in this connection, the Sonatas Opp. 28 and 31 (the latter he calls "Op. 29," as in its earliest Viennese editions) suggest that the year in question was more likely 1802.

41. "Auf eine wirklich ganz neue Manier," *Briefwechsel*, p. 126. Küthen has advanced the interesting thesis that the "wirklich neue Manier" was really a reference to a set of recently published fugues by Antonin Reicha claiming to be in "eine ganz neue Manier." Personal communication, November 1988.

42. Quoted in Tyson, "Beethoven's Heroic Phase," *MT* 110 (1969), p. 139.

43. Michael Broyles's book, *Beethoven. The Emergence and Evolution of Beethoven's Heroic Style* (New York: Excelsior, 1987), makes a concerted attempt to show that the middle-period music (which, collectively, he is willing to name "heroic") represents an amal-

gum of the "sonata-style" and "symphony-style," mentioned by eighteenth-century theorists, with elements from French Revolutionary and military music. But the categories (especially the first two), in their application to Beethoven's music, never seem very distinct, and they usurp attention that could more profitably be paid other sorts of distinctions.

44. From "Beethoven's Instrumental Music," David Charlton, ed., and Martyn Clarke, trans., *E. T. A. Hoffmann's Musical Writings: Kreisleriana, the Poet and the Composer, Music Criticism* (Cambridge: Cambridge University Press, 1989), pp. 97–98.

45. Romain Rolland, *Beethoven the Creater*, trans. Ernest Newman (New York: Harper, 1929) p. 77.

46. "Beethoven," in *The New Grove*, vol. 2, p. 382.

47. Dahlhaus, *Ludwig van Beethoven*: pp. 166–180.

48. A correspondent for the *AmZ*, reporting on a performance of the composition in Frankfurt in 1805, singled out this passage for special comment: "when the composer begins a fugato treatment of the theme in the last movement, what a shame (at least for my taste) that he gives it up too soon, and indeed at a moment of increased anticipation." See *AmZ*, 7 (1804–5), cols. 549–50.

49. This in marked contrast to the similarly situated off-key appearances of the rondo themes of Opp. 19 and 15, both of them parodic in effect. More than one writer has called attention to a procedure similar to that of Op. 37 at the analogous point in the finale of Brahms's Piano Concerto in D minor: a vigorous fugato leading to a static, lyrical section. See Tovey, *Essays in Musical Analysis*, vol. 3, p. 74, and Wolfgang Osthoff, *Ludwig van Beethoven: Klavierkonzert Nr. 3, C-moll, Op. 37*, p. 24. But there is no more to the similarity than that. This section of Brahms's movement has none of the far-reaching tonal implications of the Beethoven example; its corresponding lyrical passage is in F, the relative major.

50. But there is a possible suggestion of intermovement allusion in the tonal plan of the much earlier Piano Trio in G major, Op. 1, No. 2.

51. "The finale, or its material, not only is the key to the shape and character of the symphony as a whole but also influences its thematic material as well, especially the opening theme of the first movement Allegro." See Lockwood, "The Earliest Sketches for the *Eroica* Symphony," *Beethoven: Studies in the Creative Process* (Cambridge, Mass.: Harvard University Press, 1992), p. 136. Originally published in *MQ* 67 (1981) pp. 457–78.

52. The anomalous octave run—perhaps meant as a glissando—at the cadence ending S_2 in the first movement of Op. 15. See p. 102.

53. There is a seeming reference to it, though, in the triple trill that deceptively threatens to end the first solo section of the first movement of the Fourth Piano Concerto (mm. 183–84). And in the Triple Concerto, first movement, mm. 223–24, there is a jolly burlesque of the old convention, with all three solo instruments taking part.

54. That is, ignoring for the moment early fragments and ephemera such as the mysterious little piano piece "Lustig-Traurig," WoO 54, and the drafts of alternate movements (WoO 52 and 53) for the Sonata Op. 10, No. 1.

55. Joseph Kerman, *The Beethoven Quartets* (London: Oxford University Press, 1967), pp. 65–71.

56. The musical style of the quartet and the complete lack of sketches for it have led to speculation that this composition comes from an earlier time than its siblings in Op. 18. Riemann pointed to melodic characteristics that he said reflect the *Manieren*

of the Mannheim symphonists and suggest that some version of the quartet had been composed in the Bonn period. See TDR, vol. 2, pp. 188–90. But if this were true, if Beethoven had composed a piece of anything like these proportions in Bonn, we would expect some evidence of it to have survived. As there is no trace of such evidence, it is more reasonable to suppose, along with Sieghard Brandenburg ("The First Version," p. 127), that the quartet is approximately a contemporary of its fellows and was worked out in the missing sketchbook of 1799–1800.

57. See p. 126.

58. See pp. 140–41.

NOTES TO CHAPTER 8

1. See the admirable summary of the contents of Landsberg 6 in Rachel Wade, "Beethoven's Eroica Sketchbook," *Fontes artis musicae* 24 (1977), pp. 254–89.

2. While Carl negotiated with Breitkopf & Härtel for publication of Beethoven's music, Gottfried Christoph Härtel, director of the firm, agreed with Muzio Clementi to split the fee paid to Beethoven and grant the rights for publication in Britain to Clementi and Co. This plan to share the cost of Beethoven's compositions, "otherwise very exorbitant," according to Clementi, was apparently never implemented. See J. S. Shedlock, "Clementi Correspondence," *The Monthly Musical Record* 32 (1902), p. 142; and Leon Plantinga, *Muzio Clementi,* pp. 194–95.

3. The publications of 1803 were the three Sonatas for Piano and Violin Op. 30, two of the Piano Sonatas Op. 31, the Variations Opp. 34 and 35, the Romance for Violin and Orchestra Op. 40, the seven Bagatelles for Piano Op. 33, and a number of songs. The next year saw the appearance of the Concerto Op. 37, the Second Symphony, the *Prometheus* Overture, the Piano Sonata Op. 31, No. 3, and a few lesser works.

4. In a letter to G. F Treitschke, who revised the libretto for the final version, now called *Fidelio,* in 1814. See *Briefwechsel,* vol. 3, p. 20; Anderson, *Letters,* vol. 1, p. 455.

5. Beethoven explains this change to Friedrich Rochlitz in a letter of January 4, 1804. See *Briefwechsel,* vol. 1, pp. 205–6; Anderson, *Letters,* vol. 1, pp. 105–6.

6. No autograph for the work has survived. Preliminary sketches for the first movement in the last pages of Landsberg 6 may be dated ca. April 1804. The distribution of sketches for the concerto in Mendelssohn 15 suggests that the main part of its composition was close in time to work on the second-act finale of the first version of *Leonore,* and the beginning of act 3 (Florestan's recitative and aria "In des Lebens Frühlingstagen"). See Johnson et al., *The Beethoven Sketchbooks* pp. 140 and 149–51. This leads to the conclusion that Beethoven composed the work entirely in 1804 and completed it rather later in that year than has heretofore been assumed. Kinsky-Halm, p. 132, following Nottebohm's dating of both of the sketchbooks, assigns the concerto to 1803–4 and assumes it was completed by the time that Beethoven offered it to Breitkopf & Härtel on August 26, 1804. But Beethoven's brother Carl, it seems, had already offered the concerto ("Konzertant für alle Instrumente für Klavier, Violonzello and Violin") to that publisher in October 1803 (TDR, vol. 2, p. 620). Either that offer was made when the concerto was scarcely begun, or, conceivably, it referred to the earlier *concertante* that Beethoven had sketched in the Kessler book and written up partially in score. See p. 138.

7. J. Kerman, "Tovey's Beethoven," in *Beethoven Studies 2*, ed. Tyson, p. 188; Tovey, *Essays in Musical Analysis*, vol. 3, p. 96.

8. A. F. Schindler, *Beethoven As I Knew Him*, ed. Donald W. MacArdle, trans. Constance S. Jolly (Chapel Hill: University of North Carolina Press, 1966), p. 140. We must remember that Schindler probably had no firsthand memory of this performance, and that he is in general not trustworthy. What he and all subsequent commentators (see, for example, *The New Grove*, vol. 2, p. 395) took to be the composition's first public performance apparently was not. A correspondent's report from Vienna in the *AmZ* (10, col. 623) assigns this Augarten concert to sometime in May of 1808; another notice (*AmZ* 10, cols. 490–91) comments on a performance in Leipzig (solo parts played by "Mad. Müller, Hr. Matthäi, und Hr. Dozzauer") that had occurred before Easter of that year.

9. Czerny, *On the Proper Performance of All Beethoven's Works for the Piano*, ed. Badura-Skoda, p. 108.

10. TDR, vol. 2, p. 499. Siegfried Kross argues that the movement is influenced by Beethoven's improvisatory style, and that these melodic similarities should be seen as "transformations and extensions of a single thematic kernal." See "Improvisation und Konzertform bei Beethoven," *Beiträge '76–78*, ed. Klein, p. 136. But the themes are presented with all the requisite connections and preparations of a large-scale formal movement, forcing us to evaluate them, surely, in this context.

11. The initially fragmentary nature of these motives is essential to the idea of Beethoven's grand experiment. Their ultimate absorption into the compelling larger design of the movement has been accounted for in various ways. One approach has been the venerable one of Walter Riezler, Walter Englesmann, and Rudolf Réti, who find elaborate unifying derivations and correspondences among motives in this movement, and, indeed, in the entire composition. Quite different is Schenker's concept of interacting structural levels construed mainly as linear motions that transcend local events such as themes or motives. See the summary of this matter in Lewis Lockwood, " 'Eroica' Perspectives: Strategy and Design in the First Movement," in *Beethoven Studies 3*, ed. Tyson, pp. 85–95. Neither sort of explanation in any way overrules the fragmentary nature of the individual motives in Beethoven's exposition. Dahlhaus returns again and again to his idea of an antithesis between "processuality" or "goal-directedness" and thematic fixity. For him the *locus classicus* of the indeterminate subject is the beginning of the first movement of Beethoven's Sonata Op. 31, No. 2. Its very indeterminacy, demanding continuation, forms the "real" subject at hand. See *Ludwig van Beethoven: Approaches to His Music*, pp. 167–71. And quite specifically: "Thematic material that is 'in the service of the form' is almost always melodically rudimentary" (p. 89), and "The outstanding characteristic of the first movement of the 'Eroica' Symphony has always been felt to be that the musical form is a process in the emphatic sense, an urgent, unstoppable forward motion" (p. 173).

12. In this period themes originating in the bass occur in the *Leonore* Overtures Nos. 2 and 3, as well.

13. The effect is redoubled—and historical performance practice probably more nearly observed—if the cellist plays with a largely straight tone, as Anner Bylsma does in the fine recording with Paul Badura-Skoda, Franz Josef Maier, and the Collegium Aureum (Deutsche Harmonia Mundi, 1990).

14. In a letter of 1796 to the piano builder Streicher, Beethoven complained that the piano

was too often treated like the harp. See *Briefwechsel*, vol. 1, p. 32; Anderson, *Letters*, vol. 1, pp. 25–26.

15. Beethoven's thoughts about the cello as preeminent in this ensemble may be related to the remarkable resemblance of this finale theme to that of the Sonata for Piano and Cello in G minor, Op. 5, No. 2.

16. In mm. 17–18 the winds momentarily play a typical polonaise rhythm in a kind of military-band context.

17. Letter of December 1812. See *Briefwechsel*, vol. 2, p. 302; Anderson, *Letters*, vol. 1, p. 391. This observation comes up in reference to the Piano-Violin Sonata Op. 96, which the Archduke was to play with the French violinist Pierre Rode (who, Beethoven observed, disliked such *rauschendere Passagen*).

18. *AmZ* 10 (1807–8), col. 623.

19. *Essays in Musical Analysis*, vol. 3, p. 102.

20. In his introductory essay to the Eulenburg miniature score of Op. 56, Wilhelm Altmann says that the first concertos for this ensemble other than Beethoven's were those of the twentieth-century composers Emanuel Moor, Paul Juon, Alexander Tcherepnin, and Alfredo Casella.

21. See Barry Brook, "The *Symphonie concertante*: Its Musical and Sociological Bases," *International Review of the Aesthetics and Sociology of Music* 6 (1975), p. 13 and passim.

22. Ibid.

23. TDR, vol. 2, p. 620; *Briefwechsel*, vol. 1, p. 218.

24. See the discussion of this composition in Richard Kramer, "An Unfinished Concertante of Beethoven," in *Beethoven Studies* 2, ed. Tyson, pp. 33–65; and above, p. 138. Kramer (p. 45, n. 19) calls attention to a sketch in Landsberg 10 from sometime in 1803 that might be an idea for another abortive triple concerto; there is a remote possibility that Carl Beethoven had this in mind when he offered such a piece to Breitkopf & Härtel in October 1803.

25. Schindler, *Beethoven As I Knew Him*, ed. McCardle, pp. 111–12 and 190.

26. Anderson, *Letters*, vol. 1, p. 48; *Briefwechsel*, vol. 1, p. 64.

27. Maynard Solomon, "Beethoven's Magazin der Kunst," in *Beethoven Essays*, especially pp. 196–204.

28. There is a fairly extensive literature claiming influence from current French composers on Beethoven's works, particularly his overtures, from just after this time. See Arnold Schmitz in the *Neues Beethoven Jahrbuch* (1925), p. 104; and Boris Schwartz, "Beethoven and the French Violin School," *MQ* 44 (1958), pp. 431–47.

29. The letters are quoted in Erich H. Müller, "Beethoven und Simrock," *N. Simrock Jahrbuch* 2 (1929), 23–24 and 27.

30. Anderson, *Letters*, vol. 1, p. 106–7; *Briefwechsel*, vol. 1, p. 207.

31. In Beethoven's mind the name and notion *concertante* also attached to this composition; in the *Eroica* Sketchbook he described the sonata as "scritta in uno stilo molto concertante quasi come d'un Concerto."

32. Quoted in Müller, "Beethoven und Simrock," p. 23.

33. Ibid., p. 28.

NOTES TO CHAPTER 9

1. J. J. Rousseau, *Dictionnaire de musique* (Amsterdam: M. M. Rey, 1768), pp. 141–42. Rousseau elaborates: "The actor, in a state of agitation, transported by a passion that will not permit him to speak fully, interrupts himself, stops, hesitates, at which time the orchestra speaks for him; and these silences, thus filled out, move the listener infinitely more than if the actor himself had uttered all that is heard in the music."

2. Examples of this sort of recitative (chosen almost at random) can be seen in Handel's *Tamerlano*, act 2, scene 3; Mozart's Scena and Rondo "Ch'io mi scordi di te," K. 505; *Così fan tutte*, act 1, scene 9, and act 2, scene 7 (these last with parodic intent). Sometimes orchestral interjections of this kind occur within arias of similar affect. A familiar example is Donna Elvira's "Ah fuggi traditore" from the first act of *Don Giovanni*. Recognition of recitative and arioso in this movement of Beethoven's concerto has been surprisingly absent in the literature on the subject. Klaus Körner's article "Formen musikalischer Aussage im Zweiten Satz des G-Dur-Klavierkonzertes von Beethoven," *Beethoven-Jahrbuch* 9 (1973–77), pp. 201–16, is an exception; but here the staccato, agitated, disjunct, dotted-note figures of the strings are (quite wrongly, I think) associated with the vocal part of recitative.

3. In this section the two personae also cooperate in a rising stepwise sequence of root-position triads, from A up to E, in which parallels are averted by the time-tested pattern of $\hat{5}$–$\hat{6}$ over each bass tone.

4. Edward Cone, "Beethoven's Orpheus—or Jander's?," *19th Century Music* 7/3 (Spring 1985), p. 284.

5. Ibid.

6. "Representing a Relationship: Notes on a Beethoven Concerto," *Representations* 39 (Summer 1992), p. 90.

7. The bass note, B, drops out but must be understood as the continuing root from m. 55 all the way to m. 62, where it reappears. What is left in the intervening measures is an apparent diminished seventh, routinely described by late eighteenth-century theorists as a dominant ninth with the root suppressed—exactly the present configuration.

8. Thayer-Forbes, p. 573. Treitschke was the librettist for the 1814 version of the opera.

9. Owen Jander, "Beethoven's 'Orpheus in Hades': The Andante con moto of the Fourth Piano Concerto," *19th Century Music* 8/3 (Spring 1985), p. 196. In his tenth-anniversary reconsideration of the matter, Jander retracted the designation "program music" while retaining and expanding his opinion about the concerto's dependence upon the Orpheus myth. "Orpheus Revisited: A Ten-Year Retrospect on the Andante con moto of Beethoven's Fourth Piano Concerto," *19th Century Music* 19/1 (Summer 1995), pp. 31–49.

10. "Orpheus Revisited," p. 195. Adolf Bernhard Marx, *Ludwig von Beethoven: Leben und Schaffen* (Berlin, 1859), pp. 92–93.

11. Czerny, *On the Proper Performance of All Beethoven's Works for the Piano*, ed. Badura-Skoda, p. 110.

12. Tovey, *Essays in Musical Analysis*, vol. 3, pp. 80–81.

13. E. M. Forster, *Abinger Harvest* (London, 1936), p. 135. Kerman, who borrows this reference to Forster from Roger Fiske (*Beethoven's Concertos and Overtures* [London: Ariel Music, 1986], p. 36), uses it as a starting point for his own interesting discussion of the concerto in "Representing a Relationship," *Representations* 39 pp. 80–101. He

clouds the prehistory of Forster's inspiration a bit by putting the date of Marx's book on Beethoven from 1859 back to 1830. Ibid., p. 83.

14. See my discussion in *Schumann As Critic* (New Haven: Yale University Press, 1967), pp. 111–34.

15. Marx, *Ludwig van Beethoven*, pp. 92–93.

16. See the able discussion of these matters in Scott G. Burnham, *Aesthetics, Theory and History in the Works of Adolph Bernhard Marx*, especially chapters 1, 2, and 5.

17. NZFM 3 (1835), p. 152; *Jugendbriefe von Robert Schumann*, ed. Clara Schumann (Leipzig: Breitkopf & Härtel, 1885), pp. 286–87.

18. "Orpheus" Revisited, p. 205.

19. *Briefwechsel*, vol. 5, pp. 278, 282; *Letters*, ed. Anderson, vol. 3, pp. 1113 and 1114. The text of the Choral Fantasy, provided at the last minute, according to Czerny, by the poet Christoph Huffner, is largely an encomium to the powers of music—itself something of an Orphic theme. For Czerny's account of the composition's origins see Thayer-Forbes, p. 448.

20. Book X, lines 17–39.

21. "Orpheus Revisited," pp. 202 and 206.

22. Kerman, "Representing a Relationship," *Representations* 39, p. 100, n. 14.

23. "Orpheus Revisited," p. 205. In this article Jander does not strengthen his argument about Beethoven's reference to the Orphic myth. (See also Joseph Kerman's response to Jander in *19th Century Music* 19 [Spring 1996], pp. 286–87.) Jander's expansion of the purported connection to include more of the Orpheus story and all the movements of the concerto (the finale, for example, recalling Orpheus's destruction at the hands of raving Bacchantes, p. 44) places an intolerable strain on our credulity. And the hypothesis that the Andante con moto was originally a piece for solo piano (p. 33) is quite unsupported. The first edition rather exceptionally printed this movement on four staves in the piano part, thus explicitly underlining the separation of the two performing forces.

24. *AmZ* 11 (1820), cols. 155–56.

25. This opening theme was apparently one of Beethoven's first ideas for the concerto. It appears as a "concept sketch," probably written in early 1804, in Landsberg 6 (the "Eroica" sketchbook).

26. Some later examples are the beginnings of Schubert's well-known Impromptu in A♭ (D. 935), Schumann's *Carnaval*, and (most marvelous of all) Schubert's late Sonata in B♭, whose textural resemblance to Beethoven's opening continues in its massive doubling, with the melody followed at both the octave and the sixth below.

27. He may have been lured into this adventure by the suggestive stepwise motion after downbeats in his theme, downward in m. 2, inviting a suspension (which is done "correctly" in mm. 19 and 20), and upward in m. 3, inviting a lower appoggiatura.

28. Our ears require the tonic of m. 27 to resolve to the dominant of m. 28, an anomaly Charles Rosen points out in *The Classical Style*, pp. 387–88. But this has to do with incessant repetitions of the "question" motive, not with any doubt about what is tonic and what dominant.

29. The sketches show uncertainty about the harmonic configuration of this theme. Landsberg 10 (p. 6) has a version in which the minor segment modulates down a whole step.

30. This not as an introductory flourish to a subsequent sounding of the theme as in Mozart's D-minor and C-minor Concertos, say, but a substitution—as if the opening of the movement counts as the soloist's definitive delivery of the theme.

31. "Representing a Relationship," *Representations* 39 p. 88.

32. Among Mozart's mature piano concertos, beginning with K. 271, the only two exceptions are K. 271 itself and K. 459 in F. It hardly seems coincidental that K. 271 is the single Mozart concerto in which, as in the work at hand, the piano participates in the opening.

33. The effect is further undercut by a somewhat qualified preparation. Beginning eight measures in advance (m. 245), the bass strings and horns hold the dominant while the upper instruments effect a descent in tenths—an approximation of the falling $^6_3$ figure common at this point. But this return is less than triumphal: it remains pianissimo until the last instant, and then just as a crescendo gets underway the bass surprisingly forsakes the dominant in a disruptive chromatic upward motion to the sixth degree before making the cadence.

34. That it should continue to play at all was, as we recall, an innovation for Beethoven in the C-minor Concerto, but prefigured in Mozart's concerto in that key.

35. The occurrences of d'''' in modern scores, as at mm. 300 and 318 of the first movement, were an innovation of the Breitkopf & Härtel collected edition of the 1860s.

36. J. F. Reichardt, *Vertraute Briefe geschrieben auf einer Reise nach Wien und den Oesterreichischen Staaten zu Ende des Jahres 1808 und zu Anfang 1809* (Amsterdam, 1810), vol. 1, p. 257. A report from Leipzig in May 1809 mentions a performance of the Fourth Concerto, calling it "the most wonderful, the most distinctive, the most inventive, the most difficult of all that Beethoven has written." *AmZ* 9 (1809), col. 523.

37. *Essays in Musical Analysis*, vol. 3, p. 76.

38. *The Classical Style*, p. 392.

39. As in the move to E minor by m. 12 in the Symphony No. 99 in E♭, or the near approach to D♭ in m. 15 of the Symphony No. 102 in B♭.

40. Only two finales among Mozart's concertos having a solo-tutti ritornello begin with the tutti: the Piano Concerto K. 467 and the Horn Concerto K. 412.

41. A similarly subdued occurrence of the theme appears, remarkably, as a viola duet shortly before its third formal statement (m. 368); here it follows its usual modulatory path to the fifth above, this time E♭-B♭.

42. Tovey, *in Essays in Musical Analysis*, vol. 3, p. 82 calls the entire section "the central episode with a new theme, consisting of nothing but energetic arpeggios of tonic and dominant chords." But even if we do not grant thematic status to the arpeggios (which seems to me the point of the passage), the determined working of the ritornello theme in the "interpolations" and in the latter part of this section would seem to preclude thinking of it as an "episode." And there is no theme.

43. Ibid., p. 81.

44. "La cadenza sia corta." The cadenza that Beethoven himself supplied, presumably in 1809, recapitulates the appearances of the second theme in C and G, together with some piano figuration typical of this movement.

45. Thayer gives a good summary of eyewitness reports of this concert (Thayer-Forbes, pp. 446–48). The concert took place at the Theater an der Wien on the same evening as the annual charity event of the Tonkünstler-Sozietät at the Burgtheater, where Haydn's *Il Ritorno di Tobio* was performed by the leading singers of the city. It was something of a tribute to Beethoven that an assemblage of musical cognoscenti including Moscheles, Reichardt, Czerny, Emanuel Doležalek, and a reporter for the *AMZ* of Leipzig, should all have been there to record their impressions.

46. *Vertraute Briefe*, p. 257.

47. *Beethoven Werke*, vol. 3/3, ed. Küthen, *Kritischer Bericht*, p. 6; *The New Grove*, vol. 2, p. 395.

48. *AmZ* 9 (1807), col. 400; and *Journal des Luxus und der Moden* 22 (1807), p. 254. Only the latter mentions a concerto: "Beethoven gab in der Wohnung des Fürsten L. zwei Concerte, worin nichts als seine eigenen Compositionen aufgelegt wurden, nämlich seine vier ersten Symphonien . . . , ein Clavierconcert, und einige Arien aus der Oper Fidelio."

49. See TDR, vol. 2, pp. 527–28; *The Letters of Beethoven*, ed. Anderson, pp. 150, 152, 156, and 166. For the contract with Clementi, written in French, see *The Letters of Beethoven*, pp. 1419–20. The disruptions of Napoleon's wars were apparently responsible for the failure of Clementi's plans for publication. See Leon Plantinga, *Muzio Clementi* pp. 196–99.

50. The principal surviving sketches are in the first fifteen pages of the miscellany, Berlin, Deutsche Staatsbibliothek, Landsberg 10.

51. Matthäus Andreas Stein performed a concerto of Beethoven's, apparently the Third, in the Schuppanzigh series in the summer of 1805. The following spring both Josepha Auernhammer and a certain Herr Leidesdorfer performed the Third Concerto at their own concerts, and Czerny played the First Concerto at the Schuppanzigh series in summer 1806. See Morrow, *Concert Life in Haydn's Vienna* pp. 332–39. Beethoven's star pupil Ferdinand Ries was at this time living in Paris.

52. Wegeler-Ries, *Biographische Notizen*, trans. Noonan, pp. 102–3.

53. Thayer-Forbes, p. 450.

54. See Morrow, *Concert Life in Haydn's Vienna* p. 352.

55. Ibid., p. 351. Ries returned to Vienna from Paris in August 1808. See Cecil Hill, "Ries," in *The New Grove*, vol. 16, p. 8.

56. Vienna, Gesellschaft der Musikfreunde, A 82 b. Nottebohm gave a brief account of this manuscript in *Zweite Beethoveniana*, pp. 74–78; Paul Badura-Skoda provided some transcriptions and described its contents in much more detail in the *ÖMz* 13 (1958), pp. 418–26. More recently, Küthen has discussed it in the editorial report of *Beethoven Werke* 3/3, pp. 5–10; and it is the subject of an article (with further transcriptions) by Barry Cooper, "Beethoven's Revisions to His Fourth Piano Concerto," in Robin Stowell, ed., *Performing Beethoven* (Cambridge: Cambridge University Press, 1994), pp. 23–48.

57. The paper upon which the outer movements are written is rather thick, opaque, greenish, and in the case of the first movement, so severely trimmed as to preserve no watermarks. In the third movement, however, almost all the leaves (from pp. 179 to 276, except for pp. 207–12) show the mark "Kotenschlos"; paper from this Bohemian mill predominated in Beethoven's own manuscripts from mid-1807 to mid-1809. See Johnson, et al. *The Beethoven Sketchbook*, p. 161.

58. The editors of the Breitkopf & Härtel collected edition silently made adjustments at four points (mm. 318, 324, 327, and 329), allowing the piano to rise to d″″ by way of analogy with earlier occurrences of the same music. The Eulenburg score, edited by Wilhelm Altmann, has in all these cases restored the reading of the first edition. An optional version of m. 300 in the Breitkopf & Härtel score (with the indication "ossia"), rising to d″″, does not appear in the first edition but is retained in the Eulenburg score.

59. The transcriptions offered here differ at points from those given by both Badura-Skoda

and Cooper. Cooper has continued and supplemented Beethoven's sketchy notations in ways that are often subjective.

60. It is hard to believe that Beethoven would not have intended some ornamentation in the right hand for the later parts of this example, especially in view of the rather lavish ornament of the music it replaces. At the beginning of the example, Beethoven specifies a penultimate harmony that corresponds with neither the measures just before the cadenza nor a progression in either of the two cadenzas he later wrote for this movement.

61. This problem had already been taken care of in the version of "a₁" in the coda at m. 347.

62. Czerny later attempted a systematic description of the sorts of passages in which a ritard was usual; one such was "almost any place where the composer has written 'espressivo.'" *Vollständige theoretisch-practische Pianoforte-Schule*, Op. 500 (Vienna: Diabelli, 1839), vol. 3, p. 26. And as William Newman points out, there are at least two places in his sonatas (in Opp. 96 and 109) where Beethoven writes *espressivo* followed by *a tempo*. William Newman, *Beethoven on Beethoven* (New York: Norton, 1988), p. 114.

63. *Zweite Beethoveniana*, pp. 74–75. Küthen offers the interesting theory that the revisions were made for an arrangement for piano and string quintet, of which the string parts (alone) survive in a copy in the Berlin Staatsbibliothek. *Beethoven Werke, Kritischer Bericht*, 3/3, pp. 8–11 and 15–16. Küthen attributes this arrangement to the Viennese composer and violinist Franz Alexander Pössinger (1767–1827), who is probably referred to in a cryptic note in an unidentified hand—probably that of someone at the publishing house—on the last page of the Viennese (engraver's) copy of the concerto ("Clav. Conc. Pöss. 2 zu senden"; facsimile in *Kritischer Bericht*, p. 9). Pössinger evidently arranged *Don Giovanni* as an "Oper in Duetto für 2 Violinin" and the 1814 version of *Fidelio* for string quartet. Küthen, *Kritischer Bericht*, p. 16. A similar note on the London copy of Beethoven's Violin Concerto may possibly relate to the arrangement of that work for piano solo. See Chapter 10, note 62. Certain of Beethoven's corrections in the orchestral parts of the Vienna copy, Küthen reports, are reflected in the string parts of the revision (*Kritischer Bericht*, p. 8). But there is really no evidence that the revisions in the piano part were made specifically for the (now nonexistent) piano part of the arrangement. It is not clear why a version with string quintet would require a more elaborate and virtuoso solo part. One might rather think that a part for piano is not included with the arrangement because none was ever needed: by mid-1808 it was easily available in published form.

64. *Zweite Beethoveniana*, p. 75.

65. See Edwin M. Good, *Giraffes, Black Dragons, and Other Pianos*, pp. 82 and 91. The Piano Trio in E♭, Op. 70, composed in mid-1808 (sketched in the *Pastoral* Symphony sketchbook) also requires a range up to f⁗.

66. See pp. 125–30.

67. Barry Cooper's implication that Beethoven's revisions can be incorporated directly into a new edition or performance is misleading. Cooper, "Beethoven's Revisions," pp. 33–34. Any attempt to do so must entail a good deal of interpretation and surmise—commodities that Cooper's transcriptions provide in abundance.

NOTES TO CHAPTER 10

1. Tovey, *Essays in Musical Analysis*, vol. 3, p. 88; Tyson, "The Textual Problems of Beethoven's Violin Concerto," *MQ* 53 (1967), p. 482; The quotation in the title of this chapter is from Thomas Gray, "Elegy Written in a Country Churchyard."

2. Hans Engel, *Das Instrumentalkonzert*, vol. 2, p. 188.

3. From the time of Theocritus (fl. 3d century B.C.) the pastoral had strong associations with Sicily.

4. Tovey, *Essays in Musical Analysis*, vol. 3, p. 90.

5. Something similar happens, we recall, at the onset of the fourth tutti in the first movement of the Triple Concerto. But there the discordant gesture was not prepared in advance and seems less justified by the overall expressive context (see p. 165).

6. In the progression toward F major in m. 57, the introduction of the lowered seventh of D minor has about it an antique sound reminiscent of the Mixolydian mode; similar motions in the second theme of the first movement of the "Emperor" Concerto, as well as in the minor variation of the slow movement of the Fifth Symphony (m. 166) show the full bass and harmonic pattern of the ancient *folia*.

7. A well-known example from a slow movement occurs in the Andante con moto of the Fifth Symphony; there, in a "third variation" (mm. 185ff.) of the initial theme, its quiet gravity is turned into an exultant declaration for full orchestra.

8. Scott Burnham makes a similar point in *Beethoven Hero* (Princeton: Princeton University Press, 1995), pp. 50–52.

9. But at the pause on the dominant, the first violins hold up forward progress with a cadenza-like passage, much like that of the oboe in the Fifth.

10. Dahlhaus considered obscurity of this sort a hallmark of Beethoven's "new path" as reported by Czerny. Musical form here forsakes a pattern of "theme with commentary" for a radical "processuality" (*Prozessualität*) based upon thematic material that is, paradoxically, at the same time non-thematic. See Dahlhaus, *Ludwig van Beethoven und seine Zeit* (Laaber: Laaber-Verlag, 1987), p. 208; and Mary Whitall's translation, *Ludwig van Beethoven*, p. 167.

11. Hans Joachim Moser, "Die Form des Beethovenschen Violinkonzerts," *Neues Beethoven-Jahrbuch* 9 (1939), p. 17. Later, Moser compares the first tutti to the *Kettungstypus* ("chain-structure") exemplified by the overture to Gluck's *Alceste* of 1767 and still later (adopting the terminology of Alfred Lorenz) describes it as the first of two *Stollen* of a "sonata-bar" that "contrary to rule takes the form of a final reprise." Ibid., pp. 18 and 20.

12. At the entrance of T_2 that theme is ushered in with a three-measure extension (mm. 221–23). The surprising modulation to C major in the same section is announced with 2 + 5 measures.

13. *Beethovens Zwei Prinzipe*, p. 26.

14. *Wiener Theater-Zeitung*, Jahrgang 2 (1807), p. 27. Reprinted in Stefan Kunze, ed., *Ludwig van Beethoven. Die Werke im Spiegel seiner Zeit, Gesammelte Konzertberichte und Rezensionen bis 1830* (Laaber: Laaber-Verlag, 1987), p. 80.

15. Anticipation of the cadence in m. 3 momentarily suggests a $\frac{3}{4}$ meter. Owen Jander calls attention to a resemblance to the sarabande in "Romantic Form and Content in the Slow Movement of Beethoven's Violin Concerto," *MQ*, p. 171.

16. The romanesca, of which the best-known example is probably *Greensleeves*, typically

has a bass motion such as 3-7-1-5, 3-7-1-5-1. Chaconne basses assumed various forms, some of which Richard Hudson lists in *The New Grove*, vol. 4, pp. 101–2. While the descending tetrachordal varieties of the chaconne resemble bass patterns of the passacaglia, the former are usually in major, the latter frequently in minor.

17. This pattern of downward motion by fifths below and by chromatic steps above, yielding the intervals 3-7-3-7 etc., was a normal part of eighteenth-century compositional technique. We earlier noted a particularly beautiful example of it in the second theme of the first movement of Mozart's G-minor Symphony, K. 550, at mm. 44ff.

18. An earlier example, also in C major, of a chromatically descending bass line is the Trio of the Scherzo in the String Quartet Op. 18, No. 2.

19. Erich Schenk cites many examples from Fux, Beethoven's early teacher, Albrechtsberger, Cherubini, Haydn, and Mozart in "Barock bei Beethoven," in Arnold Schmitz, ed., *Beethoven und die Gegenwart. Ludwig Schiedermair zum 60. Geburtstag* (Berlin and Bonn: Ferd. Dümmlers Verlag, 1937), pp. 177–219, esp. 180–93.

20. Though not nearly so many as Schenk makes out in "Barock bei Beethoven," pp. 180–210. Schenk concentrates almost exclusively on instances of the descending chromatic tetrachord he finds in Beethoven's music. But his criteria are much too generous: he recognizes as "Baroque" virtually any succession of semitones (down or up), in any voice, in any harmonic context. Thus in the second act of *Fidelio*, he cites (p. 196) as an example the passage "Es ist ja bald um ihn getan" (presumably mm. 75ff.) in the trio "Euch werde Lohn." But this chromatic line (upward, and in an upper voice) occurs in the course of an ordinary modulation from D minor to F major, and there is nothing Baroque about it. The same must be said of his citation (p. 204) from the Sonata Op. 14, No. 2 (first movement, mm. 52ff.), where the upward chromatic bass line is a purely ornamental prolongation of a cadential $^6_4$ chord—and of many others of his examples.

21. Beethoven's horns, unable to play the requisite pitches above the seventh and sixth degrees in the bass, drop out in mm. 33–35; a sad thinning of the texture is aggravated as the clarinets and bassoons are reduced to unisons. This is one passage in Beethoven that might profitably be emended in modern performance (another is the point in the recapitulation of the first movement of the Fifth Symphony, mm. 303–6, where the E♭ horns, unable to play their horn call in C major, are feebly supplanted by bassoons). The opening of this passage in the Violin Concerto inexplicably exchanges viola and second violin parts; one may suspect that inexact parallels of this sort result from Beethoven's writing from memory rather than from copying.

22. The formal shape of this theme can perhaps best be seen as a "rounded binary" pattern in which the first segment, mm. 1–8, has internal repetition (with open and closed endings) but is not itself repeated.

23. This time both halves of the rounded binary form are repeated.

24. The only double stops in the concerto are in two brief parallel passages of soloistic figuration in the finale at mm. 68ff. and 242ff.

25. The Eulenburg score of 1967, edited by Alan Tyson, puts m. 83 in the higher octave, restoring the symmetry. The piano transcription of the concerto did the same from the beginning.

26. Reported from several sources in Morrow, *Concert Life in Haydn's Vienna*, pp. 340–41.

27. *AmZ* 9 (1806–7), col. 235.

28. Carl Czerny, *Vollständige theoretisch-praktische Pianoforte-Schule* vol. 4, p. 117; and

idem, *On the Proper Performance of All Beethoven's Works for the Piano,* ed. Badura-Skoda, p. 115. See also TDR, vol. 2, p. 538.

29. The Violin Concerto was probably worked out in a missing sketchbook from 1806–7 that likely also included sketches for the Fourth Piano Concerto, the *Coriolan* Overture, and the Fourth Symphony. Shin Augustinus Kojima attempts to connect the leaf in Landsberg 10 with Beethoven's stay during September and October 1806, at Prince Lichnowsky's country castle, Schloss Grätz, near Troppau in Schleswig. He notes the similarity of the paper of this leaf to that of the autograph of the Sonata Op. 57 (*Appassionata*). See "Die Solovioline-Fassungen und-Varianten von Beethovens Violinkonzert op. 61," *Beethoven-Jahrbuch* 8 (1971–72), pp. 102–3. It has sometimes been assumed that this latter manuscript was written at Schloss Grätz because, according to a notation of M. Bigot from many years later, the manuscript was soaked through in a rainstorm Beethoven encountered during the return trip from the Schloss to Vienna (the document itself, now in the library of the Paris Conservatory, attests to such a soaking). See Thayer-Forbes, p. 407. Beethoven also used that paper type (FS with three half-moons) for the autograph of the String Quartets Op. 59, now in the Berlin Staatsbibliothek; it is inscribed "angefangen am 26ten Maj-1806." But the autograph of the *Appassionata* may have been written out well before this, since Beethoven had offered it to Breitkopf & Härtel as early as August 1804. Kojima's attempt to identify the dark ink of the *Appassionata* autograph and that of the Landsberg leaf (ibid.) with the ink Beethoven used at at Schloss Grätz is not convincing.

30. *Briefwechsel*, vol. 1, pp. 288–89 and 292–93; *Letters*, ed. Anderson, vol. 1, pp. 152–53 and 156–57.

31. In support of his argument that the autograph for the concerto was not yet begun at Schloss Grätz, Ernst Herttricht mentions as well that the ink of the manuscript's first stage (light brown) is quite different from that used in the single surviving letter from this period, that of September 3 to Breitkopf & Härtel (dark brown). See *Beethoven Werke. Kritischer Bericht*, ed. from a manuscript of Shin Agustinus Kojima by Ernst Herttricht (Munich: Henle, 1995), Abt. III, Bd. 4, pp. 8–9. But of course there may have been various inks available at Schloss Grätz; the ink used in a single letter adds only minimally to the argument.

32. It has this punning inscription in Beethoven's hand: "Concerto par Clemenza pour Clement primo Violino e direttore al theatro a vienna. Dal L. v. Bthvn 1806" ("Concerto by the grace of and composed for Clement, first violinist and director at the theater in Vienna"). The theater in question was the Theater an der Wien.

33. Kojima made a cogent argument for this conclusion in "Die Solovioline-Fassungen und-Varianten von Beethovens Violinkonzert op. 61," pp. 97–145, esp. pp. 102–4. Kojima distinguished, according to color of ink, placement on the page, and cuing in of corrections, two principal stages in the solo violin part. Stage 1 (1a) together with its corrections (1b), written in light-brown ink, is virtually integral and complete. Stage 2, written in blank staves at the bottom of the page with dark brown ink, represents a series of alternatives to many of the readings of Stage 1, some of them taken up into the final published version, and some not. In addition, there are some pencil notations of ideas for the piano transcription of the concerto in the lower staves of the document. On the basis of Beethoven's use of inks in dated letters of the time, and particularly because the darker ink was used to cross out some of the sketches for the piano transcription, first commissioned by Muzio Clementi in April 1807, Kojima concluded that Stage 2 dated from the months after the first performance, and that the integral

Stage 1 was used for the copying of parts for that performance. Kojima was the editor of the text of the concerto for the *Neue Beethoven-Ausgabe* published in 1973 but died before completing the critical report for that volume. Ernst Herttrich, who finished this work based on Kojima's manuscript, reinforced these arguments as to the dating of the stages of writing in the violin part and presented all versions in schematic form (but unfortunately with serious printing errors) in *Beethoven Werke*, Abt. III, Bd. 4, *Kritischer Bericht* (Munich, 1994). In their work with the text of the concerto, Kojima and Herttricht built upon and responded to a rich tradition of scholarship on the subject. Here are the principal earlier studies, some of which are cited above: Gustav Nottebohm, *Zweite Beethoveniana*, pp. 586–90; Oswald Jonas, "Das Autograph von Beethovens Violinkonzert," *ZfMw* 13 (1931, pp. 443–50; Paul Mies, "Die Quellen des Op. 61 von Ludwig van Beethoven," *Kongressbericht Köln 1958* (Kassel-Basel, 1959), pp. 193–95; Fritz Kaiser, "Die authentischen Fassungen des D-dur-Konzertes op. 61 von Ludwig van Beethoven," *Kongressbericht Kassel 1962* (Kassel-Basel, 1963), pp. 196–98; Alan Tyson, "The Textual Problems of Beethoven's Violin Concerto," *MQ* 53 (1967), pp. 482–502; Willy Hess, "Die verschiedenen Fassungen von Beethovens Violinkonzert," *Beethoven-Studien* (Bonn/Munich-Duisberg, 1972), pp. 163–68.

34. This version first shows up in the manuscript copy B, now in the British Library, that served as *Stichvorlage* for the first Viennese edition of 1808–9.

35. The violinist Syoko Aki kindly played over and commented on many of these earlier versions for me. With one exception, all the octave passages, though treacherous, she found playable. The exception is the A♭ passage in the finale (Example 10-7b), a near impossibility for the violinist. On the more violinistic nature of the revisions see Nottebohm, *Zweite Beethoveniana*, p. 587; and Oswald Jonas, "Das Autograph von Beethovens Violinkonzert," pp. 443–44. Assuming that Clement had a hand in the revisions are Otto Jahn, "Beethoven und die Ausgaben seiner Werke," *Gesammelte Aufsätze über Musik* (Leipzig, 1867), p. 325; and Willy Hess, "Die verschiedenen Fassungen von Beethovens Violinkonzert," p. 168. Kojima ("Die Solovioline-Fassungen," p. 106) dismisses this assumption as "mere legend."

36. In a performance of what was billed as the "original version" of the concerto with the New York Philharmonic Orchestra under Dimitri Mitropoulos in 1950, Szymon Goldberg played the upper octave at this point to marvelous effect (a privately-made taping was released on compact disc in Japan in 1994). What Goldberg played adopted some earlier readings from the autograph but is far from an integral "version."

37. See p. 215.

38. In a version that probably predated the first performance (it is crossed out in the autograph), that undifferentiated passage was even longer: it began with some sixteenth-note noodling in the solo during the orchestra's playing of "b_1." In the concerto as we know it, the corresponding place in the recapitulation has the first measure of triplets (m. 469) but in the next one inexplicably reverts to the sixteenths of the earlier version.

39. In the supplementary volumes to the old Breitkopf & Härtel edition, Willy Hess published an *Urfassung* of the Violin Concerto that really consists of two versions: that of Stage 1 of the autograph; and the readings of Stage 2 with all the missing passages supplied from Stage 1. The real value of this edition is that it presents in Stage 1 the likely true first version of the work.

40. See Pamela J. Willetts, *Beethoven and England: An Account of Sources in the British*

Museum (London: Trustees of the British Museum, 1970), p. 34. Beethoven had given this manuscript to his English friend, the pianist and cellist Charles Neate, upon Neate's return to London in 1816. See *Briefwechsel*, vol. 3, p. 220; Anderson, *Letters*, vol. 2, p. 557.

41. The first edition shows a number of mistakes and misunderstandings in its replication of the text of B. This gives rise to two slightly variant texts in current use. The first is that of the old Breitkopf & Härtel *Gesamtausgabe* (1863, probably edited by Ferdinand David), which, though based upon the first edition, corrected some of its errors through a comparison with B. This is the source from which orchestral parts are commonly derived. The other source is that of all the older miniature scores, such as the undated one of Peters (plate no. 3801) edited by Wilhelm Altmann, which derive from the first edition alone. See Tyson, "The Textual Problems of Beethoven's Violin Concerto" pp. 488–89. In this article Tyson provides what is still the clearest account of the sources for this composition. He shows that the orchestral parts for the first edition are derived directly from B. He believes that the violin part, however, though very closely related to B, was apparently taken from their common source, now lost. Kojima has disputed this conclusion, pointing out that the discrepancies Tyson found between the violin parts of B and C can be explained by the existence of two separate printings of the part in C (the revised version having been undertaken to improve the page turns).

42. Fritz Kaiser, "Die authentischen Fassungen des D-dur-Konzertes op. 61 von Ludwig van Beethoven," p. 197.

43. Kojima, "Die Solovioline-Fassungen," p. 110.

44. Two notable errors in the first edition were the omission of the cellos' thematic participation in "b_1" in the coda of the first movement (mm. 529 to the end) and a missing measure (217) in the finale. Both these mistakes were caught by the editors of the old *Gesamtausgabe*, who obviously made use of copy B in addition to the first edition.

45. One point at which they differ is the figuration of the solo violin at m. 83 of the finale (in Tyson's "The Textual Problems of Beethoven's Violin Concerto," p. 499, a misprint places the problem in the *first* movement): Tyson puts the violin part up an octave to preserve parallelism with the surrounding measures; Kojima leaves it where it is.

46. See *Briefwechsel*, vol. 1, p. 316; Anderson, *Letters*, vol. 1, pp. 172–73.

47. These are described in Leon Plantinga, *Muzio Clementi:* pp. 193–96. One plan was to buy Beethoven's music from Breitkopf & Härtel for half of what the Leipzig publisher had paid the composer.

48. From a facsimile of the letter in the papers of Florence Wilshire at the Beinecke Library, Yale University.

49. The contract is printed in Thayer-Forbes, pp. 418–19.

50. In a letter of December 1808, Clementi reported to his business partner, Collard, Beethoven's claim that he had sent all the compositions in two installments. But Beethoven's payment for his music was held up, for whatever reason, until about April 10, 1810, that is, until about the time of Clementi's partial publication of the music. See Plantinga, *Muzio Clementi*, p. 199.

51. Tyson shows this convincingly in "The Textual Problems of Beethoven's Violin Concerto," p. 487. One leaf of the *Stichvorlage* for Clementi's edition seems to have survived. Among Clementi's manuscripts in the Library of Congress is a page from the first oboe part, the verso of which the parsimonious composer-publisher subsequently used to sketch a movement of his "Duettini" for piano, four hands (WoO 25). Kojima

and Herttrich surmise that the orchestral parts sent to London may have been those used in the original performance of 1806. See the *Kritischer Bericht*, p. 6.

52. Kojima and Herttricht conclude that the piano part was issued by the Bureau des Arts et d'Industrie in late summer 1808, some six months before the version for violin, which evidently appeared in the first months of 1809. See *Kritischer Bericht*, p. 7.

53. See Nottebohm, *Zweite Beethoveniana*, p. 587; Jonas, "Das Autograph," p. 444.

54. Kojima, "Die Solovioline-Fassungen," p. 106–7.

55. Other places where Stage 1 and Stage 2 differ and the piano part follows the former are: first movement, mm. 223, 388, 439, 442, 456, 465, 471, and 496; finale, m. 51.

56. Speaking of his aversion to piano concertos, E. T. A. Hoffmann wrote, "They are supposed to exploit the virtuosity of the individual player in solo passages and in melodic expressiveness, but the very best player on the very finest instrument strives in vain to equal what the violinist, for example, can achieve with little effort." David Charlton, ed., *E. T. A. Hoffmann's Musical Writings*, trans. Martyn Clarke, (Cambridge, 1989), p. 101.

57. There is a similar problem in the same movement at mm. 465ff.; in the second movement (m. 17) such attempted parallel motion results in gratuitous dissonance.

58. Another place where the tonic degree in the bass is sadly missing from the piano is in the Rondo theme of the finale—in all four occurrences of it.

59. See *Briefwechsel* vol. 1, pp. 310–11; Anderson, *Letters*, vol. 1, pp. 166–67. The "notes additionnelles" apparently refer to the extension of the keyboard to c⁗, an innovation of London piano makers in the early 1790s, and one familiar to Beethoven at least after the acquisition of his Érard piano in 1803. See above, pp. 128–29.

60. See Czerny, *On the Proper Performance of All Beethoven's Works*, ed. Badura-Skoda, p. 9; and Ries-Wegeler, *Biographische Notizen*, trans. Noonan, p. 82.

61. See pp. 239–40.

62. Kaiser thinks he knows who this person was. On the verso of the final folio of Copy B is the cryptic notation, "Pössinger pressant," a reference no doubt to the same Franz Pössinger who was a mysterious presence in the corresponding source for the Fourth Piano Concerto (see above, Chapter 9, note 63). What may have been "pressing" in regard to Pössinger we do not know, but Kaiser points to him as the arranger of both the solo violin and piano parts (though one might wonder why an urgent message about him should appear on the back of a manuscript in which both solo parts are completely written out). See Kaiser, "Die authentischen Fassungen," p. 197.

NOTES TO CHAPTER 11

1. Anderson, *Letters* vol. 1, 117; *Briefwechsel*, vol. 1, p. 219. Ries-Wegeler, trans. Noonan, p. 68; Schindler, *Beethoven As I Know Him*, ed. MacArdle, p. 116.

2. *Briefwechsel*, vol. 1, p. 265; Anderson, *Letters*, vol. 1, p. 142.

3. Letter from Napoleon to Jérôme, November 1807, quoted in George Rudé, *Revolutionary Europe, 1783–1815* (London, 1964), p. 257.

4. *Briefwechsel*, vol. 2, p. 29; Anderson, *Letters*, vol. 1, p. 203.

5. *Briefwechsel*, vol. 2, p. 40; Anderson, *Letters*, vol. 1, pp. 211–12.

6. In 1809 one gold ducat was worth about 10 florins (*Wiener Währung*); thus the proposed annuity did not equal what Beethoven reported he had been offered in Kassel. Still, an annual salary of 4,000 florins at this time would have put Beethoven's financial

status among the higher ranks of civil servants and near the top among actors and musicians. See the list of salaries among various professions in Alice M. Hanson, *Musical Life in Biedermeier Vienna*, pp. 20–22. This list, however, can be taken only as an approximate guide. The florins used as a standard unit here are of the later *Conventionsmünze* variety, having more than twice the value of the older florin (*Wiener Währung*); on the other hand, the time period represented by the list (after 1815) would likely reflect the effects of the very severe inflation that had intervened.

7. TDR, vol. 3, pp. 125–26.

8. Anderson, *Letters*, vol. 1, p. 215; *Briefwechsel*, vol. 2, p. 40.

9. Ries-Wegeler, trans. Noonan, p. 108.

10. Anderson, *Letters*, vol. 1, p. 234; *Briefwechsel*, vol. 2, p. 71.

11. "Emperor" article in *Grove's Dictionary of Music and Musicians*, ed. George Grove (London: Macmillan, 1879), vol. 1, p. 488. In 1936 Tovey called the title "vulgar" and refused to use it. See *Essays in Musical Analysis*, vol. 3, p. 84.

12. An anecdote as to Beethoven's feelings about the renewed presence of French troops in the city comes to us through Wilhelm Rust. He recalled seeing Beethoven shake his fist at a passing French officer and exclaim, "If I, as a general, knew as much about strategy as I the composer know of counterpoint, I'd give you something to do!" Thayer-Forbes, p. 466.

13. Czerny, *On the Proper Performance of All Beethoven's Works for the Piano*, ed. Badura-Skoda, p. 112.

14. Schumann, after listening to this concerto, approvingly remarked, "There is a real difference, whether Beethoven writes straight chromatic scales, or Herz does." *Gesammelte Schriften über Musik und Musiker*, ed. M. Kreisig (Leipzig, 1914), vol. 1, p. 28. Henri Herz (1803–1888) was a virtuoso pianist and composer of the Parisian school whose influence on the current musical scene Schumann considered ruinous.

15. *Essays in Musical Analysis*, vol. 3, p. 85.

16. This variation is one of those in which Corelli, like Beethoven, begins the melody on the upper third rather than on the tonic.

17. Tovey gets this backward when he speaks of "the distant keys of B minor and B major (alias C flat)." *Essays*, vol. 3, p. 85. In our tonal system the motion ♭6–5 is a familiar progression in minor; ♯5–5 is functionally meaningless.

18. See, for example, Felix Salzer, "Die Sonatenform bei Franz Schubert," *Studien zur Musikwissenschaft* 15 (1927), pp. 86–125; and James Webster, "Schubert's Sonata Form and Brahms's First Maturity," *19th Century Music* 2 (1978), especially pp. 18–22. In "Sources of the Three-Key Exposition," *Journal of Musicology* 6 (1988), pp. 448–70, Rey M. Longyear and Kate R. Covington survey a great many sonata-form expositions from before 1820 in an attempt to show that the practice had clear precedents in Classical style. This is rather convincing in the case of minor-keyed movements, where some composers (notably Muzio Clementi in the 1790s and shortly after 1800) availed themselves of both common tonal options for their second groups, namely, the relative major and the dominant minor. But expositions in major are quite another matter. In all the earlier examples Longyear and Covington cite (Mozart, String Quartet in E♭, K. 428; Beethoven, String Quartet in D, Op. 18, No. 3, and Piano Sonata in D, Op. 28) the dominant is very clearly prepared in the preceding transition and firmly established later in the second group. Thus other keys tend to be heard as momentary (and usually whimsical) diversions.

19. Showing a full acceptance of enharmonic equivalents, in these measures Beethoven

puts the piano part in C♭ and the strings in B major. Here are two other good examples of foreground use of the ♭6–5 motion in a cadential context: the ending of the soloist's initial discursus on the first theme (mm. 120–21), and the preparation for R$_2$ in the third movement (mm. 90–91).

20. Many of Beethoven's most striking effects here, as in the Fourth Concerto, avail themselves of the recent extension of the piano keyboard up to f″″.

21. There are only two chords, tonic and dominant; the melodic configuration in the woodwinds forms a common cadential pattern of descending sixths, mainly (and finally) over a dominant pedal.

22. That is, his Concerto Op. 36 in C, the one in A minor (his best known), Op. 85, as well as Op. 89 (B minor), and Op. 110 in E. Similar treatment of this section can be seen in works of other composers of the time: in concertos of Kalkbrenner, Beethoven's pupil Ferdinand Ries, and in Weber's *Konzertstück* (1821). Chopin's two piano concertos still clearly adhere to the tradition.

23. After writing those famous downward triplet scales in the autograph (Berlin, Staatsbibliothek, Beethoven Aut. 15, fol. 25), Beethoven experimented in the bottom staff with another left-hand figuration, an oscillating downward pattern in sixteenths reminiscent of the writing at the corresponding point in the first movement of the First Concerto. It was a good thing, surely, that he decided to leave the passage as it was.

24. Beethovenhaus, MS. NE39. This leaf may have belonged to a homemade sketchbook that Beethoven used in early 1809 between Grasnick 3 and Landsberg 5. Other leaves from this putative book with sketches of the first movement of Op. 73 are in Paris, Bibliothèque nationale, MSS. 72 and 73. See Johnson et al. *The Beethoven Sketchbooks*, 527–29.

25. One must be cautious about this identification, as the sketches also bear some resemblance to features of the beginning of the second tutti, similarly based on the first theme.

26. Czerny, *On the Proper Performance of All Beethoven's Works for the Piano*, ed. Badura-Skoda, p. 113.

27. Ibid.

28. Franz Kullak, again the only later editor to consult the original sources, printed the alla breve slash in the Steingräber edition of ca. 1889, and this edition was taken over by Schirmer in New York in 1902. The mistaken common-time signature still appears in the Kinsky-Halm catalogue but is duly corrected in the new *Beethoven Werke* by Hans Werner Küthen.

29. In some editions, such as the Eulenburg miniature score edited by Wilhelm Altmann, the measures in the second and third movements are numbered together. In the present discussion they are numbered separately, as in the new *Beethoven Werke*. For those using scores with consecutive numbering, it will be necessary in the finale to add 82 to the measure numbers given here.

30. Tovey calls attention to Schumann's extended reuse of a prominent rhythmic figure from this movement in the "March of the *Davidsbündler* against the Philistines" from *Carnaval*. See Tovey, *Essays in Musical Analysis*, vol. 3, p. 87. But by the time Schumann settles on this rhythm (*Molto più vivace*), the battle seems to have turned into something of a rout.

31. In the second of these presentations, that in A♭, Beethoven initially contented himself with just eight measures of this figuration; the second eight measures (173–80) he inserted into the autograph later.

32. After the concert of December 1808, Beethoven essentially stopped playing in public. In one isolated exception he took the piano part in the performance of the "Archduke" Trio at a charity concert in 1814. Louis Spohr, hearing a rehearsal for this event, reported, "It was not a treat, for, in the first piece, the piano was badly out of tune, which Beethoven minded little, since he did not hear it; and secondly, on account of his deafness there was scarcely anything left of the virtuosity of the artist which had formerly been so greatly admired." Thayer-Forbes, p. 577.

33. *AmZ* 14 (1812), col. 8. (Johann Christian) Friedrich Schneider was a highly regarded composer (especially of oratorios), conductor, and Kapellmeister of the city of Leipzig.

34. TDR, vol. 3, p. 167.

35. He also scrawled various instructions to the engraver; one such is "enter wind-instrument music into the first violin part, with expression marks" (*Hier die Blasenden Instrumente in die Violini primi einzutragen mit ausdruckszeichen*). This direction (fol. 15) occurs in the first movement, m. 107, where the violins rest as the winds accompany the piano entrance. Breitkopf & Härtel's engraver did not comply with the instruction.

36. At certain points the first edition diverges somewhat from the autograph in the notation and bass figures in the solo part during tuttis. This occurs particularly at junctures of solos and tuttis, where Beethoven carefully wrote in both functions of the solo instrument, thus sometimes doubling the rhythmic content of individual measures; the first edition simplified these places. Such discrepancies provide only one reason for thinking that the autograph for Op. 73 did not serve directly as the *Stichvorlage* for the Breitkopf & Härtel print of early 1811. The manuscript at some points contains such a thicket of corrections that only an engraver well acquainted with Beethoven's notational idiosyncracies could have made sense of it. There are, moreover, none of the engraver's markings (indicating, say, ends of pages or numbers of measures) that are usually found in *Stichvorlagen*. And while the concerto was in press (October 1810), Beethoven wrote to the publisher: "The reason I ask you to send me the manuscripts together with the proof copy is that I hardly possess any manuscripts, no doubt because some good friend here and there asks me for them. For instance, the Archduke [Rudolph] has the score of the concerto and refuses to let me have it back." Anderson, *Letters*, vol. 1, pp. 296–97; *Briefwechsel*, vol. 2, p. 162. There would seem thus to be two manuscripts of the concerto; the Archduke probably had the autograph, and what Beethoven sent to Breitkopf & Härtel was likely a copy.

37. The question of continuo realization during orchestral tuttis will be discussed in more detail in Chapter 12, pp. 281–93.

38. See note 33. Rochlitz, writing in the journal he edited, the *AmZ*, house organ of Breitkopf & Härtel, was at pains to mention that the newly published concerto was a Breitkopf & Härtel product.

39. The principle was clearly to offer these "o sia" versions for passages exceeding c''''. Both the autograph and the edition, however, miss some of them, such as the climactic scale reaching up to f'''' at the close of the piano's first solo section (m. 227) in the first movement. The corresponding passage at m. 484 supplied such an alternative.

40. We cannot be sure whether or not Beethoven prescribed this alternative passage: a gathering of the autograph is missing at this point, replaced with a later copy that omits the piano part altogether. Beethoven's own notation resumes toward the end of this passage (m. 567), and at that point these is no suggestion of an easier version.

41. *Briefwechsel*, vol. 2, pp. 104–5; Anderson, *Letters*, vol. 1, p. 261.

42. Lydia Goehr discusses this subject with considerable vigor in *The Imaginary Museum of Musical Works: An Essay in the Philosophy of Music* (Oxford: Clarendon Press, 1992). The summary and assessment in her opening chapters of the lively recent debates among philosophers as to the ontological status of the musical work is enlightening and persuasive. The main point of the book, however, that the work idea as a "regulative concept" in music emerged only in the nineteenth century, while containing a kernel of truth, is overdrawn. Particularly so is the claim that prior to this time music was thought of almost solely in connection with particular performances. One thinks, for example, of the fifteenth-century chanson repertory, evidently performed from practical documents such as scrolls, while the "works" themselves might be preserved in elaborate presentation manuscripts (e.g., the Mellon and LaBorde Chansonniers) designed for both beauty and permanence. In his later years J. S. Bach set about to put his lifework in order, compiling his contribution to the highest achievement of the composer's art, *The Musical Offering* and *The Art of Fugue*, in the tradition of the *Kunstbuch*, for which performance was almost beside the point. But the real emancipation of musical texts from particular performances surely came about with the increasingly common publication of music in the seventeenth and eighteenth centuries. The arguments Goehr marshalls against such evidence on pp. 197–203 are beset with misleading or simply erroneous claims. It was not standard practice, for example, for eighteenth-century publications of compositions to list occasions and dates of their first performance (p. 197). And that "opus" referred to a group of pieces rather than a single one (p. 201) was an artifact of the publishing business that remained standard in the nineteenth century—it hardly meant that the collection was thought of only as a single entity, an undifferentiated quantity of music. In the seventeenth and eighteenth centuries people were perfectly capable of distinguishing individual pieces; composition treatises of the period, for example, did it all the time.

43. An interesting recent discussion of this matter is Nicholas Cook, *Music, Imagination, Culture* (Oxford: Clarendon Press, 1990), pp. 122–60.

44. From a letter to Breitkopf & Härtel of November 2, 1809. See *Briefwechsel*, vol. 2, p. 88; Anderson, *Letters*, vol. 1, p. 246.

45. This incomplete movement is identified as Hess 15 after Willy Hess, *Verzeichnis der nicht in der Gesamtausgabe veröffentlichten Werke Ludwig van Beethovens* (Wiesbaden, 1957). The sixty-page partial score is Artaria 184 in the Berlin Staatsbibliothek. Sketches for the work are found in Mendelssohn 1 and Mendelssohn 6, both in the Biblioteka Jagiellońska, Krakow; the Scheide manuscript at Princeton University; and Landsberg 10 and Grasnick 20b, both in the Berlin Staatsbibliothek.

46. "Ein unvollendetes Clavierconcert," *Zweite Beethoveniana*, pp. 223–24; Lewis Lockwood, "Beethoven's Unfinished Piano Concerto of 1815: Sources and Problems," *MQ* 56 (1970), pp. 624–46.

47. A finely detailed and densely argued review of the sources by Nicholas Cook offers certain interpretations that must supersede those of Lockwood. "Beethoven's Unfinished Piano Concerto: A Case of Double Vision?" *JAMS* 42 (1989), pp. 338–74. Cook availed himself of sketches that were missing at the time of Lockwood's writing (Mendelssohn 1 and 6), and, with the extensive help of Clemens Brenneis of the Berlin Staatsbibliothek, was able to make use of recently refined methods of recognizing the original structure of manuscripts. Of the sixty pages of the partial autograph (Berlin, Artaria 184), he shows, only the first forty—together with the insertion of pp. 53–56, which sketch out the continuation of the opening cadenza—constituting the Intro-

duction, T_1, and S_1, are consecutive pages of the score. What follows reverts to sketch-like writing in score format and applies in some cases to parts of the movement that already appear written out on earlier pages in the score as now constituted. Thus a return of the opening cadenza at the putative beginning of the "recapitulation," referred to by several writers, is not supported by the sources.

But, as Lockwood points out in his response to Cook's article (*JAMS* 43 [1990], pp. 382–85), there is also scant support for Cook's hypothesis that at some point Beethoven considered excising the first tutti entirely. Such a supposition depends upon recognition of the integral continuity of leaves (pp. 57–60 of the Berlin manuscript) containing introductory material that may at one time have been inserted into the manuscript just before the first solo. But these are leaves, as Cook admitted, that he had just shown to have the status of "sketches"—hardly to be intended as a legitimate substitute for a section of the score. His attempt to find corroboration in sketches within the Scheide sketchbook for Beethoven's thought of eliminating the first tutti is similarly unconvincing: the nature of the sketching at the crucial point (just before a continuity draft for the beginning of the first solo, or possibly of the recapitulation) has no visible implications for large-scale continuity. Cook's tentative hypothesis, based on this reading, that Beethoven for a moment considered making the piece into "maybe an overture with obbligato piano" (p. 365), in any case—as Lockwood observes—has little to recommend it. And even if the "tutti exposition" were to be omitted, could the work not still have been a concerto?

NOTES TO CHAPTER 12

1. In Vienna, at least, a fair number of players performed concertos not of their own composition. See Morrow, *Concert Life in Haydn's Vienna*, pp. 159–60. Younger performers (and women performers) typically did so, and students, such as Josepha Auernhammer and Ferdinand Ries, pupils of Mozart and Beethoven, respectively, played the works of their teachers. An example of the emphasis on performance in reception of concertos is the notice in the *AmZ* of Ries's playing of Beethoven's Third Piano Concerto (1804): "It was played in masterly fashion. Herr Ries, who had the solo part, is at present Beethoven's only student and his passionate admirer; he had studied the piece entirely under his teacher's tutelage, and played in a very legato, expressive style, as well as with extraordinary facility and confidence in the easy mastery of uncommon technical difficulties." See *AmZ* vol. 6 (1804–5), cols. 776–77.

2. *E. T. A. Hoffman's, Musical Writings* ed. Charlton, p. 101.

3. Leaving out of consideration the very early Concerto in E♭, WoO 4, for which no orchestral parts survive. There is no extant autograph for the Fourth Piano Concerto, but the copy with autograph additions in the library of the Gesellschaft für Musikfreunde in Vienna shows a distinct penchant for improvisatory freedom in the piano part. See pp. 213–16.

4. This seems to be the basic aim of William Newman's (too confidently named) *Beethoven on Beethoven. Playing His Piano Music His Way* (New York: W. W. Norton, 1988).

5. In these matters I may be in partial agreement with that scourge of the historical performance movement, Richard Taruskin. His central point, endlessly repeated in his anthology of essays on the subject (*Text and Act: Essays on Musical Perfor-*

mance[New York: Oxford University Press, 1995]) is that the "authentic" historical performance movement of the twentieth century is, in its aesthetic and practice, not historical at all, but modernist. And it also fails to qualify as "authentic," not merely because it sails under false historical banners, but because Taruskin prefers to reserve the word "authentic" for use in a vaguely anthropological and entirely honorific sense to bestow approval on practices emanating directly from, and reflective of, a particular culture or tradition (even Furtwängler's "unforgettably ham-fisted continuo chords, banged out at full Bechstein blast" in a performance of the Fifth Brandenburg, [p. 106]). For the misguided attempts of the early-music movement to achieve historical accuracy, he coins the plainly pejorative "authentistic" (which he likens to "geometrical" and "dehumanized"). But a problem soon arises: if the early-music movement is in fact an unalloyed artifact of modernism, is it not then a genuine expression of that particular tradition or culture? Authentistic (bad) becomes authentic (good), and Taruskin is ineluctibly led to admit as much (pp. 143 and 151). But then why all the hostile rhetoric? ("Early music has stretched its jaws again. It is engorging Beethoven, and has announced its designs on Schubert and Berlioz," p. 202; ". . . the Early Music hardware snobs I have written about," p. 209; "The first movement [♩. = 60 by Beethoven's prescription] is set at a flabby, self-satisfied 49," p. 226.) Why assail the pianist Boris Berman, playing Prokofiev, for following his own lights (presumably modernist ones) instead of imitating the composer's recordings (pp. 188–89)?

And where does such a doctrine of "authenticity" leave conscientious musicians who wish to break free of their modernist chains and seek out elements of a genuine historical practice? (Taruskin seems to admit such a possibility on pp. 18, 19, 30, 150, 175, and on p. 214, where we find this breezy generalization about one species of historical performance: "In the nineteenth century the question seems simple enough: It [the rejection of Beethoven's metronome indications] was in favor of the inspirational *elastischer Takt*, the Wagnerian 'pure Adagio' that 'cannot be taken too slow.' ") Would such a musician be launched on a foolish quest for an authenticity that is not authentistic, but yet not authentic? It seems impossible to get from Taruskin any consistent idea as to what, if anything, he thinks a performer owes the composer by way of fidelity, to what degree *Werktreue* is to be displaced by *Selbsttreue* (this may be one of the hazards of gathering your essays into one volume, where the contradictions are laid side by side for all to see). Two statements on the subject may stand for many others: "But these are pseudo-ethics, born of a misplaced sense of obligation. A performer cannot please or move the ancient dead and owes them no such effort. There is no way that we can harm Bach or Mozart any more, nor any way we can earn their gratitude" (p. 24); and (by way of castigating Christopher Hogwood for recording an early version of the Fifth Brandenburg) ". . . to offer it as a viable substitute for what Bach offered as representative of his best and most fully elaborated work is manifestly to devalue both that work and the critical sensibility that impelled its revision" (p. 139).

6. See Hugo Daffner, "Die Entwicklung des Klavierkonzerts bis Mozart," *Publikationen der internationalen Musikgesellschaft* (Leipzig: Breitkopf & Härtel 1906), vol. 2/6, pp. 13–15; and Horst Heussner, "Zur Musizierpraxis der Klavierkonzerte im 18. Jahrhundert," *Mozart-Jahrbuch 1967* (Salzburg, 1968), pp. 165–66.

7. See Walter Lebermann, "Zur Frage der Eliminierung des Soloparts aus den Tutti-Auschnitten in der Partitur des Solokonzerts," *Mf* 14 (1961), pp. 200–8; and Charles Rosen, *The Classical Style*, pp. 189–98. Hermann Beck, editor of the first volume of the concertos for the *Neue Mozart-Ausgabe*, explains his position in the *Kritischer*

Bericht, NMA, Ser. V/15/7, p. x. A clear summary of the controversy can be had in Linda Faye Ferguson's superb dissertation, "Col basso and Generalbass in Mozart's keyboard Concertos" (Princeton, 1983), pp. 1–15.

8. An exchange between Küthen and Paul Badura-Skoda appeared in *Das Orchester-Zeitschrift für Orchesterkultur und Rundfunk-Chorwesen* (Mainz: Schott), April, 1988; and February 1989.

9. A good discussion of these developments is Ferguson, "Col basso and Generalbass," pp. 101–76.

10. See James Webster, "On the Absence of Keyboard Continuo in Haydn's Symphonies," *Early Music* 18 (1990), pp. 601–8.

11. In a correspondence report to the *AmZ,* the sharp-tongued G. L. P. Sievers wrote, "Clementi hit upon the idea of conducting from the pianoforte; but already there at the head of the orchestra was Grasset, that excellent conductor of the Italian theater; neither would take the upper hand, and the orchestra did not know whom to follow. . . . Clementi, furthermore, really played nothing—only those isolated chords which he struck as an accompaniment on the piano." *AmZ* 19 (1817), col. 461. See Plantinga, *Muzio Clementi* p. 235.

12. See Webster, "On the Absence of Keyboard Continuo."

13. Heussner, "Zur Musizierpraxis," pp. 168–69, mentions German solo keyboard transcriptions of concertos by Alessandro Scarlatti, Handel, and Vivaldi, and original compositions in this genre from as early as 1716.

14. Heussner, "Zur Musizierpraxis," p. 171, points to compositions of this sort by Johann Matthias Leffloth, Johann Agrell, and Johann Simon Löhlein. In 1763 Bernhard Christoph Breitkopf, the Leipzig publisher, put out a collection of the last-named composer's concertos with a printed keyboard part alone; parts for the other instruments could be had in manuscript copies by special order.

15. See Fritz Oberdörffer, *Der Generalbass in der Instrumentalmusik des ausgehenden 18. Jahrhunderts* (Kassel: Bärenreiter, 1939), pp. 161ff.

16. As translated in Ferguson, "Col basso and Generalbass," pp. 186–87.

17. The parts of K. 242 with Mozart's figures, now in the Memorial Library at Stanford University, come with a joint assurance by Julius André, son of the publisher of many of Mozart's posthumous works, and Heinrich Henkel, cataloguer of the elder André's Mozart collection, that "these parts were used by Mozart himself." The significance of the keyboard part is discussed in Ferguson, "Col basso and Generalbass," pp. 28–29. Mozart's pledge to supply figures for K. 466 is in a letter of January 1786, to Nannerl. Mozart, *Briefe und Aufzeichnungen,* ed. Wilhelm A. Bauer and Otto Erich Deutsch (Kassel: Bärenreiter, 1962–75), vol. 3, p. 483.

18. In one famous case, that of K. 246, Mozart wrote out something like a realization in the keyboard part. But this notation also includes some fragments of wind parts and seems to represent an ad hoc arrangement for a singular performance-situation, perhaps one in which, as Ferguson suggests ("Col basso and Generalbass," pp. 25–29), the solo keyboard cooperated with a second one in representing the orchestral music.

19. See the astute (aside from the interpretation of K. 246) and musicianly article by Paul Badura-Skoda, "Über das Generalbass-Spiel in den Klavierkonzerten Mozarts," *Mozart-Jahrbuch 1957* (Salzburg, 1958), pp. 98 and 103; and Ferguson "Col basso and Generalbass," p. 31.

20. Even C. P. E. Bach, often severe in his demands, had written in this connection, "Not every amateur [*Liebhaber*] is obliged to fulfill all these requirements. He participates in them as much as he wishes, and in as much as his natural gifts permit." See *Versuch über die wahre Art das Clavier zu spielen* (Berlin, 1753), vol. 1, p. 3. Abbé Vogler, in the introduction to the concertos included in his *Betrachtungen* of 1779 (see above, note 16) speaks of "pupils and lady amateurs in particular, blindly martyred on the torture ropes [of figured bass]."

21. Charles Rosen used Emily Anderson's misleading translation of Mozart's letter to his father of May 15, 1774, together with a very partial reading of the evidence of K. 246, to conclude that Leopold made use of continuo playing for concertos only at home, and only in the absence of winds. See *The Classical Style*, p. 193. Rosen's position— to which he may not wish to be held a quarter-century later—is effectively refuted in Ferguson, "Col basso and Generalbass" pp. 11–16, 102–3, and 234.

22. In the second edition of his *Klavierschule* (Leipzig: Schwickert, 1802), p. 150, Türk explained both uses: " 'Violino' or 'Flauto,' also 'Violoncello' etc., one sometimes finds above such passages (usually indicated in small notes) which really are not for the keyboardist but for the instruments named. These passages are entered in the keyboard part so that if necessary, in the absence of an accompaniment, one can play them on the keyboard." As translated by Ferguson, "Col basso and Generalbass," p. 179.

23. Ferguson, ibid., p. 227.

24. Lebermann, "Zur Frage der Eliminierung des Soloparts," p. 205.

25. The orchestral autograph is in the Berlin Staatsbibliothek, and the solo autograph in Bonn, Beethoven-Archiv. The use of these manuscripts for Hoffmeister's print is explained in Beethoven's letter to Hoffmeister of April 22, 1801. See *Briefwechsel*, vol. 1, p. 72; Anderson, *Letters*, vol. 1, pp. 50–52.

26. Toward the end of the first solo in the first movement, mm. 195ff., for example, his revisions and rerevisions used up the staves allotted to the piano and spilled over into the empty staff (the *"leere* Linie,") just above, reserved for corrections of that part. Beethoven resorted to drawing extra ledger-lines freehand at the bottom of the page, but all to no avail: his intent is ultimately unclear.

27. Ferguson first called attention to these markings; "Col basso and Generalbass," p. 249.

28. Lebermann, "Zur Frage der Eliminierung des Soloparts," p. 205.

29. See pp. 65–66. The autograph score, like that of the C-minor Concerto, has the typical copyist's guide numbers.

30. In each case there was apparently one intervening document, neither of which survives, that served as *Stichvorlage*. The autograph is in the Berlin Staatsbibliothek (Beethoven Aut. 15).

31. Alan Tyson has shown rather conclusively that Clementi's edition of the concerto preceded the German one by some months. See *The Authentic English Editions of Beethoven* (London: Faber and Faber, 1963), p. 19. Clementi, perhaps concluding that his customers were by and large without orchestral accompaniments, and in any case no longer adept at reading figured bass, published the piano part with the orchestral reduction alone in the tuttis, that is, without the figures and instructions for their realization. This part thus resembles those of the first editions of the Second, Third, and Fourth Concertos. Clementi specifically addressed the amateur who played alone by offering the solo part separately at a reduced price.

32. Tibor Szász, "Figured Bass in Beethoven's 'Emperor' Concerto: Basso Continuo or

Orchestral Cues?," *Early Keyboard Journal* 6–7 (1988–89), pp. 5–71; and "Beethoven's Basso Continuo: Notation and Performance," in Robin Stowell, ed., *Performing Beethoven* (Cambridge: Cambridge University Press, 1994), pp. 1–22.

33. *Beethoven Werke*, Abt. III, Bd. 3, *Klavierkonzerte* II; *Kritischer Bericht*, pp. 32–43; and "*Gradus ad Partituram*. Erscheinungsbild und Funktionen der Solostimme in Beethovens Klavierkonzerten," in *Musik als Text. 11. Internationaler Kongress der Gesellschaft für Musikforschung, 1993* (Kassel, forthcoming). I am grateful to the author for an advance copy of this article. Küthen deserves credit for perceiving the range of purposes for which published concertos were intended: to accommodate performances in which the soloist also directed the orchestra, those in which the first violinist was in charge, performance as *Hausmusik* with reduced forces, and the like. He also comments perceptively on the manifest problems of performing difficult music by an ensemble of which no member has a score. But a claim that Beethoven's figured bass indications in the "Emperor" are wholly irrelevant to any intended performance of the piece, but rather a by-product of Beethoven's use of the autograph as a kind of exercise book for his pupil, is difficult to sustain. Here are some inevitable questions: Why would Beethoven set about to teach the Archbishop figured bass in a musical genre in which (according to Küthen's claim) the practice did not apply? Why choose, for such an exercise, his own manuscript, soon to be sent for copying and engraving, thus allowing all these irrelevant markings to appear in the German edition and create confusion? (Küthen calls the appearance of the Breitkopf & Härtel edition deceptive [*trügerisch*]; *Kritischer Bericht*, p. 42. But in the long list of corrigenda Beethoven sent to the publisher in May 1811, there is no mention of the continuo figures.) And what kind of instruction is this, in which there is no sign of the student's participation? Very compelling evidence would be needed, surely, to counter such objections. What one can gather from Küthen's exposition is the following: Beethoven evidently did assemble (mainly from Türk's *Kurze Anleitung zum Generalbass-spielen*, 1791), at just about this time, some materials for teaching the Archduke figured bass. Certain slash marks in the autograph (which did not survive in any edition) resemble Türk's analytical symbols for marking off phrases (*Einschnitte*). And there are various associations between the pupil and this concerto: it is dedicated to him; he had possession of the autograph for a time; a separate copy of the piano part (with figures) was in his library; he returned from exile after Napoleon's occupation of Vienna at about the time when Beethoven would have written those figures in the later stages of work on the autograph; there may be a motivic similarity between the finales of the concerto and of the Sonata Op. 81a that expressly celebrates the Archbishop's return. But these associations of the Archduke, figured bass, and the concerto fall far short of any reasonable standard of evidence needed to make the case.

34. The string quintet version, never published, survives in a set of parts (the piano part is missing) in the Berlin Staatsbibliothek. See the full description in Küthen, *Klavierkonzerte II, Kritischer Bericht*, pp. 10–11; and above, Chapter 9, note 63. Regarding the arrangement of the Violin Concerto for piano see above, Chapter 9, note 63, and pp. 243–49. Each arrangement is closely connected with an authentic source and was probably authorized by Beethoven.

35. Ferguson has singled out the middle movement of the Fourth Concerto, that grave dialogue whose very essence is short-term alternation between piano and strings, as an exception to this general rule. For this movement the publisher of the first edition,

Mollo, took the extraordinary step of expanding the piano part to four staves, two for the solo, the other two for a reduction of the strings. Ferguson believes this highly unusual format signals that in this single case no continuo playing is expected of the soloist, and Szász agrees with her. Ferguson, "Col basso and Generalbass," pp. 265–68; Szász, "Beethoven's Basso Continuo," *Performing Beethoven*, ed. Stowell, pp. 13–15. The printed piano part does not explicitly invite this conclusion, as it presents the bass line in the tuttis entirely in large notes and the reduction of the (unison) strings above in small ones—presumably invoking the rule that the large notes are always to be played. But that other established practice of omitting the continuo in close exchanges with the orchestra might well apply here; even more pertinent, perhaps, is the unique opposition of keyboard and strings (those traditional allies) throughout this movement, providing further grounds for the soloist's silence during tuttis.

36. In 1799 the prominent music critic Friedrich Rochlitz, first editor of the *AmZ* observed that "Concerto players are given to ornament their parts, and are unable to break this habit even during the tuttis." See "Bruchstücke aus Briefen an einen jungen Tonsetzer. Dritter Brief," *AmZ* 2 (1799), col. 20.

37. Letter to Hoffmeister, *Briefwechsel*, vol. 1, p. 72; Anderson, *Letters*, vol. 1, p. 52.

38. Reported in *Caecilia* 9 (1828), pp. 219–20; quoted in Thayer-Forbes, vol. 1, p. 329.

39. Thayer-Forbes, vol. 1, p. 448. This testimony may also cast doubt upon the deduction of Richard Maunder, "Performing Mozart and Beethoven Concertos," *Early Music* 17 (Feb. 1989) pp. 139–40, that Mozart, in performances of his concertos in theaters, sat alone on stage with the orchestral players in the pit in front of it.

40. As reported in Nottebohm, *Zweite Beethoveniana*, p. 75.

41. See Chapter 9, pp. 213–16.

42. See Chapter 9, note 36.

43. Wegeler-Ries, trans. Noonan, p. 101.

44. A concise account of the matter is given in Edwin M. Good, *Giraffes, Black Dragons, and Other Pianos*, pp. 69–95.

45. *Briefwechsel*, vol. 4, p. 77; Anderson, *Letters*, vol. 2, p. 686.

46. William S. Newman, *Beethoven on Beethoven*, p. 53; Thayer-Forbes, p. 984.

47. The autographs are in Zurich and Paris; there is a fine facsimile edition, edited by Willy Hess, in *Ludwig van Beethoven: The Complete Cadenzas* (Zurich: Eulenburg, 1979).

48. And it remains so in the otherwise splendid recording of Melvyn Tan and Roger Norrington (EMI, 1989). The effect is augmented, in fact, by the strained sound of the top register of Tan's instrument, a reproduction of a Streicher piano of 1814, presumably with range to f'''', of which the cadenza uses all but the top two keys. There is a certain ease about this high range in modern pianos (which, after all, go up to c''''') that makes the top notes of this cadenza sound less radical, as in the fine recording of Alfred Brendel and James Levine (Philips Live Recordings, 1983).

49. Anthony Newman (with Stephen Simon, Newport Classics, 1987) supplies a presumably newly-composed cadenza for the first movement of the C-major Concerto that stays mainly within the range available in 1801 (there are a couple of errant a'''); but the music seems excessively dramatic and overwrought for its context. Glenn Gould's famous cadenza for this movement in his astonishingly lucid recording of 1958 (with Vladimir Golschmann, Columbia, reissued on compact disc, Sony Classical, 1992) sounds like a Stravinskian parody of a Bach fugue.

50. With Christopher Hogwood, L'Oiseau-Lyre, 1988.

51. "Resisting the Ninth," *19th Century Music* 12 (1988–9), pp. 241–56; repr. Taruskin, *Text and Act*, pp. 235–61.

52. *AmZ* 2 (1799–1800), cols. 20–21.

53. Owen H. Jorgenson has shown that the methods of tuning keyboard instruments used until the end of the nineteenth century were incapable of producing strict equal temperament. See his *Tuning: Containing the Perfection of Eighteenth-Century Temperament, the lost Art of Nineteenth-Century Temperament, and the Science of Equal Temperament* (East Lansing: Michigan State University Press, 1991), pp. 1–7. A recent discussion of this subject, including its specific application to the music of Beethoven, is Robin Rysavy, "Selected Piano Compositions of Beethoven and Schubert, and the Effect of Well Temperament on Performance Practice" (D.M.A. diss., University of Missouri, Kansas City, 1997).

54. See Mark Lindley, "Temperament," *The New Grove*, vol. 17, pp. 667–69. In his piano method of 1828 J. N. Hummel provided a rudimentary self-help method of tuning a piano in which the temperament is set simply by tuning all fifths, in turn, a trifle flat (with no checks). This method is "easier and more convenient," he says, as one cannot "assume such a sharp ear, among many who engage in tuning, as to distinguish accurately the fine variations of the various chords in irregular temperament." He complained, further, about the lack of a standard tuning, especially in wind instruments: "One is constructed according to the tuning in use in Dresden, another to that in Vienna, a third to that in Berlin." J. N. Hummel, *Ausführliche theoretisch-praktische Anweisung zum Piano-Forte Spiel* (Vienna: Tobias Haslinger, 1828), p. 442.

55. Both as quoted by Lindley, "Temperament," p. 669.

56. See Plantinga, *Schumann As Critic* pp. 69–70. Rita Steblin provides a detailed survey of characterizations of the keys from Mattheson to Berlioz in *A History of Key Characteristics in the Eighteenth and Early Nineteenth Centuries* (Ann Arbor: UMI Research Press, 1983).

57. Anton Felix Schindler, *Beethoven As I Knew Him*, ed. MacArdle, trans. Jolly, p. 368.

58. C major had two rather consistent affective associations: "completely pure . . . innocence, simplicity, naivety" (Schubart); "grandiose, military . . . serious, majestic, and tumultuous" (Francesco Galleazi, *Elementi teorico-pratici de musica*, 1796). There is less agreement about E major. Schubart speaks of "laughing pleasure and yet not complete, full delight"; Galleazi calls it "a very piercing key," and Abbé Vogler says it is "very penetrating. Has not E always been chosen in all operas where Eumenides appear?" Ab ranges from a "gentle night key" (Vogler) to "the key of the grave" (Schubart). These quotations are all from Steblin, *A History of Key Characteristics* pp. 223, 252–53, and 281. In 1813 Beethoven wrote (in his trademark faulty French) to the publisher George Thomson that the key of Ab was entirely unfitting for an air he was setting, marked "amoroso," making it seem more like "barbaresco." *Briefwechsel*, vol. 2, p. 321: Anderson, *Letters*, vol. 1, p. 406.

59. Schindler, *Beethoven As I Knew Him*, p. 423.

60. Published in the *AmZ* of December 1817, in two brochures (with assurances of authenticity) by Beethoven's publisher Steiner in 1818, and in the parallel first editions of the "Hammerklavier." A convenient listing of all the works involved, and of all the metronome markings for the symphonies and string quartets (together with the range of tempos from modern representative recordings), is given in Peter Stadlen, "Beethoven und das Metronome," *Beiträge '76–78.* pp. 57 and 69–72.

61. Schindler was among the first to find Beethoven's tempos for fast movements too fast. He speculated wrongly (in the midst of various other errors) that two models of the metronome the composer used gave very different results, and that the fast tempos for the symphonies were calculated using the larger, slower-beating machine. Schindler, *Beethoven As I knew Him*, p. 425. Stadlen, "Beethoven und das Metronom," pp. 62–67, gives an account of his extensive tests of historical metronomes (in which he even simulated the effects of repeated oiling over time with applications of a mixture of green olive oil and dust), concluding that Schindler's opinion was without merit. Willem Retze Talsma, *Anleitung zur Entmechanisierung der Musik* (Innsbruck: Wort und Welt, 1980), has postulated that for his fast movements (only) Beethoven doubled the note values he actually intended to correspond with his metronome markings (thus MM: $\half$ = 80 really means $\quarter$ = 80). For a telling refutation of this notion, see William S. Newman, *Beethoven on Beethoven*, pp. 85–86.

62. Rudolf Kolisch, "Tempo and Character in Beethoven's Music," trans. Arthur Mendel, *MQ* 29 (1943), pp. 169–87 and 291–312. One stalwart holdout in this matter is Nicholas Temperley: "Beethoven's marks are almost useless as guides to performance speeds." "Tempo and Repeats in the Early Nineteenth Century," *ML* 47 (1966), p. 323. This in the course of an interesting article on the conductor Sir George Smart's timings of performances, from 1819 to 1843, of some 140 compositions by Haydn, Mozart, Beethoven, and many other composers. Attempts to determine Smart's tempos are inconclusive, largely because of uncertainty about taking of repeats, possible cuts, and time taken between movements.

63. Johann Joachim Quantz, *Versuch einer Anweisung die Flöte traversiere zu spielen* (Berlin: C. F. Voss, 1752); trans. Edward R. Reilly as *On Playing the Flute* (London: Faber and Faber, 1966), pp. 284–86.

64. *Briefwechsel*, vol. 4, p. 130; Anderson, *Letters*, vol. 2, p. 727. Sieghard Brandenburg, editor of the *Briefwechsel*, places this letter (undated by Beethoven) in November 1817. Mosel's article was published in the *Wiener allgemeine musikalische Zeitung* at the end of November.

65. Kolisch, "Tempo and Character in Beethoven's Music"; Hermann Beck, *Studien über das Tempoproblem bei Beethoven.* (Diss. Erlangen, 1954); and "Bemerkungen zu Beethovens Tempi," *Beethoven-Jahrbuch* 2 (1955–56) pp. 25–54.

66. The relevant Chapters 2 and 3 reprinted *On the Proper Performance of All Beethoven's Works for the Piano*, ed. Paul Badura-Skoda.

67. Ibid., p. 1.

68. Gustav Nottebohm, *Beethoveniana* (Leipzig: Rieter-Bidermann, 1872), vol. 1, p. 136.

69. Newman and Stephen Simon (see above, note 49); Tan and Norrington (see above, note 48); Serkin and Ormandy (recorded in the 1950s, rereleased on CBS); Gould and Golschmann (see above, note 49). The tempo for the Serkin-Ormandy performance is from Robert Winter, "Performing Beethoven's Early Piano Concertos," *Early Music* 16 (May 1988), p. 223. Winter surveys the tempos taken for this movement among pianists over a fifty-three year period from Schnabel to Perahia; the majority played it slower, but not hugely so, than Czerny advocated. Ibid., p. 224.

70. Gould and Bernstein, 1958 (Sony Classical, 1992), $\half$ = 132; Schnabel and Dobrowen (1947; EMI, 1993), $\half$ = 138; Perahia and Haitink (CBS, 1986), $\half$ = 132; Lubin, op. cit., $\half$ = 138–44.

71. Kolisch, op. cit., p. 309.

72. Lubin and Hogwood, L'Oiseau-Lyre, 1987; Newman and Simon (Newport Classic, 1987); Levin and Gardiner (DG, 1987).

73. Ibid., p. 293. Beck more reasonably compares this movement with the Serenade for Flute, Violin, and Cello, Op. 25, and suggests a tempo of $\downarrow$ = 126. Beck, "Bemerkungen zu Beethovens Tempi," pp. 47–48.

74. As in the recordings of Ma, Zeltser, Mutter, and Karajan (DG, 1980), and of Bylsma, Badura-Skoda, and Maier (Harmonia Mundi, 1988).

75. Modern performances of the first movement of the Fourth Concerto almost unanimously favor a tempo of about $\downarrow$ = 108 (Schnabel, Gould, Perahia, Lubin), just under Czerny's 116. In the Violin Concerto, Heifetz and Munch many years ago closely approximated Czerny's $\downarrow$ = 126 (RCA reissue, 1985). Later violinists like it slower: Grumiaux and Davis (Philips, 1974) play at 112, Perlman and Barenboim (EMI, 1989) at 108. Czerny, of course, referred specifically to the piano arrangement of the concerto; the young Finnish pianist Olli Mustonen has recorded this movement (London Records, 1993), at Czerny's tempo. Kolisch, even in this piece for violin, is again the outlier, insisting that Beethoven meant the movement to be played *alla breve*, he places it in a group to which he assigns the inexplicable tempo range $\downarrow$ = 84–88.

76. Robert Winter observed that this was the case in his survey of recordings of the first movement of the first Piano Concerto. See above, note 69.

77. Winter, ibid., p. 223, claims that "there is absolutely no evidence that Beethoven thought of common time as inherently slower than ¢." But in the musical tradition of which Beethoven was a part, there was such an understanding. Two prominent theorists of the later eighteenth century, in fact, stipulated that the same values in *alla breve* go twice as fast as in common time. Quantz, *Versuch einer Anweisung*, pp. 285–86, specifically doubles the note values to which the human pulse corresponds when passing from common time to *alla breve*. Kirnberger and his student J. A. P. Schulz, in the article "Vortrag" in J. G. Sulzer's *Allgemeine Theorie der schönen Künste* (Biel: Heilmann, 1777), observed that "further, specific rates and kinds of motion belong to the individual meters. Thus a piece in *alla breve* meter is to be played 'with weight,' but twice as fast [*aber noch einmal so geschwind*] as its note-values show." And, commenting on the third movement of the Sonata Op. 31, No. 1 in G, Czerny remarked, "As the *Allegretto* is in *Alla breve* measure, the whole must be played remarkably quick, *Allegro molto*." Czerny, *On the Proper Performance of All Beethoven's Works for the Piano*, ed. Badura-Skoda, p. 42.

Bibliography

Abrams, M. H. *The Mirror and the Lamp: Romantic Theory and the Critical Tradition*. New York: Oxford University Press, 1953.

Aders, Gebhard. *Bonn als Festung*. Bonn: Ludwig Rohrscheid, 1973.

Adler, Guido. "Ein Satz eines unbekannten Klavierkonzerts von Beethoven." *VfMw* 4 (1888), pp. 451–70.

Albrecht, Theodore, ed. and trans. *Letters to Beethoven and Other Correspondence*. Lincoln: University of Nebraska Press, 1996.

Allenbrook, Wye Jamison. *Rhythmic Gesture in Mozart: "Le Nozze di Figaro" and "Don Giovanni."* Chicago: University of Chicago Press, 1983.

Anderson, Emily, ed. *The Letters of Beethoven*. 3 vols. London: Macmillan, 1961.

Anderson, Emily, ed. *The Letters of Mozart and His Family*. 2d ed. New York : St. Martin's Press, 1966.

Auden, W. H. *The Dyer's Hand and Other Essays*. New York: Random House, 1962.

Bach, C. P. E. *Versuch über die wahre Art das Clavier zu spielen*. Berlin: Henning, 1753; Winter, 1762.

Badura-Skoda, Paul. "Eine wichtige Quelle zu Beethovens 4. Klavierkonzert." *ÖMz* 13 (1958), pp. 418–27.

Badura-Skoda, Paul. "Über das Generalbass-Spiel in den Klavierkonzerten Mozarts," *Mozart-Jahrbuch 1957*, pp. 96–107. Salzburg: Internationale Stiftung Mozart, 1958.

Barth, George. *The Pianist as Orator: Beethoven and the Transformation of Keyboard Style*. Ithaca: Cornell University Press, 1992.

Beck, Herman. "Bemerkungen zu Beethovens Tempi." *Beethoven-Jahrbuch* 2 (1955–56), pp. 24–54.

Beck, Hermann. "Studien über das Tempoproblem bei Beethoven." Ph.D. dissertation: Friedrich-Alexander-Universität, Erlangen, 1954.

Beethoven, Ludwig von. *Briefwechsel Gesamtausgabe*. 7 vols. Edited by Sieghard Brandenburg. Munich: Henle, 1996.

The Beethoven Reader. Edited by Denis Arnold and Nigel Fortune. New York: Norton, 1971.

Beethoven Werke: Klavierkonzerte. Abt. III. Bd. 2–3. Edited by Hans-Werner Küthen. Munich: Henle, 1984–96 [*Kritischer Bericht*, see under Küthen].

Beethovens Werke: Vollständige, kritisch durchgesehene Gesamtausgabe. 25 vols. Leipzig: Breitkopf & Härtel, 1862–65; 1888.

Beiser, Frederick C. *Enlightenment, Revolution, and Romanticism: The Genesis of Modern German Political Thought*. Cambridge, Mass. and London: Harvard University Press, 1992.

Bent, Ian, ed. *Music Analysis in the Nineteenth Century*. Vol. 1: *Fugue, Form, and Style*. Cambridge: Cambridge University Press, 1994.

Bent, Ian, ed. *Music Theory in the Age of Romanticism*. Cambridge: Cambridge University Press, 1996.

Benton, Rita. *Ignace Pleyel: A Thematic Catalogue of his Compositions*. New York: Pendragon Press: 1977.

Biba, Otto. "Beethoven und die 'Liebhaberconcerte.'" In *Beiträge 76–78: Beethoven-Kolloquium 1977: Dokumentation und Aufführungspraxis*, edited by Rudolf Klein, pp. 82–93. Kassel: Bärenreiter, 1978.

Biba, Otto. "Concert Life in Beethoven's Vienna." In *Beethoven, Performers, and Critics*, edited by Robert Winter and Bruce Carr, pp. 77–93. Detroit: Wayne State University Press, 1980.

Block, Geoffrey. "Some Gray Areas in the Evolution of Beethoven's Piano Concerto in B-flat major, op. 19." In *Beethoven Essays: Studies in Honor of Elliot Forbes*, edited by Lewis Lockwood and Phyllis Benjamin, pp. 108–126. Cambridge, Mass.: Harvard University Music Department, 1984.

Bonds, Mark Evan. *After Beethoven: Imperatives of Originality in the Symphony*. Cambridge, Mass.: Harvard University Press, 1996.

Bonds, Mark Evan. *Wordless Rhetoric*. Cambridge, Mass.: Harvard University Press, 1991.

Borges, Jorge Luis. *Other Inquisitions*. Translated by Ruth L. C. Simms. Austin: University of North Texas Press, 1952.

Boyd, Malcolm, ed. *Music and the French Revolution*. Cambridge: Cambridge University Press, 1992.

Brandenburg, Sieghard. "The First Version of Beethoven's G Major Quartet, Op. 18, No. 2." *ML* 58 (1977), pp. 127–52.

Brandenburg, Sieghard, ed. *Kesslerisches Skizzenbuch*. Bonn: Beethovenhaus, 1976–78.

Breuning, Gerhard von. *Aus dem Schwarzspanierhause: Erinnerungen an L. van Beethoven aus meiner Jugendzeit*. Vienna: L. Rosner, 1874. Translated by Henry Mins and Maynard Solomon as *Memories of Beethoven: From the House of the Black-Robed Spaniards*. Cambridge: Cambridge University Press, 1992.

Brook, Barry. "The *Symphonie concertant*: Its Musical and Sociological Bases." *International Review of the Aesthetics and Sociology of Music*, 6 (1975), pp. 9–28.

Brown, A. Peter. *Joseph Haydn's Keyboard Music: Sources and Style*. Bloomington: Indiana University Press, 1986.

Brown, Clive. "The Orchestra in Beethoven's Vienna." *Early Music* 16 (1988), pp. 4–20.

Broyles, Michael. *Beethoven: The Emergence and Evolution of Beethoven's Heroic Style*. New York: Excelsior, 1987.

Burnham, Scott. *Aesthetics, Theory, and History in the Works of Adolf Bernhard Marx*. Ann Arbor: UMI Press, 1988.

Burnham, Scott. *Beethoven Hero*. Princeton: Princeton University Press, 1995.

Churgin, Bathia. Review of *Kesslerisches Skizzenbuch*, edited by Sieghard Brandenburg. *Israel Studies in Musicology* 3 (1983), pp. 171–77.

Citron, Marcia. *Gender and the Musical Canon*. Cambridge: Cambridge University Press, 1993.

Cole, Malcolm. "Sonata-Rondo: the Formulation of a Theoretical Concept in the 18th and 19th Centuries." *MQ* 55 (1969), pp. 180–92.

Cone, Edward. "Beethoven's Orpheus—or Jander's?" *19th Century Music* 8 (1985), pp. 283–86.

Cook, Nicholas. "Beethoven's Unfinished Piano Concerto: A Case of Double Vision?" *JAMS* 42 (1989), pp. 338–74.

Cooper, Barry. *Beethoven and the Creative Process*. Oxford: Clarendon Press, 1992.

Csendes, Peter. *Geschichte Wiens*. Vienna: Verlag für Geschichte and Politik, 1981.

Czerny, Carl. *Erinnerungen aus meinem Leben*. Strasburg: Editions P. H. Heitz, 1968.

Czerny, Carl. *Über den richtigen Vortrag der sämtlichen Beethoven'schen Klavierwerke*. Edited by Paul Badura-Skoda. Vienna: Universal, 1963. Translated as *On the Proper Performance of All Beethoven's Works for the Piano*. Edited by Paul Badura-Skoda. Vienna: Universal, 1970.

Czerny, Carl. *School of Practical Composition, or, Complete Treatise on the Composition of all Kinds of Music*. Translated by John Bishop. London: R. Cocks, 1848.

Czerny, Carl. *Vollständige theoretisch-praktische Pianoforte-Schule*, Op. 500. Vienna: Diabelli, 1839.

Dahlhaus, Carl. "Aesthetische Prämissen der 'Sonatenform' bei Adolf Bernhard Marx." *Archiv für Musikwissenschaft* 41 (1984), pp. 73–85.

Dahlhaus, Carl. "Formenlehre und Gattungstheorie bei A. B. Marx." In *Heinrich Sievers zum 70. Geburtstag*, edited by Günter Katzenberger, Tutzing: Hans Schneider, 1978, pp. 29–36.

Dahlhaus, Carl. *Ludwig van Beethoven und seine Zeit*. Laaber: Laaber-Verlag, 1987. Translated by Mary Whittall as *Ludwig van Beethoven: Approaches to His Music*. Oxford: Clarendon Press, 1991.

Dahlhaus, Carl. *Die Musik des 19. Jahrhunderts*. Laaber: Laaber-Verlag, 1980. Translated by J. Bradford Robinson as *Nineteenth-Century Music*. Berkeley and Los Angeles: University of California Press, 1989.

Dahlhaus, Carl. "Was ist eine musikalische Gattung?" *NZfM* 135 (1974), pp. 620–25.

Davis, Shelley. "H. C. Koch, the Classic Concerto, and the Sonata-Form Retransition." *Journal of Musicology* 2 (1983), pp. 45–61.

Dennis, David B. *Beethoven in German Politics, 1870–1989*. New Haven: Yale University Press, 1996.

DeNora, Tia. *Beethoven and the Construction of Genius: Musical Politics in Vienna, 1792–1803*. Berkeley and Los Angeles: University of California Press, 1995.

Deutsch, Otto Erich. *Mozart: Die Dokumente seines Lebens*. Kassel, 1961. Translated as *Mozart: A Documentary Biography* by Eric Blom, Peter Branscombe, and Jeremy Noble. Stanford: Stanford University Press, 1965.

Deutsch, Otto Erich. *Musikverlagsnummern*. Berlin: Mersburger, 1961.

Eisen, Cliff. *New Mozart Documents: A Supplement to O. E. Deutsch's Documentary Biography*. Stanford: Stanford University Press, 1991.

Engel, Hans. *Das Instrumental Konzert: Eine musikgeschichtliche Darstellung.* Wiesbaden: Breitkopf & Härtel, 1974.

Engel, Hans. "Der angeblich Beethovensche Klavierkonzertsatz." *Neues Beethoven-Jahrbuch* 2 (1925), pp. 167–82.

Epstein, David. *Beyond Orpheus: Studies in Musical Structure.* Oxford and New York: Oxford University Press, 1987.

Fétis, Francois Joseph. "Beethoven." In *Biographie universelle des musiciens.* Paris: Librarie de H. Fournier, 1837.

Forbes, Elliot. "Schuppanzigh." In *The New Grove Dictionary of Music and Musicians,* edited by Stanley Sadie. Vol. 16, pp. 871–72. London: Macmillan, 1980.

Forster, E. M. *Abinger Harvest.* London: Edward Arnold & Co., 1936.

Forman, Dennis. *Mozart's Concerto Form: The First Movements of the Piano Concertos.* London: Hart-Davis, 1971.

Frisch, Walter. *Brahms and the Principle of Developing Variation.* Berkeley: University of California Press, 1984.

Galand, Joel. "Heinrich Schenker's Theory of Form and its Application to Historical Criticism, with Special Reference to Rondo-Form Problems in Eighteenth- and Nineteenth-Century Instrumental Music." Ph.D. dissertation: Yale University, 1990.

Galleazi, Francesco. *Elementi teorico-pratici de musica.* Rome: Cracas, 1791.

Goehr, Lydia. *The Imaginary of Museum of Musical Works: An Essay in the Philosophy of Music.* Oxford: Clarendon Press, 1992.

Good, Edwin M. *Giraffes, Black Dragons, and Other Pianos: A Technological History from Cristofori to the Modern Concert Grand.* Stanford: Stanford University Press, 1992.

Grove, George "Emperor Concerto." In *Grove's Dictionary of Music and Musicians,* edited by George Grove. Vol. 1, p. 488. London: Macmillan, 1879.

Hanslick, Eduard. *Geschichte des Concertwesens in Wien.* Vienna: W. Braumüller, 1869.

Hanson, Alice M. *Musical Life in Biedermeier Vienna.* Cambridge: Cambridge University Press, 1985.

Harding, Rosamond E. M. *The Piano-Forte: Its History Traced to the Great Exhibition of 1851.* Cambridge, 1933.

Hasselt, Luc van. "Beethoven in Holland." *Mf* 18 (1965), pp. 181–84.

Hatten, Robert S. *Musical Meaning in Beethoven: Markedness, Correlation, and Interpretation.* Bloomington: Indiana University Press, 1994.

Herttricht, Ernst. *Beethoven Werke: Kritischer Bericht.* Abt III, Bd. 4. Munich: Henle, 1995.

Hertzmann, Erich. "The Newly Discovered Autograph of Beethoven's 'Rondo a capriccio,' Op. 129." *MQ* 32 (1946), pp. 171–95.

Hess, Willy. *Ludwig van Beethoven: The Complete Cadenzas.* Zurich: Eulenburg, 1979.

Hess, Willy. "Die verschiedenen Fassungen von Beethovens Violinkonzert." *Beethoven-Studien.* Bonn: Beethovenhaus, 1972.

Hickman, Roger. "Romance." *The New Grove Dictionary of Music and Musicians,* edited by Stanley Sadie. Vol. 16, pp. 123–26. London: Macmillan, 1980.

Hoffmann, E. T. A. *E. T. A. Hoffmann's Musical Writings: Kreisleriana, the Poet and the Composer.* Edited by David Charlton. Translated by Martyn Clarke. Cambridge: Cambridge University Press, 1989.

Holschneider, Andreas. "Unbekannte Skizzen Beethovens zur Cello Sonate Op. 5, WoO 36, WoO 37, und Hess Nr. 13 sind nicht im Autograph überliefert." In *Bericht über den Internationalen Musikwissenschaftlichen Kongress Bonn 1970*, pp. 444–47. Kassel: Bärenreiter, 1972.

Hopkins, Antony. *The Seven Concertos of Beethoven*. Aldershot, Hants: Scolar Press, 1996.

Hudson, Richard. "Chaconne." In *The New Grove Dictionary of Music and Musicians*, edited by Stanley Sadie. Vol. 4, pp. 100–02. London: Macmillan, 1980.

Hummel, Johann Nepomuk. *Ausführliche theoretisch-praktische Anweisung zum Piano-Forte Spiel*. Vienna: Tobias Haslinger, 1828.

Jander, Owen. "Beethoven's 'Orpheus in Hades': The Andante con moto of the Fourth Piano Concerto." *19th Century Music* 8 (1985), pp. 195–212.

Jander, Owen. "Orpheus Revisited: A Ten-Year Retrospect on the Andante con moto of Beethoven's Fourth Piano Concerto." *19th Century Music* 19/1 (summer 1995), pp. 31–49.

Jander, Owen. "Romantic Form and Content in the Slow Movement of Beethoven's Violin Concerto." *MQ* 69 (1983), pp. 159–79.

Johnson, Douglas P. *Beethoven's Early Sketches in the "Fischhof Miscellany," Berlin Autograph 28*. 2 vols. Ann Arbor: UMI Press, 1977, 1980.

Johnson, Douglas. "1794–1795: Decisive Years in Beethoven's Early Development." In *Beethoven Studies 3*, edited by Alan Tyson, pp. 1–28. Cambridge: Cambridge University Press, 1982.

Johnson, Douglas, Alan Tyson, and Robert Winter. *The Beethoven Sketchbooks: History, Reconstruction, Inventory*. Berkeley and Los Angeles: University of California Press, 1985.

Jonas, Oswald. "Das Autograph von Beethovens Violinkonzert." *ZfMw* 13 (1931), pp. 443–50.

Jorgenson, Owen H. *Tuning: Concerning the Perfection of Eighteenth-Century Temperament, the Lost Art of Nineteenth-Century Temperment, and the Sciences of Equal Temperament*. East Lansing: Michigan State University Press, 1991.

Kaiser, Fritz. "Die authentischen Fassungen des D-dur-Konzertes op. 61 von Ludwig van Beethoven." *Bericht über den Internationalen Musikwissenschaftlichen Kongress Kassel 1962*, pp. 196–98. Kassel-Basel: Bärenreiter, 1963.

Kalischer, A. Ch. "Die Beethoven-Autographe der königlichen Bibliothek zu Berlin." *Monatshefte für Musikforschung* 27 (1895), pp. 161–73.

Kastner, Georges. *Manuel général de musique militaire*. Paris: Didot Frères, 1848.

Kames, Lord Henry Home. *Elements of Criticism*. Edinburgh: Kincaid & Bell, 1762.

Kerman, Joseph. *The Beethoven Quartets*. London: Oxford University Press, 1967.

Kerman, Joseph. *Contemplating Music: Challenges to Musicology*. Cambridge, Mass.: Harvard University Press, 1985.

Kerman, Joseph, ed. *Autograph Miscellany from circa 1786 to 1799: The British Museum Additional Manuscript 29801*. 2 vols. London: Trustees of the British Museum, 1970.

Kerman, Joseph. "Notes on Beethoven's Codas." In *Beethoven Studies 3*, edited by Alan Tyson, pp. 141–59. Cambridge: Cambridge University Press, 1982.

Kerman, Joseph. "Representing a Relationship: Notes on a Beethoven Concerto." *Representations* 39 (1992), pp. 80–101.

Kerman, Joseph. "Tovey's Beethoven," *Beethoven Studies 2*, edited by Alan Tyson, pp. 172–92. London: Oxford University Press, 1977.

Kerst, Friedrich, ed. *Die Erinnerungen an Beethoven*. Stuttgart: J. Hoffman, 1925.

Kinderman, William. *Beethoven*. Berkeley and Los Angeles: University of California Press, 1995.

Kinsky, Georg. *Das Werk Beethovens: Thematisch-bibliographisches Verzeichnis seiner sämtlichen vollendeten Kompositionen*. Completed and edited by Hans Halm. Munich: Henle, 1955.

Kirkendale, Warren. *Fuge und Fugato in der Kammermusik des Rokoko und der Klassik*. Tutzing: Hans Schneider, 1966.

Koch, Heinrich Christoph. *Musikalisches Lexicon*. Frankfurt-am-Main: August Hermann, 1802.

Koch, Heinrich Christoph. *Versuch einer Anleitung zur Composition*. Vol. 3. Leipzig: Adam Friedrich Böhme, 1793.

Köhler, Karl-Heinz. "Return of Treasures to the Deutsche Staatsbibliothek." *Fonteş artes musicae* 26 (1979), pp. 86–87.

Kojima, Shin Augustinus. "Die Solovioline-Fassungen und-Varianten von Beethovens Violinkonzert op. 61—ihre Entstehung und Bedeutung." *Beethoven-Jahrbuch* 8 (1971–72), pp. 97–145.

Kolisch, Rudolf. "Tempo and Character in Beethoven's Music." Translated by Arthur Mendel. *MQ* 29 (1943), pp. 169–87.

Körner, Klaus. "Formen musikalischer Aussage im zweiten Satz des G-dur-Klavierkonzertes von Beethoven." *Beethoven-Jahrbuch* 9 (1973–77), pp. 201–16.

Kramer, Richard. "Notes to Beethoven's Education." *JAMS* 28 (1974), pp. 72–101.

Kramer, Richard. "On the Dating of Two Aspects in Beethoven's Notation for Piano." In *Beiträge '76–78: Beethoven Kolloquium 1977: Dokumentation und Aufführungspraxis*, edited by Rudolf Klein, pp. 160–73. Kassel: Bärenreiter, 1978.

Kramer, Richard. "The Sketches for Beethoven's Violin Sonatas, Opus 30: History, Transcription, Analysis." Ph.D. dissertation: Princeton University, 1973.

Kramer, Richard. "An Unfinished Concertante by Beethoven." In *Beethoven Studies 2*, edited by Alan Tyson, pp. 33–65. London: Oxford University Press, 1977.

Kramer, Richard. Review of Joseph Kerman, *Autograph Miscellany*. *Notes* 28 (1971–72), pp. 31–34.

Kross, Siegfried. "Improvisation und Konzertform bei Beethoven." In *Beethoven Kolloquium 1977: Dokumentation und Aufführungspraxis*, edited by Rudolf Klein, pp. 132–39. Kassel: Bärenreiter, 1978.

Kunze, Stefan, ed. *Ludwig van Beethoven, Die Werke im Spiegel seiner Zeit: Gesammelte Konzertberichte und Rezensionen bis 1830*. Laaber: Laaber-Verlag, 1987.

Küthen, Hans-Werner. *Beethoven Werke: Kritscher Bericht*. Abt. III, Bd. 2–3. Munich: Henle, 1984–96.

Küthen, Hans-Werner. "*Gradus ad parnassum*: Erscheinungsbild und Funktionen der Solostimme in Beethovens Klavierkonzerten." In *Musik als Text: 11. Internationaler Kongress der Gesellschaft für Musikforschung 1993*. Kassel, forthcoming.

Küthen, Hans-Werner, ed. *Ludwig van Beethoven: Klavierkonzert Nr. 3 in c*. Study score. Kassel, London, New York: Bärenreiter, 1987.

Landon, H. C. Robbins. *Haydn: Chronicle and Works*. 5 vols. Bloomington and London: Indiana University Press, 1976–1980.

Lane, Jay. "The Concertos of Carl Ditters." Ph.D. dissertation: Yale University, 1997.

Layton, Robert, ed. *A Companion to the Concerto*. New York: Schirmer, 1988.

Lenz, Wilhelm von. *Beethoven et ses trois styles*. St. Petersburg: Bernard, 1852–53. Reprint of Paris, 1909, edited with foreword by Joseph Kerman. New York: Da Capo, 1980.

Lewis, J. Lowell. *Ring of Liberation: Deceptive Discourse in Brazilian Capoeira*. Chicago: University of Chicago Press, 1992.

Lindley, Mark. "Temperaments." In *The New Grove Dictionary of Music and Musicians*, edited by Stanley Sadie. Vol. 17, pp. 660–74. London: Macmillan, 1980.

Lockwood, Lewis. *Beethoven: Studies in the Creative Process*. Cambridge, Mass.: Harvard University Press, 1992.

Lockwood, Lewis. "Beethoven's Unfinished Piano Concerto of 1815: Sources and Problems." *MQ* 56 (1970), pp. 524–45.

Lockwood, Lewis. "The Earliest Sketches for the *Eroica* Symphony." *MQ* 67 (1981), pp. 457–78.

Lockwood, Lewis. " 'Eroica' Perspectives: Strategy and Design in the First Movement." *Beethoven Studies 3*, edited by Alan Tyson, pp. 85–105. Cambridge: Cambridge University Press, 1982.

Lockwood, Lewis. Response to Nicholas Cook. *JAMS* 43 (1990), pp. 382–85.

Longyear, Rey M., and Kate R. Covington. "Sources of the Three-Key Exposition." *Journal of Musicology* 6 (1988), pp. 448–70.

Mandyczewski, Eusebius. "Beethoven's Rondo in B für Pianoforte und Orchester," *SIMG* 1 (1899–1900), pp. 295–306.

Marx, Adolf Bernhard. *Die Lehre von der musikalischen Composition*. 2d ed. Leipzig: Breitkopf & Härtel, 1841–51.

Marx, Adolf Bernhard. *Ludwig van Beethoven: Leben und Schaffen*. Berlin: Otto Janke, 1859. Reprint, Hildesheim and New York: G. Olms, 1979.

Maunder, Richard. "Performing Mozart and Beethoven Concertos," response to Robert Winter. *Early Music* 17 (1989), pp. 139–40.

McClary, Susan. *Feminine Endings: Music, Gender, and Sexuality*. Minneapolis: University of Minnesota Press, 1991.

McPhee, Colin. *Music in Bali: A Study in Form and Instrumental Organization in Balinese Orchestral Music*. New Haven: Yale University Press, 1966.

Mies, Paul. "Die Quellen des Op. 61 von Ludwig van Beethoven." In *Kongressbericht Köln 1958*, pp. 193–95. Kassel-Basel: Bärenreiter, 1959.

Milligan, Thomas B. *The Concerto and London's Musical Culture in the Late Eighteenth Century*. Ann Arbor: UMI Research Press, 1979.

Morrow, Mary Sue. *Concert Lie in Haydn's Vienna: Aspects of a Developing Musical and Social Instution*. Stuyvesant, N.Y.: Pendragon Press, 1989.

Moser, Hans Joachim. "Die Form des Beethovenschen Violinkonzerts." *Neues Beethoven-Jahrbuch* 9 (1939), pp. 16–25.

Mozart, Wolfgang Amadeus. *Briefe und Aufzeichnungen*. Edited by Wilhelm A. Bauer and Otto Erich Deutsch. Kassel: Bärenreiter, 1962–75.

Mozart, Wolfgang Amadeus. *The Letters of Mozart and His Family*. Edited and translated by Emily Anderson. London: Macmillan, 1966.

Müller, Erich H. "Beethoven und Simrock." *N. Simrock Jahrbuch*, (1929), pp. 10–62.

Müller-Reuter, Theodor. "Beethoveniana." *Die Musik* 50 (1913–14), pp. 3–15; 86–91.

Musulin, Stella. *Vienna in the Age of Metternich: From Napoleon to Revolution, 1805–1848*. London: Faber and Faber, 1975.

Nagy, Gregory. *Poetry as Performance: Homer and Beyond*. Cambridge: Cambridge University Press, 1997.

Narmour, Eugene. *Beyond Schenkerism: The Need for Alternatives in Music Analysis*. Chicago: University of Chicago Press, 1977.

Newmann, William. *Beethoven on Beethoven: Playing His Piano Music His Way*. New York: Norton, 1988.

Newman, William. "The Recognition of Sonata Form by Theorists of the 18th and 19th Centuries." *Papers of the American Musicological Society* (1946), pp. 21–29.

Nottebohm, Gustav. *Beethoveniana: Aufsätze und Mittheilungen*. Leipzig: J. Rieter-Biedermann, 1872.

Nottebohm, Gustav. *Zweite Beethoveniana: Nachgelassene Aufsätze*. Edited by Eusebius Mandyczewski. Leipzig: Peters, 1887.

Oberdörffer, Fritz. *Der Generalbass in der Instrumentalmusik des ausgehenden 18. Jahrhunderts*. Kassel: Bärenreiter, 1939.

Osthoff, Wolfgang. *Ludwig van Beethoven: Klavierkonzert Nr. 3 c-moll, Op. 37. Meisterwerke der Musik*. Heft 2. Munich: Wilhelm Fink, 1965.

Ozouf, Mona. *La Fête révolutionnaire, 1789–1799*. Paris: Gallimard, 1976. Translated by Alan Sheridan as *Festivals and the French Revolution*. Cambridge, Mass.: Harvard University Press, 1988.

Palmer, R. R. *The Age of the Democratic Revolution*. Princeton: Princeton University Press, 1964.

Perfahl, Jost, ed. *Wien Chronik*. Salzburg: Das Bergland-Buch, 1969.

Picton, H. J. *The Life and Works of Joseph Anton Steffan (1726–1797)*. Ph.D. dissertation: University of Hull, 1976; New York and London: Garland, 1989.

Plantinga, Leon. *Muzio Clementi: His Life and Music*. London: Oxford University Press, 1977.

Plantinga, Leon. *Schumann As Critic*. New Haven: Yale University Press, 1967.

Plantinga, Leon. "When Did Beethoven Compose His Third Piano Concerto?" *Journal of Musicology* 7 (1989), pp. 275–307.

Quantz, Johann Joachim. *Versuch einer Anweisung die Flöte traversiere zu spielen*. Berlin: C. F. Voss, 1752. Translated by Edward R. Reilly as *On Playing the Flute*. London: Faber and Faber, 1966.

Ratner, Leonard. "Harmonic Aspects of Classic Form." *JAMS* 2 (1949), pp. 159–68.

Reicha, Anton. *Vollständiges Lehrbuch der musikalischen Composition*. Edited and translated by Carl Czerny. Vienna: Diabelli, 1832.

Reichardt, J. F. *Vertraute Briefe geschrieben auf einer Reise nach Wien und den oesterreichischen Staaten zu Ende des Jahres 1808 und zu Anfang 1809*. Amsterdam: Im Kunst- und Industrie-Comtoir, 1810.

Reynolds, Christopher. "Beethoven's Sketches for the Variations in E-flat Op. 35." In *Beethoven Studies 3*, edited by Alan Tyson pp. 47–79. Cambridge: Cambridge University Press, 1982.

Ringer, Alexander. "Clementi and the 'Eroica.'" *MQ* 56 (1961), pp. 742–58.

Ritzel, Fred. *Die Entwicklung der "Sonatenform" im musiktheoretischen Schrifttum des 18. und 19. Jahrhunderts*. Wiesbaden: Breitkopf & Härtel, 1968.

Rolland, Romain. *La vie de Beethoven*. Paris: Cahiers de la Quinzaine, 1903. Translated by Ernest Newman as *Beethoven the Creator*. New York: Harper, 1929.

Rosen, Charles. *The Classical Style*. New York: Norton, 1972.

Rosen, Charles. *Sonata Forms*. New York: Norton, 1988.

Rousseau, Jean-Jacques. *Dictionnaire de musique*. Amsterdam: M. M. Rey, 1768.

Rudé, George, *Revolutionary Europe, 1783–1815*. New York: Harper & Row, 1966.

Rysavy, Robin. "Selected Piano Compositions of Beethoven and Schubert and the Effect of Well Temperament on Performance Practice." D.M.A. dissertation: University of Missouri, Kansas City, 1997.

Rydin, Arthur. "Zur ersten Probe des Beethovenschen C-Dur Konzerts." *Die Musik* 50 (1913–14), pp. 283–84.

Salzer, Feliz. "Die Sonatenform bei Franz Schubert." *SzMw* 15 (1927), pp. 86–125.

Scheibe, J. A. *Critischer Musicus.* Leipzig: B. C. Härtel 1745.

Schiedermair, Ludwig. *Der junge Beethoven.* Leipzig: Quelle & Meyer, 1925.

Schindler, Anton F. *Biographie von Ludwig van Beethoven.* Münster, 1840. English translation as *Beethoven As I Knew Him.* Edited by Donald W. MacArdle. Translated by Constance S. Jolly. Chapel Hill: University of North Carolina Press, 1966.

Schmidt-Görg, Joseph, ed. *Des Bonner Bäckermeisters Gottfried Fischer: Aufzeichnungen über Beethovens Jugend.* Bonn: Beethovenhaus, 1971.

Schmitz, Arnold, ed. *Beethoven und die Gegenwart: Ludwig Schiedermair zum 60. Geburtstag.* Berlin: Ferd. Dümmlers Verlag, 1937.

Schmitz, Arnold. *Beethovens Zwei Principe; ihre Bedeutung für Themen-und Satzbau.* Berlin: F. Dümmler 1923.

Scholz-Michelitsch, Helga. *Das Orchester- und Kammermusik von George Christoph Wagenseil: Thematischer Katalog.* Vienna: Böhlau in Komm., 1972.

Schumann, Robert. *Jugendbriefe von Robert Schumann.* Edited by Clara Schumann. Leipzig: Breitkopf & Härtel, 1885.

Schwartz, Boris. "Beethoven and the French Violin School." *MQ* 44 (1958), pp. 431–47.

Schwarz, Boris. *French Instrumental Music Between the Revolutions (1789–1830).* New York: Da Capo Press, 1987.

Shedlock, J. S. "Clementi Correspondence." *The Monthly Musical Record* 32 (1902), pp. 142–61.

Simon, Edwin. "Sonata into Concertos: A Study of Mozart's First Seven Concertos." *Acta musicologica* 31 (1959), pp. 170–85.

Simpson, Adrienne. "Tomášek." *The New Grove Dictionary of Music and Musicians*, edited by Stanley Sadie. Vol. 19, pp. 33–35. London: Macmillan. 1980.

Solie, Ruth, ed. *Musicology and Difference: Gender and Sexuality in Music Scholarship.* Berkeley: University of California Press, 1993.

Solomon, Maynard. "Beethoven's Magazin der Kunst." *19th Century Music* 8 (1984), pp. 199–208. Reprint in Solomon, *Beethoven Essays*, pp. 193–204. Cambridge, Mass.: Harvard University Press, 1988.

Solomon, Maynard. "Beethoven's Productivity in Bonn." *ML* 53 (1972), pp. 165–72.

Solomon, Maynard. "The Creative Periods of Beethoven." *MR* 34 (1973), pp. 30–38. In Solomon, *Beethoven Essays*, pp. 116–25. Cambridge, Mass.: Harvard University Press, 1988.

Solomon, Maynard. *Ludwig van Beethoven.* London: Granada, 1980.

Sonneck, Oscar G., ed. *Beethoven: Impressions by His Contemporaries.* New York: Schirmer, 1926.

Stadlen, Peter. "Beethoven und das Metronome." In *Beethoven Kolloquium 1977: Dokumentation und Aufführungspraxis*, edited by Rudolf Klein, pp. 57–75. Kassel: Bärenreiter, 1978.

Staehelin, Martin. "Brieffragment an Lenz von Breuning." *Beethoven-Jahrbuch* 10 (1978–81), pp. 23–33.

Steblin, Rita. *A History of Key Characteristics in the Eighteenth and Early Nineteenth Centuries*. Ann Arbor: UMI Research Press, 1983.

Steffin, Fritz F. "Ein kleiner Irrtum," *Die Musik* 50 (1913–14), pp. 281–82.

Stevens, Jane. "An 18th-Century Description of Concerto First-Movement Form." *JAMS* 24 (1971), pp. 85–95.

Stevens, Jane. "Patterns of Recapitulation in the First Movements of Mozart's Piano Concertos." In *Musical Humanism and its Legacy: Essays in Honor of Claude V. Palsica*, edited by Nancy Kovaleff Baker and Barbara Russano Hanning, pp. 397–418. Stuyvesant, N.Y.: Pendragon Press, 1992.

Stevens, Jane. "Theme, Harmony, and Texture in Classic-Romantic Descriptions of Concerto First-Movement Form." *JAMS* 27 (1974), pp. 25–74.

Stevenson, A. H. "Watermarks are Twins." *Studies in Bibliography* 4 (1951), pp. 57–91.

Stewart, Douglas. *Elements of the Philosophy of the Human Mind*. Philadelphia: William Young, 1792.

Stowell, Robin. *Performing Beethoven*. Cambridge: Cambridge University Press, 1994.

Strunk, Oliver, ed. *Source Readings in Music History*. Rev. ed. Edited by Leo Treitler. New York: Norton, 1998.

Sulzer, Johann Georg. *Allgemeine Theorie der schönen Künste*. Leipzig: Weidmann, 1771 and 1774.

Szász, Tibor. "Beethoven's *basso continuo*: notation and performance." In *Performing Beethoven*, edited by Robin Stowell, pp. 1–22. Cambridge: Cambridge University Press, 1994.

Szász, Tibor. "Figured Bass in Beethoven's 'Emperor' Concerto: Basso Continuo or Orchestral Cues?" *Early Keyboard Journal* 6–7 (1988–89), pp. 5–71.

Talsma, Willem Retze. *Anleitung zur Entmechanisierung der Musik*. Innsbruck: Wort und Welt, 1980.

Taruskin, Richard. "Another Beethoven Season?" *New York Times* (10 September 1995).

Taruskin, Richard. "Resisting the Ninth." *19th Century Music* 12 (1988–89), pp. 241–56.

Taruskin, Richard. *Text and Act: Essays on Musical Performance*. New York: Oxford University Press, 1995.

Temperley, Nicholas. "Tempo and Repeats in the Early Nineteenth Century." *ML* 47 (1966), pp. 323–36.

Thayer, Alexander Wheelock. *Ludwig van Beethovens Leben von Alexander Wheelock Thayer nach dem Original-Manuskript*. Edited by Hermann Deiters and Hugo Riemann. 3d. ed. Leipzig: Breitkopf & Härtel, 1917.

Thayer, Alexander Wheelock. *Thayer's Life of Beethoven*. Edited by Elliot Forbes. Princeton: Princeton University Press, 1964.

Thompson, Robert Farris. *African Art in Mortion*. Los Angeles: University of California Press, 1974.

Tovey, Donald Francis. *Essays in Musical Analysis*. London: Oxford University Press, 1935–39.

Türk, Daniel Gottlob. *Klavierschule, oder Anweisung zum Klavierspielen*. Leipzig and Halle, 1789. Repr. edited by E. R. Jacobi. Basel: Bärenreiter, 1962.

Tutenberg, Fritz. "Die Durchführungsfrage in der Vorneuklassischen Sinfonie." *ZfMw* 9 (1926–7), pp. 90–94.

Tyson, Alan. *The Authentic English Editions of Beethoven*. London: Faber and Faber, 1963.

Tyson, Alan. "Beethoven's Heroic Phase." *MT* 110 (1969), pp. 139–41.

Tyson, Alan. "Beethoven's Home-Made Sketchbook of 1807–08," *Beethoven-Jahrbuch* 10 (1983) pp. 185–200.

Tyson, Alan. Introduction to *Facsimile of the Autograph Manuscript in the British Library, Add. MS* 37767. London: British Library, 1980.

Tyson, Alan. "Haydn and Two Stolen Trios." *MR* 22 (1961), pp. 21–27.

Tyson, Alan. *Mozart: Studies of the Autograph Scores.* Cambridge, Mass.: Harvard University Press, 1987.

Tyson, Alan and Douglas Johnson. "Reconstructing Beethoven's Sketchbooks," *JAMS* 25 (1972), pp. 137–56.

Tyson, Alan. "The Textual Problems of Beethoven's Violin Concerto." *MQ* 53 (1967), pp. 482–502.

Tyson, Alan. "The 1803 Version of Beethoven's *Christus am Oelberge.*" *MQ* 56 (1970), pp. 551–84.

Vogler, Georg Joseph. *Betrachtungen der Mannheimer Tonschule.* Vol. 2. Mannheim, 1779. Repr. Hildesheim: Georg Ohms Verlag, 1974.

Wade, Rachel. "Beethoven's Eroica Sketchbook." *Fontes artis musicae* 24 (1977), pp. 254–89.

Wallace, Robin. *Beethoven's Critics: Aesthetic Dilemmas and Resolutions during the Composer's Lifetime.* Cambridge: Cambridge University Press, 1986.

Walter, Horst. "Haydn's Klaviere." *Haydn Studien* 2 (1969–70), pp. 256–88.

Weber, Gottfried. *Versuch einer geordneten Theorie der Tonsetzkunst.* 3d ed. Mainz: B. Schotts Söhne, 1830–32.

Webster, James. "On the Absence of Keyboard Continuo in Haydn's Symphonies." *Early Music* 18 (1990), pp. 601–08.

Webster, James. "Schubert's Sonata Form and Brahms's First Maturity," *19th Century Music* 2 (1978), pp. 18–35; 3 (1979), pp. 52–71.

Wegeler, Franz Gerhard, and Ferdinand Ries. *Biographische Notizen über Ludwig van Beethoven.* Koblenz: K. Bädeker, 1838. Supplemented by Wegeler. Koblenz, 1845. English translation by Frederick Noonan as *Beethoven Remembered.* Arlington, Va.: Great Ocean Publishers, 1987; London: Deutsch, 1988.

Wheelock, Gretchen A. *Haydn's Ingenious Jesting with Art: Contexts of Musical Wit and Humor.* New York: Schirmer Books, 1992

Wheelock, Gretchen A. "*Schwarze Gredel* and the Engendered Minor Mode in Mozart's Operas." In *Musicology and Difference,* edited by Ruth Solie, pp. 201–24. Berkeley: University of California Press, 1993.

Willetts, Pamela J. *Beethoven and England: An Account of Sources in the British Museum.* London: Trustees of the British Museum, 1970.

Winter, Robert. "Performing Beethoven's Early Piano Concertos." *Early Music* 16 (1988), pp. 214–30.

Yudkin, Jeremy. "Beethoven's 'Mozart Quartet.'" *JAMS* 45 (1992), pp. 30–74.

Zaslaw, Neal, ed. *Mozart's Piano Concertos: Text, Context, Interpretation.* Ann Arbor: University of Michigan Press, 1996.

Index

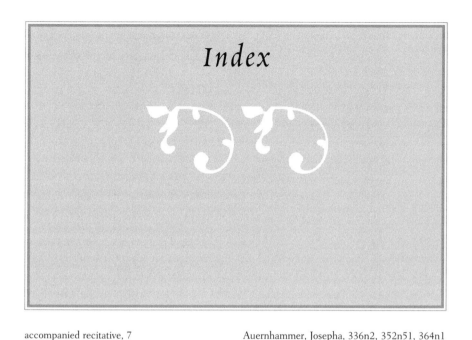

accompanied recitative, 7
Adam, Louis, 184
Adler, Guido, 86
Aeolian harp, 144, 145
affects, Baroque theory of, 190
African dance and music, 3–4
Aki, Syoko, 357n35
Albrechtsberger, Johann Georg, 48
Allanbrook, Wye Jamison, 333–34n12
Allgemeine musikalische Zeitung, 55, 107–8,
        140, 146, 180, 194, 234, 328n85,
        347n8, 351n45, 362n38, 364n1,
        369n36, 370n60
Alstädten, Court Counselor, 28
Altmann, Wilhelm, 348n20, 352n58, 358n41,
        361n29
amateur performers, 28–29, 91–92, 160, 245–
        46, 274–75, 282–84, 287, 290,
        367n20, 367n31
Anderson, Emily, 367n21
André, Julius, 366n17
André firm, 286, 341n12
aria
    parallels with concerto slow movement,
        78
    relation to concerto form, 17
    symbolism of, 311n8
Artaria & Company, 168, *169*
Aschaffenburg-am-Main, 26
Auden, W. H., 8
Auernbrugger, Franziska von, 92
Auernbrugger, Marianne von, 92

Auernhammer, Josepha, 336n2, 352n51, 364n1
Augartensaal (Vienna), 45, 46–47, 159, 160,
        174, 292
Averdonck, J. Helena, 26

Bach, Carl Philipp Emanuel, 367n20
    concertos of, 28, 342n15
    rondos of, 18, 336n41
Bach, Johann Christian
    concertos of, 4, 6, 15, 28, 223, 286, 314n11
    sonatas of, 14
Bach, Johann Sebastian, 296, 297
    autographs of, 116
    Brandenburg Concerto No. 5, 13, 225
    Concerto in the Italian Style, 284
    concertos of, 6, 11
    Goldberg Variations, 228
    keyboard transcription of string concertos,
        282
    late works of, 363n42
    Musical Offering, A, 344n32
    performance on Frederick the Great's piano-
        forte, 295
    Well-Tempered Clavier, The, 29, 33
Badura-Skoda, Paul, 344n40, 347n13, 352n56,
        352n59, 366n8, 366n19, 372n74
Bali, gamelan music in, 4
ballet, 3
bar form, 179
Barenboim, Daniel, 372n75
Baroque, concerto performance in, 282
Bastille Day, 42–43

Beauharnais, Eugène de, 253

Beck, Hermann, 300, 365–66n7, 372n72

Beethoven, Carl van (brother), 54, 60, 159, 255
  letters
    to André firm, 134
    to Breitkopf & Härtel, 113–14, 133, 182, 340n74, 341n79, 346n2, 346n6, 348n24

Beethoven, Cornelius van, 316n5

Beethoven, Johann van (father), 24, 26, 29, 318n31

BEETHOVEN, LUDWIG VAN, *167. See also* manuscripts and sketchbooks; *works categories below*
  aesthetics of, 88, 92–93, 109, 144
  as assistant court organist, 24–25
  alla breve meter, use of, 103–4, 143, 265–66, 299, 303, 372n77
  bass patterns of, 227–28
  in Bonn, 22, 24–31, 34, 36, 38, 39–41
  C-minor compositions of, 156–58
  codas of, 106–7
  compositional activity from 1782–92, 40–41
  compositional method of, 116–17, 211, 308
  concerts
    April 1800, 50, 54–55, 113
    April 1803, 113, 127, 129–30
    December 1808, 210–11, 216, 254, 291–92, 362n32
    failed concert of 1802, 113–14, 133–35, 308
  deafness of, 135, 152, 272, 362n32
  dealings with publishers, 130–31, 134, 159, 211, 235, 241, 246, 253, 275–76, 292, 295, 346n6
  Érard piano of, 128–29, 172, 184
  finances of, 253–54, 255, 359–60n6
  French influences on, 183–84
  handwriting of, 118, 307
  Hayden's influence on, 88–89
  Heiligenstadt Testament, 135, 144, 152
  heroic idealism of, 8, 151–52, 193
  instrumental recitatives of, 104, 186, 188
  key choices of, 297–98
  largo movements of, 102–3
  letters
    to Archduke Rudolph, 180
    to Breitkopf & Härtel, 182, 235, 252, 254, 255, 275
    to Gleichenstein, 254
    to Hoffmeister, 61, 67, 86, 130–31, 183, 311n5, 328n89
    to Mosel, 299–300
    to Rochlitz, 346n5
    to Sonnleithner, 184
    to Streicher, 347–48n14
    to Thomson, 370n60
    to Treitschke, 346n4
    to von Varena, 322n3
    to Wegeler, 324n25
  metronome markings of, 299–300, *301*, 302–3, 365n5
  middle period of, 151–58, 159–60, 222, 227, 250
  motifs
    horn calls or hunting, 32, 34, 56, 112, 268, 270, 272
    military, 32, 93, 95–98, 136, 138, 142, 193, 197, 205, 206, 218, 250, 256, 257, 272, 277
    pastoral, 34, 217–18, 225–26
  Mozart's influence on, 86–89, 140–42
  musical training of, 24, 29–30, 47–48, 64, 88
  patrons of, 29–30, 40–41, 43, 47, 49, 91, 160, 193, 211–12, 254, 255, 290
  as pianist, 174, 202, 272
    Bonn performances, 26–30, 41
    concerto performances, 4–7, 47–57, 62–66, 90, 113–14, 128–30, 144, 204, 210–11, 213, 215–16, 237, 280, 287, 289, 291–92
    gives up performing, 4, 211, 272, 275
  piano writing of, 32, 33–34, 36, 57, 67–68, 89, 92, 101–2, 128–29, 142, 144–46, 155–57, 179, 188, 195, 202–4, 214–16, 245, 262–63, 265, 274, 293–94
  planned trip to Paris, 183–84
  political views of, 43, 45, 252, 322n3
  presence during Napoleon's bombardment of Vienna, 255
  present-day reception of, 281
  prolongation of dissonance, 80
  reviews of, 40, 55, 107–8, 114, 140, 146, 180, 194, 225, 234, 272
  rondo movements of, 18–21, 268
  shift in attitude toward publication, 275–76, 292–93
  tours of, 1796, 48–49
  trip to Vienna, 1787, 41
  use of cyclic form, 155
  use of figured bass notation, 273–74, 282, 287–90
  use of *folia*, 259–60, 262
  in Vienna, 42–47
  view of composition as "text," 275–76
  views about piano as instrument, 293
  views about piano concerto as genre, 4–7, 216, 237, 272–73, 275–76, 280, 287–88
  violin writing of, 38, 59–60, 228, 229–30, 233–34, 235–36, 238
  as violist, 26
  Westphalia court, offered Kapellmeister position at, 253–54

women and, 36
BEETHOVEN, LUDWIG VAN: compositions of. *See also* Beethoven, Ludwig van: concertos of
"An die Hoffnung," Op. 32, 160
Bagatelles, Op. 33, 346n3
cantatas
    Der glorreiche Augenblick, Op. 136, 277
    on the death of Emperor Joseph II, WoO 87, 29–30, 40, 43, 319n35
        heroic idealism in, 8
    on the elevation of Emperor Leopold II, WoO 88, 40, 319n35
Choral Fantasy, Op. 80, 275
    premiere of, 193, 210–11, 291
Christus am Oelberge, Op. 85
    premiere of, 114, 194
    sketches for, 116, 123, 129, 132
Deutsche Tänze, WoO 8, 64
Fantasy for Piano, Op. 77, 275
Fantasy on Mozart's "Ah tu fosti il primo oggetto" from *La Clemenza di Tito* (improvisation), 53
Fidelio, Op. 72 (*See also Leonore*)
    airs from, 211
    "Euch werde Lohn," 355n20
    heroic idealism in, 8, 151–52
    "In des Lebens Frühlingstagen," 188
    March of the Guards, 250
    premiere of, 184, 253
    relationship to Joseph Cantata, 318n33
    revival of, 277
incidental music to *Egmont,* Op. 84, 194
Leonore, 166 (*See also Fidelio*)
    premiere of, 171
    publication of, 275
    récit obligé in, 179
    sketches for, 159–60, 179
"Lustig-Traurig" (bagatelle), WoO 54, 345n54
Mass in C Major, Op. 86, premiere of, 211, 291
Missa solemnis, Op. 123
    "Dona nobis pacem," 250
    figured bass in, 283
Octet, Wind, Op. 103, 319n35
Overtures
    Coriolan, Op. 62, 211, 213, 241
    Egmont, Op. 84, 275
    Leonore No. 1, Op. 138, 268
    Leonore No. 2, Op. 72, 152, 164, 257, 260
    Leonore No. 3, Op. 72, 152, 257, 260, 275
    Prometheus, 346n3
Quartet, Piano, WoO 36, 29, 40–41, 320n47
    Mozart's influence on, 342n16

piano writing in, 36, 37, 320n45, 320n50
relationship to Piano Sonata Op. 2, No. 1, 80, 92, 329n5
Quartets, String
    Minuet in A♭, Hess 33, 41
    Op. 18, 67, 151, 154
    Op. 18, No. 2, 355n18
    Op. 18, No. 3, 143, 335n33, 360n18
    Op. 18, No. 4, 116, 156–57
    Op. 18, No. 5, 342n16, 343n20
    Op. 18, No. 6, 343n20
    Op. 59, 151, 235, 241, 356n29
    Op. 59, No. 1, 152, 200, 221, 226
    Op. 59, No. 3, 153
    Op. 74, 275
    Op. 132, 186
Quintet, Piano and Winds, Op. 16, 46
Quintet, String, Op. 29, 123, 132
Ritterballet, WoO 1, 29, 30, 40
Romances, Violin and Orchestra
    Op. 40, 54, 59–60, 233, 346n3
    alla breve meter in, 143
    autograph of, 60
    Op. 50, 54, 59–60, 233, 335n29
    alla breve meter in, 143
    autograph of, 54, 60
Rondino for Wind Instruments, WoO 25, 319n35
Rondo a capriccio for piano, Op. 129, 18–19
Septet, Op. 20, 59, 343n20
    metronome markings, 302
    missing sketches for, 116
    premiere of, 55
Serenade for Flute, Violin, and Cello, Op. 25, 372n73
Sextet, Op. 81b, 275
Six Songs to poems by Gellert, Op. 48, 152
sonatas
    publication of, 5
    style in, 151
Sonatas, Piano
    Andante "favori," WoO 57 (movement), 159, 326n55
    "Kurfürsten," WoO 47, 29, 35, 40, 320n50, 335n26
    Op. 2, 59, 67, 91, 92, 103
    Op. 2, No. 1, 80, 106, 329n5, 343n21
    Op. 2, No. 2, 53, 102, 297, 343n28
    Op. 2, No. 3, 68, 102, 343n28
    Op. 7, 59, 68, 76, 102, 103, 107, 335n33, 343n28
    Op. 10, 59
    Op. 10, No. 1, 103, 156, 298, 316n26, 334n17, 335n33
    alla breve meter in, 143
    Op. 10, No. 2, 343n20
    alla breve meter in, 143

Beethoven, Ludwig van: compositions of (*cont.*)
  Op. 10, No. 3, 76, 316n26
  Op. 13 *Pathétique,* 59, 103, 144, 147,
    330n13, 343n21
  Op. 14, No. 1, 143, 339n52
  Op. 22, 59, 151
  Op. 26, 105, 144, 193, 226, 298
  Op. 27, 21, 155
  Op. 27, No. 1, 226, 343n28
  Op. 27, No. 2 "Moonlight," 132, 144, 298,
    335n29
    alla breve meter in, 143
  Op. 28 "Pastoral," 132, 218, 335n33,
    344n40, 360n18
  Op. 31, 135, 344n40, 346n3
  Op. 31, No. 1, 134, 260, 335n33, 372n77
  Op. 31, No. 2 "Tempest," 103, 144, 146,
    153, 155, 186, 188, 222, 343n21
  Op. 31, No. 3, 346n3
  Op. 49, 92
  Op. 49, No. 2, 143
  Op. 53 "Waldstein," 152, 186, 221, 227,
    326n55
    piano writing in, 102, 156, 188, 263
    sketches for, 159
    tonal structure of, 164, 260
  Op. 54, 152, 160
  Op. 57 "Appassionata," 152, 160,
    356n29
  Op. 72, 275
  Op. 78, 275
  Op. 79, 275
  Op. 81a, 275, 368n33
  Op. 90, 343n28
  Op. 109, 208, 228, 343n28, 353n62
  Op. 110, 71, 186, 343n28
  Op. 111, 192
Sonatas, Piano and Cello
  Op. 5, 51, 59, 206
  Op. 5, No. 1, 99
  Op. 5, No. 2, 348n15
  Op. 69, 143, 221, 222, 275, 335n33
Sonatas, Piano and Violin
  Op. 12, No. 1, 105
  Op. 12, No. 2, 59
  Op. 12, No. 3, 105
  Op. 30, 123, 135, 151, 346n3
  Op. 30, No. 1, 335n33
  Op. 30, No. 2, 156–58, 221, 343n28
    alla breve meter in, 143
  Op. 47 "Kreutzer," 135, 184, 233
    premiere of, 159, 174
    sketches for, 123
  Op. 96, 348n17, 353n62
symphonies
  as musical "texts," 4–5
  publication of, 5

Symphony No. 1, Op. 21
  alla breve meter in, 143
  first movement metronome marking, 302
  missing sketches for, 116
  performances of, 211
  premiere of, 55, 114
  style of, 154
Symphony No. 2, Op. 36
  alla breve meter in, 143
  first movement metronome marking,
    302
  performances of, 211
  premiere of, 114
  publication of, 346n3
  second movement, 335n33
  sketches of, 133, 134, 135
Symphony No. 3, Op. 55
  coda, 112
  first movement, 70, 80, 221, 222, 265,
    334n18
  Napoleon's relation to, 183–84, 192, 193,
    252
  performances of, 211
  premiere of, 178
  second movement, 188
  sketches for, 155, 159
  style of, 151–53
  thematic material, 89, 161, 163
Symphony No. 4, Op. 60, 241
  first movement, 335n29
  performances of, 211
Symphony No. 5, Op. 67, 152
  first movement, 221
  premiere of, 171, 210, 291
  publication of, 275
  references between movements in, 155
  second movement, 227, 354nn6–7
  sketches for, 159
  third movement, 228
Symphony No. 6, Op. 68, 86, 152
  first movement, 138, 218, 221–22, 225
  premiere of, 171, 193, 210, 291
  publication of, 275
  sketches for, 159
Symphony No. 7, Op. 92
  premiere of, 277
  second movement, 192
Symphony No. 9, Op. 125
  fourth movement, 186, 193
  heroic idealism in, 8
  third movement, 208
  timpani part, 294
Trio, Flute, Bassoon, and Piano, WoO 37,
    36, 37, 40, 321n54
Trios, Piano
  Op. 1, 67, 76, 91
  Op. 1, No. 1, 107

Op. 1, No. 2, 102, 339n52, 345n50
Op. 1, No. 3, 102, 107, 156, 343n21
Op. 70, 275, 353n65
Op. 97 "Archduke," 362n32
WoO 38, 40, 339n52
Trios, String
  Op. 3, 40, 156, 322n66
  Op. 9, No. 1, 343n20
  Op. 9, No. 3, 156, 343n20
Variations, Piano
  32 Variations in C minor, WoO 80, 227
  on a March by Dressler, WoO 63, 29
  on Righini's "Venni amore," WoO 65, 26,
    36, 40
  Op. 34, 118, 134, 135, 151, 346n3
  Op. 35, 118, 135, 151, 153, 346n3
Variations for Piano and Violin on "Se vuol
    ballare," WoO 40, 323n20
Vestas Feuer (opera project), 114, 129,
    341n79
  dropped, 160
  sketches for, 123, 159
Wellingtons Sieg, Op. 91, 252, 276–77
BEETHOVEN, LUDWIG VAN: concertos of
  Adagio in D to a concerto in A (sketches),
    48, 305, 322n64
  cadenzas for, 237–38, 294
  "Concertante" in D (project), 133–34, 308
  delayed publication of, 5–6
  form in, 9–21
  Oboe Concerto, Hess 12 (lost), 38
    sketches for, 306
  Piano Concerto fragment of 1815, Hess 15,
    4, 277–78, 363nn45, 47
  Piano Concerto in E♭, WoO 4, 27, 29, 31–
    35, 40–41, 48, 335n26
    first movement, 31–33
    manuscript of, 35
    piano range in, 33
    piano writing in, 32, 33, 36
    second movement, 33–34
    sources for, 31, 305, 364n3
    third movement, 34, 57
  Piano Concerto No. 1 in C, Op. 15, 90–112
    autograph of, 65–66, 90, 101, 103, 155,
      280, 288–89, 335n36
    Beethoven's cadenza for, 238, 294, 298
    Beethoven's performances of, 5, 48, 52–
      56, 62–66, 113, 116, 117, 131
    dating of, 63–65
    evaluation of, 92–93
    first edition, 283, 287, 290
    first movement (Allegro con brio), 93–
      102
      first solo section, 97, 98, 99–100
      first tutti, 93, 95–97, 98–99, 164
      harmonic material, 98–101, 145, 199

metronome marking, 300, *301, 302*
performance issues, 102
rhythm and meter in, 93, 95–96
second solo section, 97, 100–101, 102
second tutti, 99–100
sketches for, 99
structure of, 16, *94,* 98
thematic material, 93, 95–97, 136, 203
third solo section, 98, 100, 101
instrumentation of, 93
origins of, 62–65
piano range in, 293
piano writing in, 92, 101–2
possible cadenza draft for, 51–52
publication of, 130
reviews of, 107–8, 328n85
revisions to, 5
second movement (Largo), 102–7
  coda, 106–7
  editions of, 103
  harmonic material, 105–6, 343n28
  key of, 102, 166
  metronome marking, *301,* 303
  structure of, 21, *104*
  tempo and meter of, 103–4, 143, 266,
    303
  thematic material, 104–5
sketches for, 55–56, 63–64, 99
sources for, 65–66
third movement (Rondo), 107–12
  coda, 112
  harmonic material, 18–19, 108–9, 111–
    12, 345n49
  metronome marking, *301,* 302
  review of, 107–8
  rhythm and meter in, 108, 109, 112
  structure of, 20, 34, 108, *109,* 110
  thematic material, 21, 108–9, 268
Piano Concerto No. 2 in B, Op. 19, 67–89
  autograph of, 60, 61, 65, 280, 288, 289,
    290
  Beethoven's assessment of, 67, 86
  Beethoven's cadenza for, 238, 294
  Beethoven's performances of, 5, 60–61,
    62, 64, 90, 325n34
  dating of, 40
  evaluation of, 86, 92
  first edition of, 35, 61, 273, 287–88, 289,
    291
  first movement (Allegro con brio), 68–76
    autograph of, 76
    evaluation, 75–76
    first solo section, 71, 73–74, 76
    first tutti, 70–73, 75, 87–88, 164
    fourth tutti, 75
    harmonic material, 101, 199
    metronome marking, 300, *301, 302*

Beethoven, Ludwig van: concertos of (*cont.*)
    second solo section, 71, 74
    second tutti, 74, 75
    sketches for, 71
    structure of, *69*, 70
    thematic material, 15, 68, 70, 73, 75
    third solo section, 71, 75, 76
    third tutti, 74–75
  fragments, 31, 38–41
  influences on, 86–89, 342n16
  instrumentation of, 41, 67
  manuscripts of, 38–39
  origins and history of, 60–61, 63, 66
  piano range in, 293
  piano reduction of, 292
  piano writing in, 67–68, 89
  publication of, 67, 130
  relationship to Rondo, WoO 6, 56, 60,
    63
  revisions to, 5, 6, 48, 90
  second movement (Adagio), 76–80
    alternate movement for, 80
    coda, 80, 107
    final tutti, 80
    harmonic material, 79–80
    metronome marking, *301*
    orchestral introduction, 78
    structure of, 21, 77, 77–78, 106
    thematic material, 76–77
  sketches for, 54, 60–61, 64, 71
  sources for, 31, 305–6
  "text" of, 291
  texture in, 67–68
  third movement (Rondo), 81–86
    coda, 85–86
    evaluation of, 85–86
    harmonic material, 18–19, 345n49
    metronome marking, *301*, 302
    rhythm in, 82
    sketches for, 54
    structure of, 20, 34, 82, 83, 84
    thematic material, 81–82, 85, 268
Piano Concerto No. 3 in C minor, Op. 37,
  113–58
  autograph of, 65, 116–30, 156, *173*, 216,
    280, 288, 293, 307
  Beethoven's cadenza for, 238, 294
  Beethoven's performances of, 5, 114–15,
    118, 128–30, 144
  dating of, 55, 116–32, 150–58, 307–9
  editions of, 142, 343n30
  first edition of, 35, 116, 273, 288, 290,
    291
  first movement (Allegro con brio), 136–43
    cadenza sketches for, 129–30
    coda, 140–41, 294–95
    first solo section, 139, 140

    first tutti, 13, 138–40, 331n22
    fourth tutti, 140, 351n34
    harmonic material, 138–40, 222, 224
    meter of, 142–43, 266
    metronome marking, 300, *301*, 302
    Mozart's possible influence on, 140–42,
      158, 165–66
    second solo section, 140
    second tutti, 140
    structure of, 16, *137*, 140, 259, 264,
      278, 330n10
    thematic material, 136, 138
    third solo section, 140
    third tutti, 140
  origins of, 113–35
  performance issues, 144
  performances of, 212–13
  piano range in, 128–20, 293
  piano writing in, 34, 128–29, 142, 144–
    46, 155–57
  premiere of, 171
  publication of, 346n3
  reviews of, 140, 141, 364n1
  revisions to, 5, 147
  second movement (Largo), 143–46, *173*
    autograph of, 128, 146
    cadenza, 146
    codetta, 146
    harmonic material, 145, 298, 335n33
    metronome marking, *301*
    mood of, 143–45
    performance issues, 144
    piano figuration, 146
    structure of, 21, 145
    thematic links with Rondo, 154–55
    thematic material, 103, 144–45
  sketches for, 130–32
  sources for, 115–18
  style of, 150, 154–58
  "text" of, 291
  texture in, 57
  third movement (Rondo), 147–50
    autograph, 147
    coda, 150
    episode, 148, 154
    harmonic material, 148, 150, 154
    metronome marking, *301*
    structure of, 20, 147–48, *149*, 150, 154,
      231
    thematic links with Largo, 154–55
    thematic material, 7, 147, 205, 268
Piano Concerto No. 4 in G, Op. 58, 185–
  216, 235
  Beethoven's cadenza for, 294
  Beethoven's performances of, 6, 113, 204,
    210–11, 215–16, 291–92
  copyist's score for, 213–16

editions of, 273, 352n58
first movement (Allegro moderato), 195–204
  cadenza, 202, 237
  character of, 152
  codetta, 202, 203, 204
  display episodes, 263–64
  first solo section, 199, 201, 202, 203, 214, 345n53
  first tutti, 195–97, 199, 201
  fourth tutti, 201–2
  harmonic material, 195–97, 199, 202, 203–4, 260
  metronome marking, *301, 302*
  second solo section, 201, 203–4, 214
  second tutti, 201
  solo opening, 195, 256
  structure of, 195–97, *198,* 199–203, 236–37, 264
  thematic material, 15, 195–97, 199–200, 203, 221, 222
  third solo section, 199–201, 202, 203, 214, 215, 292
missing autograph of, 213
offered for publication, 241
performance issues, 186, 188, 203, 238
piano range, 202–3, 214–16, 293
piano writing in, 188, 195, 202–4, 214–16
premiere of, 178, 193, 210–13, 291–92
publication of, 213, 216, 273
reduction for piano and string quintet, 291, 292
reviews of, 194
revisions to, 339n59
second movement (Andante con moto), 185–94
  harmonic material, 186–88
  metronome marking, *301, 303*
  performance issues, 186, 188
  possible program of, 189–94
  structure of, 185–88
  style of, 7, 21, 204–5, 226
sketches for, 159
sources for, 364n3
text of, 213–16
third movement (Rondo), 204–10
  coda, 209–10, 298
  development in, 209
  harmonic material, 19, 205–6, 208–10, 298
  metronome marking, *301, 302–3*
  structure of, 20, 206, *207,* 208–10, 231, 270
  thematic material, 205–6, 208
Piano Concerto No. 5 in E♭, Op. 73, 251–78
  autograph of, *177,* 266, 273, 274, 289–90, 293

composition of, 255–56
"Emperor" appellation, 255–56
first editions of, 273–75, 289–90
first movement (Allegro), 256–65
  cadenza, 39, 237, 262, 264–65
  coda, 263, 264–65
  display episode, 274
  dramatic character of, 256–57, 259
  first solo section, 257, 259–60, 262, 263–64
  first tutti, 256–57
  fourth tutti, 264–65
  harmonic material, 257, 259–62, 354n6
  metronome marking, *301,* 302
  piano writing in, 156
  rhythm in, 257
  second solo section, 259
  second tutti, *177*
  structure of, 16, *258, 259*
  textures in, 262–63
  thematic material, 227, 257, 259, 264, 265
  third solo section, 261–62, 263–64
performance issues, 265–66
piano range in, 293
piano writing in, 262–63, 265, 274
premiere of, 272
review of, 272
second movement (Adagio con poco moto), 265–67
  harmonic material, 298
  metronome marking, *301*
  structure of, 21
  tempo of, 265–66
sketches for, 264
third movement (Rondo), 267–72
  coda, 272
  harmonic material, 261, 263, 270
  lack of metronome marking, *301*
  rhythm in, 267–68, 270–72
  structure of, 20, 268, *269,* 270–72
  thematic material, 268, 270
  timpani strokes, 272
Romance cantabile in E minor, Hess 13 (movement), 31, 35–37, 41
  dating of, 40
  manuscript of, 36
  piano writing in, 36
  sources for, 305
Rondo in B♭, WoO 6 (movement), 56–59
  autograph of, 57, 59, 61
  editions of, 59
  relationship to Piano Concerto No. 2, 39, 48, 56, 60, 63
  sources for, 39, 306
  structure of, 57, 58, 82
  texture in, 56–57

Beethoven, Ludwig van: concertos of (*cont.*)
  symbolism in, 7–8
  texture in, 57
  Triple Concerto in C, Op. 56, 37, 159–66,
      179–84
    evaluation of, 160–61
    first movement (Allegro), 161–66
      final section, 166
      first solo section, 163, 164–65, 166
      first tutti, 163–64
      fourth tutti, 165–66, 354n5
      harmonic material, 163–66
      lack of cadenza, 166
      metronome marking, *301, 302*
      second solo section, 164
      second tutti, 165
      structure of, *162,* 163–64, 345n53
      thematic material, 161, 163
      third solo section, 165
      third tutti, 166
    performance issues, 347n13
    piano range, 293
    piano writing in, 179
    review of, 180
    second movement (Largo), 21, 103, 166,
        179
      metronome marking, *301, 303*
    sketches for, 131, 160
    symphonie concertante genre and, 182–83
    third movement (Rondo alla polacca),
        179–82
      alla polacca designation, 179–80, 182
      harmonic material, 179
      metronome marking, *301, 303*
      structure of, 20, 179–80, *181*
  Violin Concerto in C, WoO 5 (fragment), 31,
      37–38, 41, 233, 326n45
    manuscript of, 37, 305
    possible version for piano, 38, 48
  Violin Concerto in D, Op. 61, 217–50
    autograph of, 122, *175,* 235–40, 243–44,
        339n59
    character of, 152
    copyist's score of, 239
    editions of, 242–43, 353n63, 355n25,
        358n41
    first movement (Allegro ma non troppo),
        175, 217–26
      cadenza, 225
      coda, 247
      first solo section, 220, 223–24, 248
      first tutti, 218, 220, 222–23
      fourth tutti, 220, 221, 225
      harmonic material, 218, 220, 222–24,
          354n6
      meter in, 223
      metronome marking, *301, 302*

      second solo section, 220, 224, 225, 236
      second tutti, 220, 221, 224
      structure of, 218, *219,* 220, 222
      thematic material, 7, 15, 200, 217–18,
          220–21, 222, 246
      third solo section, 220, 224
      third tutti, 220, 223, 224, 236–37
      timpani strokes, 218, 220, 223, 295
    heterophonic texture in, 233–34
    mood of, 217–18, 220–22, 225–26, 233
    performance issues, 238–41, 355n21
    piano cadenzas for, 249–50
    piano transcription of, 243–49, 262, 276,
        291, 356n33
      authenticity questions, 246–49
      sketches for, 247–48
    premiere of, 171, 234, 239
    reviews of, 225, 234
    second movement (Larghetto), 226–29
      ground bass in, 226–28
      metronome marking, *301, 303*
      structure of, 7, 21, 226
      thematic material, 226, 228–29
    sketches for, 235
    sources for, 234–43, *244*
    text of, 234–43
    third movement (Rondo), 229–33
      harmonic material, 230–31
      metronome marking, *301, 303*
      structure of, 20, 229–31, *232*
      thematic material, 10, 230
    timpani strokes, 250, 272
    violin writing in, 229–30, 233–34, 235–36,
        238
Beethoven, Ludwig van (grandfather), 23–24
Beethoven, Maria Josepha Poll van (grand-
      mother), 24
Beethoven, Maria Magdalena van (mother), 24,
      319n34
Belderbusch, Count Anton von, 24, 28, 30, 40
Belvedere Palace (Vienna), 46
"benefit" concerts, 50
Berlin, 48, 49, 51–52, 115
Berlin Staatsbibliothek, 116
Berlioz, Hector, *Symphonie fantastique,* 97
Bernadotte, Jean Baptiste Jules, 183, 184
Bernstein, Leonard, 371n70
Biba, Otto, 324nn26–27
Bilson, Malcolm, 239
Block, Geoffrey, 329n7
Bolla, Maria, 49, 51, 63, 65
Bonaparte, Jérôme, 253–54
Bonaparte, Joseph, 253
Bonaparte, Napoleon, *176,* 251–56, 276–77
  relation to *Eroica* Symphony, 183–84, 192,
      193, 254
Bonds, Mark Evan, 312–13n1

Bonn
    court of, 22–30, 251
    Electoral Palace, 23, *168*
    history of, 23
    pianists in, 28
    political upheaval in, 42–44
    salon life in, 26–29
Borges, Jorge Luis, 8
Bossler, Heinrich Philippe Carl, *Musikalische Correspondenz,* 26–27, 30
Brahms, Johannes, 334n15
    Piano and Violin Sonata in A, Op. 100, 105
    Piano Concerto in D minor, Op. 15, 345n49
Brand, Christoph, 319n34
Brandenburg, Sieghard, 340n71, 346n56, 371n64
Braun, Baron Peter von, 113–14, 160, 323n11
Brazil, *capoeira* in, 4
Brendel, Alfred, 266, 326n57, 342–43n18, 369n48
Brenneis, Clemens, 363n47
Breuning, Eleanore von, 48
Breuning, Helene von, 29
Breuning, Lorenz von, 52
Breuning, Stephan von, 323n8, 325n37
Breuning family, von, 41
Bridgetower, George A. Polgreen, 159, 174
Broadwood firm, 339n52
Brook, Barry, 182
Broyles, Michael, 344–45n43
Bruckner, Anton, Requiem of, 283
Brühl, 23, 27
Budapest, 48. *See also* Pest
Burgtheater (Vienna), 46, 55, 336n2, 351n45
Burney, Fanny, 251
Burnham, Scott, 313nn3–4, 354n8
Bylsma, Anner, 347n13, 372n74

call-and-response, 3
canzonetta, symbolism of, 311n8
capoeira, 4
Cartellieri, Antonio, *Gioas, Re di Giuda,* 51
Casella, Alfredo, 348n20
chaconne, 226–27
    symbolism of, 7
Chanson de Roland, 8
Cherubini, Luigi, works of, 234
Chopin, Frédéric, concertos of, 32, 361n22
Clasing, J. H., 194
Clemens August, Elector, 23–24
Clement, Franz, 234–36, 239, 245
Clementi, Muzio
    concertos of, 4, 28, 72, 81
    conducts own works, 282–83
    influence on Beethoven's Piano Concerto No. 2, 89
    minor-keyed movements of, 360n18

piano sonatas, 333n9
    Op. 2, 320n43
    Op. 8, No. 2, 87
    Op. 13, No. 6, 89
    Op. 25, No. 2, 87
    Op. 33, No. 1, 14, 89
    piano writing of, 33
    as publisher, 211, 241–43, 246, 249, 253, 346n2, 356n33, 358n50, 358–59n51, 367n31
    Toccata, Op. 11, 320n43
Coleridge, Samuel Taylor, "The Eolian Harp," 343n25
Collard, William, 241–42, 246, 358n50
"collective unconscious," 190–91
Cologne, Archbishop of, 22
"concept sketches," 115, 235
concert music, role of, 282–83
concertmaster, 292, 296
concerto(s). *See also specific composers and works*
    ad libitum accompaniment of, 284
    Baroque, 282
    cadenza in, 12, 13
    continuo notation in, 283–93
    discourse in, 3–4, 11–12
    first tutti in, 71–72
    genre of, 11, 279–80, 281–83
    piano reductions of, 245–46, 273–75, 276, 283–84, 288, 290–91
    public performances of, 6–7
    role in Viennese life, 287
    sacred and chamber venues for, 6
    texture in, 11–12
    as virtuoso vehicle, 4–7, 279–83
conductor, 282–83, 292, 296
Cone, Edward, 187
Confederation of the Rhine, 252
Congress of Vienna, 276–77
Conti, Giacomo, 55
Continental System, 253
continuo playing, 282–83, 296
contredanse, 270
    influence on rondo, 81, 82, 108, 109
    symbolism of, 311n8
Cook, Nicholas, 363n43, 363n47
Cooper, Barry, 353n59, 353n67
copyright, 276
Corelli, Arcangelo
    Concerto grossi, Op. 6, 6, 11
    published works of, 276
    Sonata for Violin and Continuo, Op. 59, No. 12, 259
couplet, 19
court musicians, 22, 24–27, 29–30
Covington, Kate R., 360n18
Cowper, Samuel, *The Task,* 185

Cramer, C. F., *Magazin der Musik,* 27, 28, 87
Cramer, J. B., 141
Czerny, Carl, 351n45
  completion of Beethoven's Rondo, WoO 6,
    59
  on Beethoven's childhood, 318n31
  on Beethoven's style change, 118, 151, 153,
    354n10
  on Beethoven's Walter piano, 338n52
  on Choral Fantasy, 350n19
  on form in concertos, 11, 16, 314n9
  on Piano Concerto No. 1, 102, 103, 106,
    335n23
  on Piano Concerto No. 3, 141, 143–44,
    326n50, 336n4
  on Piano Concerto No. 4, 189, 215, 292,
    353n62
  on Piano Concerto No. 5, 256, 265–66
  on piano transcription of Violin Concerto,
    246
  on principal theme, 95
  on rondo form, 20, 81
  on Triple Concerto, 160–61
  on Violin Concerto, 234–35
  performance of Beethoven's Piano Concerto
    No. 1, 352n51
  performance of Beethoven's Piano Concerto
    No. 5, 272
  studies with Beethoven, 335n24
  tempo markings for Beethoven's concertos,
    300, *301,* 302–3

Daffner, Hugo, 282
Dahlhaus, Carl
  concept of "text," 155
  on Beethoven's middle period, 153–54,
    354n10
  on Beethoven's themes, 347n11
  on *Eroica* Symphony, 334n18
  on form, 313n2
  on genre, 313n5
  on textual fidelity, 4
dating methods, 119–30
Davis, Colin, 372n75
Deane, Basil, 86, 325n45
Deiters, Hermann, 27, 36, 38, 161, 318n25
"display episodes," 13, 73–74
Dittersdorf, Carl Ditters von
  concertos of, 15, 314n8, 314n11
  symphonies of, 36
Dobrowen, Issay, 371n70
Doležalek, Emanuel, 351n45
Dramatische Blätter, 88
Dresden, 48
Dumouriez, General, 43
Duport, Jean-Louis, 51–52, 324n32
Duport, Jean-Pierre, 51–52, 324n32

Eckard, Johann Gottfried, 14
Elector, office of, 22
Engel, Hans
  concept of "display episode," 13, 73
  on Violin Concerto, 217
England, orchestral performance in, 282–
    83
Englesmann, Walter, 347n11
episode, 19–20
equal temperament, 296, 298
Érard, Sebastian, 128–29, 172
Esterházy, Prince Paul Anton, 43

Faulkner, William, 8
Ferguson, Linda Faye, 366n18, 367n27, 368–
    69n35
Fétis, François-Joseph, *Biographie universelle
    des musiciens,* 150–51
figured-bass notation, 35, 282–93
finale (concerto) form, 18–21
first movement concerto form, 12–17
Fischer, Gottfried, reminiscences of Beethoven,
    25, 27, 317n14, 319n34
folia, 227, 259
Forbes, Elliot, 316n5
Forkel, Johann Nikolaus, *Musikalischer Alman-
    ach,* 40
form. *See also specific forms; specific works
    (under composer)*
  of concerto finales, 18–21
  of concerto first movements, 12–17
  of concerto middle movements, 21
  cyclic, 155
  notion of, 9–11
  of romance, 35–36
  symbolism and, 7
  terminology for, 16–17
Forman, Dennis, concept of "piano climax," 73–
    74
Forster, E. M., on Tovey's commentary on
    Piano Concerto No. 4, 190
Frankfurt, 42–43
Franz II, Holy Roman Emperor (later Franz I,
    Emperor of Austria), 42–43, 45, 252,
    254–56
Frederick the Great, King of Prussia, 28, 51,
    295
Freimütige, 114
French Revolution, 23, 42–43, 51, 251. *See
    also* Bonaparte, Napoleon
Friedrich Wilhelm, King of Prussia, 49
funeral march, symbolism of, 7

Galand, Joel, 316n27
Galeazzi, Francesco, 11, 370n58
Gardiner, John Eliot, 372n72
Gardiner, William, 322n66

Gassmann, Florian Leopold, 50
gender issues, 311–12n8, 313n3
genre(s). *See also specific genres*
    fixed *vs.* flexible, 5
    form and, 10–11
    idea of, 313n5
Genzinger, Maria Anna von, 333n8
Gesellschaft der Musikfreunde (Vienna), 46, 59
Gewandhaus (Leipzig), 272
Gilbert and Sullivan operettas, 3
Gleichenstein, Baron Ignaz von, 254
Gluck, Christoph Willibald
    Alceste, 354n11
    Orpheo ed Euridice, 189–93
Goehr, Lydia, 363n42
Goethe, Johan Wolfgang von
    Faust, Part Two, 343n25
    Kennst du das Land, 194
    Wahlverwandschaften, 272
Goldberg, Szymon, 357n36
Golitzen, Prince Nikolas Boris, 47
Golschmann, Vladimir, 369n49, 371n69
Gossec, François-Joseph, symphonies of, 36
Gould, Glenn, 302–3, 369n49, 371nn69–70,
    372n75
Gräffer, Anton, 322n66
Grove, Sir George, 255
Grumiaux, Arthur, 303, 372n75

Haitink, Bernard, 371n70
Halm, Hans, *Thematisch-
    bibliographisches Verzeichnis,* 116, 117,
    142, 337n20, 346n6
Handel, George Frideric
    organ concertos of, 286
    published works of, 276
    Tamerlano, 349n2
Hanslick, Eduard, 51
Hanson, Alice M., 360n6
Hapsburg dynasty, 44–45, 251
harpsichord, 296
Härtel, Gottfried Christoph, 346n2
Haselt, Luc von, 26
Haydn, Franz Joseph
    1795 concert of, 49, 50, 52, 63, 65, 90
    aesthetics of, 88–89
    as Beethoven's teacher, 47–48, 88, 319n35
    concertos, 31, 223
        Hob. XVIII:3, 15
    harmonic style, 70
    influence on Beethoven, 88–89, 108–9, 151
    letters to Elector Maximilian Franz, 321n60
    piano sonatas, 34
        Hob. XVI:20, 92
        Hob. XVI:35–39, 92
    piano trios, 91
        Hob. XV:25, 327n78

pianos of, 129, 293
Ritorno di Tobio, Il, 351n45
rondo finales of, 57, 81, 111, 314n8
Schöpfung, Die, 55
string quartets
    Op. 1, No. 1, 68, 334n17
    Op. 33, 226
    Op. 33, No. 2, 89
    Op. 33, No. 5, 88–89
    Op. 33, Nos. 1, 2 and 4, 81
    Op. 74, Nos. 1 and 2, 81
    Op. 76, Nos. 2 and 5, 81
symphonies
    first movements of, 164
    instrumentation of, 295
    London performances of, 282, 295
    No. 73 "La chasse", 268
    No. 85 "La Reine", 320n53, 336n41
    No. 88, 81, 336n41
    No. 89, 81, 336n41
    No. 92, 81
    No. 94, 81, 336n41
    No. 95, 333n6
    No. 96, 81, 336n41
    No. 97, 81
    No. 99, 81, 89, 282, 336n41, 351n39
    No. 100, 81
    No. 102, 81, 336n41, 351n39
    second movements of, 36
    slow introductions of, 204–5
    sources for, 283
    trumpets and drums in, 93
    use of continuo accompaniment, 283, 295
    as Vice-Kapellmeister, 30
    views about Beethoven's C-minor trio, 333n3
    works of, 29, 51
Hegel, Georg Wilhelm Friedrich, 10
    Aesthetic Lectures, 192
Heifetz, Jascha, 303, 372n75
Heiligenstadt, 135, *170*
Heller, Ferdinand, 25
Henkel, Heinrich, 366n17
heroic (idea of), 7–8, 151–52, 193
Herttricht, Ernst, 356n29, 357n33, 359n51
Hertzmann, Erich, 327n78
Herz, Henri, 360n14
Hess, Willy, 27, 59, 357n39, 363n45
    completion of *Romance cantabile,* 320n51
    reconstruction of Piano Concerto WoO 4,
        320n45
Heussner, Horst, 366nn13–14
Hoffmann, E. T. A.
    aesthetic theories of, 192
    on Beethoven's middle period, 152–53
    opinion of piano concerto as genre, 279–80,
        359n56
Hoffmeister, Franz Anton, 61, 67, 86, 183, 287

Hogwood, Christopher, 302, 370n50, 372n72
Holschneider, Andreas, 319n38
Holy Roman Empire, 44–45, 251–52
Holz, Karl, 293
Home, Henry, Lord Kames, 332n40
Homer, epics of, 5
Honauer, Leonzi, 14
Horneman, Christian, *167*
Huffner, Christoph, 350n19
Hugo, Victor, 8
Hummel, Johann Nepomuk
    concertos of, 4, 32, 263, 264
    piano method of, 370n54

Idee concept, 192
improvisation
    in Beethoven's concertos, 4–7, 55, 215–16,
        237, 280, 289, 292
    in gamelan music, 4
individual-group discourse, 3–4
ink, 125–26, 128, 307, 329n7, 356n33,
        356nn29–30
Isidore of Seville, 6

Jahn, Ignaz, 46–47
Jahn, Otto, 315n20, 318n31
Jander, Owen
    on Piano Concerto No. 2, 330n18
    on Piano Concerto No. 4, 189, 192–94,
        312n9, 349n9, 350n23
    on Violin Concerto, 354n15
Jansen, Theresa, 89
Joachim, Joseph, 243
Johnson, Douglas Porter, 38, 51, 52, 306,
        320n38, 323n21, 325n42, 327n85,
        329n2, 333n6
    The Beethoven Sketchbooks, 60, 121, 122,
        132
    paper studies of Beethoven's manuscripts,
        39, 40, 61, 63, 64, 115, 119, 121,
        305, 321n54, 326–27n66, 328n90
Jorgenson, Owen H., 370n50
Joseph Clemens, Elector, 23
Joseph II, Holy Roman Emperor, 44, 45,
        322n70, 323n11
Josephstadt (Vienna theater), 46
Junker, Carl Ludwig, 27, 317n13, 319n35
Juon, Paul, 348n20
just intonation, 296

Kaiser, Fritz, on Violin Concerto, 239–40, 247,
        359n62
Kalischer, A. Ch., on date of Piano Concerto
        No. 3, 116, 117
Kalkbrenner, Frédéric, concertos of, 361n22
Kanne, Friedrich August, 297
    Orpheus, 189, 193, 194

Kapellmeister, office of, 24
Karajan, Herbert von, 372n74
Kärnthnerthortheater (Vienna), 46, 212–13,
        336n2
Kerman, Joseph
    on Beethoven's codas, 106
    on Beethoven's middle period, 151–52, 153
    on Piano Concerto No. 4, 188, 194, 199–
        200
    on String Quartet Op. 18, No. 4, 157
    on Triple Concerto, 160
    transcription of Adagio in D, 306
    transcription of *Romance cantabile*, 305
Kiesewetter, Raphael Georg, 4
Kinderman, William, 339n59
Kinsky, Georg, *Thematisch-bibliographisches
        Verzeichnis*, 116, 117, 142, 346n6
Kinsky, Prince Ferdinand Johann Nepomuk,
        254, 255
Kirnberger, Johann Philip, 297, 372n77
Koch, Heinrich Christoph, 11
    concept of *Einschnitt*, 266
    concept of *Takterstickung*, 68, 93, 109
    "Hauptsatz" article in *Musikalisches Lexikon*,
        95
    on form in concertos, 14–15, 16, 31,
        314nn10–11, 315n17
    on largo tempo, 103
    on rondo, 20
Köhler, Karl-Heinz, on date of Piano Concerto
        No. 3, 117, 339n59
Kojima, Shin Augustinus, 240, 241, 243–44,
        356n29, 356–57n33, 358n41, 358–
        59nn51–52
Kolisch, Rudolf, 299, 300, 302, 371n62,
        372n75
Kollmann, August F. C., 11
Kolneder, Walter, 344n40
Könnicke, Johann Jokob, 338n52
Körner, Klaus, 349n2
Kozeluch, Leopold, concertos of, 72, 81,
        332n30
Kraft (cellist), 160
Kraft, Anton, 333n5
Kraft, Nicholas, 333n5
Kramer, Richard, 321n58, 339n56, 348n24
    on Kessler Sketchbook, 133
    paper studies, 119, 121, 123, 124
Kraus, Lili, 326n57
Kreutzer, Rodolphe, 184
Kross, Siegfried, 347n10
Krumpholz, Wenzel, 151
Kullak, Franz, 361n28
    edition of Piano Concerto No. 3, 142,
        343n30
Küthen, Hans-Werner, 366n8
    Beethoven Werke: Kritischer Bericht, 51, 52,

325n39, 327n85, 328n90, 335n24, 352n56, 353n63, 368n33

Beethoven Werke edition, 282, 290, 343n30, 361n28

on date of Piano Concerto No. 3, 117, 118–19, 124, 125, 127, 133, 155–56, 307, 308, 338n37, 338n46, 339n59

paper studies, 121–22

Ländler, symbolism of, 311n8

Landon, H. C. Robbins, 93, 128–29

leader-follower paradigm, 3–4

Lebermann, Walter, 287, 288

Leidesdorfer, Herr (pianist), 352n51

Leipzig, 48

Lentner, Madame (singer), 24

Lenz, Wilhelm von, *Beethoven et ses trois styles*, 150–51, 157

Leopold II, Holy Roman Emperor, 44–45

Leopoldstadt (Vienna theater), 46

Lévi-Strauss, Claude, 190

Levin, Robert, 302

Levine, James, 343n18, 369n48

Lichnowsky, Prince Carl, 91, 356n29

Liechtenstein, Prince Johann Joseph, 46

Lindley, Mark, 370n54

Liszt, Franz
  Orpheus, 189–90
  piano concertos of, 4

Lobkowitz, Prince Ferdinand von, 47

Lobkowitz, Prince Franz Joseph von, 47, 49, 193, 211, 212, 254, 255, 291
  music room of, *178*

Lockwood, Lewis, 324n32, 363n47
  on projected Piano Concerto No. 6, 277
  study of *Eroica* sketches, 155

London, public concerts in, 6

Longyear, Rey M., 360n18

Lorenz, Alfred, 354n11

Louis XVI, King of France, 42

Lubin, Steven, 294, 302–3, 371–72nn70–71, 372n75

Lucchesi, Andrea, 25, 28

Ma, Yo-Yo, 372n74

Maelzel, Johann Nepomuk, 276, 299–300

Maier, Franz Josef, 347n13, 372n74

Malden, Ballad of, 8

Mandyczewski, Eusebius, 59

"Mannheim crescendo," 164, 166

Mannheim school, concertos of, 15

manuscripts and sketchbooks
  autographs, 1784–86, authenticity questions, 319n38
  Berlin, Staatsbibliothek, Artaria 125, 31, 305
  Berlin, Staatsbibliothek, Artaria 183, 133

Berlin, Staatsbibliothek, Artaria 184, 363n45, 363n47

Berlin, Staatsbibliothek, Beethoven Aut. 12, 328n88

Berlin, Staatsbibliothek, Beethoven Aut. 13, 326n60, 326–27n66, 331n28
  fol. 3v, 329n7

Berlin, Staatsbibliothek, Beethoven Aut. 14, 326n50
  date of, 116, 117–18, 307–9
  notation of, 125–30, 308, 339n59
  rediscovery of, 116, 307
  staff-lining of, 122–24, 308
  watermarks and paper studies of, 119, *120*, 121–24, *123*, 126, 307–8

Berlin, Staatsbibliothek, Beethoven Aut. 15, 361n23, 367n30

Berlin, Staatsbibliothek, Beethoven Aut. 28 (*See* Fischhof Miscellany)

Berlin, Staatsbibliothek, Mendelssohn 15 (*See Leonore* Sketchbook)

Berlin, Staatsbibliothek, Miscellany Aut. 19e, 116, 119, 121–22
  date of, 131

Bonn, Beethovenhaus, MS. NE39, 361n24

Bonn, Beethovenhaus, SBH 553, 60

Bonn, Beethovenhaus, SBH 606, 62, 63–64

Bonn, Beethovenhaus, SBH 609, 329n8

Bonn, Beethovenhaus, SBH 637, fol. 4r, 115–16, 129, 132, 140, 339n58

Bonn, Universitäts-Bibliothek, Velten Sammlung, f. 64, 327n71, 327n81

Eroica Sketchbook (*See* Landsberg 6)

Fischhof Miscellany (Berlin, Staatsbibliothek, Aut. 28), 117, 321n59, 329n2
  fol. 13r, 115–16
  fol. 15, 31, 38–39, 305–6
  paper types of, 119, 121

Grasnick 1, 60, 61, 117, 325n42, 331n22
  date of, 131
  fol. 2v, 54
  fols. 19ff, 54
  fol. 19v, 71
  fol. 20v, 329n8

Grasnick 2, 116
  date of, 131

Grasnick 20b, 363n45

Grasnick 24, 122, *123*

Grasnick 31, 321n54

Kafka Miscellany (London, British Library, Add. Ms. 29801), 35, 38, 39, 322n64
  fol. 46, 60
  fol. 57v, 51
  fols. 64–65, 54, 325n42
  fol. 64v, 331n28
  fol. 72v, 64
  fols. 74–80, 31, 305

manuscripts and sketchbooks (*continued*)
  fol. 75v, 31, 306
  fol. 80v, 35
  fol. 82r, 115–16
  fol. 83r, 342n17
  fol. 89, 60
  fol. 97, 327n83
  fol. 97r, 331n28
  fol. 113, 62, 63, 332–33n1
  fols. 113r and 113v, 99
  fol. 127, 61, 306
  fol. 127v, 327n83
  fol. 134, 327n83
  fol. 138, 52, 325n39
  fol. 147v, 331n28
  fol. 150, 321n60
  fol. 154v, 305
  fol. 155v, 115–16, 129
  paper types of, 117, 119
  Kessler Sketchbook (Vienna, Gesellschaft der
      Musikfreunde, A 34), 119, 133–34,
      155, 158, 182–83, 308, 338n48,
      346n6
    date of, 131
    fol. 15r, 115–16, 126
    staff-lining, 123–24
  Krakow, Biblioteka Jagiellonska, Mendels-
      sohn 1, 363n45
  Krakow, Biblioteka Jagiellonska, Mendels-
      sohn 6, 363n45
  Landsberg 6 (*Eroica* sketchbook), 159,
      338n42, 346n6, 350n25
  Landsberg 7, 119
    date of, 131
  Landsberg 10, 235, 348n24, 350n29,
      352n50, 356n29, 363n45
  Leonore Sketchbook (Berlin Staatsbibliothek
      Mendelssohn 15), 123, 131, 160,
      179, 346n6
  London, British Library, Add. Ms. 24801
      (*See* Kafka Miscellany)
  London, British Library, Add. Ms. 37767,
      119
  Paris, Bibliothèque Nationale, Ms. 61, 329n8
    fol. 2v, 31, 306
  Paris, Bibliothèque Nationale, Ms. 70, 329n4
  Paris, Bibliothèque Nationale, Mss. 72 and
      73, 361n24
  possible missing sketchbook, 116, 117,
      340n64
  Sauer Sketchbook, 308
    date of, 131, 132
  Scheide Sketchbook, 277, 363n45, 363n47
  Vienna, Gesellschaft der Musikfreunde, A 5,
      31, 305
  Vienna, Gesellschaft der Musikfreunde, A 34
      (*See* Kessler Sketchbook)
Vienna, Gesellschaft der Musikfreunde, A
      62, 327n82
Vienna, Gesellschaft der Musikfreunde, A 82
      b, 352n56
Washington, D.C., Library of Congress, acc.
      318077, SV387, 327n81
Wielhorsky Sketchbook, 116, 119, 129, 134,
      140, 155
    date of, 131, 132
    staff-lining, 123–24
Maria Theresa, Holy Roman Empress, 44,
      322n70, 323n11
Marinelli, Carl, 46
Marseillaise, 96
Martin, Philipp Jacques, 46
Marx, Adolph Bernard
    concept of *Idee,* 192
    Ludwig van Beethoven: Leben und Schaffen,
        189, 191–92
    on form in concertos, 10–11, 16, 86, 96,
        203, 313n3, 315nn19–20
Mastiaux, Johann Gottfried von, 29–30
Maunder, Richard, 369n39
Maximilian Franz, Elector, 22, 24–26, 27, 30,
      40–41, 42–44, 318n24, 318n25,
      319n35, 321n60, 322n70
Maximilian Friedrich, Elector, 22, 24, 40,
      319n34
meantone tunings, 296
Mehlgrube (Vienna dance hall), 46
Méhul, Étienne-Nicolas, 234
Mendelssohn, Felix, *Variations serieuses,* 70
Mergentheim, 26, 27
metronome markings, 299–303
Metternich, Prince Clemens Wenzel, 45
Meyer, Leonard, 313n2, 332n41
middle movement (concerto) form, 21
military symbolism, 7–8, 32, 93, 95–98, 136,
      138, 142, 193, 197, 205, 206, 218,
      250, 256, 257, 272, 277
minuet, symbolism of, 311n8
Mitropoulos, Dimitri, 357n36
Momigny, Jérôme-Joseph de, 11
Monteverdi, Claudio, *Orfeo,* 3
Moor, Emanuel, 348n20
Mörike, Eduard, "An eine Aeolsharfe," 343n25
Morrow, Mary Sue, 47
Moscheles, Ignaz, 351n45
    concertos of, 4, 32
Mosel, Ignaz Franz, 299–300
Moser, Andreas, 222
Moser, Hans Joachim, 222
Mozart, Leopold, 285
Mozart, Maria Anna (Nannerl), 285
Mozart, Wolfgang Amadeus, 26, 41
    aesthetics of, 88
    autographs of, 116

Ave verum corpus, K. 618, 335n33
Clemenza di Tito, La, 324n29
 Beethoven's fantasy on, 53
concertos
 Beethoven's performances of, 28, 286–87
 display episodes in, 263
 editions of, 282
 first movements of, 13–15, 100, 165,
   200
 first solo in, 73
 first tutti in, 72, 223
 form in, 31, 32
 Mozart's performances of, 4, 5, 6
 performance issues, 238, 285–87
 piano writing in, 101–2, 156
 rondo finales of, 19–20, 81, 82, 84, 208
 slow movements of, 78–79, 103
 thematic treatment in, 161
 third tutti in, 75
Concerto, Bassoon, K. 191, 331n30
Concerto, Clarinet, K. 622, 332n38
Concerto, Flute, K. 313 [=285c], 84, 331–
   32n30
Concerto, Horn, K. 412, 351n40
Concertos, Piano
 K. 37, 314–15n14
 K. 39–41, 314–15n14
 K. 238, 285
 K. 246, 285, 333n11, 366n18, 366n19,
   367n21
 K. 271, 68, 73, 84, 195, 256, 285,
   331n29, 351n32
 K. 413, 72, 315n18
 K. 414, 105
 K. 415, 78–79, 333n11
 K. 449, 72, 79
 K. 450, 72, 84
 K. 453, 72
 K. 456, 19, 72, 84
 K. 459, 84, 351n32
 K. 466, 19, 73, 84, 324n29, 330n20,
   366n17
 K. 467, 84, 93, 315n18, 333n11, 351n40
 K. 482, 72, 84, 331n29
 K. 488, 19, 84, 335n33
 K. 491, 73, 140–42, 158, 165–66, 285,
   321n53, 344n32, 351n34
 K. 503, 72, 73, 84, 86, 88, 333n11,
   334n20
 K. 537, 72, 84
 K. 595, 19, 72, 84, 315n18, 342n16
Concertos, Piano, Triple, K. 242, 285
Concertos, Violin
 K. 216, 331n29
 K. 218, 331n29
 K. 219, 331n29
concerts of, 324n27

Così fan tutte, 349n2
Don Giovanni, 3, 57, 87, 88, 349n2
 "Giovinette che fate all' amore," 81
 "Notte e giorno faticar," 93
Entführung aus dem Serail, Die, 87
finta semplice, La, 319n36
 grave of, 44
 influence on Beethoven, 86–89, 140–42,
   151, 158, 165–66
 letters to father, 367n21
 mature style of, 87–88
 minor-mode association with female charac-
   ters, 311n8
 as pianist, 4, 5, 6, 28, 286–87, 319n36
 piano of, 293
 Piano Sonatas
  K. 309, 19
  K. 331, 70
  K. 511, 316n27
  K. 576, 68
 Piano Trio, K. 502, 105
 piano writing of, 33
 Requiem, 344n32
 Rondo for Piano, K. 485, 20–21
 Rondo for Violin and Orchestra, K. 373,
   332n30
 as Salzburg court organist, 30
 Scena and Rondo "Ch'io mi scordi di te," K.
   505, 349n2
 String Quartets
  K. 387, 226
  K. 428, 331n22, 360n18
  K. 458 "Hunt," 105, 268, 335n33
  K. 464, 226, 342n16
  K. 465 "Dissonance," 313n2, 331n22
 String Quintet in G minor, K. 516, 87,
   205
 subscription concert series, 46
 symphonies of, 55
  K. 385 "Haffner," 331n22
  K. 425 "Linz," 105
  K. 550, 87, 331n22, 334–35n22,
   355n17
  trumpets and drums in, 93
 use of figured bass, 282, 285
 view of keyboard concerto as performance
   vehicle, 286
 Violin Sonata, K. 481, 335n33
 works of, 234
Zauberflöte, Die, 46
 "O Isis und Osiris," 78
Müller-Reuter, Theodor, 327n73
Munch, Charles, 372n75
Münster, Archbishop of, 22
Murat, Joachim, 253
Mustonen, Olli, 372n75
Mutter, Anne-Sophie, 372n74

narrative, form and, 9–12
Naumann, Johann Gottlieb, *Orpheus og Euryd-ike,* 189, 193
Neate, Charles, 358n40
Neefe, Christian Gottlob, 24, 27, 28, 29, 30, 33
Nelson, Horatio, 253
Netherlands, 26
Neue Mozart Ausgabe, 282
Newman, Anthony, 302–3, 369n49, 371n69, 372n72
Newman, William, 353n62, 364n4
Norma Edict, 323n11
Norrington, Roger, 294, 369n48, 371n69
notation, figured-bass, 35, 282–93
Nottebohm, Gustav, 300
    dating of sketchbooks, 346n6
    on abortive Piano Concerto, Hess 15, 277
    on Piano Concerto No. 1, 63
    on Piano Concerto No. 4, 214, 215
    on *Romance cantabile,* 36

Oberkassel, 26
opera
    as flexible genre, 5
    in Italy, 283
oral tradition, 5
Ormandy, Eugene, 371n69
Orpheus myth, relation to Beethoven's Piano Concerto No. 4, 189–94
Ospedale della Pietá (Venice), 6
Osthoff, Wolfgang, 150
Ovid, *Metamorphoses,* 189, 190, 193

Paisiello, Giovanni, *Il Re Theodoro,* 27
panharmonicon, 276
paper studies, 119, *120,* 121–24, 126, 308, 352n57, 356n29
Perahia, Murray, 302, 371nn69–70, 372n75
performance issues, 279–304. *See also specific works*
    "authenticity," 280, 364–65n5
    instruments, 293–96, 355n21
    soloist playing during tuttis, 215, 236–38, 279–93
    temperament, 296–98
    tempo and meter, 298–303
performer, roles of, 279–93
Perlman, Itzhak, 303, 372n75
Pest, 52, 325n34. *See also* Budapest
Pfeiffer, Tobias, 318n31
"piano climax," 74
piano reductions, 245–46, 273–75, 276, 283–84, 288, 290–91, 292
Pleyel, Ignaz
    Clarinet Concerto in C, 87
    piano trios, 318n25

Plutarch, 8
politics. *See also* French Revolution
    Napoleonic era, 251–56, 276–77
    revolutions of 1848, 45
Poppelsdorfer Schloss, 23, 27
Pössinger, Franz Alexander, 353n63, 359n62
Prague, 48, 49, 51, 53–54, 61, 63, 115
Pressburg (Bratislava), 48, 49, 51, 52
program music, 189–94
Propp, Vladimir, 190
Psyche myth, 194
public concerts, 6–7, 11, 28, 46–56. *See also specific composers and theaters*
publishing, 274–76. *See also specific works under* Beethoven
    notational practices of, 284–85, 286–87, 290–91

Quantz, Johann Joachim, notions of tempo, 299–300, 372n77

Rameau, Jean-Philippe, 296
rastrology, 122
Raupach, Hermann Friedrich, 14
Razumovsky, Count Andreas, 49
récit obligé, 7, 179, 186
recitative
    accompanied, 7
    instrumental, 104, 186, 188
    vocal, 283
Reicha, Anton, 11, 24, 30, 331n27
    treatises of, 312n1
Reicha, Josef, 24, 30
Reichardt, Johann Friedrich, 291–92, 351n45
    on Piano Concerto No. 4, 204, 211, 212
responsorial psalm-singing, 3
Réti, Rudolf, 347n11
Riemann, Hugo, 317n7
    concept of *Vierhebigkeit,* 98
    on Piano Concerto No. 2, 86
    on String Quartet Op. 18, No. 4, 345–46n56
Riepel, Joseph, 11
Ries, Anna Maria, 24
Ries, Ferdinand, 51, 52, 324–25n32, 326n50
    Biographische Notizen über Ludwig van Bee-thoven, 27
    concertos of, 361n22
    on Beethoven's 1803 concert, 114, 328n87
    on Beethoven's eradication of Napoleon's name on *Eroica* Symphony, 252
    on Beethoven's planned trip to Paris, 183–84
    on Piano Concerto No. 3, 336n4
    on Piano Concerto No. 4, 212–13
    on piano transcription of Violin Concerto, 246
    on Piano Trio, Op. 1, 91, 333n3

performance of Beethoven's Piano Concerto
No. 3, 127, 292, 364n1
Ries, Franz, 38, 317n14
Ries, Johann, 24
Ries family, 24, 30
Riezler, Walter, 347n11
ritornello, 11–12, 15–16
meaning of, 17
rondo theme as, 18, 19–20
Rochlitz, Friedrich, 369n36
on concerto playing, 292
on demise of harpsichord, 295–96
on Piano Concerto No. 5, 272, 274
on temperament, 297
Rode, Pierre, 348n17
Rolland, Romain, on Beethoven's middle
period, 153
romance (instrumental), 35
romanesca, 226
Romberg, Andreas, 24, 27, 30, 38, 49, 52–53
Romberg, Bernhard, 24, 27, 30, 49, 52–53,
325n39
rondo
character of, 20, 81
as concerto finale, 18–21
form of, 10
ritornello in, 111
symbolism of, 7, 10
terminology for, 19
Rosen, Charles, 145, 330n19, 333n4, 367n21
on Piano Concerto No. 4, 204–5, 350n28
Rösler, Johann Josef, 319n38
Rossini, Gioachino
Barber of Seville, The, 283
operas of, 4–5
Rotterdam, 26
Rouland, Carl, 59
round-song and -dance, 3
Rousseau, Jean-Jacques
concept of *récit obligé,* 186, 349n1
concept of *récitatif accompagné,* 104
political views of, 44
writings of, 7
Rovantini, Franz Georg, 317n14, 319n34
Rudolph, Archduke, 160, 180, 254, 290,
362n36, 368n33
Rust, Wilhelm, 360n12
Rysavy, Robin, 370n53

Salieri, Antonio, 48, 64
Salomon, Johann Peter, 24
Salomon, Philipp, 24
sarabande, 226
symbolism of, 311n8
Sauer, Ignaz, 132
Scheibe, Johann Adolph, on concerto form, 16,
17, 314n7

Schelling, Friedrich Wilhelm Joseph von, 10
Schenk, Erich, 355nn19–20
Schenk, Johann, 48
Schenker, Heinrich, 347n11
Schenkerian analysis, 313n2
Schiedermair, Ludwig, 24, 316n4, 317n13
Schikaneder, Emanuel, 46, 54, 61, 129, 160,
341n79
Schiller, Johann Christoph Friedrich von, 251
Schindler, Anton, 297
on Beethoven's eradication of Napoleon's
name on *Eroica* Symphony, 252
on Beethoven's tempos, 299, 371n61
on genesis of *Eroica* Symphony, 183
on Triple Concerto, 160, 165, 182, 347n8
Schlemmer (copyist), 338n49
Schmitz, Arnold, 96, 341n5
concept of "contrasting derivation," 257
on Beethoven's themes, 224
Schnabel, Artur, 302–3, 371nn69–70,
372n75
Schneider, Johann Christian Friedrich, 272,
362n33
Schobert, Johann, 14
Schoenberg, Arnold, 11
Schubart, C. D. F., 297, 298, 370n58
Vaterlandschronik, 88
Schubert, Franz
Impromptu, D. 935, No. 2, 144, 350n26
key choices of, 297
Piano Sonata in B♭, D. 960, 144, 260, 262,
350n26
Piano Trio in E♭, D. 929, 262
piano writing of, 293
Symphony in C Major, D. 944, 117
three-keyed expositions of, 260
use of lowered-sixth relation, 298
Schulz, J. A. P., 372n77
Schumann, Robert
aesthetic theories of, 190–91, 192, 194
Carnaval, 350n26, 361n30
Fantasiestücke, In der Nacht, 192
on affective qualities of keys, 297
on Piano Concerto No. 5, 360n14
Schuppanzigh, Ignaz, 46, 48, 54, 59, 60
Schütz, Heinrich, 3
Schwarzenberg, Prince Joseph von, 47
Scotch snap, 112
Seidler (violinist), 160
Serkin, Rudolf, 302, 371n69
Seyfried, Ignaz von
on Choral Fantasy, 211
on Piano Concerto No. 3, 129–30, 291,
326n50, 336n4
Shakespeare, William
Henry IV, Part 2, 73
King Lear, 194

siciliano, 217
  symbolism of, 7
Sievers, G. L. P., 366n11
Simon, Stephen, 369n49, 371n69, 372n72
Simrock, Nikolaus, 183, 184, 317n20,
    318n25
slow-movement form, 77–78, 145
Smart, Sir George, 371n62
Solomon, Maynard, 183, 317n13
  on Beethoven's Bonn output, 40–41
sonata form
  compared with concerto finales, 19
  compared with first-movement concerto
    form, 13–14, 16–17
  concerto and, 12
sonata-rondo, 82
sonatina form, 77
Sonnleithner, Joseph, 160, 184
Southwell, William, 339n52
Spina, C. A., 59
Spohr, Louis, 362n32
Stadlen, Peter, 370n60
staff-lining, 122–24, 308, 338n42
Stamitz, Carl, 317n17
Steblin, Rita, 370n56
Stein, Carl Friedrich, 212–13, 215
Stein, Matthäus Andreas, 352n51
Stepán, Josef Antonín, concertos of, 342n15
Sterkel, Johann Franz Xaver, 26, 341n5
  concertos of, 72, 81
Stevens, Jane, 315nn1718
Streicher, Johann Andreas, 51, 293
Streicher, Nanette, 293
Sulzer, Johann Georg, on principal theme, 95,
    96
symphonie concertante genre, 182–83
symphony, as fixed-text genre, 5
Szász, Tibor, 290, 369n35

Talsma, Willem Retze, 371n61
Tan, Melvyn, 302–3, 369n48, 371n69
Taruskin, Richard, 294, 312n11, 364–65n5
Tcherepnin, Alexander, 348n20
Tempelhof, G. F., 297
temperament, 296–98
Temperley, Nicholas, 371n62
tempo, 298–303
Teutonic Order, 316n2
"text," concept of, 275–76
Thayer, Alexander Wheelock, 24, 30, 43, 116,
    117, 141, 212, 316–17n7, 317n13,
    319n35, 325n39, 351n45
Theater an der Wien (Vienna), 46, 160, *171*,
    234, 253, 291–92, 351n45,
    356n32
Theater auf der Wieden (Vienna), 46, 54

"three-keyed exposition," 260
timpani, 294–95
Tomášek, Václav Jan, 328n85
  on Beethoven as pianist, 53–54
Tonkünstler-Sozietät, 50–51, 60, 63, 64, 90,
    212, 351n45
Torelli, Giuseppe, 11
Tovey, Donald Francis
  on concerto form, 73, 75, 138, 139, 164,
    314n11, 330n10
  on Piano Concerto in E♭, WoO 4, 31
  on Piano Concerto No. 3, 99, 150, 154–55
  on Piano Concerto No. 4, 189–90, 199, 204,
    209
  on Piano Concerto No. 5, 259, 266, 360n11,
    360n17
  on Schumann's *Carnaval,* 361n30
  on Triple Concerto, 160, 166, 182
  on Violin Concerto, 217, 218, 229
Trattnerhof (Vienna dance hall), 46
Treitschke, Georg Friedrich, 188
trio sonatas, 11
Trugschluss, 140
Türk, Daniel Gottlieb, 367n22, 368n33
  on rondo, 20
"Turkish" music, 34, 85
  symbolism of, 7
tutti, meaning of, 17
Tyson, Alan
  The Beethoven Sketchbooks, 60, 121, 122,
    132
  edition of Violin Concerto, 241, 355n25
  on Beethoven's "heroic phase," 151–52
  on Beethoven's middle period, 153
  on "concept sketches," 115, 235
  on date of Piano Concerto No. 3, 117,
    339n59, 340n64
  on Piano Concerto No. 5, 367n31
  on Violin Concerto, 217, 239, 240, 358n41,
    358n45, 358n51
  on watermarks, 337n28, 338n38

Vienna. *See also specific theaters*
  censorship in, 45
  concerto performances in, 364n1
  cosmopolitanism of, 44
  der Kohlmarkt in, 168, *169*
  Napoleon's bombardment of, *176*
  Napoleon's occupation of, 251–52, 253, 255–
    56
  politics in, 45
  private concerts in, 47
  public amusements in, 45
  public concerts in, 6–7, 46–56
  religion in, 44
  theater in, 46

Viotti, Giovanni Battista, Violin Concerto in A
minor, 233
Virgil
Aeneid, 8
Georgics, 189, 193, 194
Vivaldi, Antonio
concertos of, 6, 11, 12
published works of, 276
Vogler, Georg Joseph, Abbé
concertos of, 284–85, 286, 287, 367n20
on concerto composition, 14, 16, 315n17
on key associations, 370n58

Wagenseil, Georg Christoph, concertos of,
342n15
Wagner, Richard, 252
Waldstein, Count Ferdinand von, 29–30, 41
Walsh, John, 286
Walter, Anton, 338n52
waltz, symbolism of, 7
Wanhal, Johann Baptist, Concertos, Op. 14,
286
watermarks, 119, *120,* 121–22, *123,* 307,
337n28, 352n57
Weber, Bernard Anselm, 87
Weber, Carl Maria von
concertos of, 32

Konzertstück, 361n22
piano writing of, 293
Weber, Gottfried, 313n2
Wegeler, Franz Gerhard, 25, 27, 52, 90–91,
321n55, 323n8, 325n37, 327n73,
333n3
on Piano Concerto No. 1, 62–65
well-temperaments, 296–97
Westerholt-Giesenberg, Freiherr von, 36,
41
Westphalia, Kingdom of, 253–54
Wheelock, Gretchen, 311–12n8
Whitman, Walt, 8
Wiener Theater Zeitung, 225
Willem V, Prince, 26
Winter, Robert
The Beethoven Sketchbooks, 60, 121, 122,
132
on tempo in Beethoven's concertos, 371n69,
372nn76–77
Wordsworth, William, *Laodamia,* 217
Wranitzky, Paul, 55

Yudkin, Jeremy, 342n16

Zeitung für die elegante Welt, 114
Zeltser, Mark, 372n74